TOWARD A GLOBAL COMMUNITY OF HISTORIANS

Karl Dietrich Erdmann

TOWARD A GLOBAL COMMUNITY OF HISTORIANS

The International Historical Congresses and
the International Committee of Historical Sciences,
1898–2000

Karl Dietrich Erdmann

Edited by
Jürgen Kocka and Wolfgang J. Mommsen
in collaboration with
Agnes Blänsdorf

Translated by
Alan Nothnagle

Published in 2005 by
Berghahn Books

www.berghahnbooks.com

© 2005 Jürgen Kocka

All rights reserved.
Except for the quotation of short passages
for the purposes of criticism and review, no part of this book
may be reproduced in any form or by any means, electronic or
mechanical, including photocopying, recording, or any information
storage and retrieval system now known or to be invented,
without written permission of the publisher.

Library of Congress Cataloging-in-Publication Data

Erdmann, Karl Dietrich.
　　[Ökumene der Historiker. English]
　　Toward a global community of historians : the International Historical Congresses and the International Committee of Historical Sciences 1898–2000 / Karl Dietrich Erdmann ; edited by Jürgen Kocka and Wolfgang J. Mommsen in collaboration with Agnes Blänsdorf; translated by Alan Nothnagle.
　　p. cm.
　　Rev. ed. of: Die Ökumene der Historiker, 1987.
　　Includes bibliographical references and index.
　　ISBN 1-57181-434-5 (hard.)
　　1. International Congresses of Historical Sciences. 2. International Committee of Historical Sciences. 3. History—Study and teaching. I. Kocka, Jürgen. II. Mommsen, Wolfgang J., 1930–2004. III. Blänsdorf, Agnes. IV. Title.

D3.A22E7313 2005
907'.1—dc22

2005045720

British Library Cataloguing in Publication Data

A catalogue record for this book is available from
the British Library.

Printed in the United States on acid-free paper

The hope of my youth: to see the present civilization united in order to study that of the past ages …, is perhaps not a mere dream and illusion.

— *Theodor Mommsen*

Contents

Preface to the English Edition ix

Author's Preface xiii

1. Imperialism and the Network of Scholars 1
2. Prelude in The Hague, 1898 6
3. Advocates of Comparison: The First Congress, Paris, 1900 12
4. Debates on Methodology: Rome, 1903 22
5. Victorious Professionalism: Berlin, 1908 41
6. An *entente cordiale* of Historians on the Eve of the War: London, 1913 58
7. Overcoming Nationalism in the Study of History: Brussels, 1923 68
8. The Beginnings of the International Committee of Historical Sciences, 1923–1927 101
9. Cleavages and Goodwill: The "Spirit of Oslo," 1928 122
10. New Political Challenges: Warsaw, 1933 139
11. In the Shadow of Crisis: Zurich, 1938 162
12. Destruction and Revival, 1938–1947 180
13. *Nouvelle histoire* versus *histoire historisante*: Grand Debates and New Departures in Paris, 1950 196
14. Political History on the Defense—Encounters in the Cold War in Rome, 1955 220
15. The Congresses from 1960 to 1985—Politics 244
16. The Congresses from 1960 to 1985—Organizational and Structural Developments 267
17. Debates on Theory and Methodology from the 1960s to the 1980s 278
18. Debates between East and West from the 1960s to the 1980s 299

Epilogue: After the End of the Great Schism—the International
 Historical Congresses from 1985 to 2000, *by Wolfgang J. Mommsen*   313

Appendices
  I. Members of the Bureau of the International Committee of
     Historical Sciences, 1926–2000   362
 II. Members of the International Committee of Historical Sciences,
     1926–2003   367
     1. National Committees   367
     2. International Commissions   373
III. Participation of Individual Countries in the International
     Congresses, 1898–2000   377
     1. Lectures, Reports, Communications   377
     2. Congress Participants   382
 IV. Development of the Constitution of the International Committee
     of Historical Sciences, 1926–2000   389

Bibliography
  1. Archival Sources   401
  2. ICHS Publications   404
  3. Proceedings of the International Historical Congresses
     (Lectures and Discussions)   405
  4. Other Publications   407

Index   419

Preface to the English Edition

This book is about the twenty International Congresses of Historians between 1898 and 2000. It is also about the history of the International Committee of Historical Sciences (ICHS—or Comité International des Sciences Historiques, CISH), which was founded in 1926 and presently consists of historians' associations or committees from fifty-four countries as well as twenty-eight thematically specialized affiliated commissions. The book deals with the history of transnational, increasingly global, contacts between historians and the emergence of transnational, increasingly global, approaches to the study of history in the twentieth century.

There have been three phases in the history of the ICHS. In the interwar period, its main function was overcoming nationalism and bridging the deep gaps between historians from different nations who had fought one another in the First World War. From about 1950 to 1990, the Committee and the Congresses it organized served as major platforms on which historians from the communist East and the non-communist West would meet, exchange views, and engage in discussions that were frequently controversial. In the 1990s and the first years of the twenty-first century, the work of the ICHS has reflected the present trends toward globalization. It supports the emergence of new approaches to transnational history and strives to include more historians from non-Western parts of the world. By becoming more global and more universal, the discipline is changing with respect to themes and methods, questions asked, and answers offered.

The book thoroughly describes the topics, highlights, and controversies of the International Congresses of Historians that were organized in different places between 1898 (The Hague) and 2000 (Oslo). From this point of view, it presents an outline of the history of historical studies in the twentieth century. It supplies abundant information on the changing themes, viewpoints, and methods in the field, and makes clear how much the central controversies and problems of the time influenced the work of historians. It depicts the interrelation between politics and history as a discipline and presents new details about the diplomacy between practitioners and organizers of the discipline who have tried to cross borders and build bridges across deep gaps defined by different national identities, ideologies, and cultures worldwide. Many of them aimed at building a global community of historians. To some extent they succeeded; in many respects they did not. Their story is told by this book.

This is a slightly abridged and supplemented English version of a book that was first published in German in 1987. The author, the distinguished German historian Karl Dietrich Erdmann (1910–1990), mostly published on German history of the twentieth century, in a European context. At the same time, he took great interest in the history of areas outside Europe and was very active in the international cooperation of scholars. He was a member of the Bureau of the ICHS from 1970 to 1990 and its president from 1975 to 1980.[1] For the writing of this book he made extensive use of published and unpublished material from the archives of the ICHS as well as from other sources. He called his book *Die Ökumene der Historiker* (The Ecumene of Historians). The choice of title indicates the author's main perspective. Deeply convinced of the universal implications of history as a science, he was highly interested in making the discipline more "ecumenical." He was cautiously optimistic about the power of history to bring about more understanding between nations, ideologies, and cultures—despite all of the cleavages and tensions, which Erdmann knew well and described in his book. When he wrote the book in the 1980s, the East-West conflict was the most important single factor in structuring international relations, and it had a deep impact on the study and writing of history, too. Erdmann saw his task in building bridges between the two camps, both as president of the ICHS and as the author of this book. In addition, he was highly interested in the methodological controversies of the discipline, particularly in the competition and arguments between social science-oriented historians and more narrative approaches, which he liked to call "historicist" or "neohistoricist" (*historistisch* or *neohistoristisch*) and with which he sympathized.

This is the spirit in which this book was composed. Readers of the English translation cannot miss the commitment, the message, the thrust of an author who dealt with his own time with the purpose of helping to change it. But times have changed: nowadays we may have different concerns and other expectations. It testifies to the professional excellence of Karl Dietrich Erdmann that his book is packed with information, insights, and interpretations that are important and pertinent with respect to the questions historians may ask today, nearly twenty years later.

The late Wolfgang J. Mommsen, historian at the University of Düsseldorf and long-term director of the German Historical Institute in London, has added an epilogue to the book. While attempting to stay faithful to the "ecumenical" spirit of Karl Dietrich Erdmann, Mommsen brings the story up to the year 2000, when the XIXth International Congress of Historians (the official numbering regards the first Congress of 1898 as a forerunner) took place in Oslo. He relates the story to new questions and problems that are being posed and discussed in the early twenty-first century.

Compared with the German original, the English version is abridged. Extensive notes were reduced somewhat. Particularly, the last chapters of the book were closely related to debates and problems of the 1970s and 1980s more interesting to readers then than now. We have cautiously removed some of these details. But the argumentation, thrust, and substance of the book have been carefully preserved. Any omission of substantial information is indicated by an editors' note referring to the pertinent pages of the German version. Chapter titles have been added by the editors. The appendices showing the development of the ICHS and the International Congresses have been expanded in order to cover the years from 1985 to 2000, and the bibliographical entries of the German edition have been amended in accordance with the style of Berghahn Books. Finally, some selected recent works on the main issues of historical writing and thought discussed in this book have been added to the bibliography.

In the 1990s, Wolfgang J. Mommsen and Natalie Zemon Davis, who was then a member of the Bureau of the ICHS, pursued the idea of an English translation in cooperation with the Bureau. Together with Stephanie Merkenich, and with the financial assistance of the Volkswagen Foundation, Wolfgang J. Mommsen prepared a shortened version for the English translation and also had two chapters translated. However, at the time it proved impossible to find an American or British publisher, so the project was shelved until I took it up again in 2000, after being elected to the presidency of the ICHS. Wolfgang J. Mommsen contributed the epilogue. Alan Nothnagle (Berlin) translated the text. I am grateful to the Köhler Foundation (Köhler-Stiftung im Stifterverband für die Deutsche Wissenschaft) for granting the financial support that made all this possible. I am particularly indebted to Agnes Blänsdorf, a historian in Kiel who was a collaborator of Karl Dietrich Erdmann in writing this book and therefore has intimate knowledge of its genesis. Her commitment and her manifold contributions to further shortening, revising, and editing the text have been decisive. I am grateful to the historians Georg G. Iggers, Richard Vann, Irmline Veit-Brause, and Rudolf Vierhaus, who supported the work by offering encouragement when it was necessary, and by reading chapters of the translation; to Heidrun Dickson for polishing the text; to the Academy of Sciences, Göttingen, and the publisher Vandenhoeck & Ruprecht, Göttingen, who published the German edition in 1987 and, like Horst Firker, the consulted relative of Karl Dietrich Erdmann, raised no objection against using the text for an English version. I want to express my thanks to publisher Marion Berghahn, who has done so much to bridge the gap between the German-language literature in history and related fields and English-speaking audiences, and to Volker Berghahn as well. Finally, I owe thanks to my colleagues in the Bureau of the ICHS who have supported this endeavor over the years, particularly to the secretary-general Jean-Claude Robert (Montreal) and the treasurer

Pierre Ducrey (Lausanne). Jean-Claude Robert helped to update the appendices. He and Ivan T. Berend read through the epilogue.

Wolfgang J. Mommsen (born 1930) was an outstanding historian and a public intellectual with an international reputation. He was a leading expert on Max Weber and co-edited his collected works. In a cosmopolitan spirit, Wolfgang Mommsen was highly sensitive to the transnational dimensions of the discipline, and he represented German historiography well at many international occasions. He has closely cooperated with the ICHS many times. We finished most of the editing work in the summer of 2004. But he could not participate in the final steps nor read and react to the copyedited version of his epilogue. On 11 August he drowned when swimming in the Baltic Sea. His unexpected death came as a shock. The international community of historians owes him a lot.

— Jürgen Kocka

Notes

1. On Erdmann, see H. Boockmann and K. Jürgensen, eds., *Nachdenken über Geschichte: Beiträge aus der Ökumene der Historiker in memoriam Karl Dietrich Erdmann* (Neumünster, 1991), including obituaries and personal remembrances (pp. 11–54) by E. Jäckel (Stuttgart, reprint of his obituary in *Historische Zeitschrift* 252, 1991, pp. 529–539), E. Engelberg (Berlin), Th. Barker (London), J.-B. Duroselle (Paris), Hélène Ahrweiler (Paris, ICHS secretary-general), G. Susini (Bologna), H. Olszewski and J. Topolski (Poznań), D. Berindei (Bucharest), Masaki Miyake (Tokyo), Wei Hsiung (Beijing), and a bibliography of his publications by A. Blänsdorf (pp. 659–677). In the last several years, there has been a controversy on Erdmann's attitude in the National-Socialist period. See (with bibliographical references) W. J. Mommsen, "'Gestürzte Denkmäler'? Die 'Fälle' Aubin, Conze, Erdmann und Schieder," in J. Elvert and S. Krauß, eds., *Historische Debatten und Kontroversen im 19. und 20. Jahrhundert: Jubiläumstagung der Ranke-Gesellschaft in Essen, 2001* (HMRG Historische Mitteilungen im Auftrag der Ranke Gesellschaft, vol. 46, Stuttgart, 2003), pp. 96–109, here pp. 107–109.

Author's Preface

Historiography can approach its subject only through words. As a methodical inquiry into that which once was and no longer is, and as a consideration of what could be in the future but has not yet come to pass, it provides its subject matter with contemporary reality by the act of speaking about it, irrespective of its nature as an object. Both the written and the spoken word are designed for questions and answers, i.e., for dialogue. Historical dialogue is not only spontaneous, but has developed rules and organized forms in order to create propitious conditions for discussion among historians, for instance in seminars, academies, universities, and, in the course of the rapid development of historical scholarship in the nineteenth and twentieth centuries, also in historical associations at the local, regional, national, and international levels. In this book we will examine the periodic International Congresses of Historical Sciences and the International Committee of Historical Sciences (ICHS), which has been their organizer and sponsor for the past sixty years.

This book is intended as a contribution to the history of historiography. In reflecting on its own work and history, historiography pursues many paths comprising biography, intellectual and social history, philosophy of history, epistemology and methodology, and the history of institutions. The following study is focused on both the nature and the development of institutionalized dialogue among historians at the international level. They will be examined as they relate to three aspects: (1) the internal and external structure of the Congresses and the ICHS, i.e., their organizational history; (2) the external political conditions and the internal political tendencies as determining factors of the international discussion among historians; (3) the self-conception of historical scholarship as reflected in theoretical and methodological deliberation and in the themes of the Congresses. These factors interact with one another. The principal interest of this study lies in the self-conception of historical scholarship. Of course, historical congresses are not workshops for empirical, theoretical, or methodological inquiry. Their significance lies in the fact that here, the different positions connected with historical thought and writing stand eye to eye and are thus stimulated to reconsider their relationship to one another. Such congresses therefore actualize the question of whether it is possible to engage in a dialogue about history that transcends national and social divisions. The opportunity for discussion provided by the International Historical Congresses presupposes the common acknowledgement of the principle that they shall be devoted to scientific work regardless of the differences in linguistic and historical-cultural affiliations, theoretical convictions, and political or social notions of the historians participating in the dialogue.

The deeper these differences go, the more necessary the effort to ensure at least a minimal intellectual consensus, without which an institutionalized discussion would be meaningless. When this attempt is successful, the result is an "ecumenical community of historians"—which is not a neutral space devoid of all conflicting views but, ideally, a forum for intellectual freedom, tolerance, and understanding within our divided world.

The most important source for this study are the proceedings of the Congresses, which contain the text of the contributions, often in abridged form, usually along with more or less thorough reports on the discussions. They are of highly varying scope and quality. For the history of the ICHS since its foundation in 1926, the *Bulletins* edited by its secretary-generals have been essential. In addition, unpublished sources have been evaluated. Rich materials are preserved in the archives of the ICHS, which are stored partly in Lausanne, partly in Paris. Further material came from the Rockefeller Archive Center as well as from national and association archives. A number of private paper collections proved to be informative, particularly in regard to the internal history of the Congresses and the ICHS. Reports and commentaries on the Congresses in international journals were also evaluated. The study of the theoretical and methodological discussion occasionally had to go beyond the materials directly related to the Congresses and draw upon the respective contemporary literature. However, this book is concentrated on the Congresses themselves and the development of the International Committee of Historical Sciences that sponsored them. Today, numerous national committees and specialized international organizations are affiliated with the ICHS, but include their respective histories would have stretched this study beyond all boundaries and blurred its contours.

So far only a few brief studies have appeared on the history of the International Congresses. The beginnings of the ICHS were described by Halvdan Koht, one of its major cofounders.[1] Michel François, its long-term secretary-general, provided a brief outline of the organization's history on the occasion of its fiftieth anniversary.[2] As a member of the Bureau of the ICHS and its president, I myself dealt several times with the history of the Congresses and the ICHS in lectures and essays.[3] Because of the Soviet Union's ideological and political relevance, its contribution to the Congresses has been the subject of several informative studies in the GDR, the Soviet Union, and Italy.[4]

Until recently, the International Historical Congresses have sometimes been viewed by the mandarins of the historical profession—with a certain disdain—as "mass events." And yet, "questionable" though they may be, they are nevertheless an inescapable element of a living science, and they exert a sustained pull on thousands of participants from all over the world. This book will attempt to depict their scholarly significance from a theoretical and methodological point of view.

Despite all attempts at objectivity concerning the reported facts, a project of this kind cannot help but be subjective in regard to the standpoint of its author. If even a single Congress cannot be regarded as a collective individuality, but rather represents in both its program and its staging a complex network of relationships among different scientific, political, and personal factors, then this applies all the more to the long series of Historical Congresses as a whole. Only by employing a catalog of questions that has been narrowed down, which is thus necessarily selective and for which the author takes responsibility, does the subject gain in profile and become tangible. A particular fascination, which I hope is understandable, has been aroused within this German observer by the role of Germany in the Congresses' history: the classical German history of the nineteenth century, because of its importance for the history of our discipline, became an outstanding point of reference in the discussion on historical theory and methodology—through consent as well as through criticism. However, because of the two world wars and the attendant cataclysms in German history, the relationship to the international historical profession was twice destroyed and twice had to be re-established. The fact that this has been successful is of vital significance for German historical scholarship of today.

This book could not have been written without a great deal of help. For twenty years my wife has accompanied me on all my paths and detours to the Congresses and their history. Their depiction in these pages has developed from our mutual encounters, observations, and considerations. She has also made Russian journal literature available to me through her extensive translations. Dorothea Nitsche was kind enough to assume the same task for the Polish journals. Thanks to the financial assistance of the Volkswagen Foundation, my collaborator Dr. Agnes Blänsdorf was able to examine sources in archives and libraries in Europe and America, bringing in a rich yield of material. She assumed a major share of the work of assessing records, unpublished papers, and literature in all phases of the development of the manuscript from the first drafts to the final version. Thomas Mahrenholtz, Michael Matthiesen, and Lutz Sellmer provided assistance in the preparation of the bibliography and book acquisition. Christel Gerke unflaggingly copied the texts in their various phases of development. Encouragement, criticism, and assistance were given to me by many colleagues from the international historical community. Some of them—Miguel Batllori SJ (Rome and Barcelona), Charles O. Carbonell (Montpellier), Gordon A. Craig (Stanford), Aleksander Gieysztor (Warsaw), Domokos Kosáry (Budapest), György Ránki (Budapest), Bianca

Valota (Milan), and Irmline Veit-Brause (Melbourne)—assumed the burden of reading the bulk of the manuscript and commenting on it at a special meeting during the Stuttgart Congress of 1985.

I was given the opportunity to report on the structure and results of my studies at the Historical Institute of the Hungarian Academy of Sciences and the Göttingen Academy of Sciences. The names of several Göttingen historians are closely linked with the history of the ICHS. Its first General Assembly was held in this city in 1927. Thus, the "Abhandlungen" of the Göttingen Academy are an appropriate and highly welcome place of publication for this history of the International Historical Congresses. I would like to thank all those who have provided me with advice and assistance on the long path from assuming the office of president of the ICHS in 1975 to completing this contribution toward a history of historiography in the twentieth century. This study is dedicated to the dialogue partners of many years who, like the author, have been fascinated and enriched by the experiment of an ecumenical union of historians.

— *Karl Dietrich Erdmann*

Notes

1. H. Koht, *The Origin and Beginnings of the International Committee of Historical Sciences: Personal Remembrances* (Lausanne, 1962).
2. M. François, "Cinquante ans d'Histoire du Comité International des Sciences Historiques," in Comité International des Sciences Historiques, *Bulletin d'information,* ed. Michel François, secretary-general of the ICHS [hereafter: ICHS, *Bulletin d'information*], no. 10 (1976).
3. K. D. Erdmann, "Fünfzig Jahre 'Comité International des Sciences Historiques': Erfahrungen und Perspektiven," *Geschichte in Wissenschaft und Unterricht* 27 (1976): 524–537; "Die Ökumene der Historiker: Rede des Präsidenten des Comité International des Sciences Historiques zur Eröffnung des 15. Internationalen Historikerkongresses in Bukarest," *Geschichte in Wissenschaft und Unterricht* 31 (1980): 657–666, French text in *XVe Congrès International des Sciences Historiques, Bucarest, 10–17 août 1980: Actes,* 2 vols. (Bucharest, 1982), vol. 1; "Il contributo della storiografia italiana ai Congressi Internazionali di Scienze Storiche nella prima metà del XX secolo," in B. Vigezzi, ed., *Federico Chabod e la "Nuova Storiografia" italiana* (Milan, 1984); "A History of the International Historical Congresses: Work in Progress," *Storia della Storiografia* 8 (1985): 3–23, German translation: "Zur Geschichte der Internationalen Historikerkongresse: Ein Werkstattbericht," *Geschichte in Wissenschaft und Unterricht* 36 (1985): 535–553; "Genèse et débuts du Comité International des Sciences Historiques, fondé le 15 mai 1926," in ICHS, *Bulletin d'information,* no. 13 (1986).
4. L.-D. Behrendt, "Die internationalen Beziehungen der sowjetischen Historiker 1917 bis Mitte der dreißiger Jahre: Zur internationalen Wirksamkeit der sowjetischen Geschichtswissenschaften in ihrer ersten Entwicklungsphase" (Ph.D. diss., University of Leipzig, 1977); E. A. Dudzinskaja, *Meždunarodnye naučnye svjazi sovjetskich istorikov* [International scientific relations of Soviet historians] (Moscow, 1978); C. Castelli, "Internazionalismo e Storia: Gli Storici Sovietici ai Congressi Internazionali di Scienze Storiche 1928–36," *Storia Contemporanea* 12 (1981): 908–926.

Chapter 1

IMPERIALISM AND THE NETWORK OF SCHOLARS

In the age of Imperialism, international relations were characterized by two opposing trends. National aspirations for power and expansion, which dominated the picture and which led to the catastrophe of the First World War, were countered by both an economic interest in, and a quite varied cultural and scientific need for, international cooperation. This dual phenomenon was already preoccupying contemporary Marxist and liberal or conservative theorists of imperialism. However, a broad range of responses was given with regard to the relative importance accruing to cooperation on the one hand and conflict on the other. Lenin, in his famous text on imperialism, took the view that, despite all existing interconnections of interests, war was the unavoidable result of the conflict of interests within the capitalist world economy, whereas the Marxist theorist Karl Kautsky rejected the assumption that economic determinants must lead inexorably to war. The economist, historian, and philosopher Kurt Riezler, a close associate of the German chancellor Bethmann Hollweg, took a similar position in his book *Grundzüge der Weltpolitik in der Gegenwart*, published in 1914 on the eve of the First World War. Riezler left open whether the interest calculations of the powers contending with one another for economic expansion and political influence were tending more toward war or toward the prevention of war. A simple cost-benefit analysis, he said, would conclude that the elaborateness and destructive capacity of modern military technology made war unprofitable. Furthermore, "cosmopolitan" tendencies were gaining increased importance in regard to capital integration, the labor movement, international law, and the emergence of a general cultural ideal that condemned war on humanitarian grounds.

Turning to the French literature of the period, an essay by the historian and foreign ministry attaché René Lavollée on "The International Unions" merits attention, since he wrote in a similar vein on the characteristic dual

---

Notes for this chapter are located on page 5.

phenomenon of nationalism and cosmopolitanism. This text appeared in the *Revue d'histoire diplomatique* in 1887, the year of the saber-rattling stance of the French war minister, General Boulanger, and of the election victory of an alliance of right-wing parties ("Kartellparteien") in Germany, which agreed upon a substantial increase in the military budget. The *Revue* was the organ of the Société d'histoire diplomatique, which had been founded the previous year and which a decade later was to provide the initiative for the convocation of the first International Historical Congress. Lavollée's article appears to represent a certain historical-political mentality that played a role in the genesis of the International Historical Congresses.

His survey of the international tendencies of the times was tempered with skepticism, although not with hopelessness: never had respect for treaties been less secure, rivalries bitterer, hatred between peoples stronger, the instruments of destruction more terrifying. But at the same time, "in marked contrast, never have greater efforts been undertaken to bring the peoples closer together for the sake of a common humanitarian goal." He asked: "Ought we to see this twofold state of affairs as one of the forms of the struggle taking place between the last impulses of an atavistic barbarism and the modern spirit, which is a spirit of progress and peace? Or is this merely an expression of the dualism upon which our nature is founded and which expresses itself not only in the deeds of individuals but also in the lives of nations, in the history of our culture and of the human race?"[1] Whatever the future might bring, he wrote, for the present it could be seen that, hatred and war notwithstanding, a feeling of unity and solidarity was beginning to stir in the consciousness of the peoples. Lavollée reviewed some of the most important international agreements that characterized the development of this trend: the Nautical Convention of 1856; the founding of the Red Cross in 1864; the Telegraphic Union of 1865; the General Postal Union of 1878 (whereby he emphasized the recognition of the principle of obligatory international arbitration); the Convention on the International Protection of Patents and Copyrights in 1885.

As the century drew to a close, a parallel series of events reflected the nationalistic and cosmopolitan currents: on the one hand Fashoda, the Spanish-American War, the Boer War, the Boxer Uprising, and the beginning of the German-British naval rivalry; on the other, the founding of the Interparliamentary Union in Paris in 1888, the International Peace Bureau in Bern in 1891, the Hague Peace Conference in 1899, the awarding of the first Nobel Peace Prize in 1901. The cosmopolitan tendency was also evident in the field of science. The hitherto spontaneous and personal contacts within the world of scholarship were expanded through organized forms of international dialogue. Toward the turn of the century, an increasing number of international congresses were held and international associations called into being, particularly in the fields of the natural sciences and medicine, culminating in the founding of the International Association of Academies in 1899.[2] The more solid organization of the international scientific exchange was a concomitant of the intensive institutionalization of the sciences in the Central and Western European countries starting in the last decades of the nineteenth century, and it was influenced as well by the emergence of foreign cultural policy in the modern sense of the word.[3]

The beginnings of organized internationalism in historical scholarship also belong in this context. These were, however, confronted with special difficulties resulting from the deep national rooting of historical thought and writing. Whereas in the field of natural sciences, research results can be exchanged with relative ease and the usefulness of international cooperation in such areas as the exploration of the earth and the seas, astronomy, and the determination of weights and measures is obvious, the results of historical studies to a much larger degree bear the stamp of their respective national, cultural, and social origin. And while the natural sciences tend to condense their findings into brief mathematical formulas, the quintessence of historical research lies in sweeping historical description. Historical presentations gain their highest power of expression by exploiting to the full the specific literary potential provided by their respective national languages. This also applies when the most outstanding historians, such as Gibbon and Voltaire, Ranke and Croce, extend their research and their subject matters beyond national boundaries. World literature is the web of relationships between the principal expressions of individual national literatures. This also is true of history. The deep national and linguistic embedding of historiography explains why even many significant cosmopolitan historians of the various European nations had strong reservations about organizing International Historical Congresses. Of course, before and beyond all organized forms of encounter, there have always been intensive contacts among historians from different nations, founded upon common research interests. Many teacher-student relationships (such as those founded via the international appeal of the seminars of Ranke, Waitz, or Mommsen) have certainly been much more memorable for the participants than membership in international organizations or attendance at congresses. However, the fact that the International Congresses have become an essential element of the historical discipline of today, their difficult beginnings and the political vicissitudes of the twentieth century notwithstanding, can be explained by the following reasons:

1. Historians could not escape the trend toward the formation of international unions. The International Congresses reflect the two opposing tendencies of cosmopolitanism, which relates the historians' cooperation to the idea of peace, and nationalism, which uses the International Congresses as a forum for national and ideological self-promotion. Both tendencies act as a motivation for the staging of International Historical Congresses.
2. At the turn of the century, when it enjoyed its highest world standing, the study of history also experienced an identity crisis. Methodological controversies, which were being waged in nearly all European countries,

remained palpable at the early Congresses, but on the whole only played a subordinate role. Over the decades, however, the struggle for the self-understanding of history became a significant motivating factor for the Congresses. A final question was how to define a fundamental consensus on the theory and method of history, which is necessary in order to ensure that the explosive issues of history can be discussed in a scientific way in spite of theoretical and ideological conflicts. The theoretical determination of such a consensus corresponds to an elementary need of the modern technical world, which, while contracting to a global system of interactions, has at the same time fallen under the apocalyptic threat of potential self-annihilation.

3. Once brought into being, the International Historical Congresses constituted themselves as an organism that in surviving the interruptions caused by two world wars and undergoing a number of transformations, has attained a character and a momentum of its own. Participation is not limited to an elitist circle of historians. The Congresses are part of the continuous democratization of scholarship, progressing since the turn of the century, and of its worldwide expansion; in fact, the Congresses have become mass events. Increasingly, historians from Asian, Pacific, and African countries are taking part. Such a development was apparent from the European beginnings of the International Historical Congresses. It gives rise to an organizational problem that recurs periodically and does not have an obvious solution, namely, that of maintaining scientific standards, i.e., the intellectually selective character of the gatherings, during a process of democratization and globalization. The Historical Congresses are an essential field of experimentation in the search for a symbiosis of science and mass society, i.e., for appropriate modes of interaction between a small number of historical experts looking for mutual exchange and a large number of persons interested in history. The persistent confrontation with this problem and the search for an appropriate structure of the Congress programs lend dynamism and continuity to the work of the ICHS, which has prepared and sponsored the Congresses since 1926. As a result, the ICHS, along with its affiliated international commissions and associations, has become a focal point of the study of history.

Notes

1. R. Lavollée, "Les unions internationales," *Revue d'histoire diplomatique* 1 (Paris, 1887): 333–362, here p. 331.
2. B. Schröder-Gudehus, "Deutsche Wissenschaft und internationale Zusammenarbeit 1914–1928" (Ph.D. diss., University of Geneva, 1966) provides a survey on international scientific cooperation in the second half of the nineteenth century (pp. 35ff.).
3. W. Keylor, *Academy and Community: The Foundation of the French Historical Profession* (Cambridge, Mass., 1975); Ch.-O. Carbonell, *Histoire et historiens: Une mutation idéologique des historiens français 1865–1885* (Toulouse, 1976); D. S. Goldstein, "The Professionalization of History in Britain in the Late Nineteenth and Early Twentieth Centuries," *Storia della Storiografia* (1983): 3–27. For Germany, which was the earliest country to institutionalize historical research and not least for this reason was viewed as a model for other countries, see G. A. Ritter, "Internationale Wissenschaftsbeziehungen und auswärtige Kulturpolitik im deutschen Kaiserreich," *Zeitschrift für Kulturaustausch* 31 (1981): 5–16; B. vom Brocke, "Der deutsch-amerikanische Professorenaustausch: Preußische Wissenschaftspolitik, internationale Wissenschaftsbeziehungen und die Anfänge einer deutschen auswärtigen Kulturpolitik vor dem ersten Weltkrieg," ibid., pp. 128–182; L. Wiese-Schorn, "Karl Lamprechts Pläne zur Reform der auswärtigen Kulturpolitik," ibid., pp. 27–42.

Chapter 2

Prelude in The Hague, 1898

The International Congresses of Historical Sciences do not owe their inception to the academic historical profession. As so often happens in the history of historiography, this new step was initiated from outside. Political motives played a role here, as did the thirst for action and the desire for recognition on the part of the International Congresses' actual initiator, the Frenchman René de Maulde-La Clavière (1848–1902). With a doctorate from the Écoles des Chartes, de Maulde embarked on an administrative career, rising to the rank of subprefect, before he followed the example of many French noblemen and dedicated himself to the aristocratic study of history. He published works on medieval Orléans and Avignon, as well as on sixteenth- and seventeenth-century France, showing particular interest in the person of Louis XII and in diplomatic history. The doyen of the critical study of history in France, Gabriel Monod, passed a favorable judgement on these products of erudite leisure.[1]

Of greater importance for de Maulde's role in historical scholarship, however, was that he provided the initiative for founding two new institutions. In 1886 he launched the Société d'histoire diplomatique (Society for Diplomatic History) in Paris, which still exists today.[2] As secretary-general until 1899, he strongly influenced its structure and character. It was in the Society's journal that he published Lavollée's essay on "Les unions internationales." Inspired by similar ideas, he suggested convening an International Historical Congress in The Hague in 1898. Historical and political interests permeated the aims of the Société d'histoire diplomatique. According to an address by its chairman, Albert Duc de Broglie, on the tenth anniversary of the Society's foundation, it intended to counteract the biased judgement that would be inevitable if diplomatic history were to draw solely upon the sources of one's own country instead of those of all the powers involved. Thus, the Society sought to promote the publication of documents on an international scale. Diplomats, historians, and archivists of various countries were to work together within the Society. In this way, historians could profit from the practical experiences of

---

Notes for this chapter are located on page 11.

diplomats, while diplomats could benefit from the historians' knowledge. And as long as the creation of an international court of arbitration was still a distant dream, it remained the task of diplomats to preserve peace. In this endeavor, the historical study of earlier conflicts could be of assistance.[3]

The Society's goal—linking diplomacy with history, and national considerations with international perspectives—was reflected in its structure. Located in the French foreign ministry, it was supervised by a forty-member administrative council, which included a large number of diplomats and members of the Institut de France. Foreigners could also join the council. Although such membership remained the exception, there were numerous non-Frenchmen among the members of the Society. Furthermore, following the example of other learned societies, a "correspondent" was appointed for each country, who was to transmit contacts and information on research. In 1898, the year of the first International Historical Congress on diplomatic history, the Society had some 500 members in twenty-three countries—in the European states, in Russia and Turkey, in Egypt, Peru, Brazil, Central America, and the United States. The list of members contains a plenitude of illustrious names and titles: kings and members of royal houses,[4] nobles, former diplomats, representatives of the embassies in Paris or even the ambassadors themselves, current or former foreign ministers and foreign ministries as such, politicians and highly placed holders of other professions with historical interests, alongside the directors or high officials of state archives (such as the Royal Archive in Stuttgart and the national archives in Sweden and Russia), and some university libraries. The number of university professors is strikingly small. The speeches in the annual meetings of the Society, as well as the character of its journal and the letters of its secretary-general, transmit the impression of a society of historically interested notables without any serious involvement in scholarly research or affiliation with history departments. De Maulde's letters on the occasion of the International Congress of 1898[5] show how greatly he enjoyed moving within the brilliant aristocratic circles of diplomatic society.

After the Society had celebrated its tenth anniversary in 1897, de Maulde decided to advance its international aspect by staging regular historical congresses. It seems that he began implementing this plan without further consultation with the Society's president, when in September 1897 he turned to a member, the recently named Dutch foreign minister Willem de Beaufort, to suggest that he convene the first congress of this kind to be held in Holland.[6] De Beaufort accepted the suggestion and proposed early September 1898 as a possible date, when the majority and coronation of Crown Princess Wilhelmina were to be celebrated.[7] A Dutch organizing committee was formed under the chairmanship of the state councilor and jurist Asser, a staff member at the foreign ministry, who was a cofounder and member of the Institute for International Law in The Hague. Like his minister, he also belonged to the Society for Diplomatic History. It remained unclear who would ultimately be responsible for the Congress: while de Maulde wanted to avoid naming the

Society as the sponsoring authority, and endeavored to assign responsibility to the Dutch organizing committee, the latter felt that the invitation should be issued in the Society's name. The lack of clarity in this question hampered preparations. In addition, the organizing committee felt it was being drawn into a dubious enterprise, led by a man more interested in showcasing his own person than in staging a solid scholarly conference. This assumption was confirmed by de Maulde's stubborn efforts to persuade highly placed politicians and diplomats to participate in the Congress or to accept honorary memberships. The fact that de Maulde, although without success, attempted to send invitations through diplomatic channels was in keeping with the customs of the period. It was also quite usual for governments to send official delegations if an international scientific event was considered to be sufficiently important.[8] De Maulde's undertaking, however, was apparently not persuasive enough.

De Maulde took no particular pains over the program of the Congress. Aside from a few instructions for the general operation of the Congress—plenary sessions under the chairmanship of the Dutch foreign minister de Beaufort or de Maulde, the right of each country to its own section, as well as the right to use one's own language—there are no traces of thematic considerations in the preparatory correspondence or in the Congress documents. The committee took what it was offered.

The invitations to participate were issued without any system. Apparently de Maulde turned to individual members of his Society or else to various governments requesting that they send delegations. To what extent the leading professional historians were even informed of the planned Congress appears to have been a matter of personal connections between members of the Society and individual historians. In England the response was negligible. By contrast, in Germany the idea of an International Historical Congress was met with lively approval. Georg von Below and Bernhard Erdmannsdörffer, two renowned representatives of nation-centered historiography, were won over for the assembly of a "delegation" of the German historical profession. From the French side, no outstanding historians took part in the Congress. The result was a highly uneven, essentially random gathering of different nations.[9] However, the intended mixture of politics and history was successful. Among the some 300 registered participants, there were more than 100 active or former diplomats, and between sixty and seventy university professors and archivists. The national composition, too, was diverse: the French and Germans had the largest delegations, but alongside historians from other European countries and the United States, one South American, several Japanese, and one Persian took part as well.

The agenda revealed a motley array of isolated topics. Apparently, as Gabriel Monod suspected, some non-French participants, such as the twenty-two German historians (including Erdmannsdörffer, von Below, and such well-known names as Gothein and Delbrück), came to The Hague in the expectation that this was a general historical congress. If, as Monod said, many believed that there would be a debate on the "methodological controversy," i.e., the clash between Lamprecht and his critics,[10] then the presence of German historians such as Gothein and Below, who had both raised their voices in this conflict, may have contributed to this opinion. Unfortunately, neither of their lectures was published in the *Annales internationales d'histoire*, a periodical founded by de Maulde in 1899 for the purpose of reporting on this and subsequent International Congresses.[11] In fact, as far as one can gather from the *Annales* and other journals, problems of historical theory and methodology played no role at this Congress. The historians and amateurs of history assembled in The Hague in the spirit of diplomatic history were apparently not keen to be drawn into the conflict that had erupted in Germany, England, France, and Italy over whether history, in order to become a true science, should concern itself less with the state than with society, less with human actions than with historical laws. The guarded, even unyielding stance the Hague Congress took toward methodological innovations is shown by the reaction to a suggestion of Professor Vesnitsch (Belgrade), who pointed to the importance of the press as a source for the study of public opinion and urged the creation of a central press archive. This application was rejected in the plenary session after the Englishman Frederic Harrison, who participated in the Congress as an official representative of the British government, had stated simply that the press was not a scientifically usable source.[12] Diplomatic records on the other hand, being the classical source of historical studies, were evaluated quite differently. After a series of reports on relevant publications in the various countries had been given during the opening session, a resolution was passed to organize internationalized publications of records,[13] in order to bring about "an examination of historical events which is as objective and impartial as possible and excludes all one-sidedness."[14] The idea itself was not wrong, and in any case it was consistent with the aims attached to this Congress to make an attempt at international cooperation.[15] For this purpose an international bureau was formed with de Maulde as its "director." The plan failed, however, owing to insufficient preparation and the reserve of the governments that were approached on the matter.[16]

The responses to the Congress in the historical journals were quite favorable, although their views varied considerably. In addition to a thorough report in the Swedish *Historisk tidskrift*,[17] there were positive reports by Georg von Below[18] in the *Historische Zeitschrift* and by Gabriel Monod[19] in the *Revue historique*. Below compared the Hague Congress with the biennial meetings of the German historians (Historikertage), which had also recently come into being.[20] He favored the International Congress. At the German meetings, he said, pedagogical questions played too large a role. In fact, the cause for convening the first German congress in 1893 had been the didactic question of whether historical instruction at secondary schools should be relevant to the present day and linked to political goals, as the German Kaiser had demanded at the first national conference on educational policies (Reichsschulkonferenz) in 1890. In addition, Below's opponent Karl Lamprecht had strongly supported the first German meetings. The Society for Diplomatic History and the assembly in The Hague clearly suited Below's conservative tastes better. For him, the "numerous members from diplomatic circles" were "welcome elements," even if their "connection to the historical profession" left much to be desired. Both the composition of the participants and the lectures had been generally superior to those at the German meetings. The latter should take the International Congress as their model in order to upgrade their "relatively low reputation." Nevertheless, Below viewed both institutions as such valuable assets that he recommended continuing them despite the skepticism of some of his colleagues. Of course, no tangible results could be expected from such events: "What they should mainly offer is nothing more than personal interchange and the opportunity to hear a good lecture." In this regard, he held that the Hague Congress had produced, on the whole, a positive outcome.

Monod also thought it worth noting that the anticipated dispute between materialistic and idealistic conceptions of history had failed to materialize. He took a very positive view of the role of the Society for Diplomatic History, which had supplied a favorable framework for the organization of the Congress. Now that the first step had been taken, he suggested broadening the scope of future Congresses beyond diplomatic history, which had however been an excellent choice for the first Congress, because diplomatic courtesy ensured "that there would be no friction resulting from the presence of scholars of different nationalities, languages, and conceptions." In any case, diplomatic history was a good beginning for an "entente intelligente et pacifique." Referring to the first Hague Peace Congress, Monod clearly set his report in the political context of such an "intelligent and peaceful understanding." It had been a splendid idea to choose The Hague as the site of the Congress "for if arbitration among nations should ever become a reality, then Frenchmen and Germans, Englishmen and Russians, Austrians and Hungarians, Spaniards and Americans, Japanese and Chinese could doubtlessly trust the Dutch to manage a tribunal for international conflicts. Then one would see how, in a modified form, Holland would once again assume the great diplomatic role that it so outstandingly played in the seventeenth century, when Grotius laid the foundations of future international law." It was a fortuitous coincidence that the suggestion for a general conference on peace and disarmament had been under discussion in the Russian foreign ministry since March 1898 and that the invitation to the Hague Congress for Diplomatic History was issued on 29 March of the same year.

Notes

1. Obituary of R. de Maulde in *Revue historique* 80 (1902): 81ff. For more biographical information, see obituaries in *Revue d'histoire diplomatique* 16 (1902): 324ff., 346ff.
2. Today: Société d'histoire générale et d'histoire diplomatique.
3. "Discours de M. le Duc de Broglie, Président de la Société, à l'Assemblée Générale du 1er juin 1897," *Revue d'histoire diplomatique* 11, no. 3 (1897): I–VI.
4. The membership list, *Revue d'histoire diplomatique* 13, no. 1 (1899), cites among others the King of Portugal, princes from Denmark and Greece, a Russian Grand Duke, and the Prince of Monaco as honorary members.
5. See archives of Ministerie van Buitenlandse Zaken, A^1; Algemeen Rijksarchief, family archive Asser, 148 and 149.
6. Paris, 14 Sep. 1897, Ministerie van Buitenlandse Zaken, A^1.
7. Concerning this and the following, see documents from the archives of Ministerie van Buitenlandse Zaken, A^1, and Algemeen Rijksarchief, family archive Asser, 148 and 149.
8. See material in Zentrales Staatsarchiv, Merseburg, Rep. 76 V c, Sect. 1, Tit. 11, Teil VI, vol. 7.
9. See report by R. Koser, Director of the Prussian State Archives, 20 April 1899, ibid., and the published reports on the Congress as cited below in note 12; see also the short information in *Historisk Tidsskrift* (Copenhagen, 1897/1899): 576.
10. "Bulletin historique: France/Allemagne," *Revue historique* 68 (1898): 312.
11. "Underrättelser," *Historisk tidskrift* (Stockholm, 1899): 175. The *Annales internationales d'histoire* appeared in 1899 with six issues, which contained the proceedings of the Hague Congress and information on the next Congress. A new series was edited in 1900 with the proceedings of the Paris Congress.
12. *Annales internationales d'histoire: Congrès de La Haye, les 1er, 2, 3 septembre 1898* [hereafter Congress The Hague 1898: *Annales*] (Paris, 1899), pp. LXXXII, LXXXIVff.; T. Westrin, "Den första diplomatisk-historiska kongressen i Haag den 1–4 September 1898," *Historisk tidskrift* (Stockholm, 1898): 267–275, here p. 271f.
13. Congress The Hague 1898: *Annales*, p. LXIX.
14. These were the words of the Baden state archivist von Weech in a petition to the German Chancellor, 3 Jan. 1899. Zentrales Staatsarchiv, Merseburg, Rep. 76 V c, Sect. 1, Tit. 11, Teil VI, vol. 7, pp. 211–213.
15. The idea of editing diplomatic records by an international committee was realized following the Second World War in *Akten der deutschen auswärtigen Politik 1918–1945*, until this undertaking, too, was finally returned to national authority.
16. T. Westrin, W. Sjögren, and E. Wrangel, "Den internationella kongressen för jämförande historia: I Paris den 23–28 juli 1900," *Historisk tidskrift* (Stockholm, 1900): 309–328, here p. 309; report by R. Koser, 20 April 1899, Zentrales Staatsarchiv, Merseburg, Rep. 76 V c, Sect. 1, Tit. 11, Teil VI, vol. 7.
17. Westrin, "Kongressen i Haag," pp. 267–275.
18. "Notizen und Nachrichten. Vermischtes," *Historische Zeitschrift* 82 (1899): 185–187.
19. "Bulletin historique: France/Allemagne," *Revue historique* 68 (1898): 312f.
20. See K. D. Erdmann, "Geschichte, Politik und Pädagogik: Aus den Akten des Deutschen Historikerverbandes," *Geschichte in Wissenschaft und Unterricht* 19 (1968): 2–21; P. Schumann, "Die deutschen Historikertage von 1893–1937. Die Geschichte einer fachhistorischen Institution im Spiegel der Presse" (Ph.D. diss., University of Marburg, 1974).

Chapter 3

ADVOCATES OF COMPARISON

The First Congress, Paris, 1900

The Hague assembly bore the official title of Congrès International d'Histoire Diplomatique. Its initiator regarded it as a first step toward a series of regular congresses of general history. At the opening session in The Hague, de Maulde announced that this was only the beginning: "Today's assembly is our founding date. We are creating a framework for ourselves."[1] He had already given thought to how this should occur. On 17 May 1898 he had transmitted a draft set of statutes to the Dutch foreign minister, de Beaufort, under a title highlighting his own intended role as founder: "Congrès International d'Histoire Diplomatique (Fondateur: M. de Maulde). Statuts."[2] With regard to the organization's history, it is remarkable that he was suggesting an international committee as the future sponsor of the Historical Congresses at this early date. The draft statutes contained a list of eighteen prospective names for this "central committee." They were almost without exception members of the Society for Diplomatic History, and nearly half of them were members of the foreign service or the state administration. Complemented by three additional names, this group then served as the Central Committee and Bureau of the Hague Congress. The committee was composed of members from various nations. The draft statutes designated Paris as its headquarters and French as the language of the general assemblies and official announcements. Regional and local committees would form the central institution's substructure. The congresses' goal should be to treat "in common and in all their controversial aspects the questions of international history in the broadest sense."

It seems that this draft was presented to the participants of the Hague Congress in a somewhat altered form. *The American Historical Review*[3] reported that Paris was proposed as the site of the next meeting, and a self-renewing "académie internationale de l'histoire" made up of twenty outstanding scholars was recommended as the governing body of future Congresses. According to

---

Notes for this chapter begin on page 20.

the minutes of the Hague Congress, however, the draft of the statutes was not discussed in the plenary meetings. Thus, it remained unclear who would be in charge of organizing the next meeting. It seems that de Maulde's suggestions were evaluated very differently by the participants. In a critical vein, von Below advised "that someone else should take charge of things next time," not the Société d'histoire diplomatique, which contained "welcome elements among its numerous members from diplomatic circles," but was not "sufficiently connected with the academic discipline."[4] By contrast, Monod heaped praise on de Maulde and the Society, declaring that the fruits of his efforts would soon be reaped.[5] According to the published minutes, the final assembly of the Hague Congress passed a resolution stating that the next Congress should take place in 1900, without making any reference to the draft statutes, and that the Bureau, i.e., the Central Committee of the Hague Congress, would get to agree on the next site. Bucharest, Bern, Vienna, and Budapest all came up during the meeting; Paris was not included.[6] However, a report by one of the Society's secretaries,[7] probably inspired by de Maulde, went beyond what had been decided in The Hague. It described the statutes as a *fait accompli* and declared that the organization of the next Congress, and no longer just the selection of the site, would be assumed by a central committee in Paris chaired by de Maulde. In the first issue of the *Annales internationales d'histoire*, the next meeting was announced as a "Congrès International d'Histoire Comparée." In addition to international relations, it was to encompass the history of art, literature, natural science, religion, and other fields. Backed by his office as secretary-general of the Society for Diplomatic History, de Maulde seemed set to realize his intentions.

However, it was not to be. De Maulde's headstrong ways had earned him enemies. In fact, he had not even bothered asking all the members of his "central committee" if they wanted to join. The two German historians, Erdmannsdörffer and von Weech, "stated that they had been assigned to the committee as members without their assent and hereby declared their resignation."[8] Most importantly, a deep rift opened up between de Maulde and the Society for Diplomatic History. In 1899, the latter formally denied that it was in charge of organizing the International Congress in Paris. It did not even publish any information about the forthcoming Paris Congress, and later stated that it had nothing whatsoever to do with the International Congresses and wanted nothing to do with them in the future.[9] The *Revue d'histoire diplomatique* reported that "as a result of various incidents" de Maulde had been persuaded to give up his position. Thus, according to a report by the secretaries at the Society's general assembly, power struggles and uncertainties concerning competencies, "which in the past had led to more than one regrettable incident," had been eliminated.[10] De Maulde survived his resignation by only a few years. He died in 1902.

Once de Maulde had resigned, preparations for the Paris Congress proceeded on an entirely different course. Rather than handing the organization of the Congress over to an international body, the French authorities stepped in. The fourth issue of the *Annales internationales d'histoire* informed its readers that the Congress stood under the patronage of the French government, its organization having been entrusted to a French Comité Général under the chairmanship of Gaston Boissier, the secretary of the Académie Française. De Maulde was kept on for a time, but only in a subordinate role as the chairman of a French executive committee. The "central committee" that he had called into being, continued to exist in name, even listing de Maulde as its president, but it played no demonstrable role in the preparation, structure, and actual staging of the Congress. In the official Congress report, the twenty-three names that the committee now encompassed were listed alongside with the eighty-one members of the organizing committee, to which (beyond the "central committee" itself) only Frenchmen belonged.

After all the complications involved in its preparation, the Congress was finally staged within the framework of the Paris World Exposition. This was hardly a coincidence, and the organizers referred to this fact continuously. "Amid this festival of matter," the Congress's president, Gaston Boissier, proclaimed to the historians, "the spirit must also receive its due."[11] In fact, the World Exposition included a series of congresses on philosophy, psychology, social training, ethnography, and other fields. At the time, history was seen as a leading science, a "*science maîtresse*," as the Parisian law scholar Adhémar Esmein called it at the Congress.[12] Now, at the threshold of a new century, it held an unchallenged position alongside the natural sciences and technology.

The Congress for Comparative History had been given a broad program. General and diplomatic history now represented only one section among others for the history of law, economics, science, literature, art, and music. The comparative method should rule supreme. That, at least, was the objective. However, the reality of the Congress fell somewhat short. There were some 800 registrations, but only some 100 to 200 actual participants. Several journals expressed their regret that the English and German historians were almost entirely absent, and that even the French stayed on the sidelines. There were numerous representatives from Eastern Europe, and the discussion of Southeastern European problems gave the Congress a distinct accent.

The Congress did not receive much attention in the historical journals.[13] And yet, if one collects all the impressions recorded in the professional journals and in the impressive volumes of the Congress's documents, it becomes clear that distinctions must be made. The Congress had been framed within a specific methodological concept: comparative history. Whether or not this was realized depended on the individual contributions. The organizing committee had not planned the program in advance, rather, it accepted whatever it was offered. The result was a colorful, motley variety. Yet a few aspects emerge that, unlike in The Hague, highlight the methodological reflection that preoccupied historical thought at the turn of the century.

First of all, there was the repeatedly made and generally unquestioned assertion that history had encompassed and transformed the social sciences and all disciplines of the humanities. The triumph of the historical method, Congress president Boissier declared in his opening address, facilitated contacts between different branches of scholarship and eased mutual understanding even beyond national boundaries.[14] For Esmein, president of the section for comparative legal history, history was the "*science maîtresse*" because its method had had such a potent influence on the related sciences. It is this historicization of thinking in the nineteenth century, as identified by Boissier and Esmein, that is meant by "historicism." It includes the notion that history genuinely and justifiably deepens the awareness of the uniqueness and individuality of one's own nation.[15] But does not historicism, by the nationalization of thinking, lead to a national relativization of absolute values? Working on this problem later on, the German historical theoretician Ernst Troeltsch, in the quest for a European cultural synthesis, envisioned the future path toward it in "overcoming history through history." Boissier was already looking ahead in this direction when he said in his opening address in Paris: "History itself can heal the ills that it has caused." His expectations of history were informed by political optimism, and this attitude was discernable in many of the speeches at the Congress. "More than anything else, the study of history [can and must bring] the peoples closer together."[16] In a similar vein, Esmein said at the opening of the section for comparative religious history: "History, which also plays a social role to the extent that it makes men tolerant and just, that it teaches them that the future stands in solidarity with the past, and that, from the struggles and uncertainties of the present, the light will emerge, just as certainly as the dawn breaks forth from the night," enables us "to comprehend the genius of other peoples and to become aware of the natural and final harmony that will develop between them."[17]

The methodical core of historicism is the critique of sources and records. It is based on the premise that it is possible to pass intersubjectively conclusive judgements on the truth or falsity of concrete statements, independently of all value considerations that may exist as subjective motivations. At the Congress, the French historian Henri Houssaye, a member of the Académie Française and president of the section for general and diplomatic history, described this positivism of facts as the core element of historicism in eloquent terms:

> Facts, facts, facts, which contain within themselves their lesson and their philosophy. The truth, the whole truth, nothing but the truth. Oh, Messieurs, the hunt for documents, the long, yet always too short days spent over heaps of old papers and dusty records, the life that, warm in its gripping reality, emerges from this, the happy good fortune of discoveries, hypotheses confirmed by an authentic letter, a long-pursued problem whose solution suddenly jumps out of a single page, a single line, a single word—you all know how such investigations can take hold of us. You all know these sovereign joys. As far as I am concerned, I have experienced genuinely intoxicating hours of work in the Hôtel Soubise and in the War Archives, magnetically attracted by yellowed and brittle pages from which one can watch history coming to life.[18]

In contrast to this positivism of the critical method, which is an element of historicism, philosophical positivism was critically approached at the Paris Congress in the section on the history of the natural sciences. In a contribution on Auguste Comte's philosophy of science, Gaston Milhaud, professor of the history of science at the University of Montpellier, started from the verdict that Comte, counter to actual scientific development, had believed that the scientific conception of the world had largely come to a close and that, while it could be expanded, it could no longer be altered in its essential parts. This error, Milhaud said, explained Comte's conservative and rigid conception of society, as well as his assertion of a law of three stages governing the progression of history, which had come to an end in a scientific, "positive" age, beyond which he had been unable to imagine further progress leading to fundamentally different knowledge. Milhaud, secretary-general of the Society for Biology, which had been founded by students of Auguste Comte, demonstrated this by citing the impact of the evolutionary theory on biology, to which Comte had closed his eyes because of his excessive positivism.[19] Other contributions by André Lalande,[20] a professor at the Lycée Michelet, and by Daniel Berthelot, demonstrated that the Bacon-Descartes mechanism had no metaphysical validity, but merely represented a method that could not claim to exhaust reality a priori. Instead, scientific progress was achieved by the method of hypothesis formulation. It was an "absurd notion to think that modern science is a kind of closed dogma, finished, complete, without gaps and without fundamental uncertainties."[21]

A plea for the recognition of the hypothesis as an indispensable theoretical element of historical studies was made by the Romanian historian Alexandru Xenopol, rector of the University of Jassy, who together with Nicolae Iorga laid the foundations for modern historical scholarship in Romania. He was one of the pioneers and outstanding exponents of the so-called Daco-Romanic continuity theory, which gained considerable importance for the development of the historical and political self-awareness of the Romanian nation. With his book on the fundamental principles of history, which had appeared one year before the Paris Congress, he had gained recognition as a historical theoretician even beyond Romania's borders.[22] Xenopol held firm to a positivism of facts and rejected all doubts that science had its foundations "*in re*" and not just "*in intellectu.*" Science was "the knowledge of reality, a mirror reflecting the phenomena of this world in the human mind."[23] But he rejected nomothetic historical positivism, i.e., the assumption that history could only be called a science if, like the natural sciences, it endeavored to discover the laws ruling the temporal sequence of historical facts. That is why he disavowed the positivistic philosophical tradition that Condorcet, Comte, and Buckle had stood for. The use of the hypothesis as an epistemological tool of historiography was for Xenopol not an attempt at constructing historical laws, which in his opinion did not exist anyway, but rather the postulation of a causal connection between ascertainable individual facts. In Paris he demonstrated this idea using his favorite example of "Daco-Romanic continuity": Building upon the undeniable historical reality of Roman Dacia before the withdrawal of the Romans in the year AD 270, and the first historically proven appearance of Romanians in the thirteenth century, he used a series of hypothetical arguments to postulate a continuity between the Daco-Romans and the Romanians in the intervening eight or nine centuries, during which the historical development in this region could not be illuminated by any documentary evidence.[24]

The validity of this hypothesis is debatable, and it continues to be debated to the present day. Hungarian participants at the Congress, particularly Maurice Darvaï, opposed Xenopol vehemently.[25] According to Darvaï, Xenopol's historical-theoretical hypothesis really boiled down to a political thesis, and as such it needed to be confronted with "the positive scientific method, based upon proven facts and written documents." Referring to Hungarian documents from the twelfth to fourteenth centuries, Darvaï put forward his counterthesis that the continuity theory was false and that the origin of the Romanian nation had to be traced to an influx of romanized Walachians from the south. Eight decades later, this thesis and counterthesis once more played a role at the fifteenth International Congress of Historical Sciences in Bucharest in 1980. As this Parisian prelude showed, Clio has always been a fickle mistress when nationalistic claims compete with one another.

The Paris Congress had been devoted by its organizers to comparative history, "*histoire comparative*," which is concerned with methodically conducted comparisons; yet most of the Paris contributions had nothing to do with it. There were a few studies, however, and they deserve our attention for their exemplary character. The president of the section on comparative legal history, Adhémar Esmein, characterized the comparative method as a "*science d'observation*" that was predestined to thoroughly transform jurisprudence, apparently as an extension of historical hermeneutics. Comparative methods, he said, should be used not only in the social sciences, which are concerned with present times, but also for the exploration of the past.[26]

A classic example of the application of this method in the field of comparative art history was presented by Georg Dehio, professor in Strasbourg, who had received his training as a historian in the school of the constitutional historian Georg Waitz. Although Dehio did not attend the conference, he sent a contribution on the influence of French art on Germany in the thirteenth century. He practiced "observational science" in a meticulous comparison of the development of the Gothic style in France and Germany in its many variations and peculiar national manifestations, thereby demonstrating the leading creative role of France in that century. He placed the Strasbourg Cathedral and the splendid sculptures of Bamberg and Naumburg—characteristic manifestations "of the German nature and art," as Goethe once said—into the context of French influences. Dehio's statements, which were previews from still unpublished studies, impinged on national self-conceptions. Once people in the Romantic era had learned to admire the long-despised Gothic style, its origin was reclaimed by various peoples. "In England," Dehio said, "Gothic style became English, in Germany it became German. Today no person whose opinion counts can deny that Gothic art had its origin in France, and that from there it spread into other countries. It is a tribute to the scientific spirit of our age that the English and the Germans have committed themselves more strongly to this truth than the French, who, after all, should show the greatest interest."[27]

While Dehio compared two peoples in a specific historical period, the French literary historian Ferdinand Brunetière, a member of the Académie Française, took a broader perspective with regard to literary history. His splendid lecture, delivered at the opening of the Congress on 23 July 1900 at the Collège de France, dealt with the coherence of European literature[28] and was the most impressive manifestation of the methodological intentions underlying the Paris Congress. Brunetière compared Italian, Spanish, French, English, and German literature in regard to the specific contribution each had made to European literature, and arranged the high points of each national literary development into a chronological scheme corresponding to the indicated sequence of countries. By doing so he generated an image of European literature that did not rest on generalized abstractions, but depicted itself as a developmental path deriving from the peculiarities of the European national literatures. Brunetière sought to link literary criticism with history. Since the nineteenth century had explored the national literatures, he said, it was up to the twentieth century to write a comparative literary history. Sensitivity to national peculiarities was not irreconcilable with European solidarity. On the contrary, it was its true foundation. And conversely, national histories could only really be recognized as such if they were compared with one another: "You only can define yourself by comparing yourself."[29]

The comparative study of history was a path toward historical synthesis. Thus, it was in keeping with the aim of the Congress that the Frenchman Henri Berr was given the opportunity to present his newly founded *Revue de synthèse historique* in the section for the comparative history of science.[30] The founding of this journal was an event in the history of historiography. It committed itself to critical research on facts, as it had been defined by Gabriel Monod a quarter century earlier as the aim of the *Revue historique*.[31] At the same time, the new journal also sought contact with sociology. The desired historical synthesis was primarily a synthesis of methods, of hermeneutics and the comparative method, of historiography and sociology. Neither method by itself sufficed for the study of historical reality. That meant demarcation in both directions. There was delimitation from a research persisting in a positivism of facts on the one hand: "The dust of facts is nothing. According to an old formula, there is no science without generalization…. The collector of facts should not be paid more respect than the collector of stamps or shells." On the other hand, there was delimitation from sociology, particularly Durkheim and his journal *Année sociologique*, which he had founded in 1896: "As justified and important as sociology may be, does it entirely explain history? We do not believe it.... Sociology is the exploration of what is social in history: but is everything social? The role of individuals, the role of the great historical personalities, can they be neglected entirely?... The more one studies the higher forms of society, the more the significance of that which is individual perhaps grows, precisely as a result of social progress." The methodological discussion should not become a purpose unto itself in his journal, Berr said. Over time, following the clarification of basic questions, it would provide space for studies on concrete historical facts and events—studies in which the power of analysis would be combined with the spirit of synthesis. This programmatic appeal ended with a pledge to humanity, which a historiography conceived in such a way should serve: "The ideal politician is the perfect historian."[32]

What some of the other participants of the Congress presented in the way of politics appears less ideal. There were voices that sought to enlist history in the service of an unquestioned colonialism, and even some that sounded like a prelude to fascist ideas. In a contribution on "Comparative Legal History and France's Colonial Expansion," Émile Louis Marie Jobbé-Duval of the law department of the University of Paris recommended that the institutions of "backward peoples" be incorporated into comparative legal studies. The political usefulness was obvious: "Comparative legal history can provide colonization with the most valuable of services."[33] He ended with an appeal to those responsible for the training of colonial officials to arrange for courses on comparative legal history so that officials would not be confused by the apparent originality of native customs in their administrative districts.

Vicomte de Marolles, the president of the Association des publicistes chrétiens, took advantage of the section for comparative social history to present an anti-Semitic plea for the abolition of democracy, which, he asserted, merely promoted socialism and a dog-eat-dog struggle while opening the door of economic life to Jewish influences.[34] He was of the opinion that it was time to return to a corporative order, which would prevent anarchy and, like the former monarchy, guarantee peace and prosperity. Justin Godart, a lawyer at the court of appeals in Lyon, rejected this propaganda for the goals of the Action Française, which had been founded two years previously. He demonstrated that the proponents of a corporative order had fallen victim to a romantic distortion of pre-Revolutionary corporative society. The guild system, he said, had been equally unable to prevent conflicts of interest and social struggles, and the political, economic, and social conditions of the present prohibited a renewal of the pre-Revolutionary corporative order.[35]

Looking at the Congress as a whole, one is impressed by the way confidence in the future set the tone at the threshold of the twentieth century. This mood asserted itself in the self-confidence of historical scholarship in its search for new methods, as well as in the conviction that historiography was a servant of progress and reconciliation among peoples.

Notes

1. Congrès The Hague 1898: *Annales*, p. XXV.
2. Ministerie van Buitenlandse Zaken, Den Haag, A[1].
3. "Notes and News," *American Historical Review* 6 (1898/99): 201.
4. "Notizen und Nachrichten. Vermischtes," *Historische Zeitschrift* 82 (1899): 186f.
5. "Bulletin historique: France/Allemagne," *Revue historique* 68 (1898): 313.
6. Congrès The Hague 1898: *Annales*, p. LXXXIII.
7. *Revue d'histoire diplomatique* 13 (1899): 118ff.
8. H. J. Hüffer, *Lebenserinnerungen*, 2nd ed. (Berlin, 1914), p. 393; letters from Weech to Regierungsrat Kuntzen, 22 June 1899 (Zentrales Staatsarchiv, Merseburg, Rep. 76 V c, Sect. I, Tit. 11, Teil VI, vol. 7) and from Erdmannsdörffer to the president of the organizing committee for the 1900 Congress, 7 March 1900 (Zentrales Staatsarchiv, Potsdam, Erdmannsdörffer Papers 3, no. 1).
9. "Notizen und Nachrichten," *Historische Zeitschrift* 82 (1899): 381; introductory letter of the Society's secretaries E. Rott and Marquis de Barral Montferrat, 2 pages, in *Revue d'histoire diplomatique* 15 (1901).
10. "Rapport des secrétaires," *Revue d'histoire diplomatique* 14 (1900): 324.
11. *Congrès International d'Histoire Comparée, tenu à Paris du 23 au 28 juillet 1900: Procès-verbaux sommaires* [hereafter Congress Paris 1900: *Procès-verbaux*] (Paris, 1901), p. 15.
12. *Annales internationales d'histoire: Congrès de Paris 1900*, 7 vols. (Paris, 1900). Reprint in 2 vols. by Kraus Reprint (Nendeln/Liechtenstein, 1972) [hereafter: Congress Paris 1900: *Annales*], vol. 1, 2nd section, p. 8.
13. Thorough reports are to be found in "Notizen und Nachrichten," *Historische Vierteljahrschrift* 4 (1901): 155–157; *Revue de synthèse historique* 1 (1900): 196ff.; Westrin, Sjögren, and Wrangel, "Kongressen i Paris," pp. 309–328. *Historische Zeitschrift* and *Revue historique* ignored the Congress entirely.
14. *Revue de synthèse historique* 1 (1900): 203f.
15. A. Esmein in Congress Paris 1900: *Annales*, vol. 1, 2nd section, p. 5f.
16. G. Boissier in Congress Paris 1900: *Procès-verbaux*, p. 15.
17. A. Esmein in Congress Paris 1900: *Annales*, vol. 1, 2nd section, p. 5f.
18. Congress Paris 1900: *Annales*, vol. 1, first section, p. 6.
19. Congress Paris 1900: *Annales*, vol. 2, 5th section, pp. 15ff.
20. "L'interprétation de la nature dans le Valerius Terminus de Bacon," ibid., pp. 1ff.
21. Report on Berthelot's speech in "L'Histoire aux Congrès de 1900," *Revue de synthèse historique* 1 (1900): 206. His paper "Sur l'utilité de l'histoire des sciences dans l'enseignement de la physique et de la chimie" is not included in the proceedings of the Congress.
22. A. Xenopol, *Les principes fondamentaux de l'histoire* (Paris, 1899); in the following, the 2nd edition is used that appeared under the altered title *La Théorie de l'histoire* (Paris, 1908).
23. Ibid., p. 96.
24. Congress Paris 1900: *Annales*, vol. 1, first section, pp. 39ff.
25. Ibid., pp. 107ff.
26. Congress Paris 1900: *Annales*, vol. 1, 2nd section, p. 5f.
27. Congress Paris 1900: *Annales*, vol. 2, 7th section, p. 140f.
28. "La littérature européenne," Congress Paris 1900: *Annales*, vol. 2, 6th section, pp. 5ff.
29. Congress Paris 1900: *Annales*, vol. 2, 6th section, p. 36.
30. Berr's comments were not recorded in the Congress proceedings. For the following I am making use of his introductory essay "Sur notre programme" in the first issue of *Revue de synthèse historique* (1900).
31. "Avant-propos," *Revue historique* 1 (1876): 1f. On the history of historiography in France at the end of the nineteenth century, see Carbonell, *Histoire et historiens*, esp. pp. 495ff.

On Berr's journal, see M. Siegel, "Henri Berr's 'Revue de synthèse historique,'" *History and Theory* 9 (1970): 322–334.
32. Berr, "Sur notre programme," pp. 1–8.
33. Congress Paris 1900: *Annales*, vol. 1, 2nd section, p. 118.
34. "Considérations historiques sur les bienfaits du régime corporatif," Congress Paris 1900: *Annales*, vol. 1, 3rd section, pp. 13ff.
35. "Les corporations d'arts et métiers ont-elles créé et maintenu la paix sociale?" Ibid., pp. 19ff.

Chapter 4

DEBATES ON METHODOLOGY

Rome, 1903

From Paris the congress idea passed in a roundabout way to Rome. It is not entirely clear who made the decision to stage the next Congress in the Eternal City. The Parisian and Roman interpretations conflict. The official report on Paris recorded that other countries besides Italy were named at the closing session and that the assembly had given the "Bureau," i.e., the organizers of the Paris Congress, full authority to decide. But according to the Rome Congress report it was the full assembly of the Congress participants in Paris who made the decision to reconvene in Italy in 1902, either in Venice or in Rome.[1] Long beforehand, Italian scholars had come up with the idea to celebrate the new *seculum* with historians from all over the world. A circle of distinguished historians in Naples was particularly devoted to the idea. An executive committee, which included Benedetto Croce, gathered under the supervision of the ancient historian and director of the Naples archaeological museum, Ettore Pais, a pupil and friend of Theodor Mommsen. An invitation, which he issued in October 1900, only a few months after the Paris Congress, described the plan: Picking up on the Paris Congress's demand for comparative historiography, and hoping for an intensification of international scientific cooperation, the theory and methodology of historiography were to stand in the foreground of interest. The value of an International Congress was beyond doubt since contemporary historiography, "transcending national boundaries, seeks its best aid in comparison." Alongside two sections for ancient and medieval/modern history, a third section should be created to discuss the "lively controversies on the factors of history, on the theory of race, on historical materialism and economic history, on the relationships between history and sociology."[2]

However, the organizational work led to conflicts among the Italian historians and ultimately to Pais's resignation, so that the Congress, which had originally been planned for 1902 and to which the invitations had already

---

Notes for this chapter begin on page 38.

been issued, had to be canceled. Pais's unforthcoming, authoritarian nature may have played a role in this. The main reason, however, were disputes on a matter that deeply affected national feelings in Italy. The issue at stake was the prehistoric and archaic history of Rome. Pais, who had caused a sensation with the first sections of his "History of Rome" a few years earlier,[3] was one of the strongest critics of the traditional view of Roman history. A pupil of Mommsen in Berlin, he applied what contemporaries characterized as the "German" method of scientific source criticism. In particular, he radically challenged the standard Italian notions of the history of Rome before the third century BC. Scholars from the German Archaeological Institute in Rome were also drawn into the public debate. The conflict had received additional fuel through the discovery of the "lapis niger" on the Forum in 1899 and its controversial interpretations.[4] Pais's most powerful opponent was the linguist Luigi Ceci, a member of the executive committee of the Rome Congress. After the argument over the interpretation of the "lapis niger" had calmed down, the conflict between the Italian scholars flamed up once more in connection with Pais's reorganization of the Faliscan Museum in Naples, and because of the fact that Pais had allowed the German professors Helbig and Hülsen from the German Archaeological Institute in Rome to participate in the work of the executive committee of the International Congress. The *American Historical Review* had this to say: "In January 1902, an announcement of the indefinite postponement of the Congress was issued in consequence of great differences of opinion which had arisen between members of the executive committee. In Italy considerable mortification was felt over what some higher-minded people have declared to be nationally unacceptable."[5]

Some German journals were more frank. The *Internationale Wochenschrift für Wissenschaft, Kunst und Technik* wrote that Ettore Pais had been treated almost like a traitor. "The recriminations that Pais experienced due to his Germanophile stance were also transferred to the organization of the forthcoming Congress, and the unscrupulous opponents achieved so many rejections to the executive committee that the latter dropped Pais and postponed the Congress by one year."[6] The sympathy shown to Pais among German ancient historians is also evidenced by a confidential statement that Eduard Meyer sent to the board of the Verband deutscher Historiker (Association of German Historians), while Pais was still presiding over the organizing committee. Meyer spoke in favor of sending a large German delegation to the Congress, "since those elements which are striving for close contact with Germany, are in leading positions, particularly Ettore Pais (in sharp contrast to the anti-German efforts which have recently manifested themselves in the archaeological field and have been expressed by Ceci and in the discussions on the ancient inscription on the Forum)."[7]

The French ambassador in Rome considered the conflict over Pais to be so important that he reported to Foreign Minister Delcassé as follows: After the Italian rivals had challenged Pais's competence to represent Italian scholarship at the Congress, bad luck would have it that the Germans intervened. They succeeded in profoundly wounding Italian *amour-propre*. On the other hand, the ambassador felt compelled to accuse the Italian archaeologists of regarding everything associated with their country's past as their own personal property. This was "a chauvinism of a special kind, under which the archaeological missions maintained by various nations often suffer."[8]

It was the Italian government that paved over these start-up problems and made the Congress happen. First, it transferred the responsibility for preparation and management to Pasquale Villari, the president of the Roman Academia dei Lincei and the Istituto Storico Italiano. As a senator, Villari was well acquainted with public life, as minister of education he had been involved in the reform of the Italian school system, and he enjoyed international prestige as a recognized Savonarola and Machiavelli scholar. Next, Italian diplomacy was mobilized to tout the Congress.[9] After an interministerial exchange of opinions in Berlin on how to handle the Italian invitation, Germany decided to send five internationally renowned scholars as official representatives: Gierke, Wilamowitz, Harnack, Bücheler, Kehr.[10] The Italian foreign ministry placed its bureaucratic machinery at the disposal of the Congress's organization. The latter was in the hands of Giacomo Gorrini, head of department and director of the archives, an energetic and prudent man who referred to himself as a pupil of Villari and of the German medieval scholar Harry Breßlau. He was a member of the Société d'histoire diplomatique and had been formally involved in the organization of the Paris Congress as a member of de Maulde's "*Comité international permanent.*" In 1900 he had been appointed the Congress's secretary-general. Some letters from Gorrini to Villari have been discovered that show the direction in which he now wanted to maneuver the Congress. Although his name was first suggested by the Paris international committee—i.e., the circle around de Maulde[11]—Gorrini called for strict national control of the program. He found it difficult to cooperate with the Paris committee "because they intend to destroy our dignity by collecting the contributions themselves, publishing themselves our Congress reports in France, only leaving us the executive, material part and keeping the leadership for themselves.… We do not want to be dictated to in our own house! While we wish to be obliging to all, we refuse to let foreigners organize a Congress in Rome!"[12] He had a low opinion of The Hague and Paris. The Paris Committee's two Congresses had "discredited" themselves, he said. This was hardly a fair assessment. And yet, the efforts of the Italian government and scholars brought forth a Congress whose splendor and attractiveness indeed eclipsed its two predecessors.

What city could have provided a more spectacular scenery for a meeting of historians! With its Capitoline Hill, upon which the Congress was opened in the presence of the king and many representatives of the state; the Forum, which attracted ancient and modern historians in droves; with the Palatine Hill, in whose gardens and ruins the government presented the participants with a lively evening festival.[13] To be sure, the city's historical and artistic sights, the exhibits, concerts, receptions, and not least the attractive subsidized train and ship fares helped contribute to the fact that of the more than 2,000 registered persons from eighteen countries only a few hundreds participated in actual scholarly work. However, alongside President Pasquale Villari himself, these included such significant figures as Benedetto Croce from Italy, Ludo Moritz Hartmann from Austria, Paul Meyer, Vidal de la Blache, and Gabriel Monod from France, and James Bryce and Frederick Pollock from England. The German delegation, which was particularly numerous and, like that of France, included all the significant historical institutions, counted Adolf von Harnack, Otto Gierke, Paul Kehr, and Ulrich von Wilamowitz in its ranks. Focal points on the edge of the Congress were the French, Austrian, and Prussian historical institutes under their directors Abbé Duchesne, Ludwig von Pastor, and Aloys Schulte, and the German Archaeological Institute under the direction of Christian Hülsen.

Alongside the Italian foreign and education ministers and the mayor of Rome, the aged Theodor Mommsen was chosen as the Congress's honorary president *in absentia*—a fine tribute to the great historian half a year before his death, coming from a city to which he had dedicated his life's work. Mommsen, "the glory of Germany, in which Rome honors the meritorious depicter of its history and its antiquities," had been personally and urgently invited early on by the Italian minister of education.[14] Because of his great age, Mommsen did not want to make a firm commitment so long in advance. However, he was extremely pleased at the thought of participating in such an assembly.[15] A letter by Mommsen to Pais contained a guarded profession of the great common task of the historians that is impressive in its simplicity: "The hope of my youth: to see the present civilization united in order to study that of the past ages and, within the boundaries of my talent, to contribute to this immortal work, is perhaps not entirely a dream and illusion."[16]

Rome, the site of the Congress, was not only the capital of the young, secularized Italian nation-state, but also of the Roman Catholic Church. Relations were still nonexistent between the Quirinal and the Vatican, where the Pope had viewed himself as a prisoner ever since the Franco-Prussian War of 1870/71, when Rome was included into the Italian nation-state as its predestined capital. The Vatican had still not granted Italian Catholics the permission to participate in parliamentary elections. While these tensions did not detract from the Congress, they hovered in the atmosphere. In any case, Ludwig von Pastor, author of the great history of the Popes, felt the tension. As a loyal son of his church he had wanted to write a "Catholic papal history" as an alternative to the Protestant Leopold von Ranke's classic work on the Renaissance Popes.[17] As director of the Austrian Historical Institute, he was elected as the fifth vice-president of the Congress after having turned to Villari for support, alongside the four who had originally been designated—Harnack (Berlin), Meyer (Paris), Bryce (London), Modestov (St. Petersburg).[18] This was a friendly gesture toward Austria. But at the same time, it meant that one of the most loyal servants of the Roman Church had entered the inner circle of a Congress sponsored by the Italian state! From the point of view of the Church, this led to a problem of protocol when Pastor was invited to the royal table in his function as a vice-president of the Congress. Pastor himself said that he had never experienced greater embarrassment. He asked the Pope for permission. Leo XIII, a friend of history who had opened the Vatican archives, showed understanding. "Pastor could not act differently," he is supposed to have said. Monsignore Duchesne, the director of the French Institute, experienced similar difficulties.[19] It was still a long way to the later cooperation of the Vatican historians in the ICHS, and to the solemn reception given by Pope Pius XII to the International Congress in Rome in 1955.

The program of the Congress was very broad, as it had been in Paris as well. The lectures in history of states and peoples were surrounded by a garland of sessions dealing with archaeology and classical philology, the history of law, economics, philosophy, religion, and the natural sciences. This time, there was no leading methodological topic like comparative history to serve as a focal point, as had been intended in Paris and by the Naples organizing committee under Pais. As long as he paid his fee, each participant could present a "*tema*," which was then discussed, or a "*communicazione*," pending approval by the Congress's executive committee.

The "themes" largely consisted of applications for resolutions, which were presented in great number and concerned a wide range of requests regarding editorial and bibliographical issues and the preservation of historical monuments. Following a lecture by Gorrini, the desire was formulated to give access to archival material sooner and on equal standards in the various countries.[20] The Austrian historian Franz Pribram suggested the publication of an international bibliography of historical studies on the model of the bibliography of natural sciences supervised by the Royal Society in London.[21] First preparatory steps followed, but the realization of this project was left to the ICHS, which released the first volume in 1930. There also were discussions on the creation of an "association internationale des sociétés d'histoire" similar to the one considered by de Maulde, although no concrete suggestions emerged.[22] The desire for joint guidelines on the publication of papyri was one of the more practical items on the historians' wish list, and there was a touchingly unrealistic motion to develop universal pronunciation guidelines for Latin in English, French, Italian, and German schools. There were still philologists who opined that a Latin that was articulated the same way everywhere could once again "become the international language of scholars and perhaps also of the educated classes."[23]

The Italian participants at the Congress reacted violently when a matter was brought up concerning the relationship between established, institutionalized research and private scholarly initiatives. At issue was a reprinting of the venerable *Rerum Italicarum Scriptores* by Muratori, the "padre della storia italiana," a work of national significance in united Italy. A publisher, Scipione

Lapi, was financing the reprint. Scholarly supervision lay in the hands of Vittorio Fiorini and the influential literary historian Giosuè Carducci. Several volumes had already appeared. The editors and the publisher would have liked to receive some encouragement by the Congress to continue the undertaking, and proposed a corresponding motion. But they did not reckon with the Istituto Storico Italiano, which had been founded two decades earlier for the precise purpose of opening up Italian historical sources. Its staff pointed to the Institute's work on a parallel project and to manuscripts located there that were indispensable for a critical edition. However, the motion was favored by "the young historians of the world outside of the academies, who were displeased by the deliberate slowness of the Istituto Storico Italiano."[24] Both the publisher and the Institute received subsidies from the government. The competition was obvious. Now the president of the Historical Institute, Pasquale Villari, in his additional capacity as president of the Roman Congress, struck the petition by the "Muratori" publishers from the agenda. However, his opponents rejected the procedural regulations by which he justified this decision. Hotheaded debates ensued among the Italians. The foreign participants did not wish to take a position on this inter-Italian dispute. Thus, in the end, a vote was passed showing appreciation for the new edition of the "Muratori" without naming the private publisher or the Institute.

In several published commentaries and private letters one encounters the opinion that nothing of any real value emerged from the Congress. The greatest skepticism regarding the scholarly results came from Germany and England,[25] while the French, for instance Gabriel Monod, responded positively.[26] Nevertheless, everyone agreed that the journey to Rome had been worth the effort and that the Congress was a success for the organizers. In addition, there was a prevailing opinion—whether in a spirit of affirmation or resignation—that such international mass events should now be viewed as a permanent institution. Of course, these events never entail any research, and one can just as easily read the papers at home. But the fact that the new phenomenon of International Historical Congresses cannot be seen exclusively in terms of immediate results—aside from the undisputed pleasure of talking directly to colleagues from all over the world—was already evident in the tenor of Pasquale Villari's opening speech.[27]

Villari placed historiography into the general context of cultural development in the age of nationalism. He described the history of Italian unification in the nineteenth century as a striking example of the connection between the formation of national consciousness and national historiography. If, however, the development of nations in the twentieth century was heading toward denser international relationships and larger federations, as he thought, then history could not help but be drawn into this evolution. This would occur all the more as new methodological directions made themselves felt within the study of history itself. Over long periods of time, historians had mainly dealt with great, spectacular political events such as diplomatic relations, revolutions, and wars, i.e., they had concerned themselves more with the surface than with the inner organism of society. For some time, however, they had also been attempting to penetrate more deeply into the interior. In the study of history, too, the effort to move from a "descriptive to a comparative anatomy" was becoming evident. It was no longer enough to "know what happened." It rather was of importance "to know why it happened." With these allusions to Lamprecht's critique of Ranke,[28] Pasquale Villari appealed to the willingness of the international historians assembled in Rome to explore new paths of knowledge. "Today," he declared, "we are all convinced that the only way to understand ourselves and the society in which we live is in collecting all the elements of the past. History is the only solid foundation of social science."[29] From this insight, he drew the conclusion that it was becoming increasingly urgent to explain the history of one people through the history of other peoples. And yet, this declaration of belief in a comparative method open to the world and to a collaboration of historians beyond national boundaries did not lead him to make optimistic predictions.

Indeed, a dark undertone lurked beneath the celebratory mood of this speech:

> No one can foresee what consequences there will be, what problems will emerge to face the statesman and the scholar, what new dangers and what wars will arise. It is true that we here are wending our way within this dark labyrinth—through this chaos of peoples, as it has been called—cheerfully and quietly. But the pioneers and originators of the French Revolution were also quiet. Based on the works of the philosophers, they anticipated a peaceful development of society; and even when the earth was opening beneath their feet, they still hoped for the imminent triumph of justice, of brotherhood and peace. Instead, rivers of blood flowed. As Tocqueville put it so rightly, never was any such event more inevitable, more carefully prepared, and yet so completely unforeseen.[30]

How this tone differed from the optimism that the Paris Congress had proclaimed to the world just three years earlier! But whatever destiny the future might have had in store for the world, Villari was certain of the "unità intrinseca della storia" particularly for the modern peoples. From this point of view, questions concerning the practical use of such a Congress faded into the background, although Pasquale Villari did not omit them; he hoped that international cooperation would facilitate the preparation of bibliographies and source editions. A more appropriate question for the evaluation of this and the following International Historical Congresses—as confirmed by Villari's speech—is that of the self-conception and methodological consciousness that they express.

The Roman Congress was first and foremost a display of those undeniably proven methods that had been developed by critical historical research and archaeology in the nineteenth century, the great age of historical thought and writing. From among the multitude of presentations, we will single out three characteristic examples from the fields of archaeology, biographical-intellectual history, and New Testament text criticism that, according to the reports, particularly impressed the audience. On the opening day, against the backdrop of the Forum Romanum, the just completed reconstruction of parts of the "forma urbis," a map of the city from the time of the Severians chiseled into many hundreds of marble slabs, was presented to the public in a ceremonial act performed in the presence of the royal couple. The speech by Rodolfo Lancini, who had supervised the reconstruction work with the assistance of the German Archaeological Institute, is a classic example of a sober, factual report on the destruction of the old map, on the painstaking classification of the fragments, of which only a very small fraction had been discovered at all (and of which only an even smaller fraction could be properly placed), and on the fragmentary but historically informative result of this gargantuan puzzle.[31]

Gabriel Monod's brilliant lecture on "Michelet and Italy" represented a different type of historical communication.[32] This preliminary study for his later Michelet biography united the two methodological and stylistic demands that Monod had presented when he founded the *Revue historique*: precise documentation for each statement of facts combined with literary quality.[33] According to Monod, Michelet's experience of Italy represented a scholarly awakening. His thinking was set on fire by two great Italian minds, Vergil and Vico. Monod described this encounter in a convincing manner and presented a solid piece of historiographical and biographical research. His lecture also had a political aspect, however, related to a specific moment in the relations between France and Italy. Monod invoked a historically rooted solidarity between the two nations, whose fates he saw as being more closely linked than those of any other nations. The influence of the Italian Renaissance on France and France's support of the Italian Risorgimento, with which Michelet had passionately sympathized, appeared in his lecture as the essential moments in the relationship between the two peoples. In depicting this scene, he avoided everything that could have recalled conflicts between the two nations seemingly predestined for each other by Providence: the fact that, with Charles VIII's invasion in 1494, a secular struggle had arisen between the French crown and the House of Habsburg over dominance in Italy; that a reunited Italy was kept from its capital of Rome by Napoleon; and that only recently had a ten-year trade war between France and Italy been brought to a conclusion.

Now, within the power constellation of Europe at the beginning of the twentieth century, the needle of the historical compass was swinging toward a political rapprochement between the two states. In December 1900, French and Italian colonial imperialism in North Africa had found a compromise by granting each other a free hand, for France in Morocco and for Italy in Libya. And two years later, in November 1902, Italy—though belonging to a defensive alliance with Germany and Austria—guaranteed its neutrality toward France even in the case "that, as the result of an immediate challenge, France would see itself compelled to declare war unilaterally, in defense of its honor or its security."[34] Monod's speech on Michelet reflected this power-political convergence of the two laicistic states. Referring to Michelet's view that Italy, heiress of Rome, and France, harbinger of the message of the Revolution, had to bring the world a moral doctrine, he exclaimed: "Might the two nations, by him linked together through the same love, adopt this desire of Michelet as a legacy to which they must remain true." Enlisting Clio into the service of politics and inspired by ideas deriving from national interest and self-awareness: this was happening everywhere, and in the twentieth century it occurred even more unabashedly than in the educated world of the nineteenth. It should be noticed, however, that the nationalist tendencies and the European-cosmopolitan current of the time were expressed in the same breath. Monod reported that Michelet, "who wanted to teach France to the French as a dogma and a revelation," felt deeply linked to all European peoples, not only to his beloved Italians. "'From Germany,' he said, 'I received the scholarly strength that allows me to pursue my questions to their very foundation. Germany is the bread of the strong. It has founded me on Kant, it has made me heroic and it has given me greatness through Beethoven, Luther, Grimm, Gans, Herder.'... He loved England, toward which he sometimes showed himself stern to the point of injustice, because it gave him Shakespeare; Poland had given him Mickiewicz as a friend, Russia had given him Herzen. He glorified the Russian martyrs of 1825, just as he glorified the Polish martyrs of 1795 and 1830. His second wife, the daughter of a Creole from Louisiana, linked him with America."[35]

Inspired by Michelet's enthusiasm, this was an invocation of the unity of European culture against the political background of intensifying national antagonism! In the period of the first three International Historical Congresses, this great French scholar, whose words carried weight, became one of the most zealous promoters of the idea to arrange such bazaars of historical scholarship regularly and, if possible, to support them with a specific organization. It was also Monod who suggested that the next Congress should be held in Germany.[36]

Germany, the land of the Lutheran Reformation, was a center of historical-critical Bible research. The methods of biblical textual criticism and textual history have stimulated the development of a hermeneutic scientific treatment of historical texts in general. Adolf von Harnack, a researcher of early church history and one of the most significant exponents of critical Bible studies, was also one of the outstanding figures present at the Rome Congress. Vice-president of the Congress, he was elected with standing ovations as honorary president of the section on the history of philosophy and religion. Here, he presented a highly acclaimed report on his research on the origins of the New Testament.[37] Harnack had taught at the Berlin University since 1888. The appointment of this liberal and, in the eyes of many orthodox Lutherans, dogmatically suspect theologian had led to a violent confrontation between the Protestant Supreme Church Council and the Prussian Ministry of Education, which had been conducted with lively public participation. However, the orthodox forces had failed in their attempt to bar Harnack's ascent to a chair of the theological faculty, thanks to the resistance of the minister of education, who had the support of Bismarck and the young emperor William II. Harnack's appointment amounted to a declaration of belief in the freedom of historical studies and in the duty of the government to protect it from dogmatic interference. Harnack's name became a symbol. His attitude toward the topic of the lecture he delivered in Rome was characterized by the historian's critical distance from the holy text, which he objectified like any other historical relic, and by sensitivity to this text, which asks to be considered not only as a historical object, but also as truth embodied in history.

The same problem was faced by Catholic Modernism, which was standing under the influence of Protestant historical-critical Bible scholarship. The attempts to harmonize scholarly openness and adherence to the Church of Rome were particularly lively in France and Italy. On the margins of the Rome Congress, but referred to in the Congress's records, a lecture event took place in which the problem of Modernism in its tension between science and faith became manifest. Its subject matter was the so-called Babel-Bible debate, which had unleashed a broad public response one year earlier because of the presence of the German emperor at lectures by the Berlin Assyriologist Friedrich Delitzsch. The debate concerned a question touching on both historical science and the authority of the Holy Scriptures, namely, to what extent the Old Testament account of the Creation was dependent on Babylonian creation myths, and whether and to what extent it contained a unique message.[38] The speaker, a respected Italian specialist in Hebrew studies, Salvatore Minocchi, who during the Congress also presented an ambitious paper on the textual problems of the Psalm tradition, complained about Italy that it had banned "the study of religion from the university" and "so to speak expelled Christianity." He declared his belief in the "harmony of positive science and religious scholarship.... Let us profess openly and freely," he concluded, "that today, as always, the Christian ideal is the only source of morality and civic virtues, of political greatness and public welfare. The strong and genuine love that I feel for my fatherland confirms me to express the wish that Italy may once again nourish itself from the Bible and that its future greatness may be founded upon the Gospels, before it is too late for idle regret." In the following debate, which lasted three hours, critical listeners demanded a reply "in the name of positive science." It was given some time later by Paolo Orano who made a radical statement against the attempt of Catholic Modernism at reconciling religion and science.[39] The tension between objectivity and commitment, between scientific impartialness and ethical-political or religious values would occupy the later Historical Congresses again and again.

In his opening speech, Villari recommended the comparative method as a supplement to hermeneutics for a historiography that was internationalizing itself more consciously than before. It is easier to make comparisons of historical objects (such as in architecture and fine arts, language and literature) than of historical processes. This became evident in Rome in the section for legal history. In a paper delivered in Italian, Sir Frederick Pollock dealt with "The

Concept and Study of Comparative Legal History."⁴⁰ He viewed Montesquieu as the predecessor of a comparative legal history. But this farsighted genius had failed to free himself entirely from the unhistorical dogmatism of his times. For the other great predecessor from the eighteenth century, Vico, law comparison had not been an instrument of research: he merely had used it to illustrate general truths that were more metaphysical than historical. However, around the middle of the nineteenth century genuine comparative legal history had started with the founding of university chairs and historical societies dedicated to this purpose in various European countries. Pollock himself was the holder of such a chair, which had been established in Oxford in 1869. His contribution at the Rome Congress amounted to a plea for a complementary application of historical-genetic and comparative methods in legal history and in political sciences as well.

Within the same section, a lecture by the French legal scholar Raymond Saleilles on "Historical Methods and Codification of Law"⁴¹ dealt with a basic problem of historicism. It was inspired by the German civil code, which had been completed at the turn of the century. According to Saleilles, it was the German law scholar Rudolf von Ihering who had achieved the decisive intellectual turn in juristic thought leading from the backward-looking historicism of a conceptual jurisprudence and from pandectile erudition to the modern conception of law as a social phenomenon. Ihering had taught that law should be considered the product of interest conflicts. His lecture, with the evocative title "Struggle for Law" (*Der Kampf ums Recht*), which he held in Vienna in 1872 and which attracted great attention, was an echo of Darwin's notion of the survival of the fittest. Here, law was not interpreted from a dogmatic idea of justice, but in a vitalistic sense as arising from causes, purposes, and motives. This was a rejection of any idealistic legal and historical metaphysics. In his work on Roman law (*Der Geist des römischen Rechts*, 1852–1865), Ihering had brought down Roman law from its sublime pedestal and explained it on the basis of social interests. "Law is not a concept of logic, but of power," "Purpose is the author of law," "Thou shalt find thy law in the struggle"—because of such formulations, Ihering's understanding of law has justly been termed "juristic naturalism"⁴² or "social Darwinism."⁴³

Starting from Ihering, Saleilles developed a "méthode d'adaptation historique" in his lecture in Rome. Since the legal scholar as a historian was required to take a position and did not have the right to evade an evaluative interpretation of legal texts, he had to ask himself what method the interpretation should follow. Should it be exegetical, dogmatic, or "evolutionary"? This meant, according to Saleilles: "Is this interpretation to be conducted according to the original and intended meaning of the text, which means leading the text back to its historical context as in the original historical method (i.e., Savigny's method)? Is it to be conducted in regard to the agreement of the text with a rationally constructed ideal, which is characteristic of the dogmatic method? Or, finally, is it to be conducted in the evolutionary adaptation of the text to the demands of social progress? And indeed, this would be the only correct understanding of the historical method, in the sense of a method of juristic interpretation."[44] Saleilles held that such a dynamic interpretation should be orientated toward "social utility" and the "progress of the idea of justice," whatever he might have understood by these terms. He regarded economics, sociology, and law comparison as the scholarly aids that a jurist-historian should make use of for this purpose. This amounted to the pressing need for scholarship to internationalize itself. He added with appreciation that the practice of transnational law comparison was typical of the study of civil law in Italy, which regularly fell back on French and German laws and commentators.

If Saleilles's lecture expressed the naturalistic tendencies of the time, which demanded that historical interpretations of law pay more attention to conflicts of interest and socioeconomic factors than previously, then Giulio de Montemayor went one step further. In his lecture on "G. B. Vico and the Materialistic Conception of Legal History," he pledged his allegiance to the position of Karl Marx expressed in the foreword to his *Critique of Political Economy*. In the light of the materialistic conception of history, which had become indispensable, law was nothing more than the "definition, regulation, sanctioning, and preservation of a given economic order." He considered the theoretical principles of a system of laws to be "indicators of the way in which the distribution of goods is actually regulated within a society, namely, property and, with it, all of those assets which we inaccurately refer to as moral assets."[45] However doubtful his interpretation of Vico as a forerunner of historical materialism may be, more interesting is the fact that a Marxist view of history was presented in Rome for the first time. Giulio de Montemayor belonged to the Scuola Economica Giuridica of Naples, which in regard to jurisprudence adhered to the antimetaphysical, naturalistic tendency of the turn of the century.

The departure from historical idealism particularly articulated itself in a methodological subdivision of the section for medieval and modern history. The recommended alternatives to the now rejected notions of natural law and idealistic historical philosophy presented themselves in very different guises. This was shown by two prominent historians who both were on close terms with the Scuola Economica Giuridica of Naples, Ludo Moritz Hartmann and Benedetto Croce.

Hartmann,[46] the son of a German-Bohemian 1848 radical, had been introduced to the rigorous critical method in ancient and medieval history by Mommsen in Berlin and by Scheffer-Boichorst in Strasbourg. He was the author of a voluminous history of Italy in the Middle Ages, and had joined the Social Democratic Party in Vienna in 1901. As a collaborator of the *Monumenta Germaniae Historica*—he edited the *Registrum epistolarum* of Pope Gregory I—and a socialist, Hartmann was a unique figure among German historians. Together with the conservative Georg von Below, he published the respected and pioneering *Vierteljahrschrift für Sozial- und Wirtschaftsgeschichte*—a remarkable sign that, despite opposing political convictions, fruitful scientific cooperation is possible on the firm ground of factual research. In the field of public education, Hartmann later made a name for himself as the founder of the Austrian adult education centers. As a friend of the Austrian socialist leader Victor Adler and as an envoy to Berlin after the collapse of the Austro-Hungarian multiethnic state, he called for the *Anschluß* of German Austria to the Weimar Republic. In his highly estimated *Geschichte Italiens im Mittelalter*, Hartmann had moved the anonymous economic and social factors to the foreground as the driving forces of historical development, while scarcely paying any attention to the biographical and personal element. He explained his method by stating that he had striven to "create an induction as complete as possible, which, proceeding from individual economic facts, reconstructs a synthesis that reflects the real life of the time as concisely as possible. Thus, also the connections between the church reform movement, which led to the investiture struggle, and the economic development had to be deduced from this. Here the historian was clearly confronted with what is usually called a materialistic conception of history, and accordingly the individual had to be viewed as standing within the flow of mass phenomena."[47] He presented his scholarly credo at the Rome Congress in a lecture on "Historical Evolution," which he published in expanded form two years later under the title *Über historische Entwickelung: Sechs Vorträge zur Einleitung in eine historische Soziologie* (Gotha, 1905). Here he unconditionally applied Darwinistic concepts to history. Not only did he demand to exclude all theological or metaphysical teleology from the interpretation of history; he was also unwilling to acknowledge the purposeful human will—whether of the individual or with reference to a group—as a causal factor influencing the course of history. The promoter of historical development was coincidence. This was true in regard to technical inventions as well as to "social organization."

The scientific endeavor to bring history into line with the natural sciences has seldom been formulated as radically as by Hartmann. One guarantor he referred to continually was Darwin. The struggle for existence, adaptation, winnowing, and natural selection appear as the key concepts of his biologistic view of history. He suspected every appraising treatment of history by a historian as metaphysical and thus deserving of rejection. But this did not prevent him from elevating what he viewed as the essential trend of the allegedly arbitrary historical evolution, namely, progressive "socialization," to a "duty to socialize." This value, which according to Hartmann was objectively based in history, emerged as a trinity of ideals recalling the radical movement of 1848: brotherhood, work, liberty.

Hartmann's conception of history can perhaps be referred to by the paradoxical formula of an idealistic Social Darwinism. Marxist notions had been integrated in it, although they did not substantially determine his theory. Thus, Hartmann's naturalistic theory of history turns out to conceal an idealistic theory of political education. This moved him at the Rome Congress, under the impression of a lecture series on the teaching of history in various countries, to present a proposal that, however, did not meet with approval. It demanded that historical instruction be concentrated on the development of civilization, economics, and public law, and to avoid "all those means of historiography which are used—counter to historical objectivity—to stir up hatred of foreign nations."[48]

Entirely different was the intellectual development of Benedetto Croce, who delivered several addresses at the Rome Congress. Croce came from Naples, where he moved within the intellectual atmosphere of the Italian Marx and Hegel reception. His own philosophical and historical position was the result of a passionate occupation with Marx, whom he soon left behind, and with Hegel, whom he developed further from a critical stance. In 1903, the year of the Rome Congress, the first issue of *La Critica: Rivista di letteratura, storia e filosofia* appeared. Through this journal, which he edited together with the philosopher Giovanni Gentile, Croce, as a *Praeceptor Italiae,* moved for decades into the center of all philosophical, historical, and intellectual debates in his country and far beyond its borders. At the Rome Congress, he presented two treatises on "Subjectivity and Objectivity in History" and on the "Concept of Causality,"[49] alongside a lecture on literary criticism and literary history. They dealt with partial aspects of his theory of history, which were fully developed in his later systematic works. But when, with the Rome Congress and with *La Critica*, he stepped into the arena, the typical traits of his historical thought, which distinguished it from other contemporary theories of history, had already taken on a clear profile. With all due respect to his teacher Labriola, who had been the first scholar to hold a lecture on historical materialism at the University of Rome and who had declared that it represented the final and definitive philosophy of history, Croce formulated the counterthesis that historical materialism was no such thing, even if some Marxists elevated it to the status of a "metaphysical materialism." One could not simply replace an omnipotent *idea* with omnipotent *matter*. In contrast to Engels, he was also not willing to acknowledge historical materialism as a new method.

In spite of this critique, he did not deny his debt to Marx. He spoke of the enthusiasm that seized him the first time he delved into Marx's ingenious work. He spoke of how, like a shortsighted man who had been given good spectacles, his eyes were opened to economic and social matters that he had not previously seen. If one stripped historical materialism of its deterministic and teleological character, it represented a significant historiographical method well suited to correct the previous predominance of philosophy and ideology. But Marxism was lacking any philosophical significance because it was no more than a simple rule inviting the historian not to neglect what Marxists called the economic substrate and the class struggle. "A materialistic philosophy of history, however, would repeat and aggravate all the errors of the old idealistic philosophy."[50]

Croce arrived at Hegel via Marx. With Hegel, he said on one occasion, he had fared the same as Catullus with his Lesbia: he had discovered clearly and to his distress that he could neither live with him nor without him.⁵¹ At the time of the Rome Congress he was engaged in the midst of an intellectual struggle over this last great system of idealistic philosophy. He presented the result three years later under the title: "What Is Alive and What Is Dead of Hegel's Philosophy."⁵²

He viewed the metaphysical, teleological element in Hegel's philosophy of history, his *"Panlogismus"* and the "dialectic a priori" as done with and without a future. The historian Croce was in no way convinced by the speculative and artificial construction of the triad of thesis, antithesis, and synthesis into which Hegel had squeezed the course of history. Nonetheless, he viewed the fact that Hegel had placed history in the spotlight of dialectics as an everlasting cognitive gain. But Croce wanted to anchor the dialectic in empirical facts, to track it down within history, and not to put it over the course of history as the pattern of an allegedly final interpretation of its meaning. He agreed with Hegel that history and philosophy are identical, but never did he see himself as a Hegelian or as a representative of an idealistic philosophy of history. Toward the end of his life, Croce reminisced on his experience with Hegel: "For me, Hegel will always be and always remain the master; I honor him as one of my greatest teachers in the field of philosophy. But I would not be worthy of being his pupil if I had not seized every opportunity to develop his theories further, to correct and expand them,... if I had not altered the entire structure of his intellectual edifice and created a new one. It was my right and my duty to stand up against Hegel's notion of a concluding, final philosophical system and to point out the fact that in philosophy there can never be anything final."⁵³ As a liberal Italian, Croce also resented how Hegel—in his "authoritarian German temperament"—felt called upon "to subordinate the demands of ethics to the demands of the state, particularly the Prussian state."⁵⁴

To characterize his own concept of history, he adopted the term *"storicismo assoluto."* This absolute historicism was not derived from the earlier forebears of historicism, as Meinecke described it,⁵⁵ not from Herder, Niebuhr, Savigny, and Ranke, but was achieved in the critical study of Marx and particularly of Hegel. It sought its path between a final and a causal explanation of history, between metaphysics and naturalism, between idealism and materialism. Since idealism was only being treated in an epigonic fashion at the turn of the century, the main thrust of his critique was directed against the positivistic tendency of the time to submit history to the bench of natural sciences in order to prove its scientific character with altered methods and thus to provide it with legitimation. This issue was the subject of his two methodological contributions to the Rome Congress. In his comment on "The Principle of Causality in Historiography," he postulated a notion of causality peculiar to history in contrast to the natural sciences and their concept of law as "the constant antecedent." The historian's notion of causality lay in "relating the individual fact to the entirety of all individual facts." Is that science? Certainly not in the sense of the natural sciences. History as the apprehension of the individual phenomenon was more closely related to the act of intuitive cognition practiced in art.⁵⁶ He agreed with Giovanni Gentile on this point. Every attempt to transform history into a nomothetic science, he declared, was doomed to failure.

However, if history is moved into the vicinity of art, can it transmit objective knowledge at all or will it remain caught in subjectivity and indeterminacy? In his Rome lecture on subjectivity and objectivity, Croce conceived of the relationship as follows: As "the most intransigent of objectivists" he declared himself to be against any falsification of historical statements by subjectivist arbitrariness: "Truth is only achieved against the feelings and against the passions." Thus, in Croce's writings one repeatedly encounters an unconditional recognition of the methods of text and source criticism developed in the nineteenth century. He prided himself on being experienced in the application of such methods, even if he did not consider a mere "philological study" of historical facts as real scholarship. This was more than a critical examination of facts. Croce thought that it was by no means possible to grasp a historical object without the subjective moment of "idealistic criteria": for example, critical-historical research could uncover all kinds of things about Racine's *Phèdre* in regard to its origins and circumstances, the first performance, the first edition, etc. However, it was only possible to say something about this drama as a work of art, and thus to do justice to it as a historical object, if one possessed a clear understanding of what art is. This also applied to the field of political history. If one collected everything about Bismarck's work and life, one could still say nothing about his history "without judging Bismarck's work: 1) whether the goal he pursued corresponded to the ideal of society (was it progressive or reactionary, disastrous or beneficial); 2) whether he possessed the ability to achieve it."[57] Here the value judgement (*Werturteil*) appears as the genuine cognitive factor constituting the historical object.

The notion that the historical object is determined by value relations (*Wertbezug*) and that this circumstance establishes the autonomy of the cultural sciences in contrast to natural science as the study of laws, had just been formulated by the neo-Kantian Heinrich Rickert.[58] Croce referred to this epochal historical epistemology. But he was unable to free himself from the notion that science is always concerned with universality and necessity; thus for him history was knowledge, but not science, in contrast to Rickert and also Xenopol, with whom he otherwise agreed in his delimitation from natural sciences.[59] Above all, however, in his Rome lecture he made no distinction—as the neo-Kantians did—between theoretical value relatedness, which constitutes the historical object, and practical value judgement, which concerns the subjective attitude toward this object. His "absolute historicism" amounted to the renewal of Vico's thesis, which was directed against the claim to superiority of mathematics and natural sciences, and postulated the supremacy of history: *verum ipse factum*, which Croce later formulated as "History as thought and action."

Croce found an ally at the Rome Congress in the person of Giovanni Gentile. If Croce maintained the identity of history and philosophy, Gentile started from an undeniable tension between both and attempted to show that despite the differences between empirical research and the a priori of the philosophy of history, there was a meaningful relationship between history and philosophy.[60] He considered them to be two mutually independent forms of the intellectual apprehension of the same object. Following in the footsteps of idealism, Gentile defined the given reality of the historic fact ("an sich Gegebensein"), its existence independently of whether it is perceived correctly or incorrectly or whether it is perceived at all, as a question of metaphysics, of philosophy. Thus, the beauty of Homer was an a priori given fact, whether one was touched by it or not. The factual given reality of history was a postulate on which research itself was based and without which it would be meaningless. Therefore, he ascribed contingency as well as necessity to every historical fact according to whether it was seen abstracted from the context of all preceding facts or within it. For him, as for Croce, the apprehension of historical individuality was related to art, but the logic of "the necessity of the necessary" was the concern of the philosophy of history.

Compared to such impressive attempts to locate history as a science, the contribution of the American Cavour scholar William R. Thayer on the indispensability of biography was more a declared conviction than a contribution to the theory of history.[61] He presented variations on the topic "men make history" at a moment when an evolutionist conception reducing history to economic causalities was in danger of losing sight of human beings in their individuality. Looking to the historical literature of the twentieth century, one has to say that at the beginning of the century, contrary to appearances at the time, he was right in predicting a bright future for biography.

Notes

1. *Atti del Congresso Internazionale di Szienze Storiche, Roma 1–9 aprile 1903* [hereafter Congress Rome 1903: *Atti*], 12 vols. (Rome, 1907), vol. 1, p. 1f.
2. Deutsches Historisches Institut, Rome, Reg. 68.
3. E. Pais, *Storia di Roma*. Vol. 1: *Critica della tradizione fino alla caduta del Decemvirato* (Turin, 1898), vol. 2: *Critica della tradizione dalla caduta del Decemvirato all'intervento di Pirro* (Turin, 1899).
4. For a short discussion of the discovery and the controversial interpretations, see F. Coarelli, *Rom. Ein archäologischer Führer* (Freiburg i. Br., 1975), pp. 63–65.
5. H. N. Gay, "The International Congress of Historical Sciences," *American Historical Review* 8 (1902/03): 809–812, here p. 809.
6. "Publikation der Historikerkongreß-Akten," *Internationale Wochenschrift für Wissenschaft, Kunst und Technik* 1 (1907): 293. See also article by Julius von Pflugk-Harttung, newspaper clipping from *Der Tag*, n.d., Delbrück Papers, 26; further reports in *Allgemeine Zeitung* (Munich), 22 Nov. 1901 and 18 Feb. 1902; *Germania* (Berlin), 2 March 1902.
7. Notice in a circular letter to the members of the board of the Association of German Historians, 13 Oct. 1901, Historisches Archiv der Stadt Köln, Akten des deutschen Historikerverbandes.

8. Report of 9 March 1902, Archives Nationales, F¹⁷, 3092¹.
9. On this, see the correspondence between Ministre de l'Instruction Publique et des Beaux Art and Ministre des Affaires étrangères, ibid.
10. Zentrales Staatsarchiv, Merseburg, Rep. 76 V c, Sect. 1, Tit. 11, Teil VI, no. 13, vol. 1.
11. Villari Papers, correspondence, Gorrini to Villari, 6 May 1903.
12. Ibid., Gorrini to Villari, 28 Aug. 1902.
13. For the social program, see Congress Rome 1903: *Atti*, pp. 109ff., 134ff.
14. Minister of Public Education to the German ambassador in Rome, 11 March 1901, Zentrales Staatsarchiv, Merseburg, Rep. 76 V c, Sect. 1, Tit. 11, Teil VI, no. 13, vol. 1.
15. Ibid.
16. Quoted in "Theodor Mommsen und der internationale Historikerkongreß in Rom," *Berliner Neueste Nachrichten*, 26 Feb. 1901.
17. L. von Pastor, *1854–1928: Tagebücher, Briefe, Erinnerungen*, ed. W. Wühr (Heidelberg, 1950), p. 3.
18. Ibid., p. 406; Congress Rome 1903: *Atti*, vol. 1, p. 88.
19. Pastor, *Tagebücher*, p. 408.
20. Congress Rome 1903: *Atti*, vol. 3, p. XXI.
21. Ibid., p. LI.
22. G. Monod, "Bulletin historique: Italie," *Revue historique* 82 (1903): 357–362, here p. 358.
23. Congress Rome 1903: *Atti*, vol. 2, pp. XXXIIIf. Resolutions of the Congress in *Atti*, vol. 1, pp. 188ff.
24. These are the words of Aloys Schulte, who chaired the first meeting concerned with this matter, in a hand-written "Bericht über den Historikertag," 13 April 1903, Deutsches Historisches Institut, Rome, Reg. 1. See also Gay, "International Congress," pp. 809–812; Monod, "Bulletin historique," p. 359, and the report in *Rivista d'Italia* 6 (1903): 638ff.
25. Historisches Archiv der Stadt Köln, Akten des Deutschen Historikerverbandes; Delbrück papers, 26. See also the report of Pflugk-Harttung on the Congress in *Der Tag* (clipping in Delbrück papers, 26, no date).
26. Monod, "Bulletin historique."
27. Congress Rome 1903: *Atti*, vol. 1, pp. 97ff.
28. Congress Rome 1903: *Atti*, vol. 1, p. 105. Cf. K. Lamprecht, *Deutsche Geschichte*, 2nd ed. (Berlin, 1895), "Vorwort."
29. Congress Rome 1903: *Atti*, vol. 1, p. 106.
30. Ibid., p. 102.
31. Ibid., pp. 109ff.
32. "Michelet et l'Italie," in Congress Rome 1903: *Atti*, vol. 3, pp. 131ff.
33. Monod, "Avant-propos."
34. These are the words of the Italian foreign minister Giulio Prinetti to the French ambassador in Rome, Camille Barrère, in a note from 1 Nov. 1902. See French Yellow Book: *Les accords franco-italiens de 1900–1902* (Paris, 1920), p. 8.
35. Congress Rome 1903: *Atti*, vol. 3, p. 145f.
36. Report Schulte, 13 April 1903, Deutsches Historisches Institut, Rome, Reg. 1.
37. "Osservazioni storiche sulle origini del Nuovo Testamento," in Congress Rome 1903: *Atti*, vol. 11, pp. 123ff.; K. H. Neufeld, "Adolf von Harnack," in *Deutsche Historiker*, ed. H.-U. Wehler, vol. 7 (Göttingen, 1980), pp. 24–38.
38. On Modernism and the Babel-Bible debate, see the corresponding articles in *Religion in Geschichte und Gegenwart*, 3rd ed. (Tübingen, 1957), esp. "Babylonische Tradition und das AT," pp. 822ff.
39. Congress Rome 1903: *Atti*, vol. 11, p. XIII.
40. "Il concetto e lo studio della storia del diritto comparato," in Congress Rome 1903: *Atti*, vol. 9, pp. 53ff.
41. Ibid., pp. 3ff.

42. F. Wieacker, *Privatrechtsgeschichte der Neuzeit,* 2nd ed. (Göttingen, 1967), p. 562f.
43. H. Hattenhauer, *Die geistesgeschichtlichen Grundlagen des Rechts,* 2nd ed. (Heidelberg, 1980), p. 205f.
44. Congress Rome 1903: *Atti,* vol. 9, p. 13f.
45. "G. B. Vico e la concezione materialistica della storia del diritto," ibid., p. 376f.
46. For biographical information, see W. Lenel in *Historische Zeitschrift* 131 (1925): 571–574; St. Bauer, "Ludo Moritz Hartmann," in *Neue Österreichische Biographie 1815–1918,* Abt. 1, vol. 3 (Vienna, 1926), pp. 197–209; G. Fellner, *Ludo Moritz Hartmann und die österreichische Geschichtswissenschaft* (Vienna/Salzburg, 1985).
47. Quoted by Bauer, "Hartmann," p. 202.
48. Congress Rome 1903: *Atti,* vol. 3, p. XXVf.
49. "Soggettività ed oggettività nella storiografia," in Congress Rome 1903: *Atti,* vol. 3, pp. 613ff. The essay on the concept of causality was not published in the *Atti* because it had already appeared in completed form in B. Croce, *Lineamenti di una logica come scienza del concetto puro* (Naples, 1905), chaps. 4 and 5; see Congress Rome 1903: *Atti,* vol. 3, p. XLII.
50. B. Croce, "Les Études relatives à la théorie de l'histoire en Italie durant les quinze dernières années," *Revue de synthèse historique* 5 (1902): 267f.; cf. also Croce, *Materialismo storico ed economia marxista* (Bari, 1901), French edition: *Matérialisme historique et économie marxiste. Essais critiques* (Paris, 1901).
51. B. Croce, "Entstehung und Erkenntnisse meiner Philosophie," *Universitas* 7 (Stuttgart, 1952): 1009–1020, here p. 1011.
52. *Ciò che è vivo e ciò che è morto della filosofia di Hegel* (Bari, 1907), German edition: *Lebendiges und Totes in Hegels Philosophie* (Heidelberg, 1909).
53. Croce, "Entstehung und Erkenntnisse," p. 1020.
54. Ibid., p. 1015.
55. See F. Meinecke, *Zur Theorie und Philosophie der Geschichte* (Stuttgart, 1959), p. 342f. Meinecke criticized the historical philosophy of Croce, whom he esteemed highly, as "forced monism." Meinecke to Goetz, 22 March 1943, in F. Meinecke, *Ausgewählter Briefwechsel,* ed. L. Dehio and P. Classen (Stuttgart, 1962), p. 215. In a letter to H. v. Srbik, 18 Jan. 1951, Meinecke expressed the opinion that the development was heading toward a "synthesis of historicism and natural law." Ibid., p. 307.
56. He first developed this notion in B. Croce, "L'histoire ramenée au concept général de l'Art," *Academia Pontaniana,* vol. 23 (1893); cf. Croce, "La théorie de l'histoire en Italie."
57. Congress Rome 1903: *Atti,* p. 615.
58. H. Rickert, *Die Grenzen der naturwissenschaftlichen Begriffsbildung,* 2 vols. (Tübingen, 1896 and 1902).
59. See Croce, "La théorie de l'histoire en Italie."
60. G. Gentile, "Il problema della filosofia della storia," in Congress Rome 1903: *Atti,* vol. 2, pp. 607ff.
61. "Biography the basis of history," in Congress Rome 1903: *Atti,* vol. 2, pp. 573ff.

Chapter 5

VICTORIOUS PROFESSIONALISM
Berlin, 1908

Rome represented a first high point in the history of the International Historical Congresses. One could now anticipate that they would develop into a lasting institution. Some doubts remained, and until today opinions have been divided over whether scholarship is promoted by such undertakings. But as shown by the response to the Rome Congress in the professional journals, most observers were impressed by the fact that the Italians had been highly successful in organizing a genuinely international forum, with broad participation from many nations and the active involvement of a great number of outstanding historians. The publication of the Congress proceedings in twelve impressive volumes rounded off the favorable picture.

In Rome it was decided to meet again in Berlin after five years.[1] This suggestion came from French historians, which the *Historische Zeitschrift* emphasized as a "characteristic and felicitous fact."[2] Particularly Gabriel Monod supported this idea.[3] The Germans were surprised, and reactions were mixed, but the influential Adolf von Harnack spoke up in favor of accepting the suggestion. Together with Otto von Gierke, professor of legal history, and the classical scholar Ulrich von Wilamowitz-Moellendorff, Harnack immediately directed a petition to the Prussian minister of education and cultural affairs, in which he requested support for this plan. At a preliminary meeting, he wrote, a majority of Berlin historians had expressed reservations against turning congresses, whose scientific yield they saw as minimal, into a regular institution. However, "the majority of the assembled [scholars], including some members of the History Department," were of the opinion

> that however one may judge the scholarly value of such congresses, establishing professional and personal relationships among the representatives of the historical sciences of the various countries is not without use, both for scholarship and for the

---

Notes for this chapter begin on page 55.

cultivation of the international community, and that the proposal made in Rome could scarcely be completely rejected without offending against international courtesy; that even despite certain external difficulties the organization of a Congress in Berlin with a favorable outcome is not only practicable but is also desirable since in view of the current tendencies the Congress would presumably be held in another European capital and that Germany would thus be deprived of having a decisive influence on the useful delimitation and structure of the institution.[4]

It was also Harnack who spoke most clearly to the German public about the meaning and purpose of such congresses. He wrote in an advance notice of the Berlin Congress:

> Scholarship is international and has no secrets, even if it does have its own "mysteries" within each great nation. It is a common good, a world fugue, whose first movements were composed thousands of years ago, in which the voices of ever new peoples have made themselves heard and which possesses the strength to force all emerging dissonances into a final consonance. Scholarship had long been international at a time when economics still sat behind countless walls and barriers. Of course, it would remain international even without congresses, but if it does without them it would forego a practical aid that our times are placing into its hands. This aid is practical above all because it adds the living word and personal intercourse to the scholarly exchange in [the form of] publications and letters.[5]

Beyond the positivistic increase of knowledge, Harnack also saw a higher, comprehensive significance in scholarly cooperation. He had already stated his views on this subject a few years earlier in the *Preußische Jahrbücher* in an essay on "Science as a Large-Scale Enterprise." It was an appeal for an exchange of professors that he had instigated between the University of Berlin and American universities and that had been criticized in nationalistic circles. He expressly cited the international scientific congresses when, in his recommendation for the unavoidable and necessary scientific "large-scale enterprise," he included a warning and a confession of belief: "Humanity and the fraternization of peoples are in our days, when they are going to collide harder and harder in their desire for expansion, more threatened than most of us imagine. Scholarly exchange, both professional and personal, and peaceful competition in the work of science, can prevent and repair much in this respect!"[6]

However, his Berlin colleagues did not at first share Harnack's enthusiasm. When, soon after the discussion with Harnack, they realized that they would have to devote part of their time and work to the organization of the Congress, they likewise turned to the Prussian minister of education and cultural affairs with a petition stating:

> The idea of an International Congress of Historical Sciences appears to us as a failure in itself because of the boundlessness of the scholarly objectives subsumed in it.... Even if one tried to delimit the subject of the Congress to political history in the strict sense of the term, which in itself would presuppose the possibility of

finding an institution for this limitation binding for all civilized nations, the attempt would still result in a subject that is scarcely suited for international discussion in form of a congress, since history—except ancient history—, even if it is conceived of in a universal sense, is so strongly influenced by political and national differences that a common ground for international communication cannot be assumed. The discussion would probably revolve around a fruitless methodological controversy or around certain neutral marginal areas, while assiduously suppressing the central problems which deal with the struggles between the great powers and nations and which should occupy the [our] profession as such first and foremost. The experiences which have been made at such International Congresses of Historical Sciences so far by no means encourage us to continue efforts in this direction. The Congresses in The Hague and in Paris ended in abject failure, and even the last Congress in Rome can in no way be seen as proof of the viability of the institution.

The final item of the petition stated "that with the great demands that such an event makes on the otherwise more efficiently employed labor of the scholars and of the finances of the State, a rejection of the Congress lies in the public interest, assuming that this would be possible without committing an act of international discourtesy." That was at once a disclaimer and a roundabout declaration of readiness to cooperate. Indeed, three of the petition's signatories—namely, Eduard Meyer, Michael Tangl, and Otto Hintze—stated that "under the prevailing circumstances" the Congress could not be avoided.[7]

The petition is a classic document of the self-understanding that prevailed in German political historiography on the eve of the First World War. Power struggles and national conflicts were named as the focus and centerpiece of history. Their scholarly treatment appeared to be determined by national rivalries to such a degree that the historians had no expectations whatsoever from an international congress. All that remained for such a forum was the discussion of methodological problems, which they saw as unfruitful, or sidetracking to less important, perhaps even trivial "fringe areas"—by which they were probably referring to linguistic, literary, art, social, and economic history, which had been given such great attention at the two previous Congresses.

In any case, the petition by the Berlin historians, who now saw themselves faced with the task of organizing an International Congress, represented a clear rejection of those efforts at a reorientation of historical studies that had been expressed in the founding of the *Revue de synthèse historique*.

A large German daily newspaper, the *Germania* was not entirely wrong when it observed that it was owing more to political than to scientific reasons that the Congress actually did come about.[8] In a similar vein Dietrich Schäfer, bemoaning the very poor yield of the International Historical Congresses, noted in his memoirs that the Congress was promoted by the Prussian and Imperial governments "under the point of view of international reconciliation."[9] This also matched the view of Friedrich Althoff, the most important person for all university matters in the Prussian ministry of education and cultural affairs, who, convinced of the possibility of "linking the peoples together through science," was open to all initiatives for international scholarly exchange.[10] In order to popularize such ideas, he founded the *Internationale Wochenschrift für Wissenschaft, Kunst und Technik* in 1907. It was launched with an essay by Hermann Diels recommending international scientific cooperation on a large scale,[11] and as a prelude to the Berlin Congress, it published Harnack's article on the international character of historical scholarship.

Incidentally, one person who had shown as little interest in international historical meetings as the Berlin historians, the Munich professor of modern history Ritter von Heigel, was changed from a Saul to a Paul under the impression of the Berlin Congress, as he later admitted.[12] Otherwise, it is only fair to note that not only the skeptics did yield to the unavoidable, not only did they grin and bear it, but they did all they could to make the best of it. Thus, when the time came, the spokesman of the skeptics, Reinhold Koser, the director of the Prussian State Archives and biographer of Frederick the Great, who had already stated all of his reservations about such congresses to the Prussian ministry between The Hague and Paris, took the chair of the organizing committee. He was assisted by the two most significant representatives of classical studies in Berlin after the death of Theodor Mommsen (on 1 November 1903): the historian Eduard Meyer and the classical philologist Ulrich von Wilamowitz-Moellendorff. The presidency of this triumvirate was confirmed by the Congress's plenary meeting.

With regard to the structure of the program, the organizers of the Berlin Congress wanted to chart a course different from that taken in Rome.[13] They reduced the number of sections and autonomous subgroups by eliminating, among others, philology, archaeology, the history of music and theatre, historical geography, the history of natural sciences, and also—as the French *Revue de synthèse historique* noted with criticism—theory and methodology. In some cases, topics from these areas reappeared in the eight sections provided for Oriental history, Hellas and Rome, the political history of the Middle Ages and modern times, the cultural and intellectual history of the Middle Ages and modern times, church history, art history, and historical auxiliary sciences. The disappearance of methodology as a separate field was characteristic, as well as the simultaneous instruction of the Congress rules that the lectures in the various sections should "primarily deal with material communications or questions of method and scholarly activity." This is to say, the Berlin professors did not want theoretical discussions, but rather reports on practical experiences, methods, and projects in the fields of research and academic instruction.

The communications in the sections were to be followed by discussions. This, too, represented a departure from Rome, where the discussions had been restricted to "temi" that disappeared entirely in Berlin. Votes on resolutions were not planned. After all, state authorities are generally not particularly impressed by such manifestations of a common will. And yet the vote taken in Rome to accelerate the access to materials in political archives did in fact, as was communicated at the Berlin Congress, persuade Austria to open its archives up to 1848, and it also moved Prussia to loosen its restrictions. In Berlin, contrary to Rome, a plenary session was held each day. Here, eminent historians were given the opportunity to present their thoughts more extensively than in the sections.[14] These daily noon lectures, which formed the centerpiece of the Congress, were reserved for guests from abroad. None of the world-renowned German or Berlin historians spoke there. This reticence was honored as a noble gesture. However, many of those who had come from far away also regretted that German historiography did not use these lectures to present itself. Thus, Gabriel Monod stated: "With all due respect for the sensitivity that has moved such renowned Berlin scholars as Wilamowitz, Harnack, Ed. Meyer, Koser, and Schäfer to content themselves with their role as organizers in order to yield the podium to their guests, one has regretted this restraint."[15]

Nevertheless, German historical scholarship had a decisive influence on the Congress. The sections were chaired by Berlin historians such as Eduard Meyer, Dietrich Schäfer, Otto Gierke, Adolf von Harnack, and others. Several hours were set aside each afternoon for tours through the Berlin archives, libraries, and collections, guided by the respective directors. And in the end, the active participation of German historians in the sections' work was extraordinarily high. No fewer than half of all the communications, 77 out of a total of 135, were presented by Germans.[16] The French sociologist François Simiand spoke of the "compact, self-sufficient battalions of German scholarship, marching behind their teachers in their traditional cadres." His critique of the Congress corresponded to the reservations uttered by Berr and the *Revue de synthèse historique* against the "academic" historical discipline as a whole.[17]

The predominance of the Germans was to some extent caused by the fact that far fewer foreign guests attended than expected. Around 3,000 participants had been estimated, but the total number lay at around 1,000, including 150 students. No more than some 25 percent were foreigners. Russia, Italy, England, and Sweden sent the largest contingents. Only a few Americans came, although the conference date in August had been chosen in view of the American academic year, which began in September. No Poles or Czechs attended. As the *Revue historique* reported, they had remained home for political reasons. Only a few Frenchmen were present.[18] There was particular regret that half of the registered historians from France did not show up, including Monod, who had after all made the suggestion that the Congress be held in Berlin. He had promised a plenary session lecture on "Michelet and Germany," which would have continued his speech in Rome on Michelet and Italy. In the German and non-German professional and daily press there were speculations on the reasons why the French hesitated to come to the German capital. Various circumstances appear to have played a role, such as the unfavorable date in August, Berlin's lack of appeal as a holiday destination (particularly when compared with Rome), the lack of ticket reductions on the German railways, and, in individual cases, family reasons and illness. Wilamowitz, however, thought that these were nothing but excuses, and recalled the parable of the

Gospels: "I took a wife, I bought a yoke of oxen."[19] The suspicion that political motives played a role was rejected by the French journals, but it was certainly not pure invention. Maurice Prou, a French medievalist, wrote to Henri Pirenne: "I do not believe that the French scholars you mention have been restrained by patriotic reasons, for in this case they would not have registered. I think instead that they, like myself, preferred to enjoy their holidays in peace, to go walking in the woods and to bathe in the sea. However, others were held back by patriotic considerations, but then they did not register either. One of them told me that he did not want to attend a reception hosted by the Kaiser. Indeed, if I had gone as I intended to do for a moment, I would also not have wanted to participate in a reception by the Kaiser. We can have good personal and scholarly relations with the Germans, and yet Frenchmen and Germans remain enemies. Neither one side nor the other is disarming."[20]

In fact, these words about disarmament were an understatement. Instead of disarming, both states were heading toward an arms race, just like the other European great powers. In 1905/06, between the Congresses of Rome and Berlin, the first Morocco Crisis had led to a sharp German-French confrontation. The Anglo-French Entente, concluded in 1904, had survived its first great test. It had been extended in 1907 through a comprehensive elimination of non-European obstacles between England and Russia. Italy had moved closer to France since the agreement of 1902. The naval arms race between Germany and England was intensified as a result of the second German navy law in the winter of 1907/08. Thus, the power constellations leading to the World War began to take shape. In Germany, people would soon begin talking about encirclement.

The fact that, against this darkening political background, the Congress was nevertheless generally perceived to be a success, could be attributed to a large extent to the smooth organization and the generous hospitality in Berlin. Numerous receptions and dinners provided opportunities for sociable exchanges. The most representative buildings in the capital were put at the Congress's disposal: the Reichstag, the Prussian House of Lords and House of Representatives, the philharmonic hall, and the Arts and Crafts Museum. At the Congress's opening, the Imperial state secretary of the interior and vice-president of the Prussian ministry, Theobald von Bethmann Hollweg, addressed the "great scholarly community" of historians and praised history's task as "the teacher of the present ... as long as it obeys no other laws than its own."[21] The government was apparently aware of the opportunities that such a Congress provided for improving the international atmosphere, and it did its part to use them.

What about the scholarly yield of this Congress, however, and the reflection on historical methodology evidenced by it? Let us first look at Karl Lamprecht, who at that time was one of the best known and most controversial critics of the historiography of his time, and not only in Germany. The methodological controversy (*Methodenstreit*) connected with his scholarly work and theoretical demands had been touched off exactly twenty years earlier when Dietrich

Schäfer, a historian of the Hansa, in his inaugural lecture at Tübingen on "The True Field of Historical Studies" (*Das eigentliche Arbeitsfeld der Geschichte*, 1888), made a provocative plea for a decidedly political historiography. He argued that history would gain a scientific character only if it was focused on state affairs. It was false to see the essential content of history in the development of the masses, and it was useless to fill thick volumes with such insignificant matters as the history of the medieval house. Instead of dealing with manners, customs, and conditions, historiography should devote its attention to the great personalities and the political achievement of man, i.e., the state. This declaration of belief in politics as the core of history went far beyond proclaiming a legitimate personal research preference. Schäfer saw politics as the driving force and the genuine content of history itself.

Eberhard Gothein, a student of Wilhelm Dilthey and an admirer of Jacob Burckhardt, who called Gothein his heir and successor, opposed this claim to exclusivity. His place in the history of historiography is marked by a profusion of studies on economic, social, religious, political, and urban topics, all of which he subsumed under the concept of a comprehensive cultural history based on the history of ideas and psychology.[22] "Growing young sciences like history do not need to restrict their subject with fear," he had asserted in a writing on "The Tasks of Cultural History" (*Die Aufgaben der Kulturgeschichte*, 1889) that was directed against Schäfer. In his view, the state was only a peculiar form of interpersonal relationships alongside others like religion, art, law, and economics. The key to understanding historical epochs often lay outside of the political sphere. The dominance of the latter, as in Prussia, was more the exception than the rule. Moreover, the individual creative element, which Schäfer claimed for political history, might find its full realization particularly in cultural history. Gothein provided an example of this in his classic work on Ignatius of Loyola (*Ignatius von Loyola und die Gegenreformation*, 1895).

A few years following Gothein's essay on cultural history, the first volume of Lamprecht's *German History* appeared. It was also a plea for cultural history, but it was presented with excessive claims. Lamprecht believed he could reach a higher level of historical understanding if he replaced Ranke's "how it really happened" with "how it really became that way" as the task of historiography, if he substituted the deductive, genetic method for the narrative, causal analysis for description.[23] Like many of those who thought that historical studies needed sociological and economic underpinnings, Lamprecht wanted to guarantee their scientific character by bringing them closer to the nomothetic and natural sciences. That is why his "new direction" tended to see the agent of history in the masses rather than in the great historical individuals. In his early studies on German economic history (*Deutsches Wirtschaftsleben im Mittelalter*, 1885/86) and in his regional studies, he had emphasized the economic and social determinants; this induced the Marxist historian Franz Mehring to place him in the vicinity of historical materialism.[24] In his voluminous work on German history (*Deutsche Geschichte*), Lamprecht turned toward social psychology.

He sought to show that the intellectual and mental evolution of the German nation, like that of every other, proceeded in six stages according to a specific psychological law of development; in his idiosyncratic terms: symbolism, typism, conventionalism, individualism, subjectivism, and sensitiveness.

Nearly all German historians, including Franz Mehring, recoiled from Lamprecht's scientifically masked sociopsychological theories. And what about his demand that historiography finally consider collective societal factors? If one takes a look at the course catalogs of the universities, one is struck by the large number of courses on social and economic history.[25] After all, there was a powerful social history branch in German historicism deriving from Möser and Niebuhr. The apologists of historicism reproached Lamprecht for having ignored this and, moreover, having misinterpreted Ranke by accusing him of insufficient research on the underlying causes and misunderstood Burckhardt by transforming his historical types into scientific laws. Alongside the inconsistencies in his theoretical and methodological approach, it was above all the weaknesses in his empirical studies and the numerous proved errors and examples of carelessness in his statements that made him an easy target for his opponents.

When the International Historical Congress met in Berlin in 1908, the *Methodenstreit* surrounding Lamprecht had long since faded away. The *querelles allemandes* were not revisited in the presence of the foreign guests. As Gabriel Monod observed,[26] the time was past when Hans Delbrück had called Lamprecht's work humbug and, in turn, Lamprecht had called his rival Max Lenz a mediocre talent. Nevertheless, the issue itself could not be dismissed by merely renouncing mutual abuse. The momentous question of what the real subject of history is and to what extent it is a "science" was no closer to a final answer than it is today. And Lamprecht, of course, also had followers, at the Berlin Congress as well.

Lamprecht's lecture in Berlin was less concerned with methodology and theory than with didactic questions in which he had been interested for a long time. He was one of the few leading historians involved in the beginnings of the German Historikertage, which were connected with problems of school policy and the teaching of history.[27] Lamprecht used the Historikertage as a forum to enlist support for a reform of the academic study of history, most recently one year before Berlin at Heidelberg in 1907. In Berlin as well as in Heidelberg, his real topic was his Leipzig Institute for Cultural and Universal History and the studies carried out there.[28] Lamprecht would have liked to constitute cultural and world history as the basis of the entire study of history, but he realized that for the time being it was inevitable to establish them as a separate branch beside the traditional ones. In Berlin, he presented his sociopsychological scheme of development as a hypothesis whose details needed further empirical investigation, though he himself was in no doubt about its validity. It is easy to understand that—in spite of the considerable thematic expansion that his institute was to provide through the inclusion of non-European cultures and the wide interdisciplinary approach encompassing religious, art and economic history, geography, and other fields—the historical profession remained reserved. This also was true of many historians from foreign countries, although Lamprecht's institute was undeniably attractive because of its new and comprehensive conception, its wide range of publication, and Lamprecht's flair for organization.

A glance at the historical journals is revealing. There were comprehensive reports on the Congress by Ch. H. Haskins in the *American Historical Review*[29] and by T. Höjer in the Swedish *Historisk tidskrift*.[30] In the first of these, Lamprecht's name was not mentioned at all, whereas in the second his presence and the topic of his lecture were briefly referred to. The *Historische Zeitschrift* only provided a brief, general, highly positive report that did not go into detail on any of the individual lectures.[31] In his thorough report in the *Historische Vierteljahrschrift*,[32] Paul Herre briefly cited Lamprecht's lecture, though he had not himself been present. However, Hans Helmolt broke a lance for Lamprecht's methodology and his universal view of history in the *Historisches Jahrbuch* of the Görres Society.[33] He wrote that the "uncomfortable" trend of universal history had been treated in a petty fashion. "In an international event of the kind which this Congress intended to be," he wrote, the "demand for a central section on world history and methodology, embodying synthesis and preventing a dissolution into an array of separate sections, is certainly not an extravagant wish." But a section of this kind had been prevented on purpose. The result had been that lectures like Lamprecht's "had to take shelter at Oriental or literary history."

A report by François Simiand in the *Revue de synthèse historique* was similarly critical:

> None or scarcely any of the methodological questions; nor discussions on the orientation and actual meaning of historical work: the few individual contributions to this field of study, which would appear particularly appropriate to this kind of congress, were scattered in section meetings where one first had to seek them out (Professor Kurt Breysig's very interesting contribution on the concept of a comparative universal history is particularly deserving of special emphasis, as is the exposé by Professor Lamprecht on the organization of his cultural historical seminar, and finally the comments by Professor Fester on the secularization of history), while the general meetings were dedicated to reading papers on sometimes very narrow factual topics of little general interest and without discussion. It did not appear as if this meeting of historians was touched by the desire for discussion and the renewal of methods that, after all, is pervading historical work elsewhere and particularly here among us. It seemed as if they have not even taken notice of it. Without a doubt, such self-confidence can promote well-ordered and diverse work. But it also entails the danger that this work remains sterile despite its volume, and lags behind on paths and methods which elsewhere have fortunately been replaced before it was too late.[34]

Lamprecht had been in close contact with this journal since its inception in 1900. He was its "confidant" in Germany and had developed his theories there in several articles for the French public. He had also taken part in the International

Historical Congress in Paris and had noted there with pleasure that his report on "La méthode historique en Allemagne" had already been published in the first issue of the *Revue de synthèse historique*. Since Paris, he had enjoyed a good relationship with Henri Berr and Gabriel Monod. Monod, however, was decisively more critical than the *Revue de synthèse historique* toward the new "universal" conceptions of history and methodological experiments in Germany. He commented in the *Revue historique* on the Berlin Congress, even though he had only observed it from France, and Breysig and Lamprecht did not fare well. Breysig, the first volume of whose *Geschichte der Menschheit* (History of Mankind) had just appeared, had

> hurled himself head first into the scientifically dangerous movement, so loved by booksellers, which is currently bringing forth masses of works of philosophical-historical generalization in Germany. Herr Breysig has already shown in his *Cultural History of the Modern Era* that, in terms of boldness, professional historians need not take a back seat to autodidacts like Chamberlain, the inspired and eccentric author of the *Foundations of the Twentieth Century*. He explained to the somewhat irritated Congress participants the principles upon which he believes he can construct a comparative world history of mankind. But as comprehensive as Herr Breysig's knowledge and talent may be, at the present time such works are inevitably premature and superficial.

Nor did Lamprecht escape the accusation of "treating too comprehensive and too varied materials too quickly and too imprecisely." And yet, he said, Lamprecht recognized the necessity of the division of historical work. Thus, Monod praised Lamprecht's report on the Leipzig seminar in order to point out the contradiction that existed between Lamprecht's historical and political views: "despite his high intelligence and his cosmopolitan education [he is] an imperialist and a highly effusive German nationalist."[35]

Lamprecht's appearance in Berlin is worth examining within a study of the International Historical Congresses since some of the outstanding figures of the Congresses' history experienced his theory and method as a positive challenge that they critically developed in their own works. Aside from Berr, Simiand, and the circle around the *Revue de synthèse historique*, these included the Belgian Henri Pirenne, the Romanian Nicolae Iorga, and the first president of the later International Committee of Historical Sciences, the Norwegian Halvdan Koht.[36] It has been said that Lamprecht was respected more outside Germany than inside. However, it would be more accurate to say that outside of Germany, Lamprecht's sociopsychological collectivism had lasting reverberations, because in connection with the efforts to find new paths in historical thought and writing, it was perceived as a criticism of the prevailing German political historiography. The high reputation of Lamprecht lasted until his pronounced pan-German annexationist attitude during the First World War, which destroyed many an old professional contact and friendship.[37]

The relatively minor attention paid to Lamprecht at the Berlin Congress is significant in regard to the methodological self-confidence and theoretical complacency of the international historians assembled there. Even more significant is the fact that the philosophical struggle over historical epistemology, which had begun in the 1880s, had no impact on the Congress. There was no serious discussion either of Dilthey's critique of historical reason or of the thought of the neo-Kantians Windelband and Rickert, who attempted to delimitate historiography from the methods of the natural sciences by asserting that the historical object is constituted by its relatedness to values (*Wertbezug*). These were, however, epistemological notions and intellectual challenges that—especially in their continuation by Max Weber—were far more important for the self-understanding of historical thinking than all the essentially belated ontological constructions of the course of history, whether they were presented in positivistic, Marxist, or sociopsychological form.

Yet it would be erroneous to say that Dilthey and neo-Kantianism passed by the historians unnoticed. If, in Dilthey's philosophy of understanding as the specific instrument of historical cognition, as well as in neo-Kantianism, the peculiarity of the method and subject of history was ascertained vis-à-vis the natural sciences, then this corresponded precisely to the dominant self-understanding of historical scholarship vis-à-vis attempts from the fields of economics, sociology, and psychology to transform history into a nomothetic science and to bring it into line with the natural sciences. The historical profession saw itself confirmed by the new historical epistemology without bothering with it in its self-confident research work and in its self-presentation at events such as the International Historical Congress.

This self-understanding was given concise expression in several of the Berlin lectures. The American ambassador David Jayne Hill, a teacher of rhetoric, a scholar of international law, and a delegate at the second Hague Peace Conference of 1907, to whom the opening address had been entrusted, spoke about the "Ethical Function of the Historian." He distinguished between historical studies and natural science as evaluating versus measuring sciences defined by qualitative and quantitative methods.[38] There was also a clear connection to the neo-Kantian epistemology in the speech by Richard Fester, a scholar concerned with historiographical studies, entitled "The Secularization of History."[39] According to Fester, the necessary reduction of historical philosophy to historical epistemology, as asserted by Windelband and Rickert, signified the termination of the secularization process of historical thinking. Its separation from metaphysical and ecclesiastic bonds through the Renaissance and the Enlightenment represented the main subject of his Berlin lecture. He related the secularization process to two contemporary occurrences. The first referred to the Berlin Historical Congress: through secularization, there arose the "possibility of an international, interdenominational historical scholarship …, an intellectual movement …, which may one day lead to a situation where the best history of Christianity will be written by a Buddhist or Muslim, just as today we already owe the best book on Calvin to a Catholic [Kampschulte] and the best Loyola biography to a Protestant [Gothein]." His second contemporary reference strongly denounced the condemnation of Catholic Modernism through the anti-Modernist encyclical of Pope Pius X, *Pascendi dominici gregis* (1907). Some press commentaries, which were still caught up in the mentality of the conflicts surrounding the anti-Catholic Prussian laws of 1871–1875 (*Kulturkampf*), immediately accused Fester of pursuing non-scholarly goals. Unfortunately, the discussion of Fester's lecture so desired by the audience was canceled because the Congress dignitaries were invited to a reception in the Imperial residence at Potsdam.

The same happened to two Catholic scholars who spoke immediately following Fester in a combined meeting of the sections for political and church history. Their lectures were significant within the context of the denominational situation of German scholarship at the time. Since the Reformation and the Counter-Reformation, Germany had been divided more deeply than any other country in denominational terms. The conflict between the State and the Church as it emerged from the liberal *Kulturkampf* against the anti-Enlightenment Catholicism of Pius IX's *Syllabus* had been resolved step by step under Leo XIII. But the Modernism controversy, which would lead to the anti-Modernist oath forced on the clergy by Pius X in 1910, two years after the Berlin Congress, showed that the relationship between the Church and science, between dogmatic and rationally or empirically founded statements on evolution and history, was still fraught with tension. In Germany this tension tended to provoke conflicts between Catholic and Protestant scholarship. The controversy was fought with particular intensity in the domain of Reformation history—ending, however, with remarkable results. The study of the Reformation became a classic example of how scholarship can provide firm ground in the field of tension between *fides* and *ratio*. It received its decisive impulses via the centerpiece of Lutheran Reformation research, the great critical Weimar Luther edition started in 1880, and via the fertile and challenging Luther research of the Dominican Denifle and the Jesuit Grisar. Following a procedure established in Prussia by Frederick William IV, dual professorial chairs for history had been created at several universities in order to guarantee an equal representation of the denominations in this discipline, which was of such significance for the cultural peace and the public consciousness.

Yet these balancing efforts of the German states often were also combated as a sign of a reprehensible association of scholarship with religion. They were based on an understanding of science that had asserted itself in the nineteenth century, namely, that the universities were there to serve the search for objective truth, the religious or ideological convictions of scholars notwithstanding. One convincing example of the fact that interdenominational validity of knowledge was possible, even in the controversial field of Reformation history, was presented by the Freiburg holder of a Catholic historical chair, Heinrich Finke, at the Berlin Congress. His lecture on "The Current State of Research in Pre-Reformation History" need not concern us here in its details, but its reception is worth considering. The *Historisches Jahrbuch* of the Görres Society, an association founded during the *Kulturkampf* for the "cultivation of scholarship in Catholic Germany," stated: "What was generally seen with pleasure, and what is worth emphasizing here, was the apparent appreciation that Protestant scholarship evinced for the offerings brought from the Catholic side. H. Finke above all was held in high esteem in this context."[40]

The subject matter became more explosive when a priest from the Modernist camp, the Würzburg church historian and expert on the Tridentine Council Sebastian Merkle, took a critical look at "The Catholic Evaluation of the Age of Enlightenment."[41] Cautious in its argumentation and thus all the more momentous, his critique was aimed at the Catholic lack of understanding toward the complex phenomenon of the Enlightenment, despite the fact that it contained elements that, according to Merkle, merited a positive reception on the part of the Church. Merkle's lecture attracted particular attention at the Congress as well as in the press and the professional journals. The Church reacted to it with negative criticism, but in some cases also with positive words. In retrospect, Merkle declared[42] that he did not see his task as a Catholic historian in preaching or justifying: "The historian is not a preacher; he should not try to condemn or to arouse abhorrence, but seek to understand the phenomena." He joined this principle with another one concerning his allegiance to scholarly knowledge: "For all religious denominations, historical truth is only one, and I am of the opinion that it is far better to discuss these questions among men of science than to hand them over to 'the Catholic people' to decide upon in daily newspapers." Merkle's lecture received demonstrative applause. The issue of Modernism, which had only appeared on the margins of the Rome Congress, became a central event in Berlin.

The Bible-Babel debate, which had also surfaced in Rome, was expanded in Berlin by Hermann Gunkel (Gießen), who spoke on "Egyptian Parallels to the Old Testament."[43] The American Assyriologist Paul Haupt (Baltimore) supported the assertions of the popular anti-Semitic writer Houston Stewart Chamberlain, who had denied the Jewish origin of the New Testament by disseminating his thesis of an alleged Aryan ancestry of Jesus. In the heated discussion that followed, Haupt's communication was challenged by the German theologians Ernst Sellin (Rostock) and Adolf Deißmann (Berlin). Deißmann presented an indisputable argument by shoving aside all questions about the racial origin of Jesus as irrelevant and unanswerable by scientific methods: "In regard to religion, Jesus was unquestionably a Jew, and Christianity is unquestionably of Jewish origin."[44]

The profound impression left by Merkle's lecture was matched only by Erich Marck's presentation on Bismarck's youth.[45] Here, the master of the art of psychobiography and author of works on Coligny, Emperor William I, and Queen Elizabeth I of England presented a study that especially moved those German listeners who were concerned about the present political situation and looked back fondly at the heady days of the founder of the German Empire.

Biographical studies, being one of the classic forms of historiography, were repeatedly presented in Berlin. Historians from various countries spoke on

Archimedes, Emperor Constantine, William the Conqueror, Servet, Coligny, Gustav Adolf, and once more on Bismarck. But the biographical issues did not dominate. With a few exceptions, the history of foreign policy did not play a remarkable role either. As the organizers responsible for the Congress, the Berlin historians had decided not to treat the "great struggles between the nations," though they viewed them as the central issue of history. Instead, topics were presented from the fields of archaeology, Oriental and ancient history, and cultural, economic, scientific, legal, and constitutional history. Some of the lectures were given particular emphasis in the journals. For example, at the general meetings, Gaston Maspéro, the French general director of the Egyptian state antiquities department, spoke about the conservation of historical monuments in the land of the Nile; Mikhail Rostovtzev (St. Petersburg) spoke on the Roman colonate; Leone Caetani Principe di Teano (Rome), the author of a history of Islam, spoke on historical Islam research, and with particular resonance, Sir Frederick Pollock (London) spoke on "The Peculiar Phenomenon of the Committees in the Government and Administration of England."[46] In one section lecture, Henri Pirenne dealt with the constitution of the Romanic-Germanic Burgundian centralized state;[47] based on comparative studies, Kurt Kaser (Vienna) reported on the development of modern forms of government in late medieval territories and Felix Rachfahl (Gießen) on assemblies of estates.[48]

Within the spectrum of these widely scattered topics, the largest space was reserved for questions of methods—not methodological theory, but rather techniques of historical practice. Such questions were treated in various sections, for example, in ancient history and legal history, but particularly in the section for the historical auxiliary sciences. Here, information was given on the status of the work on the *Corpus inscriptionum Etruscarum* (Olof A. Danielsson, Uppsala), on a general catalog of incunabula (Konrad Haebler), on international relations in medieval diplomas (Harry Breßlau), on the linguistic atlas of the German Reich (Ferdinand Wrede), and on a plan relating to a significant piece of medieval research, the *Germania Sacra*, presented by Paul Kehr, the director of the Prussian Historical Institute in Rome, and Albert Brackmann.[49] Martin Spahn, the holder of the Catholic chair for modern history at the University of Strasbourg, read a paper on "The Press as a Source for Recent History and Current Possibilities for Its Use."[50] Whereas at The Hague it had been possible to ignore the press entirely as a serious historical source, in Berlin the problems of its methodical evaluation and collection were brought up for discussion.

The organizers' intention had been to stage a Congress that would be characterized above all by the rigor of academic historical work. They appear to have succeeded. According to a German report, the Congress was marked "more by serious scientific cooperation than by a sociability aiming mostly at general impressions."[51] Accordingly, an American participant noted that the Berlin Congress had "brought the transformation of the amateurish gathering of ten years ago into a well-organized scientific body to conclusion."[52]

Two invitations had been received regarding the next Congress: one from the Greek government and one from the academic institutions of England. At its final convocation, the plenary meeting chose London by acclamation. A letter of support for the English invitation was signed by the twenty-two British scholars attending the Congress. It was enthusiastically described by the president, Koser, as a "*momentum aere perennius*" that should be deposited in the State Archive as a symbol of the amicable rapprochement of two related and neighboring peoples.[53] As a Swedish commentator noted, the semipolitical closing ceremony distinctly served the purpose of promoting Anglo-German détente.[54]

Notes

1. Congress Rome 1903: *Atti*, vol. 1, p. 126.
2. "Notizen und Nachrichten: Vermischtes," *Historische Zeitschrift* 91 (1903): 190.
3. Aloys Schulte, "Bericht über den Historikerkongreß," Deutsches Historisches Institut, Rome, Reg. 1.
4. Petition of 7 July 1903, Zentrales Staatsarchiv, Merseburg, Rep. 76 V c, Sect. 1, Tit. 11, Teil VI, no. 13, vol. 1, pp. 146–148.
5. A. von Harnack, "Der vierte Internationale Kongreß für historische Wissenschaften zu Berlin," *Internationale Wochenschrift für Wissenschaft, Kunst und Technik* 2 (1908): 514–519, here p. 514.
6. A. von Harnack, "Vom Großbetrieb der Wissenschaft," *Preußische Jahrbücher* 119 (1905): 193–201, here p. 198. On the background, see vom Brocke, "Professorenaustausch."
7. Petition of 31 July 1903, Zentrales Staatsarchiv, Merseburg, Rep. 76 V c, Sect. 1, Tit. 11, Teil VI, no. 13, vol. 1, pp. 140–143. The other signatories were Mommsen, Hirschfeld, Lenz, D. Schäfer, Delbrück, and Koser.
8. Quoted in *Kölnische Volkszeitung*, 28 Aug. 1908.
9. D. Schäfer, *Mein Leben* (Berlin, 1926), p. 163.
10. B. vom Brocke, "Hochschul- und Wissenschaftspolitik in Preußen und im Deutschen Kaiserreich 1882–1907: Das 'System Althoff,'" in *Bildungspolitik in Preußen zur Zeit des Kaiserreichs*, ed. P. Baumgart (Stuttgart, 1980), pp. 9–118, here pp. 65ff.
11. H. Diels, "Die Einheitsbestrebungen der Wissenschaft," *Internationale Wochenschrift für Wissenschaft, Kunst und Technik* 1 (1907): 3–10.
12. Ritter v. Heigel in "Notizen und Nachrichten: Vermischtes," *Historische Zeitschrift* 101 (1908): 693.
13. *Programm des Internationalen Kongresses für historische Wissenschaften, Berlin, 6. bis 9. August 1908* [hereafter Congress Berlin 1908: *Programm*] (Berlin, 1908).
14. The Berlin organizing committee decided against publishing the lectures and discussions. It regarded the published proceedings of the earlier Congresses as "catacombs, into which only very few scholars will descend in the future," and considered it to be more practical if "each scholar publishes his lecture in a place where he expects to find the most readers." Harnack, "Der vierte Internationale Kongreß," p. 515. The most complete information on the lectures can be found in the Congress reports published in *Berliner Tageblatt*, 6–13 Aug. 1908, in the organizing committee's own daily bulletin, the *Kongreß-Tageblatt*, nos. 1–7, 5–12 Aug. 1908 [hereafter Congress Berlin 1908: *Kongreß-Tageblatt*], and in T. Höjer, "Den internationelle Kongressen för historiska vetenskaper i Berlin 1908," *Historisk tidskrift* (Stockholm, 1908): 145–169.

15. G. Monod, "Bulletin historique: Le congrès historique de Berlin," *Revue historique* 99 (1908): 298–307, here p. 299.
16. Ibid., p. 298. Congress Berlin 1908: *Programm*, indicates 69. See also below appendix III.1.
17. F. Simiand, "Récents congrès internationaux: le Congrès historique de Berlin," *Revue de synthèse historique* 17 (1908): 222–223, here p. 223.
18. The individual figures are uncertain, particularly in regard to the small number of Frenchmen. Monod, "Congrès de Berlin," p. 299, stated their number as 18; according to the official list of participants it was 22; according to the report of the Berlin organizing committee the French government had registered a delegation of nine historians. However, the registration arrived only after the end of the Congress, and only three of the delegates actually appeared. The report of the organizing committee compared this low number with the 131 Frenchmen attending the Rome Congress. The disappointment was evident. See Bericht des Organisationskomitees, n.d., Zentrales Staatsarchiv, Merseburg, Rep. 76 V c, Sect. 1, Tit. 11, Teil VI, no. 13, vol. 1. Monod, "Congrès de Berlin," mistakenly stated that the few Frenchmen contributed eleven papers to the Congress, more than the participants of any other country besides Germany. According to the advance information, it should have been 15, and 20 from Italy. See appendix III.1. In reality, only three Frenchmen spoke at the Congress: G. Maspéro (Cairo), "Ce qui se fait en Égypte pour sauver les monuments historiques"; L. Pélinier (Montpellier), "Origines et caractères généraux de la tyrannie (signoria) en Italie au 14e siècle"; J. Viénot, "La correspondence de Coligny." Simiand, "Congrès historique," p. 222, comments on this: "Il faut le dire en effet: les Français qui ont adhéré, et, encore davantage, ceux qui sont venus à ce Congrès, ont été si peux nombreux, les illustrations de l'école historique française étaient presque si complètement absentes, que les organisateurs du Congrès ont pu croire à une abstention systématique et concertée."
19. U. von Wilamowitz-Moellendorff, *Erinnerungen 1848–1914* (Leipzig, 1928), p. 311.
20. Letter of 28 Aug. 1908, Pirenne Papers, correspondence 1908.
21. Congress Berlin 1908: *Kongreß-Tageblatt*, p. 144f.
22. Among others: E. Gothein, *Politische und religiöse Volksbewegungen vor der Reformation* (Breslau, 1878); *Der christlich-soziale Staat der Jesuiten in Paraguay* (Leipzig, 1883); *Geschichtliche Entwicklung der Rheinschiffahrt im 19. Jahrhundert* (Leipzig, 1903); *Verfassungs- und Wirtschaftsgeschichte der Stadt Köln* (Köln, 1916).
23. These theoretical demands are expressed in Lamprecht, *Deutsche Geschichte,* 2nd ed., vol. 1, foreword, and in a large number of essays.
24. H.-J. Steinberg, "Karl Lamprecht," in *Deutsche Historiker*, ed. H.-U. Wehler, vol. 1 (Göttingen, 1971), pp. 58–68, here p. 59f.
25. See G. Oestreich, "Die Fachhistorie und die Anfänge der sozialgeschichtlichen Forschung in Deutschland," *Historische Zeitschrift* 208 (1969): 320–363.
26. Monod, "Congrès de Berlin," p. 304.
27. See Erdmann, "Geschichte, Politik und Pädagogik," pp. 2ff.
28. K. Lamprecht, "Die kultur- und universalgeschichtlichen Bestrebungen an der Universität Leipzig: Vortrag gehalten auf dem Internationalen Historikerkongreß zu Berlin am 11. August 1908," *Internationale Wochenschrift für Wissenschaft, Kunst und Technik* 2 (1908): 1142–1150.
29. Ch. H. Haskins, "The International Historical Congress at Berlin," *American Historical Review* 14 (1908): 1–8.
30. Höjer, "Kongressen i Berlin," pp. 145–169.
31. "Notizen und Nachrichten: Vermischtes," *Historische Zeitschrift* 101 (1908): 693.
32. P. Herre, "Bericht über den Internationalen Kongreß für historische Wissenschaften in Berlin, 6.–12. August 1908," *Historische Vierteljahrschrift* 11 (1908): 417–426.
33. H. Helmolt, "Der IV. Internationale Kongreß für Historische Wissenschaften: Berlin, 6.–12. August 1908," *Historisches Jahrbuch der Görresgesellschaft* 30 (1909): 218–222.
34. Simiand, "Congrès historique," p. 223.

35. Monod, "Congrès de Berlin," p. 303f.
36. Recalling his studies in Leipzig in 1898 and his encounter with Lamprecht, Koht emphasized his teacher's fundamental thought, which had so fascinated him and others, namely, "that history must encompass all human life, so that one must not divide it up into economic history, political history, art and literary history etc. It was the strong interconnection between all forces of human society after which he always sought." H. Koht, "Aus den Lehrjahren eines Historikers," *Die Welt als Geschichte* 13 (1953): 149–163, here p. 155. Pirenne's view was similar; see B. Lyon, "The letters of Henri Pirenne to Karl Lamprecht (1894–1915)," *Académie Royale de Belgique, Bulletin de la Commission Royale d'Histoire* 132 (1966): 161–231. In the series *Geschichte der europäischen Staaten*, ed. K. Lamprecht, Iorga published his *Geschichte des rumänischen Volkes* (2 vols., Gotha, 1905) and *Geschichte des osmanischen Reiches* (5 vols., Gotha, 1908–1913). See also Lamprecht's correspondence with foreign scholars in Universitätsbibliothek Bonn, Lamprecht papers.
37. This particularly applies to Pirenne. See B. Lyon, *Henri Pirenne: A biographical and intellectual study* (Ghent, 1974), pp. 216–219.
38. The German-language lecture under the title "Vom ethischen Beruf des Historikers" can be found in *Neue Revue* (Berlin, 1908): 1452ff.; English version: D. J. Hill, "The Ethical Function of the Historian," *American Historical Review* 14 (1908/09): 9–20.
39. R. Fester, "Die Säkularisation der Historie," *Historische Vierteljahrschrift* 11 (1908): 441–459; published under separate cover Leipzig, 1909.
40. Helmolt, "IV. Internationaler Kongreß," p. 221. Detailed report on Finke's lecture in Höjer, "Kongressen i Berlin," pp. 157ff.
41. Published in an expanded version: S. Merkle, *Die katholische Beurteilung des Aufklärungszeitalters* (*Kultur und Leben*, vol. 16. Berlin, 1909); he responded to the attacks provoked by his Berlin paper in Merkle, *Die kirchliche Aufklärung im katholischen Deutschland: Eine Abwehr und zugleich ein Beitrag zur Charakteristik "kirchlicher" und "nichtkirchlicher" Geschichtsschreibung* (Berlin, 1910).
42. Merkle, *Die katholische Beurteilung*, foreword.
43. *Berliner Tageblatt*, 8 Aug. 1908, evening edition, p. 4.
44. *Berliner Tageblatt*, 11 Aug. 1908, evening edition, p. 4.
45. Marcks's lecture "Aus Bismarcks Jugend" was adopted in his famous unfinished biography: *Bismarck: Eine Biographie*, vol. 1: *Jugend* (Stuttgart, 1909).
46. German translation: F. Pollock, "Die Kommissionsverwaltung in England," *Jahrbuch für Gesetzgebung, Verwaltung und Volkswirtschaft im Deutschen Reich* 33 (Leipzig, 1909): 65–87.
47. German translation: H. Pirenne, "Die Entstehung und die Verfassung des Burgundischen Reiches im 15. und 16. Jahrhundert," ibid., pp. 33–63.
48. F. Rachfahl, "Alte und neue Landesvertretung in Deutschland," ibid., pp. 89–130.
49. A. Brackmann, "Über den Plan einer Germania sacra: Bericht über zwei Vorträge von P. Kehr und A. Brackmann gehalten auf dem Internationalen Kongreß für historische Wissenschaften in Berlin," *Historische Zeitschrift* 102 (1909): 325–334.
50. Expanded text in M. Spahn, "Die Presse als Quelle der neueren Geschichte und ihre gegenwärtigen Benutzungsmöglichkeiten," *Internationale Wochenschrift für Wissenschaft, Kunst und Technik* 2 (1908): 1163–1170, 1202–1211.
51. Herre, "Bericht," p. 419.
52. Haskins, "International Historical Congress," p. 8.
53. *The Athenaeum*, no. 4217, 22 Aug. 1908. The report of the Berlin organization committee to the Prussian ministry of education and cultural affairs emphasized the "obliging, indeed warm attitude" of the English participants and the scholarly high-level delegation from England. See Bericht des Organisationskomitees, n.d., Zentrales Staatsarchiv, Merseburg, Rep. 76 V c, Sect. 1, Tit. 11, Teil VI, no. 13, vol. 1.
54. Höjer, "Kongressen i Berlin," p. 168.

Chapter 6

AN *ENTENTE CORDIALE* OF HISTORIANS ON THE EVE OF THE WAR

London, 1913

The London International Congress of Historical Sciences took place in the concluding phase of the first Balkan War. Two weeks before the opening of the Congress, on 18 March 1913, the Greek King George I, a brother-in-law of the King of England, had been murdered in Saloniki. Due to the assassination, Edward VII, who had assumed the patronage over the Congress, did not see himself as being in a position to welcome the participants personally to a reception at Windsor. War and terror cast long shadows over the historians' convention in London. Under the chairmanship of the British foreign secretary Sir Edward Grey, a conference of ambassadors that was also meeting in London struggled to contain the Balkan troubles. Once again, above all thanks to British-German cooperation, it was possible to prevent the European great powers from being drawn into the conflict and thus setting the continent ablaze. But even so, the disastrous fatalist notion that a general war was inescapable was gaining ground. It was against this gloomy background that the historians assembled.

At the opening of the Congress an address by the British ambassador to the United States, Viscount James Bryce, who was unable to come due to diplomatic business, was presented. Bryce had made a name for himself as an author of writings on American history and the German Holy Roman Empire. In his address, he stated that a time had come in which history could only be conceived as world history, since the modern world had become a system in which each far-reaching event interacted with all other ones around the globe. Living at the crest of the colonial era, he understood the evolution by which the modern world was becoming one essentially as a process of progressive Europeanization. The task of the historians was to serve this development through the uncovering of universal connections. Starting points were given by the expansion of range that the

---

Notes for this chapter begin on page 66.

study of history had undergone during the last decades in both time and space, for example, in prehistory, in the archaeology of the early Oriental cultures, or in ethnology. But this also applied to the fact that, alongside political history, the other activities of the human mind in economics, society, and culture were being studied with equal interest. In a world increasingly growing together, he saw the historian's allegiance to truth as a duty to serve peace through scholarly work.

> As historians, we know how few wars have been necessary wars and how much more harm than good most wars have done. As historians, we know that every great people had its characteristic merits along with its characteristic faults. None is especially blameless, each has rendered its special services to humanity at large. We have the best reason for knowing how great is the debt each one owes to the other.... May not we and the students of physical science, who also labor for knowledge in their own fields, and bow as we do before the august figure of truth, hope to become a bond of sympathy between the nations, helping each people to feel and appreciate all that is best in the others, and seeking to point the way to peace and goodwill throughout the world?[1]

His declaration of belief, "Truth, and truth only, is our aim," sounded like an echo of Henri Houssaye's appeal at the Paris Congress thirteen years earlier: "La vérité, toute la vérité, rien que la vérité." However, this confidence in science was no longer matched by political optimism. Henri Pirenne had the impression that the moving appeal to peace in this speech was at the same time an expression of hidden fear.[2] And Karl Lamprecht even felt moved to conclude his lecture on recent intellectual currents in Germany with the inappropriate threat that "if, as he did not hope, it should come to war, then one shall have to reckon with the determination of the German people."[3]

The work of the Congress remained untouched by the international situation. As far as we can gather from our sources, no reference was made to the London ambassadors' conference and the threatening world situation. Like its predecessor in Berlin, this Congress had a strictly academic character, though the sociable aspect was not forgotten. There were numerous receptions and dinners in the various institutions and colleges, including Oxford and Cambridge. The primate of the Church of England invited the historians to Lambeth Palace.

The grateful response in all countries to British hospitality was joined by a critical tone in regard to the Congress's organization. The meeting rooms of the individual sections lay so far apart that it was impossible to move from one place to another during a morning or afternoon meeting. With a total registration of some 1,000 persons, the sections often met as isolated little groups of no more than twenty to thirty participants. In contrast to Berlin, there was no daily Congress bulletin informing participants of all the events and program changes. The national representation was very uneven. Next to the Britons, who made up about two-thirds of the participants, the German historians represented the largest group, which included several of their best names so that as in Berlin, the good relationship between British and German historians was conspicuous. On the provisional list of participants, besides 65 Germans, there were 30 Russians, including Poles, 25 Austrians, 22 Frenchmen, 20 Americans, about the same number from Holland and Belgium combined, and half as many from the Scandinavian countries.[4] The fact that only a few Frenchmen came was generally remarked on—as previously at Berlin. Obviously, political motivations could be ruled out in this case. The French newspapers attributed the much-lamented shortage of French presence in London to belated and insufficient information on both the British and French sides, but also to a lack of promotion by the French authorities.[5] On the other hand, the French ministry of public instruction stated that the French historians had shown no interest and that, among others, the Collège de France and the University of Paris had responded negatively to the invitation forwarded by the ministry.[6] Whatever the reason, once again there was no representative contribution to the contemporary theoretical and methodological discussion from France.

The preparation and execution of the Congress lay in the hands of Adolphus W. Ward, president of the British Academy and master of Peterhouse, Cambridge. He was a well-known writer and political historian, not least as the editor of the world-renowned *Cambridge Modern History*. An admirer of Ranke, he was one of the founders of the modern academic study of history in England, alongside Stubbs and Seeley.[7] In his position as the chairman of the executive committee, he was supported by George W. Prothero as vice-chairman, Israel Gollancz as secretary, and James P. Withney as "secretary for papers." The *American Historical Review* cogently summed up the peculiarities of the London Congress as follows:

> The functions of government in such matters being more limited in Great Britain than in Germany, it was naturally arranged that the British Academy, in cooperation with universities, societies and other institutions interested in historical science, should undertake the organization of the congress. An organization thus based would almost of necessity lack some degree of unity and effectiveness. The general committee of organization, nearly a hundred in number, represented some eighty-four different societies and institutions; the executive committee, upon which presumably the actual work fell, was of the excessive number of sixty. It is to be expected that British individualism, which has had such brilliant results in history, should have its compensation in an organizing power, for such occasions, inferior to that of some other nations.... But while the course of the Congress was marked by some *contretemps* ... there was not a single foreign member ... for whom the sense of such defects was not quite overborne by appreciation for the abounding hospitality, kindness, and desire to make the occasion agreeable in every way to the visitors. Individuals exerted themselves valiantly to do whatever organization had not already effected, and the atmosphere of solicitude and goodwill was unmistakable.[8]

The structure of the Congress was similar to that of Berlin: some two hundred lectures were held in two general sessions and in nine sections. There was again no separate section for methodology, which was classified as a subdivision of the auxiliary sciences. Instead there was a new section for military and naval history. The Britons hoped that it would make historical experience available for a practical purpose, namely, the coordination of naval and land forces. The enhanced status of this section was emphasized by the fact that the First Sea Lord, Prince Battenberg, chaired one of the meetings, and that the papers presented there were published in a separate volume. The contributions to the legal history section directed by Paul Vinogradoff, which the Italian historian Volpe praised as the most impressive of the entire Congress, appeared in a separate publication as well. Otherwise, the Congress's organizers abstained from a collective publication of lectures and discussions, though the participants received abstracts of the papers during the Congress.[9]

It goes without saying that at such congresses strong attention is paid to the history of the host country, but apparently this was carried too far in London. The *American Historical Review* noted with some irritation: "There was a natural proclivity toward themes that might be of interest to an audience prevailingly English. Not only did forty of the British papers (which constituted more than half of the entire programme) relate to British history, but nearly twenty of the others [did too].... An American could not help thinking it to be a strange fact that, of more than a hundred papers presented by British subjects, only one was concerned wholly, and another partially, with the history of the United States, a country embracing nearly two-thirds of the English-speaking population of the globe."[10] The Italian Volpe judged the intensive preoccupation with English topics quite differently.[11] He was profoundly impressed particularly by the numerous contributions on English constitutional and legal history, since they were all related to the debate on the relative significance of the Anglo-Saxon, Norman, and Roman elements in British history, an important issue for Britain's historical-political self-conception.

The national flavor that the host country gave to the International Congress also manifested itself in regard to language. Just as French had dominated in Paris, Italian in Rome, and German—although less noticeably—in Berlin, now in London it was the turn of English. There were four official Congress languages. Two-thirds of the lectures were held in English, followed by French and German, with Italian a distant fourth. As the Congresses developed and international cooperation expanded, it became necessary to discuss a more even international distribution of the topics and language use. At the Berlin Congress, Wilamowitz had already recommended including Russian among the Congress languages. In London, Professor Bubnov from Kiev duly filed a motion on behalf of his department and university that everyone should have the right to use any language he desired. Good sense and the desire to be understood would form a sufficient check upon vagaries.[12] The inclusion of Russian was decided by the fact that at the concluding meeting, an invitation to hold the next Congress in St. Petersburg in 1918 was accepted. The Kiev proposal was certainly the most appropriate option for an ecumenical community of historians, since it counteracted tendencies toward linguistic imperialism and promised to satisfy everyone's feelings for his respective country without leading to Babelish chaos. In this context, a commentary in *The Times* can be regarded as a remarkable sign of linguistic self-criticism: it stated that of the four lectures delivered in the general opening meeting, only one was presented in English whereas the others were held in German and French. The result had been that scarcely any Britons could be found among the listeners. The *Times* did not point out this fact in order to argue that greater respect should be shown for the world language of the host country. Instead, it challenged Britain's historians to learn foreign languages. This appeal certainly was meant as a categorical imperative for all historians in all countries, and as an elementary precondition for the "better international understanding" that was proclaimed so often at this Congress.[13]

Compared to Berlin, the papers presented in London dealt more often with international relations and political events. Yet in number, such subjects lagged far behind themes of constitutional, economic, social, and cultural history. One must agree with the *American Historical Review*, which praised the generally high level of the lectures while observing that only very few of them were characterized by remarkable originality.[14] Yet several important names stand out: Harold Temperley and Charles Webster, who would later play a significant role in the history of the International Historical Congresses and who would set new standards with their editions and studies on foreign policy in the European system of powers, treated problems of colonial policy[15] and conference diplomacy.[16] One of Europe's leading legal historians, Sir Frederick Pollock, examined the evolution of the term "equity," a variant form of natural law.[17] He spoke in the legal history section chaired by the renowned legal historian Sir Paul Vinogradoff. Here Otto von Gierke, whose epochal work on natural law theories (*Althusius und die Entwicklung der naturrechtlichen Staatstheorien*, 1880) had provided decisive impulses for Pollock's work, spoke on "The History of the Majority Principle."[18] This lecture dovetailed with Gierke's studies on the German corporate bodies (*Das deutsche Genossenschaftsrecht*, 4 volumes, 1868–1913). In it the "historic-organicistic" approach was impressively stated by a proponent whose influence was felt far beyond the borders of Germany up until the World War. Adhémar Esmein, who had been the *spiritus rector* and organizer of the section for comparative legal history in Paris, examined the principle of *"legibus solutus,"* which typified the self-understanding of absolutism.[19] Aleksandr Lappo-Danilevsky, a member of the St. Petersburg Academy, spoke on the concept of state in Russia and its permutations.[20] He became the chairman of the Russian organizing committee for the next Congress, planned for St. Petersburg. The Romanian historian Nicolae Iorga, who was devoted to the idea of unity of Western and Eastern European history, delivered the first two of his many contributions to the International Historical Congresses. They suggested a universal, pan-European reinterpretation of the Middle Ages, an interpretation that should no longer be based on individual countries. Iorga was speaking here about one of his main preoccupations, namely, overcoming medieval scholars' narrow focus on Western Europe and shifting attention instead to the numerous bonds between the Southeast of Europe and the European West or South, related to each other as the heirs of the ancient world as it had been transmitted by the Eastern Roman Empire and the Western Roman Empire.[21] A study by Arnold Oskar Meyer on "Charles I and Rome" was structured on individual and psychological history, but at the same time it was an enlightening analysis of the relationship between the Roman and Anglican churches.[22]

The London Congress provided a forum for two historians whose divergent understanding of medieval economic and social history would later, and for many years, represent a touchstone for the recurring question of continuities and transformations in the transitional phase between ancient times and the Middle Ages. The Austrian Alfons Dopsch spoke on "The Money Economy in the Carolingian Era."[23] In contrast to Henri Pirenne, he advanced the thesis that the Carolingian era in no way fell back to a primitive barter economy, but that a barter economy and a money economy existed side by side. In general, however, the Carolingian period experienced an expansion of economics and trade. A direct confrontation between Dopsch and Pirenne did not take place until fifteen years later at the Oslo Congress. In London, at a plenary meeting, Pirenne dealt with another much-discussed question of economic and social history, "Stages in the Social History of Capitalism," which was viewed as the most spectacular lecture of the Congress.[24]

Pirenne's lecture represented a wide-ranging, rhetorically brilliant confrontation with German economic historians such as Max Weber and particularly Werner Sombart. While borrowing Sombart's definition of capitalism— "goods exploited by their owners with the intention of reproducing them with profit"—he rejected his thesis that capitalism had appeared as a historical phenomenon only in modern times. Pirenne thought that the social historical type of the capitalist—who creates wealth out of nothing through personal ability and intelligence via trade and speculation—could be identified from the early Middle Ages on, appearing in different situations analogous to each other in structure, and disappearing repeatedly into the landowning class through absorption. Pirenne's treatment of history in this lecture was characterized by the attempt to demonstrate the regularity of a recurring process. He was not interested in characterizing individuals but rather in a human type, the capitalist. In doing so, he examined individuals who represented, and at the same time transcended, this type. Without theorizing and without tedious speculations, Pirenne used a concrete research example—the British Saint Goderic—to show how old and new approaches, idiographic and nomothetic methods, could be linked. In another section lecture, Pirenne discussed the relationship of long-distance trade and the medieval urban economy. Here, he asserted that the generally accepted view was too strongly influenced by a focus on the guilds, and paid too little attention to the capitalist element.[25]

There were some other papers devoted to methodological issues. In a lecture on "The Organization of Academic Historical Studies," Lamprecht dealt with the necessity of reform, as he had done in Berlin. Other communications, such as those of the Britons Thomas F. Tout and Charles H. Firth, likewise emphasized the shortcomings of historical instruction at the universities. Ever since the beginning of their academic activity in Manchester and Oxford, they had dedicated themselves actively and successfully to a reform of the study of history. But the *gravamina* that they now presented in London had a different accent from those of Lamprecht. They pleaded for better training in the techniques of scholarly work and a stronger consideration of the auxiliary sciences, such as paleography and diplomatics.[26] The Englishman Whitwell suggested creating a comprehensive dictionary of Medieval Latin. It was also agreed that the numerous source editions currently underway should be entrusted to trained historians more than had been the case previously.

In a second plenary lecture, Lamprecht spoke on "The Most Recent Intellectual Currents in Germany."[27] Historiographical themes were treated by Eduard Meyer, in a survey on writings about ancient history during the past decades,[28] and by Ernst Bernheim, the author of the famous standard work on the historical method,[29] "whose pupils we all are," as one participant commented.[30] Bernheim opened the series of plenary lectures with the topic "The Interpretation of History as Influenced by Contemporary Views." He treaded the well-worn paths of a relativistic historicism.[31] By contrast, the lecture by the American Frederick A. Woods on "Historiometry" pointed toward a new field that only came to full fruition much later on, when he recommended quantitative analysis as a method securing the scientific character of history. According to the *Historische Zeitschrift*, the reflection on methodological questions took up a very large space in London, even if it was not given a section of its own: the various disciplines' methods, tasks, and techniques were discussed in all sections, at least in the introductory comments of the chairmen.[32] When the Congress's acting president, Adolphus W. Ward, recommended a "history of historians" in the opening session, it was in response to the historical profession's need to reflect its own practice and thought. He recalled Lord Acton's contribution to the first issue of the *English Historical Review* on German historiography, praised the achievements of that "group of French historical scholars to whom the idea of the Congress is due," and pointed to the book *History and Historians in the Nineteenth Century* by Acton's pupil George P. Gooch, which had appeared just in time for the opening of the Congress. In this way it was already emphasized in this early phase of the International Historical Congresses that historical scholarship ought to include the study of its own history in its reflection on its work and tasks.[33]

There was also no lack of a certain ironic distancing from the industrious pedantry of a historical profession that had blind trust in archival records. For example, Lord Morley of Blackburn, a literary critic, statesman, and author of numerous biographies, observed at a reception at All Souls College: "Today, historic science has turned taste and fashion away from the imposing tapestries of the literary historian to the drab serge of research among diplomatic archives, parish registries, private documents, and anything else provided it is not in print. As Acton puts it, the great historian now takes the meals in the kitchen."[34] Both Viscount Morley and the Congress's absent president, Viscount Bryce, can be included in that category of English—often aristocratic—writers, politicians, and historians who were more than mere professionals and about whom Wilamowitz-Moellendorff said in his London speech of greeting that, in comparison with the Continent, they represented a greater independence and autonomy of intellectual life. "The renowned German scholar," noted the *Frankfurter Zeitung*, expressed "his wish to the English colleagues that the great, isolated amateurs who substantially represent England's scholarly fame may be preserved."[35]

As the quintessence of the London Congress, the *American Historical Review* picked up an idea that had first been suggested by de Maulde in The Hague and then by Monod, namely, that the historians' "entente cordiale,"[36] as it presented itself at the International Congresses, needed to be given stronger continuity and coherence through the creation of a permanent international body:

> The executive committee, which had been in function during the six days of the Congress, had been fortified by a certain number of non-British members from the various sections. It is to be hoped, in the interest of proper future development and usefulness of the Congress as an institution, as well as in the more immediate interest of catholic judgements on matters concerning the next Congress in particular, that in its preliminary organization means may be taken toward creating at least a relatively permanent advisory committee of representatives of various nations which on each quinquennial occasion may act with the national body entrusted with the immediate proceedings. Such a step, toward which indeed some suggestion was made by the expiring committee, would aid to give continuity of regulations and policy, and might ultimately make the Congress a potent means, not merely as now of international friendship but of international achievement.[37]

The author of these words, John Franklin Jameson, editor of the *American Historical Review* and director of the historical research institute of the Carnegie Foundation in Washington, D.C., remained loyal to this idea during the ensuing war years. After the war he would help it come true.

Notes

1. *International Congress of Historical Studies, London 1913: Presidential Address by the Right Hon. James Bryce with suppl. remarks by A. W. Ward* (Oxford, 1913); also in *Proceedings of the British Academy* 6, 1913/14 (Oxford, 1920): 121–128.
2. Opening speech of Pirenne at the Brussels Congress, 1923, in *Compte rendu du Ve Congrès International des Sciences Historiques, Bruxelles 1923*, ed. G. Des Marez and F. L. Ganshof [hereafter Congress Brussels 1923: *Compte rendu*] (Brussels, 1923), p. 19.
3. Quoted in *Frankfurter Zeitung*, 11 April 1913, evening edition.
4. See Congress reports in "Nachrichten und Notizen," *Historische Vierteljahrschrift* 16 (1913): 588f.; W. Michael, "Der Internationale Kongreß für Historische Wissenschaften" (under the heading "Vermischtes"), *Historische Zeitschrift* 111 (1913): 464–469; Ch. Bémont, "Le troisième congrès international d'histoire," *Revue historique* 113 (1913): 216–218; L. S., "Den tredje internationella kongressen för historiska studier i London 1913," *Historisk tidskrift* (Stockholm, 1913): 97–104; J. F. Jameson, "The International Congress of Historical Studies, held at London," *American Historical Review* 18 (1913): 679–691.
5. H. Hauser, "A propos d'un congrès," *Revue internationale de l'enseignement* 33, no. 2 (Paris, 1913): 2ff. H. Berr shared Hauser's critical attitude; see *Revue de synthèse historique* 26 (1913): 282.
6. Correspondence between Charles Bémont, co-editor of the *Revue historique*, with Ministère de l'Instruction publique. Archives Nationales, F^{17}, 3092^1.
7. A. W. Ward, "The Study of History at Cambridge," in Ward, *Collected Papers*, vol. 5 (Cambridge, 1921).
8. Jameson, "International Congress," p. 679f.
9. *Naval and Military Essays, being read in the Naval and Military Section of the International Congress of Historical Studies, 1913*, ed. J. S. Cobett and H. J. Edwards (Cambridge Naval and Military Series, London, 1913); *Essays in Legal History read before the International Congress of Historical Studies*, ed. P. Vinogradoff (London, 1913) [hereafter: Congress London 1913: *Legal History*]. A collection of the abstracts and the printed Congress program can be found in the Koht papers, Ms. fol. 3668:3. A thorough report on the Congress appeared in *The Times*, 3–9 April 1913. A detailed scholarly report—the most painstaking and thorough report on any of the International Historical Congresses in any professional journal I know of—was provided by G. Volpe in *Archivo Storico Italiano*, reprinted in Volpe, *Storici e Maestri*, 2nd ed. (Rome, 1966), pp. 297–362.
10. Jameson, "International Congress," p. 687.
11. See Volpe, *Storici*, pp. 297ff.
12. Jameson, "International Congress," p. 688. At the Congress, a pamphlet in French and Russian was distributed, entitled: *Les Titres Scientifiques de la Langue Russe pour l'Admission de la Langue Russe dans les Congrès Historiques Internationaux* (Kiev, 1913).
13. Congress report in *The Times*, 5 April 1913. For the origins of the Kiev resolution and the early beginning of preparations for the Petrograd Congress in Russia, see A. G. Slonimsky, "Učastie russijskich učënych v Meždunarodnych kongressach istorikov" [The participation of Russian historians at the International Historical Congresses], *Voprosy istorii* 45, no. 7 (1970): 95–108.
14. Jameson, "International Congress," p. 687.
15. H. Temperley, "Some problems of British colonial policy in the eighteenth century." Abstract in Koht papers, Ms. fol. 3668:3.
16. Ch. Webster, "England and Europe 1815." Abstract in Koht papers, Ms. fol. 3668:3.
17. F. K. Pollock, "Transformation of equity." Text in Congress London 1913: *Legal History*; cf. Pollock, "La continuité du droit naturel," in Congress Paris 1900: *Annales*, vol. 1, 2nd section, pp. 109ff. In Paris he had outlined the problem tackled in London: "Il y a encore une histoire

très intéressante et qui n'a jamais été faite, c'est celle de l'influence du droit naturel dans le droit anglais, sous des noms variés comme: justice naturelle, équité, conscience éclairée."
18. Text in Congress London 1913: *Legal History*.
19. A. Esmein, "La maxime 'Princeps legibus solutus est' dans l'ancien droit public français," ibid.
20. Text ibid.
21. N. Iorga, *1. Les bases nécessaires d'une nouvelle histoire du moyen-âge. 2. La survivance byzantine dans les pays roumains* (Bucharest/Paris, 1913).
22. Text in *American Historical Review* 19 (1913/14): 13–26.
23. He developed the thoughts presented in London more thoroughly in A. Dopsch, *Die Wirtschaftsentwicklung der Karolingerzeit vornehmlich in Deutschland*, 2 vols. (Weimar, 1912, 1913).
24. *American Historical Review* 19 (1914): 494–515. Completed French version "Les périodes de l'histoire sociale du capitalisme," in *Bulletin de l'Académie Royale de Belgique, Classe des Lettres* (Brussels, 1914), reprint in *Henri Pirenne, Histoire économique de l'Occident Médiéval*, ed. É. Coornaert (Bruges, 1951), pp. 15–50.
25. Jameson, "International Congress," p. 685.
26. C. H. Firth, "The study of modern history in Great Britain," and T. F. Tout, "The present state of medieval studies in Great Britain," both in *Proceedings of the British Academy* 6, 1913/14 (Oxford, 1920), pp. 139ff. and 151ff. See also C. H. Firth, *A Plea for the Historical Teaching of History* (Inaugural Address, Oxford, 1905); Goldstein, "Professionalization."
27. Congress report in *Frankfurter Zeitung*, 11 April 1913, evening edition.
28. "Alte Geschichte und historische Forschung während des letzten Menschenalters," ibid.
29. *Lehrbuch der historischen Methode und der Geschichtsphilosophie* (Munich/Leipzig 1889, 6th ed. 1908).
30. Jameson, "International Congress," p. 684.
31. Abstract in Koht papers, Ms. fol. 3668:3.
32. Michael, "Kongreß 1913," p. 465.
33. A. W. Ward, "Introductory words" and "Closing remarks" on the speech by J. Bryce, in *Proceedings of the British Academy* 6, 1913/14 (Oxford, 1920), pp. 113–121 and 129–132.
34. Congress report in *The Times*, 10 April 1913.
35. Congress report in *Frankfurter Zeitung*, 8 April 1913, evening edition.
36. G. W. Prothero used this formula along with that of a "Concert of Europe" at the conclusion of the London Congress. See Congress report in *The Times*, 9 April 1913.
37. Jameson, "International Congress," p. 691.

Chapter 7

Overcoming Nationalism in the Study of History

Brussels, 1923

The maelstrom of the war swept away all that had grown over decades of international scholarly cooperation. As natural as it appeared that scholars, too, were willing to throw in their lot with the war efforts of their respective countries, it was still highly compromising that reason and all sense of proportion were scattered to the wind in the academic world as well. On both sides, renowned scholars fought in public declarations and manifestos for their countries' cause, unleashing "a war of minds" whose results, combined with the resentment caused by the events and outcome of the war, would reverberate long afterward.[1] "Why we are at War" was the title of a brochure published by Oxford historians in September 1914.[2] In October 1914 some 150 English academics declared that in England as well as in Belgium the war was being fought for the cause of "freedom and peace."[3] French scholars and historians discovered brutality, the hunger for power, and unscrupulousness to have been the touchstones of German politics since the Germanic migration. German scholarship, they asserted, had also succumbed to this spirit.[4]

The Germans responded with accusations aimed less against France than against "perfidious Albion" and "Russian barbarity," or else with blind justifications of the occurrences in Belgium and the conduct of submarine warfare.[5] Particular attention was attracted by an "Appeal to the Civilized World" (*Aufruf an die Kulturwelt*), which was issued in ten different languages on 4 October 1914, bearing the signatures of 93 academics.[6] Alongside the physicist Max Planck, the signatories included such respected scholars as Ulrich von Wilamowitz-Moellendorff, Adolf von Harnack, Max Lenz, and Eduard Meyer. The signatories understood this appeal as a refutation of unfounded accusations against Germany. But because of its pronounced declaration of belief in the German army and Germany's military leaders, it was viewed

---

Notes for this chapter begin on page 96.

abroad—even years after the end of the war—as proof that the educated world in Germany had also succumbed to the pernicious ideology of militarism. The mathematician and statesman Paul Painlevé declared before the Académie des Sciences on 2 December 1918 that German science was "a giant company in which, with patient servility, an entire people worked to manufacture the most terrifying murder machinery that ever existed."[7] Referring to the "Manifesto of the 93," the Académie des Inscriptions et des Belles Lettres in Paris, under the chairmanship of the historian Théophile Homolle, expelled Wilamowitz and canceled the cooperation on an edition of Greek inscriptions that had been agreed upon before the war.[8] In doing so, it followed the example of the other French academies, which had likewise dismissed their German members. The humanities class of the Belgian Academy, too, decided unanimously to expel all members from the German Empire and its allies on 3 February 1919, pointing to the "Manifesto of the 93" as a justification. They declared that all German scholars had to be equated with these 93. The "German race" had "prostituted" scholarship by placing itself "in the service of militarism and a barbarous autocracy ... whose sole aim was mastery over the world."[9]

But among both the belligerents and the neutral countries, there were voices as well who continued to argue that international cooperation and exchange were an essential precondition of scientific progress and ought to be maintained. An outstanding example of this spirit was Benedetto Croce.[10] But only a minority of historians shared this opinion, and even they doubted that international contacts in the academic world could be repaired any time soon in view of the mutual recriminations and mistrust. They were outnumbered by those who questioned the value of scientific cooperation in general, or who rejected contact with the scientific world of the respective enemy countries for the foreseeable future. In this context, one aspect that had occasionally been discernible before the war took to the foreground:[11] the international preeminence of German scholarship, which now was frequently emphasized by German scholars themselves, and the protests, particularly by the French scholars, against it. Thus did Ulrich von Wilamowitz-Moellendorff write at the beginning of the war: "We Germans will not take lightly the responsibility that has been placed upon us because we hold the leadership in sciences; the others know this too, even if they do not admit it."[12] Even Ernst Troeltsch stated in 1914 that European culture could very well be attended to by the Germans alone, although only "in an emergency," if general international cooperation should not be possible again.[13] On the other side, French and English scholars asserted as well that, like the "Pan-Germanists," the German scholars were striving for Germany's dominance over other countries and had only exploited international congresses in order to bring international scholarship under their control and to create a German "monopoly."[14]

Toward the end of the war, when heightened nationalism prevailed on all sides, efforts began to put scientific cooperation, if only rudimentary, back into motion. It is within this context that preparations were started for the founding of an International Committee of Historical Sciences, the ICHS. To illustrate the conditions of its beginnings, we will first examine what became of the International Association of Academies established before the war. Following its last meeting in St. Petersburg in 1913, the chairmanship was routinely transferred to the Royal Prussian Academy in Berlin.[15] When war broke out, the German side suggested entrusting this task to a neutral country, namely, the Netherlands, as a provisional measure. The British Royal Society agreed, but the Paris Academy objected and demanded the transfer of the chairmanship to the Netherlands as a final measure. Since the Berlin Academy did not agree to this, the Association's future remained open. Neutral countries attempted to mediate, but after the United States had joined the war these efforts dwindled away.

At the end of the war, plans for the reconstruction of an international association of academies were developed in the Entente countries, which excluded Germany and its allies. In October 1918, a conference that had been summoned by the Royal Society in agreement with the Paris and Brussels Academies of Sciences took place in London. It was attended by natural scientists from England, France, the United States, Belgium, Japan, Serbia, Brazil, Portugal, and Italy. Here it was decided to cancel the membership of all international organizations of the prewar period, and to set up an international organization of all disciplines of the natural sciences excluding the Central Powers. A resolution was passed stating that the Central Powers had offended against international law and civilization, and that they had terrorized prisoners of war and the civilian population deliberately and regularly. This guilt could not be lifted through material reparations. Cooperation required trust; this trust, however, required the rejection of all political methods leading to the war atrocities perpetrated by the Central Powers. Only when the latter had once again been accepted into "the concert of civilized nations" could international scholarly relations be restored.[16]

On the basis of these agreements, a conference convened in Paris from 26 to 29 November 1918, in which the countries represented in London were joined by delegations from Romania and Poland. There it was decided to found the International Council of Research (Conseil International de Recherches), to whose supervision and statutes the professional unions of the various disciplines, which were all to be founded anew, should be subordinated; here, too, the exclusionary clause toward the Central Powers should be enforced. At first, only sixteen nations were authorized to participate—mainly those in the wartime alliance of the Entente. New admissions would be decided upon by a three-quarters majority. These provisions were confirmed at the founding assembly of the International Council of Research in Brussels from 18 to 28 July 1919.

The neutral states were not automatically accepted. They had not been present at the preceding meetings in 1918, and apparently had not even been invited. The statutes adopted in Brussels did not provide for a general admission of the neutral states, instead naming ten nations that should be encouraged to join (including the Netherlands, Switzerland, Spain, and the Scandinavian countries). The debates at the founding conferences show that the participants viewed the neutral countries as a danger and a burden: if they did not participate, then it was to be expected that German scholarship would join with them to restore the old unions; however, if they were included, then a softening of the anti-German front was to be feared. This explains the painstaking formulation of the "exclusionary clause" and the establishment of a solid three-quarters majority for all new admission applications, with the particularly uncompromising French and Belgians taking the lead against the British and Americans to demand that the distribution of votes should occur according to the population size of the individual countries, including their colonies.

The natural sciences were followed by the humanities. Initiated by the humanities departments of the academies of the Allied countries, but including the neutral states from the beginning, an International Academic Union (Union Académique Internationale) was founded in 1919.[17] Like the Conseil International de Recherches, the Union also had its headquarters and place of assembly in Brussels. Henri Pirenne became its first president. The statutes of the Union did not decree the explicit exclusion of Germany or the Central Powers, but there was left no doubt that their scholars would not be admitted. Only the neutral states were urged to join, and a three-quarters majority was prescribed for all applications. The report on the Union's founding conference, co-authored by Pirenne, stated in emotional and ambitious terms that a new republic of scholars would be created in the spirit of friendly, trusting, freedom-loving brotherhood. Whereas the former Association of Academies had been in danger of becoming the tool of nationalistic ambitions striving for scientific hegemony over the world, the new Union was to become an intellectual League of Nations, with the goal of "making researchers accustomed to thinking like human beings and seeking nothing else but the truth."[18]

German scholars first reacted with an attempt to re-establish international scholarly contacts on their own. They succeeded in this only to a limited extent, namely, in their relationship with Spain, South America, the Baltic States, Russia, and above all Austria. Austrian scholars aligned themselves closely with the organizations of German scholarship, as in the case of the Association of Universities (Hochschulverband), the Alliance of German Academies (Kartell der Deutschen Akademien), the Relief Organization of the German Sciences (Notgemeinschaft der deutschen Wissenschaft), and the Association of German Historians (Verband Deutscher Historiker). They demonstrated their solidarity with Germany by declining to participate in the two Western international associations of academies open to them after 1922. Beginning in 1923, regular forms of cooperation were agreed upon between Germany and Russia. Russia likewise honored the German rapprochement with its own rejection of the two Brussels organizations, "out of a sense of solidarity with our German colleagues."[19] In 1925, the Soviet Union attempted to revive the old international Association of Academies as an alternative to the associations in Brussels, but without success.

The endeavors to exclude German scholarship from international institutions and events were mirrored by the attitude of a considerable part of the German scholarly community, which in turn denounced any rapprochement with the "Brussels" institutions.[20] The *Kartell* of the German Academies, which also included the Vienna Academy, rejected cooperation with the Research Council and the Union of Academies. This position did not even change when, as of 1925/26, under the influence of Locarno and thanks to the continued efforts of Italy, the Netherlands, Norway, and the United States, the prospect opened up that a German application for membership in the two Brussels organizations would achieve the necessary majority. During the entire interwar period there was not a single act of cooperation between Germany and the International Research Council, even though Germany finally joined the Academic Union in 1935.

Things looked different within the individual disciplines. The fact that the historians, despite the proximity of their profession to national politics in the 1920s, realized a comprehensive international cooperation was the achievement of a group of men who even in wartime had the courage to look beyond the resentments and pursue their vision of a truly ecumenical community of historians.

Before the First World War, the impetus for a new beginning and for new paths came not from the old centers of historical research, but rather from outside. Now a young private institution in the New World took the initiative: the Office (later Department) of Historical Research at the Carnegie Institution in Washington, D.C. The director of this Office since 1905 had been John Franklin Jameson, editor of the *American Historical Review*. In fact, the Office had been created on his recommendation. Thanks to its sponsorship of research—particularly with regard to archival works but also to the creation of biographical and bibliographical tools—and, not least, to Jameson's rich and broad correspondence, it became a "clearing house of historical interests in the United States."[21] In the history of American historiography, Jameson is remembered as an important inspirer, promoter, and organizer. His activities, however, were felt far beyond the United States. It was he who, as early as in 1913, had spoken up for giving the International Historical Congresses an appropriate permanent machinery. He was also one of the foreign historians added to the Russian organizing committee in charge of the scheduled St. Petersburg Congress of 1918. During the war he thus was in occasional correspondence with its president, Aleksandr S. Lappo-Danilevsky, who died of hunger during the Russian Revolution. Jameson wrote to him on 16 July 1917, that a "truly ecumenical gathering of historians" was not to be expected for a long time to come. And yet, it should be possible to convene a meeting of the St. Petersburg organizing committee immediately after the war. He hoped that aside from representatives of the Allied and neutral countries "it might even be possible, by tactful dealings with a few men of the right kind, to bring about some small representation from Germany and Austria, perhaps some broad-minded Slavonic-Austrian who was on good terms with the Teutonic and Magyar historians in the dual monarchy, or possibly even some German of the type of Kehr,[22] who has lived out of Germany so long as to be able to think in international terms." This could be a first step toward reconciliation.[23]

Shortly afterward, he underlined his wish to integrate the Germans with a further argument: The international cooperation of the historians should not limit itself to the convocation of Congresses. He put a series of possible joint undertakings up for discussion, for instance the continuation of the *Hierarchia Catholica Medii Aevi*, a list of ambassadors and ministers of European countries in modern times, a documentation on the Danish Sound-Dues or on the Berlin Congress of 1878, and so forth. At the same time, he asked his Russian colleague to consider the fact that "there are few international historical enterprises of which we would feel that they could be done just as well without German cooperation."[24] This scholarly attitude did not arise from any sympathy for the German cause in the war. On the contrary: His correspondence with American and British colleagues evidences that he did not view this war as a struggle between two just causes, but rather as one between justice and injustice.[25]

He was particularly touched by the fate of his Belgian colleagues Paul Fredericq and Henri Pirenne, who had bravely and openly opposed German attempts to make the University of Ghent Flemish. In consequence, they had been deported to Germany. After a few months spent in a prison camp, Pirenne was sent to the university town of Jena and from there to Creuzburg, a small town near Eisenach.[26] Here he wrote the first draft of his economic and social history of the Middle Ages. Before the United States entered the war, Jameson sought ways and means of helping the two interned Belgians. Thus, he organized a signature campaign among American colleagues in support of a similar action in Holland and sounded out prospects for setting up guest professorships for them in the United States.

All in all, Jameson developed a vigorous consciousness of the task that would devolve upon the United States in the intellectual reconstruction of Europe. He outlined his ideas in a memorandum to the director of the Carnegie Foundation:

> In any probable event of the war, the United States will emerge from it less damaged in a pecuniary sense than any other of the belligerent nations, and it will of course be far richer than any of the neutrals. I am eager to see our country appreciate and assume the responsibilities which will arise from such a state of things, do all it can to repair the ravages which war will have inflicted on scientific and learned work, bear its proper share, which means a far larger share than it has hitherto borne, in preserving and advancing civilization along all those many lines in which civilization depends upon work of research.... We are easily able, if we choose, to make good the pecuniary losses the war will have inflicted in that domain, and it is our bounden duty, our duty to the cause of civilization, to go forward with energy and generosity in that field.

The first task, he thought, was to finance the reorganization of international scientific cooperation "in an ecumenical and international spirit, as scientific citizens of the world." This was aimed at science in general, but he expressly mentioned history, which would have to seek out new perspectives and methods after the war. He suggested that the Carnegie Foundation assume the initiative and the financing for a preliminary historical congress devoted to purposes of practical cooperation, possibly in the Palace of Peace in The Hague—"Germany and Austria included, if the Germans and Austrians were prepared to come."[27]

In Jameson's concept, the cosmopolitan goal of defusing nationalism was linked with the conviction that it was now up to historical scholarship to shift the methodological accent from the previous state and nation–oriented political history to social and economic developments, because the level of international interlacements was more advanced in these areas. As Jameson put it in his picturesque and sometimes drastic words: "Standard Oil is as catholic as the pope. I often feel that our habit of studying modern European history almost entirely in its political and diplomatic aspects has emphasized unduly the national element in its growth, and obscured the great processes by which the world has coalesced into what is in many respects already one great society. If we had been devoting our attention to economic history or to the history of civilization we should not be so prone to see the world chiefly as a body of separate entities called nations."[28]

The ecumenical unity of the historians could only be approached via back alleys, and with patience. First, Jameson attempted to convene a conference of a limited number of historians from those countries that had participated in the 1913 Congress in London. Its task should lie in the discussion of joint scholarly projects of the kind he had described in his previous letters, and in the preparation of a first international postwar Congress of Historical Sciences. The "non-Russian fragment" of the organizing committee for the planned Congress in St. Petersburg, he thought, seemed suited to prepare the meeting. For this reason, he turned to the British historians George W. Prothero and Charles H. Firth and hinted at the prospect of American financial support, without referring directly to German and Austrian participation. He had become cautious in view of the exclusionary tendencies in the Western academies. But the suggestion concerning the St. Petersburg committee, which certainly included the Central Powers,[29] was clear enough. "I think that all who attended the congress in London, had great pleasure and satisfaction in it, and would wish that such meetings might recur even in the new world which is separated by so much from that of 1913."[30] The two Britons poured water into the wine. Prothero, in Paris at the time as a member of the British peace delegation, did not believe that the time had come for an initiative of this kind. Under the current conditions, he said, it was idle speculation even to think about a new Congress of historians. Everything was too chaotic and the future was too uncertain.[31] By contrast, Firth was of the opinion that plans for an International Congress could be taken up without delay. However, he added, in response to Jameson's implied question: "Most English historians will decline to cooperate with German or Austrian historians either by meeting them in a Congress or by taking part in joint enterprises. Historical Congresses for the next 20 years or so must be composed of representatives of the allies or neutrals only. Bryce does not take this view, but so large a number of prominent historians do that it must be accepted as a fact."[32]

Jameson did not lose heart. Without insisting on the participation of German and Austrian historians in the intended congress, but keeping the issue open for later, he pursued his goal cautiously and tenaciously with his friends and colleagues at the Carnegie Foundation, Shotwell and Leland.

During the war, Professor James T. Shotwell had been the chairman of the National Board of Historical Service, which had been installed to perform publicity work concerning the situation in Europe. He subsequently served as a member of the American delegation at the Paris Peace Conference. In 1919 he went to London on behalf of a documentation project by the Carnegie Foundation and took charge of the series *Histoire économique et sociale de la guerre mondiale*. Waldo G. Leland, a student of Jameson and later his assistant in the Office for Historical Research, also worked on the National Board during the war. Before the war he had been concerned with an index of sources for American history in French archives.[33] In April 1922, he returned there. He had participated in the two International Congresses of 1908 and 1913. At the end of 1919, Jameson asked Shotwell to approach Pirenne, who had by now become the president of the Union Académique. Owing to his position, his experiences during the war, and his outstanding reputation as a historian, Pirenne was destined to play a decisive role in regard to whether, where, and under what circumstances an International Historical Congress should be convened.

Jameson suggested that such a Congress be held in Brussels in 1923.[34] He considered the Union Académique to be a suitable point of departure.[35] Shotwell urged the Royal Historical Society to deal with the question, and forwarded Jameson's suggestion. Pirenne expressed strong interest and saw no difficulties as to its execution, but nonetheless he was of the opinion that now, at the beginning, "there could be no question … of any conference except Allied and neutral countries participating."[36] Prothero imparted to Jameson that he had no objection to a Congress that would at first be restricted to the Allied and neutral nations, "if for any reason it turned out impossible to make it universal." However, he did not exclude the possibility that by the time of the planned Congress, "people may be more willing to invite the Germans to attend at all events if the League of Nations gets itself established, and if the Germans are admitted to it, as I hope they may be, before that time."[37]

For the prospects of re-creating full internationality once a certain distance had been gained from the war, it was of great significance that Pirenne did not demand a definite or long-term exclusion of the German historians. Still, he believed that such a limitation was necessary "at the beginning" or "for the first meeting."[38]

At the end of 1921, two years after Jameson's initiative, the Royal Historical Society suggested to the Belgian historians that they assume the organization of the next International Historical Congress in Brussels in 1923. The Belgians agreed and conducted preliminary discussions with colleagues from France and England. The preparations began under Henri Pirenne as president, Guillaume Des Marez, the archivist of the city of Brussels, as secretary-general, and François-Louis Ganshof as secretary of the organizing committee. There was no lack of generous support by the government. The king assumed the patronage, and the prime minister took his place at the head of an honorary committee, alongside a number of cabinet members and representatives of the Academy and the universities. The Belgians regarded the fact that the convention of this Congress had been entrusted to them as a manifestation of solidarity for their country, which had been the first victim of the war and had now recovered its independence. For the historians of Belgium and France, upon whose soil the war in the West had been fought, the memory of wartime was still too much alive to accept cooperation with Germans and Austrians at the coming Congress.

Thus, in early May 1922, Pirenne informed a group of historians who attended a meeting of the Union Académique in Brussels that the academies and universities in Germany, Austria, Hungary, and Turkey should not receive invitations. However, individual historians who applied on their own initiative would be allowed to attend on an individual basis, with the stipulation that all applications from Germany be reviewed by the organizing committee to ensure that "unwelcome persons"—meaning the signatories of the "Manifesto of the 93"—could be rejected.[39] Jameson and the American Historical Association accepted this as a *fait accompli*, despite their ecumenical goals for the future.

Jameson reported later on how the American resolution on participation came about:

> Hearing from Mr. Leland that there were rumours of English abstention, I consulted individually twenty-one American historical scholars whom I thought most likely to be interested. I found that eighteen of them agreed with me that it was not reasonable to expect the Belgians so soon after the German occupation to invite the Germans to Brussels, that it was best to leave the matter of invitation in their hands and to work toward a completely international meeting in 1928, and that, toward this end, it was much better for persons of goodwill to attend the Congress and steer it in that direction rather than to stay away and leave it in the hands of such Frenchmen or Belgians or others as were intransigent. The other three Americans, one or two of them of German origin, thought otherwise, but did not feel strongly enough about the matter to take any action.[40]

Political censorship as the condition for participation in a scholarly congress was unprecedented in the history of European science. It soon became apparent that the organizers of the Brussels Congress were in danger of causing a deep rift in the international historical profession through such refusals and limitations. Leland reported on the mood in England in letters to Jameson and Shotwell in December 1922, stating that a group of London historians under Albert F. Pollard had formulated a protest letter and that similar steps were being taken in Oxford and Cambridge.[41] The petition read: "The undersigned, invited to take part in the International Congress of Historical Studies, have learnt that the organizing committee does not propose to issue invitations to historians belonging to the Central Powers. We fully appreciate how great a sacrifice of natural and legitimate feelings would be involved in extending an invitation to Germans to Belgian soil; but we would nevertheless venture to appeal to the organizing committee to render the Congress really *international,* in the fullest sense of the term. We feel convinced that such a step would be in the true interest of historical science."[42] Among those who signed on, or whose signatures were expected, were such recognized historians as Ernest Barker, George N. Clark, Charles H. Firth, George P. Gooch, Albert F. Pollard, Robert W. Seton-Watson, Harold W. V. Temperley, Arnold Toynbee, George M. Trevelyan, and Sir Adolphus W. Ward, the president of the last prewar Congress in London in 1913. This petition campaign may have been influenced by the fact that shortly before the letter was written, French and Belgian troops had occupied the Ruhr District against the will of the British government, and in this case British opinion leaned toward Germany. Leland took France's side on this issue. Like Jameson, he saw the British protests against the Brussels Congress as misguided. If the goal was to fight for full internationality in the future, then as many Britons as possible had to be present in Brussels. Leland's and Jameson's efforts to promote this tactical argument in England were successful, as the large participation in the Congress would show.

Criticism also came from Italy,[43] from the German regions of Switzerland, and particularly from Scandinavia. Historians in those countries felt passed over in the selection of Brussels and in the preparation of the Congress. There were even rumors that plans existed to organize a counter-Congress in Sweden. In Sweden and in Denmark, the academies and universities refused to accept the invitation. The Danish historian Aage Friis made uncompromising comments on the discrimination against Germany. The best one could do was to cancel the Brussels Conference, he told his American colleagues.[44] Friis had been a sharp critic of German politics in the Bismarck and Wilhelminean eras. Now he was no less critical of the postwar policies of the Western powers. He denounced the Ruhr occupation of 1923 in particularly sharp terms. When he received the invitation to Brussels in late 1922, he informed Friedrich Meinecke that he would not go there, since in his opinion it was not admissible "to hold an International Historical Congress without Germany"; and in regard to political censorship, he stated that he considered "the said restriction to be a great insult to the German historians."[45] He also tried, however, to evoke understanding for Pirenne's position. He sent Meinecke a copy of a letter from the Belgian historian[46] indicating his readiness to separate the participation of Germans and Austrians in the future from the emotions caused by the war, which at present he felt must still be taken into consideration. In this letter Pirenne wrote:

The organizing committee has sent no invitations to the scholarly bodies of Germany and Austria. This reflects not a single thought of hatred or bad intent. It is simply a result of the situation. If we had invited the scholarly bodies of Germany, we would have had to receive as delegates some of the signatories of the Manifesto of the 93, who have spread calumnies concerning Belgium not retracted as yet. This could have led to regrettable incidents. We wanted to avoid this, and otherwise the German historians are not excluded. If they want to participate on an individual basis, they will be received with courtesy. No one regrets the necessity of this measure, which we have been forced to adopt, more than I do. It was inevitable for the sake of the Congress's success. One must realize that it is taking place in Brussels, only a few steps from the palace of the King, who has assumed the patronage. One must also take into consideration that a Historical Congress is something quite different from a congress of physicists or mathematicians. Certain subjects could lead to discussions that would be difficult to keep within the bounds of a strictly scientific debate. Let us hope that the Sixth Historical Congress does not need to involve itself with such unfortunate circumstances. Let me repeat that the measure that has been taken is only a matter of expedience. Without doubt we could have invited Austria, which does not encounter the same reservations as Germany. But that would have led to the assumption that Germany has been excluded *odii causa*, and in addition that would have brought about a very difficult situation for the Austrian scholarly bodies, which we wished to avoid.

In contrast to Aage Friis, the Norwegian historian Halvdan Koht thought it advisable not to stay away, as much as he rejected the Brussels restrictions. He rather recommended strong participation by the neutral countries so as to influence the development in such a way that the internationality of the Historical Congresses could be reestablished for the next gathering. This was also Jameson's intention. Koht had known him since a trip to America in 1909, and they had occasionally exchanged letters ever since. In 1913 both of them had taken part in the London Congress. Thus, Koht had an idea of what these Congresses were and what they could perhaps become. His studies in Copenhagen, Leipzig, and Paris in 1897/98 had provided him with solid links with the historical profession outside of his country.[47] Alongside politics and language, he was particularly interested in literature (Ibsen, Björnson) and social history, whether it be that of the radical peasants' movement of the nineteenth century (*Johan Sverdrup*, 3 vols., 1918–1925), or of the development of social democracy.

This corresponded to his political involvement. At the time in question, Koht was a leading member of the Social Democratic Party of Norway. Author of a booklet on *The idea of peace in the history of Norway* (1906), he was also active in the advisory council of the Norwegian Nobel Institute and, after the war, in the Parliamentary Nobel Committee. A Norwegian patriot, he embodied the type of a historian engaged in politics, who, in the service of humanitarian and cosmopolitan ideals, is concerned with the effect of history on public life. His personal background explains why he dedicated himself to the reestablishment of the full internationality of the Historical Congresses. But he allowed political wisdom to prevail in his attempts to bring it about—if not today, then tomorrow. He tried in vain to win over his influential Danish friend Friis for this course, which would prove to be the correct one. He would have liked for Friis to urge individual German historians to apply for participation.[48] However, Friis stood by his opinion that this "Historical Congress, in the form in which it has come about, without preliminary negotiations with the neutral countries on its basic structure, is a direct anti-German manifestation."[49] But Koht met with strong support from his university in Oslo. It sent him as its official delegate to Brussels and commissioned him to invite the next Congress to Oslo. If this invitation should be accepted, it would mean the lifting of all restrictions and the reestablishment of full internationality. Koht had previously secured financial support by the Norwegian government.

While Koht was attempting to restore the ecumenical character of the Historical Congresses through the invitation to Oslo, Jameson, Shotwell, and Leland tried to achieve the same goal through the creation of an International Committee of Historical Sciences. Participation should be open to scholars from all countries. As a first step in this direction, they envisaged inviting the less-resented Austrians and Hungarians to Brussels. This could possibly be achieved by a formula under which enemy states could participate if they were members of the League of Nations. It was to be expected that Germany, too, would be admitted to the League of Nations one day or another. But perhaps at that moment the League formula seemed above all to be an appeasement measure intended to mitigate the discrimination against Germans, and to reduce reservations among reluctant historians in England and elsewhere in order to persuade them to participate. Leland devoted himself to this project. Following discussions with Shotwell and others, he wrote to Jameson:

> We think that in view of the English attitude, it is necessary for the Americans to endeavour to mediate. Shotwell will try to get the Committee of the Congress, merely as a gesture, to invite, even at this late date, all the countries included in the League of Nations. This still leaves out the Germans, but includes most of the other enemy countries. This ought to go a long way toward making the English objections less serious. In the second place we think it highly important that the place of meeting of the next Congress should not be settled at the present Congress, but should be left to a permanent international committee, to be created at the coming Congress, which should be charged, not only with arranging for the next Congress, but with any other matters of common interest left over from the present congress or coming up in the interim. This is really the beginning of an International Historical Union.[50]

If such an international committee could be formed by the nations represented in Brussels, one could assume that in regard to the site of the next Congress "the Americans, English, and neutrals would naturally outvote the French and the Belgians."[51] This was in line with Leland's strategy, which he formulated as follows: "1. Endeavour to modify the English attitude. 2. Make as much as possible of American representation. 3. Use our influence, together with the English if we can make them listen to reason, to have the next Congress held under conditions that will ensure its being all inclusive—for example, we might place it under the auspices of the Committee for Intellectual Cooperation, and have it at Geneva or Lausanne."[52]

The International Commission for Intellectual Cooperation of the League of Nations was founded in Geneva in 1922. It appeared to Leland as a possible approach for a consistent internationalization of the future Historical Congresses, because it was linked to the League of Nations and was not subject to the same exclusionary rules as the two Brussels "boycott organizations." The twelve members of the Commission did not represent their respective countries; instead, cultural regions were considered during the selection process, including Germany. Among the members was Albert Einstein, the world-renowned physicist and pacifist who, however, in 1923, under the impression of the Ruhr occupation temporarily withdrew to express his protest against the League's passivity.[53] The Viennese historian Alfons Dopsch acted as a correspondent.[54] Leland had the full support of the Polish historian Oskar Halecki, the secretary of the Commission, for his plans. Halecki suggested that on account of its non-restrictive composition, the Commission be put in charge of the formation of an international historical committee at the Brussels Congress. On Leland's urging, Halecki was invited to serve as the Commission's representative to Brussels.

Leland was keen to establish a close link to Geneva for another reason as well: he wanted to meet "English criticism that the present Congress was a slap at the League of Nations."[55] Indeed the League formula was adopted for the invitation to the Brussels Congress at the last moment. The resolution of the preparatory committee of 14 January 1923 stated "that invitations to the Congress would be sent to the learned societies and universities of all member states of the League of Nations; regarding scholars from other nations, they would be permitted to participate in the Congress subject to an examination of individual cases."[56] In accordance with this, both the Hungarians and the Austrians were invited. The Hungarians sent a delegation, whereas the Austrians refused to attend out of solidarity with their German colleagues.[57] In early February, Dopsch informed Halecki that he was "very much afraid that nobody from this country would attend, as Germany is excluded."[58]

The Brussels Congress was opened on 9 April in a sumptuous ceremony in the presence of the King, the Queen, the government and the diplomatic corps. Pirenne delivered a speech paying homage to their Royal Majesties, throughout which the audience was standing. The Congress ended on 15 April following a festive banquet for three hundred guests. The days between these two dates were filled with many lectures on a colorful blend of topics, as had been the case at earlier Congresses, and with the struggle over the future form of the Congresses. The Congress proceedings give an impression of the scholarly program, if only through concise summaries of the contributions. Individual papers were published in professional journals, as had been the case for the prewar Congresses in London and Berlin. Conveniently, the places of publication were to some extent listed in the Congress report. In order to reconstruct the historical-political debates at the Congress, we have to turn to other sources, above all to the "confidential" report by Halvdan Koht to the Senate of the University of Oslo,[59] and a letter from Leland to Jameson, complementing his Congress report in the *American Historical Review*.[60]

With some 1,000 registered participants, the Congress matched that of the last prewar assembly. The number of active participants was estimated at about 500. The Scandinavians, with a few exceptions, stayed away. The list of officially represented countries included Russia, with a separate list of emigrated historians. As before, the official invitation had been addressed to the St. Petersburg—now Leningrad—Academy (Académie des Sciences de Russie), which at the time was still regarded as a stronghold of "bourgeois" scholarship. From there, the historians Barthold, Tarle, and Ottokar attended. None of these was a communist. Among the exile Russian participants of the Union des Groupes Académiques Russes à l'étranger were Sir Paul Vinogradoff, who had already emigrated to England in 1902 on account of his liberal political opinions, and Mikhael Rostovtzev and Peter Struve, who had left their homeland in the wake of the Bolshevik Revolution. They, too, were members of the St. Petersburg Academy.[61]

With regard to the decision on the future of the ecumenical character of the Congresses, the relative number of participants of the various countries was important. The printed attendance list included a mere handful of representatives from scholarly institutions outside of the sphere of European civilization, such as Japan and Egypt. The group that wished to maintain the exclusionary policies consisted of 422 Belgians, 222 Frenchmen, and 20 Poles. The group that sought the removal of the restrictions consisted of 137 Britons, 35 Americans, and 33 Dutchmen. Added to this were 34 Italians, 18 Spaniards, 18 Swiss, and some 30 persons from other countries. Among these were three representatives of scholarly institutions from Hungary who had accepted the belated invitation. These figures show that Leland and Koht had to face considerable resistance to their goal of creating a committee that would encompass all countries, or of achieving a future Congress to which everyone would be invited. As Leland said, "The unanimous opinion of the Americans and English was that the Dutch, Swedes, and Danes had not helped the cause they stood for by staying away, but had seriously endangered it."[62]

At the instigation of the organizing committee, a printed motion drafted by Leland was handed out to all participants on the first day. It stated:

> The International Congress of Historical Sciences assembled in Brussels, does hereby request the International Committee on Intellectual Cooperation of the League of Nations to name, not later than January 1, 1925, an International Committee on Historical Sciences, consisting of one representative of each country which participated in one or more of the international historical congresses of 1908, 1913, and 1923, such representatives to be named in consultation with the appropriate academies, societies, or other bodies, of the respective countries.
>
> The Committee thus named shall meet in Geneva at a time to be appointed by the Committee on Intellectual Cooperation, for the purpose of effecting an organization,

and may thereafter hold meetings in such places and at such times as it may determine. It shall continue until action respecting it shall have been taken by the next international historical congress.

The committee … is especially charged with the preparation of a plan for the organization of an International Union of Historical Sciences, which plan, together with a report of its activities, it shall present to the next international congress.[63]

Leland had previously submitted this draft to the Société d'histoire in Paris, to which distinguished historians such as Renouvin and Homolle belonged, and which he himself had joined. The Frenchmen modified the text and presented their own draft resolution to the Brussels Congress. They discarded the American formula whereby all countries that had participated in earlier Historical Congresses should be admitted. Instead, the Commission for Intellectual Cooperation of the League of Nations should be free to assemble the committee of historical sciences as it saw fit. The latter should have only a provisional character and decide on its final composition in consultation with the historical associations "of each country." It was unclear what this meant: did it mean every country that had taken part in earlier Congresses, i.e., also Germany and Austria, or only those represented in the provisional committee? "The French version leaves something a little vague," Leland said. But despite the reluctance of the French, he was "much relieved to find that there was no opposition to the principle of including the Germans."[64]

Leland and Halecki jointly submitted to the Congress a further draft resolution that was intended to give the future international organization the more rigorous form of a "union." However, if at all, this could only be considered after the first step, namely, the creation of an international committee, had been undertaken.[65] Even Jameson, who asserted his influence from far away, thought this project was going too far for the time being. He recommended that the historians should begin with a practical task, for instance restarting and continuing, under international supervision, the annual bibliography *Jahresberichte der Geschichtswissenschaften*, which had been published in Germany until it was interrupted by the war. This was the origin of the *International Bibliography of Historical Sciences*.

As far as the next Congress site was concerned, it had previously been customary to let the prior Congress decide. In Brussels everyone knew that the selection of the site would pre-decide who would be allowed to participate. There were invitations from Amsterdam, Athens, Oslo, and Warsaw, and a recommendation from Halecki and Leland for Geneva, the seat of the Commission for Intellectual Cooperation of the League of Nations. These applications were first handled by the Congress's Bureau, which was made up of the Belgian organizing committee and seven elected foreign Congress presidents: Francis de Crue (Geneva), Bronisław Dembiński (Warsaw), Gaetano De Sanctis (Turin), Théophile Homolle (Paris), James T. Shotwell (New York), Thomas F. Tout (Manchester), and Paul Vinogradoff (Oxford).

The selection of the next Congress location concerned the scholars assembled in Brussels much more than the formation of an international historical committee. According to Leland, it became the "big fight of the Congress."[66] After all, the Oslo invitation, which was on the table in Brussels, welcomed scholars "from all countries"! From the very first day, Koht was concerned with finding allies. The Britons spoke in favor of Oslo from the beginning. The Americans were for Geneva at first. But according to Koht, this city seemed inappropriate because it was thought that the next Congress should not be held at another French-speaking location. In addition, the French Swiss had so emphatically taken sides with the Entente in the war that Geneva could not really be viewed as a neutral city. The Swiss themselves held back. They had not issued an invitation but would have been willing to host a Congress if asked. In the end, the Americans were won for Oslo. It was of particular importance that even the Belgians, who had first been in favor of Geneva, joined the Americans in deciding for Oslo. Three of the Congress presidents—the Belgian Pirenne, the Englishman Tout, and the American Shotwell—lent their support "to Oslo and the international program," in Koht's words.

The sharpest competition for Oslo was Warsaw. After Geneva was out of the running, the Pole Dembiński and the Frenchman Homolle, director of the Bibliothèque Nationale, spoke in favor of Warsaw. But since the Polish capital was scarcely a neutral city, it was rejected by both the Americans and the Britons. The Anglo-Russian president Vinogradoff found Oslo appealing, but he expressed his concern whether it was right to bring historians from the two enemy camps together again after only five years. Since Warsaw had no chance anyway, the French tried to bring Athens into play. However, at this moment the proponents of Oslo in the Bureau, who in the meantime had made sure of the agreement of Congress participants from countries like Spain, Italy, Estonia, and Lithuania, stated that either the Norwegian invitation should be accepted now or the selection postponed until later.

Since there was no clear decision for Oslo in Brussels, the debate on the next Congress's location and thus on its universality was transferred to the composition and commission of the new international committee, which would determine the site. This was Leland's special field of interest. After long discussions with Pirenne and Tout, he was prepared to modify his motion in order to yield to the objections, and agreed to a dilatory solution as suggested by the Italian Gaetano De Sanctis, who was desirous for saving the project.[67] The future committee should not be appointed by the Geneva Commission for Intellectual Cooperation of the League of Nations, as envisioned in the draft, but it should rather be constituted on a provisional basis through co-optation by the Brussels Congress Bureau. And the apodictic clause in Leland's motion, stating that the new committee should encompass representatives from all countries participating in earlier Congresses, was replaced by the more flexible statement that it should be made as representative as possible of all countries. Even this encountered opposition in the Bureau. The Americans, however, left no doubt on the consequences that a rejection would entail. In Leland's words: "Shotwell had finally to say that unless some step of this sort were taken he should have to reserve the participation of the United States in the next Congress." And he continued: "After that they all hastened to get on the band wagon."[68] On the last day of the Congress, the acting president James T. Shotwell presented the motion to create an International Committee of Historical Sciences to the general assembly in the following version:

> Whereas there have been presented to the Fifth International Congress of Historical Sciences several projects for the creation of a permanent international organization of historical sciences and for the carrying out of international co-operative historical enterprises, the congress decides that there shall be formed an International Committee of Historical Sciences.
>
> The International Bureau of the Fifth Congress shall remain provisionally in office in order to organize this committee, in consultation with the historical societies of the various countries, and with the object of making the committee as representative as possible of all countries.
>
> The International Bureau of the Fifth Congress, and succeeding it the committee as soon as it shall be organized, are charged with determining, before April 15, 1926, the place of meeting of the next Congress.
>
> The International Bureau of the Fifth Congress, and succeeding it the committee as soon as it shall be organized, are instructed to study the proposals which may be referred to it by the Fifth International Congress, or which it may consent to study upon reference from competent bodies.[69]

In the assembly, resistance once again arose against the principle of universality. A series of participants—Frenchmen and Belgians, as Koht and a Dutch observer reported—protested against the formula "of all countries." But Shotwell and Pirenne succeeded in "fending off the rising storm."[70] Koht was impressed by the equally energetic and restrained intervention with which Pirenne convinced the resisters. The motion was approved by a large majority with only a few "nay" votes. With this, the decisive step had been taken in starting the ICHS on its way.

If one asks to whom the greatest credit for this is owed, then the Americans Jameson, Shotwell, and Leland must be mentioned, along with the Norwegian Koht. Particularly Koht and Leland advanced their cause in Brussels with circumspection and tactical skill. Leland reported to Jameson with justified pride: "Pirenne seems to think that the American intervention in February produced the most important results. He said to me frequently: 'You have saved the Congress.'"[71] Henri Pirenne was the central figure throughout this process. It was not that he was an active author of the new development; rather, his agreement and his express assent to the creation of genuine ecumenical Historical Congresses based on an international institution of their own cleared the way. Occasionally, he was described as the founder of the ICHS.[72] This is just as inaccurate as the passage in his biography saying that it was only in 1927 that he finally resigned himself to the idea of admitting German historians to the next International Congress.[73] Of course, one could ask whether his repeated early statements of his readiness to invite Germans and Austrians in the future (if not yet in Brussels) was only a tactical move arising in specific discussions. But there is no reason for an assumption of this kind. Certainly, the disappointment caused by the injustice inflicted upon him and his country could not be any deeper. This disillusionment informed his image of the Germans, which he depicted in his internment memoirs, to such a degree that besides the wrongs he had to endure, he was unable to see more than mere trickery or contemptible servility in acts of kindness rendered to him as a respected scholar in Jena and Creuzburg.[74] Thus, it is all the more convincing that he used his political and scholarly prestige to clear the way for the rapid reestablishment of comprehensive internationality in the Historical Congresses. Since this occurred *contre coeur*, as everyone knew, and only in recognition of the necessity of scholarly internationality, the effect of his attitude was decisive.

The war had not only called the international cooperation of the historians into question, it had also struck a heavy blow to the historians' conception of their profession and its influence on public life. Had not the expectations, voiced at the turn of the century, that history could promote international understanding proven to be an illusion? Were the historians not called upon to reconsider their methods critically? These questions had preoccupied Pirenne during his long hours of lonely thought in the internment camp. He presented his answers at the Brussels Congress in his opening address on "The Comparative Method in History."[75]

This formulation was a program. It was a continuation of the leitmotif underlying the program of the Paris Historical Congress and Pasquale Villari's opening speech in Rome in 1903. Pirenne consciously took up the prewar endeavors to make history more universal and scientific. He particularly referred to Henri Berr, and his *Evolution de l'humanité* and the *Revue de synthèse historique*.[76] The fact that this speech became the outstanding scholarly event of the Congress did not derive from its brilliant rhetorical form alone. The profound impression that it still exerts is owing to the radical honesty with which he held up a mirror to a historical profession depraved by war: "What a moral confusion of the conscience! What an intellectual confusion of the minds!" His call for a radical change was not only aimed at historians of the former enemy countries, whom he criticized mercilessly. He generally accused the historical profession of having placed itself in the service of its respective national interests, of having all too often violated the elementary commandments of impartiality and, as he stated bluntly, of having forgotten the old truth that had been the fundamental meaning of the International Historical Congresses: that scholarship has no fatherland ("la science n'a pas de patrie"). And all this from the mouth of a historian who had become the national hero of his country and who had explored, interpreted, and presented its history for the benefit of his compatriots! To be sure, as Pirenne said, the personality of the historian is inseparable from the subject matter he studies. This is both unavoidable and entirely legitimate: "If he has studied the history of his country, how could he forget that this country is his fatherland; if it is the history of his religion, that it is the wellspring of his faith; if it is the history of his party, that this party has a claim upon his loyalty?"

Pirenne characterized such existential interests in knowledge, however, as prejudices that ought to be overcome as far as possible. He was particularly intent on denouncing a specific complex of nationalist prejudices, namely, those linked to the concept of race, which he saw as both scientifically and morally untenable. Inter alia, this was directed against the Flemish separatist movement that Germany had promoted during the war.[77] Above all, however, he spoke out against that biologically flavored national Darwinism that exploits the concepts of racial superiority and the right of the strongest. Equally inadmissible, in his view, was the historical concept of race, which had proliferated in wartime literature. According to this notion, nations were in fact products of historical development, but once molded in their individuality, they were understood as races that allegedly developed only out of themselves, following the laws of their own specific nature.[78]

This is not to say that Pirenne denied the notion of national individuality. But he asked what tangible reality lay hidden behind such collective metaphors as the soul, genius, and individuality of peoples—what could verifiably be stated about them. This is where he saw the significance of the comparative method, which examines comparable general phenomena of geographic, economic, social, and cultural conditions in order to reveal the temporal shifts, variations, peculiarities, and thus the individuality of national developments. "Il n'y a de science que du général" (There is no science without generalization) was a formula frequently repeated in the anti-individualist critique of historicism. Did this mean sociology instead of history? No, replied Pirenne: "To be sure, no one will deny that sociology provides historians with valuable services. But one must take into close consideration the fact that so far it has provided us with little more than hypotheses, which are useful, challenging, and fruitful ... but which are nonetheless too weak and conditional to make it possible to build upon them."

Pirenne was thus in no way thinking of a revolution in his discipline, even if he compared the effects of the war on the historical profession to a "*cataclysme cosmique.*" The concept of science as defined in his Brussels speech was based on the classic dichotomy of analysis and synthesis, the critical collection of facts and causal allocation. The former, he said, was the field of erudition, with the aids of auxiliary sciences, source criticism, and editions, without which history would not be a "science" but rather a literary genre. Similar opinions had been expressed by Croce in Rome and in the standard manuals on historical methodology by Bernheim and Monod. For the latter aspect—causal allocation, synthetic combination, "*construction historique*"—he availed himself of neither philosophy nor sociology. Instead, he held out the promising notion of comparative studies. What this could mean in concrete terms had been shown by comparative ethnology, particularly in the work of Émile Durkheim. It had been demonstrated at the International Historical Congress in Paris in 1900 in the fields of art and literary history. Not least, medieval studies, and particularly those by Pirenne himself, had provided viable models for research on feudalism. In Brussels, Pirenne presented an example of the comparative method in a lecture on the historical contrast between Merovingians and Carolingians, maintaining a thesis that gave rise to controversies with Dopsch and others.[79] The matter was to be debated in great detail later at the Oslo Congress.

The enthusiasm that the proclamation of the "comparative method" was able to unleash also led to misunderstandings as to what Pirenne had in mind, as for instance in the case of Henri Sée, who felt confirmed by Pirenne's speech in his comparative chronological and geographical studies on agrarian history. He shot beyond the target when he attributed to Pirenne's address the assumption that this method could make history into "a true science" capable of explaining the meaning of social development ("expliquer le sens de l'évolution de nos sociétés").[80] Pirenne himself would never have attributed to empirical historical study the capacity to make scientifically conclusive statements on the meaning of history. He even said occasionally that he thought it naïve to conceive of history as a "science" in the full meaning of the word: "Il est puéril de soutenir que l'histoire est une science."[81] More precisely, and retaining the term "science," he called history a "science d'observation," in contrast to natural science as a "science d'expérimentation."[82] In any case, Pirenne's life and work cannot be separated from the prescientific, personal decision for ethical and political values underlying his historical synthesis. The best example of this is his classic depiction of the history of his fatherland, Belgium.

Taking into account the actual scholarly importance of methodological questions, the organizing committee of the Congress had established a special section for "historical methods and auxiliary sciences." Here, Franziszek Bujak, a professor at the University of Lemberg (Lvov) and one of Poland's leading economic historians, dealt with the comparative method in the broader context of "The Problem of Synthesis in History."[83] In this paper, which was read on his behalf, he started with a pertinent observation that he expanded to a general hypothesis. Due to history's anthropological substrate, he said, there was a regular recurrence of a great number of limited processes of a biological, psychological, economic, social, and political nature. They did not permit one to speak of a comprehensive law of general historical development, but nevertheless, once they were systematically defined and classified, they would be capable of explaining the structural conditions of historical events and at the same time the events themselves to a large degree. Thus, a systematic catalog of historical concepts should be created, and subsequently their genuine content should be examined through broadly conceived comparative studies.

Bujak did not yet take into consideration the historicity of historical concepts themselves, which recent research has emphasized.[84] He formulated his thesis in opposition to the neo-Kantians, particularly Heinrich Rickert, and their differentiation between idiographic cultural sciences and nomothetic natural sciences. He shared the opinion of the French philosophers Émile Boutroux and Henri Bergson that "all phenomena of the world are individual phenomena," the phenomena of the natural sciences no less than those of the cultural sciences. In his polemic against Rickert, Bujak did not consider that for Rickert, the characteristic aspect of the cultural sciences, as opposed to the natural sciences, lies in the notion that the historical object is constituted by its relationship to values (*Wertbezug*). Despite this narrowed perspective, Bujak did not understand his theses as a rejection of the existing study of history and its proven techniques. He did not intend to pass judgement, but to invite historians to test new methods: "Even if one admits that today history is being pursued in a scientific manner, one must nevertheless note that it is less scientific than the natural sciences and even certain fields of the humanities. One could at most compare it with botany before Linné, with zoology before Lamarck or geology before Lyell."

Henri Berr spoke in Brussels on the topic of historical synthesis as well.[85] The editor of the *Revue de synthèse historique* was naturally pleased by the fact that the concept of synthesis was emphasized so strongly both in Pirenne's speech and in the Congress as a whole, even if it was not observed as a dominant methodological rule. But at the same time he pointed to the lack of precision inherent in the term. He found it noteworthy that to a great extent, scholars at German universities were dealing with historical synthesis, even if this occurred under changing labels such as practice of history, theory of history, introduction to the study of history, or even historical philosophy, whereby he emphasized the familiar distinction in Germany between content-related and formal philosophy of history, i.e., between philosophy and historical epistemology. Even if Germany was not in attendance at the Brussels Congress, one could neither ignore nor neglect its scientific achievements. For his own observations Berr took a critical look at the term "comparative method." He believed it was tenable, but, he said, one must make distinctions. Simple comparisons, groping for the identification of certain analogies in a development between groups or epochs, were not enough. This method signalized historical problems but did not represent their solution. He formulated the following program for an investigation into regular recurrences in history transcending mere comparison: "Scientific synthesis is primarily concerned with identifying factors of long duration acting upon history, and with defining precisely their nature and their relationships. Thus, one must not confuse the construction of formulas, which are merely large statements, with the investigation into explanatory causes."

With his observation that the crucial point was to determine the constant and repetitive factors as the explanatory elements of history, Berr agreed with Bujak's intentions, which, as he stated, pointed in the right direction. He was thinking of a "theory of history." It should neither be a speculation paying insufficient attention to the concrete matter of history, nor be misled by natural sciences to search for rigid and absolute laws in a dynamic past.

The concept of theory developed by the Polish historian Jean Stanisław Lewinski, as a result of his economic historical research, pointed in the same direction.[86] Lewinski presented the issue of whether economic history was determined by laws as a question, without anticipating a dogmatic answer. He drew upon material from comparative studies on economic history, referring back to Georg von Below for their problems and methods.[87] He was interested in the analogies of agrarian and urban historical development phases in various regions, as shown particularly in Russian and German research. Going beyond mere comparison to seek out the causes of analogous phenomena, he cited a number of factors that, according to him, were operating everywhere as determinant causalities, such as population growth, soil quality, the principle of the lowest expenditure and so on. The quintessence of his thoughts on the necessary correlation between theory and empirical research is contained in the following sentence: "By formulating this theory we are aware of the dangers of the comparative method and all generalizations. Only a work of long and patient empirical research can provide us with an answer to whether economic development in its essential features can really be traced to a few simple elements."

Alongside Bujak, Berr, and Lewinski, the methodology section presented a colorful palette of different opinions on the whys and wherefores of history. Gustav Fagniez—a student of the École des Chartes, cofounder of the *Revue historique,* and for some time its editor—stated his satisfaction with the current state of historical studies in France: The war had finally given full expression to the national significance of history, and, as he observed with a distinct political undertone, it had highlighted the "incurable impotence of democracy." However, it had also returned the idea of patriotism to its most basic principle, namely, the defense of one's own soil, home, and country, and thus promoted justice and equity in the attitude toward earlier history, vis-à-vis the "fathers."[88]

In contrast to this nationalist concept of history, Eugène Bacha, the director of the Belgian bibliographic service (Directeur des Services Belges de Bibliographie et des Échanges Internationaux) supported the deterministic theory that basically the same political development was occurring in all countries: "The history of the various countries demonstrates to us the same sequence of typical events which are determined by the same sequence of generative ideas."[89] He saw "laws of creation" operating in the history of nations as well as in art and philosophy. In a dialectic approach reminiscent of Croce, he described their basic pattern as a "regular sequence of contradictory ideas." From this point of view, he thought Pirenne's interpretation of history was too materialistic. It did not take sufficient consideration of the dynamic power of thought.[90] It does not appear as if this interpretation of history, which referred back to the idealistic philosophy of history, met with any noticeable response in Brussels.

Another form of idealistic interpretation of history was presented by the Polish philosopher Władysław M. Kozłowski in a paper on "The Impact of

Ideas on History."[91] He did not argue in the tradition of an ontological idealism. His sources of inspiration were the subjectivism of Enlightenment philosophy and the liberal democratic idea of progress. In a critical analysis of the thought of the French sociologist Lacombe, he declared: "It is precisely the ideas and ideals which are historical facts of the greatest importance. Their influence is greater than that of all other factors.... The problem of a comprehensive social history, which is capable of guiding reform activity, is not the search for imaginary sociological laws, but the study of the conditions under which ideas develop and spread in a society." He illustrated this through examples from recent French and Polish history, which he placed against the dark background of the inhumanity of the Russian Revolution and the attack of the German "barbarians."

Other participants saw the key to the understanding of the human condition in the concept of race. The Romanian Baron Lecca, apparently unimpressed by the warnings in Pirenne's opening speech, did not hesitate to present racial disparities as the substrate of the various European nations. Like Count Gobineau in his *Essay on the Inequality of Human Races* and Houston Stuart Chamberlain in *The Foundations of the 19th Century*, Lecca believed he had discovered where to look for what is truly valuable. "The blond race," he declared, "is the true European race ... the original and autochthonous one."[92] The Geto-Thracians, to which the Romanians belonged, were also descended from it, with a few Mediterranean additions.

Georges Blondel, however, a professor at the Collège de France and author of numerous writings on German economic and social history, considered the "Germanic races" to be highly suspect and in no way admirable. He attributed this to their "natural proclivities." He shared the belief that the history of the peoples should be understood in terms of their collective psychological determinants with the once admired Lamprecht, whose *German History* he had translated into French. In Brussels Blondel gave free rein to his racist fantasies in a paper on the German mentality.[93] He viewed virtually the whole of German history as a *massa perditionis* on account of the bad racial predisposition of the German people. The "animated discussion" that ensued revealed further unpleasant things: By the twelfth and thirteenth centuries, German philosophy already had a "herd character," and all in all the Germans had made a caricature out of the ideas that they had adopted from foreign philosophers. The Belgian archivist Alfred Hansy and the Dutch historian Van Raalte countered this philosophical hyperbole with the comparative observation "that imperialism, the idea of world domination, is to be found not only in Germany, but also in every sufficiently strong state."[94] In a report on the Congress, a Scottish participant also criticized Blondel's self-righteous condemnation of the Germans: there was "undoubtedly some truth in such a generalization, but it is not the whole truth, and to generalize the psychology of 70 millions of people is really a fanciful task. Moreover, this teaching had its representatives in all the nations more or less, for chauvinism and militarism were not exclusively 'made in Germany.'"[95]

Halvdan Koht was right when he remarked in the context of an examination of various explanatory models of the Renaissance: "One must always observe with mistrust those theories which promise to explain the given historical facts through various aspects of race or nationality.... There is no point of view which encourages more arbitrariness and contradiction than that which assumes race as an active force of history." Koht himself, in accordance with his socialist convictions, explained the individualism of the Renaissance as resulting from the capitalism of the late medieval ages.[96]

Geography as the potentially most significant of the historical auxiliary sciences was the subject matter of a paper by Charles Pergameni (Brussels). He pleaded for a *"géographie humaine"* as it had been defined by Lucien Febvre in his programmatic book on *La terre et l'évolution humaine*, modeled on Ratzel and Febvre's teacher, Vidal de la Blache. Referring to Febvre, Pergameni distinguished the intended historical anthropo-geography—a discipline investigating the interaction between man and environment—from a unilateral determinedness of the great powers by what a later research direction labeled geopolitics.[97]

Besides these contributions, a number of papers dealing with conventional topics of the historical auxiliary sciences were presented within the section for historical methods. The participants in the actual methodological discussion gained the impression that the subject was worthwhile. Upon Halecki's recommendation, they followed up on a suggestion by Berr and moved that questions of theory, methodology, and historical synthesis be given appropriate attention at the next Congress.[98]

A particularly significant event with regard to the history of historiography was the first appearance of the two protagonists of the later *Annales* at the Brussels Congress: Lucien Febvre and Marc Bloch, both professors at the newly opened humanities department in Strasbourg since 1920. They reported on clearly defined specialized themes and the methodological problems they involved. In the section for medieval studies, Bloch dealt with the question "What is a fief?" Legal definitions, he held, were just as unsatisfactory as a social delineation of the concept of fief as the "knight's reward" (*Sachsenspiegel*). He sought the answer in the economic sense that this word connoted in its late medieval usage: "The most precise definition of the fief seems to be: a fief is a lent asset that bears within it the obligation for the vassal to perform a specific service; this asset was generally, particularly at the beginning, although not always and not necessarily, a landholding."

Objections were made to this explanation from various sides. Bloch's pointed responses show some traits of his treatment of history that would later determine the character of his great works. Did he pay too much attention to the late Middle Ages, and would he have done better to start with its origins? And would he have done better to have limited himself to France? No, Bloch replied: "The state of the sources makes it possible neither to proceed by studying a single country—in the Middle Ages a country is always hard to delimit—nor to start our research at the time of the origin; one must ... proceed from classic feudalism and climb back to the origins."[99] This meant an approach starting from a broad analysis of a phenomenon's historically developed state and investigating the way back to its origins as an alternative to the genetic method. It meant international comparative study instead of restriction to one nation. Bloch did not present this as a methodological doctrine; for him, this was an approach that resulted from his practical dealings with a concrete historical problem. At the Oslo Congress in 1928,[100] he provided a more profound view of the issue he expounded in Brussels. It was perfected in his classic work on feudal society.[101] In a further paper, he provided a look into his studies on "Kings Performing Miracles," which were soon to be published as a pioneer achievement of research in the field of medieval mentality history.[102]

Like Bloch in his lecture on the concept of the fief, Lucien Febvre dealt with a methodological question concerning his attempt to clarify a specific, historically effective notion, namely, that of universal monarchy.[103] The abstract of his lecture consisted of a catalog of questions that revealed his intention to search for clarification of this concept, of great importance "for an understanding of the modern world," less in the fields of political theory at the crossover from the Middle Ages and the modern era than among those "half popular, half scientific notions" that had to be taken into account as forces determining the great political undertakings. Similar to Bloch's studies on faith in the healing power of kings, this catalog of questions pointed to what would later be called the history of mentalities.

A lively discussion arose over a journal project that Febvre suggested in agreement with Bloch. Febvre and Bloch had gained the support of Pirenne, whom they had met at the latter's frequent lectures in Strasbourg. They held him in high esteem, alongside the editor of the *Revue de Synthèse historique*, Henri Berr, as paving the way for a new approach to history. Filled with the consciousness of a new dawn in history and of the French cultural task in a redeemed Alsace, the two Strasbourg historians wanted to counter the *Vierteljahrschrift für Sozial- und Wirtschaftsgeschichte* of Georg von Below and Ludo Moritz Hartmann with a new organ. In contrast to the allegedly too traditionalistic German journal, which until 1914 had held a leading position, the new one should appeal to a younger generation of historians through the discussion of new methods and broad, up-to-date research information. Above all, the planned *Revue Internationale d'Histoire Économique* was to be "founded as a genuinely international organ … by scholars of various countries."[104] They imagined Pirenne as editor, but he declined to assume this task. It would certainly have become the international historical organization to realize such a plan, and indeed it was duly adopted in Brussels.

It may be attributed to the postwar mentality that in expounding his intentions, Febvre distorted the image of the *Vierteljahrschrift* drastically—as if its desire for international cooperation had been limited to "occasionally allowing a certain number of foreign scholars to participate, and only upon invitation."[105] The reality looked very different. From its first publication in 1903 until the war, the board of editors included several foreign historians, namely, Georges Espinas (Paris), Giuseppe Salvioli (Naples), Henri Pirenne (Ghent), and Paul Vinogradoff (Oxford). Accordingly, it published numerous essays in foreign languages, although with a declining tendency in the years immediately preceding the war. The first volume showed what was intended. Pirenne had written the introductory essay on a problem of medieval social statistics, in French. In addition, there were three French, one Italian, and one English essay, plus two French and two Italian miscellanea out of six, all in their respective languages. To be sure, the war and the postwar situation represented a bitter setback. Aside from the economic reasons, this was also due to the fact that the willingness to cooperate with German historians could only slowly assert itself against deep-seated reservations. This certainly explains why Lucien Febvre intended to limit participation in the planned journal to historians of the nations admitted to the International Historical Congresses.[106] Febvre's proposal gave rise to lively protest in the special committee set up in Brussels to discuss the project, namely, from the Dutch member, who stated that it was necessary to give the journal "a clear and entirely international character."[107] In the end, the committee did indeed drop the restrictive formula suggested by Febvre. It was decided that the journal would be open to scholars "from all countries."[108]

However, the plan could not be realized in the way the two historians from Strasbourg had imagined it. As Febvre said, this was because Pirenne attempted to interest the institutions of the League of Nations in the idea. Here, the project "sank into the miry soil of the shores of Lake Geneva."[109] But the plan to associate the journal with the intended founding of the ICHS did not fail so much in Geneva as in Washington, D.C., since the hope for support from the Rockefeller Foundation as the future patron of the ICHS failed to materialize. The reason was the condition set by the American side that the journal should be edited in "complete international cooperation," which would have meant the inclusion of a German historian in the board of editors.[110] This point, however, did not correspond to the cultural and political realities and intentions behind the Strasbourg journal initiative. After all, Pirenne, the former co-editor of the *Vierteljahrschrift* and now protector of the new journal plan, had just sharply distanced himself from German scholarship.[111] In the final result, the *Annales*—announced five years later at the Oslo Congress and founded in 1929—became an internationally oriented but nationally edited journal just as the *Vierteljahrschrift* had been, although with a different methodological focus.

The internationality of historical scholarship also meant making an attempt to expand the Europe-centered themes of the Congresses on an ecumenical basis. There were signs of this in Brussels. The internationally minded Americans, particularly Leland, introduced a separate subsection for the previously neglected "History of the American Continent." There was also a section for the "History of the Orient" in which, alongside ancient Asia Minor, questions from central and eastern Asia as well as the Indian cultural sphere were examined. But it was characteristic as well that of the fifteen contributions to this section, only a single one, concerning the interpretations of concepts related with the edicts of Asoka, was delivered by a non-European, namely, an Indian.

Finally, the principle of internationality also demanded that a path be sought toward an objective, scientific analysis of the World War. The Brussels Congress provided a separate section on the "Documentation of the History of the World During the Great War." Here, numerous reports by Pierre Renouvin, Waldo Leland, and others were presented, dealing in a professionally detached manner with questions of the gathering, organization, examination, and evaluation of sources pertinent to the war.[112] James T. Shotwell spoke on the social and economic-historical project initiated by the Carnegie Foundation. A Belgian archivist provided a well-informed survey of German document collections and libraries related to the history of the World War.

The question arose of whether at this time, when memories of the war were still so fresh and new conflicts were brewing in the Ruhr District, the historians assembled in Brussels were already able to do more than to prepare documentary information and proceed to an examination of the years of the war with specific scholarly techniques. As far as the origins of the war were concerned, Sir Charles R. Beazley from Birmingham attempted an advance against the prevailing mentality.[113] The proceedings of the Congress mention in only one brief sentence that he spoke on conflicts of interest in the Persian Gulf. The screaming discrepancy between this brief reference and the title of the paper can perhaps be explained by a certain embarrassment over the inclusion into the official record of what the Briton really said. The words of the Scottish Professor James Mackinnon, Edinburgh, in his extremely positive report on Brussels, are probably more accurate.[114] He stated that Beazley had had the courage to question the dogma of an exclusive and one-sided war guilt:

> The question of war guilt cannot yet be definitely settled from the objective point of view simply from the lack of the full documentary evidence which lies hidden in the various European chanceries. But there are already indications which tend to throw doubt on the dogma of the exclusive responsibility of the Central Powers and to lend a certain amount of support to the contention that the war was the inevitable result of the militarist system of the old European régime rather than the will and act of any single Power, and that, whatever the amount of German guilt, the assumption, for instance, of complete innocence by France, the ally of the old corrupt Russian Government, of any share of the responsibility is not a convincing one.

This was a challenge to keep political opinions caused by one's own experience suspended until the sources permitted a well-founded judgement based on historical research. It was a good sign that in Brussels at least the question was raised that would occupy the international research on the causes of the War in the coming decades, and again following the Second World War, with changing accents.

Two British contributions drew directly upon broadly based research concerning the end of the war and the founding of the League of Nations. They were delivered by Charles Webster, at that time in Liverpool, and Harold Temperley, Cambridge. Both had attended the London Congress in 1913 and would one day distinguish themselves in the study of European diplomacy following the Napoleonic Wars and following the First World War. Their Brussels papers were exemplary comparative studies in which the Congress of Vienna was contrasted with the Paris Peace Conference and the Holy Alliance with the League of Nations.[115] Temperley's paper mirrored a cautiously germinating historical optimism: The Holy Alliance, he said, failed because it did not correspond with the real situation of that time; but the League of Nations did, and "we thrust it may succeed."

The search for new paths, the doubt and self-criticism that asserted themselves so loudly at the Brussels Congress, did not determine its character as a whole. Most of the more than 350 contributions, which were presented in thirteen sections, moved self-confidently along the trails of conventional historical methods. When one surveys the entire list of topics, some ambitious challenges to the theory of history proved to be valuable and informative, along with four types of factual contributions: (1) reports on the status of research on clearly delineated topics; (2) reports on individual research, particularly when accompanied by considerations of the methods used by the authors; (3) well-founded new interpretations of previously known subjects; (4) forward-looking proposals regarding future cooperation. To list only a few examples: Philippe Sagnac and Alphonse Aulard spoke about research on the French Revolution, while Carl R. Fish spoke on studies on the United States. Examples of papers from historical workshops that later led to major works include the already mentioned contributions of Bloch, Webster, and Temperley. Stimulating interpretations were presented by Pirenne on the "historical contrast between Merovingians and Carolingians"; by the French historian Jules Gay—in a remarkable turn against the Germanophobe bias—on the "alleged foreign domination" of the Hohenstaufen rulers over Italy; by the Warsaw professor Marceli Handelsman on Eastern European feudalism; and by Louis Halphen from Bordeaux on the unity of Asian and European history, a unity constituted by mutual interaction. The motions that found consideration and led to significant results included Febvre's journal project, the suggestions by Jameson and the Hungarian Eugen Horvath on the creation of an international bibliography, and above all the Americans' initiative to found an international historical committee.

The Brussels Congress generally received high marks in the professional historical journals, to the extent that they covered it at all.[116] Georg von Below, irritated by the exclusion of the "historians from those states against which the Entente waged war," wrote a brief critical notice in the *Historische Zeitschrift* on "The So-Called Fifth International Historical Congress."[117] Henri Berr published a critical evaluation for other reasons in the *Revue de synthèse historique*.[118] He was not critical toward the organizers, who, as he wrote, had done their best, but rather against the general state of historical scholarship, which had yet to become a "science" and whose current chaotic condition had only just become apparent in Brussels: "Allowing everyone who registers to choose the topic that he likes; allocating the same half hour for the tiny little discovery of some scholar and for the thoughts of a man like Pirenne on economic development; providing the same possibilities—or the same strangulation—of discussion in both cases; determining the use of time by the clock and not by the scope of the subject—this means ensuring success rather than profit. A Congress should not evoke the idea of a sort of intellectual marketplace, where everyone freely peddles his wares." An assessment worthy of consideration! There were surely limits to an all-too-rigid thematic restriction in a freely developing scholarly community with multiple interests of knowledge. And yet, structuring future Congresses through a focus on a few central themes presented itself as an essential task of the future.

Notes

1. See K. Schwabe, *Wissenschaft und Kriegsmoral: Die deutschen Hochschullehrer und die politischen Grundfragen des Ersten Weltkriegs* (Göttingen, 1969); Schröder-Gudehus, "Deutsche Wissenschaft," pp. 51ff., with a comprehensive bibliography. H. Kellermann, ed., *Der Krieg der Geister: Eine Auslese deutscher und ausländischer Stimmen zum Weltkriege 1914* (Dresden, 1915).
2. *Why we are at War: Great Britain's Case*. By Members of the Oxford Faculty of Modern History (Oxford, 1914).
3. *The Times*, 21 Oct. 1914.
4. Schröder-Gudehus, "Deutsche Wissenschaft," p. 70f.
5. Declaration by twenty-one German scholars of international law in *Zeitschrift für Völkerrecht* 9 (1915/16): 135–137, 430.
6. See B. vom Brocke, "Wissenschaft und Militarismus: Der Aufruf der 93 'An die Kulturwelt!' und der Zusammenbruch der internationalen Gelehrtenrepublik im Ersten Weltkrieg," in W. M. Calder III, H. Flashar, and Th. Lindken, eds., *Wilamowitz nach 50 Jahren* (Darmstadt, 1985).
7. Quoted in Schröder-Gudehus, "Deutsche Wissenschaft," p. 75. Clemenceau was still dealing with the Manifesto of the 93 in 1930; see G. Clemenceau, *Grandeurs et misères d'une victoire* (Paris, 1930), chapter 15.
8. Wilamowitz-Moellendorff, *Erinnerungen*, p. 313.
9. *Académie Royale de Belgique. Bulletin de la Classe des Lettres et des Sciences Morales et Politiques 1919* (Brussels, 1919): 89.
10. B. Croce, *Randbemerkungen eines Philosophen zum Weltkriege* (Zürich/Leipzig/Wien, 1922). For further examples, see Schröder-Gudehus, "Deutsche Wissenschaft," pp. 70ff.
11. See the chapter on the "challenge" of French scholarship by Germany in Carbonell, *Histoire et historiens*.
12. U. von Wilamowitz-Moellendorff, "Der Krieg und die Wissenschaft," *Internationale Monatsschrift für Wissenschaft, Kunst und Technik* 9 (15 Oct. 1914): 101–106, here p. 103. Response from the Académie des Sciences, 3 Nov. 1914, in Schröder-Gudehus, "Deutsche Wissenschaft," p. 73.
13. E. Troeltsch, "Der Krieg und die Internationalität der geistigen Kultur," *Internationale Monatsschrift für Wissenschaft, Kunst und Technik* 9 (15 Oct. 1914): 51–58.

14. Schröder-Gudehus, "Deutsche Wissenschaft," p. 87.
15. On the following, see ibid., pp. 89ff.
16. Text extract ibid., p. 91, note 6; a résumé of the London Conference and the exact wording of the resolution are to be found in *Académie Royale de Belgique. Bulletin*, pp. 49–62.
17. On the following, see *Union Académique Internationale. Compte rendu de la Conférence préliminaire de Paris. Statuts proposés par le Comité des Délégués, 15 et 17 mai 1919* (Paris, 1919); idem, *Compte rendu de la seconde Conférence académique, tenue à Paris les 15–18 octobre 1919* (Paris, 1919); idem, *Comptes rendus des sessions annuelles du Comité*, 1–15 (Brussels, 1920–1934).
18. *Académie Royale de Belgique. Bulletin*, p. 627f.
19. Schröder-Gudehus, "Deutsche Wissenschaft," p. 203f. The most detailed description of German-Russian cooperation is to be found in Behrendt, "Die internationalen Beziehungen," pp. 119ff.; see also R. Stupperich, "Die Teilnahme deutscher Gelehrter am 200jährigen Jubiläum der Russischen Akademie der Wissenschaften, 1925," *Jahrbücher für Geschichte Osteuropas* 24 (1976): 218–229; *Mitteilungen des Verbandes der deutschen Hochschulen* (Halle 1921ff.), and the documents concerning the Union Académique Internationale in the papers of Koht, Brandi, Friis, Leland, and De Sanctis.
20. See K. Düwell, *Deutschlands auswärtige Kulturpolitik 1918–1932: Grundlinien und Dokumente* (Köln, 1976), pp. 154ff., 232ff.
21. L. F. Stock, "Some Bryce-Jameson Correspondence," *American Historical Review* 50 (1944/45): 261–298, here p. 261; on Jameson's biography, see above all E. Donnan and L. F. Stock, eds., *An Historian's World: Selections from the Correspondence of John Franklin Jameson* (Philadelphia, 1956); M. D. Rothberg, "'To set a standard of workmanship and compel men to conform to it': John Franklin Jameson as Editor of the American Historical Review," *American Historical Review* 89 (1984): 957–975.
22. Paul Kehr, director of the Prussian Historical Institute in Rome from 1903 to the beginning of the war.
23. Donnan and Stock, *An Historian's World*, p. 211f.
24. 3 Aug. 1917, ibid., p. 214f.
25. Ibid., esp. pp. 174 and 209f. (Jameson to Bryce, 12 Nov. 1914 and 18 June 1917).
26. Ibid., pp. 195ff.; cf. H. Pirenne, *Souvenirs de captivité en Allemagne: Mars 1916–Novembre 1918* (Brussels, 1920); Lyon, *Pirenne*, pp. 227ff.
27. Jameson to Woodward, 24 May 1918, in Donnan and Stock, *An Historian's World*, p. 223.
28. Jameson to Dwight W. Morrow, an American businessman, 18 March 1919, ibid., p. 233.
29. The committee's composition is not known in detail. At least, Jameson himself and Prothero, probably also Firth, belonged to this never-acting committee.
30. Letter to Firth, 19 March 1919, in Donnan and Stock, *An Historian's World*, pp. 233ff.; similar in letter to Prothero, 28 Feb. 1919, Jameson papers, file 1368.
31. Prothero to Jameson, 23 March 1919, Jameson papers, file 1368.
32. Firth to Jameson, 15 April 1919, in Donnan and Stock, *An Historian's World*, p. 235.
33. W. G. Leland, *Guide to Materials for American History in the Archives and Libraries of Paris*, 2 vols. (Washington, D.C., 1932, 1943).
34. Jameson to Shotwell, 26 Nov. 1919, Jameson papers, file 1531.
35. Jameson to Prothero, 11 Dec. 1919, Jameson papers, file 1368.
36. Shotwell to Jameson, London, 31 Dec. 1919 and 2 Feb. 1920, Jameson papers, file 1531.
37. Prothero to Jameson, 24 Dec. 1919, Jameson papers, file 1368.
38. Shotwell to Jameson, 31 Dec. 1919 and 17 March 1920, Jameson papers, file 1531.
39. On this meeting, see Koht to Friis, Oslo, 3 May 1922, Friis papers, I, 1.
40. Jameson to Friis, 4 March 1927, Jameson papers, file 584. For the contents of the American resolution, see Jameson to Leland, 23 Dec. 1920, Jameson papers, file 992.
41. Leland to Jameson, 18 Dec. 1922, Jameson papers, file 992; Leland to Shotwell, 18 Dec. 1922, Leland papers, box 26. See also Pollard to his parents, 14 and 28 Jan. 1923, Pollard papers.

42. Quoted in letter of S. E. Morison to Jameson, 22 Jan. 1923, copy in Leland papers, box 21.
43. C. Barbagallo in *Corriere della Sera*, 19 April 1923; similar comments were published in *Tribuna*, 17 April 1923; both quoted by G. von Below in "Vermischtes," *Historische Zeitschrift* 128 (1923): 556.
44. See his letter to Westergaard, quoted in Leland to Jameson, 9 Feb. 1923, Jameson papers, file 993.
45. Friis to Meinecke, 30 Sep. 1922, Meinecke papers, 11.
46. Pirenne to Friis, 17 Sep. 1922, copy, ibid.
47. Koht, "Lehrjahre."
48. Koht to Friis, 3 May 1922 and 17 Sep. 1922, Friis papers, I. 1.
49. Friis to Koht, 2 June 1922, Koht papers, 386.
50. Leland to Jameson, 5 Jan. 1923, Jameson papers, file 992.
51. Leland to Westergaard, 19 Jan. 1923, Leland papers, box 28.
52. Leland to Jameson, 18 Dec. 1922, Jameson papers, file 992; cf. also Leland to Shotwell, 18 Dec. 1922, Leland papers, box 26.
53. See Schröder-Gudehus, "Deutsche Wissenschaft," p. 147f., and Ph. Rank, *Einstein: Sein Leben und seine Zeit* (Munich, 1949), p. 328f.
54. As a "correspondent," not as a "member." Leland to Jameson, 21 Feb. 1923, Jameson papers, file 993.
55. Leland to Jameson, 5 Jan. 1923, Jameson papers, file 992.
56. Congress Brussels 1923: *Compte rendu*, p. 8f.
57. Bulgaria became a member of the League of Nations in 1920, Turkey in 1932. Neither country was represented at the Brussels Congress.
58. Halecki to Leland, 7 Feb. 1923, Leland papers, box 19.
59. Til Det Akademiske Kollegium. Fortrolig. Kristiania 24 April 1923. Copy in Friis papers, II, 86; see also Koht, *The Origin*, pp. 3–5.
60. Leland to Jameson, Paris, 20 April 1923, Jameson papers, file 993; W. G. Leland, "The International Congress of Historical Sciences, held at Brussels," *American Historical Review* 28 (1922/23): 639–655.
61. Congress Brussels 1923: *Compte rendu*, p. 38.
62. Leland to Jameson, 20 April 1923, in Jameson papers, file 993.
63. Leland papers, box 40.
64. Leland to Shotwell, Paris, 6 April 1923, ibid., box 26.
65. Text of this "Projet de statuts pour une Union internationale des sciences historiques" in Congress Brussels 1923: *Compte rendu*, pp. 533ff. According to Halecki, it was presented on behalf of the Polish Historical Society, too. The Polish contribution to the origins of the International Committee of Historical Sciences—generally attributed to the Americans alone—was emphasized by Oskar Halecki, "VI Międzynarodowy kongres nauk istoryczny" [The VI. International Congress of Historical Sciences], *Przegląd Powszechny* 180 (1928): 115f. Cf. also Halecki, "V Międzynarodowy kongres historyczny" [5th International Historical Congress], *Kwartalnik historyczny* 37 (Lvov, 1923): 262.
66. Leland to Jameson, 20 April 1923, Jameson papers, file 993; see also Koht, *The Origin*, p. 3f.
67. Cf. report by De Sanctis to the Minister of Public Instruction on the meeting of the Brussels Committee of 15 and 16 May 1924. De Sanctis papers, Congresso storico internazionale.
68. Leland to Jameson, 20 April 1923, Jameson papers, file 993.
69. Text in Congress Brussels 1923: *Compte rendu*, p. 470.
70. M. S. de Boer in *Tijdschrift voor Geschiedenis* 38 (1923): 304.
71. Leland to Jameson, 20 April 1923, Jameson papers, file 993.
72. M. Lhéritier, "Henri Pirenne et le Comité International des Sciences Historiques" (speech, 1932), in *Henri Pirenne, Hommages et Souvenirs*, vol. 1 (Brussels, 1938), pp. 88–89.
73. Lyon, *Pirenne*, p. 294.
74. Pirenne, *Souvenirs*.

75. "De la méthode comparative en histoire," in Congress Brussels 1923: *Compte rendu*, pp. 19ff.
76. In a number of notes in the printed text of the speech.
77. Lyon, *Pirenne*, pp. 316ff.
78. In succession to Lamprecht, this concept of race was particularly articulated by Nicolae Iorga at the International Congress in Zurich 1938, see p. 173 below.
79. "Un contraste historique: Mérovingiens et Carolingiens," in Congress Brussels 1923: *Compte rendu*, p. 97f. See also chapter 9, note 14.
80. H. Sée, "Remarques sur l'application de la méthode comparative à l'histoire économique et sociale," *Revue de synthèse historique* 36 (1923): 37–46.
81. Quoted from a letter to the French historian Prou, 16 March 1898, in B. and Mary Lyon, "Maurice Prou, ami de Henri Pirenne," *Le Moyen Age* 71 (Brussels, 1965): 71–107, here p. 96.
82. Ibid., p. 97, note 52.
83. "Le problème de la synthèse dans l'histoire," Congress Brussels 1923: *Compte rendu*, p. 403f.; complete text in *La Pologne au Ve Congrès International des Sciences Historiques*, published by Comité National Polonais du Ve Congrès d'Histoire (Warsaw, 1924) [hereafter Congress Brussels 1923: *La Pologne*]. On Bujak, see St. Arnold, "En Pologne: un maître, une école," *Annales d'histoire économique et sociale* 5 (1933).
84. Cf. R. Koselleck, Introduction to *Geschichtliche Grundbegriffe: Historisches Lexikon zur politisch-sozialen Sprache in Deutschland*, ed. O. Brunner, W. Conze, and R. Koselleck (Stuttgart, 1972).
85. "La synthèse en histoire," brief abstract in Congress Brussels 1923: *Compte rendu*, p. 405; for a more thorough presentation, see H. Berr, "Le Ve Congrès International des sciences historiques (Bruxelles, 8–15 avril) et la synthèse en histoire," *Revue de synthèse historique* 35 (1923): 5–14.
86. J. S. Lewinsky, "L'Évolution économique est-elle déterminée par des lois?," Congress Brussels 1923: *Compte rendu*, p. 288f.; complete text in Congress Brussels 1923: *La Pologne*, pp. 171ff.
87. G. v. Below, *Probleme der Wirtschaftsgeschichte: Eine Einführung in das Studium der Wirtschaftsgeschichte* (Tübingen, 1920), pp. 7ff.
88. G. Fagniez, "Les variations de l'esprit public et les historiens en France," Congress Brussels 1923: *Compte rendu*, p. 399f.; complete text in *Revue Universelle* (Paris, 1923).
89. E. Bacha, "Les multiples évolutions politiques sont déterminées par une loi," Congress Brussels 1923: *Compte rendu*, p. 402f.; a more detailed version can be found in E. Bacha, *La Loi des Créations* (Brussels/Paris, 1921).
90. On Bacha's critique of Pirenne, see Lyon, *Pirenne*, p. 297, note 26.
91. W. M. Kozlowski, "L'action des idées en histoire," Congress Brussels 1923: *Compte rendu*, p. 402f.; complete text in Congress Brussels 1923: *La Pologne*.
92. Baron Lecca, "Les anciennes races Europeénnes et le substratum des nations modernes," Congress Brussels 1923: *Compte rendu*, p. 419f.; idem, "Sur la vieille race européenne des hommes blonds," in *Bulletin de la Société royale belge de Géographie* (Brussels, 1923).
93. "L'évolution de la mentalité allemande à l'époque contemporaine," Congress Brussels 1923: *Compte rendu*, p. 325f.; complete text in *Revue militaire générale* (Paris, 1923).
94. Congress Brussels 1923: *Compte rendu*, p. 326.
95. See note 114 below.
96. H. Koht, "Le problème des origines de la Renaissance," *Revue de synthèse historique* 37 (1924): 107–116, here p. 109.
97. Congress Brussels 1923: *Compte rendu*, p. 441f.; complete text, entitled "Géographie historique et géographie humaine," in *Bulletin de la Société royale belge de Géographie* (Brussels, 1923).
98. See Halecki, "V Międzynarodowy kongres," p. 262.
99. Congress Brussels 1923: *Compte rendu*, pp. 103ff.
100. See below, pp. 127–129.
101. M. Bloch, *La Société féodale*, 2 vols. (Paris, 1939, 1940).

102. "Une contamination de croyance: les rois de France, guérisseurs d'écroulles, saint Marcoul et les septièmes fils," Congress Brussels 1923: *Compte rendu*, p. 315f.; M. Bloch, *Les Rois Thaumaturges* (Paris, 1924).
103. "L'idée moderne de domination universelle," Congress Brussels 1923: *Compte rendu*, p. 328f.
104. "Projet de création d'une Revue internationale d'histoire économique," presented by Febvre, De Sanctis papers, Congresso storico internazionale; see also Congress Brussels 1923: *Compte rendu*, pp. 291–293. On the correspondence with Pirenne on this subject before the Congress, see Lyon, *Pirenne*, p. 339; on the founding of the *Annales* in 1928 also P. Leuilliot, "Aux Origines des 'Annales d'histoire économique et sociale' (1928): Contribution à l'historiographie française," in *Méthodologie de l'Histoire et des sciences humaines. Mélanges en l'honneur de Fernand Braudel* (Toulouse, 1973), pp. 317–324. On the political and historiographical milieus surrounding the planned journal foundation, see Ch.-O. Carbonell and G. Livet, eds., *Au Berceau des Annales: Le milieu strasbourgeois. L'histoire en France au début du XXe siècle* (Toulouse, 1983).
105. See Febvre's exposé in the economic history section of the Congress, Congress Brussels 1923: *Compte rendu*, p. 292.
106. Ibid.
107. Congress report by M. S. de Boer, *Tijdschrift voor Geschiedenis* 38 (1923): 304.
108. Congress Brussels 1923: *Compte rendu*, p. 303.
109. L. Febvre, *Combats pour l'histoire* (Paris, 1953), p. 398.
110. This conclusion results from Leland's letter to Pirenne, Paris, 4 March 1924, Leland papers, box 24, where Leland discusses the perspectives for financing both undertakings (International Bibliography: *Jahresberichte*; International Review of Economic History: *Vierteljahrschrift*): "These two projects ... will I think receive ... support in the form of recommendations to the trustees of the Rockefeller Fund. There are however, I am convinced, certain conditions which would have to be fulfilled in order to secure this support, the chief of which is an assurance that the enterprises should be carried on through a complete international cooperation—in other words that the German scholars should have their representation in the direction of those undertakings. This would require the addition of a German member to the board of editors of the International Review of Economic History."
111. H. Pirenne, "De l'influence allemande sur le mouvement historique contemporain," *Scientia: Rivista Internazionale di Sintesi Scientifica* (Bologna, 1923): 173–178.
112. Congress Brussels 1923: *Compte rendu*, pp. 425ff.
113. "Some clues to the origin of the war of 1914," Congress Brussels 1923: *Compte rendu*, p. 445.
114. *The Glasgow Herald*, 16 April 1923. Mackinnon had contributed a paper on "The Claim of the English Church to Jurisdiction over the Church of Scotland in the 12th Century," Congress Brussels 1923: *Compte rendu*, pp. 215ff.
115. Ch. Webster, "The Congress of Vienna and the Paris Peace Conference: A comparison and a contrast"; H. Temperley, "The Congress and Conference system and its breakdown." Both in Congress Brussels 1923: *Compte rendu*, pp. 142ff. Complete text in *The Congress of Vienna 1814–15 and the Conference of Paris 1919. 1. A comparison of their organization and results ... By Professor C. K. Webster. 2. Attempts at international Government in Europe; the period of the Congress of Vienna, 1814–15, and the period since the Treaty of Versailles, 1919–1922. By H. W. V. Temperley*, Historical Association, Leaflet no. 56 (London, 1923).
116. The most thorough reports were those by Leland in *American Historical Review* 28 (1922/23): 639ff., and M. S. de Boer in *Tijdschrift voor Geschiedenis* (1923): 303ff.
117. "Vermischtes," *Historische Zeitschrift* 128 (1923): 555f.
118. Berr, "Le Ve Congrès," p. 7.

Chapter 8

THE BEGINNINGS OF THE INTERNATIONAL COMMITTEE OF HISTORICAL SCIENCES, 1923–1927

In order to carry out the Brussels resolution of 15 April 1923 calling for the formation of an international historical committee, the Congress Bureau convened in Brussels on 15/16 May 1924 at the same time as a meeting of the Union Académique Internationale. The United States was represented by Shotwell's replacement, Waldo Leland, who had dedicated himself with consummate skill and enthusiasm to the re-creation of a comprehensive ecumenical community of historians and, in this context, to the founding of the ICHS. Now he was pushing for its rapid realization. Not everyone wanted to move forward as quickly as he did, so backing from the Carnegie Foundation was all the more important. His correspondence shows the pains he took to ensure that his activities were in concert with Jameson's instructions and suggestions. Thus, he reported to him on 16 November 1923 from Paris: "Pirenne is rather inclined to adjourn any decision respecting German membership in the committee, but I think that when the permanent committee is formed a definite place must be left for a German member. If that is not done, the English and most of the Americans and all the Scandinavians will hesitate to go on with the organization."[1]

Pirenne's hesitation can be explained both by the deep disappointment he had experienced during the war and by his respect for the popular mood in Belgium and France. In Leland's view it was also connected to contemporary predictions about Germany's political perspectives. The Franco-Belgian efforts to create autonomous states in the Rhineland seemed to be closer than ever to realization. Pirenne, Leland said, "argues that the only hope for a permanent peace in Europe is a Germany broken up into several parts."[2] One could hardly expect that a person who saw the division of Germany as a desirable outcome would raise his voice in favor of an expedited representation of an undivided

---

Notes for this chapter begin on page 118.

Germany in the future international historical committee. Nonetheless, Leland succeeded in persuading Pirenne to include a few additional historians at the Brussels Bureau meeting in May 1924, if only in an advisory function, instead of discussing the proposed expansion at this meeting first, as Pirenne would have preferred.[3] Among those whom Leland invited personally was the Austrian economic historian Alfons Dopsch, the founder of the famous Vienna Seminar for Economic and Social History. As a proponent of the thesis of an economic continuity from ancient times to the Middle Ages, he was Pirenne's equal, and his antipode, in one of the major historical controversies of contemporary medieval studies. Because of his position as president of the Austrian section of the Commission for Intellectual Cooperation of the League of Nations he was predestined for cooperation in the future international historical committee, for in contrast to Germany, Austria had decided to join this Commission.[4]

For Leland, who was struggling to gain Pirenne's assent, the high estimation that Dopsch enjoyed in this body provided an argument against the allegation made by a number of French historians that Dopsch was a pan-Germanist. "And anyhow," he wrote to Pirenne, "a converted Pangermanist is worth half a dozen internationalists who need no repentance." Other Frenchmen (he mentioned the influential Société d'histoire moderne to which he himself belonged and which had just admitted two Austrians) and both British and American colleagues loudly applauded Dopsch's invitation.[5] Upon encountering Dopsch in Paris in December 1923, Leland had tried to persuade him to cooperate in the future international historical committee. He described his argumentation as follows:

> I asked him then if it would not be possible to persuade the Austrian scholars to take part at once in the work of the international Committee without waiting for the Germans to be invited, or without even demanding a promise that the Germans should be invited. I explained that it was a bad time at present to lay down such conditions, that I had no doubt but that the Germans would be invited to the next congress, that I thought as a practical procedure the question would be settled indirectly by selecting a place for the congress where there would be no question about inviting the Germans, and that I thought Austrian cooperation now might help materially to prepare the way for German cooperation at the earliest possible moment. I also assured him that in fact the Americans and English were in a position somewhat similar to that which the Austrians would occupy if they came in with us, in that we were not at present demanding any promises as to the future but that we were determined not to take part in another congress unless it should be organized on an all inclusive basis. This seemed to make an impression on him and I judge has had its effect on his colleagues.[6]

And indeed, he was successful. Dopsch conferred with his colleagues in Vienna, Graz, and Innsbruck and then provided the assurance: "We are prepared to assume the mediation on behalf of the Germans as you requested under the condition that they be invited to the Congress as before and that the German language be admitted there on equal terms."[7] Leland gave the ambiguous term "condition" the more precise definition of "assumption": "If I translate his letter correctly he says they are ready to cooperate on the *assumption* that the Germans will be invited next time and that the German language will have equal rights with the other languages. If the Germans are there, of course their language will enjoy equal rights, and if the Germans are not there, or rather are not invited, I assume that the English and Americans will not be there either, nor the Scandinavians or Swiss, so it seems to me the Austrians have nothing to fear." On the basis of this preliminary agreement, and after the American Historical Association had promised to pay the travel costs, he invited Dopsch to participate in the Brussels meeting.[8]

It was also on Leland's initiative that Michel Lhéritier, the later secretary-general of the ICHS, attended the meeting. Lhéritier had embarked on a career as historian with a number of small studies and a doctoral thesis at the Sorbonne on topics concerning the history of Bordeaux in the Ancien Régime and at the time of the French Revolution. He subsequently turned to the history of Greece[9] and wrote popular studies on French and Greek history as well as a schoolbook on the history of Europe and France (together with Georges Pagès). As a collaborator on the preparatory work for the Paris Institut International de Coopération Intellectuelle, set up in 1925, he stood in contact with the cultural enterprises of the League of Nations. In 1926 he became a professor at the École des Hautes Études Sociales in Paris. His fields of scholarly interest were primarily the history of Eastern and Southeastern Europe (Greece and Hungary), French administrative and urban history, and benevolent despotism. In numerous essays over the following years, for example, in the *Revue de synthèse historique*, he dealt with questions of international cooperation, particularly in the field of historical instruction, which lay close to his heart. Leland respected this enthusiast of reconciliation, not least for his broad knowledge of modern languages, but also for representing that segment of French historians who were ready to cooperate with Germany, in contrast to his countryman Homolle, France's representative in the international historical Bureau.

It was of great significance for the ensuing course of events that Leland also included Halvdan Koht as a "consultant." With his invitation to hold the next Congress in neutral Oslo, Koht had firmly supported Leland's ecumenical efforts. A meeting of the Scandinavian historians in July 1923 had placed itself shoulder to shoulder with his intentions. When he arrived in Brussels in May 1924, Koht brought with him letters from Aage Friis and from Johan A. Almquist, director of the Swedish national archives, confirming the Danish and Swedish historians' opinion.[10] The expanded Bureau, meeting in Brussels in May 1924—with Pirenne, Homolle, De Sanctis, Vinogradoff (at the time still a member of the Leningrad Academy and regarded as a representative of Russia, although he had been living and working in Oxford since the prewar period), Dembiński, Powicke (as a representative for Tout), Leland, and the additionally invited persons—constituted itself without delay as the provisional International Committee of Historical Sciences,[11] with Pirenne as president and Leland as secretary-general. According to Koht's report, the Brussels meeting of May 1924 demonstrated that the atmosphere had changed since the Congress of April 1923. If back then the French had had a hard time accepting the thought that they could be pressured to meet with German historians again such a short time after the war, now it was evident that they had got used to the idea.

This corresponded to the changing political situation. The Ruhr struggle and the impending separation of the Rhineland had been followed by international negotiations that cleared the way for a new conjoint settlement of the reparations question in the Dawes Plan of 1924 and ultimately led to the Locarno Treaties of 1925 and Germany's entry to the League of Nations in 1926. This reduction of the inner-European tensions matched American interests. Leland knew how to exploit this situation when the moment was right. The establishment of an international historical committee was unthinkable without financial start-up assistance from America. But this money would not be handed over unconditionally. Thus, he told Pirenne that he and Shotwell had asked the Rockefeller Foundation to support the undertaking, and that there were good chances of receiving funds. The Rockefeller Foundation was "interested in promoting historical and social studies in Europe as a means of hastening the return to a more normal state of affairs in the intellectual world." And he added, "There are, however, I am convinced certain conditions which would have to be fulfilled in order to secure this support, the chief of which is an assurance that the enterprises should be carried on through a complete international cooperation—in other words that the German scholars should have their representation in the direction of those undertakings."[12] He was thinking particularly of the international bibliography and—as already mentioned in the previous chapter—of the international review for economic history.

Thus, it was not the Austrians who were able to make "conditions" in regard to a future German participation, and even less the Germans, but rather Leland himself, the "moteur essentiel de toute l'organisation," as Pirenne once addressed him.[13] And yet, Leland's own political reservations toward Germany were no smaller than Pirenne's. "I think it quite evident," he wrote to Jameson, "that from the beginning there has been in Germany a determination to avoid the terms of the treaty of Versailles and gentler treatment would not have softened this determination at all. I think that Pirenne's view of Germany is pretty nearly correct."[14]

It was under these conditions that the provisional committee approached the task of drafting its final constitution on 15 May 1924. Leland was entrusted with drawing up the draft statutes and writing invitations to the historians of those countries that had taken active part in the earlier Congresses. He apparently had considerable freedom of decision in regard to the selection of the persons to be invited, and he made good use of it.

The invitations were sent from Washington, D.C., to 27 (almost exclusively) European countries.[15] Two years later, 19 of them took part in the constituent meeting in Geneva on 14/15 May 1926.[16] Chile, Finland, Greece, Hungary, and Yugoslavia failed to respond to the invitation. Special problems and uncertainties arose in regard to the Russian delegation. In a letter to Shotwell, Leland wrote that "we must deal directly with Russian scholars in Russia and not adopt the fiction that they can be represented by Russian scholars outside Russia." It was absurd, he said, to proceed from the viewpoint that Vinogradoff, for example, who had been teaching in Oxford since 1903 and still represented the Leningrad Academy and thus "Russia" in the Union Internationale Académique, or that Rostovtsev, who was living in the United States, could represent the interests of Russian scholarship in the international historical committee, as both of them were probably stuck in their new homelands for the duration. However, he told Pirenne that Vinogradoff, who had already taken part in the meeting of the expanded Bureau in May 1924, should be invited to the inaugural assembly as a representative of Russia.[17] In any case, an invitation was indeed sent to the Leningrad Academy of Sciences. But no representative could come to Geneva, since Switzerland had not yet recognized the Soviet Union. From the reply sent by the secretary of the Leningrad Academy, Sergei F. Oldenburg, Lhéritier gathered that the Russian historians were prepared to take part in principle.[18] Argentina had accepted the invitation, but her delegate could not be informed in time. The two Britons Tout and Temperley were prevented from traveling by a general strike in England.

The most noticeable change since Brussels was the participation of historians from Germany. On Dopsch's suggestion, Leland had directed the official invitation to the Association of German Historians (Verband Deutscher Historiker) and also, with cover letters, to its chairman Georg Küntzel and to Hermann Oncken. The form and content of these letters had scattered all German reservations.[19] German scholars felt wounded by their far-reaching exclusion from international cooperation with the former enemy nations—not only from the "boycott organizations" in Brussels, namely, the Research Council and the Academic Union, but also from numerous professional associations. At first they were even distrustful of Leland, who, like Shotwell, had been an "ardent promoter of the scholarly anti-German propaganda campaign" and who was currently representing the American Council of Learned Societies in the exclusionary Union Académique. Such misgivings were raised by the German ambassador to the United States, Ago von Maltzan, the former state secretary and promoter of the Rapallo Treaty, in a letter to the Foreign Office, only to be dissipated at once. He recommended that the German historians participate in the International Committee of Historical Sciences in close cooperation with the Austrian Alfons Dopsch.[20]

The Nobel laureate Fritz Haber, the director of the Kaiser-Wilhelm-Institute for Physical Chemistry, sent a thorough report on international scholarly cooperation to the German chancellor Luther.[21] In his view, the "general tendency" in both England and France pointed so strongly to a reestablishment of scholarly relations, that the only problem remaining to be resolved was "the bridging of the German-French conflict." Positive signs of this were emerging in France. Above all, the resumption of scholarly relations—a question that would be on the agenda, impending with the near entry of Germany to the League of Nations—should not be made dependent on the previous fulfillment of certain stipulations. Demands of this kind had been raised in a resolution of the Association of German and Austrian Academies, stating that Germany would only join the two Brussels organizations on the condition "that the boycott of German scholarship be withdrawn in a form which is satisfactory to Germany, that the organizations stay clear of all political tendencies forever, that the German language be given equal status etc."[22] Haber accurately perceived what was appropriate and possible when he said: "Within the small orbit of the scientific world, the demand to reestablish the previous status as a precondition of our reconciliation with the earlier war adversaries would lead to the same impossible situation that would have occurred in the larger orbit of foreign policy if the German government had officially demanded the effects of Locarno as the preconditions of the agreement, and had tried to impose this with the participation of the press." The German historians' concerns were dispelled thanks not least to the letter by Leland to Hermann Oncken assuring that despite Leland's membership in the Brussels Union Académique, there were no relations whatsoever between this organization and the future ICHS.[23]

The founding of the ICHS would not have succeeded without a considerable dose of goodwill on the part of all participants. The driving force in every respect was the Americans, particularly Waldo Leland. This applied no less to their efforts for financial assistance than to their organizational preparations. As start-up assistance, the Laura Spelman Rockefeller Memorial Foundation approved the sum of $25,000, in care of the American Historical Association. But this was not to be all. The documents of the Rockefeller Foundation show that in the entire interwar period from 1926 to 1940, the ICHS was granted no less than $96,000.[24] Why should such generous assistance have been granted to historians? Some of the formulations from the official application of the American Historical Association, upon which the approval was based, reveal the Americans' considerations and expectations. It stated that Europe's material troubles were not the guiding motive.

> Of greater concern are the spiritual wounds of war and the cessation of cooperative efforts in history and social sciences. The first sign that these rifts might be closed seems ... to have come in the field of history. This is highly significant and important. The Council of the American Historical Association finds that the success of the attempt to renew international cooperation will depend on the efforts of our group. We attach importance to this from the standpoint of historical work, but we are even more impressed with the responsibility that rests on this experiment as pointing the way for all groups in the social sciences, now divided on national lines and impotent to carry on the cooperative study and discussion of social, economic and political problems that are international in scope.[25]

One of the foundation's internal statements concerning the application resumed this argument: "It presents the need to support the first of the group of social sciences (or any science) that is attempting to bridge the War gap and get together on a truly international basis."[26]

In his capacity as director of the Carnegie Endowment for International Peace, Division of Economics and History, Shotwell supported a later extension application made by Leland with the assertion that historical scholarship could fulfill the international task incumbent upon it only if it was provided with a corresponding international organization:

> The World Conferences of Historians which have been meeting every five years, furnished a very proper base upon which to build. But the organization of these Conferences was open to very serious criticism. Each meeting was left to be arranged by the historians of the country in which it was to take place and there was no provision against nationalist over-emphasis and no certainty that the sounder aspects of objective scientific work would not be obscured by transitory and more popular influences. National jealousies have played their part in historical scholarship with lamentable results. The work which Mr. Leland has achieved in the formation of this International Committee, in the very heart of post-war Europe, is therefore all the more important, and the whole-hearted cooperation of the different national representatives in the organizing Bureau is a fact of much greater significance than might be apparent at first. The maintenance of this work for the next five years is an essential element in the restatement of the social sciences in Europe. The alternative might mean a reversion to pre-war conditions with a post-war psychology which would be nothing short of a calamity for European historiography.[27]

Leland anticipated that the founding of an international historical committee would also favorably influence the development of historical methods: "With money," he said, "I have no doubt that the international committee would get into production and would turn out very valuable work. But still more than that would be the influence which such a committee would have on the point of view in historical work. I rather think that the comparative study of history is going to be the pace of the next half century. The study of history from the international point of view, the study of institutions and phases of life which are common to many nations, instead of the study of national institutions from the nationalistic point of view."[28]

On 14 May 1926, Pirenne opened the Geneva inaugural session in his capacity as president of the still provisional committee. The meeting, and the better part of the participants' travel costs, were financed through the subsidies administered by the American Historical Association. Waldo Leland, supported by Lhéritier, worked as the organizer and secretary of the gathering. The fact that Pirenne, in his opening address, now pledged his support for an unlimited "Internationale" of historians was a good prelude to this goodwill assembly. Not without pride—and not without justification—he pointed out that this time, the historians were not running behind events, but were indeed in the vanguard: "Faster than the League of Nations was founded, we here in Geneva have reestablished our league of historians, which is more complete than the other one."[29] The draft statutes were discussed first. Leland had passed them out to the participants beforehand asking for their opinions. While presenting his draft in Geneva, Leland—taking into consideration German and Austrian concerns—dropped formulations suggesting possible cooperation with the Brussels Union Académique and the International Commission for Intellectual Cooperation.[30] With the memories it aroused, the meeting room in the Athenäum, which the Société des Arts had placed at their disposal, appeared to be a good omen. The Red Cross had been founded in the same place in 1863.

The foundations of the organization, laid down at that time, have proven themselves to the present day, albeit with a number of modifications: collective membership, then still by national committees and not yet by international organizations specialized in particular fields of historical study; equal membership dues for all; an executive committee (Bureau) made up of a president, two vice-presidents, a treasurer, a secretary-general, and four (later on six) assessor members; the replacement of the president and the partial renewal of the board according to the rhythm of the quinquennial Congresses. On the suggestion of the Germans, article 2 included a stipulation that non-sovereign states such as dominions, protectorates, colonies, and mandated territories could also be represented in the ICHS with a seat and a vote. The sponsors of the motion were thinking of Danzig. Similar wishes were soon presented by Canada and Algeria.[31]

The founding of the ICHS had a remarkable impact on the organization of the individual nations' historical discipline. In countries such as the United States and Germany, the already existing national historical associations, which were based on individual membership, assumed the function of the national committees provided for by the statutes. In other cases, as in France, England, Italy, and Denmark, a national representation of historical studies came about only through the impulse of the international union. In France this occurred in the form of an organization integrating local, regional, and national institutions concerned with the cultivation, research, and teaching of history. In England, Italy, and Denmark, loose committees were created or national representation was transferred onto an already existing institution.[32]

The location of the ICHS led to some discussion. The Institut de Coopération Intellectuelle in Paris had placed office space at the disposal of Lhéritier, whom Leland envisioned as secretary-general.[33] Leland thought it very appropriate that the ICHS be given such a "lift in the organization" by an institute associated with the League of Nations.[34] However, the German side did not agree with the logical conclusion that Paris could then also become the seat of the ICHS. These objections were not directed against Lhéritier himself, though; from the beginning he had sought successfully to develop a relationship of mutual trust with the German members of the ICHS. Nor were they directed against the working arrangement between the Institute and the secretariat. On the contrary, Brandi urged the German Foreign Office to abandon its previous reserve toward the Paris Institute upon Germany's admission to the League of Nations.[35] As a way out of this situation still overshadowed by war resentment, Washington, D.C., was selected as the provisional headquarters for legal acts, administration, finances, and the archive. This solution seemed plausible since Leland was expected to become the treasurer, and the ICHS depended on American support in its early years.

Even more pressing was the decision on the site of the next Congress. Would it be located in a neutral state or in one of the wartime countries? The participants agreed that the choice of location should determine the choice of the first president. The invitation to Oslo, for which the Scandinavian countries, the United States, and Germany had been pushing against strong French reservations,[36] was vying with another from Warsaw, since Athens, which the French and Italians had favored, had been dropped because no Greek was present to advocate the invitation to Athens. An agreement was made in the sense that Warsaw should withdraw its invitation for 1928. This decision was probably influenced by the news of Marshal Pilsudski's military coup.[37] After this, the vote for Oslo was unanimous. At the same time, upon Koht's motion, the assembly—the Germans abstaining—resolved to consider Warsaw as the site of the 1933 Congress.[38] Like so many other decisions that helped set the ICHS on its way, this happy solution to a difficult question came about thanks to Waldo Leland. A year earlier, Leland had written to Pirenne that apparently the French favored Warsaw. It could be taken into consideration for 1933, but the Americans had committed themselves to "a truly neutral place" for 1928. Warsaw would possibly be attended only by Belgium, France, and the Eastern European allies of France, while financial support from America would only be provided to a Congress open to all countries.[39]

After the decision was made in favor of Oslo, Halvdan Koht was duly elected president. This was the first and last time in the history of the ICHS that the selection of the congress site and of the president's nationality were coordinated. On a recommendation from the Scandinavians, presented by Aage Friis, Pirenne and Dopsch became vice-presidents, Leland became treasurer, and Lhéritier—whom Pirenne called Leland's "alter ego"[40]—became secretary-general. Meinecke (Germany), Temperley (England), De Sanctis (Italy), and Dembiński (Poland) were chosen as assessor members of the Bureau. When Meinecke declined, Karl Brandi was confirmed via correspondence.

Under Koht's chairmanship, the Committee immediately began discussing two publication tasks that had been entrusted to it by the Brussels Congress. These were an international bibliography, for which Lhéritier had prepared a comprehensive memorandum, and an international journal of economic history corresponding to the recommendations of Lucien Febvre and Marc Bloch in Brussels.

The creation of the bibliography, which went back to a suggestion made by Jameson, had been financially guaranteed by support from the Rockefeller

Foundation, even before a clear concept had been developed. It was intended to replace the German *Jahresberichte der Geschichtswissenschaft* (Annual Reports on Historical Studies), which had ceased publication during the war. After it had been announced in Geneva that the *Jahresberichte* would reappear under the title *Jahresberichte für deutsche Geschichte*, restricted to German history, a general problem arose regarding the distinction between the planned international bibliography and national bibliographies appearing in various countries. Should a selection from the national bibliographies be published in the international bibliography, or should it be devoted to fields that had been insufficiently covered so far? International relations and organizations, as well as interdisciplinary fields such as economic and social history, were taken into consideration. The idea of comparative historical research was suggested as a guiding principle by Pierre Caron, an archivist at the Archives de France and secretary of the International Commission for Bibliography set up by the Geneva assembly. Aage Friis, its chairman, who had originally considered making a selection from the national bibliographies, summed up the outcome of the discussion in 1927: "Thus it will be up to our International Committee to see that excellent national bibliographies are available in every country. But what we now want is something different, [namely] the possibility of promoting surveys of research."[41]

A clear and convincing distinction was not arrived at, and today, after the *International Bibliography* has been in operation for many decades, we can see that it has not gained the status of an indispensable tool for historical research, regardless of its significance as a reference work, particularly for those countries that do not have a comprehensive bibliographical apparatus of their own. However, it is worth recalling from the discussions surrounding the start of this project that it was viewed as a symbol for the ongoing task of the ICHS to promote historical thought and knowledge beyond national bias and ideological narrow-mindedness. It is in this spirit that Chabod, one of the later presidents, called the *International Bibliography* the banner (*"le drapeau"*) of the ICHS.

Concerning the second project, the founding of an international journal for economic history, Pirenne presented a report stating that this journal was not intended as a rival to the German *Vierteljahrschrift für Wirtschafts- und Sozialgeschichte*. It would mainly publish critical bibliographical articles, and it should be edited not by the ICHS itself, but rather with its consent. Leland's earlier suggestion to create an index of diplomatic representatives met with approval. All of these tasks were transferred to the Bureau or to special commissions for further processing. The list of diplomats and the bibliography were actually realized.[42] The journal, however, became an autonomous undertaking under the title *Annales d'histoire économique et sociale*, which was introduced by its editors at the Oslo Congress of 1928.

The statutes assigned two tasks to the ICHS: to "promote the historical sciences through international cooperation," and to organize the International Congresses. As the later developments show, the focal point of its work always lay with the Congresses. They gained significance in the history of the historical discipline as manifestations of the self-awareness of historical scholarship in their time. The ICHS's own publications, however, were no more than technical aids. The ICHS gained the desired organizational conjunction with the practical work of the ever-ramifying branches of historiography only through the gradual inclusion of autonomous specialized international associations, which had and have publications and journals of their own.[43]

The strongest impression that the participants took away from the Geneva inaugural assembly was the fact that historians from previously hostile countries had been able to approach one another again in the service of history. In a report to the Rockefeller Foundation, Leland rightly emphasized the "spirit of amity and courtesy" that had dominated in Geneva: "It was not merely a matter of a correct attitude on the part of all the delegates, which might indeed have been expected from cultivated gentlemen, but a very real sentiment of mutual sympathy and esteem, which animated all the discussions and conversations, and which produced an atmosphere of confidence and friendship. It is safe to believe that a step of the utmost importance has been taken which will lead to far-reaching results, the significance of which it would be hard to overestimate."[44]

The test case for whether and to what extent joint scholarly interests could also be brought to bear on the personal level was the relationship between the French and German participants. Brandi spoke of "very agreeable impressions." In his report to the German Foreign Office, Reincke-Bloch, chairman of the Association of German Historians, reveals ambivalent feelings, praising the accommodating treatment of the Germans but viewing it as "obvious that despite all the wooing of German historical scholarship," the real intention was "to integrate them in the framework of French cultural relations."[45] Reservations and mistrust toward France had in no way disappeared from the German side, despite the favorable impression of Geneva.

On the other side there were the examples of Gustave Glotz, professor at the Sorbonne, member of the Institut de France, and chairman of the French national committee, and Lhéritier, secretary of the French committee and now of the ICHS as well. According to a letter by Lhéritier, Glotz traveled to Geneva with considerable skepticism and reservations. The French national committee, Lhéritier continued, had first thought of merely inviting the Germans as guests, similar to the advisory status of Dopsch at the meeting of the preparatory committee in May 1924. Their feelings were highly ambivalent, as they were on the German side as well. "It is certain," Lhéritier wrote in his letter, "that our International Committee will only be truly international if the Germans are admitted. But it is just as certain that it will only be truly international if it serves neither German nor any other national propaganda, if it has nothing else in view besides purely disinterested study of history.... We must elevate history above prejudice and passion."[46] This appeared to have succeeded in Geneva. After the first day of negotiations Glotz said that it showed "what was possible when reasonable men came together determined that their actions should be governed by good sense and reason rather than by sentiment."[47] As Brandi noted with satisfaction, Glotz spoke of a "victory of reason."[48]

Alongside Leland, Koht contributed significantly to the fact that the negotiations ran as smoothly as among good colleagues. He ensured, too, that the use of languages corresponded to the international character of the assembly. The official languages were German, English, French, Italian, and Spanish, although French dominated as the language shared by the greatest number of participants.[49] Koht reported: "It has to be noted that all the transactions of the first day were conducted in French. Personally, however, I was anxious to see established from the start that the other languages recognized as officially legitimate should also be used in practice. Therefore, for a while during the second day, I left the presidency to Dopsch and asked him to lead the discussion in German. Later, during my service as president of the Committee, I took up the practice of changing regularly from one language to another." For the meetings of the Bureau, however, another solution was adopted. "Before opening the transactions," Koht wrote, "I wanted to raise two practical questions regarding the meetings of the bureau. The first one was that of the languages to be employed in the discussions. I thought it essential that there should be no need of interpretation and translation, and I asked all the members what languages each one of them was able to understand and to speak. It turned out that French was the only language serviceable to everybody, and therefore that was determined for use within the bureau."[50]

Lhéritier chose a handy formula to characterize the spirit of the founding assembly of the ICHS. In a letter to Reincke-Bloch he called Geneva the "Locarno de la science historique."[51] At a reception at the building of the League of Nations given by Dr. Nitobe, one of the secretaries of the League, who also represented Japan in the ICHS, the proud founding fathers were solemnly shown the originals of the Locarno documents.[52] During the Briand-Stresemann era, everyone on both banks of the Rhine who was interested in peace placed his hopes in the spirit of Locarno and in the attempts at a *rapprochement franco-allemand*. The first years in the development of the ICHS up to the Oslo Congress in 1928 must be viewed in the context of these widespread feelings. The first Bureau meeting took place in 1926 in Paris on the invitation of the French national committee, and the first General Assembly took place in Göttingen in 1927.[53] The fact that France and Germany were the first two countries in which the ICHS and its Bureau convened underlines the spirit of goodwill surrounding the start of the organization's work.

The Göttingen assembly assumed the very character of a Franco-German meeting of reconciliation. The decision made by the Bureau in Paris to hold the first General Assembly in this old German university town was described in Brandi's opening speech as a gratefully perceived courtesy. There was no state representation, but the academic and private hospitality were all the more sincere. The American, Belgian, French, and Italian delegates, who were accompanied by their wives, were hosted by the Göttingen professors. At a reception given by the Göttingen Academy, the polyglot secretary of its Philological-Historical Class, the archaeologist Hermann Thiersch, gave an address shifting from German to French to English and to Italian. He recalled how Göttingen had remained free of the burdens of war during the occupation of Hanover in the Napoleonic era:

> Listen to what war minister Berthier said to General Martier, the commander of the French troops who had occupied the electorate of Hanover in the Year 11 of the French Republic: "The University of Göttingen, Citoyen général, has at all times provided the greatest services to the natural sciences and humanities, and the Institut National de France has awarded it a special sign of its high estimation by accepting a member of this university into its ranks. It is the will of the First Consul that you provide its facilities and its members with particular protection; let them know that the clatter of weapons shall not interrupt their peaceful pursuits, and that the French nation honors the scholars and scientists of all countries."

And Thiersch went on to say: "On the very same soil of our little town, which was once so uniquely honored through the noble generosity of the French nation, we today can hope to find once again the same just estimation and conciliatory understanding, the same nobility, the same magnanimity of thought." These words were understood and were spontaneously reciprocated. Among those who responded was the venerable French ancient historian Gustave Glotz, president of the Académie des Inscriptions et Belles Lettres, who had originally been so skeptical toward cooperation with his neighbors from across the Rhine. Now, in a heartfelt speech, he listed the names of the numerous scholars from Göttingen who had been accepted into the French academies over the course of history.[54]

Lhéritier founded his hopes for the future development of the ICHS on this good understanding between German and French historians.[55] "We French," he wrote to Thiersch,

> who were at first somewhat amazed, somewhat moved, to find ourselves in Germany, feeling not like passing strangers but rather like invited guests; we felt at ease. It is scarcely possible to express the satisfaction we felt when we listened to you in the university library on 13 May, in these unique surroundings, under these Gothic arches, with these thousands of books, with the busts of your great men, in the society of your colleagues, and among all these lovely flowers. As I wrote to Mr. Brandi: In that moment, France approached Germany; Monsieur Glotz approached you, dear Mr. Thiersch, and we must express our gratitude to you for having understood how to create, for this one moment, the atmosphere of direct, desirable and necessary rapprochement.[56]

And in a letter to the chairman of the Association of German Historians, he said: "Although we are Germans and Frenchmen, I think that from now on, if you agree, we may view one another as friends.... For me the most beautiful moment was the reception in the library with its warm-hearted speeches. Monsieur Glotz was very enthusiastic."[57] "The French and the Germans are perfectly happy together," Leland commented on the developing cooperation after the Paris meeting of the bibliographical commission.[58]

Although this may have been true of the ICHS, the situation was not as promising everywhere. Thus, it proved impossible to surmount the psychological barriers still blocking Germany's admission to the Union Académique. An attempt at mediation was undertaken on the margins of the Göttingen General Assembly by Koht, Leland, and the Dutchman Colenbrander, who, on behalf of their countries, intended to appeal to the Union Académique to offer Germany membership. The issue was discussed at a meeting attended by representatives of the academies of Berlin, Vienna, and Göttingen—among them Wilamowitz, Dopsch, and Brandi—as well as the president of the Union, the Italian De Sanctis, who, like Koht and Leland, played an important role in the ICHS and who from the beginning had stood up just as firmly as the two others for Germany's inclusion.[59] There was no difficulty in agreeing on practical matters of scholarly cooperation. The Union would not interfere with the ongoing *Corpora* of ancient inscriptions in Berlin, and an agreement was reached on the delimitation of work areas between the German *Thesaurus linguae latinae* and a new *Du Cange*. However, there remained insurmountable obstacles in the area of national sensitivities and resentments. The Germans and Austrians resented the fact that, according to the statutes of the Union, its permanent seat was Brussels. They desired that "the rationale for the exclusion of the Central Powers be rescinded in a form satisfying to us,"[60] that meeting sites be regularly shifted, and, in addition, that the German language be admitted as equal alongside French, which was the language of official business. However, the opposing side was not prepared to accept such desires as conditions for the German entry to the Union. In his disappointment, Leland wrote to Koht that the Germans seemed to be less interested in cooperation than in political prestige.[61] Koht was disenchanted to see that on both sides, the bitterness resulting from the war still acted as a barrier against international academic cooperation.[62] Koht, Leland, and Pirenne were all of the opinion that the initiative would now have to lie on the German side. But the Germans were not ready to apply for admission before the questions of language and meeting place had been settled. Dopsch and Brandi, however, the Austrian and German Bureau members of the ICHS, would have liked different conduct on the part of the German and Austrian academies for the sake of scholarly cooperation, which they hoped could also provide a new basis for a successful support of political concerns.[63]

There was another political issue, namely, the question of Russian membership in the ICHS. Did not the Soviet understanding of historical studies view history as an instrument of the Party and the state, destined for justification of the political system and ideological propaganda? At the time of the Göttingen meeting, the uncertainties in regard to Soviet participation had not yet been resolved. The Leningrad Academy had been invited, but no Soviet representatives took part. On 28 October 1926, Oldenburg and Tarle had surprisingly appeared for a brief moment at a meeting of the Commission for the International Bibliography, convened on the occasion of the Paris Bureau meeting.

Then the contacts with the Leningrad Academy were severed.[64] A whole array of problems began demanding a solution: What about the Russian historians living in the West? What position would the Leningrad Academy, which was still informed by the tradition of bourgeois historiography, be given in the Soviet delegation? What position would be granted to the Moscow Academy, which had been created as the fulcrum of Soviet-Marxist scholarship? According to Brandi, the Pole Dembiński had pointed out the tensions to be expected between emigrated and Soviet historians at the Paris Bureau meeting in October 1926. He had attempted "to prevent the invitation of the Soviet Republic to Oslo, or at least—under the slogan 'Il y a deux Russies'—to draw attention to the misgivings that an encounter between the Soviet representatives and the true scholarly Russia of the émigrés would engender." Brandi added: "As I myself, not only the president but also the rest of the entire eight-member Bureau, without hesitating, were of the opinion that in international dealings there is only one Russia today, namely, Soviet Russia."[65] Koht, the president of the ICHS, sought contact with the official Soviet scholarship through a Société pour les rapports scientifiques de l'U.R.S.S. avec l'étranger in Moscow.[66] However, until shortly before the Oslo Congress, he was not sure whether Soviet scholarship viewed itself as a member of the ICHS.[67] It was only after the Oslo Congress, where the historical profession of the Soviet Union was represented by communist and one or two "bourgeois" historians, that Mikhail N. Pokrovsky, the head of the new school, informed the secretary-general that the Soviet historians wished to take part in the activities of the ICHS. Aside from himself, Professor Oldenburg from the Leningrad Academy was designated as the official representative.[68]

The entrance of Soviet Russia into international cooperation in historical studies was launched by a German-Soviet congress held in Berlin 7 to 14 July 1928, to which the Deutsche Gesellschaft zum Studium Osteuropas (German Society for Eastern European Studies) under Otto Hoetzsch had issued invitations.[69] At its first appearance abroad, the Soviet historical discipline presented itself as a pluralistic picture. Alongside Marxist historians like Mikhail N. Pokrovsky, Isaac I. Mints, and Sergei M. Dubrovsky, representatives of the pre-Revolutionary historical studies such as Sergei F. Platonov and Dmitrii N. Egorov were given a voice. This corresponded to Pokrovsky's conviction of the usefulness of coexistence, which to him meant a constant confrontation between bourgeois and Marxist social sciences as a condition for the ultimate victory of the latter. He still believed that, in the final result, the bourgeois historians could spontaneously be won over for the new Marxist conception and research. In the eyes of Pokrovsky and his school, bourgeois and particularly German historiography functioned as an essential and significant preliminary for the development of Soviet-Marxist scholarship. Although Marxism was dominant in Russia, it nevertheless had no intention of intolerantly suppressing other points of view, Mints declared in his report on Berlin and Oslo. The relative openness that the Soviets displayed appeared as a favorable sign for future discussions between Western and Soviet historians, particularly in view of the coming International Congresses.

Alongside the question of whether and how it would be possible to bring historians from mutually hostile nations and ideologically antagonistic societies together in scholarly discussion, the ecumenical self-perception of the ICHS led to the subsequent task of more intensively integrating non-European history into the theme catalog of Europe's modern historical studies at future Congresses, and also of recruiting non-European historians for active participation. However, the first General Assembly in Göttingen was attended only by Europeans and Americans, namely, by scholars from Germany, Austria, Belgium, Bulgaria, Denmark, Spain, the United States, Finland, France, Great Britain, Greece, Hungary, Italy, Norway, the Netherlands, Poland, Portugal, Sweden, Switzerland, Czechoslovakia, and Yugoslavia. Cancellations came from Argentina, Brazil, and Japan, although they were already members of the organization. The ecumenical ideal was still in the distant future.

What impact did such general interests as peaceful scholarly cooperation among the former war enemies and new ideological challenges have on the planning of the impending Oslo Congress—the first Congress organized under international supervision? It would be hard to argue that the Bureau meeting and the General Assembly of the ICHS in Paris and Göttingen were successful in explaining what the specifics of the International Historical Congresses should be. In order not to disturb the desired harmony, it was decided to exclude politically controversial themes, above all the issue of war guilt, regardless of how much the historians of individual countries were actually dealing with it. This safeguard did not demonstrate great confidence in the ability of scholarship to objectify debate on historically and politically contentious questions. And yet, for a goodwill enterprise like the Oslo Congress, such restraint was probably appropriate.

One positive innovation was the intention to distinguish between "*rapports*" and "*communications.*" While the "communications" were to present individual research results or interpretations, loosely grouped in different sections, the "reports" were given a task more fitting to the international character of the Congresses. Lhéritier, who had developed this idea and persuaded the Bureau to accept it, explained it as follows: "Under reports we understand presentations of the same length as the communications, but with an entirely different content. Our reports assume that the respective matter is known, and restrict themselves to providing the most important bibliographical aids and to outlining the current research situation, including the accepted results, the questions that are yet to be answered, and the means with which to clarify them."[70] The subjects of the "reports" were to be recommended by the national committees, but the Bureau should assume a stronger leadership role in their selection and coordination than the organizing committees of the earlier Congresses had done.[71] Lhéritier would have liked to insert a clear statement on the task of the "reports" in the invitation sent from Oslo. He wrote to Koht: "The Congress participants would in this way be informed on what a report is; they would feel moved to furnish such reports, and in this way what is probably the most fruitful innovation of your Congress would be realized, namely, the methodical study of general, but precise and well-defined questions, in place of those ineffective and disordered sessions which hitherto were the characteristic feature of even the least badly organized Congresses."[72] Unfortunately, the invitation to the Oslo Congress included no corresponding definition of the "reports." Nevertheless, the Congress itself was to yield several outstanding examples, above all from the French and Polish side and from the president himself.

But were the Congresses and their preparation really the essential task of the ICHS? The American initiators and financial benefactors had thought that the ICHS should also (if not primarily) be active in internationally based edition and research projects. If one reads the reports on the Paris and Göttingen meetings, one can note that the organization and program of the Oslo Congress occupied relatively little space next to the discussion of all kinds of projects. Between Geneva and Oslo, it was not only the list of diplomats and the international bibliography that were under discussion, but also the following projects: an international journal, an iconographical documentation, the gathering of constitutional texts, a chronology of world history, an index of the publications of diplomatic records, and a new edition of the *Bibliotheca Historica Medii Aevi (Potthast)*. The first issues of the *Bulletin* published surveys on the organization of historians, on historical atlases, and on historical bibliographies in the various countries. This corresponded to the purpose of the ICHS as Leland had intended it in his first draft of the statutes. Its first article said: "It will suggest and encourage historical studies and publications; it will place new tools at the disposal of historiography, such as bibliographies, information pamphlets etc."[73] As secretary-general, Lhéritier had gone looking for possible projects with zest. For some people this was too much.

Thus, the British and Germans declared their opposition to the creation of more and more study teams and commissions.[74] Pirenne particularly warned against too much industriousness. He did not want the ICHS to compete with the academies in the field of historical research. But this was precisely Lhéritier's intention. "In no way do I share Pirenne's opinion on the role of our Committee," he wrote to Koht. "According to Pirenne, our task should be restricted to managing short-term business and leaving the large projects in the hands of the academies. I for my part, on the contrary, think that in the field of history both the large and small projects belong to the International Committee. The bibliographical yearbook, even the list of diplomats are by no means humble endeavors, and yet we have taken charge of them. If we know how to procure the funds ... we can undertake important publications. History should not exclusively belong to the academies." The task of the academies should lie in fields in which several sciences worked together. Historical studies, however, should entirely be the responsibility of the Committee.[75] Aage Friis took a conciliatory standpoint. He believed that the academies were better suited to the supervision of classic editions than the ICHS.[76] Since Koht also thought that "Göttingen was, to a certain extent, a rather bad experience"[77] in regard to insufficiently prepared project suggestions, Lhéritier latched himself all the more onto Leland. "Without you, without your active participation," he implored him, "our Committee will lose the foundation of its existence. As far as I myself am concerned, you know that it is your help alone which keeps me going."[78]

Notes

1. Jameson papers, file 993.
2. Ibid.; on the political background, see J. Bariéty, *Les relations franco-allemandes après la première guerre mondiale* (Paris, 1977).
3. Leland to Pirenne, 4 April 1924, Leland papers, box 24.
4. See "Alfons Dopsch," in S. Steinberg, ed., *Geschichtswissenschaft der Gegenwart in Selbstdarstellungen* (Leipzig, 1925), pp. 51–90, here 36f.; O. Brunner, "Dopsch," in *Neue Deutsche Biographie* 4 (Berlin, 1959), p. 77. On the opposition to the Commission for Intellectual Cooperation of the League of Nations in Germany, and on the varying opinions within the Commission as to whether a German cooperation was even worth striving for, see Schröder-Gudehus, "Deutsche Wissenschaft," pp. 227ff., and J. R. von Salis, *Grenzüberschreitungen: Ein Lebensbericht. Erster Teil 1901–1939* (Frankfurt a. M., 1975), pp. 164–177.
5. Leland to Pirenne, 17 March 1924 and 29 April 1924, Pirenne papers, Président du Comité International des Sciences Historiques, 1923–1929.
6. Leland to Shotwell, Paris, 4 March 1924, Leland papers, box 26.
7. Dopsch to Leland, Vienna, 28 Feb. 1924, Leland papers, box 17.
8. Leland to Shotwell, Paris, 4 March 1924, Leland papers, box 26; Leland to Dopsch, Paris, 10 March 1924, Dopsch papers.
9. Cf. inter alia his doctoral thesis *Tourney (1695–1760)*, 2 vols. (Paris, 1920), and his two volumes in the series *Histoire diplomatique de la Grèce de 1821 à nos jours*: vol. 3, *Le règne de Georges Ier avant le traité de Berlin, 1862–1878* (Paris, 1920), and vol. 4, *Suite du règne de Georges Ier jusqu'à la Révolution turque, 1878–1908* (Paris, 1926).
10. Report by Koht to the Academic Collegium Oslo, 22 May 1924, Friis papers, II, 8b; also with regard to the following.
11. This list is derived from Koht's report. Further names on the list of the provisional committee: the Belgians Delehaye SJ and Ganshof, the Swiss de Crue, the American Shotwell, the Englishman Tout, the Frenchman Mirot; ICHS, *Bulletin* 1: 2f. On the meeting itself, see also the report made by De Sanctis to the Italian ministry of culture and public instruction, De Sanctis papers, Congresso storico internazionale.
12. Leland to Pirenne, Paris, 4 March 1924, Leland papers, box 24. See also chapter 7, note 110, and Leland to Jameson, Paris, 26 Feb. 1924: "[I]n order to secure that support it must be completely internationalized,… it must have a German representative." Jameson papers, file 994.
13. Pirenne to Leland, 10 Feb. 1925, Jameson papers, file 994.
14. Leland to Jameson, Paris, 4 April 1924, ibid.
15. According to ICHS, *Bulletin* 1: 3, the list included: Argentina, Austria, Belgium, Brazil, Bulgaria, Chile, Czechoslovakia, Denmark, Finland, France, Germany, Greece, Great Britain, Hungary, Italy, Japan, Netherlands, Norway, Poland, Portugal, Romania, Sweden, Switzerland, Spain, USSR, the United States, and Yugoslavia.

16. List of participants ibid., p. 4f.
17. Leland to Shotwell, 2 June 1925, Leland papers, box 26; Leland to Pirenne, 25 June 1925, Pirenne papers, Président du Comité International des Sciences Historiques, 1923–1929. However, in a letter to Tout and Pollard of 6 March 1926, Leland described the recently deceased Vinogradoff as a representative of England. Archives CISH, dossier 1926.
18. Oldenburg to Lhéritier, 6 May 1926; Lhéritier to Oldenburg, 10 June 1926. Archives CISH, dossier 1926–1927/Pays.
19. Hermann Reincke-Bloch, Breslau, Küntzel's successor as chairman of the *Verband*, in a report on Geneva to the German Foreign Office, Breslau, 6 June 1926, Politisches Archiv, Nr. 607, VI w, vol. 1. Leland to Küntzel, 8 March 1926, and to Oncken, 6 March 1926, Archives CISH, dossier 1926.
20. Maltzan to the German Foreign Office, Washington, D.C., 20 Jan. 1926. Politisches Archiv, Nr. 607, VI w, vol. 1.
21. Haber to the German Chancellor, Berlin, 8 Dec. 1925, Bundesarchiv, R 43/I, 817, vol. 1.
22. Report on a meeting concerning international scholarly cooperation on 13 Jan. 1926 in the German ministry of the interior. Bundesarchiv, R 73/19.
23. See note 19 above.
24. Rockefeller Archive, RFA, box 88, series 100 R, F 816.
25. Rockefeller Archive, LSRM, Series III, Sub. 6. "Memorandum on the needs of the International Committee of Historical Sciences, submitted to the Laura Spelman Rockefeller Memorial Foundation by the Executive Council of the American Historical Association," Washington, D.C., 26 March 1925.
26. Statement signed by Guy Stanton Ford, 1 April 1925, Rockefeller Archive, LSRM, Series III, Sub. 6.
27. Shotwell to Dr. Edmund E. Day, Laura Spelman Rockefeller Memorial Foundation, New York, 1 May 1928, ibid.
28. Leland to Jameson, Paris, 9 April 1924, Jameson papers, file 994.
29. ICHS, *Bulletin* 1: 7.
30. Preliminary draft by Leland, Leland papers, box 40; report by Reincke-Bloch to the German Foreign Office, 6 June 1926, Politisches Archiv, Nr. 607, VI w, vol. 1.
31. ICHS, *Bulletin* 1: 112 and 195.
32. See "Enquête sur l'organisation des historiens," ibid., pp. 55–77, 197–216, 362–400.
33. Leland to Lhéritier, 6 March 1926, Archives CISH, dossier 1926.
34. Leland to Shotwell, 2 June 1926, Leland papers, box 26; Leland to Pirenne, 6 March 1926, Archives CISH, dossier 1926.
35. Brandi to Geheimrat Soehring, 15 July 1926, Politisches Archiv, Nr. 607, VI w, vol. 1.
36. "Oslo est rejeté par les Français, Varsovie par les Anglais et les Américains." Pirenne to Glotz, 17 July 1925, Archives Nationales, 70 AJ 159.
37. Koht, *The Origin*, p. 10.
38. Report by Reincke-Bloch to the German Foreign Office, 6 June 1926, Politisches Archiv, Nr. 607, VI w, vol. 1.
39. Leland to Pirenne, 17 March 1925, Pirenne papers, Président du Comité International des Sciences Historiques, 1923–1929.
40. ICHS, *Bulletin* 1: 8.
41. Friis in General Assembly Göttingen, 13 May 1927, ICHS, *Bulletin* 1: 321; see also report on the founding assembly 1926, ibid., pp. 32–39, 45–48; meeting of the Commission de Bibliographie, Paris, 21–22 Oct. 1926, ibid., pp. 128–157. Defense of the German *Jahresberichte* in the report by Reincke-Bloch to the German Foreign Office, 6 June 1926, Politisches Archiv, Nr. 607, VI w, vol. 1.
42. See the bibliography of ICHS publications on p. 403f. below.
43. See the list of affiliated international organizations in appendix II.2. Survey on their activities and publications up to 1940 in the minutes of the General Assemblies 1927–1939 in

ICHS, *Bulletin*, and from 1953 to the present in ICHS, *Bulletin d'information*, particularly in no. 12 (1985).
44. Report by Leland, "Organization of the International Committee of Historical Sciences, Geneva, May 14–15, 1926," Rockefeller Archive, LSRM, series III, sub. 6.
45. Report by Reincke-Bloch to the German Foreign Office, 6 June 1926, Politisches Archiv, Nr. 607, VI w, vol. 1.
46. Lhéritier to Leland, 27 July 1925, Leland papers, box 22.
47. Report by Leland, "Organization of the International Committee of Historical Sciences, Geneva, May 14–15, 1926," Rockefeller Archive, LSRM, series III, sub. 6.
48. K. Brandi, "Aus 77 Jahren. Lebensgeschichte und wissenschaftliche Entwicklung," p. 162 (typescript in the possession of the Brandi family).
49. Report by Reincke-Bloch to the German Foreign Office, 6 June 1926, Politisches Archiv, Nr. 607, VI w, vol. 1.
50. Koht, *The Origin*, pp. 11 and 12.
51. Lhéritier to Reincke-Bloch, n.d. [1926], Archives CISH, dossier 1926–1927; also in the daily *L'Oeuvre*, 30 June 1926 (clipping ibid.).
52. Brandi, "Aus 77 Jahren" (typescript, Brandi family), pp. 162ff.
53. Minutes of the Paris and Göttingen meetings in ICHS, *Bulletin* 1: 159ff., 297ff.; report by Brandi to ambassador Freytag, 14 May 1927, Brandi papers, 51.
54. Text of both speeches in ICHS, *Bulletin* 1: 328ff.
55. Lhéritier to Brandi, 29 Aug. 1927, Brandi papers, 42.
56. Lhéritier to Thiersch, 10 June 1927, Archives CISH, dossier 1927.
57. Lhéritier to Reincke-Bloch, undated letter draft, Archives CISH, dossier 1926–1927/Pays.
58. Leland to Jameson, 26 Oct. 1926, Jameson papers, file 1007.
59. Minutes of the discussion in Göttingen, 14 May 1927, in Brandi papers, 51. Participants: Koht (Oslo); Leland (Washington, D.C.); Colenbrander (Leiden); Baxter (St. Andrews); De Sanctis (Turin); Ussani (Pisa); Wilamowitz, Lüders, Norden (Berlin); Reisch, Dopsch (Vienna); Stille, Thiersch, Brandi, Reitzenstein, Pohlenz (Göttingen). There are numerous letters in the Koht, Leland, Brandi, and De Sanctis papers relating to the issue of German membership.
60. Statement by the *Kartell* of the German and Austrian Academies, cited in Dopsch to Koht, 11 Jan. 1926, Koht papers, Ms. fol. 3722: 1–6.
61. Leland to Koht, 18 May 1928, ibid.
62. Correspondence between Koht and Dopsch, Thiersch, Pirenne, 1925–1931, ibid.
63. Brandi to Marcks, n.d., Brandi papers, 42; "Denkschrift über den Beitritt der Deutschen Akademien zu Union und Conseil," Brandi papers, 51. Cf. also M. Rothbarth, "Die deutschen Gelehrten und die internationalen Wissenschaftsorganisationen," in H. Konen and J. P. Steffes, eds., *Volkstum und Kulturpolitik* (Festschrift for Georg Schreiber), (Cologne, 1932), pp. 143–157.
64. Archives CISH, dossier 1926–1927/Pays.
65. Brandi to Geheimrat Terdenge (German ministry of the interior), 6 June 1928, Brandi papers, 51.
66. Koht to Lhéritier, 11 Sep. 1927, Archives CISH, dossier 1927.
67. Koht to Lhéritier, 1 July1927, Archives CISH, dossier 1928.
68. Pokrovsky to Lhéritier, 20 Aug. 1928, ibid. For the resolution on cooperation, see M. N. Pokrovsky, "Doklad o poezdke v Oslo" [Report on the trip to Oslo], in *Vestnik Kommunisticeskoj Akademii* [Bulletin of the Communist Academy] 30, no. 6 (Moscow, 1928): 231–237, here p. 234.
69. See Castelli, "Internazionalismo e Storia," p. 908f.; Behrendt, "Die internationalen Beziehungen," pp. 153ff.; H. Jonas, "Die russische Historikerwoche und die Ausstellung 'Geschichtswissenschaft in Sowjetrußland 1917–1927' in Berlin," Osteuropa 3 (1927/28); G. M. Enteen, "Marxists versus Non-Marxists: Soviet Historiography in the 1920s," *Slavic Review* 35 (1976): 91–110; I. I. Mints, "Marksisty na istoričeskoj nedele v Berline i VI Meždunarodnom kongresse

istorikov v Norvegii" [Marxists at the historical week in Berlin and on the VIth International Historical Congress in Norway], *Istorik Marksist* 9 (Moscow, 1928): 84–85.
70. Lhéritier to Brandi, 29 Aug. 1927, Brandi papers, 42.
71. Bureau meeting, Paris, 25 Nov. 1926, ICHS, *Bulletin* 1: 169.
72. Lhéritier to Koht, 9 Sep. 1927, Archives CISH, dossier 1926–1927.
73. "Projet de statuts," ICHS, *Bulletin* 1: 9.
74. Tout to Lhéritier, 11 Oct. 1927, Archives CISH, dossier 1927; Reincke-Bloch to Lhéritier, 21 March 1927, Archives CISH, dossier 1926–1927/Pays.
75. Draft of letter from Lhéritier to Koht, 22 May 1927, Archives CISH, dossier 1927.
76. Friis to Lhéritier, 2 Oct. 1927; Lhéritier to Friis, 7 Oct. 1927, Archives CISH, dossier 1927. Friis, in a report on the Göttingen assembly, registered a strong conflict between Pirenne and Lhéritier, which had erupted over a question pertaining to the international journal. Friis papers, II, 8a, Lag 1.
77. Koht to Lhéritier, 18 May 1927, Archives CISH, dossier 1927.
78. Lhéritier to Leland, 8 Dec. 1927, ibid.

Chapter 9

CLEAVAGES AND GOODWILL
The "Spirit of Oslo," 1928

In 1926, the founding year of the ICHS, the Nobel Peace Prize was awarded to four statesmen whose names symbolized a policy of reason and international conciliation: Briand, Chamberlain, Dawes, and Stresemann. In August 1928, the same month in which the first Congress organized by the ICHS took place, the Kellogg-Briand Pact, a solemn rejection of war as a tool of national politics, was signed in Paris. The climate was favorable for an encounter of historians from the former enemy countries. Just as the rapprochement between French and German historians since Geneva, Paris, and Göttingen had smoothed the way to Oslo, a particularly large contingent of historians from both banks of the Rhine came to the Congress in the Norwegian capital.[1]

The French contributed by far the greatest number of "reports" and "communications" to the Congress.[2] This was certainly an indication of France's particularly strong interest in cultural representation within this new international organization. Lhéritier emphasized with pride that the Chambre des Députés was unusually willing to approve a considerable subsidy.[3] In this regard, it was certainly also an important fact that Lhéritier combined the office of secretary-general of the ICHS and that of secretary of the French national committee. As he proudly wrote to his president: "The parliament had never before approved subsidies for a scientific Congress; we have received [such subsidies].... For the first time we are organized. It is no longer the way it was before the war."[4] France was also impressively represented in Oslo in regard to language use. No fewer than 52 percent of the "reports" and "communications" were composed in French, compared with 27.7 percent in German, 14.7 percent in English, and 5.5 percent in Italian.

Without any doubt, the dominant figure of the Congress was the Norwegian Halvdan Koht, who impressed his colleagues with his scholarly contributions and his language skills, and above all with his winning charm. He was the true

---

Notes for this chapter begin on page 135.

embodiment of the will to mutual understanding within the historical profession that was often referred to as the "spirit of Oslo"—an expression coined by Hermann Oncken at the Congress's opening.[5] The Norwegian state, with the royal house at the top, the city of Oslo, the university, and the academy, did everything possible to supply this manifestation of the new spirit with a generous and hospitable framework. To be sure, deeply rooted political and scholarly reservations existed among the participants, and according to the reports on Oslo in the journals and newspapers, these were by no means eradicated by the Congress. And yet, as many participants noticed, the relationship among the historians underwent a transformation during the Congress. At the beginning, the historians approached one another timidly and with suspicion. The members of the former enemy nations tended to conceive of themselves as "delegations," and to regard the Congress as an appropriate forum for the representation of national interests. The forming of "delegations" with varying degrees of internal regimentation and discipline was most evident among Fascist and Soviet historians. The decisive factor for most participants, however, was the experience of the communicative force of scholarship as such. It became evident that the interest in controversial factual problems asserted itself in such a way that divisions caused by non-scholarly concerns took second place.

The structure of the scientific work of the Congress corresponded to that of its predecessors, apart from a certain number of peculiarities. Five of the fifteen sections were devoted to the different periods of history, in chronological order; two of them were designated according to geographical regions (the Nordic nations and, summed up under "The History of America, the Far East and Colonization," everything not subsumed under European history); five sections were destined for certain branches of history (religious and church history, legal and institutional history, economic and social history, history of science, literature, and art). In addition, there were two sections for auxiliary sciences and historical methodology, and finally, as an innovation, a section for the teaching of history.

In view of the political constellation of "Locarno Europe," as well as of the intentions of both the founders of the ICSH and the organizers of this Congress, two issues that were discussed more than any other at the Congress are of particular interest: the concept of the nation, and its role in history. Koht addressed this topic in his opening speech on "National Spirit and Sovereignty of the People" in the first plenary session, and a special session dealt with "History and National Identity"; the issue was approached in the section for recent history as well. Besides Koht, three Poles and one German, one Austrian, and one Frenchman spoke on this topic.[6]

The methodological accent of all the contributions lay in intellectual history. Koht sought the origin of the concept of nation in a transformation of consciousness in the eighteenth century, and described it as an "idea that divides us and unites us all." Louis Eisenmann (Paris) placed it into a process of increasing "spiritualization." Like Koht, he pointed to the close connection between nation and democracy. Koht did so with a proud mention of the fact that Norway was the first country in which the national sovereignty of a people had definitively asserted itself, namely, in the constitution of 1814. For Tadeusz Walek-Czernecki (Warsaw), who dealt with "The Role of the Nation in Ancient History," the national idea was a "psychological" phenomenon that was in no way primarily linked to the state. As he said, we must "always distinguish between the nation and the state, even in the case of the nation-state.... A society cohering only by adherence to a state" was not a "nation."[7] His fellow countryman Marceli Handelsman (Warsaw), who spoke on "The Role of the Nation in the Middle Ages," also tried to define the concept of nation more comprehensively by detaching it from the nineteenth-century idea of the nation-state, namely, as a "profound feeling that binds the individual to the larger social group through common race and language, through common moral and material interests, through a spirit of solidarity in the common defense."[8] Using the example of medieval France, he first discovered this feeling of solidarity within provinces. Evolving under the influence of religious factors such as crown, church, and cult (St. Denis), it expanded into the later notion of the nation-state. Another fellow countryman, Bronisław Dembiński (Poznan), treated "The Problem of the Nation in Modern History." Restricting his exposition to the Renaissance, he presented Italy as an example of why the nation had to be distinguished from the nation-state: if political unity generally promoted the formation of nations, then in Italy it was precisely the lack of political unity that inspired and awakened national feelings in the period of the Renaissance, thanks to intellectual power.[9]

This recalled Meinecke's well-known distinction between a nation constituted by common culture (*Kulturnation*) and the nation-state (*Staatsnation*). In a lecture on "German Intellectual Influences in the European National Movements of the Nineteenth Century," Hermann Oncken (Berlin) drew attention to Herder and the rooting of national feelings in pre-rational historical phenomena. He placed Herder's national introspection—"each nation has its center of bliss within it, just as every sphere has its center of gravity"[10]—into the context of the development "from cosmopolitanism to the nation-state" as it had been expounded by Meinecke in his book *Vom Weltbürgertum zum Nationalstaat*. Oncken, however, held that one principle did not replace the other, but rather that both—the "drive toward international interlacing" and the "need for the development of a national identity"—necessarily corresponded with each other at present. The emergence of a national consciousness during the nineteenth century had been determined by Herder's influence as well as by Schiller's ideas of humanity and the universal ideas of 1789. The Austrian Harold Steinacker (Graz), attached to the tradition of German historical thought, delivered an address on "People, State, Homeland and the Relationship among them in the Romanic-Germanic Peoples." He saw two factors at work in the formation of nations: nature and consciousness. "As soon as an ethnic group, which has naturally evolved, has attained consciousness of itself, this consciousness will become the strongest among the forces shaping its later history. The strongest one, but not the only one. For the original, natural factors of its formation remain alive deep down." Like Walek-Czernecki, he attributed the decline of the ancient world to its "disregard for the national principle." His conclusion from this premise—"may Pirenne forgive me"—was that the "reappearance of the national principle in world history [represented] the boundary between the ancient times and the Middle Ages."[11] And as far as the present was concerned, he agreed with Koht when he asserted that the nation had in no way been replaced by the new idea of class.

These seven papers give the impression that despite all the dismal experiences that Europe had had with an excessive nationalism, and that Pirenne had castigated at Brussels in the shadow of the Great War, the idealistic concept of nation remained the meaningful center of world history for the historical consciousness of the time of Oslo. There was neither a theoretical critique of the principle of nation, nor an analysis of its sociohistorical premises. Nevertheless, it should not be overlooked that even if the Oslo papers did not challenge the validity of the national idea, they pointed to possible correctives and feasible transformations.

In no way had the creation of an East-Central European belt of states on the western border areas of the former tsarist empire and the dissolution of the multinational state of the Danube Monarchy led to the formation of homogeneous nation-states. The intermingling of different ethnic groups in Eastern and Southeastern Europe had led to a situation where national minorities, sometimes of a considerable size, were frequently incorporated in the new states. Treaties for the protection of ethnic minorities, imposed upon these states after the war and guaranteed by the League of Nations, represented a first attempt to protect the language and culture of ethnic minorities within nation-states by international law. Eisenmann (Paris), who was familiar particularly with the history of Central and Southeastern Europe, understood this as an indication that the "logic of history" would overcome the "assimilatory and intransigent concept of the nation-state,"[12] which still had many adherents in Europe. The meaning of this development, he said, lay in the ultimate overcoming of the conflict between the national and the transnational state. Despite all the imperfections of the current implementation of the laws protecting minorities, he saw the League of Nations as a precursor of this idea.

Steinacker, too, agreed with a transferal of the primary meaning of nation from the state to the linguistic-cultural sphere. Nostalgically referring to certain efforts within the Habsburg Empire, fallen to ashes in the fire of nationalistic antagonisms, he maintained that beyond the guarantee of individual human rights, cultural autonomy ought to be secured as a natural right of ethnic groups. The greatest confidence in the idea of nation was expressed by the Pole Walek-Czernecki: "If there was need of any negative evidence of the unique value of the national factor, then it would be given conspicuously by the fate of the cosmopolitan and un-national culture of Antiquity. And positive evidence is given by the fact that the highest civilizations of the ancient world were national civilizations, the achievements of nations and the expression of their historical individuality. Thus, if today we see prophets of bad tidings standing up to shout out the end of our civilization, similar to that of Antiquity, the current vigor of the nations and the national idea is suited to supplying us with certainty that these dark prophecies will not become reality."[13]

The concept of nation was at the fore of the program of the Oslo Congress, but it was not a topic that aroused agitated debates. True, this may to some degree have been due to the fact that the vast number of papers left no time for discussion. The most spirited discussion, conducted in the "spirit of Oslo," was once again triggered by a lecture delivered by Pirenne. It dealt with a purely scientific question that had no political relevance but was significant for understanding the coherence of European history. Pirenne spoke on the expansion of Islam and the beginning of the Middle Ages during the opening meeting. He had already touched on this topic in Brussels; now he described it in greater detail. It was to become the theme of one of his major works, published posthumously, whose epochal importance is familiar to every historian concerned with the periodization of the transition from ancient to medieval Europe.[14] His thesis was, in the concise formulation of the summary he presented in Oslo:

> Up to the beginning of the eighth century, the dominant feature of European civilization as a whole was its Mediterranean character. The Germanic invasions did not fundamentally alter this fact. Both before and after, the Western world remained oriented on the Mediterranean, as in the Roman Empire. This can be seen in both the socioeconomic and the moral-intellectual realms. Only when the dominance over the Tyrrhenian Sea fell to the Muslims was the Mediterranean unity of the European world destroyed. Relations to the Byzantine Empire were disrupted, Europe's gravitational center moved northward, the trade and significance of the cities vanished, and the Germanic influence began to play an important role. These transformations manifested themselves at the same time that the Carolingian epoch began. This means that one must consider the latter event as the beginning of the era that is known as the Middle Ages.[15]

A fortuitous organizational glitch, namely, the absence of all the other speakers who had been scheduled for that day's medieval section, provided interested persons with the opportunity to discuss Pirenne's theses without time limits. Distinguished names like Dopsch and Halecki, Iorga, Handelsman, and Marc Bloch figure in the sober and brief report on this discussion.[16] Oskar Halecki considered it to be the most interesting discussion of the entire congress.[17] Years later, Lucien Febvre recalled with enthusiasm: "In the evening the greatest historians in the world assembled spontaneously in order to discuss the speech of the Belgian master with passion—a unique event in such an environment. We had never experienced anything of that kind before, and we have never experienced it since."[18] Pirenne's assumption that the Arabian expansion in the Mediterranean region was of epochal significance for the course of European history met with general approval. But, questioning his thesis of a strict caesura, his critics pointed to elements of continuity between the ancient Mediterranean and the Germanic-Romanic period. Thus Handelsman objected: "The Arabian invasion was not a break, but rather an important event that changed the development of European conditions." On the other hand, Pirenne's periodization, which was deduced from observations of economic history, was countered by Nicolae Iorga with the assertion that the transformation of church-state relations was the characteristic phenomenon for the delineation between ancient times and the Middle Ages: "The Middle Ages begin when the [Christian] Church becomes the imperial Church." Above all, Pirenne's observations, in his own field of economic history and Mediterranean trade, were corrected by Alfons Dopsch. He held fast to the migrations of the Germanic peoples as the epochal boundary between ancient times and the Middle Ages, asserting that there was no cultural turning point between the Merovingian and the Carolingian eras.[19] Marc Bloch made very precise objections. "He pointed out that trade had already been in decline since the end of the Roman Empire, and that the trade balance of the West with the East was negative at that time. Trade declined further after the Arabian expansion, but the Danube route was never interrupted, and the Germanic peoples continued to navigate through the Mediterranean after the Arabian invasion. And as far as urban life was concerned, it had been withering long before the appearance of Islam."[20]

In a section dedicated to a problem of methodology, Marc Bloch returned to the same issue. Like Pirenne, he saw a clear distinction between Merovingian and Carolingian society. But unlike Pirenne, he did not look to the economic effects of Islamic Mediterranean rule, but rather to transformations in the relationship between church and crown. "The Merovingians were never particularly concerned with placing power into the service of the Church. This was very different under the Carolingians. Without refraining from treating the clergy like schoolchildren and using their assets for political purposes, they obviously saw themselves called upon to impose God's law on earth. Their legislation was essentially oriented on promoting religion and morality." Aside from that, he also referred to a social transformation: Under the rule of the Merovingians, personal relationships that secured protection already played an important role in society, but they were only marginally referred to in the laws. The Carolingians, by contrast, recognized and sanctioned these relationships, and both defined and limited the cases in which a vassal could leave his lord. They were concerned with utilizing these personal relationships to secure public peace. Bloch quoted a sentence from a capitulary of the year 810, which he evaluated as a concise statement of Carolingian social policy: "Every lord shall exert authority on those who stand beneath him that they may better learn to obey and embrace the imperial orders and instructions."[21]

Bloch was one of those who regarded Pirenne with the highest esteem. As we have already seen, he had tried to win over Pirenne for the editorship of the new journal he was planning with his Strasbourg colleague and friend

Lucien Febvre. Pirenne had refused the position of editor-in-chief, but he did join the editorial board. The appearance of the journal was now announced in Oslo. The Congress proceedings merely reported that before beginning his lecture on problems of medieval agrarian history[22] in the section on social and economic history, Bloch distributed a prospectus on the impending *Annales d'histoire économique et sociale*, which was to start in January 1929, and made a few comments about it. A discussion scheduled for the following meeting failed to materialize due to the absence of those most interested in the project.[23] Thus, the announcement of an event of the first magnitude for the history of historiography passed by virtually unnoticed.

According to the Congress proceedings and the journal reports, there also was no deepened discussion on Bloch's lecture in the medieval section, in which he pleaded for a comparative history of medieval societies, though it was of great significance for the specification of the comparative method.[24] Bloch did not intend to announce a new program. Rather he wanted to show what the comparative method could achieve if it was regarded as a "technical instrument which can be used efficiently and which promises positive results," and if it was not understood as a "chapter of the philosophy of history or of general sociology, schools of thought which researchers sometimes honor and sometimes regard with a skeptical smile, depending on their way of looking at things, but which they usually avoid practicing." What distinguishes Bloch's Oslo lecture is the method it demonstrates: he conducts comparisons of data from medieval social history and adds an accompanying theoretical reflection, which draws attention to each step of the procedure observed and examines its potential cognitive results. One could develop this extraordinarily dense and rich lecture into a *vade mecum* of the comparative historical method!

Starting from medieval history, this method led Bloch to a critical conclusion with regard to the idea of nation, namely, that the geographical lines delimiting areas that are similar or dissimilar to one another in linguistic and social historical respects are in no way identical to the national borders of the Modern Age. He provided the following examples:

> Studying the French cities of the Middle Ages at the moment of the urban renaissance would mean blending two objects that are dissimilar in all but name: namely, the old Mediterranean cities, traditional centers of rural life, "*oppida*," which were at all times resided in by the ruling groups, namely, the lords and "knights"—and the cities in the rest of France, which were above all populated by merchants and reinvigorated by them. And how could we separate this latter type of cities by an arbitrary cut from the analogous type in Rhenish Germany? Finally, the "*seigneurie*" in medieval France: when a [French] historian who has begun studying feudalism north of the Loire leafs through texts in *langue d'oc*, does he not often feel more abroad than when he looks at documents from the Hennegau or the Moselle region? If we wish to find our way out of the arbitrary, we must seek the geographical framework appropriate for each aspect of European social history and for each moment of its development.[25]

From such observations, Bloch proceeded to skeptical comments that did not concern the spirit of Oslo itself, but the chances for its realization, and the fragility of its foundations:

> At this Congress, I believe, there will be much talk about a reconciliation of the peoples by means of history. Do not worry: I do not intend to improvise a speech on this delicate theme. Comparative history, as I understand it, is a thoroughly scientific matter. It is concerned with knowledge and not with praxis. But what would you say to a reconciliation of our terminologies and our methods of asking questions?... In a word, let us finally stop speaking from one national history to another without understanding one another. A dialogue between the deaf, each of whom answers without regard to the questions the other has posed. That is an old comedy trick very appropriate for getting a public to laugh that is willing to be amused, but it is not an exercise of the intellect to be recommended.[26]

This was an all too justified skepticism. But reflections on sociohistorical links were ill-suited to overcoming the realities of historically grown national individualizations and antagonisms as well as the virulence of national feelings. That is why the "spirit of Oslo" as an appeal to the will to restrain excessive nationalism retains its significance for what was possible at that time and what should remain possible—in the sense of Immanuel Kant, who said that peace is not a state of nature among human beings but must be created.

In the scholarly journals that reported on the Oslo Congress, two names are mentioned repeatedly whose lectures (aside from Pirenne's) particularly impressed the listeners: Karl Brandi and Alfons Dopsch. Like Pirenne, both presented provisional appraisals of ongoing research projects that would materialize into major works several years later.

In the plenary session at the opening of the Congress, Brandi spoke on "Charles V: The Governing of an Empire."[27] This was a topic that—like Pirenne's research—was perched at a turning point between two epochs. It concerned the period between the Middle Ages and the Modern Age, which—with its overlapping of the old and the new—was to be presented in the form of a biography. Brandi reported on the fate of the governmental documents of Charles V, which were scattered across the European archives, on the collections of correspondence reassembled through the joint efforts of many scholars, on the reconstruction of the *modus operandi* of his chancery, and on the status accruing to his personal letters and the great political testaments, a genre that first began with him. These were all questions pertaining to the classic method of historical source study, and concerning a subject that possessed international significance and befitted an International Congress. The medieval notion of the Emperor, rooted in the idea of the universal Church, once again—and for the last time—took shape in the dynastic interests of a wide-reaching Empire, but ultimately the inherent multiform tendencies of the states incorporated resisted the overarching imperial idea and doomed it to decline. What Brandi presented in Oslo was a preliminary study for a broadly conceived biography, which remained significant for all later research, even when interpretations varied from Brandi's.[28]

There were only a few other biographical contributions at the Oslo Congress.[29] Papers on social and economic history, understood in the broadest sense possible, were much more prominent. These included Alfons Dopsch's lecture on "Barter Economy and Money Economy in World History," which he delivered at the concluding plenary session.[30] Dopsch described his method as "synoptic," since he endeavored to incorporate into his observations the results of the related sciences, from ethnology and prehistory to linguistics. This was an example of what Bloch referred to as the long-range comparative method ("méthode comparative à longue portée"), namely, a type of research based on the gathering of testimonies from all four corners of the world ("rassemblement de témoignages empruntés aux quatre coins du monde").[31] Dopsch presented a critical examination of all varieties of the theory of economic development stages that assumed a systematic evolution in the sequence of different societal forms of economic activity. For this purpose, he drew together a vast amount of material from all areas of available historical knowledge, in order to substantiate his thesis that payment in kind and money economy had always existed side by side in varying degrees of interaction. This was directed against the classics of German political economy, like Bücher and Sombart; in more concrete terms, however, against Pirenne's theory of a break between the Merovingian and Carolingian eras. With the appearance of these two men in Oslo—one of them at the opening plenary session, the other at the closing assembly—one of the great controversies in modern historiography was brought into view at an International Congress.[32]

It is not surprising that the Oslo Congress again brought up the old question, which recurred at later Congresses as well, of whether the program had been designed appropriately. Henri Berr was of the opinion that, with all due respect for the Congress's scholarly level, too many disconnected topics had been offered, just as in Brussels. He demanded that a broader space should be made for questions concerning historical synthesis at the beginning and end of future Congresses, for the scientific character of all sciences, and thus of history as well, existed only in the exploration of what is general, and not of what is special and unique. "How can we come together," he asked,

> if we work separately? Will we, at the Historical Congresses, always see before us an image of how excited participants run from one hall to another, sometimes from one building to another, only to miss the end of one lecture and the beginning of another? Or how they start tearing their hair because in four or five simultaneous sections subjects are discussed that they find equally interesting? There is a certain irony in this "general regulation" of the Oslo Congress: each participant has the right to take part in all the assemblies, if he so desires. If they had only taken the opportunity to counteract this fragmentation, e.g., through the general sessions! But the general sessions themselves were nothing more than official events guided by the rules of protocol and not by the greater interests of science.[33]

This was unfair, and despite the justified desire to pay appropriate attention to problems of theory and method, it was blind to the sparkle that Pirenne, Bloch, Brandi, Dopsch, and others had given the Congress.

I think that Oslo distinguished itself by providing space for the "great speech" in which a historian can fully develop his ideas. Thus, there was no lack of voices recommending the opposite, for instance, the Belgian medievalist François L. Ganshof, who had served as the secretary of the Brussels Congress and now in Oslo was dealing with a highly specialized question of the medieval judiciary system. He considered the lecture by his teacher Pirenne together with the ensuing discussion to be one of the most sensational results of the Congress. He also heaped praise on the contributions by Brandi and Dopsch. And regarding the great number of disparate communications, he believed that they were what represented the actual life of the Congresses. He warned:

> A different danger threatens the next Congress, in the shape of the "theoreticians" of history. Nothing is further from our mind than to question their usefulness and importance; Mr. Henri Berr, who is the most representative and sympathetic personality among them, has provided significant services to history, both then and now, which are well known and do not need to be emphasized. But we are told that the "theoreticians"—those who concern themselves with periodization, with historical vocabulary, with the relationships between history and time and space—dream of ensuring a particularly privileged status for their section. Some of them are said to have the ambition of suspending the work of the other sections while the theoreticians hold their own highly important meetings so that everyone can take part in their work, which, as they think, takes first place in the hierarchy of the historical sciences. However, we greatly fear that the majority of the Congress's participants would prefer to use such an interruption of the meetings in order to dissipate in cabaret shows. History should not withdraw from the facts; as useful and interesting as it is to talk about methodology—provided we stay close to the facts—, our interest is ultimately distracted and exhausted when lectures and discussion take on a philosophical attitude. That is, in any case, the perception of a great number of historians.[34]

In Oslo, the historians encountered a challenge of a new kind, namely, the confrontation with Soviet historical scholarship as a special variety of Marxism. The Marxist approach to history had already been the subject of methodological considerations at the Rome Congress of 1903, as mentioned in a previous chapter. Let us recall the School of Law and Economics in Naples, and Labriola, Croce, and Hartmann. But that first phase of discussion remained a mere episode. As far as we can gather from the International Congresses, the historians had hardly considered Marxism to be a serious intellectual challenge. Now it took the stage in Oslo as an ideology providing the rising Soviet state with historical justification, and confronting the other directions of historiography labeled all together as "bourgeois."

The dispute between Soviet and "bourgeois" historians would come to be a problem informing the International Congresses after the Second World War.

But at this first appearance of the Soviet historians, the challenge was more a programmatic one, since the Russian contributions did not particularly manifest any new modes of practicing historiography. And it was not only Marxist historians who were sent to Oslo by Moscow, even though the leadership of the delegation lay in the hands of the outstanding representative of Soviet Marxist historiography, Mikhail Pokrovsky. On behalf of the Bureau of the ICHS Halvdan Koht, guided by a liberal notion of science, had emphatically requested that Soviet historians present their specific contribution at the Congress. It was "a need and a duty to do everything possible in order to complete the international cooperation of the historians through the inclusion of our Russian colleagues," he imparted to them. He himself was planning a lecture on "The Importance of the Class Struggle in Modern History," and he exclaimed: "How much you could tell us on this issue!"[35] When Koht called himself a Marxist, the Soviet side noted it with a certain irony. The weak development of the class struggle in Norway allowed "the liberal bourgeoisie the luxury of playing with Marxism."[36] Pokrovsky expressed himself in a more benevolent way in a report to the Communist Academy in Moscow. Whether Koht could really be regarded as a Marxist in a communist sense was questionable, he wrote. But without a doubt he was a remnant of the dying type of honorable bourgeois radical, an upright democrat. In any case, he was expecting the Soviet side to strengthen the left wing in the ICHS and to take a more or less energetic stance.[37]

At the closing session of the Congress, Pokrovsky delivered a lecture on the origins of Russian absolutism from a Marxist point of view. The summary, included in the official edition of the Oslo papers,[38] began with the statement that "the bourgeois historians" had seen everything wrong. Namely, Russian absolutism was in no way a military dictatorship that stood above the classes and that could be explained out of the need to ward off the nomads of the steppes, but rather an agent of trade capital in its struggle for markets in Eastern Europe and Asia. This was an explanation worthy of consideration. Pokrovsky's contribution concerned an issue that Lhéritier, too, had dealt with in a report on benevolent despotism. The lively discussion that ensued, in which Pokrovsky participated, led to a vote to form a special commission for the further study of this question.[39]

Other Soviet contributions also fit well into the field of specialized, positivistic historical studies. To name but a few: Vladimir V. Adoratzky reported on the "Central Archive of the RSFSR" (Russian Socialist Federative Soviet Republic), Boris L. Bogaesky on "The Gods of Pottery of Minoan Crete," Evgenii A. Kozminsky on "The Medieval Village in England."[40] A certain ideological coloration could be seen in such contributions as that by Sergei M. Dubrovsky on "The Peasants' Movement in Russia in the 20th Century," or by Vyacheslav P. Volgin on "Socialism and Egalitarianism in the History of Social Theories."[41]

No heated controversies emerged during the working sessions. However, contrasting positions collided intensely on the sidelines of the Congress. After Pokrovsky had been elected as one of the Congress's presidents in the opening meeting, the ancient historian Rostovtsev, who had emigrated from Russia following the Revolution and who now had traveled from the United States to Oslo, gave an interview to the Norwegian newspaper *Aftenposten* on the participation of the Soviet scholars. From a political point of view, he said, such an invitation might have been desirable, but with regard to scholarly work it was a mistake. Pokrovsky's election to the Congress's presidium was incomprehensible. After all, he had participated in the expulsion of non-Bolshevik scholars from Russia. Scholarship, he continued, was the search for truth, while the Soviet historians believed from the outset that they already possessed it. What they were pursuing was thus not research but theology.[42] As a result of this attack, Rostovtsev was formally ejected from the Leningrad Academy. Two days following the interview, *Aftenposten* printed a response by Pokrovsky. In Russia, he asserted, nobody was persecuted because of his political opinion. In Oslo, as in Berlin previously, Russian scholarship was represented by both Marxist and some "bourgeois" historians. Of course it was true that a number of scholars had been expelled, but this occurred on account of their political attitude. He had had to endure the same experience at an earlier time: during the tsarist regime he had been deported for political reasons, not because of his scholarly work. In any case, "in Russia under the dictatorship, scientific research, including historical research, is entirely free."[43]

The liberal style of this interview concealed the real situation in Russia: when selecting the delegation to Oslo, Pokrovsky had done the best he could to ostracize the "bourgeois" historians of the Leningrad Academy as far as possible. The remnants of the "old" historical profession in the Soviet Union would only be tolerated for a short time longer, and for Marxist scholarship, which was about to organize itself more strictly, participation in the Oslo Congress represented the prelude to an intensified struggle to assert its absolute authority. Koht played the incident down. Rostovtsev's statements, he said, expressed only a personal opinion. Pokrovsky found the situation convenient. Rostovtsev, he later stated before the Communist Academy, had essentially done the Soviet delegation a great service. "With our nearly complete silence we were not paid attention to. But following the interview people spoke about us."[44] Pokrovsky was of the opinion that the Soviet delegation had left a great deal to be desired. It was too small, and the lectures were rhetorically poor in many cases. It was extremely unfortunate, he told the Academy, that there was not at least one Soviet delegate in each section. However, it was even more unfortunate that this tiny fraction had stubbornly remained silent. "We come from the country that was the first to introduce the dictatorship of the proletariat, we come, sit, and remain silent. That was our big mistake, the biggest of all. Of course, whether or not someone delivers a lecture has to be firmly agreed on. But in any case, he must make an appearance in his field of history with two or three critical contributions and prepare for them. I stood up twice, not particularly aggressively, but others remained entirely silent."[45]

An entirely different picture of the Soviets' conduct in Oslo was painted by Isaac I. Mints, who was not a professional historian and thus did not officially belong to the Soviet delegation. He announced news of battle and victory: "Not only did our delegation deliver lectures, but also contributions to the discussions, constituting a contrast to the deadly boredom of the idealistic interpretation of history thanks to the vigorous and fruitful method of Marxism."[46] Here, a new type of Congress report appeared that conveyed the impression that the Historical Congresses were less concerned with scholarship than with struggles for position and prestige.

Like the Soviet Marxists, the Italian Fascists were a new and unaccustomed element at the International Historical Congress. Both the Soviet and the Italian participants were expected to form closed, disciplined delegations, but this was more a desire than a reality. Pokrovsky's criticism of his colleagues had its counterpart in a report by Gioacchino Volpe, who enjoyed high standing as a medieval expert and social historian, and who had joined the Fascist movement. The German or Polish historians, he said, and particularly the "phalanx" of the French historians' group, faced only a few Italians, and from among these even fewer took an active part in the Congress's work. It would only make sense to send delegations to future Congresses after appropriate and timely preparation.[47] All the same, there were sixteen papers from the Italian side. They generally kept their distance from politics and stuck to the traditional paths of archaeology, genealogy, literary and art history, or history of science; or else they dealt with specific themes of Italian national history, such as the prehistory of Italian unification. There was only one explicitly Fascist paper, namely, the contribution of a representative of the Italian naval ministry who went on about the necessity of Italy's colonial expansion and cultural mission in the heroic struggle against the African barbarians.[48] Volpe himself gave an instructive report on the publication of parliamentary documents of the separate Italian states and a survey of Risorgimento research over the preceding fifty years[49] with a kowtow to the "new Italian state," which had been accepted by all "without reservation." The sharpest confrontation to occur at the Congress, however, arose between him and the secretary-general of the ICHS, Michel Lhéritier, on a political and historical question.

After the war, diverse initiatives had been launched to put the teaching of history in schools into the service of peace. Lhéritier was a keen proponent of such endeavors. At his suggestion, the ICHS and its Bureau had decided to constitute a commission for historical instruction. Its main concern was the revision of schoolbooks.[50] In Oslo, Lhéritier outlined his intentions in the section on historical instruction, which had been scheduled specifically for the discussion of this issue. Volpe wrote in his report: "Lhéritier wanted to turn historical instruction into propaganda for internationalism and peace." [51] During the discussion, he fiercely rejected Lhéritier's comments and disputed the ideal of peace itself: "The educators teach peace, to be sure, but certainly they teach war as well, if necessary.... Order or disorder, peace or war, this has nothing to do with scholarship and history.... In order to improve or to preach peace, we could very well introduce a new catechism into the schools, if we so desired, but we should not bother the sciences and history.... History gives us as much truth as possible, a truth that is not in the least denied by the fact that it is promoted in different ways; education endeavors ... to form human beings well endowed with all the abilities for doing good deeds, prepared for peace and prepared for war, [prepared] to live powerful and, if necessary, to die powerful."[52]

At the conclusion of the Oslo Congress, everyone agreed that the ICHS had passed the test. "Even the most stubborn nationalists," Aage Friis wrote, "are forced by our international cooperation to take account of the truth as it is understood by others. 'Quand-même, la raison est en marche.'"[53] Koht was once again elected president. It was decided that the next Congress should take place in Warsaw in 1933, as it had already been envisaged at the founding assembly of the ICHS in Geneva in 1926. The Austrian historian Dopsch was confirmed as vice-president, and was joined in this office by the Polish historian Bronisław Dembiński in place of Pirenne, who had resigned. Dembiński presented the invitation in the name of the Polish government and his colleagues. Taking up the words of Oncken in a friendly gesture, he promised that "the spirit of Oslo" would prevail in Warsaw, too.[54]

Notes

1. Materials on the preparation of the Congress in "Le Congrès d'Oslo," ICHS, *Bulletin* 1: 409–434; texts of the "reports" available at the start of the Congress in "VIe Congrès International des Sciences Historiques, Oslo 1928: Rapports présentés au Congrès," ICHS, *Bulletin* 1: 559–753 [hereafter Congress Oslo 1928: "Rapports"]; summaries of other papers in *VIe Congrès International des Sciences Historiques, Oslo 1928: Résumés des Communications présentées au Congrès* (Oslo, 1928) [hereafter Congress Oslo 1928: *Communications*]; topics on Scandinavian history in *Rapports présentés au Congrès International des Sciences Historiques, publiés par Historisk Tidsskrift* (Oslo, 1928); Congress report in "Organisation du VIe Congrès International des Sciences Historiques," ICHS, *Bulletin* 2: 5–21, and "Compte rendu du VIe Congrès International des Sciences Historiques" [hereafter Congress Oslo 1928: "Compte rendu"], ICHS, *Bulletin* 2: 25–211. On the special publication of the Polish papers as well as on the section "La nationalité et l'histoire," see note 6 below. The list of participants indicates 950 active persons from 38 countries, among them 132 from France and 121 from Germany (plus 5 from Danzig). See below, appendix III.2.
2. Seventy-seven contributions out of 307. See below, appendix III.1.
3. Lhéritier to Koht, 31 March 1928, Koht papers, 386.
4. Ibid.
5. See Koht, *The Origin*, especially p. 18. Alongside its documentary value, this work is impressive as a testimony to this "spirit of Oslo."
6. Texts in *La nationalité et l'histoire: Ensemble d'études par Halvdan Koht, Louis Eisenmann, Marcel Handelsman, Hermann Oncken, Harold Steinacker et T. Walek-Czernecki* (Paris, 1929), and in ICHS, *Bulletin* 2: 217–320. Abstracts of the papers by Walek-Czernecki and Handelsman as well as a report by Dembiński, "Séance spéciale: Histoire et nationalité. Le problème de la nationalité dans l'histoire (Époque ancienne, époque médiévale, époque

moderne)" were published in advance (July 1928) as "reports" in Congrès Oslo 1928: "Rapports," pp. 559–571. The contributions by Handelsman and Dembiński are also included in *La Pologne au VIe Congrès International des Sciences Historiques, Oslo 1928*, published by Société polonaise d'histoire (Warsaw/Lvov, 1930) [hereafter: Congress Oslo 1928: *La Pologne*].
7. ICHS, *Bulletin* 2: 305.
8. Ibid., p. 236.
9. Congress Oslo 1928: "Rapports," p. 568.
10. ICHS, *Bulletin* 2: 254.
11. Ibid., pp. 275–278.
12. Ibid., p. 233.
13. Ibid., p. 320.
14. The Brussels lecture in 1923: "Un contraste historique: Mérovingiens et Carolingiens," in Congress Brussels 1923: *Compte rendu*, p. 97f. It was based on an essay entitled "Un contraste économique: Mérovingiens et Carolingiens," *Revue belge de philologie et d'histoire* 2 (Brussels, 1923): 223–235. Summary of the Oslo lecture: "L'expansion de l'Islam et le commencement du Moyen-Age," in Congress Oslo 1928: *Communications*, p. 4f. Complete text in Pirenne, *Histoire économique*; concluding formulation of these preliminary studies in H. Pirenne, *Mahomet et Charlemagne* (Brussels, 1937), posthumous.
15. Congress Oslo 1928: *Communications*, p. 5.
16. Congress Oslo 1928: "Compte rendu," pp. 61–64.
17. Congress Oslo 1928: *La Pologne*, p. 80. See also Halecki, "VI Międzynarodowy kongres," p. 119f.
18. "Un maître de l'histoire vivante," in *Les Nouvelles Littéraires*, 9 Nov. 1935, quoted in Lyon, *Pirenne*, p. 327, note 26.
19. Dopsch had presented his conceptions in two major works: *Die Wirtschaftsentwicklung der Karolingerzeit, vornehmlich in Deutschland*, 2 vols. (Weimar, 1912, 1913); *Wirtschaftliche und soziale Grundlagen der europäischen Kulturentwicklung aus der Zeit von Cäsar bis auf Karl den Großen*, 2 vols. (Vienna, 1918, 1920).
20. Congress Oslo 1928: "Compte rendu," p. 63.
21. M. Bloch, "Pour une histoire comparée des sociétés médiévales," in Congress Oslo 1928: *Communications*, pp. 119ff.; completed text: "Pour une histoire comparée des sociétés européennes," *Revue de synthèse historique* 46 (1928): 15–50, here p. 24f.
22. M. Bloch, "Le problème des systèmes agraires envisagés particulièrement en France," Congress Oslo 1928: *Communications*, p. 264f.
23. Congress Oslo 1928: "Compte rendu," p. 105f.
24. Bloch, "Histoire comparée."
25. Bloch, "Histoire comparée," p. 44f.
26. Ibid., p. 49f.
27. Congress Oslo 1928: *Communications*, p. 3f. Complete text in *Preußische Jahrbücher* 214 (1928): 23–31; the later work: *Kaiser Karl V.*, 2 vols. (Munich, 1937, 1941).
28. For example, P. Rassow, *Die Kaiseridee Karls V: Dargestellt an der Politik der Jahre 1528–1540* (Berlin, 1932).
29. These were twelve out of a total of 300 lectures dealing with European rulers (Philip of Macedonia, Emperor Frederick II, Philip II of Spain, Louis XIV, James I of England, and Napoleon), medieval theologians (Ruisbroeck, Thomas of Bradwardine), historians (Michelet, Sismondi), the painter Dürer, and the composer Saint-Saëns.
30. Congress Oslo 1928: *Communications*, p. 6f.; full text in A. Dopsch, "Naturalwirtschaft und Geldwirtschaft in der Weltgeschichte," *Archiv für Rechts- und Wirtschaftsphilosophie* 22/23 (1929), reprinted in Dopsch, *Beiträge zur Sozialgeschichte: Gesammelte Aufsätze, zweite Reihe* (Vienna, 1938), pp. 85–94. The complete work: *Naturalwirtschaft und Geldwirtschaft* (Vienna, 1930).

31. Bloch, "Histoire comparée," p. 18f.
32. An excellent collection of the most important essays in this long and wide-ranging controversy was edited by Paul Egon Hübinger in the series *Wege der Forschung*, published by the Wissenschaftliche Buchgesellschaft Darmstadt: *Bedeutung und Rolle des Islam beim Übergang vom Altertum zum Mittelalter* (1968); *Kulturbruch oder Kulturkontinuität im Übergang von der Antike zum Mittelalter* (1968); *Zur Frage der Periodengrenze zwischen Altertum und Mittelalter* (1969); *Spätantike und frühes Mittelalter: Ein Problem historischer Periodenbildung* (1972).
33. H. Berr, "Quelques réflexions sur le VIe Congrès International des Sciences Historiques," *Revue de synthèse historique* 46 (1928): 8f.
34. F. L. Ganshof, "L'évolution du Mallus en France au Xe siècle," in Congress Oslo 1928: *Communications*, p. 243f.; Ganshof, "Le Congrès historique international d'Oslo," *Revue belge de philologie et d'histoire* 7 (Brussels, 1928): 1685–1692, here p. 1691.
35. Letters of 21 Dec. 1927 and 5 April 1928, quoted in Behrendt, "Die internationalen Beziehungen," p. 196f. Brief abstract of Koht's lecture in Congress Oslo 1928: *Communications*, p. 145, complete text in *Journal of Modern History* 1 (Chicago, 1929): 353–360; discussion in Congress Oslo 1928: "Compte rendu," p. 75.
36. Mints, "Marksisty," p. 95.
37. Pokrovsky, "Doklad," p. 234.
38. "Les origines de l'absolutisme russe au point de vue du matérialisme historique," in Congress Oslo 1928: *Communications*, p. 7f.
39. M. Lhéritier, "Le rôle historique du despotisme éclairé, particulièrement au XVIIIe siècle," in Congress Oslo 1928: "Rapports," pp. 601–612; discussion in Congress Oslo 1928: "Compte rendu," p. 71f.
40. Congress Oslo 1928: *Communications*, pp. 19f., 80f., 270f.
41. Ibid., pp. 144 and 289f.
42. "Professor Rostovtzeff om bolsjevikenes deltagelse i historiker-kongressen," *Aftenposten*, 15 Aug. 1928.
43. "Professor Pokrovsky uttaler sig til 'Aftenposten,'" *Aftenposten*, 17 Aug. 1928. It is difficult to identify how many of the fifteen Soviet historians on the list were "bourgeois" or "Marxist." The literature contains contradictory information. For example, according to K. F. Shteppa, *Russian Historians and the Soviet State* (New Brunswick, 1962), p. 43, the ratio between the members of the "old" and the "new" directions was fairly balanced (5:6). However, a more recent Marxist work states: "The eleven-member Soviet delegation in Oslo consisted entirely of Marxists with only one exception. (In Berlin four bourgeois historians were still among the ten Soviet participants.) ... Through its unified appearance, they showed the new profile of historical studies in Russia more clearly than in Berlin." L.-D. Behrendt, "Zu den internationalen Beziehungen der sowjetischen Historiker in den zwanziger und dreißiger Jahren," in E. Donnert, H.-T. Krause and W. Schaaf, eds., *Die sowjetische Geschichtswissenschaft: Leistungen und internationale Wirksamkeit*, part 4 (Halle, 1979), pp. 29–37, here p. 33. Behrendt, "Die internationalen Beziehungen," pp. 198 and 206f.: The non-party members were almost all considered to be "Marxists within their sphere of activity."
44. Pokrovsky, "Doklad," p. 234.
45. Ibid., p. 233.
46. Mints, "Marksisty," p. 95. A similar report was given by N. Lukin in *Pravda*, 15 Sep. 1928, long extract in S. N. Harper, "A communist view of historical studies," *Journal of Modern History* 1 (Chicago, 1929): 77–84, here pp. 78–84.
47. Volpe to the president of the Italian House of Deputies, 1 Sep. 1928, Archivio Centrale dello Stato, Rome: Presidenza del Consiglio dei Ministri, 1929, Facs. 14/3, no. 3432.
48. A. Tosti, "L'opera civile della Marina Italiana in favore della colonizzazione africana," Congress Oslo 1928: *Communications*, p. 175f.

49. G. Volpe, "Gli Atti dei Parliamenti Italiani anteriori all'Unità e la loro recente pubblicazione," ibid., p. 255f.; Volpe, "Il risorgimento italiano negli studi dell'ultimo cinquantennio," ibid., p. 142f.
50. [Ed. note: For detailed information on the discussion of this issue within the ICSH and at the Oslo Congress, see the German edition of this book, pp. 183–188.]
51. Volpe to the president of the Italian House of Deputies, 1 Sep. 1928, Archivio Centrale dello Stato: Presidenza del Consiglio dei Ministri, 1929, Facs. 14/3, no. 3432.
52. Congress Oslo 1928, "Compte rendu," p. 145.
53. Friis to Koht, 1 Sep. 1928, Koht papers, 386. Friis presented a thorough report on Oslo to the Royal Academy of Sciences, 2 Nov. 1928. The aspects he criticized—as in his letter to Koht—included particularly the tendency to form delegations, which he noted especially among the French and Italians but to a lesser degree among the Germans as well. Friis papers, II 8b.
54. General Assembly, 18 Aug. 1928. ICHS, *Bulletin* 2: 366.

Chapter 10

NEW POLITICAL CHALLENGES
Warsaw, 1933

Dembiński's promise was kept. "The international atmosphere of the Congress was excellent," the *Revue historique* reported, "perhaps even a shade better than five years ago in Oslo. All relations, whether between groups or individuals, were polite and sincere. It was like a finale of the harmony when the German historians of Danzig invited all the participants to conclude the Congress as their guests in Zoppot and Danzig."[1] On the German side, as summarized in Friis's impressions, Brandi set the tone and as a result "everything went harmoniously."[2] German reports emphasized that both in Warsaw and Cracow separate Polish-German conversations had taken place, in which the promotion of mutual scientific and personal exchanges was discussed.[3] No matter the journal, no matter the language, everyone heaped praise on the Congress's atmosphere.

This universally acknowledged appreciation was at the same time an expression of relief and surprise. After all, the development of the international situation since the Oslo Congress had not been conducive to hopeful forecasts for a meeting of historians that was intended to serve not only professional purposes but also mutual understanding. The economic crisis spreading from America had plunged the European countries into financial shocks, economic recession, and mass unemployment. With regard to economics, the crisis had led to an increase in protectionist tendencies. In social terms, it had brought an intensification of the class struggle, and politically a swelling tide of conservative and revolutionary nationalism, particularly in Germany. In this climate, Briand's almost desperate attempt of 1929/30 to unite the drifting states of Europe in a federal league had failed. In addition, Franco-German relations had come under increasing pressure in 1931—in France as a reaction to the customs union agreed on by Germany and Austria, and in Germany as a reaction to the French objection to the intended union. This had led to a decision

---

Notes for this chapter begin on page 159.

by the European Court in The Hague that defeated the union by eight to seven votes. Finally, in January 1933, practically on the eve of the Warsaw Congress, National Socialism had triumphed in Germany.

In some of the member countries, the historical discipline was subjected to totalitarian interventions. This confronted the ICHS with the question of whether it should remain silent for the sake of harmony or speak up for the sake of truth. In Italy in 1925, the renegade liberal Giovanni Gentile, a former friend and collaborator of Benedetto Croce, had published a manifesto of Fascist intellectuals. Croce responded to it with a countermanifesto that met with broad approval. In order to counteract this, and to align the nonconformists at the universities with the Fascist educational goals, Italian professors were forced in 1931—once again on Gentile's instigation—to swear an oath in which they committed themselves, above and beyond their loyalty as civil servants, "to educate citizens faithfully devoted to the Fascist regime." Twelve professors refused to swear, including Gaetano De Sanctis, co-founder of the ICHS and a member of the Bureau from the beginning. This resulted in his resignation from his professorship in Rome and also from his office in the international organization.[4]

How would the ICHS respond to the news of his withdrawal? Koht intended to show his colors and to suggest to the General Assembly that it should condemn, clearly and unmistakably, this violation of scholarly freedom by the Fascist government: "It may become inevitable for our Committee to protest against this oppression; otherwise we would assume a portion of the responsibility upon ourselves."[5] But Lhéritier thought that it was not desirable that the relations between the ICHS and the Italian national committee, the Giunta Centrale, and its president Fedele should be burdened with an explicit condemnation of De Sanctis's expulsion. He even recommended that De Sanctis's letter of resignation not be transmitted to the members of the ICHS in its actual wording. Instead, the notification should be confined to a circumlocution ("*périphrase*"), whereupon Fedele should immediately be admitted to the Bureau as De Sanctis's successor.[6] Waldo Leland's attitude was similar. He wrote to Lhéritier that the discharge of the twelve professors was an act of despotism, but that "there is no way to improve or reestablish the situation from outside by means of protest."[7] And finally, he added shortly afterward, "most of us think that those professors who have refused to swear the oath were perhaps a little more scrupulous than was necessary."[8] Thus, de Sanctis was criticized because he took the issue of the Fascist oath too seriously! Let us recall what he himself wrote to his Danish colleague Aage Friis in response to the expression of sympathy he had received from Friis: "A historian who subordinates his work as a scholar and teacher to the random interests of a party or a regime is not worthy of the name of scholar."[9]

At the same time, Koht was profoundly unsettled by news reaching him from Russia and France on the Soviet "cultural revolution" and its effects on historical scholarship in the Soviet Union. While a few non-Marxist Soviet historians had been allowed to participate in Berlin and Oslo and had been paraded about as evidence of the freedom of science in Russia, they were now excluded from scholarly life and persecuted. To name just a few examples, Platonov was ejected from the Academy, Oldenburg lost his position as Academy secretary and was withdrawn as a representative of the Soviet Union in the ICHS, and Tarle was charged with alleged participation in an international conspiracy. He and several other historians were punished by deportation.[10] None other than Pokrovsky himself had stated in a *Pravda* article shortly after Oslo that there was a connection between the anti-Marxism inside the Soviet Union and outside, and that it was therefore the duty of Soviet historians to lead this struggle on an international level as well.[11] This primarily concerned the ICHS and the Congresses.

An evaluation of the experiences of Oslo had led to a series of rules for the conference tactics with which Soviet historians were to comply in the future. Some of these requirements, which "afterward and up to the present have determined and still determine [the behavior] of the Soviet scholars at the Congresses," have been summed up as follows: (1) discussion contributions in all sections, to be prepared alongside the papers; this required "outstanding language abilities"; (2) "'complete unity and agreement within our own ranks,' since differing opinions would immediately be used by the enemy to discredit Soviet scholarship"; (3) the unmasking of the "aura of objectivity" surrounding "bourgeois" historians; this required "excellent mastery of the tactic of scholarly work"; (4) persistent efforts aimed at "gathering Marxist forces and forces close to Marxism" after the failure of such an attempt in Oslo; (5) in the search for "allies," joining forces with the historians of the Slavic countries, whereby Bulgaria and Yugoslavia were to be given particular attention; (6) viewing the Commission for Historical Instruction and the Commission for the History of Social Movements (founded in 1930 upon the initiative of the Soviets) as the preferred arenas of the ideological class struggle.[12]

The strategic evaluation of the scholarly situation corresponding to this tactical catalog of behavior contained two paradoxical elements. First, the "bourgeois" study of history had reached its end: "That which yesterday was considered science, today is no longer science, but in the best instance a certain preparation for science, a certain gathering of materials etc."[13] This formulation of Pokrovsky's is reminiscent of similar ones by Henri Berr[14] and other protagonists of the New History in the West. Second, "bourgeois" historians were gathering their forces for an active anti-Marxist conspiracy in the name of historical "synthesis." The forces within Western historiography searching for new paths, and especially Henri Berr, were viewed as the real challenge to Marxism, as would become particularly obvious in Warsaw.

It was thus to be expected that in Warsaw, the international historical profession would have to reckon with a more strictly organized, more combative delegation of Soviet historians than in Oslo. But what was most noticeable in the years between these two Congresses were the measures taken against "bourgeois" historiography in the Soviet Union, as difficult as it was to see through the particular incidents.

In an exchange of letters between Koht, Lhéritier, Leland, and Pierre Renouvin, who had recently assumed the position of secretary of the French national committee, the Bureau of the ICHS became convinced that an official protest would do more harm than good to both the affected persons and to international cooperation, which they under no circumstances wished to endanger. Therefore, the ICHS contented itself with a declaration of principle, without calling the Soviet purges and the Italian Fascist oath by name. Lhéritier would have liked to avoid even this step. The declaration was formulated in such an appeasing way that even the Fascist and Soviet representatives agreed to it at the General Assembly in The Hague on 6 July 1932. Even so, although it avoided direct charges, it represented an unambiguous profession of the freedom of scholarship challenged by totalitarianism. If the ICHS did not want to give up on itself, it had to defend this principle for the sake of the International Historical Congresses. On account of the significance of this "charter of the International Historical Congresses," as I would like to call it, I will cite the decisive sections from the minutes of the Hague General Assembly. In his opening speech of 4 July 1932, President Halvdan Koht proclaimed:

> Freedom is one of the essential conditions of international brotherhood and cooperation. There are reasons to recall this before this assembly. For unfortunately we see how around us the political, social, and national struggles of our times tend to limit intellectual freedom, even that freedom which is the most precious to us, and which represents the vital condition for all our activities: the freedom to pursue scholarly research and to publish that which appears to each of us to be the truth evidenced by our research. Today we must say out loud that without this freedom the relations between scholars of different nations, the exchange of thoughts on scholarly problems would lose much of its value, and that we can never cease to demand categorically that every serious student must have the free opportunity to pursue his research and to present his results without being hindered for political reasons.[15]

Concerning the resolution passed on 6 July 1932 the report stated:

> Mister Koht, the president of the ICHS, then reads the suggested declaration, which has been approved by the Bureau, and introduces it with the following presentation of motives: "In my opening speech I pointed to the dangers that appear to be resulting from the political, social, and economic struggles of our times and that manifest themselves in various countries inside and outside of Europe.
> The Bureau believed that it was the moral duty of this organization of scholars from all over the world to raise its voice against every attack on the complete freedom of our work, and it thus suggests to you that you decide on the following declaration, which in its opinion expresses the wishes of all historians:
> "The International Committee of Historical Sciences, convinced that the complete freedom of research, a principle which has been secured in the course of the past century, is an imperative condition for the constant progress of science and

scholarship, and in view of the fact that the political, economic, and social struggles of the present have a tendency to restrict this freedom, calls upon the governments of all civilized nations to demand that they maintain the freedom of research and of researchers to the fullest extent, guided by the conviction that truth, which is the ideal goal of all scholarly work, can only result from diverse studies by different people." The declaration was unanimously adopted by the assembly.[16]

On Koht's initiative, this appeal was sent to all national committees with the request that they should forward it to their respective governments.

Over the years in which the Warsaw Congress was prepared, the ICHS was also concerned about Germany. An unspectacular event, which passed unnoticed in the public, strained the relationship between the German historians and the ICHS. A meeting of the Association of German Historians, which finally failed to materialize due to financial difficulties, had been planned for October 1931 in Koblenz and Bonn. The selection of these sites amounted to a nationalist demonstration. For the first time since the war, historians intended to meet again in the Rhineland, which had been freed of its occupying forces in 1930, following the withdrawal of the last French troops—five years earlier than stipulated by the Versailles Treaty. This early liberation of the Rhineland was a late result of the conciliatory Locarno policies of Stresemann and Briand. Was it not only natural that Lhéritier, who had celebrated the "Locarno of the historians" in Geneva, wanted to attend the German congress? But he received a negative reply. Robert Holtzmann, the chairman of the bibliographical commission of the ICHS and until recently chairman of the Association of German Historians, wrote to Lhéritier that he advised against a visit, "at least to the Koblenz convention"—Koblenz had been the headquarters of the French occupying forces—"since the mood in such a celebration of liberation, quite naturally, will not be such that a foreigner would feel comfortable."[17] Holtzmann might have been right, given the tenor of the official speeches marking the event, which contained not the slightest recognition of the French concession. Nevertheless, it was an insult to give the cold shoulder to the secretary-general of the ICHS, who had done more than anyone else for reconciliation and cooperation between the German and French historians.

But responsibility for the deterioration of the climate for international cooperation did not rest solely with one side. French scholars again did all they could to prevent any concessions in the International Academic Union that would have made it possible for the Germans to join. Koht believed that the French were endangering the very existence of the Union Académique. He told Pirenne that the Oslo and Copenhagen Academies were seriously considering a withdrawal from the Union because it was *"trop francisante"* (too Francifying).[18] Friis wrote to Leland: "My impression of the situation in the Union is anything but positive, particularly after my conversation with the French members, and as far as I can see we Danes and perhaps others too will have to abandon collaboration with them. If the French members and their followers in the Union want to persist in their mentality of the first post-war years, then it is time that something be undertaken."[19] Leland feared that a German refusal to participate in the Warsaw Historical Congress could be the result.[20] This impression was conveyed to him by a letter he had received from Brandi: "You know the state of our economical affairs today and I am sorry that the German payment shall be the last contribution to our International Committee of Historical Sciences, because I fear that it shall be impossible for us—morally and in fact—to stay here futurely. All German peacefulness and all our sense of international communion and scientific relations seem in vain for the French policy and public opinion. We have contributed our best toward our work, and I should be so glad if we might perpetuate it. But I think that all German historians feel the same vexation and the greatest disappointment." Moved and disappointed, Leland responded that "the cancellation of German cooperation would deal the Committee an appalling blow and crush" the work built up over the past ten years.[21]

On 1 August 1931, Brandi wrote to the secretary-general that the political background was "so gloomy that our entire work is endangered and the preparations for Warsaw are becoming increasingly difficult,"[22] upon which Lhéritier implored him: "The interpretation of the current events varies, I believe, from country to country. And I believe that our International Committee and the gatherings it organizes, such as the Congress of Warsaw, must stand above the various statements of opinion. As a member of the Committee, I believe that neither you nor I nor our colleagues on the Committee are or will be politicking."[23] Finally, after much hesitation and wavering, the German historians passed a decision at an association meeting in Göttingen from 2 to 5 August 1932 to attend the Warsaw Congress a year later. The more official character of Germany's participation, as compared with earlier Congresses, was emphasized by the fact that a General Committee of German Historians (Allgemeiner Deutscher Historikerausschuß) had been constituted following Oslo, in close cooperation with the ministry of the interior.[24] It included representatives from the most important historical institutions, such as the Historische Reichskommission, the Historical Commission of the Bavarian Academy of Sciences, the Görres Society, and also the Association of German Historians. The delimitation of the areas of responsibility between these institutions and the new Allgemeiner Historikerausschuß remained unclear in many respects. This contrasted with the opinion, stated with "complete unanimity," "that it is desirable to give the German participants the character of a closed delegation—similar to the Fascist organization of the Italians, which one could observe in Oslo."[25]

This will to put up a more united, coordinated front in Warsaw than at the previous Congresses had political motivations. The German participants should be prepared for discussions on the controversial German-Polish border, as it had been drawn at Versailles, and on its historical backgrounds. This topic was not included in the Congress program, but it was anticipated that it would inevitably arise on the periphery of the Congress. For this purpose, a "vade mecum" was composed in the form of questions and answers.[26] The director of the Prussian State Archives, Albert Brackmann, sent this training material to all German historians attending the Congress "for personal confidential information." Under the editorship of this highly esteemed medievalist, a thorough, scholarly collection of essays on "Germany and Poland" was published, with contributions by renowned German experts on Central and Eastern European history. Alongside Brackmann himself, these included Hermann Aubin, Josef Nadler, Karl Brandi, Robert Holtzmann, Otto Hoetzsch, Gerhard Ritter, Hermann Oncken, Fritz Hartung, and Hans Rothfels.[27] As Brackmann wrote to his collaborators in a circular letter of 1932/33, he had intended "neither a polemical nor a defensive book." It would rather be in accordance with "the peculiarity of our German historical scholarship ... if we attempted to adhere to a universal view of things and thus to adopt a standpoint beyond national conflicts."[28]

If one reads this work today, with a distance of more than half a century and with an eye on the entirely transformed map of Eastern Europe, one has to admit that it examined the history of the two neighboring peoples on a scholarly basis and tried to avoid the revisionist tendencies of the times. The reaction in the Polish journals was lively, mostly critical, but not without respect for the scholarly intentions. Oskar Halecki, who—in view of the Warsaw Congress—had already presented his own understanding of Polish national history in 1932, praised the essays by Ritter, Oncken, and Hartung as "the starting point for a scholarly, unbiased discussion."[29] There were a number of controversial matters, such as the early settlement history in the area inhabited by Germans and Poles, the position of Silesia between Poland and the German Empire, the ethnic struggles of the nineteenth century and so on. The differing perceptions on both sides, however, also resulted from different opinions about the adequacy of the concept of nation in the East-Central European border regions between the German people and its Eastern neighbors. The German historians deduced from the dovetailing of German and Polish settlements, as it still existed at that time, that the Western European idea of nation, which strives for the identity of state and ethnicity, was not applicable to that region. From their perspective, the new Polish state was not a nation-state but rather a multinational state, which in this respect was comparable to the former Habsburg Empire. From the Polish perspective, however, resurrected Poland was the ultimate fulfillment of the dream of an independent nation-state nurtured since the partition, even if this state contained some national minorities within its borders.

After Hitler's seizure of power, the attitude of the German historians who, despite certain reservations, demonstrated a loyal stance toward the new regime, appeared highly questionable. The Danish historian Aage Friis, who had taken such a benevolent view of the Germans ever since the founding of the International Committee, recorded some of the private conversations during the Congress in Warsaw. His notes show the doubts and troubled premonitions that were concealed beneath the cordial and cultivated atmosphere of the Congress. Friis spoke confidentially and in depth with Brandi, Mommsen, Rothfels, and Brackmann, and briefly with Holtzmann and Brandenburg. When he told Holtzmann that the situation of scholarship in Germany was a great worry to the Danes, Holtzmann answered brusquely that "there was no reason to worry. Hitler had stated categorically that there was no talk of infringing on the freedom of science, and there was no reason to assume that this would not be kept to. I then maintained a demonstrative silence." Friis continued: "Brandenburg was extraordinarily moved by what had happened, and apparently could hardly bear to speak about it. His words demonstrated with great clarity how moved and bitter he was, and that he held fast to his democratic principles and views." Friis was dismayed at the "compliant and weak" attitude of his German colleagues toward the Hitler regime. Their attempts to explain what had happened amounted to a "quiescent defense." "The main argument they made was that as bad as things were, one should not forget the positive sides that had to be appreciated even from a democratic perspective." For example, "German unity had taken a major step forward, and Germany was not returning to the Wilhelminian system or to the rule of the Junkers and capitalists, or to the Prussian bureaucratic state." In the social realm, the community of all young people, as promoted by the Reich Labor Service, represented massive democratic progress toward a "genuinely organic national community [*Volksgemeinschaft*]." Friis's observations on the nationalism spreading throughout the entire German educational system were played down. When he said "that the entire system, with its struggle against Jews and other foreigners, with the abolition of the rule of law etc. etc., was a break with the primitive human concepts of rights and with the elementary achievements of civilization, they all admitted vaguely that this was of course correct, that they deeply regretted the many deplorable things that were occurring, but quickly returned to the assertion that these phenomena had already been restrained and would certainly disappear gradually. Of course, in the Jewish question they all tried to point to the well-known unfortunate facts, but they naturally could not avoid the core of the matter, namely, the equally foolish and criminal racial hatred."

The discussions went round and round and came to nothing.

> My definition of German nationalism as a vile cultural regression translated into facts and an obvious danger to Europe's future was always countered with hopes, assumptions, etc. Concerning the position of scholarship, Brackmann (who provided most of the positive and placatory statements) explained that official requests had been made to Hitler—it is not clear by whom, whether by representatives of the Berlin University or the Berlin Academy—who had expressed his profound astonishment that anyone could even imagine an attack upon the freedom of science. From [Brackmann's] and Brandi's statements it became evident that a certain number of efforts have been undertaken to save individuals and to create special arrangements for individual researchers who are in danger, and that this has been successful in some cases.[30]

A report made by Brandi on such discussions on the margins of the Congress shows the extent to which conservative illusions could cloud the perception of what was looming in Germany, and how much clearer the view was from the outside. "The Italians," Brandi wrote, "showed themselves, as before, to be extremely guarded in political matters and apparently uninterested in Germany. By contrast, among our Scandinavian and English friends there was more interest than faculty of understanding." They had interpreted the notion of *Volksgemeinschaft* "democratically."

> When one tried to draw them further into the actual German-Social idea, they followed along as far as the goal was concerned, but they denied that Germany could achieve this goal and maintained that Germany, like Fascist Italy or Bolshevik Russia, would remain on the level of a party state. They are then surprised to hear that the views and opinions of the party are also profoundly felt outside of the current party organization, perhaps there most of all, and that among university professors, too, the same conviction was prevailing.... In the interest of our educational work, it was good and effective that, with the express permission of the Prussian educational administration, Prof. Koebner from Breslau was present as a speaker and Prof. Rothfels from Königsberg as a discussion contributor, and that they both moved among us in respected positions, because these examples could show in practical terms how little harm is inflicted on our non-Aryan lecturers.[31]

Despite such declarations of national loyalty, however, the Warsaw Congress had political repercussions for Brandi personally, such that all illusions concerning the true character of the new regime were dispelled. On 18 January 1934, the ancient historian Ulrich Kahrstedt gave the academic speech on the occasion of the anniversary of the founding of the German Reich at the University of Göttingen. He used this opportunity in the most contemptible manner to attack those historians involved in international cooperation. In a provocative departure from Ranke's principle that the task of history was "to say what really happened," he called upon the Göttingen *Civitas academica* to abandon "research for research's sake," "international scholarship," and the "international republic of scholars." There followed a sort of apology by the rector and a letter from the German minister of the interior Frick, as a result of which Brandi saw himself more or less rehabilitated. He was also allowed to speak before the university senate. "However," as Brandi wrote in a resigned tone, "the senate took note of everything, but did not go one step further, and information to the public and the students remained within the most restricted of boundaries."[32]

The political conversations in Warsaw that Friis and Brandi reported on were private ones. In regard to the Congress's official work, the organizers avoided all discussions of contemporary issues liable to inflame political passions. This applied above all to the war guilt question, which had already been excluded in Oslo. Thus, a suggestion by the Austrian historians, presented by Dopsch, to include it in the program this time had been rejected. Alongside Koht and Leland, the French national committee had particularly objected to the Austrian suggestion, namely, in a detailed memorandum that Lhéritier sent to Leland for his private information.[33] It brought forward two arguments against the discussion of the war guilt question at the Warsaw Congress: that it was inexpedient, and scientifically premature—inexpedient because a debate about this issue would inevitably be politically charged, and thus spoil the atmosphere at the Congress. "This would doubtless be the end of the institution of the International Congresses." Similar concerns were expressed by Koht and Leland. Only three decades later did a discussion of this question become possible, namely, in a controversy among German scholars at the International Historical Congress in Vienna in 1965. The second argument was that the matter had not yet reached the state of maturity necessary for rigorous research. Too many documents were still unknown. How, under such conditions, could one draw precise and honest conclusions about the causes of the war and, which was more sensitive, pass judgement on who was responsible? Nevertheless, such hesitations did not prevent the French historians from participating in bilateral conferences with their German colleagues in order to bring about a revision of history textbooks, and to formulate together with them what could be said according to the evidence of accessible documents. Two years after Warsaw, balanced recommendations for historical teaching were agreed on, which have still lost nothing of their scholarly significance.[34]

Upon seeing how their suggestion was received, the Austrian historians had no choice but to forgo an inclusion of the war guilt question in the Warsaw program. With only a few exceptions, they did not participate in the Congress in the end, probably on account of the tense relations between the clerical-fascist Dollfuss regime in Austria and the Hitler regime in Germany.[35] With regard to the Congress program, however, they successfully demanded that if the war guilt question was not to be dealt with, then other politically explosive topics from the time of the World War should also be rejected, including those referring to revolutionary upheavals.[36] That is why a lecture by Renouvin on the cooperation of the general staffs was canceled, as well as a Polish contribution on the administration of the Polish mines during the years of German occupation. Over the long term, of course, it was impossible to exclude the historical questions connected with revolutionary unrest. The Soviet historians had suggested early on that an international commission should be formed to deal with the history of social movements, particularly those associated with the agricultural and industrial proletariat.[37] The Soviet application presented to the General Assembly of the ICHS in Cambridge and London from 28 April to 3 May 1930, had described the underlying political and historical interest as follows: "The current history of mankind, the history of the past ten years, is developing under the sign of the social question. With new and powerful strength, the war and the post-war epoch demonstrate the significance of social problems, the growing role of the working masses in the life of all countries and, even more, their role in the construction of the future."[38] This commission, which would come to develop a very lively activity in the coming years, was constituted in Warsaw under Koht's chairmanship.[39]

Thus, some dikes had been built in order to keep the waves of political turmoil from inundating the quiet waters of the scholarly Congress. The goodwill demonstrated by most participants also helped. With regard to the Congress's program and structure, the organizers had thought long and hard about how to arrange this mass gathering. The minutes of the Bureau meetings and the General Assemblies of the ICHS in Venice in 1929, in Cambridge/London/Oxford in 1930, in Budapest in 1931, and in The Hague in 1932 are full of such considerations. They found their expression in a circular letter to the national committees authored by Koht and Lhéritier, as well as in a special Congress issue of the monthly journal *La Pologne Littéraire* on 15 August 1933, in which contributions by Bronisław Dembiński, the president of the organizing committee, his secretary Tadeusz Manteuffel, Marceli Handelsman, deacon of the philosophical faculty of the University of Warsaw, and Michel Lhéritier were published. The program of the Oslo Congress had been arranged primarily by the historians of the host country. In the preparations for Warsaw, however, some non-Poles were delegated to the Polish organizing committee, including Lhéritier and Vigander, the secretary of Oslo, and the ICHS exerted greater influence on the structure of the program than previously. This particularly applied to the "*rapports*," the research reports. They were to be given the major weight compared with the "*communications*" as well as with the "*interventions*" (discussion contributions), which were to be announced in advance but did not have to be submitted in writing. Lhéritier spoke of the "*triomphe des rapports*," which he published at the expense of the ICHS, at a total of nearly 500 pages. The Poles published two volumes of abstracts of the "communications" with over 500 pages, plus the complete text of all Polish contributions in three volumes with a total of nearly 1,000 pages. Finally, the minutes of the Congress were published in a volume of the *Bulletin*—all in all, a documentation of extraordinary meticulousness.[40]

Another innovation lay in the fact that the national committees assumed a greater role in the Congress's preparation than they had in Oslo. In principle, no papers were accepted without their consent. However, there remained a number of exceptions. The final decision on the acceptance of papers and on the structure of the program within the prescribed outline lay with the organizing committee, not with the ICHS. This arrangement inevitably led to certain frictions between the Polish members of the organizing committee and the expansive energy of a man like Lhéritier. The latter showed "tendencies to subordinate the future organization of the Congress entirely to the Committee," Handelsman wrote in a concerned letter to Dembiński. One would "have to oppose him with delicacy."[41] The affiliated international commissions, too, were asked to take the initiative in regard to the program of the Congress—a first step toward their later integration into the ICHS as members with equal rights. And this path was the correct one, despite the criticism that was voiced and continued to be voiced from opposite sides. One side, led by the Frenchmen Berr and Bloch with their influential journals, wanted more organization and planning. Others, such as the Belgian historian Ganshof, who had been involved in the organization of Brussels, were skeptical toward further regulation. For this reason, Ganshof refused to join the Warsaw organizing committee out of "fear of an organization that he [considered to be] too far-reaching."[42] Two opinions remain worthy of note, namely, Brandi's comment that a Congress should offer the opportunity "to listen to the masters," and that of Pirenne, who insisted that the Congresses should retain their character of a "festival of the mind."[43]

To some extent, these remarks were also aimed at Lhéritier and his zealous organizational style. In addition to the traditional, nearly unaltered section scheme—this time with a special section for Eastern European history, analogous to the Scandinavian history section at Oslo, and with the integration of the theory of history into the methodology section in response to a suggestion by the *Revue de synthèse historique*—the program included a series of sessions devoted to special themes. To compare with Oslo: demography, historical geography, and military history were present in both Oslo and Warsaw; "history and nationality" was dropped. New themes included instead: benevolent despotism, great journeys and discoveries, colonial history, the history of banks and bills of exchange, social movements, feudalism, humanism, the history of the Jews, and oriental history. This framework was filled by 286 personally presented "reports" and "communications" (compared with 307 in Oslo). Despite the poor international economic situation, the number of active participants was high. It amounted to 1,031 (950 in Oslo), including 542 Poles.[44] Among the foreign registrations, the majority consisted of the French (108), Italians (86), Germans (59), and Britons (51). Among overseas nations, only the United States sent a large number (47; Leland's absence was particularly regretted), plus a few individual historians from other North and South American countries. Three participants each from Turkey and British India also attended. The special section on oriental history did not quite materialize.[45] The Congress was still far from an "ecumenical community" in geographical terms. But it had moved a step closer to the realization of the ecumenical ideal, namely, to be an institution as comprehensive as possible with regard to contradictory interpretations of the world and of human life. After Soviet-Marxist historiography had taken the stage at the Oslo Congress, two representatives of the Vatican participated in Warsaw. The archbishop of Warsaw, Msgr. Godlewski, brought greetings from Pope Pius XI, recalled the opening of the Vatican Archives by Leo XIII, and declared that the Church had always been committed to historical truth.[46]

The Congress as a whole bore a salient Central and Eastern European accent. Despite political restraint and the avoidance of current issues, it paid homage to resurrected Poland, which, proud of its history and its newly recovered statehood after centuries of partition, treated its guests to stylish and generous hospitality in the presence of the highest representatives of the state.

Topics on Polish history constituted the largest block of the program, to which 41 papers by Polish and 39 by non-Polish historians were dedicated. One can identify two reasons for this extraordinary attention paid to the history of the host country. The awareness of history as a powerful element capable of guaranteeing the continuity of a nation over a long era of partition and statelessness made Poland a uniquely fascinating subject of historical recollection. Secondly, the profound changes ensuing from war and revolution had increased the general interest in Eastern European history, which had previously often been viewed as a marginal field of academic studies. Before a large audience Jaroslav Bidlo (Prague) examined the question: "What is Eastern European History?"[47] His answer was that it was restricted to the sphere of Byzantine-Orthodox culture. A spirited discussion followed, because many listeners felt that this criterion, derived only from intellectual and church history, was too one-sided.[48] Following the Second World War, this question posed itself once more in an ideologically divided Europe, namely, as the problem of the cultural and historical identity of the East-Central European countries and their respective alignment within the East-West polarity. In Warsaw the lively interest in Eastern Europe was also reflected in a generally praised exhibition of historical maps prepared by historians from Poland (W. Semkoviez), Belgium (F. L. Ganshof), and Germany (F. Curschmann).[49]

Among those who presented their contributions to Polish history at the Warsaw Congress were three historians who had committed themselves to the preparation and execution of this Congress, and who symbolized the relations between Polish historiography and the ICHS: Oscar Halecki, Bronisław Dembiński, and Marceli Handelsman. In an essay on Poland and the oriental question, Halecki presented a vivid description of Poland's heroic role in the European resistance against the Turks. Dembiński painted a sensitive picture of the last Polish King, Poniatowski, a great friend of the arts and literature who, through his Constitution of 1791—the last attempt to consolidate a state struggling for its existence—earned the admiration of Burke, but who lacked the leadership qualities necessary to ward off his country's fate. Handelsman presented a meticulous report on the wide-ranging correspondence and activities of Prince Adam Czartoryski, the "secret king of Poland," as he was called, who had lived in Paris after the Polish uprising of 1830. His efforts had been aimed at advancing the struggle for national independence in the Danube principalities, as well as the national revolutionary movements against Russian dominance. In 1848/49 this led him to the idea of transforming Kossuth's revolutionary Hungary into a federal state with equal rights for the various nationalities living there.[50]

The problem of the nation remained a major focal point of historical interest at the Warsaw Congress. As in Oslo, this issue had been given a section of its own. In addition, it resurfaced again and again as one of the Congress's leitmotifs. This applied particularly to the Italian papers. Federico Chabod and Gioacchino Volpe provided significant contributions on Risorgimento research, and Pietro Fedele presented arguments supporting the continuity of the Roman Senate in the Middle Ages. Georges Pagès (Paris) provided a survey of the source material on Napoleon III's foreign policy and showed how difficult it was to gain a reliable picture of the motives underlying his policies. Louis Eisenmann, also from Paris, dealt with the nationality problems of the multiethnic Austrian-Hungarian Empire prior to the World War. Erich Brandenburg (Leipzig) presented his theses on imperialism and elicited a lively discussion about its relationship to nationalism. Gerhard Ritter (Freiburg) tried to explain the separate development of Germany's intellectual history in comparison to Western Europe, and sought the causes for this in the Reformation era, particularly with Luther. The Romanian Nicolae Iorga delivered a lecture on the national idea in Southeastern Europe at the Congress's opening session, including critical observations, presumably in regard to the nationalistic excesses of the various fascisms: "C'est un peu en se barbarisant qu'on se nationalise" (One turns somewhat barbaric once one is nationalizing).[51]

The wide-ranging consideration of national questions also included a special session on the history of the Jews.[52] At issue here was what approaches should be used to understand the history of the Jewish diaspora. The factors of national self-assertion, social environment, and religion were assessed with regard to their specific relevance. A controversial discussion ensued following the paper by Rafael Mahler (Warsaw) on the "Theory of Jewish Cultural Development in Jewish Historiography," which had emphasized external conditions. F. Friedmann (Lodz) particularly accused Mahler of being a proponent of "historical materialism," and stated that this theory had yet to provide a satisfactory interpretation of Jewish history. Culture and religion, he concluded, were more significant for its development than socioeconomic factors.[53]

A special session was devoted to the "History of Social Movements." There were three papers, all by Soviet authors.[54] The subject matter was in keeping with an international commission called into being on Soviet initiative and now constituted in Warsaw. The Soviets intended to use this commission as a special forum for the implementation of Marxist methods in historical studies. In addition, in the section for economic and social history, a report by Anna Mikhailovna Pankratova on the "History of Factories in the Soviet Union" stood out. It gave an impression of the range of studies supported by the Soviet government, although a Czech critic held that it brought nothing new in comparison to earlier studies of this kind in other countries, aside from their quantitative and ideological aspects.[55]

Among the remaining contributions on social and economic history, the Belgian historian Émile Lousse's paper is worth mentioning because of the stimuli it provided for future research. Lousse dealt with the emergence of estates and assemblies of estates. His report represented the very model of what a *"rapport"* on the state of research, available source material, and desiderata can achieve. The lively discussion it provoked led to the formation of a permanent international commission for research on the origins of estates.[56]

This project was based on historical comparison. Pirenne, who had recommended this method so strongly at the Brussels Congress, was among the initiators of the new commission. In Warsaw, "comparative method" was an often-heard watchword. It was used by Hermann Aubin to characterize the Germanic and Arab invasions of the ancient world, by Halvdan Koht in a reappraisal of the phenomenon of united kingdoms typical of the late Middle Ages, by Gerhard Ritter for the genesis of the intellectual differentiation of Germany and Western Europe, and in special sessions on benevolent despotism in the various European countries and comparative research on demographic developments. In the generation since the Paris Congress of 1900, which had proclaimed *"l'histoire comparative"* as its program, the comparative method had become an unchallenged and much-used component of historiographical techniques, alongside an unbroken tradition of the still prevailing hermeneutic-critical method.

Discussions on methodology in the narrow sense of the word, i.e., considerations of the instruments and procedures of research, were scarce in Warsaw. Dembiński acted in full conformity with the prevailing methodological consciousness when, at the Congress's opening session, he quoted Fustel de Coulanges: "[F]or one day of synthesis years of analysis are needed," and then continued: "That is our destiny and our good fortune."[57]

The real meaning of the much-cited notion of synthesis was examined in the section "Historical Methods and Theory of History" under the direction of Henri Berr. This discussion led to a clear confrontation between the ideas of Western and Soviet historians. The American Fred Morrow Fling stated in his paper entitled "Historical Synthesis":[58] "Only the creator of a synthesis is an historian. The scholars who gather and edit texts, criticize sources or establish facts (*Jahrbücher*), but do not complete the work of the historian by constructing a synthesis, are not historians. They are *érudits*, as Langlois called them, the assistants who procure material and prepare it for the creative artist." But if critique of sources and erudition are not an integral component of historical knowledge, one must ask, then what is history? Is it related to art, as Wilhelm von Humboldt perceived it? Or is it philosophy, as Croce taught? In any case, Fling said, history was entirely different from sociology, "and never the twain shall meet." Already thirty years previously, when the discussion on a New History oriented around sociology was starting in America, Fling had published an essay in the *American Historical Review* (9, 1903) on "Historical Synthesis." Referring to the neo-Kantian distinction between nomothetic and idiographic methods, he did not deny the possibility of establishing laws of societal evolution, but asserted that these were not historical laws. According to him, Rickert had shown "that it is possible to observe society from the standpoint of natural sciences and that one can perhaps even formulate laws of social development—but such laws are not historical laws, they are not the laws of a unique series. A historical law, a law concerning that which occurred once and which cannot occur again, is a *contradictio in adiecto*." For Fling, the historical object was constituted by its value relatedness (*Wertbezug*). With the help of the concept of values, he developed his notion of historical synthesis now in Warsaw. Referring to the idealistic "philosophy of life" (*Lebensphilosophie*) of Rudolf Eucken (*Der Kampf um einen geistigen Lebensinhalt*, 1896), he stated: "Historical synthesis is concerned with the development and application, in human relations, of a system of values.... The historian deals with the values involved in his synthesis as a hierarchy of values, rising from economic institutions at the bottom, to mysticism and human personality at the top. The hierarchy is based on an understanding of the profound significance, for the transformation of man from an animal to a spiritual personality, of the saying, 'What shall it profit a man, if he gain the whole world and lose his own soul.'" "Synthesis" obviously covered a great number of different conceptions and techniques of history, ranging from Pirenne's empirical comparative method to Fling's historical metaphysics of a hierarchy of values.

The problem took yet another turn in a paper on "Historical Materialism or Synthesis?" read by Wilhelm Keilhau, a lecturer in economic history at the University of Oslo.[59] For him, synthesis meant a certain choice of methods, and not philosophical or economic speculation on the course of history. He recommended psychology as its basis. A comprehensive causal explanation of historical processes had to take into account the entire spectrum of the drives embedded in human nature, and examine them in their respective interactions, from the elementary instinct of self-preservation to the "dream-related transcendental drive." His view of historical synthesis was directed against historical materialism; his notion of the latter, however, certainly was wrong. He shared a common misunderstanding by viewing it as a kind of economic determinism. He was pushing at open doors by noting in his critique of historical materialism that economic phenomena themselves consisted of a "complicated entirety of phenomena ... that demand a precise analysis. Thus, human decisions enter into every economic chain of causality as important elements. However, in human decisions we perceive a process that is not determined by 'causes' but by motives, and decisions in the economic sphere are often influenced by considerations that are of political, religious or purely personal nature.... Between economic and extra-economic factors of development there is a relationship of continuous interactions." These assertions could not be seen as directed against Marx himself, but at best against a vulgar or doctrinaire Marxism.

Thus, it was not difficult for Marxist historians to counter Keilhau's thesis. Since this argument reappeared at later Congresses, let us record verbatim the response of the historicism theorist Evgenii A. Preobrazhensky of Moscow:

> Mr. Keilhau maintains that historical materialism traces all the driving forces of history to economic facts. One can call that economism, but it is not historical materialism. Mr. Keilhau notes correctly that such economism is not capable of explaining ultimate historical enigmas because the economy itself is a many-sided phenomenon requiring analysis. It is very strange that Mr. Keilhau has not found

this analysis in Marx. It is also very strange that in his comments on historical materialism, Mr. Keilhau failed even to mention the fundamental concept—that of the productive forces.... Marx did not take all the manifold economic phenomena as the basis of the historical process, but specifically the productive forces.[60]

But Preobrazhensky, too, strayed from the realm of historical and anthropological empiricism and entered that of speculation when he postulated that the various human drives, such as the drives for dominance and sociability, were not rooted in fundamental anthropological conditions, but rather were products of social development, i.e., secondary phenomena.

Two other Soviet historians rejected the Western conceptions of historical synthesis more fiercely. Nikolai M. Lukin examined the neo-Kantian distinction between natural and cultural sciences, as it had been outlined by Windelband and Rickert, who had defined one as concerned with laws, the other as concerned with values. He compared this conception with Marx's "historicism," which made a distinction between the laws concerning society and those concerning nature, but in both cases held such developments to be of an "inevitable necessity." Lukin rejected theories of a mechanical or naturalistic determinism, but he held on to the conviction that history was governed by lawful processes. The existence of such a system of laws, he said, allowed predictions that had found "striking confirmation" in the development of capitalist society. At that time, Marxist historicism, as it presented itself at the Historical Congresses, drew a sense of superiority from the apparent crisis of capitalist economy and "bourgeois" society, and sometimes expressed it in keen terms, as, for example, when Lukin's colleague Vyacheslav P. Volgin from Leningrad observed that Fling's theory of a progressive hierarchy of values, if pursued to its logical conclusion, required the existence of a divine being. Volgin then continued: "We historical materialists are proud that we do not need this hypothesis.... And if someone in the twentieth century takes refuge behind it, then we call this an expression of scientific reaction, which is a reflection of the reactionary mood of the respective social class." This was a denial of the elementary fact that both atheistic and theistic beliefs are anchored beyond science, and it was inappropriate to the scholarly discourse of the historical community that the conflict between two contrasting historical worldviews degenerated into political discrimination. However, Volgin's statement that in Warsaw, "for many of the historians present, synthesis has become a banner beneath which a struggle against historical materialism is being waged" was quite accurate.[61] But he did not question the methodological value of synthesis. For Marxism itself, as he explained at the closing session, had resulted from "a synthesis based on the findings of Utopian thought, bourgeois political economy in England, and German philosophy."[62]

How did Henri Berr, the pioneer of "synthesis" and chairman of the methodological section, respond to all this? The minutes remain silent, aside from a few keywords concerning a short paper in which he presented a definition of synthesis. To the extent that synthesis was understood as a hypothesis, he ascribed to it an indispensable methodological value, for without the guidance of a hypothesis, analysis might become blind and end up groping in the dark. This explained why the analytical-synthetic approach was open in all directions. He caught the tenor of the international historical gatherings when he emphasized their fundamental tolerance and the potency of ideas in history:

> Nationalist or internationalist history? "Bourgeois" or "proletarian" history? Idealistic or materialistic history? Truth is neither tendentious nor exclusive. Materialism or idealism? No. Materialism and idealism! Certainly, the significance of the economic factor, which sometimes so painfully hits us in the eyes in today's world, has forced itself upon our minds in this Poland that has resolved such immense difficulties and must resolve many more. But within the miracle of this *Polonia rediviva*, how could one fail to recognize the role of another element? It is not economic interests which have reawakened Poland. It is not economic interests which, in the years of trial when Poland's body was torn apart, preserved the unity of its soul: it was spiritual forces.[63]

In Warsaw, a number of questions of historical theory as well as of Eastern European history attracted a large audience, especially from among the younger generation. The lecture on "Historical Materialism or Synthesis" led to a genuine "migration of peoples" (*Völkerwanderung*), it was said.[64] Therefore, there was considerable regret when it was announced that two addresses by Soviet historians, Nikolai I. Bukharin and Anatolii V. Lunacharsky, could not be delivered because their authors were not in attendance. Both had considerable scientific and literary merits, and they held important positions in the political system of the Soviet Union. Bukharin had been a member of the Politburo until 1929, and chairman of the Comintern and editor of *Pravda*, until he came into conflict with Stalin and was relieved of all duties. From 1933, he stood under constant surveillance, and he was sentenced to death in the course of the purges in 1938. At Warsaw, he wanted to speak as an economic theoretician on "The Methodology of Historical Knowledge." Unfortunately, only a brief outline is available. It shows that Bukharin intended to include a discussion of the ideas of Max Weber, which, despite their great significance for historical theory, had so far been neglected at the Historical Congresses.[65]

There also was no discussion about a further remarkable report on methodological issues presented by the Swiss historian Hans Nabholz, who was to bear the main responsibility for the organization of the next International Historical Congress in Zurich in 1938, and afterward would serve as the president of the ICHS during the difficult years of the Second World War. In his lecture at the final meeting of the Congress in Cracow "On the Relationship between Political and Economic History"[66] he inquired into the logic of this relationship. His answer: They interact like "end and means. Economics is primary, politics is secondary." For this reason he spoke against a historiography concentrated on political processes. To be sure, the driving forces of history also included ideas; Humboldt and Ranke, he said, had the merit of having emphasized their potency. However, they had not concerned themselves with the origin of ideas, but had taken them as a given. For his part, Nabholz believed that ideas could be traced back to economic conditions and causes, which sounded like Marx. However, that is not how he wished to be understood. He saw the dividing line in his conviction that "the intellectual and the psychological," and not only the physical, were original needs of mankind. We will leave open whether Nabholz's conception of Marx was accurate or not. In any case he, like many another "bourgeois" historian of the time, sympathized with the Marxist interpretation of history, as did Halvdan Koht, the first president of the ICHS. To illustrate both his proximity to and his distance from Marx, Nabholz referred to Ernst Troeltsch, the theologian and critic of historicism, whom he quoted as follows:

> It remains a fact that the socioeconomic substructure indeed underlies all historical life as the firmest and most lasting lower stratum, which is the most difficult of all to move and which, if it moves, revolutionizes everything else.—The great periods of cultural history can indeed be characterized best with the features of this substructure; and this characterization will be all the more well founded if we can show that the foundations of this substructure itself already contain a certain mentality typical of the respective cultural area, which has already given the most elementary way of life specific colorations and patterns of future trends; or if we can show that certain economic upheavals only receive their meaning and force through the supervention of psychological attitudes.[67]

Did it not appear as if, in the course of future Historical Congresses, it might become possible to at least build bridges of mutual understanding between "bourgeois" and "Marxist" historicism, even if the conflicting views could never be entirely reconciled?

Building bridges of understanding—Nabholz was concerned with doing just that in regard to the language barrier. The fact that there is no *lingua franca* common to all intellectuals has burdened and continues to burden the scholarly discourse at the International Historical Congresses. Improved means of communications are particularly urgent for languages that are only spoken within a restricted geographical area. In Europe this applies to the Scandinavian languages, Polish, and Hungarian, among others. Even though the historians of these countries impress their foreign colleagues with their polyglot abilities, nevertheless the historical literature of their respective linguistic areas remains largely unknown. It lay in the logic of the ecumenical historical community to seek means of better information and understanding. For this reason, at the General Assembly of the ICHS in Budapest in 1931—the first one to take place in an Eastern European country—Nabholz had filed the following motion: The ICHS should arrange the translation of important works and publications of abstracts of historical essays into commonly intelligible languages.[68]

Hungary was suitable terrain for such an initiative, aimed at a better integration of small countries with narrowly restricted languages into international cooperation. At that time, the Hungarian Historical Society was directed by Alexander Domanovszky, a leading exponent of a nationally inspired historiography, who maintained a lively personal relationship with a number of Polish historians and with Nabholz. Thus, it was no coincidence that the participation of the Hungarian historians in the Congresses in Warsaw in 1933 and in Zurich in 1938 increased considerably, as was shown by the number of their reports and communications. Nabholz's suggestion of creating annotated bibliographies and, if possible, translations with the help of the ICHS, met with lively support in Budapest. The Hungarian historians, whose territory had been shrunk by the Treaty of Trianon, were guided by strong nationalist impulses and imbued with the task of correcting alleged errors being spread abroad concerning Hungarian national history. A young historian of the Domanovszky school, Tibor Baráth, was assigned to the Paris Secretariat of the ICHS as an assistant for the publication of the *Bulletin*. He fulfilled this role in constant correspondence with Domanovszky. In subsequent years, summaries of Hungarian, Danish, Norwegian, and Swedish historical literature from the second half of the 1920s were published in the *Bulletin*.[69] But this undertaking remained fragmentary. The war put an end to it, and after the war the *Bulletin* was not continued in its previous volume.

The means of information provided by the concerned countries, under their own initiative and on their own responsibility, were more continuous and thus more effective. At the Congresses of Brussels and Oslo, the Poles had been the first to publish a collection of their reports and communications verbatim, in one of the Congress languages. They did the same at the Warsaw Congress.[70] On the occasion of the General Assembly in Budapest in 1931, Imre Lukinich, secretary of the national committee, published the first information on Hungarian historical studies, namely, an annotated bibliography on the publication of sources on Hungarian history, which had been pushed vigorously after the First World War.[71]

Such efforts to promote the spread of information on the historical oeuvre of small countries also led to the formation of a federation of Eastern European historical societies, which can be traced to a Polish initiative in 1927. Societies, institutes, and academies from nearly every country in this region belonged to it, including Russian émigrés. Alongside the use of their respective mother tongues, French served as the common vehicle of understanding. Two scholarly undertakings were prepared: information on the development of historical studies in Eastern Europe through the help of a bulletin, and a reference work on Slavic antiquities. Above all, however, it was felt that personal exchange among historians interested in the cross-border problems of this area should be promoted. This federation differed from the organizing principle of the ICHS in its regionally restricted membership. However, their tasks were complementary, and it was only natural that a conference of the Eastern European historians was held in conjunction with the International Congress in Warsaw.[72]

Notes

1. R. Lisbonne, "Congrès internationaux," *Revue historique* 172 (1933): 405.
2. Friis to Leland, 5 Sep. 1933, Leland papers, box 40.
3. Report by Brandi to the German Foreign Office, "Vertraulicher Bericht über das Comité International des Sciences Historiques und über die Tätigkeit der deutschen Delegation auf dem VII. Internationalen Historikerkongreß zu Warschau und Krakau, 21.–29. August 1933," Zentrales Staatsarchiv, Merseburg, Rep. V c, Sect. 1, Tit. 11, Teil VI, no. 13, vol. 3. Brandi had nothing but praise for the behavior shown by the Polish professors toward their German colleagues. Similar comments in report on the Congress by the German ambassador in Warsaw, ibid., and in Brackmann to Meinecke, 30 Aug. 1933, Brackmann papers 1/21.
4. De Sanctis to Koht, 2 Jan. 1932, in G. De Sanctis, *Ricordi della mia vita*, ed. Silvio Accame (Florence, 1970), p. 242.
5. Koht to Lhéritier, 10 Jan. 1932, Archives CISH, dossier 1932.
6. Lhéritier to Koht, 7 Jan. 1932, ibid.
7. Leland to Lhéritier, 26 Jan. 1932, Archives CISH, correspondence Koht/Leland.
8. Leland to Lhéritier, 20 April 1932, Archives CISH, dossier 1932.
9. De Sanctis to Friis, 19 March 1932, in De Sanctis, *Ricordi*, p. 255.
10. For detailed information on this, see Shteppa, *Russian Historians*, and Castelli, "Internazionalismo e Storia."
11. M. N. Pokrovsky, "Klassovaja borba i ideologiceskij front" [Class Struggle and the Ideological Front], *Pravda*, 7 Nov. 1928, cited in Castelli, "Internazionalismo e Storia," p. 904.
12. Behrendt, "Die internationalen Beziehungen," pp. 209ff. Behrendt was permitted to evaluate the Pokrovsky papers and other Soviet documents.
13. M. N. Pokrovsky, "Institut istorii i zadači istorikov-marksistov" [The Institute for History and the Tasks of Marxist Historians], *Istorik Marksist* 14 (1929): 3, cited in Enteen, "Marxists versus Non-Marxists," p. 108. Enteen writes that Pokrovsky's interpretation became, with minor variations, "the standard Soviet version." This assumption has often been confirmed by the Historical Congresses.
14. Cf. p. 18 above.
15. ICHS, *Bulletin*. 5: 817.
16. Ibid., p. 823f.
17. Holtzmann to Lhéritier, 28 June 1931, Archives CISH, dossier 1931. Holtzmann resigned as chairman of the bibliographical commission half a year later because a journal essay by the Innsbruck historian O. Stolz was removed from the *International Bibliography* on the instigation of the Italians. The essay dealt with the history of the German schools in South Tyrol. See Holtzmann to Lhéritier, 26 and 31 Jan. 1932, Archives CISH, dossier 1932.
18. Koht to Pirenne, 31 May 1931, Koht papers, 386.
19. Friis to Leland, 5 June 1931, Friis papers, I, 1.
20. Leland to Lhéritier, 19 Aug. 1931, Archives CISH, dossier 1931.
21. Brandi to Leland, 16 July 1931, Brandi papers, 46; Leland to Brandi, 24 July 1931, ibid., 44.
22. Brandi to Lhéritier, 1 Aug. 1931, Archives CISH, dossier 1931.
23. Lhéritier to Brandi, 3 Aug. 1931, Brandi papers, 46.
24. Minutes of the founding session of 17 Nov. 1931 and of the following ones in Brandi papers, 46.
25. Report on the meeting of the Allgemeiner Historikerausschuß 19–20 June 1931, Brandi papers, 51; cf. also the minutes of the meeting of the Ausschuß des Verbandes Deutscher Historiker, 10–11 June 1933 in Eisenach, Brackmann papers, III/87.
26. "Vademecum für die historisch-politische Auseinandersetzung zwischen Polen und Deutschland," published by Publikationsstelle des Preußischen Geheimen Staatsarchivs, Berlin, Bundesarchiv, R 153/723.
27. A. Brackmann, ed., *Deutschland und Polen: Beiträge zu ihren geschichtlichen Beziehungen* (Munich, 1933).

28. Oncken papers, 50.
29. O. Halecki, *La Pologne de 963 à 1914: Essai de synthèse historique* (Paris, 1932). In France as well there appeared a series entitled *Problèmes politiques de la Pologne contemporaine* (Paris, 1931–1933). It met with sharp criticism on the part of German historians and was one of the motivations for the German essay collection; see Holtzmann to Brandi, 3 Feb. 1933, Brandi papers, 46. On the German view of this discussion, see A. Brackmann, "Ein Wort zur geistigen Auseinandersetzung zwischen Deutschland und Polen," *Geistige Arbeit. Zeitung aus der wissenschaftlichen Welt*, no. 5, 5 March 1934.
30. Optegnelse om tyske Historikeres Stilling til Hitlerregimentet, efter Indtryk under Historikerkongressen i Warschau August 1933. Friis papers, II, 8 b.
31. K. Brandi, "Vertraulicher Bericht über das Comité International des Sciences Historiques und über die Tätigkeit der deutschen Delegation auf dem VII. Internationalen Historikerkongreß zu Warschau und Krakau, 21.–29. August 1933," Zentrales Staatsarchiv, Merseburg, Rep. V c, Sect. 1, Tit. 11, Teil VI, no. 13, vol. 3.
32. Brandi, "Aus 77 Jahren," typescript, Brandi family, p. 173f. Complete text of Kahrstedt's speech in *Göttinger Tageblatt*, 19 Jan. 1934; see also W. Petke, "Karl Brandi und die Geschichtswissenschaft," in H. Boockmann and H. Wellenreuther, eds., *Geschichtswissenschaft in Göttingen* (Göttingen, 1987), pp. 287–320; C. Wegeler, "Wir sagen ab der internationalen Gelehrtenrepublik" (Vienna, 1996), pp. 147–162 [revised ed. of Ph.D. diss., University of Vienna, 1985].
33. Koht to Lhéritier, 23 March 1931, and Leland to Lhéritier, 6 April 1931, Archives CISH, dossier 1931. Text of the memorandum: "La Discussion au Congrès de la Kriegsschuldfrage," n.d., ibid.
34. "Accord franco-allemand pour les manuels d'histoire," in ICHS, *Bulletin* 9 (1937): 405–408, and vol. 10 (1938): 142–144, 738f. By contrast, the German-Polish deliberations on history textbooks from 1936 to 1938, suggested by the Poles following the German-Polish non-aggression treaty of 1934, led to no result. They were successfully resumed in the late 1970s.
35. Friis to Leland, 5 Sep. 1933, Friis papers I, 1. The Austrian government paid no travel subsidies. Some Austrian historians, to whom Germany had offered subsidies, felt unable to accept them. Steinacker to Brandi, 7 Aug. 1933, Brandi papers, 44.
36. Bittner (director of the Austrian Haus-, Hof- und Staatsarchiv and secretary of the ICHS Commission for the list of diplomats) to Lhéritier, 17 July 1931, Archives CISH, dossier 1931.
37. Lukin to Lhéritier, 30 April 1930, Archives CISH, dossier 1930.
38. "Projet d'une commission pour l'histoire des mouvements sociaux," ICHS, *Bulletin* 3: 249f.
39. ICHS, *Bulletin* 5: 901.
40. "VIIe Congrès International des Sciences Historiques: Rapports présentés au Congrès de Varsovie," ICHS, *Bulletin* 5 [hereafter Congress Warsaw 1933: "Rapports"]; *VIIe Congrès International des Sciences Historiques: Résumés des Communications présentées au Congrès, Varsovie 1933*, ed. for the Organizing Committee by T. Manteuffel, 2 vols. (Warsaw, 1933) [hereafter Congress Warsaw 1933: *Communications*]; *La Pologne au VIIe Congrès International des Sciences Historiques, Varsovie 1933*, ed. for the Société Polonaise d'Histoire by O. Halecki, 3 vols. (Warsaw/Lvov, 1933) [hereafter Congress Warsaw 1933: *La Pologne*]; "Procès-Verbal du Septième Congrès International des Sciences Historiques, Varsovie 1933," ICHS, *Bulletin* 8: 361ff. [hereafter Congress Warsaw 1933: "Procès-Verbal"].
41. Handelsman to Dembiński, 12 Feb. 1930, Handelsman papers, t. 249.
42. Ganshof, Assemblée Générale London, 2 May 1930, ICHS, *Bulletin* 3: 198; Ganshof to Lhéritier, 4 Dec. 1931, Archives CISH, dossier 1931.
43. Both in Assemblée Générale London, 2 May 1930, ICHS, *Bulletin* 3: 197.
44. Report by Handelsman with a statistical appendix, Assemblée Générale Paris 1934, ICHS, *Bulletin* 7: 136ff.
45. See the report in ICHS, *Bulletin* 8: 580.
46. Congress Warsaw 1933: "Procès-Verbal," p. 371.
47. Congress Warsaw 1933: *Communications*, vol. 2, pp. 197ff.

48. Some Polish conference reports concerning this: Ks. St. Bednarski, "VII Miedzynarodowy Kongres Nauk Historycznych" [VIIth International Congress of Historical Sciences], *Przegląd Powszechny* 190 (1933); K. Tymieniecki, "VII Miedzynarodowy kongres historyczny" [VIIth International Historical Congress], *Roczniki Historyczne* 9 (1933).
49. See ICHS, *Catalogus mapparum geographicarum ad historiam pertinentium Varsoviae 1933 expositarum*, (The Hague, 1934).
50. O. Halecki, "La Pologne et la question d'Orient de Casimir le Grand à Jean Sobieski," in Congress Warsaw 1933, *La Pologne*, vol. 1; B. Dembiński, "Stanislas-Auguste et ses relations intellectuelles avec l'étranger," ibid.; M. Handelsman, "Le Prince Czartoryski et la Roumanie 1834–1850," ibid., vol. 2.
51. Congress Warsaw 1933: *Communications*, vol. 2, p. 270.
52. Ibid., pp. 453–472.
53. Congress Warsaw 1933: "Procès-Verbal," p. 578f.
54. G. S. Zaidel, "Bakounine et Marx à l'époque de la Révolution de 1848"; N. Lukin, "L'Internationale et la Commune de Paris"; S. M. Dubrovsky, "Die Bauernbewegung in der Revolution der Jahre 1905 bis 1907," in Congress Warsaw 1933: "Rapports," pp. 645–684.
55. Ibid., pp. 153ff.; discussion in Congress Warsaw 1933: "Procès-Verbal," p. 451f.
56. É. Lousse, "La formation des États dans la société européenne du moyen-âge et l'apparition des assemblées d'États: Questions de faits et de méthodes," in Congress Warsaw 1933: "Rapports," p. 85f.; discussion in Congress Warsaw 1933: "Procès-Verbal," pp. 431ff.; on the history of the commission, see ICHS, *Bulletin* 8: 595, and ICHS, *Bulletin d'information, no* 11: 96ff.
57. Congress Warsaw 1933: "Procès-Verbal," p. 366.
58. Congress Warsaw 1933: *Communications*, vol. 2, pp. 168ff.
59. Ibid., pp. 166–168.
60. Congress Warsaw 1933: "Procès-Verbal," p. 494.
61. Congress Warsaw 1933: "Procès-Verbal," p. 496f.
62. V. P. Volgin, "De Babeuf à Marx," in Congress Warsaw 1933: *Communications*, vol. 2, p. 406.
63. *Revue de synthèse* 3 (1933): 202.
64. Thus Bednarski, "VII Miedzynarodowy Kongres."
65. Congress Warsaw 1933: *Communications*, vol. 2, p. 165f. Lunacharsky's paper, "La méthode du matérialisme historique dans l'histoire de la littérature," in Congress Warsaw 1933: "Rapports," pp. 388ff.
66. Congress Warsaw 1933: "Rapports," pp. 430ff.
67. Ibid., p. 442, quoted from E. Troeltsch, *Über den historischen Entwicklungsbegriff und die Universalgeschichte. Gesammelte Schriften* vol. 3 (1st ed. 1922, new ed. Aalen, 1961), p. 349f.
68. ICHS, *Bulletin* 4: 410f.
69. See St. Hajnal, "Über die Arbeitsgemeinschaft der Geschichtsschreibung kleiner Nationen," in I. Lukinich, ed., *Archivum Europae Centro-Orientalis*, vol. 9/10 (Budapest, 1943/44), pp. 1–82.
70. See chapter 7, note 83; chapter 9, note 6; this chapter, note 40.
71. I. Lukinich, *Les éditions des sources de l'histoire hongroise, 1854–1930* (Budapest, 1931). On this and further efforts to disseminate information on Hungarian historiography, and on the problems of an isolated language in general, see the foreword by Domokos Kosáry in *Études historiques hongroises publiées à l'occasion du XVIe Congrès International des Sciences Historiques* (Budapest, 1985).
72. See M. Handelsman, "Les organisations internationales dans le domaine des sciences historiques," in *La Pologne Littéraire*, 15 Aug. 1933 (Warsaw).

Chapter 11

IN THE SHADOW OF CRISIS
Zurich, 1938

In the five years between Warsaw and Zurich, the development of world politics did not at all correspond with the reconciliation invoked at the International Historical Congresses. In 1935, Italy invaded Abyssinia. In 1936, a three-year civil war broke out in Spain. In 1937, the incident on the Marco Polo Bridge unleashed the Sino-Japanese War. In 1938, following the *Anschluß* of Austria to the German Reich in March, Hitler ordered the *Wehrmacht* on 30 May to start preparations for the crushing of Czechoslovakia, and in the autumn, the struggle for the Sudetenland reached its climax. Hitler's pretext was that Germany demanded the implementation of the principle of national self-determination that had been denied to the German-speaking border area of Bohemia-Moravia in 1919. In reality, however, he intended to gain strategic bases for his geopolitical aims in Eastern Europe. On 27 August 1938, one day before the opening of the Zurich Historical Congress, the chief of the German General Staff, Major General Beck, resigned out of protest against these military plans. All indicators pointed to war. Against this background, the historians attempted to hold a Congress that should once again be a forum for understanding and reconciliation, even though the enthusiasm of Geneva, Göttingen, and Oslo had long since evaporated.

A new Bureau was elected in Warsaw. Halvdan Koht was replaced as president by Harold Temperley (Cambridge), one of the leading European historians in the field of foreign policy. Through him, British historiography, which had so far remained more or less in the background at the Congresses, reasserted itself. After he had acquainted himself with his duties and the general state of affairs, Temperley avowed that he was impressed by the results achieved so far, and "which I, at least, had hitherto but incompletely realized."[1] He sought his specific task in an intensive effort to transcend the ICHS's limited European-American horizon. On a journey to Japan, China, and India he tried to recruit Asian historians for participation in the work of the ICHS. He reported to the

---

Notes for this chapter begin on page 176.

Bureau that he encountered great willingness, but saw the difficulties as well. What advantages could non-European members expect from cooperating in an international organization "whose main interest is and remains European?" He called upon the Bureau's members to give serious thought to developing forms of cooperation that could also satisfy non-European interests—"otherwise the enthusiasm evident in China and India today will simply die away."[2] He committed himself to creating a Commission for East-Asian History in which Dutch India, French Indochina, and Portuguese Goa should work along with Japan, China, and India. He also recommended the establishment of a national committee for Palestine, which should apply for membership at the coming Congress.[3] It was the emigration of Jewish professors from Germany that induced him to make this suggestion. In Zurich, however, he saw no chances of realizing it in the face of intensifying persecution of Jews in Germany,[4] virulent anti-Semitism in Poland (which even a scholar like Handelsman felt threatened by[5]), and the new anti-Jewish racial laws in Italy.

As vice-presidents, a Pole and a German were placed at Temperley's side—Bronisław Dembiński and Karl Brandi—a well-considered gesture meant to demonstrate that scholarly cooperation was possible independently of national conflicts. The Swiss historian Hans Nabholz assumed Waldo Leland's office of treasurer. As a result, the official seat of the ICHS was temporarily moved from Washington, D.C., to Zurich. The transfer of financial management from the United States to Europe also indicated that in the near future the Europeans would have to take greater responsibility for financing the ICHS and its activities. Along with membership fees, support from American donors continued to represent the lion's share of its income. But the annual payments were declining, and the partial devaluation of the dollar aggravated the situation.[6] Nevertheless, the ICHS retained its financial mobility. It remained in a position to support the various special commissions created by or affiliated to it through modest contributions. No fewer than twelve "internal" and thirteen "external" commissions presented their reports at the General Assembly in Zurich in 1938, and five others were acknowledged.[7] Through some of these commissions, or with their assistance, the ICHS was able to release a series of publications up to the eve of the Second World War.[8] Another sign of the ICHS's vitality was its further growth. In Zurich, China and—at Cardinal Tisserand's instigation—Vatican City joined the organization, as did Ireland. It is remarkable that Ireland acquired membership as a cultural unity, i.e., with a joint representation of historians from both parts of the politically divided country.

Thus, the ICHS remained true to its ecumenical ideals against the currents of the time. This self-assertion was certainly not free of inner tensions that more than once endangered its survival. Individual members made threatening gestures of a national or ideological kind. For example, Nicolae Iorga, the undisputed head of the Romanian historians, announced that he would lay down his chairmanship in the national committee, which would likely have led to Romania's withdrawal from the ICHS, if the General Assembly of 1936 were not held in Bucharest. But invitations had also been issued by Prague and Moscow, and the members of the ICHS had decided on Prague by a large majority. Iorga felt deeply wounded in his image of himself. He was one of those outstanding historians who were committed to their national contexts and at the same time, through their scholarly development, research, and academic lecture activity, also had particularly strong international connections. He had cooperated early on with Lamprecht's Institute for Cultural and Universal History in Leipzig, he delivered regular lectures in Paris, and he was closely connected with Italian research and international Byzantine studies through the Romanian Research Institute in Venice, which he had founded. Since 1910, he had been actively involved in the politics of his country as the founder of the National Democratic Party, and from 1931 to 1932 he rose to the office of Prime Minister. He expected that a General Assembly of the ICHS in Bucharest would give the national importance of both Romania and the historian Iorga visible international recognition.

Iorga did not only have friends, though. Among those who took a skeptical view of him were Koht, Friis, Temperley, and Domanovszky, who, as the most representative historian of Hungary, was at that time a member of the Bureau. Their misgivings were confirmed by unusual behavior on Iorga's part. Through diplomatic channels, he moved the Czech government and the Czech national committee to withdraw the invitation to Prague in favor of Romania. But the Czech renunciation was formulated in such an embarrassed way that the president and the secretary-general of the ICHS felt compelled to bring about a decision by the members. Lhéritier, though he did not approve of Iorga's actions, leaned toward the Romanian side. To be on the safe side, he contacted the French national committee. In a letter to its president, Coville, he wrote: "Of course, this is all a mistake on the part of Monsieur Iorga, who severely intervened with the Czechs without informing us, with the intention of presenting us with a *fait accompli*. However, since I have always endeavored to defend French interests both in this matter and generally—although some of my countrymen persistently insist on calling my work in the international secretariat 'foreign service'—I would like to know to what extent, in your opinion, I should engage myself for Monsieur Iorga's sake."[9] Lhéritier's conduct led to profound discord between him and Temperley. Iorga issued threats. A refusal to assemble in Bucharest would lead to a situation "where Romania, more than once despised and neglected, will withdraw from the International Committee of Historical Sciences. I shall propose such a decision to our [national] committee in a few days, and if the majority holds a different opinion, then I shall request my replacement [as chairman]."[10] But it never went this far. A renewed, clear renunciation on the part of the Czechs, Lhéritier's zeal, and a survey among the Bureau's members led to Iorga having his way. In April 1936 a General Assembly was held in the Romanian capital.

On another occasion, a resignation threat came from Italy. In April 1935 Fedele, the president of the Fascist Giunta Centrale per gli Studi Storici, announced that some Italian members of the international commissions affiliated to the ICHS were to be withdrawn and replaced by others. This unleashed a discussion within the ICHS as to whether such outside interventions in the scientific work of the commissions were permissible.[11] A written enquiry on the Italian request was conducted, and most members joined Nabholz in his view that the commissions' members could be withdrawn only if they themselves had declared their resignations, which in this instance had not been the case. Lhéritier, however, pointed out that the Italian Ussani, who in Warsaw had assumed De Sanctis's seat in the Bureau, had expressed the threat that the cooperation of his country might be terminated. The *Giunta,* as he said, demanded that only historians enjoying its confidence should be allowed to cooperate in the ICHS in the name of Italy. The question was suspended, and remained undecided in principle at subsequent meetings of the Bureau and the General Assembly, probably because Ussani resigned from the Bureau in 1936 for other reasons. His successor in the Bureau was Volpe, who was particularly committed to enhancing the traditionally strong position of Italy in the ICHS. The Soviet Union had often shifted members in and out of the international commissions without unleashing a fundamental discussion. The development was irreversible. To the degree to which the participation of scholars in international bodies became the affair of governments—i.e., to the degree that a free national committee became a state-guided *Giunta* after the Italian model—the autonomy of international scholarly cooperation came under pressure.

This was also evidenced by what occurred in the commission responsible for assembling the *International Bibliography*. In 1937, when the volume for the year 1935 was ready to go to press, the Soviet correspondent of the commission, the Academy member Lukin, demanded that no fewer than 83 titles be withdrawn from the 354 Soviet entries, to be replaced by 110 new ones. Caron, the secretary responsible for editing the bibliography, replied: "I will not conceal the fact that I am irritated by the vacillating, hesitating style of your participation. Why does this work and that article, which were considered worthy of inclusion six months ago, suddenly stop being so? Why shall essays that have appeared in the journal directed by yourself be no longer cited? This leads me to the suspicion that non-scholarly reasons are involved."[12] In response he first received a threatening telegram from the Academy secretary Deborin, stating that the Soviet side would stop cooperation in the *Bibliography*. This was followed by a written statement with a more detailed explanation: "We consider ourselves justified in undertaking corrections in the book lists in cases where an author, who has been selected and named, loses the right to be recommended as an historian of the USSR.… When we checked the lists for the year 1936 we noticed that Soviet historians are expected to be listed side by side with the name—not of an historian—but of a criminal person, the fascist Trotsky, who is contemptible and hateful."[13] Of course, there was no break, although during these years the actual participation of Soviet historians was reduced to a nearly imperceptible minimum on account of the events in Russia. The mutual interest in continuing the cooperation was great, as difficult as it may have been at times. However, in order to prevent the worst manifestations of political and pseudo-scientific pamphlet literature of Soviet, Fascist, or National Socialist origin, with Temperley's backing no further chapters about the literature on the period after 1919 were adopted in the following volumes.[14]

All of these difficulties were insignificant compared to the acute threat to freedom and scholarship issuing from Germany. Those eminent members of the International Committee who had committed themselves to overcoming old enmities were now all the more concerned. Disappointment and horror are reflected in the correspondence of Koht, Leland, and Friis. "What is currently taking place in Germany," Friis wrote to Leland in view of the persecution of the Jews, "is, in its injustice, unbelievable maliciousness; in its hypocrisy without parallel in the history of civilized humanity. And we are all powerless, particularly we Danes, who have this bestiality directly at our door. But we must fearlessly do what little we can in individual cases."[15] Both endeavored to find employment opportunities for persecuted Jewish colleagues abroad. At the request of several German colleagues, Friis interceded particularly on behalf of Hans Rothfels, who had still been allowed to participate in Warsaw.[16] But they all still wanted to avoid a break.

Since De Sanctis had fallen victim to his refusal to swear the Fascist oath, the ICHS had made it a rule to avoid direct interventions, arguing that they were doomed to failure from the start and would do the affected persons more harm than good. A helpless feeling of ineffectiveness was expressed in a letter from Nabholz, moved by the fate of the Cracow professor Stanisław Kot, who had delivered a paper at the Warsaw Congress. Kot had been dismissed for "political reasons," as Nabholz assumed. "The example of Germany seems to become more and more usual," he wrote. And he added: "I do not see how we can help him. We cannot interfere in Poland's internal affairs." The only possibility he saw was to assist Kot personally by perhaps supplying him with a position at a university outside Poland.[17] An appeal for assistance in favor of the Kiev historian Hrushevsky, who had been registered as a member of the Soviet delegation in Oslo but was not allowed to participate, went unheard. A Ukrainian committee in London requested an intervention on his behalf.[18] Hrushevsky, they said, had been dismissed and deported. Old and blind, he now lived in Moscow, ill of health and in the most abject poverty. Here, too, the ICHS showed no reaction.

It seems that there was only one case where a direct intervention was brought about, not by the Bureau itself but by its members, who appealed to the Austrian chancellor Schuschnigg on behalf of Alfons Dopsch. The government had been planning to retire him prematurely in early 1935. The reasons for this are not entirely transparent. The financial difficulties of the country and Dopsch's age— he was sixty-eight at the time—as well as academic rivalries may have played a role. It seems likely that his political attitude, too, annoyed the Austro-Fascist regime. Dopsch was committed to forming a Pan-German study commission within the framework of an institutionalization of regional research suggested by Temperley. The latter referred to him with palpable distaste as "großdeutsch."[19] Nevertheless, the members of the Bureau, who certainly were not to be suspected of Pan-German sympathies, gave him their support for scholarly reasons, and they were successful, though only for a short time.[20]

Since the ICHS saw no way of providing effective help in such cases, it was left only with the option of emphasizing the principle of freedom of scholarship as the vital element for the ecumenical community of historians, and of preserving the International Congresses as a free and open forum as long as the circumstances of the time allowed.

Despite the difficult circumstances, this was still the case in Zurich. Two seemingly contradictory lessons were derived from the experience at Warsaw concerning the establishment of the program. On the one hand, international responsibility was expanded. An organizing committee was formed in which, alongside the host country, all the countries that had hosted one of the seven previous Congresses were represented.[21] On the other hand, the question Ganshof raised in this body, namely, "who should select the topics and the speakers," led to the decision that this was to be the responsibility of Nabholz as the chairman of the Swiss national organizing committee.[22] These two decisions amounted to excluding the secretary-general from the preparation of the program. His reaction was correspondingly piqued.

With regard to the structure of the Congress, the essential difference between Zurich and Warsaw lay in the fact that the distinction between "reports" and "communications" was removed. Ganshof regarded the published *rapports* from the Warsaw Congress as nothing more than a worthless heap of rubbish. One could have spared the Poles the printing costs, he said.[23] Such a verdict against the disliked Lhéritier was unjust, and yet it met with approval insofar as the organizing committee now unanimously adopted Nabholz's suggestion to subdivide the contributions in a different way: "Morning lectures of general interest, *discorsi* or *Vorträge*, and afternoon communications, *communicazioni* or *Mitteilungen*."[24] It was agreed that the extensive lectures giving an individual historian full opportunity to present himself as a researcher and speaker should determine the Congress's image, and that such lectures should be gathered into thematic groups. They also should be limited in number. All this was placed under Nabholz's responsibility. How did he proceed? How far-reaching was his authority?

At first, the national committees were asked to submit suggestions within a preselected catalog of sections. Out of these, a list of major themes was assembled and passed on via a circular letter. Those who wanted to deliver "lectures" or "communications" had to apply for admission of their topics via their respective national committees, which were envisaged as a sort of sieve. Of course, the number of applications was greater than the number of contributions that could be considered. This is where difficulties surfaced. It was already problematic enough to assign certain quotas to the different countries; reducing the overflowing number of applications in negotiation with the respective national committees demanded as much firmness as tact. In the final result, the number of contributions was higher than planned, but nevertheless lower than at the two previous Congresses organized by the ICHS: 248 in Zurich in contrast to 286 in Warsaw and 307 in Oslo.[25]

However, no thematic or even qualitative selection took place under Nabholz's direction. Instead, the ball was played back to the national committees. They were entitled "finally to determine their countries' program."[26] But whether a contribution would be scheduled among the long "morning lectures" or the shorter "communications" at the afternoon sessions remained the decision of the Swiss.[27] Thus, at this Congress, too, events were to a large degree determined by chance. It became clear that this procedure, which concentrated the competence for the organization of the program on one person, could not be the final solution. But it was certainly to the Congress's benefit that the Swiss placed so much emphasis on the major lectures of the morning sessions. They were particularly convincing when it was possible to connect several contributions on the same problem. For example, the professional journals heaped praise on a morning session of the medieval section, where the Frenchman Louis Halphen, the Italian Raffaello Morghen and the German Robert Holtzmann discussed the conceptions of empire and rulership of the Holy German emperors.[28]

Equally remarkable was the great attention turned to research on diplomatic history. Perhaps this interest reflected the tense international situation on the eve of the Second World War. Various themes from the prehistory of the First World War were discussed. Such outstanding experts as Renouvin, Webster, Temperley, and Friis participated.

The program contained many topics dealing with the nation. This issue proved to be of undiminished significance, particularly for Europe's smaller states. Thus, there were lectures on Bulgaria, Hungary, Greece, Finland, Belgium, and Luxembourg. Marceli Handelsman's presentation on the "Renationalization of Silesia in the 19th Century" unleashed a controversial discussion.[29] A lecture by Alexander Domanovszky on "The Hungarian Nation-State in the Middle Ages" once again ignited the old Hungarian-Romanian quarrel over the history of the Danube-Carpathian region.[30] The history of Switzerland—a federal state encompassing several languages and nationalities—naturally took an appropriately large position at the Congress with many references to great Swiss historians such as Jacob Burckhardt. However, the tactful organizers did not push Switzerland's national history into the foreground.

Armando Sapori (Florence), who was one of the pioneers of the new social and economic history, presented an exemplary report on the results of his research on the history of trade in the late Middle Ages in a convincing confrontation with Sombart's theses on the late beginnings of modern capitalism.[31] In this endeavor he was strongly supported by the Hanse researcher Fritz Rörig (Berlin).[32] There was also a spirited and controversial discussion in the section for ancient history, where the issue was the perennial question of the decline of the Roman Empire.[33]

Yet the Zurich Congress fell short of its two predecessors in the absence of Soviet historians. It is difficult to make out exactly why they did not attend. At that time there were no diplomatic relations between the two countries.[34] In the Soviet Union the Stalinist purges, which also affected the historical profession, were not yet at an end. Financial questions and the exchange rate may also have played a role. The salutary mutual challenge of "bourgeois" and Soviet-Marxist historiography that had begun in Oslo was interrupted.

The absence of Soviet historians was particularly regretted by the German émigré press, which turned it into one point of its criticism of the Zurich Congress.[35] Despite good and solid performance in individual cases, it was said, the Congress had lacked an essential element; for if one could expect historiography to contribute to our understanding of the world we live in, then the Zurich Congress had failed precisely in this endeavor, by the absence of the Soviet Union as well as by the lack of concern with contemporary history. For pragmatic or political reasons it may have appeared expedient or even necessary to avoid including post-1914 history in the Congress's work. The experiences of the *Bibliography* commission served as a warning. Ganshof was right when he explained this *terminus ad quem* as follows: "One must avoid like the plague everything that even from a distance could appear as a national demonstration or an act of political or social propaganda."[36] Nevertheless, a certain unease remained.

What was offered by Italian and German historians in Zurich was partially burdened by the ideologies that held sway in both countries. Giovanni Gentile, who had once been a friend of Benedetto Croce, spoke in pathetic words of the right of the nation that was realized through struggle and death.[37] An insignificant historian of literature from Berlin called Koch was equally unpersuasive. In a lecture on "The Organicistic Worldview in German Poetry," he celebrated a completely distorted Herder as the father of biological thinking and highlighted Kolbenheyer as one of the greatest contemporary writers, while not even mentioning Thomas Mann, who at that time lived in exile and embodied the Other Germany.[38]

The Italians appeared with a broad range of "lectures" and "communications" that demonstrated that Italian historiography continued to work in a methodologically flexible and productive manner in both old and new thematic areas. The mere fact that a person had sworn the Fascist oath in no way meant that he did not remain committed to historical truth or that he did not know how to prevent his statements from sliding into ideological confessions and heroic bombast in front of the skeptical international audience. Thus, Italian historiography, in spite of everything, maintained a leading position in Europe.

The number of German contributions was considerably small, in spite of the relative high number of participants.[39] The reason for this lay in severe inner conflicts within the German historical profession.[40] Soon after the Warsaw

Congress, Karl Brandi and his colleagues, who had represented the German historians there, were exposed to the most disgraceful abuse. For two years a general attack was launched against the "clique of dignitaries" (*Geheimratsclique*), i.e., against those conservative, liberal, or democratic professors who until then had been responsible for international cooperation within the German historical discipline, and who had set the tone in the Historische Reichskommission. Its place was assumed by the Reichsinstitut for History of the New Germany under the direction of Walter Frank, a protégé of Alfred Rosenberg, the Party official responsible for ideological training and the author of the anti-Christian defamatory book on the *Myth of the 20th Century*. The Reichsinstitut was the crystallization point for a "young," ideologically reliable generation of historians who marched behind Walter Frank's banner in order to finally put an end to "bourgeois" historiography, which they had declared dead already. This also affected suspected historians' cooperation in the work of the ICHS. Wilhelm Mommsen, whom the Nazi historians viewed as a notorious democrat, was compelled to lay down his office as secretary in the Commission for the History of the Press, and Fritz Curschmann was withdrawn from the Commission for Historical Geography.

The most spectacular victim—aside from the Jewish and Socialist professors who were forced into exile—was Hermann Oncken, who had coined the inspiring term "spirit of Oslo." He was a pillar of the University of Berlin and co-editor of the leading professional journal *Historische Zeitschrift*. Exposed to the vilest disparagement, he was pushed out of his professorship and the editorial board of the journal. Alongside Friedrich Meinecke, Gerhard Ritter was one of the few who spoke up for him. He demanded that the *Historische Zeitschrift* rehabilitate Oncken, and when this request was not fulfilled, he announced his resignation. Frank tried to prevent Ritter's participation in the Zurich Congress. Indeed, Ritter's application for a lecture was rejected by the Allgemeiner Deutscher Historikerausschuß, which had been in charge of coordinating Germany's Congress participation since Oslo.[41] Yet he was able to attend the Zurich Congress and distinguished himself as a discussion speaker.

This occurred when the Kiel historian Otto Scheel, like Ritter a well-known Reformation scholar, held a lecture on "Luther's Concept of the People" in the section for religious and church history.[42] Scheel placed the political Luther in the foreground, and quoting his words of the "sound hero and performer of miracles," he interpreted the reformer as a revolutionary with a divine calling who also had the right to shatter the existing legal order and create a new order of the people. The reference to the present conditions was more than obvious. In the discussion, Ritter refuted this interpretation. Luther, he said, could only be understood on the basis of his religious message. Luther knew nothing of any exceptional rights of the heroic individual. His national attitude was limited by a rigid criticism of the nation from a religious point of view that rejected all human self-aggrandizement, and his patriotism was just as much colored by universalism as the patriotism of any other German in the sixteenth century, including the humanists.

The controversy, conducted in a genteel manner, attracted considerable attention, and not only in a negative way. The most remarkable aspect of this dispute was that, upon the open stage of the Congress, an obviously pro-regime German historian was contradicted by another German. For tactical reasons and in order to protect Ritter, Karl Brandi—who after considerable hesitations had once again been appointed head of the German delegation because of his international reputation and his Congress experience—, emphasized in his report on the Congress that the possibility of such free and open discussion among German historians had made a favorable impression on the foreign participants.[43] He did so to Frank's great displeasure. Both Frank and the crew of young Nazi historians he brought with him scarcely attracted any attention at the Congress. Aside from Koch's literary lecture, only two other lectures are worth mentioning, namely, those by Ernst Anrich and Adolf Rein, which dealt with Bismarck, the founder of the Reich and the initiator of German colonial policy, in a manner typical of the spirit of the times. Both received virtually no consideration. Frank reacted all the more angrily to Gerhard Ritter, whom he accused of a "behavior damaging to the Reich" in a petition to the ministry of education. Ritter's contribution in Zurich had been an "insolent demonstration" of "a Confessing Church-oriented [bekenntniskirchlich] opposition going hand in hand with political liberalism."[44] Brandi, too, was inculpated. He had not made the slightest effort, Frank said, to point out to Ritter "his scandalous behavior." On Frank's instigation, Ritter was forced to renounce further lecture trips abroad after Zurich, although there was no shortage of invitations.

Aside from the Ritter-Scheel controversy, there was another paper at the Zurich Congress that led to a confrontation among Germans. George W. F. Hallgarten, who was living in American exile and who had made a private application to Nabholz for admission to the Congress, delivered a lecture on "The Relationship between Banking and Industrial Capital in German Foreign Policy During the Wilhelminean Era." It was one of the most interesting presentations to be held at the Congress, with regard to methodological questions. Instead of the usual diplomatic historical treatment of foreign policy events, he had analyzed the impact of economic factors, of financial and industrial capital. He had taken the manuscript book of these studies into exile and entrusted it for safekeeping to Pierre Renouvin, the director of the Museum of the World War in Vincennes and secretary of the French national committee.[45] When this book was published soon after the war,[46] its method and assertions promoted lively discussions. Hallgarten's lecture in Zurich had already had the same effect.[47] Hans Mayer (Geneva) regarded it as a "significant attempt at socioeconomic historiography" that continued what had been initiated by the French school and particularly Henri Hauser, who in Zurich also dealt with the interrelation between politics and economics.[48] Hallgarten's assessment of the origins of economic imperialism met with agreement from Veit Valentin, who had emigrated from Germany to London, but it encountered passionate opposition from another German émigré, Georg Solmssen, the former president of the Central Association of German Banking Houses (Centralverband deutscher Banken), who was now living in Switzerland.

Hallgarten's lecture and the discussion about it were concerned with the deeper causes of the politics leading to the First World War, and referred to different methods of historical research: socioeconomic analysis confronting or completing the analysis of individual motivations and actions. Was the existence of such divergent views of history and methodology, which had become apparent also in other papers at the Zurich Congress, evidence of a crisis of historical studies? Henri Berr did not think so. He preferred to speak of a "transformation," of a search for a new path leading from history as novelistic depiction and erudite knowledge of facts, which he regarded as only a preliminary stage, to history as a science. If there was a crisis, he said, then it consisted in the penetration of history by political tendencies, in a pragmatism that put a politically guided interpretation on historical facts. However, history as a "science" must retain its "explanatory" character and develop it further: "L'histoire doit être explicative."[49] But what does "explain" mean? For Berr, as he had often stated, it was not to assign events to the operation of general laws after the model of the natural sciences. For the historians of the *Annales*, the answer lay in a well-reflected and precise application of the comparative method as it had been demonstrated by Marc Bloch at the Oslo Congress.

Nicolae Iorga provided his own answer to the problem of history as a science. In Zurich he spoke on "Les permanences de l'histoire" (permanent factors in history).[50] His work, which is permeated by a romantic notion of development, has been assessed as a prefiguration of the methodological experiences of the *Annales*.[51] At Berr's request, Iorga had written contributions to his journal for years. Both agreed that "synthesis" was the goal of all historical research. The national pedagogue of the Romanian people, who could not see his people's individuality in any other way than as integrated into the context of Southeastern European history and of European history in general, had delivered lectures and communications at all International Historical Congresses since London in 1913. His complete work can be described as the search for a synthesis encompassing national and universal history. A brief retrospective on his earlier contributions to the Congresses reveals characteristic traits of his historical thought. At London, he presented the provocative thesis that previous medieval studies had generally come to a wrong understanding of the Middle Ages. They projected a nation-state perspective back onto an entirely different period and had thus been unable to comprehend its specific character. Iorga saw the Middle Ages as a pre-national phenomenon formed by the continuing influence of the idea of imperial Rome and—as he emphasized particularly—of its most impressive embodiment in Byzantium. It was his goal to develop a new conception of universal history, which would raise the East and Southeast of Europe to their due position on the same level as Western Europe.

No one viewed Eastern and Western European history more persistently as an interacting unity than Iorga. That was his special topic in Oslo. In counterpoint to this universal topic, he dealt with the history of *Romania* (peoples of East Romanic languages and culture) in Southeastern Europe, particularly in the Danube-Carpathian region. Wherever written records were lacking, he fell back on folk art as a historical source, breaking new methodological ground in his lecture at Brussels. As the master student of Xenopol, who had impressively represented the rising Romanian historical profession at the inception of the International Historical Congresses, he also continued the latter's studies on the Daco-Romanic roots of Romanian history. For him the nation, particularly in Southeastern Europe, was a late phenomenon. This was the issue of his lecture in Warsaw. The nation was not a characteristic component of medieval history, he said. Its appearance, which he defined as the emergence of the awareness of a distinct historical identity, marked the end of the Middle Ages, which was characterized essentially by universal ideas. Though he identified so strongly with his own nation, Iorga coined a skeptical phrase about the relationship between nation-building and loss of civilization in Warsaw: "C'est un peu en se barbarisant qu'on se nationalise" (One turns somewhat barbaric once one is nationalizing).

This reservation about the concept of nation may explain a certain observable distance between him and some of those who still believed in an unbroken harmony of nationalism and cosmopolitanism. Another reason for this may have been that his attempt at a universal synthesis of history was received with distinct coolness by the scholarly world at the end of the 1920s.[52] Despite personal compliments, his lecture on factors of long duration in history, which he delivered in Zurich in a session presided over by Berr, received rather critical comments. Iorga listed three elements of long duration: geographical conditions, race, ideas.[53] These terms, which Iorga used with self-confident nonchalance, could not help but appear extremely suspect to his listeners on account of the political misuse they were being subjected to by others. Their objections were not alleviated by the fact that Iorga endeavored to explain his terms in such a way that they were set off from contemporary distortions. Space: the oscillation of his notion between compulsions and temptations emanating from geographical regions—interpreted as neutral environment, climate, soil, natural preconditions of extension or isolation, *"terra mater"*—recalled to some extent Montesquieu's thought, but his conception also approached the geopolitical thought of the Sweden Kjellén and the German Haushofer. Race: for Iorga it was a product of the environment and was thus subject to transformations. He spoke clearly against contemporary racism: "Nowadays people speak a great deal about race and racism; a certain kind of politics wants it that way. But in fact, there is no race that is crystallized once and for all and that one would have to defend against infiltrations." Idea: clearly discarding historical materialism, he defined ideas as "states of mind that dominate everything. In them, which have more than once forced a nation to proceed against its own interests, even toward its own destruction ... lies the driving force of every historical movement." As the crowning achievement of his life, Iorga imagined a comprehensive survey of history, a "historiology," as he called it. But his planned four-volume work remained a fragment. A murderous attack by members of the Romanian Iron Guard put an end to the life of this hated opponent of the fascists on 27 November 1940.

For Iorga, the will and the capacity to create a historical synthesis was a matter of courage, personal responsibility, broad education, and human stature. Only those historians who took full part in the cultural and political life of their people could be called upon to interpret history. The activity of the historian was related to art and literature and was thus necessarily subjective. Whenever a historian shied away from taking such responsibility or proved incapable of assuming it, Iorga spoke scornfully of "objectivity as an excuse," an objectivity that was nothing more than "the impotence to be subjective."[54] This was the quintessence of the self-understanding of a historian who possessed a firm foundation in stupendous erudition. Ranke was among Iorga's favorite authors. At the last International Historical Congress before the Second World War, he embodied a historicism grown from old idealistic roots.

The participants of the Zurich Congress, however, were not primarily moved by questions of historical methodology or theory. The Sudetenland crisis, which was approaching its climax, hung heavily in the air. Although contemporary issues had been excluded from the program, a political undertone could be found in numerous historical papers, such as those by Gentile and Koch, Scheel and Ritter, Hallgarten, and Iorga. The political tensions endangered what many saw as the most important aspect of the Congresses, namely, the readiness to engage in an open exchange of ideas among historians of different languages, nations, and political convictions. This particularly applied to the relationship between "fascist" historians—although by no means did all German and Italian historians fall into this category—and their colleagues from the democratic countries. A report from the *Pariser Tageszeitung*, a German émigré journal, exposed the scene to sharp criticism:

> The Germans, "historicizing Stormtroopers," were kept apart from the other participants at the social events merely by their obvious lack of language skills as if by an empty space, just as all the delegations, except for those from unambiguously democratic countries, faced each other with mistrust. Hitler and Fascist salutes were gestures with which each Congress guest became well acquainted, and the scholarly lectures by the numerous gentlemen with the Lictor bundle in their buttonholes sounded like gramophone records from the Palazzo Venezia—sometimes even in phonetic terms. All in all, the Congress was a clear symptom of the decline of scholarship and of its stagnation even in non-fascist countries under the influence of the neo-fascist barbarity.[55]

How difficult individual communication across the political trenches had again become was depicted by a member of the Swiss organizing committee almost four decades later:

After the Congress had begun, we noticed how little the historians from the various national camps socialized with one another, how frostily they faced each other. We Swiss, conscious of our duty to negotiate, attempted constantly to establish contacts, but with little success. Most of the lectures by the Germans were only attended by their fellow countrymen and political friends, and the same unfortunate spectacle repeated itself in the presentations by the representatives of other nations as well as in the social events organized by them. On one evening I was sitting with the Frenchman Pierre Renouvin, whom I knew from my student days in Paris, and with the Austrian Heinrich von Srbik, who had once visited me on his return trip from Geneva (he was a member of the Committee of Intellectual Cooperation of the League of Nations). I introduced them to each other, whereupon they extended their hands with demonstrative reserve. But I did not succeed in starting a conversation between the two colleagues who would have had so much to say to each other. Renouvin explained that he couldn't speak German, and Srbik said he didn't understand French (the biographer of Metternich!). What was the point of coming together at an international conference if people didn't want to talk to one another? The statutes of the International Committee defined the association's purpose as follows: "Travailler au développement des sciences historiques en procédant par voie de coopération internationale" [to strive for development of the historical sciences through international cooperation]. In the sultry and menacing pre-war atmosphere—if I remember correctly—the news of Mussolini's decree against the Jews came as something like a thunderbolt, whereupon a large part of the Italian delegation left the Congress. Throughout this turbulence, Nabholz kept a remarkably cool head; even after the tensest moments I never saw him nervous or tired. That was his great strength. Srbik usually appeared at the events with a train of young German historians, whom we maliciously called his "*Knüppelgarde*" [clubbing guards]. Näf and I had intended to ask him why Meinecke had been dismissed so silently from the editorial board of the *Historische Zeitschrift*. His hesitant answer astounded us: "Well, isn't it true, after all, Meinecke had quite a number of Jewish students." All these experiences left such a bad impression that we—still young—Swiss decided not to attend the next International Congress.[56]

An impression of the underlying tensions that were palpable in Zurich because of events in Germany is conveyed by notes written by Aage Friis during the Congress:

> In order to request my help for Rothfels, I was addressed by: Brandi, Schramm, Rein from Hamburg, Kähler from Göttingen, [Gerhard] Ritter from Heidelberg, and finally Srbik, too. I promised them to help Rothfels in any way, but took the opportunity to express to all of them, in the sharpest words, my profound outrage on the development taken by German culture, which we all regarded with high esteem, in the barbaric treatment of the Jews, which violates all the values of culture and morality. Toward Steinacker, who had nothing to do with Rothfels, I expressed the same opinion in extraordinarily sharp terms and emphasized how doubly shameful it was that such things could occur in view of the complaints that the Germans had made with regard to the oppression of the Germans in South Tyrol. I told both Srbik and Steinacker: Now you have handed hundreds of thousands of Tyroleans to the Italians, and now you let hundreds of thousands of Jews starve to death in Germany

with refined maliciousness, which is worse than when the Bolsheviks kill their enemies straight away at one blow. And this is not occurring in barbaric Eastern Europe, but rather in countries that we view as centers of human culture.[57]

In spite of such dark perspectives, and in spite of all external and internal threats, the Congress managed to go forward in the forms of international politeness, and to maintain a remarkable scientific standard. To this the atmosphere of Zurich and the unpretentious, obliging hospitality of the Swiss contributed much. With a certain amount of contrariness and defying the spirit of the times, the responsible members of the ICHS did not give up their conviction that the act of holding such a Congress as a forum for the free exchange of ideas possessed intrinsic value, particularly in view of the offensiveness of the totalitarian menaces. Waldo Leland, who was elected president in Zurich, ended his closing address with the beseeching wish, accompanied by demonstrative applause, that the ICHS commit itself more than ever before to intellectual freedom and ward off all temptations by those in power to enlist science into their service for whatever economic, political, or social purposes.[58] He reiterated his concerned appeal to "knowledge" and "conscience" a few days later in Geneva, where he presented the public with a memorial inscription that was placed above the entryway to the hall in which, twelve years earlier, in a time of hope, the ICHS had been founded.[59] It would be another twelve years before—following a time of horror even worse than that of the First World War—new attempts to reestablish the international community of historical scholarship could be realized.

Notes

1. Temperley to Leland, 15 Sep. 1933, Archives CISH, dossier 1933.
2. Temperley to members of the Bureau, 12 April 1937, Archives CISH, dossier 1937. On the other hand, D. Kosáry maintained that the chief task of the ICHS lay in Europe, and warned against an endless expansion of themes. See his report on the Zurich Congress in the journal *Századok* (Budapest, 1938).
3. Lhéritier to Koebner (professor in Leipzig until 1933, thereafter in Jerusalem), 18 April 1937, Archives CISH, dossier 1937.
4. Temperley to Lhéritier, 12 March 1938, Archives CISH, dossier 1938.
5. Temperley to Lhéritier, 15 Nov. 1937, Archives CISH, dossier 1937.
6. Leland presented a comprehensive financial report to the General Assembly in Warsaw, where he transferred his office to Nabholz. See ICHS, *Bulletin* 7 (1935): 74–84. It showed that the Rockefeller Foundation approved two subsidies in the sum of 25,000 and 30,000 dollars for 1926–1933. The ICHS had filed a new application for 20,000 dollars. For more information concerning the actual, if reduced, support by the Rockefeller Foundation, see the financial reports by Nabholz, Zurich 1938, and Woodward, Luxembourg Bureau meeting, May 1939. For the fiscal years (since 1938 starting on 1 April) from 1938/39 to 1940/41 there was a special grant of 16,800 dollars. ICHS, *Bulletin* 11: 34ff. and 581.

7. See below, appendix II, 2.
8. See below, Bibliography, Publications of the ICHS, and the following publications supervised by the respective commissions: *Bibliographie de l'histoire coloniale, 1900–1930* (Paris, 1932); J. G. van Dillen, ed., *History of the Principal Public Banks* (The Hague, 1934); *Répertoire chronologique des littératures modernes*, ed. under the direction of P. Van Tieghem (Paris, 1935); H. Nabholz and P. Kläui, eds., *Internationaler Archivführer* (Leipzig-Zurich, 1931); E. Déprez, ed., *Bibliographie des grands voyages et des grandes découvertes* (Paris, 1937); *Organisation corporative du Moyen Âge à la fin de l'Ancien Régime*, 4 vols. (Louvain, 1937); *La Costituzione degli Stati nell'Età moderna*, ed. under the direction of G. Volpe, 2 vols. (Milan, 1933; Florence, 1938); M. Jaryc and P. Caron, eds., *World List of Historical Periodicals and Bibliographies* (Oxford, 1939).
9. Lhéritier to Coville, 18 March 1935, Archives CISH, dossier 1935. This file also contains a voluminous correspondence concerning these events, including letters from Temperley, Iorga, Lhéritier, and the Czech historian Stloukal. They are completed by the Iorga papers, correspondence 1935–1936. Romanian nationalist sentiments were also confronted with those of the Hungarians. Thus Domanovszky imparted to Temperley that he could not agree to a decision in favor of Romania on account of political reasons, namely, because of the treatment of the Hungarian minority in Romania. "A journey to Romania, under the present circumstances, would be very humiliating for us Hungarians." Domanovszky papers, n.d. [19 May 1936].
10. Iorga to Lhéritier, 23 March 1935, Archives CISH, dossier 1935.
11. Correspondence on this event in Archives CISH, dossier 1936 and 1937.
12. Caron to Lukin, 20 Nov. 1937, Archives CISH, dossier 1937.
13. Deborin to Lhéritier, 27 Sep. 1938, Archives CISH, dossier 1938.
14. Memorandum by Caron, 17 Nov. 1934, Archives CISH, dossier 1934.
15. Friis to Leland, 14 Nov. 1938, Friis papers, I, 1.
16. See p. 175. Friis took the opportunity to visit Rothfels in Berlin on his return trip from Switzerland. On Friis's efforts on Rothfels's behalf, see the Friis-Lhéritier correspondence in Archives CISH, dossier 1938; Friis papers, I, 1 and II, 8 c, Lag 1.
17. Nabholz to Temperley, 7 Oct. 1933, Archives CISH, dossier 1933.
18. 29 May 1935, Archives CISH, dossier 1935.
19. Temperley to Lhéritier, 22 Feb. 1935, Archives CISH, correspondence Temperley 1932–1935.
20. After his dismissal had first been postponed, the government retired him on 31 July 1936. The Bureau's intervention on Dopsch's behalf was initiated by his assistant Erna Patzelt, who had turned to Aage Friis on 25 Jan. 1935 with a request to support Dopsch. Friis intervened immediately with Temperley (Friis papers, I, 1). In a letter to the president, the Bureau's Hungarian member, Domanovszky, pointed to the significance of Dopsch's Institute for Economic and Social History at Vienna for Hungarian scholarship (Domanovszky to Temperley, Budapest, 18 Feb. 1935, Domanovszky papers). Petition of the Bureau members, 18 May 1935, in ICHS, *Bulletin* 7: 209. On Dopsch's dismissal, see R. Neck, "Alfons Dopsch und seine Schule," in *Wissenschaft und Weltbild. Festschrift für Hertha Firnberg*, ed. W. Frühauf (Vienna, 1975), p. 377; see also material of the Austrian ministry for education, copies put at my disposal by the Verband österreichischer Geschichtsvereine. According to these documents, Dopsch's pupils, his colleagues, and the university supported Dopsch's cause, but without success.
21. Members of the organizing committee formed at the General Assembly in Paris, 21–23 March 1934: Lhéritier, Ussani, Brandi, Temperley, Ganshof, Koht, Handelsman, and Nabholz. ICHS, *Bulletin* 7: 125.
22. Zurich meeting, 7 Sep. 1934, ibid., p. 273.
23. Ibid., p. 296.
24. Ibid., p. 273.
25. See appendix III, 1 and 2. The Zurich Congress is documented in "Eighth International Congress of Historical Sciences, Zürich 1980, Scientifc Reports I–II: Communications

présentées au Congrès de Zurich, 1938," in ICHS, *Bulletin* 10 [hereafter Congress Zurich 1938: "Communications"]; "VIII. Internationaler Kongreß für Geschichtswissenschaft 28. August–4. September 1938 in Zürich unter dem Patronat des Herrn Bundespräsidenten. Protokoll," in ICHS, *Bulletin* 11 [hereafter Congress Zurich 1938: "Protokoll"].
26. G. Hoffmann, secretary of the organizing committee, to Renouvin, secretary of the French national committee, 7 Oct. 1937, Archives Nationales, 70 AJ 159, dossier Zurich 1938.
27. Comité organisateur, Paris, 19 May 1937, ICHS, *Bulletin* 9: 403.
28. Congress Zurich 1938: "Protokoll," pp. 315ff.
29. "Le procès de la renationalisation de la Silésie au XIXe siècle," in Congress Zurich 1938: "Communications," p. 370f.; discussion in Congress Zurich 1938: "Protokoll," p. 344f.
30. Congress Zurich 1938: "Communications," pp. 240ff.; Congress Zurich 1938: "Protokoll," pp. 327ff.
31. "Il commercio internazionale nel medioevo," in Congress Zurich 1938: "Communications," pp. 526ff.
32. Congress Zurich 1938: "Protokoll," p. 387.
33. Papers were presented by: K. Zakrzewski (Warsaw), "Le rôle du christianisme dans la ruine du monde ancien"; T. Walek-Czernecki (Warsaw), "Les causes profondes de la ruine du monde antique"; A. Alföldi (Budapest, not attending), "Aspekte des Übergangs vom Altertum auf das Mittelalter"; O. Bertolini (Rome, not attending), "Il passaggio dal mondo antico al mondo medioevale"; H. Zeiss (Munich), "Kontinuitätsproblem und Denkmälerforschung"; A. Stein (Prague), "Das Fortleben des römischen Principatsgedankens"; all in Congress Zurich 1938: "Communications," pp. 179–193; discussion in Congress Zurich 1938: "Protokoll," pp. 298–307.
34. Nabholz referred to diplomatic difficulties as the reason for the Russians' absence. See Temperley to Lhéritier, 12 July 1938, Archives CISH, dossier 1938.
35. Congress report by G. W. F. Hallgarten in *Zeitschrift für freie deutsche Forschung* 1, no. 2 (Paris, Nov. 1938); cf. also the Congress report in *Pariser Tageszeitung*, 6 Sep. 1938.
36. ICHS, *Bulletin* 7: 296f.
37. "Il concetto di nazione nel Mazzini," in Congress Zurich 1938: "Communications," pp. 646ff.
38. Ibid., pp. 623ff.
39. See below, appendix III.
40. On the following, see Heiber, *Walter Frank*.
41. Record of Reichsministerium für Wissenschaft, Erziehung und Volksbildung, on a conversation with Platzhoff and Schröder, 30 Nov. 1937, in Zentrales Staatsarchiv, Potsdam, 2842. The German delegation was once again led by Brandi. But in early 1937 he had transferred his position as chairman of the Allgemeiner Deutscher Historikerausschuß to Walter Platzhoff (Brandi to Dölger, 26 Jan. 1937, and to Nabholz, 17 Feb. 1937, Brandi papers, 46). The Ausschuß also included Walter Frank. See report on Zurich by Brandi to Reichs- und Preuß. Minister für Wissenschaft, Erziehung und Volksbildung, n.d., Brandi papers, 51. Immediately following Austria's annexation to the German Reich, the Austrian historians were incorporated into the German national committee. This was accompanied by a hasty reorganization of the Austrian contributions to the Zurich Congress. At the same time, a wave of repression and dismissals passed over the Austrian historical profession. The victims included August von Loehr, secretary of the International Commission for Numismatics, and Dopsch's pupil Erna Patzelt. See correspondence in Archives CISH, dossier 1938.
42. O. Scheel, "Der Volksgedanke bei Luther," *Historische Zeitschrift* 161 (1940): 477–497; discussion in Congress Zurich 1938: "Protokoll," p. 360f.
43. Brandi to Reichs- und Preuß. Minister für Wissenschaft, Erziehung und Volksbildung, n.d., Brandi papers, 51.
44. Frank to Harmjanz (Reichsministerium für Wissenschaft, Erziehung und Volksbildung), 28 Sep. 1938, quoted in Heiber, *Walter Frank*, p. 754f.

45. Hallgarten to Nabholz, 27 Jan. 1937, Nabholz papers, 35, together with copy of a letter from Hallgarten to Renouvin, 9 Jan. 1937.
46. G. W. F. Hallgarten, *Imperialismus vor 1914: Theoretisches, soziologische Skizzen der außenpolitischen Entwicklung in England und Frankreich, soziologische Darstellung der deutschen Außenpolitik bis zum ersten Weltkrieg* (Munich, 1951); 2nd revised ed. under the title *Imperialismus vor 1914: Die soziologischen Grundlagen der Außenpolitik europäischer Großmächte vor dem ersten Weltkrieg*, 2 vols. (Munich, 1963).
47. Congress Zurich 1938: "Communications," pp. 378ff. (text); Congress Zurich 1938: "Protokoll," pp. 339ff. (discussion). See also Hallgarten's memoirs: *Als die Schatten fielen* (Berlin, 1969), pp. 256ff., and his critical report on Zurich in *Zeitschrift für freie deutsche Forschung* 1, no. 2 (Paris, Nov. 1938). Similar criticism in *Pariser Tageszeitung*, 6 Sep. 1938.
48. "Richelieu et le commerce du Levant," in Congress Zurich 1938: "Communications," p. 543f.
49. Congress Zurich 1938: "Protokoll," p. 417.
50. Abstract in Congress Zurich 1938: "Communications," p. 690f.; long extract in Congress Zurich 1938: "Protokoll," pp. 39ff.; complete text in *Revue historique du Sud-Est européen* (Bucharest, 1938): 205–222.
51. For example, by B. Valota Cavallotti, *Nicola Iorga* (Naples, 1977).
52. N. Iorga, *Essai de synthèse de l'histoire de l'humanité*, 4 vols. (Paris, 1926–1929); cf. M. Berza, "Nicolas Iorga, Historien du Moyen Âge," in *Nicolas Iorga, l'homme et l'œuvre* (Bucharest, 1972), p. 149. On Iorga's work and historical thought, see also Valota Cavallotti, *Iorga*; on his contributions at the International Historical Congresses L. Boia, "Nicolae Iorga si congressele internationale de istorie," *Revista de istorie* 31 (Bucharest, 1978): 1825ff.
53. Congress Zurich 1938: "Protokoll," p. 39f., and Congress Zurich 1938: "Communications," p. 690.
54. Quoted from *Essai de Synthèse* and *Istoriologia umană* in Valota Cavallotti, *Iorga*, pp. 226 and 236.
55. 6 Sep. 1938.
56. Edgar Bonjour to the author, 17 March 1976.
57. Friis papers, II, 8b, notes in Danish, comments on Srbik and Steinacker in German.
58. Congress Zurich 1938: "Protokoll," p. 453.
59. Ibid., p. 69f.

Chapter 12

DESTRUCTION AND REVIVAL, 1938–1947

It was a difficult task for the ICHS to develop the appropriate form for the mass events of the Congresses. It experimented from one Congress to the next and attempted to evaluate the results. In the end, it was always faced with the same question: how best to "rein in the chaos." Following Zurich, the Swiss organizing committee presented a self-critical assessment. There had still been too many lectures. The attempt to influence the selection of subject matters by means of a topic catalog had shown little success. The reality had fallen short of what the Swiss organizers had hoped to achieve when they decided to assume total responsibility for preparing the Congress's program. Allowing more time for long, detailed lectures in the mornings, however, had turned out to be a success. For the future, the Swiss committee suggested that the program commission should once again be assembled on an international basis, and that it should select the topics of the morning lectures and the appropriate speakers.[1] The Bureau agreed to these suggestions and decided to assume the task of the organizing committee.[2]

The success of this arrangement depended to some extent on the composition of the Bureau. At Zurich, the ICHS elected Leland as president, and Iorga and Nabholz as vice-presidents. The British historian Ernest L. Woodward took over Nabholz's office as treasurer, with the result that the ICHS's seat was relocated to Oxford. Lhéritier was confirmed in his office as secretary-general. The minutes of the electing meeting included the statement that he would "yield this function in five years."[3] Because this comment was added by Temperley, who still acted as president during this meeting, it was perceived by Lhéritier as a gratuitous commitment and a clear act of criticism. Leland also considered it superfluous. In fact, Lhéritier had announced such an intention to resign, but only in reaction to growing reservations about him personally. In addition, his professorship, which he had exercised in Dijon since 1935,

---

Notes for this chapter begin on page 193.

made it impossible for him to dedicate himself to his tasks as secretary-general to the same degree he had in the first years. While his critics held that he was too busy and not substantial enough as a scholar, others appreciated his energy and industry as the "*animateur*" of the ICHS.[4]

Criticism of his practical accomplishments concerned three areas where he had shown particular commitment. First, there were the international commissions. Leland and the American benefactors, who had supported the ICHS since its foundation in 1926, were of the opinion that permanent international scholarly undertakings should be its major focal point. Regular reports on the commissions' activities were presented at the meetings of the ICHS. But they were not always convincing. There was a widespread opinion that, in a wave of pioneer spirit, the organization had done too much, and now it was time to start weeding the garden. One commission was especially controversial, namely, the Commission for Historical Instruction, which was particularly dear to Lhéritier. Useful work for the improvement of schoolbooks was performed in bilateral conferences that were convened outside of the ICHS, though under the influence of impulses emanating from it. But its own commission did not succeed in accomplishing more than to generate noncommittal surveys and statements of intent.

Furthermore, there was dissatisfaction with the periodical of the ICHS, the *Bulletin*, to which Lhéritier had dedicated the lion's share of his activity. Forty-five issues, gathered in eleven thick volumes, had appeared in the thirteen years since the founding of the ICHS. They contained minutes, sometimes also documents, of conferences, assemblies, and commission activities, together with surveys, statistics, and reports on the historical literature of languages of small geographical range, plus the occasional scholarly paper. The *Bulletin* was not a scientific periodical—it lacked the necessary profile and thematic direction—and as an informational organ it was too voluminous and impractical. Thus, after Zurich a separate commission was formed to take charge of the *Bulletin*. Lhéritier should no longer be its editor-in-chief. He grasped the consequences and announced a new working style. "The general secretariat," he wrote to the new president, Leland, "as it functioned until August 28, is dead. My personal work in the Committee ... is thus at an end. In order to oblige you ... I shall continue to run the general secretariat, which the Nominating Committee and the General Assembly wish me to retain. But I will exercise it in a different way that will make it easier for you to select a successor for me. I understand the new manner of discharging my office as follows: I will efface myself, and I will take it easy with my duties.... I will limit myself strictly to my general secretariat as an executive instrument of your decisions as president by leaving all important questions pertaining to the Committee's responsibilities to you."[5] In reality, however, Lhéritier had no intention of "effacing" himself, least of all in regard to questions that faced the ICHS in the intensifying international situation and then during the war. He was even left with considerable freedom of action, because during the war Leland was not able to provide the ICHS with the firm leadership that had been expected from him.

The last Bureau meeting broke up in Zurich, "after it had been decided to assemble again in the second half of the following May in Prague, and ... after Mr. Volpe had been advised of the resolution to recommend to the [General] Assembly that they accept the invitation by the Italian historians for the next Congress."[6] The acceptance of the invitation to a Bureau meeting in the capital of Czechoslovakia was a manifestation of sympathy for the threatened country, a hope against all hope. A few weeks after the Congress, this decision was swept away by Munich. Even before Prague fell into German hands, the Czechs no longer saw themselves in a position to maintain the invitation. Lhéritier turned to Luxembourg, which was not yet even a member of the ICHS.[7] From 22 to 24 May 1939, two months after the occupation of Czechoslovakia, three months before the invasion of Poland, this small, hospitable country, which presented itself as an Eldorado of peace, hosted the last Bureau meeting before the outbreak of war. Here, despite many reservations, a resolution was passed to hold the next Congress in the capital of Fascist Italy.[8]

The Italian invitation issued in Zurich had caused some embarrassment.[9] The General Assembly at the closing of the Congress had been unable to arrive at a decision, which would have been the standard procedure. On the one hand, the members of the ICHS did not want to refuse. That would have meant Italy's withdrawal and, perhaps, the end of the ICHS itself. On the other hand, a simple yes was impossible, firstly due to the fundamental conflict between the totalitarian self-conception of the Fascist state and the liberal principles of intellectual freedom upon which the International Congresses were based; secondly and above all, because it was not even certain whether participation in a Congress in Rome would be open to everyone. The announcement of discriminatory racial laws in Italy on the Nazi model had caused a shock. In order to gain time for deliberations on these issues within the various national committees, a written survey was carried out. The Giunta Centrale was irritated but provided appeasing guarantees. In a letter to Lhéritier, Volpe stated: "I can guarantee you that at the next Congress, should it take place in Rome, there will be no restrictions, neither in regard to the USSR nor in regard to foreign scholars of non-Aryan race."[10] The restriction implicit in this sentence was clear enough: an express guarantee for the participation of "non-Aryans" only if they came from abroad—there was no corresponding guarantee for Italian Jews. What were the reactions in the ICHS? There were so few responses to the written survey that the necessary quorum of two-thirds of the members was not reached. A second written survey, for which only the participation of half the members was necessary, brought a clear majority for the acceptance of the Italian invitation.[11]

In some of the national committees the vote was preceded by controversial discussions. Everyone who voted with yes knew what this meant. In the discussions, as far as they are mirrored in letters and minutes, three different positions can be distinguished. First there was the positivistic conviction that science and politics are separable and, in this case, had to be separated. This argument often coincided with the second, pragmatic consideration that only such a separation could prevent a break in the organization. And finally, as a third argument against the other two: There are ethical demands upon which scholarship itself rests that may not be yielded up under any circumstances.

Lhéritier and Leland maintained the positivistic and the organizational argument most succinctly. Lhéritier wrote: "If we do not accept their invitation, then I fear that they will withdraw from the Committee. Since, as long as the Committee has existed, I myself have practiced a policy of unanimity both toward the Soviets and the fascist states as well as toward all the other countries, I do not believe that I would have the courage to remain in an organization that, after having created unanimity among historians, would begin to dissolve itself.... For us, this is not a matter of listening to opinions on ideologies which are currently opposing one another. We have much better things to do. And our Committee must remain above politics."[12] On another occasion, Lhéritier said that all countries had to be treated the same way, whether they were communist, fascist, or democratic. "I will continue to represent this policy of unanimity so long as I belong to the Committee.... And I also believe that politics must be carefully kept out of cultural relationships."[13] In this regard, Leland completely agreed with Lhéritier. "I confess, my dear Michel," he wrote to him, "that for these difficult times I have adopted the principle which you yourself have followed since the organisation of the Committee, namely, that the Committee cannot allow itself to be disrupted by political or other considerations that do not affect its scientific work. It is exceedingly hard to maintain such a line of conduct, for our emotions are deeply stirred."[14] He had brought the affair before the executive committee of the American Historical Association and asked for its assent to his reasons for accepting the invitation to Rome, without suppressing his doubts as to whether full and unlimited freedom would really prevail: "The Italian historians give us assurances that there will be complete freedom of access to the Congress, and that 'non-Aryans' and citizens of the Union of Soviet Socialist Republics will not be excluded. (I do not understand, however, that this freedom of access will apply to exiled Italians.)" He cited the following reasons for an affirmative consent despite such reservations: "moral support to scholars of the totalitarian states who look with disfavour (although fearing to express it) upon the excesses of their respective governments"; and: "a refusal ... may bring about the disruption of the International Committee."[15] In the executive committee of the American Historical Association there were differing opinions, but in the end Leland and Shotwell, the second American representative in the ICHS, were empowered to vote as they thought best. Shotwell opposed Leland and voted no.[16]

The chairman of the Danish national committee, Friis, took an entirely different view of the situation. "This is above all a purely moral question," he wrote to Lhéritier. "What is at issue is not politics, but rather the simple question of whether an international organization which encompasses all historians may conduct general Congresses in a country where individual groups of historians are defamed, as is now the case for our Jewish colleagues. I, for my part, do not agree to this: it is an insult to historical scholarship and to individual persons. If the Bureau has no reservations against conducting Congresses in countries like Italy, Germany or Russia, then I no longer wish to take part in international cooperation."[17] In no way did he agree with Leland's actions:

> I am sorry that you have thought it necessary to put the question on the order of the day for the recent [vote]; after my opinion it would have been the only natural standpoint to postpone for the present any [decision] regarding further Congresses. In such a crisis the greatest possible passivity is necessary. I cannot agree with your reasons for accepting the Italian invitation, as this standpoint of course includes a principle agreement to the eventual holding of a congress in Germany or in Moscow. The fact pointed out by you: the regard to certainly many fair-minded histor[ians] in the dictator countries, seems less essential to me. And the guarantee given by Volpe or others for free admission for all of the histor[ians] is still less significant. Firstly, you cannot rely on anything, even if you presume the *bona fide* of the Italian histor[ians]; on the other hand these promises do not concern the matter. What would become of Ferrero,[18] if he would come to Rome? And I wonder whether any Jewish histor[ians] beyond the dictator countries could think of coming to Rome, where they are dishonoured etc. etc.! Under the present circumstances all these promises seem to me a downright bluff. But finally deciding for me is the real moral question which we have to cling to more than ever in times as these, provided external powers don't make it perfectly impossible. We can by no means invite our Jewish (or non-Aryan) colleagues, however few or many of them there are, to a meeting in Rome or Berlin, where they are defamed without the slightest guilt.[19]

However, the Danish national committee did not share Friis's view. It voted for Rome. Friis drew the consequences. He laid down the chairmanship and withdrew as the Danish representative to the ICHS.[20]

Halvdan Koht also expressed severe reservations. Like Friis, he considered the way in which Leland had handled the affair to be wrong. He felt that a delicate question like this had to be discussed in a General Assembly of the ICHS, and could not be left to the national committees.[21] After some deliberations, the Scandinavians came to an agreement and issued a conditional yes. They assented to accepting the invitation in the expectation that no one would be prevented from participating in Rome. The Belgian national committee also expressed strong reservations against Italy, particularly on account of the anti-Semitic measures. It did not intend to "secede," however, "if the other countries do not share [our] reservations."[22] The attitude of the British historians was reported on by Webster, who spoke in favor of accepting the invitation to Rome: "There was a great difference of opinion in our Committee and as you no doubt also know Temperley was strongly against accepting the invitation, but I am sure that we have done the right thing, though in the world in which we now live it may very well be that the Congress never takes place."[23] His own motive was to preserve "the ecumenical character" of the ICHS and its Congresses.[24] The outcome of the vote in the British national committee was five for acceptance, four against.[25]

The French national committee, Lhéritier wrote to the secretary of the *Giunta* Dupré, voted for Rome and sought to do everything it could to bring about a generally positive decision. That is why he would soon inform the other members of the ICHS of the French vote. And—far from "effacing" himself—Lhéritier asked Dupré to impart to the president of the *Giunta* "that it will be one of the great joys of my secretariat when finally, despite the difficult situation, the majority of the neutral countries in our International Committee will declare themselves in favor of your invitation."[26] When he was certain that the decision would come out in support of Rome, he gave his sympathies free rein: "Please forgive me if, without any ulterior motives, I am pleased with this result as a Gallo-Roman, i.e. as a Latin; for if there is one race and one brotherhood for the Germans and for the Slavs, I do not see why there shouldn't be one for us Latins, too."[27]

Thus it was decided in Luxembourg that the historians would go to Rome, and that the Bureau would take the scholarly preparation into its own hands. The war spared the ICHS the embarrassment of conducting a Congress that could not have been free of an unpleasant taste of racial discrimination. The guiding maxim of the Bureau remained the imperative to prevent the breakup of what had been built in the course of thirteen years. In 1939/40, Leland traveled throughout South America to canvass for the ecumenical historical union, as Temperley had previously done in Asia, and instructed Lhéritier to start preparing for the Rome Congress.[28] Even after the outbreak of the war, as the radius of action became increasingly constricted, Lhéritier received a number of encouraging letters from the neutral and Western countries, among others from Domanovszky in Hungary, and particularly from Webster and Woodward in England, as well as from German historians. They all advised him to continue his work as far as possible.[29] Even in March 1940, during the *drôle de guerre*, six months after the attack on Poland and a few weeks before the German attack in the West, Woodward, as ICHS treasurer, applied for a grant from the Rockefeller Foundation. In his application, he wrote that the Bureau had decided to do everything within its power to keep the ICHS intact "in order that, after the war, we might have our organization ready to play its part—an important part—in restoring international cooperation." This step was expressly approved by both English and German historians.[30] But while the Bureau of the ICHS tried to pursue its scholarly business, the first phase of the war already showed what bestialities lay in store for Europe.

The bombing of Warsaw by the German Luftwaffe inspired pure horror. Even the cautious Lhéritier found clear words. In a circular that he directed to the Bureau members in November 1939, he wrote: "We, for our part, cannot help but to lament endlessly the destruction of Warsaw, of that center of world culture, with which we have been on such close terms since we held our penultimate Congress there. And we hope that the German historians will also one day deplore it with us. Profoundly moved, we salute this martyred city."[31] Leland, however, who did not abandon the hope that there were other

Germans with whom cooperation could be continued in the future, thought that Lhéritier's remark regarding the German historians went too far. "I think perhaps it would have been better in that paragraph not to make a direct reference to our German colleagues, for it seems to imply that they may approve of the destruction of Warsaw at the present time but that later, when they come to a better state of mind, they will disapprove of it. I like to think that all of the members of the Committee are men of goodwill, and have much the same sentiments about such things. In our correspondence with regard to the Committee, we must make the greatest effort not to draw any distinctions between the scholars of the different countries."[32]

Among those who did not believe that it still made sense to pretend that the work of the ICHS could be continued under wartime conditions was Iorga. But he, too, was unwilling to condemn the Germans once and forever: "Internationalism, this beautiful thing, is at an end! How could we, even if it were to Italy, invite scholars from nations who are engaged in killing one another? We must postpone, postpone everything, and who knows if we will ever again be able to become active as we once were! The madness of a single human being has brought all this about. This scoundrel who dreams of being the master of the world has broken all the bonds that were precious to us. For I do not doubt that men like Brandi and Holtzmann regard with horror and repugnance what their Leader or seducer has done at the expense of humanity."[33] Woodward, however, who was serving as a captain in the British army, expressed decisiveness and the certainty of victory in his numerous letters to Lhéritier.[34]

Of the many voices reaching Lhéritier in these difficult times, that of Nabholz deserves particular mention because of the role he was to play in the later history of the ICHS. "Now the worst has become reality," he wrote following the invasion of Poland. "An insane criminal is tipping Europe into another abyss. And the middle and small powers—Switzerland included—sit and watch while England and France, with endless sacrifices in human beings and material goods, attempt to free Europe from this man! I am not at all proud of Switzerland's neutrality. Now a joining of forces with the two great democracies would be a moral duty."[35]

The condemnation of Hitler's Germany among the historians of the Western and neutral countries was unanimous, particularly under the impact of the first news about the fate of the Polish historians. Lhéritier's conduct, too, was unambiguous at first. However, the collapse of France and the occupation of Paris by German troops created a new situation. A continuation of the earlier international intellectual cooperation seemed possible only on a transatlantic basis, with the backing of England, Canada, and particularly the United States. This was also the opinion of Henri Bonnet, the director of the Institut International de Coopération Intellectuelle in Paris, who had been able to escape to the United States before the German occupation, and who took refuge with Leland. Shortly after his arrival, he asked Shotwell to ensure that the United States would continue the work of the ICHS. Cooperation with Nazi-occupied

Europe, he held, was no longer possible.[36] Leland, who at the beginning of the war had spoken out so strongly for the continuation of the ICHS's work, including Germany, changed his attitude entirely following the defeat of Belgium and France. He no longer wished to place the funds approved by the Rockefeller Foundation at Lhéritier's disposal, since he would be able to continue his work only under German domination. Instead, Leland wanted to use these funds to support ICHS members who had found their way to the United States, above all the Jewish Austrian Jaryc, who had lived in Paris until 1940 and then fled from the Nazis. In Paris he had worked on the *International Bibliography*, and he was now to continue this work in the United States.[37] As president of the ICHS, Leland thought it best to let all questions regarding the ICSH rest until the end of the war in order to prevent its complete disintegration. Webster and the British national committee agreed to this.[38]

Lhéritier, whose offices had long been housed at Bonnet's International Institute for Intellectual Cooperation, oriented himself in an entirely different direction. Like some employees of the Institute following Bonnet's escape, he sought to save the organization entrusted unto him with the help of the German authorities.[39] He received the support of the Vichy Government and the new authorities in Paris. Nabholz informed him that Brandi and Holtzmann desired the continued existence of the ICHS. Woodward, however, warned against cooperating with the Germans during the war, even before the occupation of Paris: "I do not feel a personal resentment against men like Brandi and Holtzmann. I remember how miserable Holtzmann was at Luxembourg last May, but the fact remains that the German historians allowed themselves to be made the instruments of the Nazi Party long before the war began, and it would be the greatest possible mistake to allow them, after the war, to continue the membership of the International Committee as though nothing had happened.... If we could get now a meeting of the International Committee, I should like to propose expelling the Germans from membership."[40]

Lhéritier's most important contact in Paris was Karl Epting, director of the newly created German Institute. As a longtime Paris representative of the Deutscher Akademischer Austauschdienst (German Academic Exchange Service), Epting was well acquainted with Parisian cultural life and was himself a critical admirer of French literature. Through his Institute, he did a great deal to promote Franco-German cultural and intellectual cooperation. He and his friends saw the meeting between Hitler and Pétain in Montoire as the symbol of a possible Franco-German rapprochement. In doing so they misunderstood Hitler's intentions, and they underestimated the depth of the rift that had been torn open by the war and could not be paved over through the promotion of theater, music, and new literary works.[41]

The projects promoted by the German Institute included the *Bulletin of the International Committee of Historical Sciences*. During the war, Lhéritier published issues 46 and 47 as parts 1 and 2 of volume 12 (1941 and 1943).[42] Since there was nothing more to report on the activity of the ICHS, the *Bulletin* published randomly collected essays, including some by renowned authors. These included the French Orientalist René Grousset ("État actuel des études sur l'histoire gengiskanide"), the Ukrainian historian Mikhailo Hrushevsky (posthumously, "La principauté de Kiev au moyen-âge"), Nicolae Iorga (posthumously, "Talleyrand et Reinhard. Un chapitre de l'ancienne diplomatie"), and Wolfgang Windelband, Berlin ("Bismarcks Ägyptenpolitik"). Lhéritier also inserted some of his own essays, including his introduction to a series of lectures at the Sorbonne, in which he dealt with revolutions in modern and recent history. In these articles, he expressed the hope for an enduring reconciliation between Nazi Germany, France, and Europe, "a synthesis between authority and freedom, between the continent and the ocean, between nationalities and Empires, between the Center of Europe and its border regions."[43] Since he had received this lectureship under the aegis of the German occupation authorities, made suspiciously friendly comments concerning the foreign rulers and committed himself to the organization of a congress of French and German historians during the war, Lhéritier fell into the category of "collaborator."[44]

What were the intentions of the German occupation authorities toward the ICHS? Epting's benevolent conduct toward Lhéritier and the *Bulletin* brought about a series of considerations in Berlin between 1940 and 1942 regarding this and other international scholarly organizations. In this discussion, which was initiated by the ministry for science and by the cultural department of the Foreign Office, the prevailing opinion was that following the war the French, Belgian, and American influence should be pushed back, but no immediate measures should be taken. In regard to history, Platzhoff, in his capacity as leader of the German national committee, the Allgemeiner Deutscher Historikerausschuß, recommended exercising restraint, watching the developments, and deferring the question until after the war. Dedicated National Socialists were of the opinion that the German humanities had to be renewed from the ground up before the reconstruction of international organizations could be examined.[45] In this context, the transfer of the general secretariat of the ICHS to Germany was also considered, but did not occur, not least because of an intervention by Brandi and Holtzmann.[46] There were also no efforts to undertake steps that would predetermine this question for the future. In the meantime, the backing that Karl Epting and his friends were giving the *Bulletin*, and Lhéritier's willingness to cooperate, had the result that following the liberation of Paris, Lhéritier was suspended from his teaching position for three years. The French national committee, which discussed the "Lhéritier case" at its first meeting after the end of the war, felt that he no longer was acceptable as secretary-general of the ICHS.[47] This opinion was shared by the British national committee, the American Historical Association, and those who were responsible for the ICHS in the Rockefeller Foundation. Four months after the war, Leland, who like Koht had lost all confidence in his associate of the first hour, urged Lhéritier to withdraw from his office as secretary-general.[48]

The latter saw the writing on the wall and resigned. In a long letter to Koht, to whom he expressed his admiration for the heroic resistance of the Norwegians, he emphasized that he had no regrets: "You know my creed. I wanted to keep history and the Historical Committee above politics."[49] After his suspension from the teaching position had expired, he received a chair in history at the university of Aix-en-Provence in 1949.

Despite the developments during the war and the obvious political failure of the secretary-general, in the light of its previous work the ICHS proved sufficiently viable and needed by the historical discipline. Immediately following the war, efforts were started to reestablish old contacts and to start planning a new Congress. Upon Leland's request, the secretary of the French national committee, Albert Depréaux, assumed the duties of the secretary-general on an interim basis. During the war, Western, neutral, and also German historians had repeatedly suggested that the ICHS should resume its activity as soon as possible after the war. Leland took the initiative six months after the end of hostilities. In a circular letter to Depréaux, Nabholz, Woodward, Ganshof, and Koht (leaving out Holtzmann and Volpe), he declared that the Bureau was ready for business.[50] He proposed to examine the idea of organizing a Congress in Paris in 1948. The French national committee immediately consented to this and suggested a General Assembly of the ICHS in Prague in 1947—picking up on the resolution in Zurich to accept an invitation from Czechoslovakia for the next assembly.[51]

Then Leland remained silent for more than a year. Neither Depréaux nor Nabholz, who was the last surviving vice-president following Iorga's death, nor Woodward, the ICHS's treasurer, heard anything from him. It was not until November 1946 that contact was reestablished between him and the French national committee. Its new president was Robert Fawtier. As a member of the Résistance, he had been sentenced to life in prison in 1942 and had been detained most recently in the Mauthausen concentration camp; following the end of the war, he became a professor at the Sorbonne. He informed Leland in December 1946 that the French national committee had appointed Charles Morazé, a professor at the École Pratique des Hautes Études et des Sciences Politiques, to act as secretary-general.[52] Morazé belonged to the circle of young historians around the *Annales* who enjoyed wide-ranging opportunities in postwar France and found firm institutional support in the Sixième Section of the École Pratique des Hautes Études, founded and led by Lucien Febvre. Morazé served as *Directeur d'Études*. Self-confident, and with the intention of contributing to a new beginning in the study of history, he began placing new accents on the ICHS's activities. As a member of the French UNESCO delegation, he endeavored to make good use of his connections to this comprehensive cultural organization of the United Nations for the historians' international work.

Leland gave the French committee a free hand for the next steps. "My intention is," he wrote to Fawtier in his power-of-attorney letter, "to leave the management of the ICHS in the hands of your Committee, since it is impossible for me to maintain direct control over it. Your Committee has power accordingly to do what may be necessary to assure the good functioning of the International Committee."[53] Shortly thereafter he retreated entirely. On account of "circumstances beyond my control" he declined to attend the meeting of the Comité Restreint scheduled by the French national committee in Royaumont near Paris from 3 to 5 June 1947. At the same time, he handed in his resignation as president of the ICHS, "impressed ... by the fact that its president is unable, because of distance, to give adequate attention to its affairs at this critical time."[54] He had previously asked Nabholz to assume the office of president on an interim basis. The latter was confirmed in this office in Royaumont pending the new election by the General Assembly at the next Congress. Nobody, least of all Nabholz, knew precisely why Leland resigned. "Against my desires and my will," Nabholz wrote his friend Domanovszky, "I have had to assume the leadership of the International Committee ... until the next International Congress. Leland declared his resignation without providing any reasons."[55]

Later on, Leland occasionally took part in administrative meetings of the ICHS, though he never again participated in the Historical Congresses. But he observed from afar and said what was on his mind, sometimes even adjusting his own opinions. For example, he forwarded his recommendation that if the ICHS really intended to reduce the proliferating number of commissions in order to maintain only those that were really useful for scholarly work, then the *International Bibliography* should not be spared either. He himself had promoted it, even during the war, but had now joined his American friends in the conviction that it simply was not worth the bother.[56] Inevitably, the question arose of how to deal with Germany, Italy, and Japan. In late 1945 Leland, who after the First World War had spoken so passionately in favor of integrating the former enemy nations, still shared the opinion prevailing in the Western national committees that this was not possible "in any predictable future."[57] He made only one exception: De Sanctis, who had refused to swear the Fascist oath and who had now been reinstated as professor in Rome and named special commissioner for historical studies. In May 1947, however, when he announced his resignation, Leland saw things differently. Now he warned: "The guiding principle should be the desire of the committee to bring the historians of *all* countries together in friendly and useful collaboration. Care should be taken not to do anything at the present moment that might make this difficult or impossible."[58]

The Bureau and the Comité Restreint dealt with both questions—interim presidency and membership roll—in Royaumont between 3 and 5 June 1947. The meeting was attended by one or two historians respectively from Belgium, Denmark, the United States, France, Great Britain, Greece, Luxembourg, Switzerland, and Czechoslovakia.[59] Nabholz was confirmed as interim president, and Morazé was confirmed as interim secretary-general. The Committee's publications underwent a critical review. The *Bulletin* would not be continued. Occasional information brochures were considered for the future. However, after a long debate the *International Bibliography* was retained. Likewise, the diplomats' list and the constitutional studies were to be continued.

In regard to membership, a magnanimous and tolerant resolution was passed, entirely in Leland's spirit, stating that nothing should be changed ("qu'il n'est apporté aucune modification à la liste"). Thus, in contrast to the situation in Brussels in 1923, the former adversaries were not expelled! The formal reintegration of Germany and Japan was to be postponed until the General Assembly at the next Congress. No reservations were expressed toward Italy, Austria, and Spain. The reintegration of Austria was prepared by Nabholz, together with von Loehr and Dopsch, in Zurich and Vienna starting in October 1947. On 22 September 1949, the Austrian Historical Association was constituted with the purpose of immediately starting cooperation with the ICHS.[60] As far as Italy was concerned, the only problem was Volpe. After Royaumont, Nabholz contacted De Sanctis in order to reestablish relations with the Italian national committee, emphasizing that Volpe still had to be considered a member of the Bureau. De Sanctis, however, countered by pointing out that, with all due respect for Volpe's scholarly achievements, the Italian national committee was not prepared to accept him as its representative on account of his political behavior before 1945.[61]

The astonishing resolution to reestablish the complete historians' Internationale a mere two years following the end of the war must be understood against the backdrop of the altered world situation. The East-West wartime alliance against Germany and Japan had become inoperable. The first indications appeared of Germany's integration into the Western world and of the economic reconstruction of Europe with assistance from the United States. The most important dates: On 6 June 1946, the American secretary of state Byrnes delivered his famous speech, which for the first time raised new hopes in Western Germany. On 19 September 1946, in his Zurich address, Winston Churchill called for a union of Europe around a Franco-German core. And on 5 June 1947, as the ICHS met in Royaumont, the American secretary of state Marshall announced his economic recovery and reconstruction plan.

The initiative behind all this lay in the West. The Comité Restreint, however, endeavored to include the Eastern countries as well in the recommencing international activities. During the discussion on the new composition of the Bureau in Royaumont, a seat was specifically reserved for "a member to be named by the USSR." Fawtier informed the Soviet ambassador in Paris that the ICHS was back in operation. It would take years, however, before the socialist countries of Eastern Europe would once again participate fully in the Congresses. The USSR remained deaf to all calls to participate. In 1948 relations with Hungary, Poland, and Czechoslovakia were disrupted, even though the historians of these countries had manifested their profound interest in cooperating in the ICHS.[62] It was a long-term task to re-create a community of historians of the scope that had existed in Warsaw, and to complete it through the incorporation of non-European countries in a continuation of the East Asian and Latin American initiatives of Temperley and Leland.

The first task of the re-created board of the international historical organization was to legitimize it as the international representation of the historical profession by an appointment of its executive organs according to the statutes, and through the reestablishment of its substructure, the national committees. It also had to ensure the financing of their work and to decide when, where, and how the first postwar Congress would be held. Only a duly constituted General Assembly could decide on these issues. It was resolved in Royaumont that such an assembly should be convened in Paris at Easter 1948. Negotiations should be conducted with the Rockefeller Foundation and UNESCO concerning the necessary financial support of the Committee, and Morazé was granted authority to establish a general secretariat able to act.

The historians assembled in Royaumont dealt at length with the issue of the next Congress. Fawtier reported that the French government was inviting the historians to convene in Paris for the hundredth anniversary of the Revolution of 1848, and that it was prepared to place the necessary funds at their disposal. However, reservations arose immediately because of the date. Webster, it is recorded in the minutes, was restive "due to the political character of 'Forty-Eight.'" Woodward reacted similarly. He considered it "most unwise that our first postwar international Congress should be associated in this way with a political glorification in which there will be floods of oratory but very little science."[63] The British apparently wanted to avoid the danger of the first postwar Congress becoming a festival of revolution. Other concerns were stirred by the murky international situation. Would it not be better to wait? Some historians finally pointed out that, as shown by previous experience, it took at least two years to prepare a Congress thoroughly. A vote in the Comité Restreint had the following outcome: France, Belgium, and Switzerland were in favor of a Congress in 1948, whereas the other five nations were against it.[64] It was decided that the Congress should be scheduled for 1949 or 1950 in France, though there was no invitation on the table.

Even more important was the question of how the program of a new Congress should be structured in view of the transformed political situation of the world and of the mixed experiences of the previous Congresses. Everybody agreed that future Congresses should be different from the previous ones: Methodological questions should be given more attention, and there should be regulations for the hitherto unlimited number of "communications."

Royaumont documented the desire for a new beginning. With Charles Morazé, a representative of a young and dynamic generation of French historians imbued with a sense of efficiency and mission had advanced to the key position in the ICHS. He intended to shape future Congresses according to new organizational and methodological considerations, in correspondence with the demands articulated by the *Revue de synthèse* and the *Annales* in their criticism of the previous Congresses.

Notes

1. ICHS, *Bulletin* 11: 470.
2. Luxembourg meeting, 23–24 May 1939, ibid., pp. 574 and 577.
3. Ibid., p. 16.
4. Friis to Lhéritier, 29 Sep. 1939, Archives CISH, dossier 1939.
5. Lhéritier to Leland, 10 Sep. 1938, Leland papers, box 42.
6. ICHS, *Bulletin* 11: 26.
7. Correspondence in Archives CISH, dossiers 1938 and 1939.
8. ICHS, *Bulletin* 11: 563ff.
9. On the following ibid., p. 17; Friis papers, II, 8c, Lag 1; Giunta Centrale per gli Studi Storici, Comitato Nazionale: Report on the meeting of the national committee, 5 Jan. 1939; Archives CISH, dossier 1939.
10. Volpe to Lhéritier, 16 Dec. 1938, carbon of a copy sent by Lhéritier for information, Webster papers, 7/1.
11. ICHS, *Bulletin* 11: 568. Comprehensive material on the details in Archives CISH, dossier 1938–1939.
12. Lhéritier to Leland, 23 Oct. 1938, Archives CISH, dossier 1938.
13. Lhéritier to Leland, 3 Dec. 1938, ibid.
14. Leland to Lhéritier, 31 March 1939, Archives CISH, dossier 1939. See also Leland to Webster, 18 March 1939, Webster papers, 7/1: "My own feeling is that we can do more good by holding a Congress in Rome at which we will maintain a real freedom of speech and discussion than by refusing to go there, and this feeling is supported by the conviction that it is above all important to keep these international bodies in existence."
15. Leland to Buck, 3 March 1939, copy, Archives CISH, dossier 1939.
16. Leland to Lhéritier, 16 March 1939, ibid.
17. Friis to Lhéritier, 29 April 1939, ibid.
18. Guglielmo Ferrero, who had emigrated from Italy, was a professor of history in Geneva since 1930.
19. Friis to Leland, 6 April 1939, Leland papers, box 42.
20. Friis to Lhéritier, 29 March 1939, Archives CISH, dossier 1939.
21. Koht to Webster, 26 Jan. 1939, Webster papers, 7/1.
22. Van Kalken to Leland, 4 May 1939, Leland papers, box 42.
23. Webster to Leland, 5 April 1939, Leland papers, box 28.
24. Webster to Lhéritier, 27 March 1939, Archives CISH, dossier 1939.
25. Minutes of the meeting of 2 Feb. 1939, Webster papers, 7/1.
26. Lhéritier to Dupré, 24 Jan. 1939, Giunta Centrale per gli Studi Storici, Comitato Internazionale di Scienze Storiche.
27. Lhéritier to Dupré, 27 March 1939, ibid.
28. Leland-Lhéritier correspondence, Archives CISH, dossier 1939.
29. Archives CISH, dossiers 1939 and 1940.
30. Woodward to Lhéritier, 23 Feb. 1940, Archives CISH, correspondence Woodward 1938–1940. Woodward to Rockefeller Foundation, 14 March 1940, copy, Archives CISH, dossier 1940. Webster to Lhéritier, 11 April 1940, Webster papers, 7/1. On the German desire to continue the work of the ICHS, see Holtzmann to Lhéritier, 5 Nov. 1940 and 26 Aug. 1941, Archives CISH, dossier 1940–1944.
31. Archives CISH, dossier 1939.
32. Leland to Lhéritier, 18 Dec. 1939, ibid.
33. Iorga to Lhéritier, 4 Nov. 1939, Archives CISH, correspondence Iorga.
34. Letters of 1939/1940, Archives CISH, correspondence Woodward. Following the outbreak of fighting in the West, he requested on 16 May 1940 that Lhéritier restrict the still remaining

ICHS funds strictly to England, the United States, and France. He should send nothing to the neutral countries, and above all, nothing to Germany.
35. Nabholz to Lhéritier, 17 Sep. 1939, Archives CISH, dossier 1939.
36. Bonnet to Shotwell, 28 June 1940, Shotwell papers.
37. Notes by J. Marshall, Rockefeller Foundation, on a conversation with Leland, 9 Aug. 1940 as well as letters and notes from 1941 on the same question in Rockefeller Archive, RFA, Box 88, Series 100 R, F819. For 1942, see Box 89, Series 100 R, F 821.
38. Leland to Webster, 28 April 1941; Webster to Leland, 14 Nov. 1942, Webster papers, 1/22 and 1/23.
39. Archives CISH, dossier 1940–1944, particularly Lhéritier's activity report for 1940–41 from 10 May 1941.
40. Woodward to Lhéritier, 16 May 1940, Archives CISH, dossier 1940.
41. A former collaborator of the German Institute reported on the type and scope of this promotion: G. Heller, *Un Allemand à Paris* (Paris, 1981); on the general political and intellectual background, see H. Amouroux, *La grande histoire des Français sous l'occupation*, vol. 3: *Les beaux jours des collabos juin 1940–juin 1942* (Paris, 1979).
42. Politisches Archiv, Bonn, Akten der ehemaligen Deutschen Botschaft Paris; Zentrales Staatsarchiv, Potsdam, 49.01, 3191, file IX/13.
43. ICHS, *Bulletin* 12: 7f.
44. In a letter to the secretary of the French national committee he sought to defend his conduct with patriotic motives: "Je ne peux que déplorer votre changement d'avis. Pour moi, je suis essentiellement Français, et je m'intéresse à tous les pays, sans être spécialement, dans les circonstances actuelles, ni pour ni contre aucun. D'autre part, avec ma mentalité d'historien, il m'est impossible de faire la politique d'hier, pas plus que celle de demain; je me contente de celle d'aujourd'hui. J'estime que nous ne pouvons pas rester dans l'état où nous sommes, avec nos revues suspendues sine die, pour ne parler que d'elles. Et je pense que nous devons tout essayer pour sortir de cet état, c'est-à-dire pour maintenir la France. Nous avons notamment à replacer notre pays en face de l'Allemagne, quelle que soit l'impression pénible que nous puissions actuellement en ressentir." Lhéritier to Depréaux, 8 Aug. 1942, Archives Nationales, 70 AJ 159.
45. Record by Scurla, Reich Ministry for Science, on a meeting at the "Ausschuß für die Frage der internationalen wissenschaftlichen Organisationen," 2 Jan. 1941, Zentrales Staatsarchiv, Potsdam, 49.01, 3191; further material on this question ibid., 3190–3191, and in Politisches Archiv, Bonn, Akten der ehemaligen Deutschen Botschaft in Paris, 1940–1943.
46. Minutes of a discussion on this question on 12 Nov. 1940 in the science ministry, Zentrales Staatsarchiv, Potsdam, 49.01, 3191.
47. Minutes of the committee meeting of 11 June 1945, Archives CISH, box 31.
48. Leland to Lhéritier, 10 Sep. 1945; Leland to the president of the French national committee Petit-Dutaillis, 10 Sep. 1945; Leland to the Bureau members Nabholz, Woodward, Ganshof, Koht, to Webster as president of the British national committee, to G. S. Ford, secretary of the American Historical Association, and J. Marshall, Rockefeller Foundation, 10 Sep. 1945, all in copies in Nabholz papers, 29/5. In the latter circular, Leland explained his decision concerning Lhéritier as follows: "I have not reached this decision on the basis of the action of the French Committee alone, although that would suffice. I have learned through independent sources of information that he has sought to make capital for himself out of the emergency situation and has been dangerously close to a position of collaboration with the German authorities. He took no part in the Resistance movement, and a long editorial that he printed in *Bulletin* No. 46 of the International Committee of Historical Sciences spoke with respect of Hitler and his 'generous gesture' in the return of the ashes of Napoleon's son. Monsieur Lhéritier tried to ingratiate himself with the officers of the Rockefeller Foundation in Paris, presenting unsolicited memoranda. He endeavored also to ingratiate himself with the German authorities, and very clearly, although indirectly, attempted to get himself

appointed by the Germans to the Directorship of the Institut International de Coopération Intellectuelle in Paris. He patronized the appearance at the University of Dijon of Professor Schmitt, German cultural propagandist, and succeeded in having himself appointed chargé-de-cours at the Sorbonne, without the consent of the faculty, through support of Abel Bonnard, a notorious collaborationist. He also agreed, at the behest of the Germans, to organize a Franco-German Congress of Historians at Wiesbaden, using his position as Secretary-General of the Comité International in his effort to bring into the Congress French historians who served on various sub-committees of the Comité International. The unanimous refusal of the French historians made the proposed Congress impossible." Further material on this question in Rockefeller Archive, RFA, Box 89, Series 100 R.

49. Lhéritier to Koht, 10 April 1940 and 14 Oct. 1946, Koht papers, 386.
50. Leland, circular of 26 Oct. 1945, Nabholz papers, 29/5.
51. Minutes of 15 Dec. 1945, Archives CISH, box 31.
52. Fawtier to Leland, 21 Dec. 1946, Leland papers, box 42. Further material on the revival of the ICHS after the end of the war in Rockefeller Archive, RFA, Box 89, Series 100 R.
53. Leland to Fawtier, 24 Feb. 1947, Leland papers, box 42.
54. Leland to Fawtier and Morazé, 17 May 1947, ibid.
55. Nabholz to Domanovszky, 25 Oct. 1947, Domanovszky papers.
56. Leland to Koht, 3 Jan. 1948, Leland papers, box 22.
57. Leland to Petit-Dutaillis, 30 Nov. 1945, Leland papers, box 42.
58. Letter of 17 May 1947, ibid.
59. Compte rendu de l'Assemblée du Comité International des Sciences historiques, tenue à Royaumont les 3–5 juin 1947, Nabholz papers, 29/6.
60. Mikoletzky to Nabholz, 31 Oct. 1949, Archives CISH, box 26.
61. Archives CISH, box 26.
62. Material in Nabholz papers; Archives Nationales, 70 AJ 160; Webster papers (CISH 1946–1948); Koht papers.
63. Woodward in a report on Royaumont to Stevens, Rockefeller Foundation, 6 June 1947, Rockefeller Archive, RFA, box 89, Series 100 R, F 821.
64. A French Congress on 1848 was indeed staged in 1948 in Paris with international participation, including historians from Hungary, Poland, and Czechoslovakia.

Chapter 13

NOUVELLE HISTOIRE VERSUS *HISTOIRE HISTORISANTE*

Grand Debates and New Departures in Paris, 1950

The assembly of Royaumont in 1947 was swiftly followed by a General Assembly in Paris in 1948 and two meetings of the Bureau: in Copenhagen in 1948 and in London in 1949. Representatives from eighteen national committees convened in the French capital on 5 and 6 June 1948.[1] Aside from the United States, Canada, and Algeria/Tunis, this was a European event. It also included representatives from Poland, Czechoslovakia, and Hungary, and from Austria and Italy. The Soviet Union did not react to the invitation. Japan and Germany were not invited, since in accordance with the resolutions of Royaumont, the decision on their reintegration was postponed until the next Congress. China had to be left out of consideration because of civil war and revolution. A number of former member states had lost their independence, such as Lithuania, Latvia, and Estonia. Others were unable to attend due to currency and travel difficulties. Twelve of the countries represented in Paris had taken part in the founding assembly of the ICHS in 1926. It was the same European-American core that had supported the founding of the organization after the First World War and that now, after the Second World War, felt responsible for its reactivation.

Among the historians who had shaped the character of the Congresses in the interwar period, several had become victims of the fascist terror. Toward the end of the war, Marceli Handelsman, the guiding spirit of Polish underground university, was denounced to the Nazis and died in a German concentration camp. Nicolae Iorga, the universal humanist and visionary interpreter of Southeastern European history who, in his brief term as head of the Romanian government, had banned the Iron Guard in 1932, was murdered by Romanian legionaries in November 1940. Marc Bloch, the ingenious seeker of new paths in historiography, an officer in both world wars and a fighter in the Résistance, fell into the hands of the Gestapo in June 1944. He was tortured and shot to death.

Notes for this chapter begin on page 217.

Immediately following France's collapse in June 1940, Marc Bloch had drafted an analysis of the "Strange Defeat."[2] This work was the moving testament of an ardent patriot who, bereft of all illusions, felt forced to render account—"I belong to a generation that has bad conscience"—for himself and for the military, political, social, and intellectual reasons for the defeat of his country. In his examination of his own scholarly discipline some maxims stand out that can be viewed as the legacy of the founder of the *Annales* to the succeeding generation of historians.

It may appear surprising that Bloch, who rejected any conception of historiography as art for art's sake and demanded that history make a contribution to informed action in the present, warned against too much contemporary history. His argument was that a historian who only looks at the present or the recent past loses the ability to explain the world in which he or she lives. Without knowledge of the distant past, there can be no understanding of the present; the historian is deprived of the broad field of comparative observation, and the sense of the distinctive and of historical change is impaired. For the same reason, Bloch warned against too much history of political events, which particularly asserts itself in the preoccupation with the present and the recent past.

Starting with its founding fathers, the *Annales* circle has always regarded political history skeptically as "*histoire événementielle*" (history of events), "*histoire historisante*" (historicizing history), or "*histoire narrative*" (narrative history), and has pushed it to the margins of historical interest and investigation. In response to the challenge of the *Annales*, the question of whether the "event" is nevertheless an indispensable and central part of a historiography concerned with reality was put up for discussion as a basic problem of orientation at the Congresses of Paris, in 1950, and of Rome, in 1955.

Alongside this internal issue of Western historical studies, the relationship between Marxist and non-Marxist historiography gained increasing significance for the meaning and purpose of international historical cooperation. As an introduction to these problems and because of the broad interest the *Annales* encountered in Western and Eastern Europe, particularly in Poland and Hungary, it is worthwhile quoting Bloch's own words on his relationship to Marx as recorded in his testament:

> I myself have the greatest admiration for the work of Karl Marx. As a person, I fear, he was intolerable, as a philosopher he was undoubtedly less original than many would like to believe, but as a social analyst no one is more convincing. If future historians, disciples of a newly conceived science, should decide to erect an ancestral portrait gallery, then the bearded bust of the old Rhenish prophet would occupy the first position in the chapel of their guild. But are his teachings sufficient to be considered a model of each doctrine for all times? Outstanding scholars, who in their laboratories believe in nothing besides experience, have written physiological and physical essays "in the Marxist sense." What right would they then have to make fun of "Hitlerian" mathematics? Parties preaching the changeability of economic forms excommunicated those ill-advised who refused to swear an oath on the word of the master. As

if theories that were developed in the 1860s and that were based on the sociological knowledge of a scholar of that time could still be valid in the year 1940![3]

A similar relationship to Marx—high esteem for his methodological approach and reservations about an ossified doctrine of history—was characteristic for the school of the *Annales* in general, though individual opinions about historical materialism differed greatly.

Koht and Nabholz attended the General Assembly in Paris in 1948. After Leland's resignation, Nabholz had become president of the ICHS. Koht—who had been Norway's foreign minister before the occupation, remaining in this position in the London exile government until 1941 before going to America, where he spent the rest of the war—represented the Norwegian historians. Both were a personification of continuity within the ICHS beyond the war. France was represented both by Pierre Caron, secretary of the Bibliographical Commission for many years and thus also thoroughly acquainted with the tradition of the ICHS, and by Robert Fawtier, the chairman of the French national committee. As a long-term prisoner in a German concentration camp, Fawtier had suffered greatly in the war. Convinced that a radical reorientation in the ICHS and the Congresses was necessary, he shielded Morazé's activities as secretary-general from all criticism, which came—as will be shown below—from two Bureau members, Hans Nabholz and the treasurer Ernest L. Woodward. The reservations of the latter went so far that he lay down his office during the General Assembly of Paris in 1948, although without making an issue out of it.[4]

What had happened? Differing concepts of the future path of the ICHS collided with each another. The first question at stake was whether the Rockefeller Foundation would be prepared to continue providing support. The foundation's decision would to some extent be determined by its policy toward international organizations in general, which might change with the altered political conditions. Therefore, it was essential to convince the donors that the previous payments to the historians had been money well spent, and that the ICHS's future plans warranted further subsidies. Neither argumentation seems to have been successful. The behavior of the secretary-general Lhéritier, who had been on its payroll during the war, had profoundly shocked the foundation. Furthermore, virtually nothing had come of Leland's and Lhéritier's original idea to transform the ICHS into an international clearing house for historical study activities and to entrust it with diverse long-term tasks of research and publication, aside from the list of diplomats and the *International Bibliography*. The latter had regularly received subventions from the Rockefeller Foundation. But even the value of this showpiece of international scholarly cooperation was being questioned. Had the ICHS, which had once been founded with so much hope, not failed before the great tasks of its time? Should it not perish in the general European disaster and give way to more effective forms of international cooperation, which UNESCO appeared to offer? On the other hand, the dynamic and youthful secretary-general Morazé inspired new hope among the relevant staff members of the Rockefeller Foundation for a renewal of the study of history. During a term as visiting professor at the University of Wisconsin in the summer of 1947, he gained the impression that the foundation would be prepared to provide further support.[5]

What did Morazé think about the future modus operandi and purpose of the ICHS? In his discussion with the representatives of the Rockefeller Foundation he painted a highly negative picture of its previous activity. One of the members noted: "Morazé spoke very openly about the Committee's situation. He said that before assuming the position as international secretary he had looked into the Committee's history. As far as he could gather from it, he had to conclude that its activities were not well considered and carried out. From the report on the International Congresses, he offered a number of amusing examples of what the freedom of speech granted to all participants might lead to. In the final result, the Congresses appeared rather useless and more ceremonial than serious undertakings. He is convinced that more young people should be involved in the International Committee and in the Congresses themselves."[6] For the future he was planning Congresses "which would be genuinely and seriously concerned with the problems of contemporary historical studies." He expected them to provide exact information on progress in historical research. It was agreed that he would present his plans to the foundation in a memorandum. He submitted it in August of 1947. Here, he recommended the continuation of both the *International Bibliography* and the Congresses, which enjoyed a certain popularity in all countries, "particularly among historians of a certain age." In the future, the ICHS could gain increased significance. "Its basic purpose should be to act as a focus for historical work throughout the world" in a much tighter and more regular international cooperation than in the past. He hoped to win UNESCO's support for the continuation of the previously started activities of the ICHS. The foundation, however, should promote new and forward-looking activities:

> In principle, the Foundation's money should be used to establish the secretariat, which is designated to become the largest clearing house for history in the world. It is our intention to begin, in close association with the *International Bibliography*, a comprehensive international index of historians, their writings, their methods and of the applied and available sources. This extensive enterprise will take several years and probably require a stronger organization than that which was available to us in 1939, which, however, we will be content with at the beginning. We even believe that the quality of a few people dedicated to the task can represent a compensation for our scarce resources. Young historians throughout the world will surely show enthusiasm for voluntary cooperation in an undertaking which we know will have great significance for the development of a global culture.[7]

With this paper in hand, although now more skeptical and with a number of reservations, John Marshall from the Rockefeller Foundation proceeded to Paris to speak with Fawtier and Morazé. Fawtier, who became acquainted with Morazé's memorandum only on this occasion, agreed with Marshall's judgement that it was "hardly specific enough to be the basis for the R[ockefeller] F[oundation]'s action"—whereupon Morazé declared his willingness "to clear up at once a more precise statement."[8] Besides the organization of the Congresses, the continuation of the *Bibliography* and the completion of publications started before the war, the second memorandum listed as worthwhile new tasks for the ICHS the creation of a "world index of historical research workers," the publication of a "Bulletin on historical methods in view of a general inventory of references and working possibilities," and cooperation in a cultural history of humanity that was being suggested by UNESCO. This program catalog of Morazé's, whose far-reaching new suggestions derived from his personal ideas and were not covered by any discussions or even decisions within the ICHS, were passed on to the Rockefeller Foundation by Nabholz, who added his own clear criticism.[9]

In the meantime, Nabholz—who, as president of the ICHS, did not at all agree with the unauthorized proceedings of his secretary-general—had sent his own memorandum on work plans and financial needs, dated 11 October 1947, to the director of humanities at the Rockefeller Foundation, D. H. Stevens. His application was aimed at promoting current publication projects, but not at supporting the secretariat to which Morazé wished to assign these wide-ranging new tasks. Morazé's program was also criticized by the treasurer of the ICHS, Woodward, as immature and scarcely practicable, whereas Morazé himself was highly esteemed by the foundation's staff as the representative of new ideas and of a young generation of historians in whom they placed their hopes after the European collapse. Those who were to decide on the foundation's subsidies found themselves in a difficult position. Who had the say in the ICHS—the president or the secretary-general? The latter was supported by the influential Fawtier, the former by the equally well-respected Woodward. The end of the story was that the Rockefeller Foundation lost interest in continuing the financing. As John Marshall summarized the results of the deliberations, the foundation was not inclined to finance "academic undertakings" such as the bibliographical or biographical reference books suggested by Nabholz. While these could certainly be useful working instruments for the historians, "our interest in the Committee is aimed at what it can do as an international clearing house in order to stimulate and maintain the growth of historical scholarship." The ICHS did not seem to offer a sufficient guarantee of this.[10] Even a special visit that Fawtier and Morazé made to the United States to reiterate the request had no effect.[11] Although the foundation helped the ICHS to start its activities again with a number of installment payments amounting to $5,000, all subsidies were halted starting in 1950.[12]

These events revealed contradictory conceptions of the ICHS's tasks and abilities. The letters of several older historians, who had essentially contributed to its work in the interwar period, reveal a profound unease. Ganshof turned away in resignation. Nabholz emphasized how satisfactory the earlier work in the ICHS had been under Koht and Temperley. He had jumped into the breach as interim president only out of a feeling of duty, and he was happy to be able to place the office into other hands after the Paris Congress. Leland had withdrawn, and Woodward had resigned because he felt incapable of working with Morazé. Koht, the addressee of such complaints, shared many of the practical and personal reservations, but he also tried to ease tensions with firmness and skill.

The tensions within the ICHS led to Morazé's resignation at the Paris Congress of 1950. His plans to transform the ICHS, with a well-staffed and well-equipped secretariat, into an instrument of international historical research could not be realized. Following the First World War, Leland and Lhéritier had pursued similar ideas, but then as well as after the Second World War the organization of the International Congresses emerged as the central task of the ICHS. The planning and structure of long-term research requires firm institutional backing that can be provided only by the state. It was thus understandable that the Rockefeller Foundation, which was perfectly willing to support new trends in research, preferred to give its support to the Sixième Section rather than to the ICHS. The ICHS's proper task, which it was able to handle as a loose association and as the interface of a number of different interests, lay more clearly than ever in organizing the Congresses with the purpose of making them as ecumenical as possible.

Internationality, as complete as possible in the domains of culture, science, and education—this was also the goal of UNESCO, the cultural organization of the United Nations, which had been founded in 1946 and which, like the ICHS, had its headquarters in Paris. Besides the proximity of location, there were also personal links. Both Fawtier and Morazé worked in the French UNESCO delegation. Both endeavored to ensure the flow of funds for the ICHS, which became all the more urgent as the Rockefeller Foundation withdrew its support. They were successful. UNESCO financed the first postwar volume of the *Bibliography* as well as the publication of the "reports" for the International Congress of 1950. That was the first step in a long series of subsidies that the ICHS subsequently received and still receives from UNESCO. However, the link to UNESCO has always been indirect: at its General Assembly in April 1948, the ICHS decided to join a loose umbrella organization of humanities associations that, at the request of UNESCO, was to assume the task of clarifying and mediating research wishes and allocations. The first, highly influential secretary-general of this "International Council for Philosophy and Human Sciences" (ICPHS) was Fawtier, who, together with Morazé, succeeded in convincing the reluctant General Assembly that the ICHS would lose nothing of its independence through such a link to UNESCO.[13]

The test question for the efficiency and future character of the ICHS would be the success of the Paris Congress of 1950. Fawtier and Morazé rendered great services to its preparation and planning. With perseverance they did all they could to counter the division of Europe and the world into two antagonistic social and political systems by making possible the participation of historians from the Eastern European countries. They enlisted the French foreign ministry and the embassies of the Eastern European countries in Paris in the drive to achieve their goal. Moscow did not respond to their repeated invitations.

The Soviet Union also kept its distance from UNESCO until 1954. Poland (J. Dabrowski, T. Manteuffel), Hungary (F. Eckhart, D. Kosáry), and Czechoslovakia (Marie Husowa) had still participated in the Paris General Assembly of April 1948, and they all had intended to take part in the Congress. However, none of them could come. Yugoslavia also canceled at the last moment.[14] In the years from 1948 to 1950 these states underwent profound political transformations resulting in the creation of people's democracies firmly integrated into the system of states led by the Soviet Union. Poland and Hungary, however, demonstrated their desire for cooperation with the ICHS by maintaining their membership dues. The president of the Belgrade Academy wired his regret that the Yugoslav delegates saw no possibility of coming to Paris. Conversely, the General Assembly of the ICHS, which met at the Congress, manifested its readiness to ensure cooperation between East and West by creating a commission for Slavic studies. As Fawtier said, this decision was "suited to show that the International Committee of the Historical Sciences cares for Slavic studies and that it is hoping to see the historians from the countries of Eastern Europe participate once again at its Congresses."[15]

The list of some 1,400 participants in Paris, almost twice as many as at the last prewar Congress in Zurich, included historians from thirty-three countries.[16] At the General Assemblies held during the Congress, twenty-four national committees were represented.[17] In addition, Spain returned into the ICHS, and Israel was admitted as a new member. In a letter, Japan expressed its desire to resume its previous cooperation, and one historian from this country took part in the Congress.

The readmission of Germany represented a particularly delicate problem. As mentioned above, Germany was never deleted from the list of members. The willingness to allow its active participation one day had been clear since Royaumont. The question was merely who could credibly represent Germany after all that had happened, and whether Germany should be readmitted immediately. The actual process of reintegration occurred simultaneously with Germany's admission to UNESCO during the years from 1948/49 to 1952, like the admission of Japan to the ICHS and UNESCO. Since at that time the Soviet Union kept its distance from both international organizations, the admittance of the recently founded Federal Republic of Germany—in the political situation of 1950, characterized by the Monet Plan for the founding of a European iron and coal union and the Korean War—had as its context Western Germany's integration into the Western world. But despite the favorable political circumstances, the reintegration of the German historical profession into the ICHS resulted in complications.[18] One could expect that historians from countries that had suffered from the war and the German occupation would have misgivings. It was encouraging that such a powerful opponent of Nazi Germany as Aage Friis sought to reestablish old contacts with the German and Austrian historians immediately after the war, and that he taught others to make distinctions because "many Germans resisted Hitler under the very worst of circumstances."[19] It was all the more shameful that some German historians planted stumbling blocks on the road to return into the international community of historians. Addressing themselves to the French occupation authorities, they denounced the president of the newly founded Verband der Historiker Deutschlands (Historians' Association of Germany) as politically suspect and described the *Verband* itself as a clique of his followers that had no authority to speak for the German historical profession.

The *Verband*, after it had been checkmated by the Nazis, could not have been reconstituted more correctly than was actually the case. On 12 October 1948, members of the Historical Commission of the Bavarian Academy of Sciences and the board of editors (Zentraldirektion) of the *Monumenta Germaniae Historica*, the two historical institutions with the richest tradition in Germany, assembled in Munich and decided to re-create the historians' Association. They did so in the knowledge that German representation in the ICHS would soon be on the agenda. They had been informed that the reactivation of German cooperation in the *International Bibliography* was desired. An Austrian historian (von Loehr), who had participated in the Paris General Assembly of April 1948, had reported that the International Congress would deal with the readmission of Germany. Encouragement also came from Sweden and not least from Hans Nabholz, the president of the ICHS.[20] In 1949, a German Historikertag convened in Munich, attended also by archivists, history teachers, and regional historians. Here, the provisional founding resolution was sanctioned with the full support of all the participants. Historians from the Soviet occupation zone also joined the *Verband*. Nabholz's presence at this first postwar German congress confirmed the German initiative. Gerhard Ritter was almost unanimously elected chairman of the *Verband* in a secret vote, and in this office he was, as previously, to represent German historians in the international bodies.

Ritter was predestined for this office like no one else, on account of both his scholarly and his political reputation. With his Freiburg friends and as a dedicated member of the Confessing Church, he had been on close terms with the Resistance group surrounding Goerdeler. He had been arrested following the assassination attempt on Hitler and had spent the last six months of the war in prison. Among his colleagues there was no one who had similar experiences. Fawtier turned to Ritter with the request to make a list of German historians, from among whom a small number should be selected and personally invited to take part in the Paris Congress. But General Schmittlein, the general director of the office of cultural affairs in the French High Commission for Germany, prohibited this direct communication between Fawtier and the professor of the University of Freiburg, which lay in the French occupation zone. He considered this step to be bypassing his authority. In addition, he said, Ritter was running the Verband der Historiker Deutschlands in an authoritarian manner, and the formation of a united German association contradicted the federalist notions on which France's German policy was based in the first postwar years.

Schmittlein also suspected Ritter of extreme nationalism and inveterate enmity toward France.[21] Two essays of Ritter's from the war years, which had been placed into his hands, served as evidence. Fawtier was called upon to deal with the issue. He asked Pierre Renouvin to write an expert report. Renouvin saw no reason whatsoever to dissociate from Ritter because of the incriminating pieces.[22] But Schmittlein insisted on his rejection, and Fawtier received a notification from the foreign ministry stating: "As far as Dr. Ritter is concerned, the High Commission, after having taken your and M. Renouvin's point of view into account, stands by the opinion that you already know. Under these circumstances, any decision you might make to invite this professor can only occur upon your personal responsibility."[23] This was not a direct prohibition, hardly even a cautioning. Furthermore, Fawtier believed that the French foreign ministry disapproved of Schmittlein's behavior toward Ritter and that soon everything would become easier "since François-Poncet will become High Commissioner, even if Mr. Schmittlein has not yet been shown the door."[24] Nevertheless, during the meetings of the Bureau and the General Assembly at the Congress, Fawtier did not respond immediately to the Germans' application to reactivate their membership, though it was strongly supported by Nabholz. Instead, he decided to gather further information, beginning during the Congress with a sort of interrogation of the German participants assembled for this purpose in a lecture room.[25] Then a German memorandum on the founding and structure of the *Verband* had to show that it was legitimatized to represent the German historians in the ICHS.[26] The General Assembly of 3 September 1950 then authorized the Bureau to collect existing and further information regarding the decision on final readmission. This decision was taken in Stockholm at the Bureau meeting in June 1951 without any further discussion.[27]

After twelve years of National Socialism and the moral and material devastation of the war, the fact that the readmission of Germany occurred so soon, much sooner than after the First World War, can to a large degree be attributed to Fawtier, who steered the reintegration with magnanimity, tactical skill, and single-mindedness. What this meant for German historians, despite the limited scope of their participation,[28] was testified by personal notes and a report of Hermann Heimpel.[29] He expressed his joy over the new freedom of academic exchange regained with the help of French colleagues, and he recalled the consternation he felt at the sight of a marble tablet in a lecture hall of the Sorbonne with the inscription: "À Marc Bloch, professeur d'histoire économique, fusillé par les Allemands" (To Marc Bloch, professor of economic history, shot by the Germans).

The memory of Marc Bloch and the presence of historians linked to the *Annales*, such as Lucien Febvre, Fernand Braudel, and Ernest Labrousse, dominated the intellectual climate in which Robert Fawtier and Charles Morazé prepared the program of the Congress.[30] *Rapports* on the state of research and problems of historical investigation were to take center stage. This idea was not a new one. Lhéritier had already issued suggestions of this kind for the 1933 Warsaw Congress, although without any decisive effect. The Bureau had made similar plans for the scheduled Congress in Rome in 1943.[31] This time, as before, reservations were expressed during the preparatory meetings of the ICHS. They came from historians who did not regard the social historical approach of the *Annales* as the key to all historical knowledge, and who wanted to ensure a place at the Congress for traditional individual research in the fields of political history and the history of ideas. "Why change that which has been successful?" Webster asked. Koht said that the Congress should be limited to a few general themes, "since Fawtier's suggestion was 'an ideal' of which one could at best attempt 'to realize a part.'"[32] The minutes record the following outcome of the Copenhagen deliberations of 1948: "Despite the doubts and concerns that were expressed in the discussion, the Bureau's members accept the organization of the reports in principle. However, they express their desire that the topics should not be exclusively limited to the presentation of the state of research, but that important historical events should also be studied and discussed in regard to their origin and their influence on the future."[33] Thus, the Bureau members agreed that the program for the Paris Congress should represent a sort of compromise between "Annalistes" and "traditionalists," while the French historians would have the last word in shaping the scholarly structure of the Congress. It was to be expected that the spirit of the *Annales* would impose itself on the Congress and that it would be used for presenting history as a *science de l'homme*, together with the new methods of this approach.[34] To what extent was this idea realized?

The Paris Congress was a genuine working meeting.[35] The participants flocked to the lecture halls of the Sorbonne to attend the discussions of the morning "reports." This time the organizers had actually succeeded in sending the text of the *rapports* to the participants several weeks in advance. Thus, the speakers limited themselves to presenting their text with only a few brief comments. The chairmen generally were well-informed, and some of them managed to give the discussions a certain profile, even if they were far removed from Morazé's ideal: the best *rapporteurs* are the best chairmen.[36]

Sociability did not play a large role in Paris. There were a few official events and receptions, but they lacked the glamour of the earlier Congresses. There was also a dearth of opportunities for spontaneous, informal encounters. After they had completed their day's work, the participants went their separate ways.

The reports were of consistently high quality, and they were elaborated with scholarly expertise. The authors had been asked to present the status of research on the basis of the literature of the preceding ten years and to assess its results. The object was to present precise information on methods, theses, and problems in order to provide an empirical basis for the examination of the present position and self-awareness of historical studies. The reports approached this task in very different ways, and the *rapporteurs* did not always keep to the instructions they had been given. Some of them analyzed the most important controversial questions and presented their own point of view. Others endeavored to provide broad surveys of the scholarly literature. A third type examined an individual question from the field of study assigned to them.

The absence of Eastern Europe did not mean that at this Congress, which was so thoroughly influenced by the *Annales* group, the presence of Marxist historiography was not expressed in other ways. Several of the reports included Soviet historical literature. However, there were only two that can genuinely be described as Marxist. Both were written by Polish authors who were not allowed to attend the Congress.[37] However, some of the other participants occasionally introduced Marxist points of view, for example, Eric J. Hobsbawm, Fellow of King's College, Cambridge, and Pierre Vilar from the *Annales* group. In Paris, as the Polish historian Aleksander Gieysztor remarked in a later comment, "the spirit of the *Annales* had waved its rather red banner."[38]

Instead of structuring the program according to historical regions and epochs, the organizers had ordered it according to partial aspects of historical research. Thus, there were sections for "Anthropology and Demography," "Ideas and the History of Mentalities," "Economic History," "Social History," "Cultural History," "Institutional History," and a section on "The History of Political Facts," which had been added at Webster's request. The organizers intended to present the practical historical work going on in the various special areas, and all in all they reached their goal. However, the program did not provide the opportunity of placing the whole of an epoch or an event or a figure in the center of interest. Thus, a specialization concerning methodological questions and research literature in the different branches of historiography determined the scholarly style of the Congress. A future "*science de l'homme*," in the sense of a comprehensive historical anthropology as it had been envisaged by the organizers, did not emerge from the papers and discussions. In addition, the Congress was almost entirely restricted to European history.

Despite such limits, Paris nevertheless represented an important step in the development of the theoretical self-awareness of historical scholarship. Ever since the convocation of the first International Congress at the time of the "*Methodenstreit*" at the turn of the century, the traditional "historicist" historiography with its characteristic elements—textual criticism, hermeneutics, intellectual history, politics, events, individuals, narrative—had been challenged by ethnology, sociology, economics, psychology, and quantificational approaches. Under their influences, a methodological direction had developed that sought to transform history into a "historical social science." This "New History" or "*Nouvelle Histoire*," as its adherents liked to call it, defined its self-conception in opposition to a historicizing history ("*Histoire historisante*") or a history of events ("*Histoire événementielle*"). In the following, the Paris "reports" will be examined with regard to their understanding of the relationship between historicism and New History. Do they assess them as mutually exclusive opposites where only one side can win? Or rather as two positions that attempt to take each other into account? This points to another question, namely, how this polarized Western historiography viewed its relationship to historical materialism. Was a "life and death struggle" emerging, as some historians thought?[39] Or did the community of historians prove to be so elastic and durable that it provided room for both sides, despite the ideological gap dividing the world? This issue was not approached at Paris because of the absence of the Eastern Bloc, but it would be put to the test at future Congresses.

Although the historians of the *Annales* school dominated in Paris, they did not monopolize the floor. About half the "reports" were from authors who in a narrower or broader sense belonged to this circle, most of them Frenchmen: Aymard, Boutruche, Fourastié, Francastel, Friedmann, Lefebvre, Renouard, Varagnac, and Wolff (France), Cipolla (Catania), Dhont (Belgium), Postan (Cambridge), de Roover (United States), and Sapori (Florence). Within this group, there was a wide range of opinions. Their common denominator was the conviction of a paradigm shift from historicism to historical social science. They saw the relationship between the objects and methods of the "new" and the traditional approach, however, in very different ways. The point at issue was a matter of priorities, not of "either or," and thus a matter that in its essence was not at all a new one in the course of the "traditional" historiography. At Paris, a number of papers dealing with social history in the broadest sense had also been entrusted to historians who were not part of the *Annales* circle. One of these was Louis Chevalier. His studies on social classes in Paris attracted considerable attention owing to their link between demography and social history.[40] He was a sharp critic of the *Annales*. At the Congress, he stated: "The discovery of Man! An easy topic for the new passionate zeal in history. But many of the reservations we have voiced are aimed at saving research, which is necessarily strict and tedious and which can only be conducted in concert, from the lyrical temptation and joy of precipitous syntheses."[41] Does Chevalier belong to the "New History"? This question has received different answers. In any case, it became apparent in Paris that, despite the undeniable paradigm shift between the different trends of historical thought and writing, it would be wrong to draw rigid boundaries.

Some of the "reports" limited themselves to literature or research information, without revealing the methodological orientation of the author. In others, characteristic positions were emphasized. The first among those I wish to mention here is a contribution by Robert Boutruche,[42] a medieval scholar in Strasbourg and a student of Marc Bloch. He had taken the "report" on the Middle Ages in the section on the "History of Institutions," but he confined it to a special topic, the relationship between feudalism and the manorial system. His paper presented a thorough evaluation of the literature and precise formulations of the social historical problems involved in his field of research. It was well received by historians of all tendencies. According to the professional journals, it showed convincingly how effective the rigorous application of a methodology based on Bloch's approach could be.

Boutruche's Strasbourg colleague Pierre Francastel, however, delivered a "report" on the cultural history of the Modern Age that aroused controversy.

He saw cultural history as a new discipline whose aim was to explore "the intellectual structures of Man" by a synthesis of all the branches concerned with human history. "Our goal is to analyze all economic, literary, artistic, and technical features that represent the work of generations, by no longer viewing them as evidence of conflicting ideas, but rather as different modes of living, feeling, thinking, and expressing oneself."[43] Thus, for him, cultural history was a history of human behavior. Compared to it, the great intellectual and political questions of the past appeared relatively insignificant.

During the discussion, Gerhard Ritter countered this notion of cultural history with three objections. He firstly considered a comprehensive approach of such proportions to be an excessive demand. Without denying the usefulness of interdisciplinary research activities on a broad scale, he asserted that a new science, with epistemological goals of its own, could not be brewed out of them. Nonetheless, he pointed out that there already were a few wide-ranging cultural historical syntheses of high status, such as Burckhardt's *Culture of the Renaissance* and Huizinga's *Autumn of the Middle Ages*. Thus, his misgivings about a cultural historical synthesis were more of a pragmatic than a logical nature.

Ritter's second objection was more fundamental. "But what do '*mode de vie*' or '*façon de vie*' [way of life] really mean?" he asked. "In the end, every distinctive, strong individual has his own '*mode de vie*,' his own way '*de se comporter*' [way of behavior]. If one removes everything that represents individual distinction, then what is left as a common 'style'? Scarcely more than a pallid general notion of the 'Renaissance man,' the 'baroque' or 'romantic' man—a mere '*Begriffsgespenst*' [conceptual ghost] by which practically nothing (or at least very little) is gained for the deeper understanding of historical reality."[44] These reservations were rooted in a different set of priorities: Which is historically more significant, individual or typical, general features? Both possible answers can refer to the traditions of historicism and to such pioneers as Ranke and Burckhardt.

Ritter's third objection was based on his philosophical-idealistic and Lutheran profession of faith, according to which not everything in history is historical:

> The highest creations of the human spirit, such as the great works of art or the philosophical systems, undoubtedly tower high above mere history. That which is historical is that which is transitory, but the spirit in its highest creations is eternal, and religion understands itself as the revelation of the eternal. Of course, every great intellectual creation also has a historical side: its form depends on its time, and its development is only possible under certain unique conditions, which must be examined by historical research. But for us, this historical side of its existence is far less significant than the timeless one. The masterpiece of St. Peter's Cathedral in Rome certainly has a building history, which one must know, and this building history stands in a close relationship with the general history of the Papacy in the sixteenth century. But what this cathedral with its wonderful dome really seeks to express, what makes it into a great work of art, cannot be learned from its

artistic and cultural history, but rather from its architecture. A person who is not profoundly aware of the essential laws of architecture will ultimately miss the point of the thing itself.... In the end, there is no successful study of Reformation history without theological expertise, no successful analysis of the great political thinkers like Grotius, Hobbes, Locke without thorough training in legal-philosophical thought. That is why the philosophers, the philologists and literary scholars, the scholars of art and music, the theologians and legal scholars and national economists are the best cultural historians—each in his own field.[45]

It is probably correct to say that the more radical historicism—the unreserved reduction of all intellectual-artistic phenomena in history to their spatial-temporal-social conditions—was to be found not in the "traditionalist" Ritter, but rather in his "annalistic" adversary Francastel.

A "report" on historical anthropology by André Varagnac stood in close proximity to Francastel in terms of methodology.[46] Varagnac was concerned with introducing his concept of "*Archéocivilisation*" into archaeology and anthropology. He had founded an institute with this name in Paris in 1947 together with Henri Berr, the veteran of historical synthesis, as honorary chairman. Like Francastel, Varagnac strove to establish a "*discipline synthétique*," in his case with particular attention to prehistory and anthropology. The object of this branch of historical studies should be research into long-term patterns of behavior and perception, as they can be found in the daily life of the broad masses of the population. It was obvious that he had read Lucien Febvre and Fernand Braudel when he distinguished three levels for each culture: at the bottom there were the hardy "practical conditions" (*statuts techniques*), above them the organization of production and exchange of goods, and finally at the top the culture of the elite. To uncover their mutual interactions, he said, was a historian's real task. Worth mentioning was his reference to the rapidly growing interest in archaeological research in the Soviet Union and the Eastern European people's democracies. He attributed this to a general Marxist effort to provide a realistic depiction of the conditions of human life and to the needs of assuring national identity by history. In this context, he pointed out what it meant for the divided world that the common faith in history survived on both sides and—something that was particularly important to him—that there was a newly aroused interest in preindustrial ("*prémachinistes*") conditions.

This was an aspect that was dealt with in Georges Friedmann's contribution on contemporary cultural history, which stood out from the other "reports."[47] Friedmann worked on the *Annales* editorial team alongside Braudel, Morazé, and Lucien Febvre. Instead of talking about methodological issues or providing a survey of the state of research, he presented a refreshingly provocative essay on the impact of technology and industry—"*machinisme*"—on culture. Arnold Toynbee, the English universal historian and philosopher of history who led the discussion, expressed the questions raised by Friedmann's report in a pointed formulation referring to the international problems of the moment:

> What is the relation between modern technology and the western bourgeois civilization that has conjured this technology into existence? Are these two things indissoluble, or are they separable? Is it possible, in the long run, to reject the individualism and retain the technology? Does the triumph of technology actually spell the death of individualism as the Marxists maintain? Is the technological element in our modern western civilization going in any case to become the heritage of the whole of Mankind? If the whole world adopts a uniform technology, is the whole world then also bound to adopt one uniform social system? Or could a communist technological civilization and an individualist technological civilization co-exist peacefully side by side?[48]

As far as I can tell, this is the first time that the notion and the term of "coexistence" were mentioned at the International Historical Congresses. The ensuing, rather stormy discussion was concerned with "remedies" for "depersonalization." Halecki spoke of religion, Talmon spoke of freedom, and Varagnac spoke of the preservation or resurrection of the remains of preindustrial behavioral patterns, touching on such contemporary questions as reduced working hours and leisure problems. An English student finally defined the generally diagnosed ailment as "alienation" and observed that this was the central question in the sociology of both Karl Marx and Max Weber.[49]

In the Paris program, the history of culture ("*civilization*") and of ideas ("*idées-sentiments*") were allocated in different sections. This fact raised occasional criticism, for it is impossible to exclude the history of religious or philosophical or scientific thought, which endeavors to provide orientation for human actions and perceptions, from a cultural history concerned with collective modes of behavior and mentalities. Georges de Lagarde (Paris), who presented a brilliant report on the research into intellectual history in the Middle Ages,[50] asserted that cultural history and intellectual history signified different scientific interests and shifts of emphasis rather than fundamental contradictions. Lagarde was the author of a multivolume work on the medieval origin of the "*esprit laïque*" (secular thinking), a modern collective mentality whose origin he tried to discover among the philosophers and theologians of the thirteenth and fourteenth centuries, always taking into account the context of political and social life.[51] Now in Paris, dealing with the history of medieval philosophy, he pleaded for studying the "authentic thinkers" alongside the "ideas and feelings of the various groups making up medieval society."[52] After all, there was an interaction between the thinking of individuals and the social and intellectual climate in which they lived. In regard to historical methodology, he provided a persuasive definition of understanding: "The golden rule for an intellectual historian must indeed be the constant and sometimes painful endeavor to extricate himself from his own intellectual world, i.e., a persistent will to live with the people whose convictions he is researching, to make their prejudices and concerns into his own, to think with them, to yield to the same feelings and fears and to succumb to the same collective compulsions of their thinking."[53] I do not see that such presentations of "New History" differ greatly from the historicists with regard to the notion of "understanding" as the cardinal virtue of the historian since the time of Herder and Ranke.

As holds true for intellectual history in general, the history of science was particularly affected by social scientific conceptions. This was shown in a report by Henry Guerlac (United States).[54] He emphasized, on the one hand, how new and incomplete this discipline, which had first emerged at the Paris Congress of 1900, still was. On the other hand, he thought the time was ripe to develop a "sociocultural history of science." Others objected that, in view of the sketchiness of knowledge concerning the development of science itself, such a project was somewhat premature.[55] However, they all agreed to recommend the formation of a separate section for the history of science at future Congresses, as had been the case in Paris half a century earlier.

The differences between New History and historicism were naturally most visible in the sections for economics and social science. In a discussion following a presentation by Jean Fourastié (Paris), the problem of determinism in history was raised. Fourastié asserted that "an event from the past interests us to the extent that it determines or at least helps determine our present or our future. In our opinion, historical investigation only becomes scientific to the extent that it attempts to uncover deterministic processes and factors."[56] This dogmatical and restricted definition was narrowed down by Fourastié to the fields of social developments and economics, where, however, he wanted to ascribe to them a predictive potential, e.g., in the struggle against unemployment. This historical empiricism, which was conscious of its limitations, was too narrow for the Marxist tastes of Pierre Vilar: "Every determinism that does not encompass the whole of history," he said, was "impotent."[57] On the other hand, the social scientist Émile Coornaert of the Collège de France expressed his skepticism toward the scientific viability of determinedness in general. Statistical methods—of course. However, they do not transform the previous modes of historical studies but rather complement them. Is there not a danger that in the end the historian sees only material objects and not man? One must not lose sight of the fact that behind, for instance, price movements there stands the weight of moral factors, habits, and mentalities, whose significance had been highlighted by Marc Bloch and Lucien Febvre. Like other participants in the discussion, the Swiss historian Jean Halpérin underscored the "often very subjective character of statistical documents."[58] And when, in his "report" on economic history in the Middle Ages, the Englishman Michael Postan applied the term "*longue durée*" to medieval economic developments—expansion until the fourteenth century, contraction thereafter—Émile Coornaert denied that such a broad generalization was possible for the Middle Ages. In this era, personal factors had played a decisive role, and they were what the historian ought to examine in the first place.[59] In this discussion, Ernst Labrousse lent the entire weight of his scholarly competence as head of the new economic history direction in France to an attempt at mediation. He agreed with Fourastié, but he only granted his findings on deterministic factors "a certain character of probability." He also agreed with Postan, but nevertheless thought it necessary to warn against doctrinaire simplifications and to plead for "a great infusion of historical thought into economic theory."[60]

Marxist notions were given greater attention in the social science section. The report by the absent Polish historian Marian Malowist[61] was discussed under Hobsbawm's supervision. Malowist provided a factually rich survey of the results of economic-historical research on the economic situation of the nobility, the peasants, and the middle classes in Poland at the beginning of the modern era. While his paper claimed to be Marxist, it was not dogmatic. Thus, the Polish émigré Halecki, who was living in the United States, could state that he "saw nothing in the presentation of the facts which was directly contradictory to other methods."[62] However, in contrast to Hobsbawm and Vilar, he and other participants rejected the concept of class as the key to social history. The assertion that social history could have a much broader significance than the mere examination of social strata and conflicts was illustrated by Adolf J. C. Rüter from the University of Leyden. He confronted the continental view of social history, centered on the concept of class, with Trevelyan's understanding of social history as the "history of a people under the exclusion of political events."[63]

The relationship between political and societal history was the subject of the section "History of Political Facts." For ancient history there was a collective report by three authors (Masson-Oursel, Aymard, Palanque), which was presented by André Aymard (Paris).[64] If political history was today being shoved into the corner as the "Cendrillon du travail historique" (Cinderella of historical work) or even "la reine déchue" (the dethroned queen), then, thank God, this certainly was not so noticeable in the case of ancient history. Here the ideal that history was to encompass all aspects of life was still in force. Aymard received lively agreement from Henri-Irénée Marrou, who vehemently protested against any fragmentation of ancient history into arbitrary compartments.[65] Apparently, the "new" history had not yet found its way into ancient history.

Things looked different for the Middle Ages. In his diagnosis on the status of political history, Yves Renouard (Bordeaux), who delivered the "report," declared: "Political history is only one of the goals of modern historians and one to which they feel least committed. And yet it is the oldest form of history."[66] Systematic studies on it were only going on at a few old research centers, such as the École des Chartes (from whence the next secretary-general of the ICHS would come!). At present political history was still important, but he could not guarantee it any chances for the future. Its real task lay only in making itself superfluous. In an unbroken positivistic understanding of science, he arrived at the following conclusion:

> When all the documents of the kings and princes have been published or cataloged, when the dating, the sequence of events, of treaties, of heads of states, and of governments have been incontrovertibly determined, when local, regional, and national histories have been written coherently and with scholarly methods, then political history will have fulfilled its task and it will have provided general cultural history

with the initially necessary ancillary services that the latter expects from it. Future historians, relying on the final works of their predecessors, will no longer deal with it, and the International Congresses can drop the superfluous section. The fact that it still exists today will one day serve to position our own, by then remote generation in the course of history.[67]

A swan song for political history, but a bit premature! For it returned with unbroken vitality into the arena of the Paris Congress. The "report" by Pierre Renouvin on "Histoire des faits politiques, époque contemporaine" was one of the most brilliant contributions to the Congress. Renouvin restricted his survey review of research literature to political electoral sociology, administrative history, and biography in the more important Western countries. The lasting value of his instructive presentation lay in the way he defined the place of political history within the field of historical studies. He saw it in an intermediate position between two poles of historical methodology, which he characterized with the names Seignobos and Febvre/Morazé. From Seignobos's *Political History of Europe* he took the distinction between historical phenomena of depth ("*phénomènes profonds*") and of superficiality ("*phénomènes superficiels*"). He placed economic, social, and intellectual factors in the first category, political events in the second. But in contrast to Seignobos, he fully included "*forces profondes*" in the study of the causes of political phenomena. He agreed with Febvre and Morazé that it was extraordinarily questionable to give political events primacy over economic, social, and intellectual developments. Therefore, one must "delve beneath the surface and try to take hold of the 'depth phenomena,' as Seignobos called them, even if this search often gives considerable space to hypotheses."[68] Here a door was opened for the entrance of economic and social history and theory into political history. And yet Renouvin sketched a clear dividing line between himself and Morazé, who had brought Lucien Febvre's concepts into an "extreme form."[69]

Morazé's new historical method, Renouvin said, reduced history to economic and social conditions. With the help of statistical research, the historian was to be enabled to recognize economically determined general movements and in this way to explain human behavior, a method for which, in Morazé's own understanding, "both the date and the fact lose their value."[70] Renouvin countered this disdain for the "time and event factor" in historiography with the following observation:

> Economic development cannot explain everything. For example, has it not been proved that in France social groups with analogous economic interests have differed in their behavior in political life, simply because they have been divided by questions of faith? In the comparative study of the development of two states, does one not notice that social forces of the same type produce divergent political behavior? Is it possible to explain the entire movement of the national minorities in Central and Eastern Europe exclusively on the basis of economic or social forces? The fact that these forces exerted their influence on one region or another is obvious. But have

there not been cases in which the political protest of a national minority ran counter to its own material interests? When Bismarck launched the *Kulturkampf*, when Gladstone after the vote on the agrarian laws took sides in the issue of Home Rule, where was the deterministic role of the economy?[71]

The report on the ensuing discussion, which was supervised by Webster, the initiator of this section, indicates no comments by Morazé. As secretary-general he participated in the Congress, but obviously he did not rise to the challenge. Thus, the discussion comments were all delivered in a conciliatory tone. Renouvin's position between Seignobos and Febvre/Morazé appeared to be generally convincing, even for Labrousse. As a representative of the "New History," he did not in the least differ from Renouvin when he sought to give "mentalities" a central position between economic and political history. "Labrousse," the report says, "demonstrates his belief in the conciliatory potential of the New History, which denies nothing which once was, but which wants to write large new chapters.... The convergence at the finishing line is of greater significance than the divergence at the start."[72]

The methodological conception of the study of history as defined by Renouvin, in which the elements of "traditional" and "new" historiography are combined, constitutes a type of history that I would like to term "New Historicism." At the Paris Congress, this "New Historicism" asserted itself conspicuously. In general epistemological considerations did not play any important role in the discussions on what the preferred object of history should be, how the relationship between political and social history was to be understood, and what historical synthesis might mean. There was, however, one exception: Henri-Irénée Marrou, professor of the Sorbonne and a specialist for late Antiquity, who contributed the "report" on ancient cultural history.[73] He used Toynbee's notion of ancient culture as really existing from prehistoric times to the fall of late Rome in order to examine the value of this synthetic general term, and he arrived at the conclusion that it did not stand up to historical reality. Instead, he suggested that three periods be distinguished—the Greek era, Hellenism, and the late ancient period—giving them the names Polis, Peidaia, and Theopolis. In doing so, he admitted that such general cultural historical concepts could never signify idealistically or realistically conceived entities. He defined himself as a nominalist and characterized the epistemological function of such syntheses making use of Max Weber's notion of the "ideal type." Marrou turned the concept of the "ideal type" not only against historical idealism and realism, but also against the notion that historical synthesis exhausted itself in the combination of the knowledge drawn from the various cultural and social historical disciplines. "If cultural history has its own special object, then it must investigate the relationship between the various possibilities of observing the past, namely, between the history of ideas, economics, politics, art, social matters, and religion, and if possible, it must reveal the common inspiration behind all of them, the principle to which they can be traced back."[74] However, this principle, such as the "*Cité antique*" of Fustel de Coulanges, can never cover the whole of reality, and it requires constant correction in keeping with historiographical progress. As Marrou stated in his fine description of the interaction between subject and object in historical understanding: "The only authentic knowledge of history is that which emerges from a long acquaintance with the sum of documents of all kinds from an epoch and which allows this milieu to develop gradually in the thinking of an attentive, skilled, patient historian; of a historian who is sufficiently gifted to communicate with the people of that epoch and that milieu and who ultimately becomes just as well acquainted with the people of 'his' era as with his own contemporaries."[75]

Just as Paris represented a crucial orientation point for an appraisal of the methodological discussion at mid-century, far-reaching organizational and personnel decisions were being made for the ICHS.[76] The number of the assessor members of the Bureau was raised from four to five in order to improve its geographical and linguistic composition. A further change in the statutes addressed the admission of the specialized international organizations ("*organismes internationaux*") to the ICHS. Alongside the national committees, they now received full voting rights except in resolutions on changes in the statutes. This made it necessary for the ICHS to decide which of the numerous internal and external commissions of the interwar period should be brought back to life and were capable of surviving in the future. The alteration inaugurated a development that finally led to the result that, through the growing number of affiliated organizations, specialized historical research received equal responsibility for the work of the ICHS. This far-reaching innovation was brought about by the ICHS's relationship with UNESCO, specifically, it resulted from its membership in the latter's humanities suborganization, the ICPHS (International Council for Philosophy and Human Sciences). Membership meant entitlement to occasional subsidies. The ICPHS, however, as its secretary-general Fawtier explained, opposed an increase in direct memberships. Thus, the ICHS was given a monopoly position for all branches of historical scholarship. If other professional historical organizations wanted to establish a relationship with the ICPHS, then the only path went through the ICHS.

A third change in the statutes was related to the election of the Swiss Largiadér as treasurer at the Paris General Assembly of 1948 following Woodward's resignation. Whereas the legal headquarters of the ICHS had previously only been of a provisional nature—Washington, D.C., because of Leland as treasurer, later London because of Woodward—it was now decided that they should be located in the city where the assets of the ICHS were deposited. This was Lausanne, a city in the economically stable and transfer-friendly country of Switzerland. It was logical that the office of treasurer would be delegated to a Swiss in the future as well.

The general secretariat also stabilized itself in Paris. That it would do so was in no way certain after it became apparent at the Paris Congress that Morazé would resign and Robert Fawtier become president. In order to avoid a concentration of offices in Paris, Fawtier suggested transferring the general secretariat to London. Vice-president Sir Charles Webster's plea for Paris was all the more remarkable. "I believe myself," he wrote to Fawtier, "that the secretariat should, if possible, be in Paris. If it is not in Paris, then I think that Brussels would be the obvious place. It is essential that the secretary has a complete command of French, and very few Englishmen are in that position, as you know."[77] Fawtier was elected president, and the Bureau was approved in its new composition by acclamation on 27 August. Michel François, the 47-year-old Conservateur adjoint aux Archives Nationales and member of the Commission d'Histoire au Centre National de la Recherche Scientifique, was elected secretary-general. He had been jointly recommended by Fawtier, who had originally wanted to retain Morazé, and Renouvin.[78] His three-year administrative experience as the former Directeur des Beaux-Arts with the French military government in Baden-Baden was given particular emphasis in Renouvin's letter of nomination. He had received his training as an archivist and a historian at the venerable École des Chartes, whose director he was to become between 1970 and 1976.

During his three decades in office, François' thoughts, actions, and goals were so closely linked with the international historical organization that "Monsieur CISH" actually appeared to personify it. He did not share Morazé's visionary zeal of scholarly and organizational reform. However, he dedicated his inexhaustible, conscientious, and diligent labor to the full service of the organization. He had no assistant to help him, making do with only a part-time typist at his disposal. He received no material compensation for his sacrifice of time and energy. In the study of his private apartment there stood a heavy iron file cabinet: this was the entire special equipment of one of the world's best-administered international scientific organizations. He was proud of his achievements for the ICHS, with which he identified himself completely, and he was justified in this pride. As a scholar whose monographs and editions were mostly concerned with the late Middle Ages and the early modern era, Michel François embodied an *"histoire historisante"* (to use this term coined by his critics) characterized by the critical examination of documents and records, facts and events. The École des Chartes, an element of the old Sorbonne, was viewed by the disciples of the *"Nouvelle Histoire"* as a "bastion of traditional historiography in the middle of the 20th century."[79] François stood by this tradition consciously, and occasionally, despite all the correctness of his official statements, he spoke dismissively of the *Annales* school. Thus, it is remarkable that Fawtier, who held Morazé in high esteem, supported François as his successor in the office of secretary-general. This was probably not only an expression of Fawtier's tolerance, but also evidence of his grasp of reality, for his new task was to preside over an organization in which the most varied historiographical tendencies crossed. The ICHS could not have made a more fortunate choice.[80]

Notes

1. Minutes and report by Edward F. D'Arms on a conversation with Nabholz, 18 April 1948, Rockefeller Archive, RFA, box 89, series 100 R, F 822.
2. M. Bloch, *L'Étrange Défaite: Témoignage écrit en 1940. Avant-propos de G. Altman* (Paris, 1946). In this context, see also his uncompleted work, written in the period between the defeat and the Résistance and edited by L. Febvre: *Apologie pour l'histoire ou métier d'historien* (Paris, 1949).
3. Bloch, *L'Étrange Défaite*, p. 170f.
4. See Woodward to Marshall, 19 March 1948, Rockefeller Archive, RFA, box 89, Series 100 R, F 822.
5. On the entire process, the concepts for the ICHS and support from the Rockefeller Foundation, there is comprehensive material in Rockefeller Archive, RFA, box 89, Series 100 R, F 821 and 822, and in the Nabholz papers.
6. Notes by John Marshall on a discussion with Edward F. D'Arms and Morazé in New York, 17 June 1947, Rockefeller Archive, RFA, box 89, series 100 R, F 821.
7. English translation of 18 Sep. 1947, ibid.
8. Notes by J. Marshall, Paris, 16 Oct. 1947, ibid.
9. Nabholz to Stevens, 1 Nov. 1947, ibid.
10. Marshall to Leland, 8 Sep. 1948, ibid.
11. Nabholz to Koht, 1 Jan. 1949, Koht papers, Ms. fol. 3928:1.
12. See Rockefeller Archive, RFA, Box 89, Series 100 R, F 822.
13. Minutes of General Assemblies 1947–1950, Archives CISH, box 26, and Nabholz papers, 28/3.
14. Correspondence in Archives CISH, box 26.
15. "Procès-Verbal 3 Septembre 1950," copy in Giunta Centrale per gli Studi Storici, Comitato Internazionale di Scienze Storiche.
16. By contrast, François speaks of "1,100 inscrits," ICHS, *Bulletin d'information*, no. 10: 11.
17. An information brochure of UNESCO (UNESCO Archive), probably written by Morazé, names the following countries: Algeria, Argentina, Austria, Belgium, Brazil, Canada, Denmark, Egypt, Finland, France, Great Britain, India, Ireland, Italy, Luxembourg, Mexico, Netherlands, Norway, Portugal, Sweden, Switzerland, Turkey, the U.S., and the Vatican.
18. On the following, comprehensive material is preserved in Nabholz papers 36/2; Ritter papers; Rockefeller Archive, LSRM, RF, RG 2—1950/100; Archives Nationales, 70 AJ 160; Archives CISH, box 26.
19. Friis to Dopsch, 4 June 1947, Dopsch papers.
20. Minutes of the founding assembly, Munich 1948, in Aubin papers, 18.
21. See G. Ritter to R. Schmittlein, 16 June 1949, in Ritter, *Briefe*, no. 159, and Ritter to R. Fawtier, 16 June 1949, Archives Nationales, 70 AJ 160.
22. The titles of Ritter's essays were *Zur politischen Psychologie des modernen Frankreich* (*Lehrbriefe der Philosophischen Fakultät der Universität Freiburg* 2, Freiburg i. Br., 1943); *Der Oberrhein in der deutschen Geschichte* (*Freiburger Universitätsreden* 25, Freiburg i. Br., 1937). On Renouvin's judgement, see his letter to Fawtier, 2 March 1950, Archives Nationales, 70 AJ 160: "Dans la première ... je ne vois vraiment rien de choquant, et je trouve même beaucoup de remarques très justes. Ces pages sont de 1940: or, pas d'accent de triomphe insolent, pas de trace de haine. Sans doute, il reproche à la politique française d'avoir été brutale en 1919–1924. Mais je ne peux m'étonner qu'un Allemand ait un point de vue différent du nôtre!" In the second work, Ritter argues that the Rhine and the Alsace are German: "Mais combien de professeurs allemands connaissez-vous qui aient expressément professé le contraire?... En somme, Ritter est un nationaliste. Il n'y a pas lieu d'en être surpris, ni indigné. S'il n'y a pas à son dossier d'autres textes que ceux-là, je ne vois pas pourquoi nous l'écarterions. Aurions-nous donc le dessein de n'admettre au Congrès que les historiens allemands qui, entre 1919 et

1940, auraient abdiqué tout nationalisme? Ils risqueraient de n'être pas nombreux, et de n'être pas non plus très 'représentatifs' de la 'science historique' allemande!"
23. Archives Nationales, 70 AJ 160.
24. Fawtier to Nabholz, 10 Aug. 1949, ibid.
25. Notes by Hermann Heimpel on the Paris Congress, made available to me for the purpose of this study.
26. Paris, 30 Aug. 1950, supplement to the minutes of the General Assembly of 3 Sep. 1950, Koht papers, 3668:2, complemented by a letter from Ritter to Fawtier, 26 Oct. 1950, Archives CISH, box 26.
27. Documents of 1950 and 1951, Archives CISH, box 26.
28. Ten historians from the Federal Republic, two from the Saarland, none from the GDR. The Germans delivered no lectures, except one by K. Handfest from the Saarland.
29. H. Heimpel, "Internationaler Historikertag in Paris," *Geschichte in Wissenschaft und Unterricht* 1 (1950): 556–559, here p. 557; on Heimpel's notes, see note 25 above. Cf. also L. Dehio, "Der internationale Historikerkongreß in Paris (IX. congrès international des sciences historiques)," *Historische Zeitschrift* 170 (1950): 671–673, here p. 673.
30. See "Proposition de Monsieur Fawtier pour l'organisation du IXe Congrès International des Sciences Historiques," n.d., 16 p., Nabholz papers, 36/1.
31. Nabholz pointed this out at the Copenhagen Bureau meeting, 9–10 Oct. 1948, "Procès-Verbal" in Archives CISH, box 26.
32. Ibid.
33. Ibid.
34. See the UNESCO brochure cited in note 17 above.
35. Two volumes of proceedings were published: *Comité International des Sciences Politiques—International Committee of Historical Sciences: IXe Congrès International des Sciences Historiques*. Vol. 1: *Rapports* (Paris, 1950); vol. 2: *Actes* (Paris, 1951) [hereafter Congress Paris 1950: *Rapports*; idem: *Actes*]. They present the "rapports" verbatim and summarize the discussions. As far as the "communications" are concerned, only the titles and the eventual places of publication are indicated. See Congress Paris 1950: *Actes*, pp. 287ff.
36. See Morazé's summary of the Paris Congress, in Congress Paris 1950: *Actes*, p. 282.
37. M. Malowist, "Histoire sociale. Époque contemporaine," Congress Paris 1950: *Rapports*, pp. 305ff.; W. Kula, "Histoire des institutions, Époque contemporaine," ibid., pp. 472ff. Kula's report did not fit with a scientific meeting because of its political declarations in the style of the Cold War and was not discussed. See Congress Paris 1950: *Actes*, p. 193.
38. A. Gieysztor, "O kongressach historycznych nauk" [On the Historical Congresses], *Kwartalnik historyczny* 73 (1966): 481–495, here p. 481.
39. W. Hofer, "IXe Congrès International des Sciences Historiques," *Schweizer Monatshefte* 30 (1950/51): 457–461, here p. 461.
40. L. Chevalier, *La formation de la population parisienne au XIXe siècle* (Paris, 1950); id., *Classes laborieuses et classes dangereuses à Paris dans la première moitié du XIXe siècle* (Paris, 1958).
41. Congress Paris 1950: *Rapports*, p. 108; Chevalier was one of five "rapporteurs" in the "Anthropology and Demography" section. On his historiographical position, see H. Coutau-Bégarie, *Le phénomène "Nouvelle Histoire": Stratégie et idéologie des nouveaux historiens* (Paris, 1983).
42. Congress Paris 1950: *Rapports*, pp. 417ff.
43. Ibid., pp. 341ff., quotation p. 355.
44. "Zum Begriff der Kulturgeschichte: ein Diskussionsbeitrag," *Historische Zeitschrift* 171 (1951): 293–302, quotation p. 295; in this article Ritter worked out his Paris discussion comments (Congress Paris 1950: *Actes*, p. 264f.) in detail.
45. Ibid., p. 297f.
46. Congress Paris 1950:, *Rapports*, pp. 38ff.
47. Ibid., pp. 367ff.
48. Congress Paris 1950: *Actes*, p. 171.

49. Ibid., p. 178.
50. Congress Paris 1950: *Rapports*, pp. 160ff.
51. G. de Lagarde, *La naissance de l'esprit laïque au déclin du moyen âge*, 2 vols. (Paris, 1934); vols. 3–4 (Vienna, 1942); 2nd ed. 2 vols. (Paris, 1948); new revised ed. 5 vols. (Paris, 1958–1963).
52. Congress Paris 1950: *Actes*, p. 75.
53. Congress Paris 1950: *Rapports*, p. 174.
54. Ibid., pp. 182ff.
55. Congress Paris 1950: *Actes*, pp. 83ff.
56. Congress Paris 1950: *Rapports*, p. 217.
57. Congress Paris 1950: *Actes*, p. 107.
58. Ibid., p. 103f.
59. Ibid., p. 113.
60. Ibid., p. 113.
61. "Histoire sociale. Époque contemporaine," Congress Paris 1950: *Rapports*, pp. 305ff.
62. Congress Paris 1950: *Actes*, p. 150.
63. Congress Paris 1950: *Rapports*, p. 296.
64. Ibid., pp. 510ff.
65. Congress Paris 1950: *Actes*, p. 229.
66. Congress Paris 1950: *Rapports*, p. 541.
67. Ibid., p. 559f.
68. Ibid., p. 576.
69. Renouvin referred to Ch. Morazé, *Trois essais sur histoire et culture* (*Cahier des Annales*, No. 2, 1948), and Morazé, *Les méthodes en histoire moderne* (*Congrès historique du Centenaire de la Révolution de 1848)*, (Paris, 1948).
70. Congress Paris 1950: *Rapports*, p. 575f.
71. Ibid., p. 576.
72. Congress Paris 1950: *Actes*, p. 250.
73. Congress Paris 1950: *Rapports*, pp. 325ff.; see also Marrou, *De la connaissance historique* (Paris, 1954).
74. Congress Paris 1950: *Rapports*, p. 326.
75. Ibid., p. 330.
76. See typewritten minutes of the General Assemblies of 27 Aug. and 3 Sep. 1950, along with the report by secretary-general Morazé of 27 Aug. 1950, in Giunta Centrale per gli Studi Storici, Comitato Internazionale di Scienze Storiche.
77. Webster to Fawtier, 2 May 1950. Archives Nationales, 70 AJ 160.
78. Renouvin, as a member, to Koht as chairman of the "Commission de nomination," 7 July 1950, Koht papers, Ms. fol. 3668:1.
79. J. Le Goff, "L'histoire nouvelle," in Le Goff, ed., *La Nouvelle Histoire* (Paris, 1978), 210–241, here p. 213.
80. See obituary of Michel François, who died in 1981, by his successor in the office of secretary-general, Hélène Ahrweiler, in ICHS, *Lettre d'information*, no. 1 (1982).

Chapter 14

POLITICAL HISTORY ON THE DEFENSE—ENCOUNTERS IN THE COLD WAR IN ROME, 1955

In Paris, invitations had been presented from Rome and Stockholm. The ICHS decided on Rome, since this location had been intended for the 1943 Congress that had failed to materialize because of the war. In exchange, Stockholm was to be given priority treatment for the following Congress.

As they prepared for Rome, the Bureau and the General Assembly reviewed the experiences of Paris. The newly elected members of the Bureau included an Italian as assessor member, Salvatorelli at first, and then, after 1952, Federico Chabod, who played an outstanding role in the scholarly preparation and, as a member of the Giunta Centrale, in the organization of the Congress. The Brussels General Assembly of 1952, which took the basic decisions on the program of the Rome Congress, convened once more without representatives from the Eastern European countries, with the sole exception of Yugoslavia.[1]

The Paris Congress, which had been so heavily influenced by the French historians, met with some criticism, particularly in England. Therefore, this time the members of the ICHS were again more strongly included in the preparation of the program. The national organizing committee should no longer, as in Paris, decide on topics and *rapporteurs*.[2] The principles formulated to this end have remained largely unchanged to the present day, namely: establishment of guidelines by the General Assembly, suggestions for topics and scholars who were to treat them by the national committees and the international affiliated organizations, final decision on the program by the Bureau of the ICHS, execution by the national organizing committee. This was not a simple *modus operandi*. However, it had the advantage of allowing sufficient space for initiatives by both the member organizations and the Bureau, which bore the ultimate responsibility.

The distinction between "reports" and "communications" was retained. With regard to the structure of the program, however, the ICHS returned to

---

Notes for this chapter begin on page 240.

the traditional division into ancient times, the Middle Ages, the early and late modern era, with a preceding section for methodology, general problems, and auxiliary sciences. Time once again appeared as the basic category of history. The return to the conventional periodization scheme offered an opportunity to counteract the fragmentation of history according to the various historical subdisciplines by assembling their contributions within comprehensive chronological sections. In this regard, the Rome Congress came closer to the vision of "global history" as an essential goal of a "New History" than the Paris Congress had done. The proponents of "New History," particularly the *Annales* school, took part in the reports, contributions, and discussions, although not in such a dominant way as at the Paris Congress. Nevertheless, the French sent the largest delegation: 463 of the nearly 1,600 active participants, more than the Italians themselves. This was an indication of the steady interest that France continued to show toward the International Historical Congresses.[3]

A felicitous innovation, which unfortunately was not followed up at any of the later Congresses, were the Rome "reports": internationally renowned historians accepted the invitation to present orientation reports on the scholarly literature of the past ten years regarding the four main periods of history. These were Arnaldo Momigliano (London and Turin) for ancient history, Fernand Vercauteren (Liège) for the Middle Ages, Gerhard Ritter (Freiburg) for the early modern era, and Pierre Renouvin (Paris) for the late modern era. The four reports were scheduled for the section on methodology, but—largely because the manuscripts arrived late—they could not be included in the corresponding first volume of the *Relazioni*, which was to be delivered to the participants before the Congress; thus they could not be put up for discussion. Instead, the authors were asked to evaluate the results of the Congress in the light of their reports at the closing session.[4] Their assessments, too, were not subjected to any discussion. In other words, the reports, a capital opus of 388 printed pages, represent monologues. Nevertheless, they can be viewed as key documents of the Rome Congress. All four reports concurred in the observation that economic and social historical approaches had stepped into the foreground, and that powerful stimuli had emerged from recent French research and particular from the *Annales* school. However, the ascertainment of this historiographical fact was accompanied by different commentaries and critical considerations resulting from the peculiarities of the respective field of observation.

In his report on ancient history, Arnaldo Momigliano provided a survey of research tendencies and problems. The study of ancient history, he said, was imbued with fresh activity. One characteristic feature was the expansion of the field of interest through prehistory and early history. In this regard, he pointed to the intensified archaeological research inspired by social scientific questions, but he particularly emphasized the significance of two linguistic feats, namely, the decoding of Linear-B for the examination of the Minoan culture and the decoding of the Hittite hieroglyphs for the understanding of the ancient Middle East. For studies striving for a comprehensive cultural history, the concept of "*civiltà*" had become a symbolic word; meanwhile, political and institutional history had not lost its significance. The contemporary feeling of crisis had stimulated the quest for the reasons for the decline of ancient culture. Answers were being sought in very different directions, either in the internal social conditions of the late Roman Empire, or in the external events of the barbarian invasions, or in a combination of both. In the investigation of the internal conditions, concepts and techniques of social history were increasingly applied, and for the first time, statistical and quantifying methods had been used in the prosopographical studies of R. Syme. Repeatedly, Momigliano referred to Rostovtzev, who had died three years earlier, and to his exemplary economic and social historical interpretation of ancient history, which had not yet been attained again. The social historical approach—like biographical studies—is faced with particular difficulties in ancient history, resulting from the nature of the available sources. Social history tends toward statistics. However, establishing such statistics, Momigliano said, was possible only in a few areas, and then only to a very limited degree. On the other hand, with a very few exceptions, there was a lack of sources for well-documented biographical research. From this he derived general methodological observations that illustrated the situation of historiography, and certainly not only that of ancient history, ten years after the Second World War. One difficulty was "to distinguish between the certain, the probable, the possible, and the improbable.... If it is true that historical research always develops between the two poles of the discovery of new facts and the interpretations of established facts, then a great deal still must be done to develop and spread a more secure method of discovery and interpretation. It is a good sign that today circumspect ancient historians like E. Bickermann and H. I. Marrou (*De la connaissance historique*) are endeavoring to give serious thought to historical methodology."[5]

If once before, some 150 years ago, ancient history had provided the methodological model for the study of the Middle Ages and the modern era, then today the situation was reversed. This modest statement by Momigliano at the closing session of the Congress appeared in Fernand Vercauteren's report on medieval research from 1945 to 1954 as a self-confident introductory thesis. Indeed, the largest lecture hall of the Congress had been reserved for the medieval section. Vercauteren's report was aimed more at providing general information on the literature in the form of an annotated bibliography than an analysis of the research situation. He grouped this information according to the various subdisciplines of historiography, resuming the classification principle of the sections at the Paris Congress. In the chapter dedicated to political history, his statement is worth noting that "*histoire politique pure*," i.e., "*histoire événementielle*," as the sociologist Simiand had branded it, hardly existed anymore. In the present, political history had to be defined as the history of nation-building and of constitutions: "Political facts no longer appear in isolation: they are generally examined as a function of economic and social life, and in connection with the religious, moral, and emotional atmosphere."[6] The role of the individual was not ignored, as demonstrated by various biographical studies. However, almost all of them endeavored not to isolate the person being examined. The prevailing feature was the will to "total history."

Vercauteren was unable to present his report at the closing session. This was done by Yves Renouard, who had reported on medieval research in Paris and had there announced the impending end of political history.[7] Now he was appalled that his prognosis had been realized so quickly. He warned: "It would be dangerous to advance too quickly along this path. We must become aware of the gaps in our documentation and begin to fill them: it is essential that at least one scholarly monograph be dedicated to each of the reigns of the kings in the various countries; but we are still far away from this. Before we continue on this path, onto which the new forms of history whose methods we discuss with such passion are beckoning us, we must first make sure of our foundations, publish texts and prepare the comprehensive, thorough monographs that place persons and events into their chronological framework."[8]

In his report on "Achievements, Problems and Tasks of International Historical Writing on Recent History (16th–18th Century)," Gerhard Ritter started with a survey of the literature of the various countries, which was followed by an analysis of the interrelation between social history and the history of the State. Two general statements stood out in his report. First, the bulk of publications in all countries were still dedicated to nationally defined topics—as a shining counterexample of this he pointed to the British historian George P. Gooch. Transborder knowledge and cooperation was all too rare, not only in the East-West relationship, but also among the Western historians. Ritter himself provided an example of such cooperation by pointing to the *Archiv für Reformationsgeschichte*, which he published on behalf of the Verein für Reformationsgeschichte and the American Society for Reformation Research. Second, Ritter's survey of research in the various countries showed how he assessed the universally perceptible effects of social history. He registered the growing significance of such studies in the United States: "The former one-sidedness of the legal and constitutional point of view, as it dominated in the so-called 'John Hopkins School,'" had been overcome long since. For England, he noted a tendency toward an "economic interpretation" of the Revolution of the seventeenth century (for example, in the work of Richard H. Tawney), which, to be sure, had triggered controversies and had not been able to reduce the great traditional role that biography continued to play in the English historiography on the early modern era.

Of course, it is of particular interest to note how Ritter evaluated the chief proponents of the new historiographical direction in France. He heaped praise on Lucien Febvre's study on Rabelais and above all on his book on Luther. Febvre exhibited "a finer and deeper understanding for the uniqueness of his genius" than any earlier French author known to him.[9] His reaction to Braudel's book on the Mediterranean, however, was restrained. He extolled the extraordinary diversity of his historical analysis, but as far as the history of maritime trade and politics was concerned, the work provided new information only in regard to the Corsar and Turkish wars. And how could one understand the era of Philip II without showing the king—on his knees—wrestling with God for the unity of the Church! The reservations Ritter expressed toward Ernest Labrousse were still stronger. He warned against overestimating the significance of statistical investigations for the understanding of the general course of history. In his view, the zeal of a young generation of French historians with regard to economic history could best be explained by the fact that this branch of historiography had started in France at a late date and thus was considered something particularly new.

His comments on Germany were formulated in a thoughtful and critical tone. Ritter hoped to elicit understanding for the general circumstances that German research had to cope with: its fate in the war, wartime destruction, and the incipient reconstruction. At the same time, he repeated the "call for a fundamental revision of the German conception of history," which he had raised along with Meinecke, Dehio and others.[10] After the nation had gone astray, such a reconsideration of Germany's political history certainly could not occur by delving into cultural and social history while suppressing the history of the State, but neither could it be achieved by a history of political events reduced to a mere narrative without an analysis of their economic, social, and intellectual background. Here, Ritter once more examined the possibilities of a historical synthesis, developing further his earlier Paris contribution.[11] In his rejection of a mere history of events limited to the chronological sequence of occurrences, he agreed with the historians of the *Annales*. He considered the polemics on this issue to be outdated, since no historian in the world was inclined "to contradict the inclusion of all human spheres of life into the field of historical observation and to view an isolated observation of *faits politiques* as 'historiography' in the full sense of the word."[12] His own answer to the question of how historical synthesis was possible was that it could be achieved by taking the State as the center of a dynamic history and revealing the cultural historical circumstances and interconnections by which it is conditioned from the perspective of this center. This was a clear alternative to the conception of history as a historical social science. According to Ritter, it would be disastrous to turn away from the great issues of political history. Together with other critics, he shared a general unease over the fact that the great world-shaking questions of the present were not being approached at the International Historical Congresses. Historians should not shrink from the task of making their own contribution to an intellectual and political understanding of the present. Only a historian who was involved in his own times, who was prepared to make value judgements and to take sides, was in a position to understand the intellectual and political conflicts that were the driving factors of history.

Ritter thus resumed the problem of subjectivity and objectivity, which had already been brought up by Benedetto Croce at the first Rome Congress and by Nicolae Iorga in Zurich. For Ritter, as for them, this was less a matter of epistemology than of scientific ethics and historical experience. Ritter held fast to the ideal of "objective truth" and also to the conviction that progress in scholarly knowledge was possible. He described the inherent postulate of scientific objectivity as a regulative idea in words that characterize him as a historian both rooted in tradition and critical of it, and as a politically committed contemporary:

> Objectivity is nothing other than a certain conduct on the part of the historian, a certain direction of the will: it is the endeavor for unconditional truthfulness, it is the uncompromising love of truth that fears no correction if the situation demands it.... Precisely this is the approach of the scientific historian: the unconditional willingness to test his own historical conception against the undoubtedly secured body of historical facts and original sources. Such a test can be very uncomfortable, and the appearance of new historical facts in the sources can be very irritating if they contradict a painstakingly developed general view, even more: when they come into conflict with certain prejudices, wishes, inclinations of the observers. Every historian, above all of recent history, can tell you a thing or two about that.[13]

And Ritter, the biographer of Goerdeler and a participant in the Resistance movement against Hitler, added: "I am speaking from my own fresh experience: In the preliminary work for my most recent publication (*Carl Goerdeler und die deutsche Widerstandsbewegung*, 1954) I continually encountered documents that were extremely inconvenient for me (with my passionate dedication to the subject and to the fate of the central figure of the book, who was known to me personally), even disappointing. Nevertheless, I could not conceal, embroider or cover up the smallest part of it. For only in this way can objective history emerge instead of tendentious history, only in this way can a presentation of a historical problem or period be really convincing."[14]

The general report on current tendencies in contemporary historical research was presented by Pierre Renouvin, whose view of history was close to that of Ritter. This report was an extension of what Renouvin had presented in Paris on the "*faits politiques*" insofar as he now dealt with the various branches of historical studies, as Vercauteren had done, and compared the situation in the individual countries. Alongside France, the United States appeared as the country of the Western world in which economic and social historical research was being pursued most intensively.[15] This cannot be examined here in detail. However, it is worth emphasizing that Renouvin—like Ritter—pleaded for a methodological pluralism. His advice was not to lose sight of the political and the individual as significant historical factors, and he warned against any dogmatic interpretation of history.

> I for my part do not believe that historical research guided by an exclusive or dominant hypothesis can satisfy the mind. Surely economic and social explanations are often valid; but they are not always so. The historian is faced with an entire scale of possible hypotheses, and among them there are the economic and social. But he must forego them if he does not find any solid confirmation for them in the sources.

However, many among us already know beforehand what results they wish to attain. In this case, one can no longer really speak of historical research. It is precisely in the diversity of hypotheses that the interest of research lies. Giving one of them preference in advance means foregoing the best which we are striving for: in such a case we are no longer dealing with historical research but merely with the search for arguments in support of a preconceived thesis. Every one-sided explanation, however, leads to arbitrary simplification, for in reality the influence of economic and financial conditions, currents of collective psychology, and finally individual initiatives complement and interpenetrate one another in the life of human societies. Let us recall that, in the words of Werner Sombart, we should never "lose sight of the endless diversity of motivations which manifest their effectiveness in history."[16]

All four general speakers had the impression that the Rome Congress had corroborated the tendencies that they had pointed out in their reports. It turned out that the different methodological orientations were not to be understood as mutually exclusive opposites but rather as complementary approaches— though the emphasis might be shifted to the one or to the other side—since the disciples of the New History nevertheless were building upon the traditional critical methods of history, and those who were more firmly rooted in the traditions of historicism were not closing their minds to new approaches. In this regard, the Rome Congress offered rich and colorful illustrations.

First, there were three instructive contributions on American historiography. Since the four general reports were centered on French historiography, it was a wise idea to include information on related tendencies in the American historical profession, which this time, with twenty-four contributions, was more strongly represented than at any previous Congress.[17] Oscar Handlin (Harvard) gave a survey of "The Central Themes of American History." Throughout the nineteenth century and continuing into the twentieth, narrative history dealing with political institutions had dominated according to the principle "history is past politics" (Freeman). The emphasis on the development of the Constitution and the government corresponded to the Americans' general interest in politics as well as to the "the general belief then current that most significant achievements of the United States had been connected with political democracy."[18] This historiographical tradition had been challenged by two different approaches. The first was represented by Frederick Jackson Turner's epochal lecture on the significance of the frontier in American history. This topic received a universal-historical expansion at the Rome Congress by Owen Lattimore (Johns Hopkins University) in a lecture on "The frontier in history." Lattimore emphasized that by defining the continually westward-moving frontier instead of the Constitutional tradition as the real integrating factor of American history, Turner had introduced an alternative methodological approach toward an understanding of the specific process of nation-building in America. In this context, the question had arisen as to whether it was geographical factors as such, or the social imprint of the groups of people facing the challenge of the frontier, that was decisive.[19] The "frontier interpretation" became a leitmotif of American historiography, but according to Handlin some of Turner's more dogmatic followers had misunderstood him. His real intention had been to warn against the traditional error of treating "the institutions of politics, of economics, or of religion as if their development were entirely self-contained and self-generating."[20] Translated into French terminology, this was a plea for a "*histoire globale.*"

As the second starting point for the criticism of the traditional view, Handlin referred to "New History." Its proponents, too, "at first misapprehended the true nature of their criticism. It was not really the excess of concern with politics that troubled them, but rather the fact that the institutional historians accepted the phenomena of politics at face value as if they were entirely self-explanatory. Like Turner those who argued for a New History were seeking a technique for demonstrating the connections among social, cultural, economic, and political events; and if at first they rather neglected politics as a subject, it was out of the conviction that other fields long overlooked needed more immediate attention."[21] These were arguments not for the overcoming, but rather for the deepening of political history. They perfectly corresponded with the positions of Ritter and Renouvin. Handlin's survey of the great achievements of American regional, minority, intellectual, social, and economic history contained a number of critical reservations. "Intellectual history" had not always withstood the temptation "to view ideas as no more than reflections of the context or rationalizations of interests."[22] All things considered, "New History" had yielded a vast quantity of facts, "but the conception of history has not really been changed."[23] Thus, it was an advantage that in the discussion on this report Dietrich Gerhard, who taught German history in the United States and American history in Germany, pointed out that "New History" was far ahead of historical studies in Europe, particularly in the field of industrial history.[24]

Concerning the American "New History," Henri Berr had said that it was "syncretism" rather than "synthesis."[25] In a report on "History and the Social Sciences," however, Thomas C. Cochran (University of Pennsylvania) gave convincing examples of what could be achieved in historical practice through cooperation with adjacent disciplines. He maintained that a Gibbon, molding a past world according to his own tastes in his lonely study, was no longer possible. "In his endeavor to be a social scientist, [the historian] is largely the slave of other people's knowledge and hypotheses, a humble supplier of data which are to be tested against theoretical models."[26] Historical understanding was by no means as unique and immediate as, for example, Collingwood had believed. Referring to several instructive examples from his own research in industrial history, Cochran suggested that the historian, in consultation with scholars from the neighboring disciplines, should expand the catalog of questions for his empirical research with problems and theoretical models from the synthetic social sciences.

The themes selected for presentation at the Rome Congress gave evidence of the almost complete withdrawal of pure political history. A breakdown of the "reports" provides the following picture: social and economic history 7, intellectual and religious history 5, history of political institutions 4, cultural history 2, political history 1.[27] In these reports, however, which had mostly been prepared by international teams, the political phenomenon was definitely present, though rather in terms of political institutions than events.

Three of these reports deserve particular attention. One of them dealt with a topic on the social and political history of institutions, namely, the status of research on representative assemblies.[28] It was the product of the International Commission for the History of Estates, which had been suggested at the Warsaw Congress of 1933 and formally founded in 1936 (since 1973 it has borne the name "Commission for the History of Representative and Parliamentary Institutions"). It represents a prime example of what continual international cooperation in an affiliated international commission can contribute to the Congresses. Another example was the contribution by Bourgin, Maîtron, and Demarco on "Social Problems in the 19th Century," a research report of the affiliated Commission for the History of Social Movements.[29]

It provided a survey of the history of the social question and of attempts to find solutions for it, largely with reference to the industrial working class. The task of this commission was expanded in Rome at the instigation of Ernest Labrousse. He argued that the history of social movements, which was essentially a history of "social agitation," required a history of "social structures" as an explanatory background. In response to this request, the name of the commission was changed to Commission internationale d'histoire des mouvements sociaux et des structures sociales.[30] Labrousse was elected chairman of the commission in Stockholm five years later. Thenceforth, an unusually productive group regarded the dual notion of movement and structure, which was so characteristic of the *Nouvelle Histoire,* as the guiding line of its work. In a report on new methods for a history of the Western middle classes, Labrousse explained at the Rome Congress how he wanted the highly controversial term "structure" to be put into practical operation.[31] In place of the deductive, theory-guided construction of a general definition, he pointed toward the opposite method of taking a careful inventory of the differences within a thoroughly inhomogeneous class that, on account of the diversity of professions and social standards, appears to include many groups and hierarchical ranks. For this kind of research, new source material that previously had scarcely been examined promised to be useful: voting and tax lists, demographic and professional statistics, notary records. This was an advocacy for historical empiricism based on a subtle observation of differences and peculiarities—for social historical structural research oriented primarily toward positive facts and only secondarily toward the formation of general concepts. As Labrousse had stated in his discussion with Renouvin at the Paris Congress, this structuralist approach should be understood more as a complement to, and less as a contradiction of, the traditional study of history.

Finally, the joint report by Jacques Godechot (Toulouse) and Robert R. Palmer (Princeton) on the history of transatlantic relationships[32] was of particular political and methodological interest. If there had been complaints that the great historical problems of the present scarcely affected the International Historical Congresses, this subject matter was different indeed. The Atlantic Charter of 1941 and the founding of NATO in 1949 had immediately met with scholarly response, most recently at the Paris Congress of 1950 in a contribution by the Swiss Max Silberschmidt on "Economic Aspects of Recent History: The Atlantic Community."[33] The report on the Atlantic at the Rome Congress took Braudel's book on the Mediterranean as its methodological example. In the words of the two authors: "Braudel wanted to show the 'durable links between history and space.' He states that the history of the Mediterranean is tightly interwoven with that of the continents surrounding it: 'Its history can no more be separated from that of the continents surrounding it than clay can be shaped without the hands of the potter.' Can we not say the same of the Atlantic, at least for recent times, in which the rapid means of transport have so uniquely abbreviated distances? Can we not attempt to grasp the 'Atlantic of history,' similar to the way Braudel endeavored to define the 'Mediterranean of history'?"[34] The two authors maintained, however, that the question of whether and to what extent there existed an Atlantic community beyond common political and strategic interests could not yet be examined in the same way that Braudel's book had treated the Mediterranean due to the lack of preliminary archival studies. Thus, they tried to provide a discursive problem study, presenting arguments and counterarguments, which, however, precisely because of this workshop character, unleashed a lively discussion. Is the Atlantic our modern Mediterranean? Can one speak of an Atlantic civilization?

This "extremely pressing problem" (Palmer) was very controversially discussed by no fewer than fourteen historians. The American Donald Mac Kay, who as a member of the Bureau of the ICHS had suggested this report as well as the previous one on American historiography,[35] emphatically advocated the idea of an American-European community in history as well as in the present day. The Pole Leśnodorski (Warsaw) held that the sharp distinction between Eastern and Western Europe underlying the report was historically untenable. The English Marxist Hobsbawm wanted to banish this topic from the Congresses once and for all, which triggered a violent rejoinder: "This is a dangerous and confusing argument that could lead to all kinds of bad implications. It presupposes that there are 'right' and 'wrong' questions on history and that any attention to the wrong ones must be at the expense of the right ones. I should deny that any of us can say what is right or wrong until the matter is examined through one's own research and public debate; and I can only hope that future historical congresses will open their doors to problems of this kind without prejudice, leaving to both advocates and critics the opportunity to state their positions."[36] For obvious reasons, the Soviet historians, too, rejected a division of European history into an Atlantic and a non-Atlantic section.[37]

The main political and scientific event of the Rome Congress was the participation of historians from the Soviet Union and the socialist states of Eastern

Europe. The first General Assembly of the ICHS dealing with the preparation of the Rome Congress (Brussels, June 1952) had reiterated the decision to invite the Eastern European countries.[38] Since the registrations were submitted at a very late date,[39] when the program was already complete, only a few papers from the countries beyond the "Iron Curtain" could be inserted. Even so, one Soviet and one Polish report on historical research[40] and a dozen communications were published in the *Relazioni* immediately before or during the Congress. Furthermore, the Soviet Union, Poland, Hungary, Czechoslovakia, Bulgaria, and also Yugoslavia presented the Congress with essay collections containing their contributions. The Eastern European historians took a very active part in the discussions. Russian was allowed as a Congress language, although it was only used occasionally.

Both the participants and the professional journals in the East and the West firmly welcomed the fact that scholarly contact had finally been established. The international situation matched this mood. A number of events pointed to détente. The Korean War had been ended, and the adversaries were negotiating in Geneva. In Europe, the resolution of the Trieste conflict between Italy and Yugoslavia, the completion of the Austrian Staatsvertrag, and the progressive inclusion of the two German states into the economic and political alliances of the East and West showed that the conditions ensuing from the war were beginning to consolidate. "Peaceful coexistence" became a familiar term of political rhetoric in the years after Stalin's death. The scholars assembled in Rome were aware of the political significance of building bridges between historians in a divided world. To be sure, the term "peaceful coexistence," as it was used in Marxist parlance and defined by Khrushchev at the Twentieth Party Congress, also meant that there could be no pause in the ideological struggle. But if historians were going to meet for mutual discussion, at least some basic rules of scholarly exchange had to be accepted as binding upon all participants. Thus, the departing president Robert Fawtier, who in Paris five years earlier had tried in vain to bring about the participation of the socialist countries, emphasized the "ecumenical character" of this assembly at the opening of the Rome Congress. On the same occasion the president of the Italian *Giunta* Aldo Ferrabino pointed to the principle of intellectual freedom as the basic law of science, which by nature had to be observed at the Congresses above and beyond all kinds of conflicts: "Our work in the coming days will be filled with controversies and hypotheses. The Congress enters into them with its unanimous postulate, the formula that profoundly binds us all: the guarantee and demand of the freedom of the historian."[41] Starting with Rome, historians from the Soviet Union and the socialist countries of Eastern Europe participated in all subsequent Congresses. What political and scientific barriers stood in the way of an ecumenical cooperation between "bourgeois" and "Marxist" historians, and what chances did it have of being realized?

One of the first questions the organizers of the Rome Congress had had to decide was whether to allow historians who had emigrated from the socialist countries to participate. It was to be expected that their inclusion would give rise to sharp polemics endangering the peace of the Congress. Such concerns were expressed in the correspondence exchanged in the preparation of the Congress.[42] The organizers proceeded as they had done after the First World War: individual participation was possible for each historian, but organized delegations of émigré scholars were not to be permitted, in keeping with a repeatedly used formula that the "actual diplomatic situation" had to be respected.[43] At the Congress itself, the personal relationship between emigrated historians and those who had remained in their countries was distant. According to Halecki, it was also affected by consideration for those who presented themselves as Marxists but whose hearts were not in it.[44] There were individual cases of sharp polemics, which were largely ignored by the official Congress report, but there were also tentative attempts to approach one another. One of these was an appeal by Halecki included in his critique of Bogusław Leśnodorski's report on Polish historical research after 1945. He complained that this report had passed over the non-Marxist historical literature published in Poland in the first post-war years and the exile literature. If the author of this report declared "that it is desirable to cooperate with the historians of the other countries," then "a cooperation between the representatives of the various directions in Polish historical studies" was even more desirable. To this, Leśnodorski replied that the Polish émigrés were not a homogeneous group. One had to distinguish between those researchers who contributed serious works and "those writers who in reality often pursue political purposes in the guise of a historical or similar study." The historians working in Poland "should follow with interest the work of those Polish scholars in exile who are worthy of the term scholars."[45]

Cooperation proved to be least problematic in the area of the historical auxiliary sciences and empirically ascertainable facts. This was especially true for archaeological research. In his report on "Archaeological Questions at the Historical Congress in Rome," Aleksander Gieysztor (Warsaw) pointed out when and where archaeological problems had been examined. He regretted that this discipline, which was so fruitful for international cooperation, had not been given more attention.[46] Regarding another element of factual research, the access to archival materials and their publication, various historians in Rome directed a most urgent appeal to the Soviet Union to permit the study of documents that were indispensable for research on contemporary history. This appeal was particularly aimed at documents concerned with the failure of the British-Russian negotiations in August 1939, the Hitler-Stalin Pact, and the attached secret protocol on the demarcation of mutual spheres of interest in the Baltic States, Poland, and Southeastern Europe.[47] The Swiss historian Walther Hofer reported:

> I pointed out that the secret agreement of August 23, 1939, which divided Poland and the Baltic States into a German and a Soviet sphere of influence, is entirely ignored by the so-called historical scholarship of the Soviet Union, and that in this

way the depiction of the beginning of the Second World War is completely distorted. I called the suppression of such an important document a falsification of the greatest degree, which is completely irreconcilable with the concepts of scholarship and objectivity in the Western sense.[48] After Sidorov at first attempted to evade this question, I insisted that the leader of the Soviet Russian delegation take a position on it.... Only after this second attempt was Sidorov finally ready to say that the Soviet historians had no reason to deny this agreement.[49]

This incident did not appear in the official report of the *Atti*, probably because the accusation had been so severe and Hofer had been called to order by the vice-chairman of the session, Heinrich Felix Schmid (Vienna).[50] Its importance lies in the fact that for the first time in an international scholarly forum the existence of this document shrouded in such political secrecy was not denied by a leading Soviet historian. Thus, Schmid noted as the result of this confrontation that "in his response, Sidorov admitted the existence of the mentioned secret treaty."[51] The explosive nature of this issue is revealed by an essay published thirty years later in the leading historical journal of the GDR. It did not mention the real result of the debate at all and reduced the incident to the simple formula of a "provocation" by historians from the Federal Republic and West Berlin[52]—at that time Hofer was employed at the Friedrich Meinecke Institute of the Free University of Berlin.

In another case, a Soviet scholar showed great openness in reaction to factually based criticism. Anna Mikhailovna Pankratova had mentioned Benedetto Croce in a short paper on historicism.[53] She included him along with Spengler in a list of cultural pessimists, and maintained that his subjectivism and pessimism led to the negation of history as a science. During the discussion, Italian historians set this "distortion" of Croce's theory straight (F. Gaeta). Charles Webster praised Croce as a historian who had always been a brave advocate of liberal thought. In her reply, Pankratova readily admitted her limited knowledge of the great Italian's work.[54]

According to the voluminous report of the *Atti*, the historians from the two halves of the divided world spoke to one another in an objective, if usually controversial, manner during the discussions of the reports and communications, which were almost exclusively written by Western European and American authors. There were scarcely any direct political attacks. Labrousse aptly described the prevailing atmosphere when he appropriated the slogan of the time to speak of a "coexistence of delegations and schools."[55] Of course, there were occasional "vulgar Marxist" arguments, such as the assertion that the church was an "instrument of the ruling class to suppress dependent persons,"[56] or clichés that went unnoticed, such as that of the class character of the Renaissance.[57] The fundamental theoretical issues relevant to the relationship between Western and Eastern historians repeatedly surfaced in the course of the Congress, particularly in some of the reports on the current state of research. But a deepened discussion of these questions did not materialize. There was no more than the exchange of theses and antitheses, for example, in regard to the problems of determination and freedom, or partisanship and objectivity, and the expression of mutual reservations about the scholarly character of "Marxist" or "bourgeois" approaches. As far as the debate on Western and Eastern theories of history was concerned, Rome only formed the prelude.

A counterpoint to the presence of Marxist-Leninist historians, and a major event of the Congress, was a reception given by Pope Pius XII. Vatican City had announced its affiliation to the ICHS at the Zurich Congress in 1938. Starting with the Rome Congress of 1955, it confirmed its membership through official participation in the General Assembly and later also through cooperation in the Bureau. How the situation had changed since the Rome Congress of 1903! At that time, the still existing alienation between the Pope and the secular Italian state had also affected the Congress. Now, the Pope held a festive address to the historians assembled in the Aula della Benedizione of the Vatican! The subject matter of his speech was the historical self-conception of the Church. It aroused much attention that the Pope spoke in favor of the ideas of tolerance and freedom of conscience and declared the theocratic teachings of Boniface VIII on the relationship between church and state to have been overcome. Picking up the term "coexistence," he professed the "coexistence of the Church and its believers with the powers and people of another belief," and he emphasized that the Church was "not bound to any particular culture," not even to that of the West, but that in all the historical transformations of its appearance it always held fast to a substantially immutable truth. In this context, he took up the term "historicism" in order to reject it: "The word 'historicism' signifies a philosophical system that in the entire intellectual reality, in the knowledge of that which is true, of religion, moral concepts, and justice, merely sees transformations and developments and thus rejects everything that is perpetual, valid, and absolute throughout eternity. Such a system is without doubt irreconcilable with the Catholic worldview, and with every religion that recognizes a personal God."[58] This definition of historicism recalls the *storicismo assoluto* of Benedetto Croce (which, however, is not the only understanding of historicism). Therefore, the Pope's statement was critically examined by disciples of Croce during the Congress. In its distinction between the temporal and the eternal, it almost exactly corresponded to what the Lutheran Gerhard Ritter had said in his report. And yet Ritter certainly belonged to the tradition of "German historicism," despite all the critical distance that he repeatedly expressed against the historical idealism of Ranke and against Friedrich Meinecke's concept of historicism.[59]

With the participation of the Marxist-Leninists and the Pope's address, the ICHS had taken a significant step closer to realizing its goal of an ecumenical community of historians. Vatican City and Brazil were inducted as new members, and Japan took up its place again. The number of international historical organizations affiliated to the ICHS grew with the Union of Roman institutes and an association of Renaissance historians.[60] The ICHS now encompassed twenty-seven national committees and five specialized organizations. Gerhard

Ritter, the Dutchman Isaak J. Brugmans, and the combative but adaptable Anna Mikhailovna Pankratova were admitted to the Bureau. Federico Chabod became its new president. As a researcher and director of two historical institutes in Naples and Rome, he took center stage in Italian historical studies and was considered to be one of the most significant historians of his time. He could not be classed with any particular methodological tendency. Significant elements of his scholarly education had been his intensive occupation with Benedetto Croce, his encounter with Friedrich Meinecke in Berlin, and the ideas he received from Gioacchino Volpe. At the same time, he was open to the efforts of social historians in Italy and France. His main scholarly interests concerned the Italian Renaissance and the Risorgimento. In the last phase of the war, he had taken active part in the Resistance struggle against the German occupiers. Born in the French-speaking Aosta Valley, he fought for the autonomy of his province within the Italian state, struggling against separatist efforts and Italian cultural centralism alike. His guiding principle was "harmony in diversity."[61] He had repeatedly contributed scholarly papers to the International Congresses. As a member of the Bureau of the ICHS since 1952, he had been involved in the preparation and organization of the Rome Congress. In regard to the next Congress, which was planned for Stockholm in 1960, his most important task, to which he committed himself entirely, was to continue and deepen cooperation between East and West. However, the year following Rome would bring with it a crucial test for both him and the ICHS.

The response that the Rome Congress encountered in the international professional journals was the most positive of any Congress so far. The scholarly level of the reports, the pertinent structuring of the program, and the exemplary organization by the Italian hosts were praised without reservation. Particular attention was accorded to the fact that communists and the Church had taken such an active part. However, many observers regretted that despite all the felicitous personal meetings between historians from the East and the West, there had been no profound scholarly exchange across the ideological barriers.

The assessment that the Congress was given in the Soviet Union is of particular interest. The Rome Congress took place at a time of ideological reorientation in the Soviet Union. The struggle between different political trends that had begun after Stalin's death in 1953 ended with the epochal Twentieth Party Congress of the CPSU in February 1956. On that occasion, Khrushchev proclaimed the principle of "peaceful coexistence" as the guideline of Soviet foreign policy. It meant that the Soviet Union should strive "to transform the already achieved moderation of international tensions into a lasting peace" and—as a means of realizing this goal—"for an expansion of contacts and cooperation in the field of culture and science."[62] Under the direction of Pankratova, the editors of *Voprosy istorii* dedicated themselves to the service of this policy. They requested evaluations of the Rome Congress and suggestions for concrete measures to intensify international relations from the Bureau of the ICHS. The replies from the Bureau members Ahnlund, François, Ritter,

Schmid, and Webster were published in the journal,[63] including passages that clearly criticized unfruitful doctrinaire conflicts. These letters expressed an unusually positive appraisal of the Congress. In addition to the Congresses, the authors saw the following possibilities for promoting scholarly East-West contacts: the exchange of professors, of journal articles, and of photocopied archival materials, as well as meetings of historians at international conferences with a limited number of participants (a suggestion by Fawtier). This was an encouragement of a process that was already in motion. Since then, the nexus of bilateral encounters between socialist and Western historians has become denser, and cooperation within the professional associations affiliated with the ICHS has been practiced constantly and successfully.

Aside from these letters, *Voprosy* provided a survey of the comments published by the international professional journals.[64] The author, N. N. Melik-Taikazov, aptly stated that the response to the Congress was stronger in the socialist journals than in the Western ones. And, one should add, nowhere was it stronger than in *Voprosy* itself. The journal correctly noted the "prejudice" that Marxist-Leninist scholarship had encountered in Rome: that it had committed itself too schematically to the interpretation of history from the point of view of economic interests and class struggles and ignored historical facts. *Voprosy*'s countercriticism was that most of the bourgeois historians avoided an examination of lawful processes in history. As a particular *gravamen*, *Voprosy* resumed the assertion of socialist journals that the Vatican historians, as "militant reactionaries," had endeavored to link historical scholarship with religious issues. From among the articles of bourgeois tendency, a report by Gerhard Ritter had—according to the journal—offered the most complete picture.[65] More than anyone else, he had emphasized the significance of the participation of historians from the Soviet Union and the other socialist countries. Stating that in many cases "historical thought and writing of the West, too, is far removed from genuine clarity and decisiveness," he had called for the development of new methodological principles, while other bourgeois historians had not seen the need for such discussions. The Congress had found its weakest response in England and its strongest in Italy, particularly among Marxist historians. For the Soviet historians the encounter with British historians around the Marxist journal *Past and Present* and with the Italian Marxists of the Gramsci Institute had been especially fruitful. The significance of the Gramsci Institute and Italian Marxist research for historical studies was also emphasized by the Poles.[66] *Voprosy* devoted particular attention to the critical attitude of the Italian Marxists toward the Eastern communist behavior at the Congress. "Even if many of their contributions stood out due to their earnestness and their powerful criticism," the journal quoted from one Italian report, "in the positive part of their presentations, the prevailing tendency was to confine themselves to the area of general problems, scarcely indicating the direction of concrete investigation."[67]

In addition, *Voprosy* repeatedly dealt with the Rome Congress in contributions by Soviet authors. Immediately before the Congress a brief survey of the previous Congresses and the Russian or Soviet participation at them was presented;[68] immediately afterward, the journal published a report on the Congress itself,[69] and finally, Maria Pankratova made a summary.[70] It was based on the usual dualistic model. Proceeding on the principle that "the ideological struggle ... can never end," she examined the reports presented in Rome from an ideological perspective. However, like all Eastern and Western comments on the Congress, she also emphasized that minimum of common commitment to academic studies—namely, the interest in historical facts and in information on historical research—which was already as such an argument for the legitimacy of the Congresses: "Of course we take entirely different methodological positions from the bourgeois scholars. But regardless of this, we have a common ground for scholarly cooperation. This ground is: historical facts. The true scholar sees his task in ascertaining precise, verifiable historical facts."[71]

The historiography of historical materialism is anything but a homogeneous, monolithic block. That is why it is worth mentioning some Marxist comments on the attitude toward non-Marxist scholarship that were self-confident and self-critical at the same time and were particularly apt to promote future dialogues. The leading Polish historical journal noted:

> We often lack a comprehensive orientation about the differences that typify this or that research direction in the capitalist countries and about the standpoints of their proponents. On the other hand, the existing tendency to simplify and reduce everything to a common denominator, occasionally also the negation of and contempt for the concrete results of historical studies in these countries, makes it difficult to utilize the actual yield of their research, particularly in regard to sources. This also leads to a detrimental process of being put at ease and of ideological disarmament on our part in the undoubtedly difficult but nevertheless essential task of exchanging ideas and experiences and of research competition on a world scale, and thus to ossification and intellectual stagnation. On the other hand, a deepened orientation about everything which occurs in the scholarship of the capitalist countries, in the contemporary humanities as a whole, about everything which is at least not indifferent there, can preserve us from the aforementioned detrimental tendency toward an uncritical evaluation of scientific standpoints and results that we find in these countries. Superficial enthusiasm and precipitous generalization can lead to the attempt to adopt not only actual results, but also false theories and opinions, which are far removed from the truth, or which are to some extent unclear.[72]

Marxist criticism of a Marxist conception of history, although a politically and not scientifically motivated one, was also made at the Twentieth Party Congress of the CPSU in February 1956. The impact of the reassessment of Stalin's historical role and of the Stalinist epoch on the self-conception of Soviet historiography is beyond the scope of this study. However, there was a direct reference to the International Historical Congresses in the reappraisal of the Soviet historian Pokrovsky. When Soviet historians had participated for the first time at an International Historical Congress, in Oslo in 1928, Prokrovsky had led the delegation as the unchallenged head of Soviet historiography. By his death in 1932, he had already been disgraced, and some years later he was condemned posthumously. Following the Bolshevik Revolution, Pokrovsky had published documents on imperialistic tsarist foreign policy, and he had criticized it—along with the tsarist colonialism in Central Asia—mercilessly, without any nationalist or patriotic reservations. This had no longer conformed with the Stalinist conception of history, which had imposed a patriotic reevaluation of Russia's entire history. Even at the Rome Congress, the Soviet historians still felt moved to distance themselves expressly from Pokrovsky and his "abstract sociologizing" (Sidorov), and from his view that history is "politics projected onto the past" (Sidorov, Pankratova).

Shortly thereafter, however, the conception of Russian history was reconsidered, and together with it the appraisal of Pokrovsky. At an extraordinarily lively conference of *Voprosy* editors and readers in January 1956, problems of Russian and Soviet history were discussed back and forth, and considerable criticism was aimed at official historical studies.[73] For example, objections were raised that Soviet historiography tended to confuse the proclamation of general theses with deep analysis, that it lacked an understanding of economic theory and praxis, that the depiction of the two Russian revolutions was insufficient due to a lack of analysis of class forces, that some authors appeared to have forgotten to what extent tsarist Russia had been a "prison of the peoples," that the history of the Second International should not be presented only as the history of opportunism. As far as Pokrovsky was concerned, one of the managing editors of *Voprosy* declared that his work also contained valuable elements. In any case, one must not "count him among the bourgeois scholars, as many authors do." At the Twentieth Party Congress, which was convened shortly after this historians' conference, Maria Pankratova—as the most outstanding historian—was chosen to deliver a self-critical speech.[74] Her description of Soviet historiography was very different from the one she had presented at the Rome Congress. She spoke less about achievements than about failures.

During the Rome Congress, the General Assembly of the ICHS had accepted an invitation by the Soviet historians to conduct the next meeting in Moscow in 1957. But between the Rome Congress and the intended General Assembly in the Soviet Union, the world was shaken by the uprising in Hungary and the intervention of the Red Army in the internal affairs of this country. The president of the ICHS, Federico Chabod, reacted quickly and decisively: One could not travel to Moscow, he said, both for reasons of political ethics and to prevent a split between the members of the ICHS. In order to forestall the protests against an assembly in Moscow, which were indeed later raised by the Scandinavian, Dutch, and Belgian historians, and after a survey among the Bureau's members, the president had to assume personal responsibility for moving the assembly to a different city.

Lausanne, the seat of the ICHS in Switzerland, lent itself to this purpose. The correspondence between the president Chabod, vice-president Webster, and secretary-general François gives evidence of the various evaluations of the situation among the members of the Bureau of the ICHS, and of the different views on the interrelation between politics and scholarship. "If we went to Moscow," Chabod wrote to François, "then, both in content and form, we would be taking sides with those who are massacring the Hungarians.... As far as I am concerned, my decision has been made: I will never go to Moscow and preside there."[75] The response from the secretary-general lacked such decisiveness. Although he declared that he agreed with Chabod in his fundamental evaluation of the occurrences, he advised him to do nothing, but rather to watch how things developed and wait for a possible initiative on the part of the Soviet historians, who might themselves take these difficulties into account and withdraw the invitation to Moscow.

When François thus advised patience, he was also moved by other political considerations. At the same time that the Soviet invasion of Hungary was shaking the world, England, France, and Israel were waging a war of intervention against Egypt in response to the nationalization of the Suez Canal. Might not this manifestation of an anachronistic colonialism on the part of the leading powers of Western Europe lead to embarrassing comments if the Bureau conducted a survey on the relocation of the conference out of protest over Soviet intervention in Southeastern Europe? But Chabod stood by his opinion: "The politics of 'wait and see' could only be applied in a single case; i.e., if we wanted to go to Moscow in spite of everything. Gaining time in the hope that the intended path could be resumed once the climax of the crisis is overcome, would be advantageous in this case. But such an orientation would entirely contradict the course I am determined to follow. For me the assembly cannot be held in Moscow; the situation is irreversible."[76] He also explained his decision to Halvdan Koht: "A convocation of the assembly in Moscow would now assume a political meaning: it would be futile to deny it: it would remain in the general judgement. The Soviets would be the first to exploit such an event occurring after November 1956."[77] In a letter to Webster, he expressed similar sentiments.[78] Webster shared François' opinion that the Bureau should not be consulted since it was not even certain if it had the right to decide on the relocation of the General Assembly. Would it not be better to cancel the 1957 assembly altogether?

Chabod was also aware of this legal question, so he assumed a tactically flexible position by answering that after consulting the Bureau members he would also seek the opinion of the national committees. But against the advice of the vice-president and the secretary-general, and also of his predecessor in the office of president, Fawtier—who in his protest against Chabod's actions went so far as to send him his resignation as a Bureau member—he stood firmly by his decision not to wait but rather to act in his personal responsibility. He was even ready to risk the withdrawal of the Soviet historians from the ICHS. Eventually, the majority of the Bureau voted for Lausanne. Everything now depended on how the Soviet historians behaved. A letter from Maria Pankratova resolved the crisis. In a realistic evaluation of the situation, and showing concern for the continuation of the cooperation, she informed the president that the Soviet national committee "confirms its suggestion to hold the General Assembly in Moscow, but has no objections to Lausanne if the majority of the Bureau should decide upon this city."[79]

The attitudes shown in this critical situation by the two leading historians of the ICHS, the president and the secretary-general, reflect two different views of history. In the opinion of Michel François, "the scholarly sphere must be clearly distinguished from the political."[80] That is understandable if one is convinced that history—to the extent that it is science—is essentially limited to the critical processing of positive facts. Moreover, the secretary-general felt responsible for the historians of the socialist countries of Eastern Europe who wanted to continue their newly reestablished relationships with the West. Relocating the General Assembly from Moscow to Lausanne because of the Hungarian events entailed the risk of severing the bonds between the historians of the East and West, but holding the assembly in Moscow despite the events in Hungary meant the risk of a split among the Western historians. This explains the secretary-general's advice, which was supported by the former president Fawtier, to wait and do nothing. In his opinion, the study of history could and should remain above the political conflict. For Chabod, such a separation of scholarship and politics, of thought and action, was not possible. He made this clear in a letter to Michel François:

> This is no longer a "political" question where an international organization, which is keeping clear of the conflict, has nothing to decide. Today it is about much more: namely, about a fundamental question of human morality, in which on the contrary all who are concerned must come to a basic agreement, even if we want to cooperate in a strictly scholarly field. The question is to know whether respect for the fundamental right of individuals and nations to select the course that they desire to take, represents a compulsory starting point which is the indispensable precondition that people of different political convictions and different, even virtually contrary scholarly ideas can nevertheless work together on an international level in regard to some joint undertakings. Today we must answer this with yes or no.[81]

The unity of knowledge and conscience, as Chabod lived it, was a convincing manifestation of the tradition of intellectual freedom connected with the names of Croce and De Sanctis in the history of the International Congresses and the ICHS. But the fact that the ICHS did not break apart despite the political pressures of the time was due not least to the Soviet historians, who respected the Bureau's majority vote to move the General Assembly meeting to Lausanne.

Chabod and François were to face a new challenge stemming from the occurrences in Hungary when, in November 1957, it became known through a report in the newspaper *Le Monde* that Domokos Kosáry, who had been one of Hungary's representatives at the 1948 General Assembly in Paris, had been arrested. The reason was that he had prepared a documentation of the events of 1956, which he had deposited in the university library. It was expected that he would be convicted and sentenced to a very long term in prison. Encouraged by the success of an intervention by intellectuals in favor of the writer Tibor Dery, whose death sentence had been commuted to nine years in prison, and encouraged by Fawtier and Renouvin, Chabod directed an appeal to Kadar, which he classified as a "private" communication—since the Bureau could not be involved because the presence of its Soviet member would prevent a unanimous decision—but signed it as "president of the International Committee of Historical Sciences."[82] A few months later he wrote to François, who had suggested a renewed intervention for Kosáry, that his appeal had received no direct response but that he had been informed that, thanks to his letter, Kosáry had got away with a relatively mild sentence of four years.[83] Later on Kosáry, the current president of the Hungarian national committee, was fully rehabilitated.

Notes

1. The attendance list registered participants from "Belgium, Denmark, Germany, France, Great Britain, Ireland, Italy, Yugoslavia, Luxembourg, Netherlands, Norway, Austria, Sweden, Switzerland, the U.S.; Association internationale des Études byzantines, Commission internationale des Études slaves"; see note 2 below.
2. The General Assembly decided, among other things: "La responsabilité des Comités nationaux et Organisations internationales membres du CISH est directement engagée dans la préparation du Congrès. Le choix des sujets qui seront traités dans les rapports ne sera determiné qu'après consultation des Comités nationaux et Organisations internationales.... Les propositions adressées au Secrétaire general seront soumises au Bureau du CISH qui les examinera.... Aucune communication ne pourra être retenue qui n'aura pas été présentée par l'intermédiaire du Comité national ou de l'Organisation internationale dont relève son auteur." ICHS, *Bulletin d'information*, no. 1 (1953): 21. Alongside this abbreviated report on the assembly in Brussels, 14–16 June 1952, there are thorough minutes, together with minutes of the previous Bureau meeting from 12–13 June 1952, in Archives CISH, boxes 40 and 30.
3. Comparative figures for the participants from other countries: Italy 357; Great Britain 260; Germany (including a few participants from the GDR) 206; the U.S. 102; Yugoslavia 77; Switzerland 67; Japan 4; Latin America as a whole 11; USSR 24; Poland 12; Czechoslovakia 6. Numbers according to D. C. Mac Kay, "Tenth International Congress of Historical Sciences," *American Historical Review* 61 (1955/56): 504–511, here p. 504. The Congress was documented in an exemplary fashion in *Comitato Internazionale di Scienze Storiche. X Congresso Internazionale di Scienze Storiche, Roma 4–11 settembre 1955*. Vols. 1–6: *Relazioni*; vol. 7: *Riassunti delle Communicazi-oni* (Florence, [1955]); *Comitato Internazionale di Scienze Storiche: Atti del X Congresso Internazionale, Roma 4–11 settembre 1955* (Rome, [1957]) [hereafter Congress Rome 1955: *Relazioni*; idem: *Riassunti*; and idem: *Atti*].
4. Text of the reports in Congress Rome 1955: *Relazioni*, vol. 6; closing session in Congress Rome 1955: *Atti*.
5. Congress Rome 1955: *Relazioni*, vol. 6, p. 37f.
6. Ibid., p. 78.
7. Cf. p. 212f. above.
8. Congress Rome 1955: *Atti*, p. 860.
9. Congress Rome 1955: *Relazioni*, vol. 6, p. 189.

10. Ibid., p. 215.
11. See p. 208f. above.
12. Congress Rome 1955: *Relazioni*, vol. 6, p. 298.
13. Ibid., p. 325f.
14. Ibid., p. 326, n. 1.
15. Ibid., pp. 331ff. Completing comments in P. Renouvin, "L'histoire contemporaine des relations internationales: Orientation de recherches," *Revue historique* 211 (1954): 233–255.
16. Congress Rome 1955: *Atti*, p. 870.
17. See comments by Bureau member Mac Kay, ibid., p. 57.
18. Congress Rome 1955: *Relazioni*, vol. 1, p. 152.
19. Ibid., p. 135.
20. Ibid., p. 155.
21. Ibid., p. 155f.
22. Ibid., p. 160.
23. Ibid., p. 156.
24. Congress Rome 1955: *Atti*, p. 55.
25. H. Berr in a memorial article, "Le cinquantenaire de la revue," *Revue de synthèse* 21 (Jan.–June 1950): 61.
26. Congress Rome 1955: *Relazioni*, vol. 1, p. 481.
27. Alongside the only "report" on political history by M. Toscano, "Origine e vicende diplomatiche della seconda guerra mondiale" (Congress Rome 1955: *Relazioni*, vol. 5), the following "communications" also dealt with foreign policy history: B. E. Schmitt, "July 1914, Unfinished Business" (Congress Rome 1955: *Riassunti*); V. M. Khostov, "L'alliance franco-russe et sa portée historique" (ibid.).
28. H. M. Cam, A. Marongiu, and G. Stökl, "Recent work and present views on the origins and development of representative assemblies," Congress Rome 1955: *Relazioni*, vol. 1.
29. "Les problèmes sociaux au XIXe siècle," Congress Rome 1955: *Relazioni*, vol. 5.
30. Congress Rome 1955: *Atti*, p. 739f.
31. The often cited opening words are: "Définir le bourgeois? Nous ne serions pas d'accord. Allons plutôt reconnaître sur place, dans ses sites, dans ses villes, cette espèce citadine, et la mettre en état d'observation.... D'abord, l'enquête. D'abord, l'observation. Nous verrons plus tard pour la définition." E. Labrousse, "Voies nouvelles vers une histoire de la Bourgeoisie occidentale aux XVIIIème et XIXème siècles (1700–1850)," Congress Rome 1955: *Relazioni*, vol. 4, p. 367.
32. "Le problème de l'Atlantique du XVIIIème au XXème siècle," Congress Rome 1955: *Relazioni*, vol. 5.
33. M. Silberschmidt, "Wirtschaftshistorische Aspekte der neueren Geschichte: Die atlantische Gemeinschaft," *Historische Zeitschrift* 171 (1951): 245–261.
34. Congress Rome 1955: *Relazioni*, vol. 5, p. 178.
35. Congress Rome 1955: *Atti*, p. 566.
36. D. S. Landes, ibid., p. 574.
37. V. M. Khvostov, ibid., p. 573f.
38. Notes in Archives CISH, box 17.
39. The Soviet registration is dated 16 Dec. 1954.
40. A. L. Sidorov, "Hauptprobleme und einige Entwicklungsergebnisse der sowjetischen Geschichtswissenschaft"; B. Leśnodorski, "Les sciences historiques en Pologne au cours des années 1945–1955"; both in Congress Rome 1955: *Relazioni*, vol. 6.
41. Congress Rome 1955: *Atti*, p. 7.
42. Archives CISH, box 17.
43. Statement by Fawtier at the General Assembly at Brussels 1952 and by François at the Lausanne Bureau meeting in 1954, notes in Archives CISH, box 17 and 30. Cf. also Chabod's response to the request of Polish émigrés to exhibit their literature at the Congress: "Chabod

si oppose, per non irritare la delegazione dell URSS, che rappresentava la novità del Congresso." Quoted in Vigezzi, *Chabod*, p. 355.
44. Congress Rome 1955: *Atti*, p. 121.
45. Ibid., pp. 122 and 126.
46. "Zagadniena archeologiczne na rzymskim kongresie historików," *Kwartalnik historyczny* 63, no. 3 (1956): 221–227.
47. Congress Rome 1955: *Relazioni*, vol. 5, p. 30f. (M. Toscano); Congress Rome 1955: *Atti*, p. 626 (B. E. Schmitt), p. 628f. (W. L. Langer), p. 671 (G. H. N. Seton-Watson), and others.
48. The term "falsification" was a response to the title of a brochure published by the Soviet Information Bureau in 1948, *Geschichtsfälscher* [Historical falsifiers], in which the American documentary publication *National Socialist Germany and the Soviet Union 1939–1941: Documents from the Archive of the German Foreign Office*, ed. E. M. Carroll and F. Th. Epstein (Washington, D.C., 1948; German edition 1948) was criticized because it had not included the negotiations between Germany and Great Britain in the summer of 1939. See G. von Rauch, "Der deutsch-sowjetische Nichtangriffspakt vom August 1939 und die sowjetische Geschichtsschreibung," *Geschichte in Wissenschaft und Unterricht* 17 (1966): 472–482, here p. 479.
49. Hofer to Thieme, quoted in K. Thieme, "Möglichkeiten und Grenzen west-östlicher Historikerbegegnung: Zu den 'Akten' des internationalen Historikerkongresses (Rom 1955)," *Geschichte in Wissenschaft und Unterricht* 8 (1957): 593–598, here p. 595. See also W. Hofer, "Historikerkongreß im Zeichen der Koexistenz," *Nationalzeitung Basel*, 25 Sep. 1955, and Hofer, "Geschichtswissenschaft im totalitären System," *Neue Zürcher Zeitung*, 10 Aug. 1956.
50. Chairman of the session was N. Ahnlund (Sweden). In 1960, Schmid was elected president of the ICHS.
51. Schmid in response to Thieme's "appeasement" accusation, in "Zum Thema: 'Möglichkeiten und Grenzen west-östlicher Historikerbegegnung,'" *Geschichte in Wissenschaft und Unterricht* 10 (1959): 114–119, here p. 116.
52. H. Haun, "Der X. Internationale Historikerkongreß 1955 in Rom und die Geschichtswissenschaft der DDR," *Zeitschrift für Geschichtswissenschaft* 34 (1986): 303–314, here p. 309.
53. A. Pankratova, "Le problème de l'historisme et la période contemporaine," Congress Rome 1955: *Reassunti*.
54. Congress Rome 1955: *Atti*, p. 94; critical comment on Pankratova's paper by the Italian Marxist Delio Cantimori in his Congress report "Epiloghi congressuali," *Società*, 5 Oct. 1955, included in Cantimori, *Studi di Storia* (Turin, 1959), p. 843f.
55. Congress Rome 1955: *Atti*, p. 530.
56. Ibid., p. 478.
57. Ibid., pp. 540–542.
58. *Osservatore Romano*, 9 Sep. 1955.
59. On Ritter's concept of "historicism," see Ritter to Meinecke, 7 Oct. 1936, in Ritter, *Briefe*, no. 73. Thirty years later, at the International Historical Congress in Stuttgart, the president of the Papal Committee for Historical Studies, Msg. Michele Maccarrone, mentioned this reception by Pius XII in connection with his comments on the promotion of historical studies by the Holy See and the further opening of the Vatican Archives for research. M. Maccarrone, "L'apertura degli archivi della Santa Sede per i pontificati di Pio X e di Benedetto XV (1903–1922)," *Rivista di Storia della Chiesa in Italia* 39 (Rome, 1985): 341–348.
60. Unione degli Istituti d'Archeologia, di Storia e di Storia dell'Arte in Roma, Association "Humanisme et Renaissance."
61. A. Dupront, "Federico Chabod," *Revue historique* 85, no. 225 (1961): 261–294.
62. Khrushchev, *Rechenschaftsbericht des Zentralkomitees der KPdSU an den XX. Parteitag* (East Berlin, 1956), p. 47f.
63. *Voprosy Istorii* 31, no. 5 (1956): 217–220.
64. Ibid., pp. 212–217.

65. G. Ritter, "Der X. Internationale Historikerkongreß in Rom, 4.-11. September," *Historische Zeitschrift* 180 (1955): 657-663.
66. "Niektore spostrzeżenia i wniowski z X Kongresu Nauk Historycznych w Rzymie" [Some comments and conclusions concerning the Xth Congress of the Historical Sciences in Rome], no author, *Kwartalnik historyczny* 63, no. 1 (1956): 3-11, here p. 4f.
67. Quotation from a report by Paolo Alatri, *Rinascita* 13, no. 9 (Rome, 1955): 570. The highly interesting Congress report by G. Manacorda, "Le Correnti della storiografia contemporanea al decimo Congresso di scienze storiche," ibid., was published by *Voprosy Istorii* 31, no. 2 (1956), 214-219, in an almost complete translation, including critical remarks on the Soviet historians' treatment of history.
68. *Voprosy Istorii* 30, no. 8 (1955), pp. 230-233.
69. Ibid., no. 10, pp. 179-180.
70. A. M. Pankratova, "K itogam Meždunarodnova kongressa istorikov" [On the results of the International Historical Congress], *Voprosy Istorii* 31, no. 5 (1956): 3-16.
71. Ibid., p. 3.
72. "Niektore spostrzeżenia," p. 4f.
73. "Konferencija čitatelej žurnala *Voprosy istorii*" [Conference of the readers of the journal *Voprosy Istorii*], *Voprosy Istorii* 31, no. 2 (1956): 199-213.
74. "Unsere ruhmvolle Geschichte—wichtige Quelle des Studiums," in *Diskussionsreden auf dem XX. Parteitag der KPdSU 14.-25. Februar 1956* (East Berlin, 1956), pp. 364-375.
75. Chabod to François, 7 Nov. 1956, Archives CISH, box 11; here, as in box 17, there is a thorough correspondence concerning these events.
76. Chabod to François, 18 Nov. 1956, ibid.
77. Chabod to Koht, 20 Dec. 1956, Koht papers, Ms. fol. 3928:1.
78. Chabod to Webster, 19 Nov. 1956, Webster papers 19/32.
79. This communication is contained in a letter from Chabod to Koht, 5 Feb. 1957, Koht papers, 386.
80. François to Koht, 29 Dec. 1956, ibid.
81. Chabod to François, 7 Nov. 1956, Archives CISH, box 11.
82. Letter of 9 Jan. 1958, Archives CISH, box 14.
83. Chabod to François, 12 Aug. [1958], ibid. Kosáry was freed after two and a half years in prison.

Chapter 15

THE CONGRESSES FROM 1960 TO 1985—POLITICS

Six Congresses took place in this quarter century:

Stockholm	1960, 21–28 August	The eleventh Congress
Vienna	1965, 29 August–5 September	The twelfth Congress
Moscow	1970, 16–23 August	The thirteenth Congress
San Francisco	1975, 22–29 August	The fourteenth Congress
Bucharest	1980, 10–17 August	The fifteenth Congress
Stuttgart	1985, 25 August–1 September	The sixteenth Congress

In a departure from the chronological principle used in this study so far, the Congresses from Stockholm to Stuttgart will be presented in a summary account that, in view of the main aspects of this book, will deal with the impact of politics, the development of the organization's structure, and the discussion on the theory and methodology of history. There are several reasons for this.

The basic political configuration of international relations under which these Congresses were held remained constant. The antagonism between the two competing political systems, which nonetheless rely on cooperation and seek it also in the field of history, is an element of the "long-term" perspective. It has had its impact on the Congresses. But at the same time, they have been influenced by surface events fluctuating between the behavioral patterns of the Cold War and de-escalation. A further political parameter modifying the basic configuration of polarity and convergence has been the gradual emergence of a pentarchy—the United States, the Soviet Union, Japan, China, and Europe—overlying the political world dualism of the two hegemonic powers. This has corresponded with a distinctly "ecumenical" evolution of the Historical Congresses in this period that has well suited to the defusing of ideological tensions.

Notes for this chapter begin on page 262.

In their organizational structure and in the conception of their programs, the post-Stockholm Congresses developed a form that was modified in consideration of local conditions, without however undergoing any fundamental changes.

The discussion on theory and methodology gained in importance between Stockholm and Stuttgart despite clear fluctuations in the interest it attracted, and in its scholarly level. The most important issue for the self-conception of historical scholarship since Paris and Rome has been the intensifying debate on the relationship between structural history and the modes of historical thought and writing surviving from the historicist tradition, and on the relationship between these two "neohistoricist" directions and Marxist-Leninist historicism. The discussion of these questions during the last six Congresses was a coherent process. An analysis transcending the individual Congresses thus appears appropriate.

A more analytical than narrative presentation of this period is also motivated by the nature of the source material. Scarcely any private papers are accessible for the contemporary history of the Congresses. Even when they are accessible, for example, in the Archives of the ICHS, their proximity to those who still are members of the ICHS or participate in the Congresses demands discretion. Thus, it is not possible to report on background events to the same degree as in earlier phases of the Congresses' history. We have to stay largely, although not entirely, with published Congress materials and journal articles. The concentration on the theoretical and methodological discussion is justified by such considerations, as well as by the fact that these debates are the most interesting aspect of a history of the International Historical Congresses that is conceived as a contribution to the history of historiography, and as an attempt to explain its present condition.

The political atmosphere in which the historians assembled in Stockholm in 1960 was much more fraught with tension than it had been during the Rome Congress. While in Rome the peaceful component of "coexistence" had been emphasized, five years later the political and ideological antagonism that this term also denotes, prevailed. The events of Hungary, Poland, and Suez in 1956 were still fresh in everyone's memory when once again a German problem gave rise to international tensions. In 1958, Khrushchev's ultimatum demanding that West Berlin be cleared of American, British, and French troops and declared a "free city" inaugurated a long crisis that ended in 1961, when Germany's capital was divided by a wall. In Cuba, the Soviet-American conflict mushroomed into a crisis that was to lead both countries to the brink of war in 1962. As the Polish historian Žanna Kormanowa stated, it was precisely because of this "historical moment, with the shift in international power relationships," that Marxism and the debate about it played such a large role in Stockholm.[1]

The particularly fierce "*querelles allemandes*" emerging at the Congress had another, special aspect that directly concerned the ICHS. Since 1952, the Verband der Historiker Deutschlands (Historians' Association of Germany), to which some forty "bourgeois" historians and archivists from the GDR still belonged at the time of the Stockholm Congress, had been recognized as the national representation of German historical studies. This claim was disputed by the Deutsche Historikergesellschaft (German Historical Society), founded in the GDR in 1958. Its chairman, Ernst Engelberg, filed vicious accusations against the allegedly expansionist and militarist intentions of the West German historical profession with the secretary-general in December 1958, during the first phase of the Berlin Crisis. A year later, a "national committee of the historians of the GDR" applied for membership. This demand corresponded to the GDR's desire to be recognized as a sovereign state. The Verband der Historiker Deutschlands and Gerhard Ritter, in his capacity as a member of the ICHS Bureau, resisted the East German request. They were given full support by the president, the Bureau, and the Swedish organizers of the Congress. In Stockholm the Bureau decided not to put the application before the General Assembly during the Congress. This was a political decision. For Federico Chabod and Michel François, the following considerations were decisive: Germany was not the only divided country. There was also Ireland, and there were Vietnam and Korea. Ireland had and still has a joint delegation from Eire and Ulster in the ICHS. Until then, Germany had had the same arrangement. Why should this not remain so? The Bureau had already been presented with applications from the national committees of North Vietnam and North Korea in 1957, who had been told to include representatives from the southern sections of their countries, because "[t]he examples of Germany and Ireland prove that there can be unity in the field of scholarship independent of political conditions."[2] This was pure wishful thinking. It did not take into account that in countries divided into competing social systems, history was involved in the ideological dispute with such bitterness that there was no common ground for scholarly cooperation or understanding as long as "political contingencies" did not allow it.

Only a few weeks before the beginning of the Stockholm Congress, the circumspect and vigorous president Chabod succumbed to a long illness. The direction of the Congress fell to Sir Charles Webster, the first vice-president of the ICHS. Torvald Höjer, the second vice-president and organizer of the Congress, stood at his side. Supported by certain energetic chairmen of the Congress's sections, such as the American Hans Kohn, and borne up by the sympathy of the Congress, they did their best to defend its scholarly character against the tide of ideological conflict. They were not always successful because such attacks were launched in certain situations and against certain individuals with tactically organized regularity.

The response to the Congress in Eastern and Western reports was marked by triumph, or by dismay and resignation. According to one commentator, "the Marxists attacked on all fronts in Stockholm," even though "the form" of their "critical intervention sometimes was not quite appropriate yet."[3] "In the Shadow of Marx" was how Ernst Engelberg titled a report on the Congress, which had demonstrated the "growing influence of the Marxist school of thought in international historiography" and the "superiority of historical materialism."[4] The leading professional journal of the Soviet Union published similar self-confident remarks.[5] Western historians felt deeply disturbed by the contentious atmosphere that had dominated the entire Congress. Paul Harsin spoke of "non-scientific, if not to say anti-scientific debates, which are not encouraging for the organizers of future Congresses,"[6] and even Michel François, who had been so keen on seeking harmony, said that the clash of ideologies had led to a "hopeless" quarrel.[7] Marx, Engels, and Lenin, a West German report said, had "dominated—or, if you prefer—tyrannized the Stockholm Congress.... For the Congress, this conflict, which from a distance recalled the irreconcilable sensibilities of the Wars of Religion ... represented a heavy burden.... Even Western historians could not focus their attention on the factual contributions of their own colleagues because the limited time was barely sufficient to ward off the most massive polemics."[8]

The list of such statements could be extended. What was to be done? It was certainly nostalgic to recall earlier Congresses, where historians appeared and crossed swords with one another merely as individuals, and which had had nothing to do with "delegations" who sent their speakers on "the attack" on "all the fronts of Stockholm." Should the ICHS simply drop the Congresses and instead content itself with a series of small, specialized colloquia, as was considered here and there? That would not have been a solution. After all, it hardly lay in the interest of the pluralistic historical thought of the West to avoid the debate with Marxist-Leninist historians for fear that the Congresses could degenerate into public spectacles. It rather was, and is, in its interest to seek the unavoidable scholarly-ideological debate, if possible in a way that guarantees that the scholarly discourse conforms to those manners and methodological rules whose general validity results from the history of historical research and criticism. In this regard, Theodor Schieder's comments are worthy of mention: The intrusion of ideological conflicts into the Congress should not be condemned in advance. Western scholarship, however, was risking "self-alienation" by adapting itself to the style and vocabulary of the other side. There was "no other way but to fight for every inch of historical knowledge, to uncover all contradictions and inconsistencies and to pose questions concerning the facts from the standpoint of a superior scientific attitude, which continually challenges and critically verifies its own premises." It was certainly an illusion to believe that the ideological system as such could be shaken in this way. Nevertheless, there was the "weak hope that greater objectivity and less dogmatism could gain ground in individual cases."[9]

In any case, it seemed possible—and the subsequent Congresses have proven that it was possible—to return to an urbane style of writing and speaking. Violations of this elementary rule were rare even in Stockholm. Most of them arose from the conflict among the Germans, and it is not worth recalling them in detail. It would anyhow be wrong to depict the Stockholm Congress only in terms of political scandal, since the politically controversial commentaries that were ignited by historical topics usually concerned factual matters and not persons. Such controversies particularly emerged in Section I, "Methodology," as will be shown below, but almost all the topics in the chronological sections gave rise to political clashes as well. However, when the press generally concentrated on politically interesting or scandalous aspects of the Congress rather than on its scholarly merits, it did not do justice to the Stockholm Congress as a whole. There were contributions that remain of lasting value: presentations akin to the previous "*rapports*" dealing with concrete subject matter and providing information on the state of literature and research problems,[10] and papers that presented the results of individual research projects[11] or examined a controversial historical problem in the light of a clear and well-founded judgement.[12]

On this foundation, there was agreement even between scholars of conflicting scholarly and political convictions. In some private reports it was noted that especially Soviet and Western participants sought a cordial relationship. The fact that this was possible was to a large degree due to the hospitable atmosphere provided by the Swedes. A reception hosted by the Swedish king, concerts and theater performances, the style of the opening and closing sessions, and at the end, a visit to the venerable University of Uppsala gave the Congress a festive quality that recalled the Oslo Congress in 1928. Halvdan Koht, whose name was linked with the enthusiasm of the ICHS's founding, was present in Stockholm for the last time.

In Vienna five years later, the ideological confrontation was as impassioned as before. "No compromise is possible," declared the pugnacious Polish émigré Halecki. Christian philosophy, he argued, emphasized "the primacy of the spiritual, as opposed to the Marxist belief in the primacy of the material." This was a conflict that went much deeper than the conflict between socialism and capitalism.[13] In response to this view, a report on the Congress by the other side noted that "not a trace could be found of ideological coexistence between Marxist and bourgeois historians."[14] But how much had changed all the same! First, the world situation had changed: China, the other potential communist world power, was seeking its own path; Beijing had broken with Moscow; Albania had seceded. Romania found the courage to launch a distinct policy of national autonomy. In Cuba, the Soviet Union had been forced to dismantle its missile threat against the United States. West Berlin had not been abandoned by the Western powers, and finally Khrushchev had been toppled. To the degree that, with the increased military and economic integration of the West, political coexistence between the two rival social systems turned out to be a permanent situation and not only an intermediate stage, the historians, too, had to seek a *modus vivendi* or, more accurately, a *modus parlandi*. And in this respect Vienna represented genuine progress. The participants avoided severe moral accusations and strove for objectivity. In Vienna, it was said in the East, real scholarly discussions took place; the scene was illuminated by the soft light of coexistence, it was stated in the West.

The altered Congress atmosphere, however, was not exclusively the result of the altered political relationship between the East and the West. Another significant factor was the burgeoning awareness of a specific scholarly process: The simple scheme of a historiography divided along Marxist-bourgeois lines no longer fit. In Vienna, the participants from Socialist countries were irrefutably shown the degree to which social and structural research and the theoretical element contained within them had developed in the West. Marxist-Leninist scholarship had no monopoly over this field. It was faced with a serious challenge and encountered it in different ways. The simplest response was to declare that all "progressive" developments in Western historical writing could be traced to Marxist influence, although they were essentially designed to mislead. Thus, Gerhard Becker and Ernst Engelberg observed that "bourgeois historiography" saw itself forced to overcome its animosity toward theoretical thought by the progress of Marxist historiography. But they urged caution, because this was basically nothing more than "pseudo-theoretical sophism," an attempt to "counter the ideological offensive of historical materialism with an evasive maneuver."[15] Another response, with a positive evaluation, was given by Soviet historians who spoke of "a process of partial rapprochement" not only with the "increasing progressive part of world science," above all the school of the *Annales,* but even with "those trends that oppose Marxist historiography not only in its initial methodological premise, but also in the estimation of the main historical processes and events."[16]

The scheme of rigid polarization was also made questionable by the fact that within the Western historical profession, there were more than a few critical, undogmatic Marxists or socialists who took active part in the Congresses, including Gastone Manacorda, Leo Valiani, Pierre Vilar, Albert Soboul, Ernest Labrousse, and Eric J. Hobsbawm. The fact that the house of Marxism contained many mansions became visible in the comments made by a communist Hungarian historian in support of a Soviet report on historiography in the twentieth century. In order to understand the present situation of historical thought, Gyula Tokody (Debrecen) said, one also had to consider "the changes that have occurred within the Marxist conception of history." Particularly notable was "the elimination of the theoretical distortions of the cult of personality, the condemnation of the rigid conduct by which Marxist historians closed their minds to the achievements of bourgeois historiography.... We are actually speaking of loosening up the theoretical petrification that Marxism has suffered from in recent times and that has also led to a theoretical shallowness in the field of historical thought. The theoretical purge, which is the most important trait of historical thought on an international scale as well, would be unthinkable without the inner purge and the development of Marxist thought."[17]

During the festive opening ceremony in the reconstructed Vienna Opera, President Jonas stated that, thanks to its history and geographical location, the reconstituted Republic of Austria was called upon to perform a task of European proportions. Against the backdrop of the former Habsburg capital, the Vienna Historical Congress was undoubtedly one of the most glamorous and eventful of all. The great themes from the history of the host country, however, were not addressed. Recent Austrian history remained hidden in occasional statements cloaked in the mythical fog of half-truths that the Moscow declaration of 30 October 1943 had spread. This is not to say that there was any shortage of historical questions that were politically motivated. But the emotional debates emerged from issues affecting feelings of national self-awareness, rather than from controversial problems of Marxist or "bourgeois" theory and methodology.

The Congress's longest discussion was sparked by the report by the American historian Hans Kohn on "Nationalism and Internationalism in the nineteenth and twentieth centuries."[18] A series of speakers objected that the paper was too strongly oriented toward political and intellectual history, and that Kohn had not sufficiently thought through the socioeconomic conditions of the emergence and development of the nation and of nationalism. But the main emphasis of the discussion lay less on such methodological arguments than on the comments made by historians from the successor states of the former Habsburg monarchy and other Eastern European countries. They asserted their various national points of view, and distinguished between a legitimate and an illegitimate nationalism—that of the dominated and that of the dominant peoples. They shed no tears for old Austria. Democratic and federalist reforms, such as those attempted by the Austro-Marxists, had foundered on the conditions of their time.[19] And yet several speakers perceived the Danube monarchy as an outdated but nevertheless impressive manifestation of a transnational state, which remained worthy of recollection and at the same time constituted a political challenge. Kohn expressed this in the words of the young Ranke, who had seen Austria as the sole state of a truly European character, which "represents as it were visibly the unity of Europe for it unites all the races of the continent into one state."[20] Milivoj Mostovac (Ottawa), a Croatian-born historian living in Canada, made this bold assertion: "If the Danube monarchy had been reformed in due time and according to the wishes of its member peoples; if its government had been composed of authentic representatives of the peoples … then it could have become the nucleus of a united Europe."[21]

The Congress's president, Friedrich Engel-Janosi, came to feel the strong emotions still aroused by the remembrance of the final phase of the Danube monarchy. Since the *Actes* remain silent on this, let us quote from his memoirs:

> If the "Congress of Vienna" had no acknowledged highpoint, there was at least an "*éclat*." It came in connection with the discussion of my paper on Emperor Charles's peace efforts during the First World War, which I consider to be an undeniable historical fact, without regarding them as a particular accomplishment on the part of the monarch.… But there were South Slav historians who disputed any peaceful motives on the part of the Emperor or of German Austrians, while according to their own view, all the South Slav military formations serving in the Austrian Army

sought to end the war by revolution. I spoke up against this latter claim and pointed to the extraordinary military valor of the Bosnian regiments during frontal attacks. In an interpretation that is not easy to understand, my comment was taken as a dangerous insult against the national honor of the Bosnian regiments, which, since it came from the president of the assembly, demanded a very serious, if not "bloody" revenge. The three remaining days of the Congress just sufficed to cool the tempers that had been heated to the boiling point.[22]

Those who witnessed this scene know how cool this report is compared with the actual event.

In the same section on "Political Problems of the First World War," the opponents in the German controversy over the July crisis of 1914 and the German war aims presented their views: Fritz Fischer (Hamburg), Egmont Zechlin (Hamburg), and Karl Dietrich Erdmann (Kiel), who filled in for Gerhard Ritter.[23] The latter had prepared a paper on "The Political Role of Bethmann Hollweg During the First World War," but was prevented from attending due to illness. The discussion in Germany had been followed outside of Germany with considerable interest. In Vienna this was evidenced by the great number of listeners, around 800, more than at any other session. Scholarly and political interest dovetailed with the underlying question of whether Germany had not only planned and unleashed the Second World War, but the First World War, too—deliberately, and in pursuit of hegemonic goals. Coinciding with the Vienna Congress, the weekly journal *Die Zeit* published an essay by Fritz Fischer, in which he presented this thesis pointedly. Here, he went far beyond what he had maintained in his book *Griff nach der Weltmacht* (Germany's Grasp for Power), which had caused a sensation and was translated into many languages. A Polish participant aptly reported that in the discussion of the issue at Vienna, "various standpoints were presented, and the majority of the speakers spoke in favor of Fischer's theses."[24] For whatever reasons, Western European and American historians did not participate in this discussion. At a Franco-German colloquium in Dijon a few days beforehand, Fritz Fischer had suggested to his French colleagues that they seek to change the Franco-German recommendations of 1951 for historical instruction by deleting the statement: "The documents do not permit us to ascribe to any government or any people the conscious will to wage a European war in 1914." Pierre Renouvin, who did not attend the Vienna Congress, Jean Baptiste Duroselle, and Jacques Droz had rejected abandoning this balanced formulation in favor of the thesis that Germany had pursued the intention of unleashing a general war for years in advance—a thesis not supported by the available documents.[25]

The unanimous acceptance of the Soviet invitation to hold the next Congress in Moscow and thus for the first time in a communist country demonstrated that Marxist-Leninist historiography had gained a firm place within the ICHS and the Congresses, and that Western historians, whose representatives held a large majority in the ICHS, were willing to take up the permanent ideological challenge resulting from this situation. However, the path from Vienna to Moscow was not smooth. The violent suppression of the Czech reform communists through the invasion of the Red Army and its allies on 21 August 1968 caused a profound shock in the Western world, and also among historians. The situation was reminiscent of 1956, when the president of the ICHS, Federico Chabod, and finally the entire Bureau had refused to comply with the Committee's previous acceptance of the invitation to hold a General Assembly in Moscow. Should one, and could one now prepare an International Congress in the Soviet capital as if nothing had happened? Opinions within the ICHS were divided.

The British position was unambiguous. The national committee thought that it was not right to hold the Congress in the Soviet Union, and passed a resolution requesting that the Bureau locate it in another country, or cancel it if that should not be possible. The British national committee would not participate in a Congress in the Soviet Union.[26] This resolution was presented to the other forty-one national committees and the press, together with a statement that denounced the Soviet action as an "unprovoked aggression," as an "attack particularly aimed at the freedom of speech and writing," but at the same time declared that the British committee did not intend to call for a general boycott of the Congress and that it did not claim to speak for all British historians since there were also arguments against staying away.[27] The American Historical Association also came out against Moscow.[28] The Dutch likewise made an "official démarche," stating that the principles of the ICHS prohibited holding the Congress in Moscow.[29] The national committees of other countries, including France,[30] expressed reservations without raising such objections. By contrast, Italian and Austrian historians warned against the consequences of preventing the Congress.[31] The West German historians refrained from taking a position because they anticipated the admission of the GDR as a new member, and believed that their absence from the Moscow Congress would not be in the German interest, "since in this way the GDR would practically be made the sole representative of German historical scholarship."[32]

Despite his condemnation of the Soviet intervention in Czechoslovakia, Boyd Shafer, the American second vice-president of the ICHS, did not share the opinion of the American Historical Association. "I fear now that the very existence of ICHS is at stake," he wrote. "There might come a complete break between the 'west' and the 'east,' which in itself would be disastrous, or there would come many withdrawals of support whatever is decided about Moscow." Therefore, he called upon the Bureau to "assume a certain leadership role in this crisis."[33] This applied particularly to the task of the Belgian medievalist Paul Harsin, who had been elected president in Vienna. In contrast to François, Harsin felt that the Bureau ought to act as it had done twelve years earlier with regard to the occurrences in Hungary, and call the Moscow Congress into question. It was in this spirit, he said, that he had been officially approached by the Dutch national committee, and privately by some French historians. It would be necessary to present the question to the Bureau and the ICHS.[34] He thus turned to Aleksandr Guber, president of the Soviet national committee and first vice-president of the ICHS, with the request that the invitation to the Moscow Congress be temporarily withheld. He wrote that he intended to ask the Bureau's members for their opinion and to conduct an "international consultation."[35] The Soviet historians, who were just as eager to avoid a break, proved to be conciliatory and postponed the first circular letter concerning the invitation to the Congress. Upon receiving the British protest note, Guber showed that he did not seek a collision course: he confirmed that the Soviet historians accepted the invitation to a conference with British colleagues scheduled for September 1969 in London.[36]

As in the Hungarian crisis of 1956, François once again used his tactical skill to avoid a break. He was certain that he did so in accordance with the wishes of the Eastern European historians. French colleagues who had visited Warsaw informed him of the Poles' worries that they could once again be cut off from the West, "to which they had always looked."[37] For this reason, he wanted to avoid the "international consultation" that Harsin had announced in his letter to Guber. With varying arguments, he tried to prevent "categorical statements of position"[38] and to delay the survey, although Harsin insisted on it. Not until 10 December—a month after the Britons had informed the national committees of their resolution—did he send a circular letter to the Bureau members, in which he requested that they state their position regarding a consultation of the national committees. The responses and discussions with individual members clearly showed that most of them did not intend to undertake anything that could endanger the Moscow Congress. Aside from the exceptions mentioned above, the national committees, too, did not wish to disturb the normal course of events. The Bureau and the ICHS acted according to a maxim that François repeatedly used during those months: to continue preparations for the Congress "comme si rien n'était" (as if nothing had happened).[39] François felt confirmed in his policy by the fact that the Western powers did nothing to interfere in Czechoslovakia. After the defeat of the reform movement, when the Czechoslovakians were left with no option other than to adapt, he confided to the secretary of the Italian national committee that "one must not be more royalist than the king," and that thus he "did not have to be more Czechoslovakian than the Czechoslovakians" who had yielded to Moscow's dominance. And criticizing the British behavior, he added that he had always sought a clear separation of politics and scholarship.[40]

The fact that the two areas were nevertheless indissolubly intertwined was demonstrated by a question raised from different sides, namely, whether the ICHS had the duty to speak openly and clearly on the events in Czechoslovakia as far as they affected the freedom of scholarly work, and all the more so if it was of opinion that the Congress in Moscow should not be canceled. Thus, Jean d'Ormesson, the chairman of the International Council for Philosophy and Human Sciences, recommended issuing a proclamation of sympathy with

Czechoslovakia, while leaving open the question of whether the Congress could be held in Moscow. If the Soviets then decided to cancel the Congress, they would be the ones responsible for the break.[41] The American Historical Association took a similar position. If no other Congress location were possible, then they would go to Moscow, "but at the same time present our views that we condemn the restraints upon intellectual activity in Russia and Czechoslovakia."[42] A firm and open statement seemed all the more appropriate since the international community of historians was directly affected by the fact that a considerable number of Czech historians had been ousted from their positions and from academic work for political reasons.

When some 3,000 historians, a larger number than ever before, assembled on 16 August in the Great Hall of the Kremlin, Paul Harsin, in his carefully phrased opening address, mentioned the hundredth anniversary of Lenin's birth, which was being celebrated that year, in due form—Lenin, "who, through his thought and actions, brought about the most profound transformation of living conditions on nearly half the globe"—, and combined this with a comment on the great unease caused in the ICHS by the "crisis of the summer of 1968." A number of national committees had withdrawn their promise to participate, and the Congress's preparation had been delayed by several months. "We hope," he continued, "that all participants will show understanding for the moral scruples that the historians of some countries have felt and that others have only overcome with difficulty. For the first essential precondition for scholarly research is intellectual freedom, the possibility to express critical judgements in scholarly work. It would be meaningless to promote the encounter of historians from countries of different, or even antagonistic systems if there was no guarantee that each individual may represent his own point of view."[43]

A representative from the Federal Republic of Germany, Eberhard Jäckel (Stuttgart), made use of this freedom. In a discussion contribution to a paper by Ernst Diehl (GDR) on the October Revolution, he declared:

> As I stand here before you, I cannot help but direct the attention of the Congress to the fact that currently many of our colleagues in that country [Czechoslovakia] are subjected to a certain political persecution, that in the past weeks fifteen members of the Historical Institute of the Czechoslovakian Academy of Sciences have been dismissed, and that many of our colleagues whom we listened to at the Congress in Vienna five years ago, are not in attendance this year. I believe that a Congress like ours cannot decently take place without an open discussion of these facts. I want to express my protest and my hope that at the next Congress we will be able to talk with all our colleagues who wish to come, and I conclude with a quotation from Rosa Luxemburg, spoken in connection with the October Revolution, which states: "Freedom is always the freedom of dissenters."[44]

Once the passionate storm of protest caused by these words had subsided, the discussion leader, Karl Dietrich Erdmann, stated that the open confrontation of opposing opinions was inherent in the Congresses' very nature, as had been successfully proved right there in Moscow. In a later official comment, a member of the Soviet organizing committee, A. O. Chubaryan, expressed virtually the same view. He said that "the fierce debates were rooted in this topic's unresolved problems. However, the Soviet historians were happy about this open discussion and about the fact that it took place right in Moscow."[45]

The prudent behavior of the Soviet hosts, who attempted not to exacerbate the conflict, had a specific political background. A few days before the Congress's opening, a German-Soviet treaty had been signed in Moscow inaugurating the new "Eastern policy" (Ostpolitik) of the Federal Republic of Germany initiated by the Brandt/Scheel government. It was an element of the general détente policy of the 1970s, which was based on de facto recognition of the political situation and zones of influence created by the war. This influenced the Congress's atmosphere. There was a deliberate endeavor to establish contact despite the existing tensions, even though the Congress hardly lacked for historical and political confrontations. These were particularly harsh in the discussion of a lecture by the Hungarian Miclos Lackó on fascism in Eastern Europe that did not fit into the rigid Marxist theory of fascism because of its attempts at differentiation. Fierce disputes also arose from some assertions by the Norwegian Torolf Rafto about the communists' responsibility for the division of the labor movement, with all its bad consequences, and about the collective security policy of the Soviet Union in the interwar period.[46]

In order to prevent such disruptions of unanimity during the Lenin Symposium that was running parallel to the Congress, not a single non-Marxist Western speaker had been invited. Evgenii M. Zhukov's address at the Congress's opening ceremony on "Lenin and History" formed a prelude to this.[47] It was a speech that would have fit well into the *Acta Sanctorum*, as a Church historian observed. There were others who perceived such declarations of unconditional, uncritical admiration of a great historical personality as a "congratulatory ceremony of Byzantine proportions."

Since the political events preceding the Moscow Congress amounted to the acceptance of the East-West relationship as created in the wake of the Second World War, the ICHS decided to change its previous stance toward the politically divided countries. The impetus had been provided by South Korea's application for admission presented to the Bureau at its Liège meeting of July 1969. Inevitably, the question had come up as to whether the previous applications for membership from divided countries such as Germany and Vietnam had to be submitted as well to the General Assembly at Moscow. The Bureau decided "to consider the candidacy of the national committee of South Korea, but to present it at the General Assembly of 1970 within the framework of the question of principle concerning all the divided countries." The national committees of those countries were informed that their candidacy would be taken into consideration, provided they maintained it.[48] North Korea filed an application; the two Vietnams did not. Thus, the General Assembly of 15 August 1970 in

Moscow discussed the admission of the German Democratic Republic and the two Koreas. The public vote brought the following result: GDR, 26 for, 3 abstentions; South Korea, 21 for, 2 against, 6 abstentions; North Korea, 27 for, 3 abstentions. The representative of the Verband der Historiker Deutschlands, Karl Jordan (Kiel), abstained from voting.

This affair had an internal sequel in regard to West Berlin. In the list of participants, grouped by countries, that the Soviets had drawn up and distributed shortly before the end of the Congress, the historians from "West Berlin" were listed separately from the historians from the "Federal Republic of Germany." The political intention was obvious. It contradicted the actual mode of the German historians' representation in the ICHS by the Verband der Historiker Deutschlands, which rests upon individual membership and includes the historians from West Berlin. A lengthy correspondence with the secretary-general of the ICHS was required before he agreed to insert a corresponding correction in the *Bulletin d'information*.[49] Later lists of participants were handled correctly.

A few months after the Congress, the Bureau was deeply affected by the death of its newly elected president, Aleksandr A. Guber. This highly respected, polyglot scholar convincingly combined Marxist-Leninist vigilance on political and ideological issues with the ability to seek openhearted contact with colleagues of all nations and points of view. Since he had been able to exercise his office of president for only a short time, some Bureau members were of the opinion that it would be fitting to recommend a Soviet historian as his successor at the planned 1972 General Assembly of the ICHS in Herzeg Novi. But there was resistance to this idea both inside and outside the Bureau. The American Historical Association imparted that it considered the election of a Russian to be "inappropriate."[50] Others thought the same way. Why should not the first vice-president perform this function until the next Congress, as after the deaths of presidents Chabod (1960, succeeded by the vice-president Webster) and Schmid (1962, succeeded by the vice-president Guber)? But if the presidency was to remain in Soviet hands, then it appeared desirable to nominate several candidates, in agreement with the Soviet national committee, in order to make the election appear like a real election.

However, Moscow had decided on only one name: Evgenii Mikhailovich Zhukov, who had given the hero-worshipping Lenin speech at the opening of the last Congress. It could be assumed that the General Assembly would see his sole candidacy as an imposition. In discussions conducted in Moscow at the behest of the Bureau, the second vice-president Erdmann expressed the fear that sticking to this sole candidacy would not lead to the desired majority or even unanimity with which all previous presidents had been elected. This concern proved to be justified. The election took place with only a one-vote majority (40 votes cast, 21 for Zhukov, 1 for Shafer, 17 blank ballots, and one invalid ballot).[51] Independently of this, the Bureau had chosen the first vice-president Boyd C. Shafer as president of the San Francisco Congress. This was the good result of a bad procedure: Giving the Soviet Union the presidency for the entire period from Moscow to San Francisco was in keeping with the world-political situation and the scholarly constellation in the ICHS, and Shafer, who was well acquainted with the affairs of the ICHS, would serve as the president of the next Congress.

Despite the disagreement about the election of its president, the scholarly cooperation within the historians' Internationale continued to develop under the favorable conditions of an increasing global détente. Following the *Ostverträge* of the German Federal Republic (Moscow Treaty in 1970, Warsaw Treaty in 1971, *Grundlagenvertrag* with the GDR in 1972), the Four Powers Agreement on Berlin (1971), and the SALT I Treaty on the reduction of nuclear weapons (1972), the conclusion of the Conference for Security and Cooperation in Europe (CSCE, Helsinki 1975) a few months before the San Francisco Historical Congress represented a climax in the process of détente.

In San Francisco, a further defusing of the political tensions was noticeable within the international historical community. Commentaries in both the East and the West attested that the climate of the scholarly dialogue had increasingly improved. Of course, this did not mean that antagonistic political interpretations of historical facts did not collide with one another. Topics like revolution or reform, the character and cause of migratory movements, or international security in interwar Europe provided plenty of opportunities.[52] As in Moscow, the most interesting yield for the history of historical studies was provided by the contributions on theory and methodology. Typical of the emergence of a new constellation was a discussion comment made by a Hungarian participant "who stated openly that Marxism was not a closed system, but merely a scientific method; not a conclusive answer to historical questions, but rather a special way of posing such questions."[53]

The San Francisco Congress was the first one to take place outside of Europe. The number of participants was rather low, as compared to the increasing attendance of the three previous Congresses. Relatively few American historians took part, even from the neighboring universities of Berkeley and Stanford. Many of them preferred instead to attend a historical meeting of the Western states of the United States that was staged in another location at almost the same time. Historians from the old continent were astonished by the utter indifference with which the Congress was received by the public. The press took scarcely any notice at all of the events in the elegant Fairmount Hotel on Nob Hill, the historical founding site of the United Nations. The political establishment ignored the Congress. But that was only one side of the coin. On the other were the unusual activity of the American Historical Association's organizing committee under the direction of Richard Schlatter (Rutgers), which had gathered all the funds for this undertaking from private donors and foundations, and the unique experience of a hospitality provided by a private citizens' initiative. On one evening all the foreign participants were invited into the homes of American families who, in most cases, had no professional link to history. To experience the Americans' warm-hearted and open hospitality, and a country built on its free citizens, meant more in political terms than all the undelivered speeches.

Perhaps the restraint shown toward this Congress can be explained by the fact that, following the experiences of Stockholm, Vienna, and Moscow, it was expected to be a showcase of Marxist-Leninist propaganda. It is hardly surprising that it was indeed viewed as such afterward in the Soviet historical journals. Thus, the *Voprosy* emphasized the success achieved on the "propaganda podium for the materialistic understanding of history," and the *Vestnik Moskovskovo Universiteta* proudly announced: "The activities of the scholars of the Socialist countries transformed the Congress into a platform for the propaganda of Marxist historical understanding."[54] However, a warning "not to cross the line beyond which a historical discussion mostly or exclusively becomes a political polemic" appeared in the leading Polish historical journal.[55] The overall impression of this Congress is that the propagandistic orchestration of the ideological confrontation had declined in volume over the course of the Congresses, to the great benefit of the scholarly debate.

On the margins, but in the immediate vicinity of the Congress's events, the participants were reminded of the Czech historians who had been driven from their positions. Amnesty International distributed information on their fates and on the work that they continued to perform under great pressure. Later, in Bucharest and Stuttgart, this task was assumed by colleagues from a number of different Western European countries.[56]

In San Francisco, for the first time in the history of the ICHS, a German, Karl Dietrich Erdmann, was elected president (results of the en bloc vote on the new composition of the Bureau: yes 27, no 3, abstentions 7).[57] This election and the subsequent positive cooperation with those national committees that presumably had voted against him or abstained are evidence that in the field of institutionalized international cooperation, it was possible to reduce the burden with which Germany was encumbered because of its history during the years from 1914 to 1945. Just like the departing president Zhukov before him, the newly elected president referred to the political perspective of Helsinki in the Congress's closing session. The solemn commitment made by so many countries from the North and South, from the East and West, to respect intellectual freedom and tolerance recalled Article 19 of the United Nations Declaration of Human Rights, which guarantees each person the inalienable right of freedom of thought and speech. The president's address therefore reminded his audience of the many colleagues who had been deprived of this right. However, his hope, expressed against all expectations, to be able to welcome them at the next International Congress was ahead of its time. The coexistence slogans of Helsinki lacked political precision and binding force. Did the historians possess opportunities of their own to promote the formation of an ecumenical community committed to peace at least within their own profession?

The Helsinki CSCE conference led to a continuous process of information and discussion among the countries involved concerning the realization of the principles agreed on in 1975. The first successor conference took place in Belgrade in 1977, and the second was meeting in Madrid when the Historical Congress of 1980 convened in Bucharest. The discussion on arms limitation also appeared to progress. SALT II was signed in 1979, though it was not ratified.

At the turn of 1979/80, the Red Army invaded Afghanistan. Yet this blow against the policy of détente had no impact on the working climate of the Bucharest Congress. The International Congresses had gained their own inner momentum, which tended toward increasing objectivity. This was also manifested five years later. The renewed arms race had again led to such a level of international tension that it was possible to speak of a second Cold War, and yet the Stuttgart Congress in 1985 managed to take another step toward the realization of a genuine ecumenical community of historians. This, too, was influenced by external factors: the general awareness of a permanent nuclear stalemate ("response capability") consolidating itself despite the new arms race; the peaceful development of trade relations between the East and the West despite a number of disruptions and threatening political or military gestures on both sides; the development of a certain degree of solidarity between the two German states, achieved in the awareness of their mutual national interest in peace; and finally the incipient transformation of the world-political balance of power. The United States had suffered setbacks and a severe inner shakeup through the unsuccessful end of the Vietnam War and the Watergate affair, while in Angola, Mozambique, and on the Horn of Africa the Soviet Union had managed to gain new positions equivalent to the American system of bases. Even more significant was the fact that the People's Republic of China was starting to present itself as a potential economic and political world power and had abandoned its long cultural self-isolation. China's return to the world system had begun with President Nixon's visit to Beijing in 1972. The gradual establishment of scientific contacts by the People's Republic made it possible in 1980 to win China back to the ICHS, after some Chinese historians had already participated at the last prewar Congress in Zurich in 1938. As a guest of the Chinese Academy, the president of the ICHS held lectures in Beijing and Shanghai on the development of the International Historical Congresses. On the invitation of the Romanian government, which strongly supported the efforts concerning the attendance of Chinese historians, a Chinese delegation took part in the Bucharest Congress. It subsequently applied for membership in the ICHS. It was no coincidence that Romania promoted the Chinese participation. Against the backdrop of the rupture between China and the Soviet Union, this was a clear manifestation of Romania's desire for a policy of national autonomy.

In contrast to San Francisco, the Bucharest Congress was perceived as a public event in the national interest. Smooth organization, generous hospitality, and the strong participation of representatives of the government, the Party, the academies, and the Church, as well as lively reporting in the press, ensured that for a week the international historical profession was present in the public life of Romania—even if newspaper reports and interviews also were aimed at inducing leading historians from all over the world to make statements *ad majorem gloriam* of Romania's exalted president and party leader Nicolae Ceaușescu. Five impressive volumes of reports on the Congress were published, carefully prepared by Dan Berindei. In contrast to Moscow and San Francisco, they included the discussions, which were presented as clear documentation of controversial historical-political positions. The national history of Romania was depicted in lectures at the opening and closing sessions[58] within the framework of a "major theme" on Eastern Europe[59] and in events on the margins of the Congress. The familiar topic of the "Dacian-Romanic continuity," which had already been presented at several previous Congresses, was orchestrated with many variations. Romania was celebrating the creation of the "first centralized and independent Dacian state 2,050 years ago." In this context, the national significance of rich archaeological research became particularly evident. In a similar vein, Bulgaria presented its history, to which a special evening session was dedicated. It commemorated the founding of the first Bulgarian state 1,300 years earlier.[60] The inclusion of this session represented a friendly gesture on the part of Romania toward its neighboring country, which would have liked to host the Congress itself. Both cases showed the national importance attached to international cooperation in Southeastern Europe.

In a communication to the Congress, Ceaușescu appealed to the historians to place their work in the service of peace, and asked emphatically that the national sovereignty and independence of the smaller peoples be defended. When the newly elected Polish president of the ICHS, Aleksander Gieysztor, returned to this motif in his closing speech, the reference to the actual political situation was unmistakable to all listeners. At this moment and in this place, in the capital of Romania, such appeals, as irrelevant as their political efficacy may be, had concrete political meaning. What, however, is the specific and genuine contribution that the "Internationale of the historians" can provide for the promotion of mutual understanding, rapprochement, and peace? The Congress's president sought an answer to this question in a survey on the history of the ICHS, which he subsumed under the notion of an "ecumenical" community of historians.[61]

The issue of peace was one of the "major themes" of the Congress.[62] In this attempt to put the general idea of peace into concrete historical forms, antagonistic political convictions collided when issues like imperialism and disarmament, the five principles of Bandung in 1954 (non-intervention!), the concept of "just war," historical constructions of peace utopias, or the assessment of war causes and significant peace treaties were approached. The treaties ending the First World War in particular gave rise to a pointed scholarly controversy. Was the Versailles system fundamentally flawed because it contained the seeds of a new war within it (Fritz Klein, East Berlin), or should it instead be viewed as an attempt to let reason prevail and seek a balance of conflicting interests (Fritz Fellner, Salzburg)?

The reports on the Congress generally highlighted the matter-of-fact negotiating climate. The East German journal *Zeitschrift für Geschichtswissenschaft* accurately reported that "the debates between Marxist and bourgeois historians ... were generally to the point, the exchange of opinions fruitful," while maintaining that it had become clear in Bucharest "that there can be no ideological coexistence."[63] The Soviet journals took a sometimes approving, sometimes critical view of the notion of an "ecumenical" historical union. Some of the authors misinterpreted it as an appeal for the "depoliticization of historical studies."[64] If the president's speech warned against unproductive polemical declamations of irreconcilable ideological positions, this did not mean that he denied the interrelation between history and political values, or the political motivation of historical research, for "objectivity and partisanship need not contradict one another." It is, however, a decisive question for the objectives and purposes of the Congresses whether the normal scholarly dialogue can rely on a minimal consensus between liberal and communist historians concerning the basic methodical principles of the historical discourse.[65]

At the opening of the Stuttgart Congress of 1985, the president of the German Federal Republic, Richard von Weizsäcker, placed the term "ecumenical community of historians" at the center of his welcoming speech on "History, politics and nation." Well acquainted with theological thought, he considered the term "ecumenical," which denotes the common ground and difference among the churches, as a "felicitous name" for the historians' task of conducting a dialogue, "which presupposes the otherness of the other" just as much as "faithfulness to oneself, to one's own solid foundation." But what was the "solid foundation" of the German hosts who, like their predecessors, sought to show something characteristic from their own history? In no other European country is the concept of nation as discredited as in Germany. As Christian Meier, chairman of the Historians' Association of Germany, said in his opening address: "Where else do we find this: a society which in addition to encompassing only three quarters of a people, has a deep split running between itself and its history? Which, historically, defines itself essentially through the negation of a brief historical period immediately preceding the founding of its state?"[66] Would not Berlin have been the fitting "solid foundation" upon which to visualize German history, many a participant asked himself. So far, with one exception, the Congresses had always been held in the capitals of the host countries. In any case, Berlin would have illustrated the split in German history, and thus its reality, more graphically than Stuttgart, the capital of Baden-Württemberg. Berlin was forsaken in order to avoid loading a discipline as politically sensitive as history with additional emotional tensions by exposing the Congress to the sight of the barbarian Berlin Wall. In Stuttgart, far from the frontier dividing Germany, it was easier to respect the "otherness of the other." With a few exceptions not worth mentioning, the conversational atmosphere was more matter-of-fact than ever before, even in the relationship between the historians of the two Germanys.

Politically relevant aspects were included in the session on "Resistance to Fascism, National Socialism, and Japanese Militarism." The topic had been suggested by the West German side. The intention was a comparative analysis of the economic, social, political, and intellectual preconditions and capacities of the Resistance movement in the three countries.[67] No such study existed at that time. Unfortunately, the subject matter was expanded beyond all bounds, so that precise comparative studies failed to materialize. The contributions either repeated well-known information or stayed within the narrow national frameworks, and sometimes they presented a mythical elevation of a general Resistance of the people whereas in reality only small, dedicated minorities were at work. The main difference between the two introductory reports by François Bédarida (France) and Miroslav Kropilák (Czechoslovakia) also lay in their quantitative appraisals of the Resistance movements.[68] Bédarida sought to develop conceptual distinctions and to introduce greater precision. In doing so, he also arrived at an appropriate appraisal of the loyalty conflicts within the German military Resistance during the war that "stands at the center of the controversy." Unfortunately, Kropilák failed to include a corresponding assessment of the conflict experienced by the communist Resistance in Germany and Czechoslovakia during the cooperation between Hitler and Stalin in the period from 1939 up to the German attack on the Soviet Union. However, the speakers corroborated one another in a joint declaration that different interpretations "are the salutary and normal reflections of the pluralism that is necessary within the international community of historians." Furthermore, they declared that they agreed on three crucial points in their appraisal of the Resistance movement, namely, that it was aimed at "the defense of Man," the "will to peace and harmony," and the conviction of the "necessity of international cooperation."[69]

Notes

1. Ž. K[ormanowa], "Na marginesie obrad XI Międzynarodowego Kongresu Nauk Historycznych" [On the margins of the discussions of the XIth International Historical Congress], *Kwartalnik historyczny* 68, no. 1 (1961): 268–271, here p. 271.
2. Minutes of the Bureau meeting in Lausanne, 18–21 June 1957, Archives CISH, box 17. Rich material on the entire problem in Archives CISH, Box 17, esp. correspondence Chabod-François.
3. J. Macek, director of the Historical Institute of the Czechoslovakian Academy of Sciences, in *Literární noviny*, 29 Oct. 1960.
4. *Neues Deutschland*, 16 Oct. 1960.
5. "XI Meždunarodnyj kongress istoričeskich nauk v Stokgol'me" [The XIth International Historical Congress in Stockholm, no author], *Voprosy istorii* 35, no. 12 (1960): 3–29, here p. 4. See also A. A. Guber, "Nekotorye problemy novoj i novejšej istorii na XI meždunarodnom Kongresse istorikov v Stokgol'me" [Problems of modern and recent history

at the XIth International Historical Congress in Stockholm], *Novaja i Novejšaja Istorija*, no. 1 (1961).
6. *Extrait du Bulletin de l'Académie royale de Belgique (Classe des Lettres): Séance du 5 décembre 1960*, p. 679.
7. François to Ritter, 15 Oct. 1960, Ritter papers, 383.
8. E. Jäckel, "Der XI. Internationale Historikerkongreß in Stockholm," *Geschichte in Wissenschaft und Unterricht* 11 (1960): 700–705, here p. 703.
9. Th. Schieder, "Der XI. Internationale Historikerkongreß in Stockholm: Ein Nachbericht,"*Historische Zeitschrift* 193 (1961): 515–521, here p. 516f.
10. Some examples: S. Stelling-Michaud (Geneva), "L'histoire des universités au moyen âge et à la renaissance au cours des vingt-cinq dernières années," in *XIe Congrès International des Sciences Historiques, Stockholm 21–28 août 1960: Rapports* [hereafter Congress Stockholm 1960: *Rapports*], 5 vols. (Uppsala, 1960), vol. 1; G. Le Bras (Paris), "Les problèmes des Institutions de la chrétienté médiévale," Congress Stockholm 1960: *Rapports*, vol. 3; G. Johannesson (Lund), "Die Kirchenreformation in den nordischen Ländern," Congress Stockholm 1960: *Rapports*, vol. 4; E. Sestan (Florence), "La città comunale italiana dei secoli XI–XIII nelle sue note caratteristiche rispetto al movimento comunale europeo," Congress Stockholm 1960: *Rapports*, vol. 3; Earl J. Hamilton (Chicago), "The history of prices before 1750," Congress Stockholm 1960: *Rapports*, vol. 1; F. Thistlethwaite (Cambridge), "Migration from Europe overseas in the nineteenth and twentieth centuries," Congress Stockholm 1960: *Rapports*, vol. 5; H. Haag (Louvain), "La social-démocratie allemande et la première guerre mondiale," ibid.
11. For example, A. L. Sidorov (Moscow), "Les problèmes de la structure de l'industrie à la fin du XIXe siècle en Russie," in *XIe Congrès International des Sciences Historiques, Stockholm 21–28 août 1960: Résumés des Communications* (Uppsala, 1962) [hereafter Congress Stockholm 1960: *Communications*]; V. M. Khvostov (Moscow), "La politique extérieure de l'Allemagne dans les années quatre-vingts du XIXe siècle à la lumière des sources des archives russes," ibid.; W. Norman Brown (Pennsylvania), "Traditional Culture and Modern Developments in India," Congress Stockholm 1960: *Rapports*, vol. 5.
12. For example, H. Holborn, "Power Politics and Christian Ethics in Early German Protestantism," Congress Stockholm 1960: *Communications*; H. Rothfels, "Nationalität und Grenze im späten 19. und frühen 20. Jahrhundert," ibid.
13. *XIIe Congrès International des Sciences Historiques, Vienne 29 août–5 septembre 1965: Actes* [hereafter Congress Vienna 1965: *Actes*] (Vienna, [1968]), p. 512f.
14. G. Becker and E. Engelberg, "Der XII. Internationale Historikerkongreß in Wien," *Zeitschrift für Geschichtswissenschaft* 13 (1965): 1309–1322, here p. 1315.
15. Ibid., p. 1311.
16. M. V. Nechkina, V. T. Pashuto, and E. B. Chernyak, "Evolution of historical thought in the middle of the XXth century," in *XIIe Congrès International des Sciences Historiques, Vienne 29 août–5 septembre 1965: Rapports* [hereafter Congress Vienna 1965: *Rapports*], 4 vols. (Vienna, [1965]), vol. 4, pp. 57–67, here p. 64.
17. Congress Vienna 1965: *Actes*, p. 512, commentary on the report cited in note 16 above. Ideological divergences were also manifest in the contributions of Henryk Katz (Lodz) and Josef Kowalski (Warsaw), ibid., pp. 540, 111f.
18. Congress Vienna 1965: *Rapports*, vol. 1, pp. 191–240.
19. See esp. a discussion contribution by H. Mommsen, Congress Vienna 1965: *Actes*, pp. 91–93.
20. Congress Vienna 1965: *Rapports*, vol. 1, p. 211f. Cf. L. Ranke, "Aus den Papieren eines Landpfarrers" [1818], *Historische Zeitschrift* 137 (1928): 231–244. Reprint in Ranke, *Aus Werk und Nachlaß*, vol. 3: *Frühe Schriften*, ed. W. P. Fuchs (Munich/Vienna, 1973), pp. 467–483, here p. 481f.
21. Congress Vienna 1965: *Actes*, p. 99.

22. F. Engel-Janosi, ... aber ein stolzer Bettler. Erinnerungen aus einer verlorenen Generation (Graz, 1974), p. 283. Further details in J. Matl, "Einige Bemerkungen zum XII. Internationalen Historikerkongreß in Wien," Der österreichische Standpunkt 3, no. 2 (1966): 17.
23. Congress Vienna 1965: Actes, pp. 717–748 (lectures and discussion); see also E. Zöllner, "Bericht über den 12. Internationalen Historikertag," Mitteilungen des Instituts für Österreichische Geschichtsforschung 73 (1965): 437–445, here p. 443; T. Jedruszczak, "Sprawy niemieckie na XII Kongresie Nauk Historycznych" [German affairs at the XIIth Historical Congress], Kwartalnik historyczny 73 (1966): 496–501.
24. Jedruszczak, "Sprawy niemieckie," p. 499.
25. See K. D. Erdmann, "Internationale Schulbuchrevision zwischen Politik und Wissenschaft," Internationale Schulbuchforschung 4 (Braunschweig, 1982): 249–260.
26. The resolution of 1 Oct. 1968 was signed by F. Wormald, Chairman, and Al. Dickens, Honorary Secretary. Text in Institute of Historical Research, papers of the British national committee.
27. Daily Telegraph, 15 Nov. 1968.
28. Letter of the Executive Secretary of the AHA, Ward, to François, 24 Oct. 1968, confirmed by François on 12 Nov. 1968, Archives CISH, unnumbered box.
29. Notice by François concerning a letter by Brugmans (Amsterdam) to Harsin, 27 Aug. 1968, and a message from François to Shafer, 14 Dec. 1968. Archives CISH, unnumbered box.
30. François to Harsin, 31 Aug. 1969, and to Reinhard (Sorbonne), 7 Sep. 1968. Archives CISH, unnumbered box.
31. For example, G. Vitucci, secretary of the Giunta Centrale, and F. Engel-Janosi. See François to Harsin, 31 Aug. 1969, Archives CISH, unnumbered box.
32. Minutes of the meeting of the executive board and committee of the Verband der Historiker Deutschlands, Cologne, 25 Oct. 1969, in the possession of the author.
33. Shafer to François, 11 Oct. 1968, Archives CISH, box 73.
34. Harsin to François, 30 Aug. 1968, Archives CISH, unnumbered box.
35. Harsin to Guber, 31 Aug. 1968, Archives CISH, unnumbered box.
36. Guber to Wormald, 19 Dec. 1968, Archives CISH, unnumbered box. See also letter from François to Shafer and Harsin, 31 Aug. 1968, about his visit to Moscow, ibid.
37. François to Harsin, 5 Oct. 1968, Archives CISH, unnumbered box.
38. François to members of the Bureau, 7 Sep. 1968, Archives CISH, unnumbered box.
39. See letters to H. Michel, 30 Sep. 1968, and to Biaudet, 5 Oct. 1968, Archives CISH, unnumbered box.
40. François to Vitucci, 25 Nov. 1968, Archives CISH, unnumbered box.
41. J. d'Ormesson to François, 21 Oct. 1968, Archives CISH, box 73.
42. Shafer to François, 21 Oct. 1968, Archives CISH, box 73.
43. XIII Meždunarodnyj kongress istoričeskich nauk. Moskva, 16–23 avgusta 1970 goda. Doklady Kongressa I [hereafter Congress Moscow 1970: Doklady], 7 vols. (Moscow, 1973), vol. 1, p. 19.
44. Jäckel's text was published in Christ und Welt 36, 4 Sep. 1970. An official record of the Congress discussions was not published. A relatively thorough report on this session can be found in D. Grille, "Der XIII. Internationale Historikerkongreß in Moskau: Bericht und Kommentar eines Teilnehmers," Deutsche Studien 32 (Lüneburg, 1970): 406–416.
45. According to Grille, "Historikerkongreß in Moskau."
46. Text of the lectures in Congress Moscow 1970: Doklady, vol. 6; report on the discussions by W. Malanowski, "Das ist doch alles zu dogmatisch," Der Spiegel 24, no. 36 (1970); H. Mommsen, "Der Internationale Historikertag in Moskau im Rückblick," Geschichte in Wissenschaft und Unterricht 22 (1971): 161–173; communist views: A. A. Guber (president of the Soviet organizing committee of the Congress and new president of the ICHS), "XIII Meždunarodnyj kongress istoričeskich nauk v Moskve" [XIIIth International Historical Congress in Moscow], Voprosy istorii 46, no. 6 (1971): 3–16; A. L. Narochnitsky (vice-president of the organizing committee), "K itogam XIII Meždunarodnogo kongressa istoričeskich nauk" [About the results of the XIIIth International Historical Congress],

Novaja i novejšaja istoria (1970, no. 6); in the same vein of Marxist-Leninist judgements G. Becker, M. Krause, and D. Lange, "Der XIII. Internationale Historikerkongreß in Moskau," *Zeitschrift für Geschichtswissenschaft* 19 (East Berlin, 1971): 165–179; ibid., pp. 242–265, reports on individual sections and commissions (E. Anderle et al., "Die Sektionen und Kommissionen auf dem XIII. Historikerkongreß").

47. "Lenin i istorija," Congress Moscow 1970: *Doklady*, vol. 1.
48. Minutes of the Liège Bureau meeting, 16–17 July 1969, Archives CISH, box 79; ICHS, *Bulletin d'information*, no. 9: 101.
49. The correspondence on this and on a similar incident of 1974 is in the possession of the author.
50. Ward to François, 7 Feb. 1972, Archives CISH, box 80.
51. Minutes of the General Assembly of Herzeg Novi, 21–22 July 1972, ICHS, *Bulletin d'information*, no. 9: 117.
52. For the San Francisco Congress, too, an official record of the discussions was not published. As for Moscow, one must therefore rely on the journals or detailed newspaper articles, such as G. Rhode, "Historiker am Pazifik—ganz unter sich," *Geschichte in Wissenschaft und Unterricht* 27 (1976): 420–435; H. A. Winkler, "Kein Historiker entrinnt seiner Gegenwart. Ost-West-Dialoge auf dem Weltkongreß der Geschichtswissenschaft in San Franzisko," *Frankfurter Allgemeine Zeitung*, 3 Sep. 1975; A. Bauerfeind et al., "Der XIV. Internationale Historikerkongreß in San Francisco," *Zeitschrift für Geschichtswissenschaft* 24 (1976): 442–467; A. M. Sakharov and S. S. Khromov, "XIV Meždunarodnyi kongress istoričeskich nauk" [XIVth International Historical Congress], *Voprosy istorii* 51, no. 3 (1976): 14–32; A. M. Sakharov, "O nekotorych metodologičeskich voprosach na XIV Meždunarodnom kongresse istorikov: zametke delegate" [On some methodological problems at the XIVth International Historical Congress: notes of a delegate], *Vestnik Universiteta Moskovskovo*, no. 3 (1976): 3–22; S. L. Tikhvinsky and V. A. Tishkov, "Problemy novoj i novejšej istorii na XIV Meždunarodnom kongresse istoričeskich nauk" [Problems of modern and recent history at the XIVth International Historical Congress], *Novaja i Novejšaja Istoria* 20, no. 1 (1976).
53. According to Winkler, "Kein Historiker."
54. Sakharov, "Metodologičeskich voprosach."
55. T. Jedrusczak, "Z prac Komitetu Nauk Historycznych" [From the work of the Committee of Historical Sciences], *Kwartalnik historyczny* 83 (1976): 476–480, here p. 479 [followed on pp. 480–490 by other reports under the same headline].
56. Czechoslovakian historians assembled the following document collections: *Acta persecutionis: Presented at the XIVth International Congress for Historical Sciences* (San Francisco, 1975); Vilém Prečan, ed., *Acta creationis: Vorgelegt dem XV. Internationalen Kongreß für Geschichtswissenschaften* (Bucharest, 1980). It contains a bibliography of "independent historiography in Czechoslovakia 1969–1980." See also "Une contribution tchécoslovaque: des 'Acta persecutionis' aux 'Acta creationis,'" *Le Monde*, 14 Aug. 1980. For Stuttgart, two volumes of collected historical essays were duplicated under the title "Independent Historiography in Czechoslovakia."
57. Minutes of the General Assembly of San Francisco, 21 Aug. 1975, *Bulletin d'information*, no. 10: 124.
58. St. Pascu, "La genèse du peuple roumain. L'origine et le développement historique du peuple roumain," in *XVe Congrès International des Sciences Historiques, Bucarest, 10–17 août 1980: Actes* [hereafter Congress Bucharest 1980: *Actes*], 2 vols. (Bucharest, 1982), vol. 1; V. Cândea, "La place du peuple roumain dans l'histoire universelle," *Congrès Bucarest 1980: Actes*, vol. 2.
59. "L'Europe de l'Est, aire de convergence de civilizations." Rapporteurs E. A. Condurachi and R. Theodorescu (both from Romania); text and supplementary reports in *XVe Congrès International des Sciences Historiques, Bucarest, 10–17 août 1980: Rapports* [hereafter Congress Bucharest 1980: *Rapports*], 3 vols. (Bucharest, 1980), vol. 1, discussion in Congress Bucharest 1980: *Actes*, vol. 1, pp. 57–122.
60. D. Angelov, "Das bulgarische Reich und das europäische Mittelalter," Congress Bucharest 1980: *Actes*, vol. 2.

61. See pp. 307–309 below.
62. "Formes et problèmes de la paix dans l'histoire. 1. Moyen âge," *rapporteur* R. Manselli (Italy); "2. L'époque moderne et contemporaine," *rapporteurs* L. Diez del Corral and A. Truyol Serra (Spain). Text of the reports and supplementary reports in Congress Bucharest 1980: *Rapports*, vol. 1, discussion in Congress Bucharest 1980: *Actes*, vol. 1, pp. 123–196.
63. G. Becker, "Der XV. Internationale Historikerkongreß in Bukarest 1980," *Zeitschrift für Geschichtswissenschaft* 29 (1981): 507–537, here pp. 508 and 513.
64. I. R. Grigulevich, Z. V. Udalcova, and A. O. Chubaryan, "Problemy novoj i novejšej istorii na XV Meždunarodnom kongresse istoričeskich nauk" [Problems of modern and recent history at the 15th International Historical Congress], *Novaja i Novejšaja Istorija* 25, no. 4 (1981): 24; similar in S. L. Tikhvinsky and V. A. Tishkov, "XV Meždunarodnyi kongress istoričeskich nauk" [XVth International Historical Congress], *Voprosy istorii* 55, no. 12 (1980): 3–23, here p. 5.
65. See p. 308 below.
66. Chr. Meier, "Zur Lage der Geschichtswissenschaft in der Bundesrepublik," *Geschichte in Wissenschaft und Unterricht* 37 (1986): 71–73.
67. K. D. Erdmann in Bureau meeting (Andorra, 1981).
68. *XVe Congrès International des Sciences Historiques, Stuttgart, du 25 août au 1er septembre 1985: Rapports* [hereafter Congress Stuttgart 1985: *Rapports*], 2 vols. (Stuttgart, 1985), vol. 1.
69. "Conclusion commune," ibid., p. 145. [Ed. note: In Stuttgart, a purely political theme was treated in a round table discussion on the historians' responsibility in the nuclear age, organized by S. L. Tikhvinsky. See German edition of this book, p. 374f. The session resulted in a resolution calling for disarmament and peace, which was proposed by Tikhvinsky and supported by the Bureau members T. C. Barker (U.K.) and G. A. Craig (U.S.). The resolution was adopted "unanimously" by the c. 400 attendants of the round table. Text with a brief introduction in "Historiker für den Frieden," *Zeitschrift für Geschichtswissenschaft* 34, no. 3, (1986): 23.]

Chapter 16

THE CONGRESSES FROM 1960 TO 1985—ORGANIZATIONAL AND STRUCTURAL DEVELOPMENTS

At first glance, the attendance at the ICHS General Assemblies and the active participation in the work of the Congresses still appears to involve primarily European and American scholarship. This corresponds to the fact that the geographical space in which all Congresses have taken place, and in which the next one will be held, with Spain as the host country, has been staked out amid Oslo in the north, Rome in the south, Moscow in the east, and San Francisco in the west. When the eleventh Congress convened in Stockholm in 1960, the organization encompassed six international organizations for the study of special fields and themes (international affiliated organizations or *organismes internationaux affiliés*) and 34 national committees.[1] With only a few exceptions, all of these were located in Europe and North America. In addition, only Japan, Mongolia, Turkey, and Uruguay were represented at the two General Assemblies in Stockholm. The utter dominance of European and North American historians was even more apparent in the statistics of the contributions to the Stockholm program: out of a total of 159 items, only 8 came from historians outside of Europe or North America (Japan 4, Israel 2, Turkey 2). But during the twenty years from Stockholm to Stuttgart, there has been a clear shift.

At the time of the Stuttgart Congress, the ICHS encompassed sixteen national committees from Asia, Africa, Latin America, and Australia out of a total of forty-seven.[2] Eleven countries from these continents were represented at the two General Assemblies.[3] In addition, some of the international affiliated organizations have a non-European regional character[4] through which the non-European component of the ICHS has been reinforced. In 1960, 1965, 1970, and 1985 a Japanese, in 1975, 1980, and 1985 an Indian, and in 1950 and 1980 a Mexican were elected to the Bureau. Ernesto de la Torre Villar (Mexico)

Notes for this chapter begin on page 276.

assumed the office of president in 1985. The Islamic world of the Near and Middle East, however, has so far found no adequate representation.

The active participation of the continents in the Stuttgart Congress was the following: of a total of 182 contributions, 26 were provided by authors from outside of Europe and North America. This is a relative improvement compared with Stockholm (159:8), but the major share of the organization and Congress work remains with Europe and North America. This corresponds with the fact that the critical modern study of history had its origins in Europe, that it developed here and only later spread to the other continents. Therefore, one must beware of the term "eurocentrism." When used properly, it refers not to the geographical region in whose culture historical scholarship is rooted, but rather to historical interests and perspectives. In any case, the ICHS cannot take the quantitative principles of the UN or UNESCO as its model and aim at representing as many states as possible in the here and now. Membership in the ICHS is linked to the qualitative condition that genuine historical scholarship must actually exist in the respective countries. At the same time, the composition of the Bureau shows that the ICHS is consciously opening up toward the other continents, particularly toward the ancient cultures of Asia and Latin America.

The reinforcement of the ecumenical tendency can be observed step by step in the development of the Congresses' programs. A first departure can be identified following the thoroughly Europe-centered Congresses of Paris in 1950 and Rome in 1955. There, alongside a number of short "communications" on individual questions of ancient Middle Eastern, Islamic, Chinese, and Latin American history, there were two major "reports" on non-European developments. One of these examined the influence of modern Western science and technology on East Asia, while the other presented a survey of the history of the modern Arab world.[5] The authors of these papers themselves came from the Western world.

In Stockholm as well, only two major reports dealt with topics of Asian history. An American reported on the result of a research group from the University of Pennsylvania that had been examining an issue central to modern India: modernism, i.e., the interpenetration of traditional culture and Western influences.[6] The second report[7] dealt with a problem of Chinese history of the middle centuries. It had been prepared by a Japanese research group. Three more communications on East Asian history were presented by Japanese historians. These contributions, however, remained isolated within the transactions of the Stockholm Congress. In the ensuing discussion, in which Soviet historians strongly participated, it was agreed that comparative East-West studies must be given an adequate place at future Congresses.

Thus, a special section on "The History of the Continents" was established for Vienna. It included reports on premodern Chinese history,[8] decolonization, ancient Central American civilizations,[9] the sources on the history of black Africa,[10] and the structures of the Spanish administration as the foundation of the Latin American nations.[11] Furthermore, a Mongolian historian[12] dealt with the historiography of his country in a report that was guided by a Marxist understanding of history and led to vehement political controversies, as did another one on decolonization prepared by Soviet historians.[13]

The intensified inclusion of non-European cultures could not fail to raise the question of whether and how world history was possible. Marxist and Western historians agreed that the process of globalization demanded a reassessment of worldwide historical interrelations. Let us quote two statements made during the discussion of a report by Louis Gottschalk (Chicago) on projects and conceptions concerning world history. They started from different theories of history but converged in their perception of the problem itself. Theodor Schieder observed: "Our current situation differs greatly from that of earlier times: a world history of mankind is no longer a speculative goal toward which past history has been oriented, but rather it is a current experience calling for confirmation by history." A new picture of history had to be achieved through the comparison of different cultures. "In this context, European-Western culture is one among others, and yet it is the one whose dynamics have drawn modern mankind together into a tension-filled unity. This must not be overlooked. This goal cannot be reached in one attempt, but rather it requires that the cultural units from which the world history of mankind is assembled become better known and better researched and that their relations to one another become more clearly illuminated. It is no longer national histories which form the basis of world history, as in the nineteenth century, but rather the history of great cultures, of continents."[14] Departing from this conception, and yet showing agreement, D. Bárta (Prague) defined the relationship between the current worldwide interconnection and world history as follows:

> One can only speak of a unity of human development if one thinks of a certain progression corresponding to laws of social development.... The various ethnic groups, nations, and cultural zones have developed in almost complete isolation for a long time without any possibility of deeper knowledge and mutual influence. Only when the contact between the nations became more intensive and frequent could historical studies gain an expanding horizon. The development of these relationships also depended on the development of production, industry, means of communications, trade, and that which we today call "media."... The development of the world market and international relationships have created world history and, indeed, a world historiography.[15]

Five years after Vienna, world-historical comparative studies were a leitmotif of the Moscow Congress. Particularly appropriate to this was the major theme "Nationalism and Class Struggle in the Modernization Process of Asia and Africa." Here two German authors demonstrated an empirical comparative approach in their reports on continuity and the formation of elites, both based on research literature and limited to intra-African developments.[16] A third paper delivered by the Swiss H. Lüthy dealt with the temporarily emerging idea of India's participation in imperial rule over East Africa.[17] In contrast to these three sophisticated treatises, a conventionally Marxist line of interpretation lacking any awareness of the problems involved was pursued in three other reports by a Japanese, a Czech, and a German historian.[18] The intention of the ICHS to promote comparative studies was realized by some exemplary papers on problems of the recent social history of Latin America, namely, on the social situation of dependent peasants, peasant movements, and guerrilla warfare.[19] Early Asian history, without which a modern concept of world history cannot be developed, was only approached by two Japanese papers dealing with "Special features of Japanese feudalism"[20] and "The Circulation of Silver in the Far East During the 16th and 17th Centuries," a topic that appeared rather isolated in the context of the Congress program.[21]

One of the above-mentioned papers on Latin America, presented by P. Vilar, was part of a study on peasant movements since the late eighteenth century, in which several scholars had participated.[22] At the Moscow Congress, five French historians who also belonged to this research group delivered reports on such various aspects as feudalism (A. Soboul), traditional agrarian society (Ph. Vigier), market economy (P. Barral and Y. Tavernier), and national movements (J. Droz). Their common feature was that, although they started from European history, they took into account related phenomena on other continents as well. This *enquête* had been promoted by a particularly active organization affiliated to the ICHS, the International Commission for the History of Social Movements and Structures. The results presented here provide a compelling example of what an international group of researchers who continue their work in the five-year intervals between the Congresses can achieve when dealing with a transcontinental question demanding the cooperation of many historians. But it is also characteristic that there were only six non-Europeans among the forty-five scholars who had prepared these reports.[23]

Five years later in San Francisco, a group of Japanese historians presented the results of their work on revolutionary events in Asia and Africa. The significance of this informative survey for the history of the Congresses lies in the fact that it depicted world history from an Asian view, and applied it to its appraisal of Western historiography as well.[24] This report, which was based on Marxist thought, and a voluminous French contribution on contemporary Chinese history by Lucien Bianco[25] were given an outstanding position at the Congress by their inclusion into the "major themes." In his thorough social-historical analysis, Bianco, well-known for his studies on the Chinese revolution (*Les origines de la Révolution Chinoise*, 1967), assessed the national revolutionary and the agrarian social revolutionary elements as driving forces motivating the revolutionary movement. He ascribed greater importance to the nationalist aspirations that sought to make China into a predominant world political power, thus going far beyond mere liberation or "anti-imperialism." In a persuasive prognosis, Bianco spoke of a "nationalism that is open to foreign influences," and of a "march into modernity, which, however, shall by no means follow the path taken by the capitalist West." It remains to be seen what interpretation of their national history the Chinese historians themselves will present after their decision to join the international historians' community a few years ago. Nine other papers on Asian history were scattered within the chronological sections of the Congress, dealing with Korea, the Kushan Empire, the Chinese Ming Dynasty, Ottoman Turkey, and nomadic peoples. The reports on the latter constituted a cleverly composed, cohesive group. Starting with a bibliographically well-endowed survey of the Eurasian nomadic peoples (C. C. Giurescu, Romania), nomadism was discussed in relation to the cities (A. Haneda, Japan), to feudalism (Sh. Natsagdorj, Mongolia), and finally the Golden Horde (B. Spuler, Germany).

Two papers in San Francisco dealt with the policy of conquest (T. Gökbilgin, Turkey) and state centralism (J. Perényi, Hungary) in the Ottoman Empire, thus moving Turkey into the focus of the Historical Congresses.[26] The Bucharest Congress picked up this topic with a paper on the ethnic composition of the empire (Th. Papadopoulos, Cyprus). The foundation myth of the state created by Kemal Atatürk reaches back to the Hittite Empire. The feudal character of the latter was the subject of a further Turkish contribution (F. Kinal). A Japanese report dealt with Islamic expansion in China (S. Imanaga), and N. Cagatay (Turkey) examined rationalism in ninth century Asia Minor.[27] In one of the "major themes" of Bucharest dedicated to the problems of peace, Asian questions were treated in two papers. Y. Amino (Japan) showed that in Japan there were institutions analogous to the medieval right of asylum in Europe. In contrast to this informative, scholarly study, a more political than historical presentation on the peace-preserving role of the "people" in Asia, which was laced with anti-American remarks, provoked sharp criticism.[28] In addition, there were some very informative contributions by African historians on "oral history" in the methodology section.[29]

More than at any previous Congress, the sessions organized by international affiliated organizations came to the fore in Bucharest. Some of them contained significant contributions to non-European history. On behalf of the Pan-American Institute of Geography and History, Guillermo Morén (Venezuela) developed a comprehensive project for a general history of the Americas.[30] Within a session devoted to the legal institution of marriage, the International Association for Legal and Institutional History presented two studies on the Muslim world (M. El-Shakandiri, Egypt) and on Central Africa (Eyi Engusa Yangasa, Zaire).[31] These contributions showed that the affiliated specialized commissions, through personal contacts and well-defined subject matters, are capable of achieving persuasive results also for the ecumenical expansion of the Congresses' fields of interest. It would be a valuable enrichment of the Congresses, if the two young organizations of Arab and African historians who discussed their projects at special sessions in Bucharest would one day add coordinated studies to the efforts for a universal conception of history.

The Stuttgart Congress accomplished—in the words of Hélène Ahrweiler, the secretary-general of the ICHS—a genuine "globalization" of the program.[32] This first applied to the three "major themes." Satish Chandra (India) had coordinated cooperation within a virtually global research project on the Indian Ocean as chief *rapporteur*. Papers came, inter alia, from Denmark (N. Steensgard), Belgium (Ch. Verlinden), India (S. Bhattacharya), Sri Lanka (L. Goonawardhane), and Japan (O. Kondo). Here, an oceanic, transcontinental approach was convincingly realized, recalling in some respects the Atlantic topic discussed in Rome.[33] The second major theme, "The Image of the Other," directed and introduced by Hélène Ahrweiler, involved historians from Upper Volta (Ki-Zerbo), China (G. Wangzhi), Japan (H. Kotani, K. Nagahra, T. Kuroda), Israel (R. Barkai, E. Menelsohn, S. Simonsohn), and others. The third major theme, on the Resistance movements, also included non-European papers (Q. Hua, China, and F. Kanda, Japan). For the methodology section, the German delegation had suggested considering the relationship of "Archaeology and History," not least in regard to the spectacular archaeological research being undertaken in the People's Republic of China. Finally, the section on Max Weber included a discussion of his conception of world history; here, critical examinations of his statements on the Asian cultures were presented by Y. Shiba (Japan) and S. Munshi (India).

Scattered throughout the chronological sections, a number of non-Europeans dealt with various topics of non-European history, for example, Buddhist issues (Ji Xian-Lin, China; Ki-Baik Lee, Korea), the culture of the nomadic peoples of Central Asia, and the role of Protestantism in Korean nationalism (Young Ick Lew, Korea). The densely composed section on motorization and road traffic under the direction of Theo C. Barker (London) contained two contributions on Japan (K. Shimokawa) and Zaire (E. Sh. Tshund'olela and U. Mafulu). This section had planned to include non-European history right at the beginning of its work like other sections within the chronological part of the program, for instance the one on "Social Changes in the Developing Countries," where non-European historians examined Indian (G. S. Bhalla and D. D. Narul) and Latin American (E. Cardenas, Columbia) problems, or the section on "The Role of Religions in Africa," where K. T. Mashaury from Zaire delivered a paper. The perennial issue of absolutist monarchy was oriented entirely on a European-Asian comparison this time. Roland Mousnier (France) continued his contributions to earlier Congresses with a pointed analysis of the question of whether the European absolute monarchies were fundamentally different from those in Asia. This topic was also approached by an Indian (S. N. Hasan) and a Japanese (H. Tsuda and J. Sasaki) contribution. Finally, there was a roundtable discussion organized by the Japanese Hiroyuki Kotani in connection with the major theme "The Image of the Other." Here a number of stereotypical, and increasingly criticized, views of the older Asian history were debated, such as "Asian despotism" in comparison with democracy in Europe, "Asian village community" as the foundation of "Asian despotism," and the stagnation of Asian society as a result of both. This discussion was the kind of intellectual challenge one would like to see more of in the treatment of world historical problems at future Congresses.

Past experiences with the various methods that have been chosen for dealing with non-European history provide a basis for the appropriate structuring of the Congress programs as a whole. For it turns out that the most fruitful contributions to the Congresses have been those that resulted from coordinated preparation among a number of collaborators. Various forms of cooperation and coordination have developed.

First there are the "major themes." They go back to a suggestion presented by Heinrich Felix Schmid (Vienna), who was elected as president of the ICHS in Stockholm, at the meeting of the Bureau in Istanbul in 1961. He was thinking of reports prepared in international cooperation by several researchers. The "major themes" arose from the realization that the constantly growing number of topics proposed for the Congresses could no longer simply be scheduled successively. The call for synthesis and comparative methods, which had already been raised at the turn of the century, became more urgent the more the field of historical interest expanded in time and space. A first attempt to meet this demand had been the Rome Congress's great survey reports on research and literature, structured according to the conventional periodization of history and presented by eminent experts. It was obvious that this experiment could not be repeated every five years.

Repeatedly, there had also been valuable reports by individual authors dealing with problems or the state of research of delimited topics. In view of the purpose of the ICHS, however, the reports prepared in joint international work appeared to be most promising. The major themes should be dedicated precisely to this kind of contribution. Their first realization at the Vienna Congress attracted a certain amount of criticism, and they fared no better at the next four Congresses. There were cases of appalling misuse of the Congress podium for political declamations, and of a lack of willingness to look beyond national and ideological boundaries, but more important was the fact that the ICHS only gradually became aware of its unavoidable coordination task. All too often the selection of the collaborators for a specific topic was guided more by accidental suggestions from the national committees than by criteria of professional qualifications. The results sometimes were of such poor quality that the reputation of the ICHS was at risk. By now, the Bureau has found the courage to assume a stronger responsibility in the preparation of the program and—essential to success—to ask individual members to take charge of a "major theme." This procedure was applied for the first time in organizing the Stuttgart Congress. It meant that the respective Bureau member held personal responsibility for both the form and structure of the reports and the enlistment of competent collaborators. The same was done for the section on theory and methodology. Wherever it was possible to arrange interim meetings of the respective research groups, this proved to be helpful. Thus, cooperative reports were successfully prepared for Stuttgart, with a high degree of thematic coordination that warranted scholarly standards even where harsh debates arose on specific facts.

A counterpoint to the major and methodological themes in the Congresses' structure, as it has developed since Stockholm, are the contributions of the international affiliated organizations. They represent specialized historical research and provide the Congresses with the experience of constant international cooperation, which continues during the five-year intervals. Thus, the large assemblies are interspersed with a number of small, often overlapping circles whose members know each other from continuous transnational and cross-ideological cooperation. The consistent inclusion of these international commissions into the program of the Congresses is relatively recent. At Vienna in 1965, they were granted a section of their own for the first time.[34] At the previous Congresses, they had usually held their colloquia and meetings one or two days earlier, or parallel to the actual Congress work, always remaining outside of the official Congress program.[35] Meetings on the periphery of the Congresses gave rise to several of the most active international commissions, which after some time, sometimes first via the status of "internal commissions," acquired membership in the ICHS.

The establishment of international research groups necessarily arose from the trend toward scholarly specialization and practical international cooperation within particular fields of research. And yet, when a special section was provided for the commissions in Vienna, this decision was not welcomed by everyone. In an understandable desire to reduce the profusion of papers presented at the Vienna Congress, the official organ of the East German historians suggested removing the commissions from the program. To some extent this actually happened, though only during a limited time. At Moscow in 1970, the Commissions for Social Movements and for the History of the Second World War were the only ones to figure officially in the program and in the report volumes.[36] In San Francisco in 1975, there was again a special section assigned to the "internal" and "affiliated" international commissions, and many of them participated. But as in Vienna, the frequent overlapping of commission events and those of the other sections were felt to be disturbing. Therefore, two entire days were dedicated exclusively to the commission meetings at the Bucharest Congress in 1980. The Stuttgart Congress of 1985 maintained this regulation.

A long-overdue change in the statutes corresponded to this development. In 1950, the affiliated international organizations were admitted as members of the ICHS, but with limited voting rights: decisions on changes in the statutes, i.e., on changes in the structure of the ICHS, were reserved for the national committees. This restriction was lifted at the General Assembly in Puerto de la Cruz in 1977.[37] The increasing influence of specialized research represented by the affiliated organizations is a guarantee that the Congresses reflect the scholarly level achieved by the different branches and institutions of historical research.

Alongside the comprehensive major and methodological themes, and the specialized sessions of the affiliated bodies, the traditional chronological sections have maintained their place. More consistently than before, they are now grouped thematically. A coordinator (*"animateur"*) takes responsibility for each one. In order to provide room for individual initiatives, round tables have been established. Only by subdividing the Congresses into many meetings of the utmost variety is it possible to create the preconditions for making these mass meetings of 2,000 and more participants both scientifically productive and rewarding for those who attend them or are involved in their work.

One problem that has grown in difficulty with the increasing participation of many countries from all continents has been that of language. This question had already emerged at the turn of the century. The *Revue de synthèse historique* reported that the participants at the Paris Congress of 1900 spoke in favor of a "universal scientific language." Some pleaded for Latin; apparently no other suggestion was made. It was resolved to transfer the decision to another institution, namely, the International Federation of Academies via the Institut de France.[38] From among the living languages, French dominated at first. This was understandable in view of its outstanding cultural significance and because of France's initiative in the convocation of the first Congresses. Thus, French was made the official language in the Congress rules of 1900. However, Latin, German, English, Italian, and Spanish were also permitted, and the use of further languages was allowed, under the condition that a French summary be provided afterward.[39] Naturally, the fixation on a single Congress language could not be maintained. All the languages that were "permitted" in Paris were thereafter viewed as "official." In Rome, Berlin, and London, the respective national languages moved clearly into the foreground. In addition, as already reported, the London Congress decided to expand this language group in view of the planned Congress in St. Petersburg by including Russian. In the interwar period the Congresses stuck to German, English, French, Italian, and Spanish. Russian was permitted as a Congress language in Rome in 1955. But since the equal status of these languages by no means corresponded to their equal utilization as a conference medium, and since the official privileged status of a few European languages essentially ran counter to the ecumenical character of the Congresses, a decision was made in Stuttgart to allow participants to speak in any language they wished, provided they could make themselves understood. In Stuttgart, as at all previous postwar Congresses, these languages were English and French, and—according to the host country, or the respective language's regional prevalence as a second language—Italian in Rome, Russian in Moscow, German in Bucharest and Stuttgart, and at the next Congress it will certainly be Spanish. This presupposes that in this age of an emerging world history, a historian's qualifications must include proficiency in at least two foreign languages.

Notes

1. Report by the secretary-general at the first General Assembly in Stockholm, 19 Aug. 1960, Congress Stockholm 1960: *Actes*, p. 277. For the following indications concerning membership and participation in the Congresses, see below, appendices I, II, and III.
2. ICHS, *Bulletin d'information*, no. 12.
3. Japan, South Korea, Mongolia, China, India, Israel, Egypt, Mexico, Cuba, Venezuela, and Australia.
4. Commission internationale des historiens latino-américanistes; Union des historiens arabes; Association des historiens africains.
5. J. K. Fairbank (U.S.), "The influence of modern western science and technology on Japan and China" (a report prepared by a study group at Harvard University); F. Gabrieli, "La storia moderna dei popoli arabi," both in Congress Rome 1955: *Relazioni*, vol. 5.
6. W. N. Brown, "Traditional culture and modern developments in India," Congress Stockholm 1960: *Rapports*, vol. 5.
7. T. Yamamoto, "From T'ang to Sung," Congress Stockholm 1960: *Rapports*, vol. 3.
8. S. Nishijima and T. Masabuchi (Tokyo), "Characteristics of the unified states of Ch'in and Han," and N. Niida (Tokyo), "Chinese Legal Institutions of the Sui and T'ang periods," in Congress Vienna 1965: *Rapports*, vol. 2.
9. Including P. Kirchhoff, "The fundamentals of mesoamerican history," W. Jiménez Moreno, "Mexico, Toltec and Mixtec History," I. Bernal, "The classic Period in the central area," and H. Berlin, "La historia maya," all from Mexico. Congress Vienna 1965: *Rapports*, vol. 2.
10. H. Moniot (Paris) in cooperation with thirteen other European historians, "Le problème des sources de l'histoire de l'Afrique noire jusqu'à la colonisation," Congress Vienna 1965: *Rapports*, vol. 2.
11. J. M. Ots Capdequi (Valencia), ibid.
12. Sh. Bira (Ulan Bator), "Mongolian Historiography," in Congress Vienna 1965: *Rapports*, vol. 4; discussion in Congress Vienna 1965: *Actes*, pp. 577–586.
13. A. A. Guber and A. F. Miller, "Changements politiques et économiques dans les pays d'Asie et d'Afrique au XXe siècle," in Congress Vienna 1965: *Rapports*, vol. 2; discussion, in Congress Vienna 1965: *Actes*, pp. 281–309.
14. Congress Vienna 1965: *Actes*, p. 525f.
15. Ibid., p. 527.
16. F. Ansprenger (Cologne), "Probleme der Kontinuität afrikanischer Staaten während und nach der Periode europäischer Kolonialherrschaft"; I. Geiss (Bremen), "Die Entstehung der modernen Eliten in Afrika seit der Mitte des 18. Jahrhunderts," both in Congress Moscow 1970: *Doklady*, vol. 2.
17. "India and East Africa: Imperial partnership at the end of the First World War," Congress Moscow 1970: *Doklady*, vol. 2.
18. S. Imahori (Japan), "Nationalism and class conflict in China"; A. Palat (Czechoslovakia), "Qualitative changes in the development of Asian countries after World War II"; W. Markov (GDR), "Wege und Formen der Staatsbildung in Asien und Afrika seit dem Zweiten Weltkrieg." Congress Moscow 1970: *Doklady*, vol. 2.
19. M. Mörner (Sweden), "Tenant Labour in Andean South America since the eighteenth century, a preliminary report," Congress Moscow 1970: *Doklady*, vol. 2; P. Vilar (Paris), "Mouvements paysans en Amérique latine," Congress Moscow 1970: *Doklady*, vol. 7; G. Kahle (Cologne), "Ursprünge und Probleme lateinamerikanischer Guerilabewegungen im 19. Jahrhundert," Congress Moscow 1970: *Doklady*, vol. 2. On the same topic, although based more on the Marxist classics than on research questions, see A. H. Glinkin (USSR), "Latinskaja America i mirovoj istoričeskij process v XIX i XX vv" [Latin America and the worldwide historical process in the XIXth and the XXth centuries], Congress Moscow 1970: *Doklady*, vol. 2.

20. H. Matsuoka, in Congress Moscow 1970: *Doklady*, vol. 4.
21. A. Kobata, in Congress Moscow 1970: *Doklady*, vol. 5.
22. "Enquête sur les mouvements paysans dans le monde contemporain (de la fin du XVIIIe siècle à nos jours)," Congress Moscow 1970: *Doklady*, vol. 7.
23. Congress Moscow 1970: *Doklady*, vol. 7, p. 131f.
24. S. Kimbara, "Tradition and innovations in Asia and Africa." Several Japanese organizations were mentioned as participants: Historical Science Society, Society for Japanese History, Council for Teachers of History; see Congress San Francisco: *Reports*, vol. 1, pp. 550ff.
25. L. Bianco, "La Révolution chinoise." Congress San Francisco: *Reports*, vol. 1, pp. 220–263.
26. T. Gökbilgin, "La politique ottomane devant la réforme," in Congress San Francisco: *Reports*, vol. 2, pp. 1083–1102; J. Perényi, "The Ottoman Expansion and the Rise of the East-European Centralized States," ibid., pp. 1103–1117.
27. Th. Papadopoulos, "Le modèle ethnohistorique de l'Empire ottoman," in Congress Bucharest 1980: *Rapports*, vol. 2, pp. 258–271; F. Kinal, "Der hethitische Feudalismus," ibid., pp. 55–60; S. Imanaga, "The Islamites in Ch'ing Dynasty of China," ibid., pp. 288–298; N. Cagatay, "Les courants de la pensée rationaliste dans le Proche-Orient au XXe siècle," ibid., pp. 105–114.
28. Y. Amino, "Muen, kugay, raku: Freedom and Peace in Medieval Japan," in Congress Bucharest 1980: *Rapports*, vol. 1, pp. 187–190; B. Eguchi and N. Nishikawa, "Peace and People in Asia in the 20th Century," ibid., pp. 231–235.
29. Boubacar Barry (Senegal), "La chronologie dans la tradition orale du Waalo—Essai d'interprétation," in Congress Bucharest 1980: *Rapports*, vol. 1, pp. 516–519; E. J. Alagoa (Nigeria), "Oral Tradition," ibid., pp. 520–535. Cf. p. 290 below.
30. G. Morén, "Sintesis del informe Proyecto de Historia general de America," in Congress Bucharest 1980: *Rapports*, vol. 3, pp. 21–32; discussion in Congress Bucharest 1980: Actes, vol. 2, pp. 1019–1021.
31. M. El-Shakandiri, "Le mariage dans le monde islamique," in Congress Bucharest 1980: *Rapports*, vol. 3, pp. 79–84; Eyi Engusa Yangasa, "Le mariage africain: hier et aujourd'hui," ibid., pp. 107–112.
32. See the detailed report by I. Geiss, "Außereuropäische Geschichte," in "Bericht über den 16. Internationalen Kongreß der Geschichtswissenschaften in Stuttgart (25. 8.–1. 9. 1980)," *Geschichte in Wissenschaft und Unterricht* 37, no. 2 (1986): 105–115. All the reports mentioned in the following can be found in Congress Stuttgart 1985: *Rapports*, vols. 1 and 2.
33. Geiss, "Außereuropäische Geschichte," p. 109f. See also the presentations by Ch. Verlinden (Belgium), "The ancient period and the middle ages," and N. Steensgard (Denmark), "The Indian Ocean network and the emerging world economy c. 1500–c. 1750."
34. Congress Vienna 1965: *Rapports*, vol. 3, Commissions; Congress Vienna 1965: *Actes*, pp. 351–507.
35. Reports on these varied activities can be found, e.g., in Congress Rome 1955: *Atti*, pp. 727ff., and in Congress Stockholm 1960: *Actes*, pp. 287ff.
36. Congress Moscow 1970: *Doklady*, vol. 7.
37. On the development of the statutes, see appendix IV.
38. *Revue de synthèse historique* 1 (1900): 207f.
39. Congress Paris 1900: *Annales*, vol. 1, p. IV.

Chapter 17

Debates on Theory and Methodology from the 1960s to the 1980s

For a time at the middle of the century, it may have looked as if there were two camps within Western historical studies, facing each other suspiciously and restricting mutual communications to censorious messages. The issue at stake was the question of what the true subject of history is: the specific or the general, the individual or the typical, the unique or the recurring, events or structures. Should the historian's methods be interpretative and hermeneutical, or quantitative and analytical? Should his first and foremost field be the history of the State and of ideas, or economic and social history? Already in Paris in 1950, in the crucial discussion between Renouvin and Labrousse, and then in Rome in 1955, in the positions taken by historians like Momigliano, Chabod, Ritter, and again Renouvin, it had become apparent that by no means had the impulses arising from the older, "historicist" or "positivistic," traditions of historiography been displaced, even if they no longer dominated the scene. At the same time it became obvious that the two camps differed not because of a fundamental epistemological conflict, but rather because of diverging interests of knowledge and, as a result, diverging methodological priorities. Renouvin had sought a synthesis of political and social history under the priority of his interest in the history of domestic and foreign politics. The Congresses of Paris and Rome had been permeated by the search for a convincing definition of the relationship between structural history and the history of events, between social and political history, or even for an integration of the two—for a "New Historicism," as I would like to denote it. These endeavors were continued at the subsequent Congresses.

In Stockholm in 1960 it still looked as if the two camps were facing each other as strangers. This impression grew sharper at the first International Colloquium of Economic History, which—like all the sessions of the international affiliated organizations—convened at Stockholm independently of the actual Historical Congress, and which met with a particularly strong response. It had

---

Notes for this chapter begin on page 295.

been organized spontaneously by a still provisional commission under the initiative of Michael Postan (Cambridge). The great number of distinguished collaborators and the 300-plus participants were proof of an eminent scholarly interest.[1] The conference tackled two main topics: "Industrialization as a Factor of Economic Growth after 1700," and "Large Agricultural Holdings since the End of the Middle Ages."

It was not only the protagonists of structural history who heaped praise on this colloquium. What the ICHS had to offer at the Congress itself seemed less remarkable, aside from the fact that this or that political provocation provided journalists with welcome headlines. As Braudel said in the *Annales*, the Congress as a whole would have been outdated and boring if the Marxists hailing from the Democratic Republics of the Eastern Bloc had not blown some fresh wind into "l'histoire de papa" (daddy's history). Compared to the Paris Congress of 1950, which he praised as an unattainable model, Rome appeared to him as an "*antithèse*" designed "to allow conventional history, which died away more than a half century ago ... and which yet continues to survive itself, in and outside of France, thanks to the miracle of the force of habit and the element of inertia, to claim victory."[2] Despite his harsh judgement, Braudel did not deny the right of existence to "certain humanities," for which some of the economists assembled in Stockholm put in an occasional good word, for instance the French Marxist Pierre Vilar. The Italian communist Gastone Manacorda thought this so remarkable that in a report on Stockholm, he quoted Vilar as saying:

> The necessity of a rapprochement between economics and history is felt more strongly now, if still in an unclear way. It is aimed at confronting two manners of thinking—which is the opposite of opposing them—two kinds of analysis, the economic and the historical, which are often motivated by similar curiosity, but are characterized by very different habits and stances. If an economist classifies a study as "historical" or "descriptive," then that is paramount to a condemnation. If a young historian uses the word "theoretical," then he will feel shattered by a glance from the masters of his discipline. This antagonism is disastrous for the building of a science concerned with the transformations of human society.[3]

In regard to the relationship between the two directions at the Stockholm Congress, it is worth mentioning a report by the Spanish historian J. Vicens Vives (Barcelona) on the administrative structures of the state in the sixteenth and seventeenth centuries.[4] Impressed by the Paris Congress, Vives had increasingly turned to social scientific studies. His Stockholm report was a result of this orientation, but at the same time he reassessed traditional political history. His paper dealt with the emergence and nature of absolutism, a topic that frequently recurred at the International Congresses and on which Lhéritier had already suggested comparative studies at Oslo.[5] A detailed report on the problems of absolutism had been presented to the Rome Congress by Fritz Hartung and Roland Mousnier.[6] The joint French-German authorship is remarkable, not least because of the fact that in the *Annales*, Lucien Febvre had severely criticized an article by Hartung on the dictum "L'état c'est moi" published in the first issue of the *Historische Zeitschrift* after the Second World War. In Febvre's view, the constitutional and legal historical method practiced by Hartung was hopelessly antiquated.[7] Hartung's conception of history is comparable to that of Mousnier. In France, the latter is viewed as one of the innovators of research on political history enriched by social historical points of view.[8] In their Rome lecture, Mousnier and Hartung started from the self-perception of absolutism and the theories surrounding it, i.e., from intellectual history, which the structuralists considered passé. Subsequently, they had elaborated different types of absolute rule. This was followed by a survey on the various intellectual, economic, social, and geographic causes, whose interactions needed to be considered for an understanding of absolutism. The authors placed the greatest emphasis on the development of standing armies and the need to finance them. As far as the significance of the remaining conditions was concerned, Mousnier answered a critic by asking: "[D]o the intellectual and psychological causes of absolutistic monarchy really have less significance than the economic and social ones? That is one of the fundamental questions of history. One can come with a priori answers for philosophical or political reasons, but the state of purely historical studies does not yet provide us with a clear solution."[9]

Even more strongly than Hartung and Mousnier, Vives emphasized the significance of war—war against both internal and external enemies—for the development of the military and administrative organization of absolutism in his Stockholm paper. By contrast, he ascribed little significance to intellectual and institutional factors. It was necessary, he said, to discard the traditional conception of absolutism based on intellectual history and the theory of politics. Instead, he asked about the concrete forms of the exercise of power—namely, through the landlords, the municipal administration and jurisdiction, and the princes—and suggested that studies on absolutism should concern themselves above all with the characteristic tool of princely power: the bureaucracy. For this purpose he sketched out a research program that was open to economic, social, and mentality perspectives.

According to the reports on the Stockholm Congress in the professional journals, Vives's report was not paid any particular attention—perhaps because his paper was available only in Spanish and could not be presented by Vives himself (he had died some weeks before the Congress), and certainly also because the shrill dissonance of the ideological contention blotted out the gentle voice of science. This does not diminish the value of this contribution as an indicator of the methodological constellation of the time: it shows that there were bridges leading from the "old" state and event history to the "new" social and structural history. Although this question did not dominate in Stockholm, a thorough Congress report by the Swiss historian Alain Dufour[10] ascribed central significance to Vives's paper: it "stood at the heart of the Stockholm Congress" as a description of "an extremely modern study of political history at the interface of demographical, economic, social, intellectual, and legal history." The remaining papers presented in Stockholm ranged from "modernistic" contributions on price history or demography[11] to a "traditionalistic," intellectual historical treatment of historiographical topics.[12] In addition, a type of research considered by the avant-gardists to be the very symbol of an outdated study of history, namely, sweeping erudite compilations planned for the long term, also attracted considerable attention among Church historians.[13]

At the Vienna Congress of 1965, Jean Glénisson, the secretary-general of the French national committee, stated in a report on contemporary French historiography that "erudition," with its predilection for source editions and philological-historical text criticism, was making a comeback even in France, despite the undoubted triumph of the *Annales* and its conception of history.[14] The names he listed as representatives of "erudition" in France included Michel François, the secretary-general of the ICHS, as well as Robert Fawtier, its former president, and Robert-Henri Bautier, later the president of the French national committee. In the final result, Glénisson observed, the traditional mode of historical studies had greatly profited from the challenge by structural history. The new questions posed by social history had expanded its range of activity and renewed its methods.

This official report is remarkable in the way it characterized the prevailing trend, and in regard to the nomenclature it used. The *Annales*, Glénisson said, inaccurately referred to the opposite direction of historical studies as "positivistic history." Earlier, the *Revue de synthèse historique* had coined the term "historicizing history." Historical positivism and historicism thus appeared here as equivalent terms. But what does positivism mean in this case? Glénisson distinguished between the historical thought and practice described by this label, and positivistic historical philosophy, which he rejected with a reference to Collingwood, the proponent of a modern historicism. In reality, the "positivistic" conception of history "represents the legacy of the erudition of the sixteenth to eighteenth centuries. It has been victorious without rival because the intellectual climate of the nineteenth century favored its spread."[15] His second assertion: Proceeding from the observation that "positive" or, more accurately, empirical historiography in France generally viewed philosophical syntheses, which outlined the general course of history, with extreme skepticism, he sought to explain the nonspeculative "synthesis" of a rationalist and empiricist like Henri Berr, the patriarch of *Nouvelle Histoire*. His result: no metaphysics, no "nuées en théorie" (clouds of theory), no a priori, no historical philosophy, no utopias—instead, just "generalizations on the basis of the state of knowledge," resting on the comparative method. Berr's decisive achievement was that he had defined historical synthesis as a mutual completion of scholarly knowing and worldview, developing itself in scholarly discourse.[16] Glénisson's formulations recalled the radically historicizing statements made by Thomas S. Kuhn three years earlier, according to which the criteria of truth—both in the humanities and the natural sciences—were determined by a societal phenomenon, namely, the historically conditioned "scientific community," and the ideas or values accepted in its critical discourse.[17]

Glénisson's third assertion was that the paradigm shift from the history of events to the history of structures, achieved in *Nouvelle Histoire*, corresponded to the awareness of the relativity of all historical knowledge. Glénisson cited one of the fathers of the *Annales* as his prime witness: "Lucien Febvre minted formulas that today every French historian preserves in his memory—from 'history, the daughter of its time' to the famous dictum: 'There is no history. There are historians.'"[18] Awareness of the relativity of historical knowledge granted historians the freedom to opt between the different interpretations of history that their own times offered them, or else to suggest new ones. In doing so, the principles of learned criticism, as transmitted by Ranke and the philologists, were indispensable.[19]

And a last observation by Glénisson: for a long time, the philosophical and epistemological evolution of historicism had been only casually noticed in France. Raymond Aron's attempt to make "contemporary historicism, particularly as it was represented in Germany by Dilthey, Rickert, Max Weber," available to historical thought in France could not be achieved because of the war. However, in the ten years following the war, in a transformed world situation and in connection with the spectacular upswing of historical study in France, it was necessary to rethink the questions of historical epistemology and methodology. Some (A. Piganiol et al.) had picked up on the methodology of historical positivism developed by Langlois and Seignobos; the Marxists had countered the relativistic thought of historicism with the thesis that historical objectivity was possible in analogy to natural science. Glénisson located the climax of the theoretical discussion in the mid 1950s, when challenging contributions on the theory and method of a "new history" appeared, including Lucien Febvre's *Combats pour l'histoire* (1954), Philippe Ariès's *"Le temps de l'histoire"* (1954), and Fernand Braudel's *La longue durée* (1958). This was the moment when the ancient historian Henri-Irénée Marrou published his treatise on the theory of historical knowledge (*De la connaissance historique*, 1954). It was based on the premise of a relativist mode of thinking as embodied in the names of Dilthey, Weber, Croce, Collingwood, and Aron. In this sense, his work represented the counterposition to the classics of historical positivism, Langlois and Seignobos. The notion of a non-positivistic historicism was thus for the first time thoroughly incorporated into the French discussion on the theory of history.

To this report, Jacques Godechot added a personal commentary in the name of the French national committee.[20] He distinguished three tendencies in his country's historiography. On the political right he saw conservative historians who predominantly dealt with political, sometimes religious history, while largely neglecting economic and social problems. On the other side, Marxists trained in the best historical methods and attracting a mass audience devoted their attention to such topics as economics, society, and class struggle. Between these two tendencies, which placed historiography in the service of political goals, Godechot identified a third, "which encompasses the greatest number of historians in the French universities." Earlier, in the first half of the century, the academic discipline of history had been split by the harsh controversies between the positivistic school and a group that was inexactly called the *Annales* school. This conflict had now been settled, as shown by Glénisson. The historians of the third camp were ready to take Marxism seriously, as a method directing attention to the significance of infrastructures. He referred to Renouvin as an example, emphasizing his notion of "slow and deep currents" in economic, social, and mentality history, including religious history. The history of politics, international relations, ideas, institutions, and also biography were not neglected, but placed more than before into the greater context of social development. Particularly characteristic of this group was "its attempt at objectivity, its refusal to write with the intention of favoring one political viewpoint or another." It was noteworthy that the tendency toward convergence, which could be noted as a promising, if marginal, phenomenon at the Paris Congress fifteen years earlier, was now presented as prevailing in France. A discussion comment by the American Louis Gottschalk in Vienna pointed in the same direction with regard to historical studies in his country.[21]

Now, it would be misleading to infer from such voices that there was a balance of forces between the old and new tendencies at the Congress. At many sessions, the mere formulation of the topics already revealed the prevailing interest in social and structural history.[22] This particularly manifested itself in regard to the major theme "The World in 1815"—a topic that appeared to call for a political and event-oriented historical treatment of the Vienna Congress 150 years earlier. However, that was not how it turned out. The ICHS had intended and officially announced presentations by historians from five different countries—England, Italy, the Soviet Union, Canada, and the Federal Republic of Germany[23]—but a few weeks before the Congress it was communicated that five French historians had assumed this task. All of them were close to the *Annales*. At the Congress, this change led to sharp commentaries by the ejected *rapporteurs* Gerald S. Graham (London), Lewis Hertzman (Canada), and Aleksei L. Narochnitsky (USSR).[24] The papers delivered by the French authors concerned demography (Marcel Reinhard), economics (Ernest Labrousse), institutions and political structures (Jacques Godechot), society (Albert Soboul), and ideology (Louis Trénard).[25] This division corresponded to the sections of the 1950 Paris Congress. And as in Paris, political history was missing!

The presentations were excellently coordinated and impressive in their cogent, though one-sided approach, but at the same time they were centered on France as the "guiding nation"—the "*nation pilote*"—and they did not deliver a satisfactory appraisal of the developments between 1789 and 1815 in their entirety. Essential aspects were lacking. For example, what about the political experiences and problems that had kept imposing themselves on political thought since the Napoleonic era: the cycle of revolution, the transformation of freedom into despotism, and of wars of revolution into wars of conquest? What about the relationship between European unity and national freedom, land power and sea power, peace, conservative order, and revolution? In the discussion about these contributions, a number of participants pointed out that the Congress of Vienna itself, and the problem of a stable peace settlement, were not discussed at all. The Soviet historian Narochnitsky deplored that the simultaneously revolutionary and counterrevolutionary character of the Napoleonic regime, or the "transformation of the patriotic and just wars of the Revolution into wars of conquest," had not been considered, and that England's leading role in the economic development of Europe had been neglected. Charles W. Crawley (Cambridge) likewise held that the papers should have paid much more attention to the fact "that the driving force of the industrial change in this period came from England," that the European liberals looked far more to England and to America than to France, that even the French Constitution of 1814 was oriented on the English model of 1660, and that after the experiences of the war, "for some nations the new principles spelled conquest, conscription, heavy taxation, and even plunder."[26] Such evaluations of events of the revolutionary period indicated that a social-historical and structural approach was by no means sufficient for the assessment of an epochal event such as the French Revolution.

The ICHS subsequently published a volume with some of the ejected contributions on the topic of 1815:[27] They dealt in the "traditional" way with the now unchallenged British naval dominance (Graham, London), the influence of the progressive and conservative forces between 1815 and 1848 (Hertzman, Toronto), and the contradictory political and social ideas at the end of the Napoleonic epoch (Manfred, Moscow). In addition, the volume contained a report by Narochnitsky (Moscow) on the historical significance of the British continental blockade, which presented the state of research in an exemplary way and developed a well-considered evaluation of the interaction between economic, social, and political factors. There was another remarkable contribution that appeared separately, by the Hungarian historian Domokos Kosáry,[28] on the history of the historical writing about the Congress of Vienna and the Metternich system. He described the wishful manner of thinking in which the national and liberal forces had interpreted the European condition created in 1815, and showed how, in reaction to the growing political radicalism in the second half of the nineteenth century, Metternich's image was positively transformed until it was totally rehabilitated through the great Metternich biography by Srbik in 1925, and then changed entirely again, despite the generally high esteem shown toward the multinational order of 1815 (e.g., by R. A. Kann), which Kosáry critically examined in turn.

Reservations toward a too one-sided approach restricted to social historical analysis were also expressed in other sections of the Vienna Congress. The dismay concerning the reports on 1815, and the general impression that there was a primordial historiographical and methodological problem demanding clarification, may have been the reason for the decision of the ICHS to establish a special section at the Moscow Congress of 1970 dealing with the relationship between "History and Social Sciences." Out of the seven contributions in this section, one came from the Hungarian Marxist Lajos Elekes.[29] The others had been entrusted to Western historians. This corresponded to the fact that the Western historical profession was particularly concerned with this issue.

A radical challenge to the methodology of historicism was "quantification." Its position in the social sciences and in history was examined by the American Jack H. Hexter. His report on "History, the Social Sciences and Quantification"[30] is one of the most witty and imaginative contributions to be found in the many volumes documenting the Historical Congresses. Hexter's relationship to the social sciences was one of well-meaning, irreverent curiosity. He did not deny their usefulness, but he did not believe that they provided the philosopher's stone. The core of his report is a warning against an uncritical use of computers, faulty programming, and incorrect interpretation of the results. He concluded with an energetic appeal to social scientists to realize that there could not be a value-free science of Man comparable to mathematics or the natural sciences. The two oldest scholarly disciplines of Man, history and jurisprudence, had always known this. And even if it should be logically possible to analyze any given value systems or value-determined actions in a value-free manner—Hexter left this Weberian aspect of *Wertfreiheit* open—the language in which such knowledge was formulated and passed on could not help but be related to values. Among the examples he cited were the following: "Should we call the military action of 400,000 troops of a large nation on the strife-torn land of a small East Asian country 'support of the legitimate government,' 'a policy war,' or 'imperialism'? Should we call the unresisted crossing of the borders of a small Central European state by 600,000 unwelcome troops 'comradely assistance,' or 'intervention,' or 'invasion'? How does one neutralize such terms as 'policy war,' and 'imperialism,' as 'intervention' or 'invasion'?" History, he concluded, was a "literary narrative" and a "humanistic interpretation."[31]

The Cypriot historian Theodore Papadopoulos also dealt with the role of the quantification method in his attempt to define the relationship between the social sciences and historical studies.[32] The field of its application was expanding constantly, he said. Its proper areas of applicability were population, economics, and society, but with the use of electoral statistics and voter sociology it was extended to political history. Certain fields of history included processes governed by laws that were to be studied with social science methods. Challenging Popper,[33] he even believed that historical predictions could be made when limited to these sectors. But the coherence of history could never be entirely explained through the concept of determination. The origins and the effects of those determined components, and especially the actions of Man, were the domain of the historical method. Neither the freedom of individual decisions nor chance could be eliminated from political history and the history of international relations. The social sciences and history had to be regarded as different disciplines, even if there was a "mutual methodological and hermeneutic interaction" between them.

The economic historian Alfred Dubuc (Canada) recognized the enrichment history had gained through the social sciences, but he also felt moved to warn against a "new positivism in history": "Quantifying everything, counting everything, measuring everything, putting everything into a computer, and submitting information to every possible statistical and mechanical-graphic treatment: this is what is being attempted today." History, from which all the other sciences of Man had been derived, should never merely follow in the wake of the social sciences. Citing Dilthey, the "German historical school," and Croce, he pleaded for an "understanding history." Collingwood, he said, had been right when he asserted that all history is history of thought ("qu'il n'y a d'histoire que de l'esprit").[34]

In a paper on the "Differences between the Historical and the Social Scientific Method," Theodor Schieder (Cologne) assessed the distinguishing and the common features of history and social sciences more cautiously and in a more positive perspective.[35] He limited his observations to social history, without referring to political and intellectual history, although his main historiographical achievements lay in these areas. Schieder, a pupil of Hans Rothfels, had taught at the university of Königsberg until the end of the war. The first scholarly task with which he had been entrusted after the war was the supervision of a comprehensive documentation of the expulsion of the German population from Eastern and Southeastern Europe, and from the eastern provinces of the former German Reich. It was based on methods of social science research—opinion polls, interviews, critical comparisons, quantitative examination, and data distribution—since they offered a way to cope with demographic and social historical occurrences of such proportions. Methodological reflections on structural and social history continued to preoccupy Schieder. His suggestions were developed further by his pupils. A new direction of research that defined itself as Historical Social Science came into being. It was strongly influenced by the *Annales* and the American New History, and like the *Annales* in its early days, it saw itself in strict opposition to everything that in its view was associated with the older, "historicist" tradition of historical thought and writing in Germany.

In his Moscow paper, Schieder attempted to define the specific quality of a historical social science method as compared to the social sciences, and exemplified their distinctive and their common features by contrasting the concepts of "model" and "type," "experiment" and "comparative method." Both disciplines converged on the techniques they used, and on the basic questions of epistemology. For the latter, he primarily referred to Max Weber. The contrast between "explaining" and "understanding," which had caused long controversies in the past, had become obsolete. The natural sciences' "nomothetic" notion of law could no longer be applied without modifications, and at the same time, it was no longer possible to seek the meaning of social acts solely in their value reference or in the intentionality of conscious behavior through an exclusively hermeneutic approach. The range of historical problems had been expanded through psychoanalysis and demography, and many conceptions had been set into motion. The quintessence of Schieder's paper was: "History and social science are sitting in the same boat. They can no longer solve the questions of our time in isolation, but only in concert."

Ernesto Sestan, one of the grand seigneurs of the historical profession in Italy and a friend and companion of Federico Chabod, moved toward a clear confrontation with the *Annales* and the "storiografia dei tempi nostri." He presented a paper on "The History of Events and Structural History" in Moscow, and five years later in San Francisco, another one on "Historiography as Historical Science."[36] Without questioning the high value of Braudel's "masterpiece" on the Mediterranean, he did not restrain his criticism: Braudel had only been partially successful in his attempt to demonstrate a clear historical connection between the diverse structural elements he had examined in great detail, and the history of events. He had neglected the importance of "mental structures" and events, and the impact of both of them on long-term structures, for example, on the political and economic situation of seafaring Venice and the Venetian mentality.

In addition, Sestan presented his objections to modernistic conceptual language in general. "Structure" was "a particularly dark and complex term."[37] Upon closer examination, it meant little more than what had previously been called "system" or "organism." He saw the wave of historical structuralism and its terminology as a temporary phenomenon. It could be explained "on the one hand by the attractiveness of 'the scientific,' on the other hand by the economic and social thought dominating the political concepts of the present." The scientific character of history, however, did not rest upon the method of historical structuralism, nor on quantification, which certainly had its value in particular fields. Historians often had an "inferiority complex" in regard to the scientific character of their work. This explained their readiness to adopt methods promising a higher degree of scientific rigor. Indeed, ever since the beginning of the century, the question of whether history is a science has been discussed again and again. In this debate, the natural sciences, as sciences concerned with the discovery of laws, appeared as an imposing and unattainable model. Sestan held that it was time for the historians to bid farewell to their bad conscience. After all, it had since been demonstrated that the natural scientists' conception of laws and the regularities examined by the historian were not at all that far apart from one another: "The natural sciences adopt the principles of uncertainty and relativity, and we should ask ourselves seriously whether this is not an element that could link all types of research with one another, whether we are dealing with physics and biology or with the sciences of Man, which include history."[38]

Similar observations regarding the concept of law were made by several historians at Moscow and San Francisco, for instance by Schieder. The Italian

Paolo Brezzi, who treated the same issue in San Francisco in a paper on "Historiography as a Historical Science," wrote: "The deterministic axiom of the mathematical natural sciences has vanished.... The factor of the subjective, the concept of relativity, a different understanding of time, the notion of evolution, the theory of errors and probabilities, have replaced mechanism and causality. Beyond that, scientists speak less of laws than of working hypotheses, which can be verified and developed further."[39] The possible and necessary convergence of history and of the social sciences, which are oriented on the observation of laws—like Schieder, Brezzi speaks of mutual penetration—means on the one hand bidding farewell to an idealistic historicism fixated on the individual factor, as defined by Dilthey, Troeltsch, Meinecke, and Croce, while on the other hand recognizing that a "valid account of history" nevertheless must be "concrete, realistic, individualized."[40]

While the relationship between history and social science was discussed intensely at the Congresses, the contemporary debates on a general theory of science were only occasionally touched on, for instance in the papers of Schieder, Sestan, and Brezzi. But what about the relationship between judgements on facts and value judgements, what about the postulates of value-free research and political responsibility as problems that are particularly pressing for the historian and that, as the Congresses' history shows, have unavoidably presented themselves under changing political challenges? The Dutch historian Anton G. Weiler dealt with this issue in San Francisco, in a paper on "Value Reference and Value Judgement in Historiography."[41] It was a relatively thorough presentation of the various responses that had been given to this question in the contemporary debate on the theory of science. For Weiler, who oriented himself on Max Weber, the former dualism between nomothetic and idiographic sciences, as the neo-Kantians viewed it, had been overtaken by the modern theory of science. He shared the conviction of the proponents of analytical philosophy that scientific judgements on fact as such are devoid of value references. Nevertheless, he viewed historical statements on facts as being linked to value judgements in various ways: (1) as a distinction between that which is worth being known and that which can be known, between the "important" and the "unimportant"; (2) as a theoretical value relationship, without which human actions, which are guided by motivations, norms and values, goals and expectations, cannot be understood; (3) as an estimate of the differing weight allotted to the various motivational factors. Such an estimation is dependent on the historian's own conception of human life, "for instance, when he considers the religious and ideological components of events to play more of a determining role, and so to be historically more important, than the economic and social factors"; (4) as a "commitment" of the historian, who is responsible to his time when he performs "the public function of historiography." On this point, Weiler pointed to political-ethical values that he defined as "fundamental conditions of existence," namely, "the abolition of wars, poverty, racial and national hatred, restraint of freedom."[42]

Observations of this kind on the development of historical thought since the Second World War, to the extent that they were mirrored in the International Congresses, induced the president of the Bucharest Congress of 1980 to speak of a "New Historicism": "new" because the conflict between the idiographic and nomothetic methods as emphasized by the neo-Kantians is overcome insofar as the study of history by necessity has to include nomothetic elements, and therefore is broadly susceptible to impulses from the social sciences; "historicism" in the sense that the historical discipline continues to be concerned with the thinking, acting, responsible human being, and therefore is beginning to move events, politics, and ideas more into the center of its interest once again. What is at issue is not a new doctrine, but rather—according to terms used at the Congresses—a "tendency," a process of "osmosis" or "interpenetration," a "convergence" of historicist, or positivistic, and social scientific approaches in historians' work. Thus, it seems appropriate to speak of a metamorphosis of historicism taking place in the atmosphere of the social sciences. Other historians have used the terms "reconstituted historicism"[43] and "analytical historicism"[44] to define this metamorphosis.

It is no coincidence that at the 1980 Bucharest Congress, in the methodological section "The Language of the Historian," the rhetorical element inherent in historical studies, the historical narrative, and the interpretation of linguistic sources were approached. In his paper on "The Rhetorical Dimension of the Language of the Historian," Karl-Georg Faber described the point of departure of this discussion as follows: "On the one side [we have] those who hold fast to the demand of a scientific language that is as independent of context as possible in the interest of historical truth, even if it is only in the sense of a regulative idea; on the other side, [we have] those who plead for a rehabilitation of historical-political rhetoric in historical writing so that it does not fail to fulfill its public task." He saw both positions as too one-sided, since they missed the "ambivalent character" of history. "The alternative sketched out here—rhetoric on the one side, scientific language on the other—is in danger of dissolving the unity of history as thought and action, as Croce said, in favor of a more or less illusionary division between knowledge and action. But the point is to find a conception of historiography that serves both aspects without equating them indiscriminately."[45]

Pietro Rossi, who dealt with "The Language of the Historian between Colloquial and Scientific Language,"[46] said that historiography was increasingly borrowing its concepts, explanatory schemes, and methods from the social sciences. But "only a small portion of these are actually useful for historians." Historical research was developing its own theoretical-conceptual apparatus, which was not identical with that of the social sciences. Rossi pointed out two characteristic features of the historians' language: its relatedness to events— "The historical context is a sequence of sentences that contribute to the classification of an event within a process"—and its "individualizing tendency, i.e., the tendency ... to express the unique and specific aspects of an event."

He emphasized the narrative character of historical writing as an account that is simultaneously an explanation and for this purpose makes use of "regularities" deriving from colloquial speech or referring to a philosophical conception of history or to the "laws" of the social sciences. History could "certainly not adopt the scientific standards of other disciplines as its model." Therefore, he rejected the "neo-positivistic claim of being able to take the language of the historian and above all his explanatory techniques back to the unity of a scientific language" as an error, while he wished to hold on to the "semantic polyvalence" of historical concepts.

Historical studies are largely based upon written texts, but not all linguistic sources are recorded in writing. The "traditional" sources for the history of cultures that are not based on writing and literature are oral traditions. Furthermore, in recent decades, with the help of modern recording devices, interviews and surveys have developed into a distinctive branch of historical methodology. One of the "major themes" in Bucharest was devoted to these matters. Maclyn P. Burg (U.S.) presented a report on "Problems and Methods of Oral History,"[47] complemented with papers from Senegal, Nigeria, Spain, Great Britain, Hungary, and Norway. They were followed by an unusually lively discussion.[48] If one of the tasks of the International Congresses is to inform historians of new developments in historical research and to transmit new impulses, then in this case the participants' expectations were entirely fulfilled. Oral history, said Theodor C. Barker (Great Britain), is not a new field of history but rather a specific method whose problems and productivity must be systematically examined. His lucid report on "Oral History in England"[49] showed that an obvious area for the application of this method can be found in social history. Broadly based surveys uncover the life experiences of population strata that normally do not articulate themselves in written form. The Bucharest reports and discussion contributions on this subject provide a unique collection of information on the development of Oral History in various countries, and they contain an entire catalog of practical experiences. At the same time, this session included valuable contributions from various African countries, and thus gave evidence of the ecumenical expansion of the historians' cooperation.

At the Bucharest Congress, the intensified interest in a critical evaluation of the tendencies currently competing within historiography induced a Franco-Italian group to suggest the founding of the "International Commission for the History of Historiography." Five years later, at the Stuttgart Congress, this commission was granted full membership in the ICHS as an "affiliated organization." In the meantime, it had already begun lively activity. A journal appeared that enjoyed considerable attention from the beginning.[50] A congress in Montpellier in 1983 dealt with the "methodological controversy"[51] at the turn of the century. A colloquium held at the University of Milan on "Federico Chabod e la 'Nuova Storiografia' Italiana" examined the work and achievement of this politically involved historian, who had played a significant role in the history of the International Congresses.⁵² In Stuttgart, the commission staged its own program under the title "Narrative and Structural History: Past, Present, Perspectives,"⁵³ thus resuming the methodological discussion of the Bucharest Congress. One of the results was—not surprisingly—that the examination of structures in history was not all that new after all. Let us recall that the gateway to the path of historicism, which moved the thinking and acting human being into the center of historical interest, is flanked by two works that analyze the structural conditions of human existence in order to offer an explanation for its historical peculiarities. These were Justus Möser's *Osnabrückische Geschichte* (2 vols., 1768) and particularly Barthold Georg Niebuhr's *Römische Geschichte* (2 vols., 1811/12, 1832). Had the latter not already seen the task of historical studies above all in presenting "a complete picture of the [general] condition" that he held to be "the actual substrate of the historical events"?⁵⁴ In reviewing the history of historiography, the Stuttgart session revealed that narrative and theoretical-structural elements had always permeated each other. The director of the *Annales*, Marc Ferro, outlined the methodological approach developed by this journal. In a comment, Glénisson remarked that it was not possible to identify the *Annales* with a specific, clearly defined theoretical position. According to Charles-Olivier Carbonell (Montpellier), the president of the commission for historiography, it seemed more appropriate to classify it as a "*sociologie rétrospective*," in the tradition of French positivism. Another Frenchman, Hervé Coutau-Bégarie, criticized the hegemonic claims of the *Annales* circle.⁵⁵ If, at the Paris Congress of 1950, the *Annales* had presented themselves with the challenging claim of being able more or less to shove aside the history of events in favor of a "scientific" structural history, the Stuttgart Congress witnessed "something like the swan song of the new beginnings of those days."⁵⁶

In this context the contemporary state of historical methodology was considered as well. The "wind of neohistoricism" was blowing into the faces of the analytical, theory-oriented historians, Jürgen Kocka stated.⁵⁷ He referred to Gordon A. Craig, the vice-president of the ICHS, who had called upon historians to engage in the art of vivid and interesting narrative.⁵⁸ What is the motive behind this new quest for more narrative, Kocka asked. He pursued this question by examining a specific manifestation of neohistoricism, namely, "everyday history," and listed a series of observations that showed from whence came the irritation toward structural history and the desire for more historical narrative: (1) empirical studies had become too overgrown with theory in many cases. He thus urged a certain abstinence here, and suggested a balanced mixture of theory and narrative; (2) theory-oriented history had usually presented itself as being politically committed. The general climate of the times, however, was no longer that of the 1960s and early 1970s. There was no particular interest in theory anymore, not even in the field of politics. Kocka moved his argumentation on historical methodology on to a general critique of the times, identifying some collective-psychological phenomena that he viewed as typical of the contemporary situation in Germany: fear, pessimism, a fin-de-siècle mood, and a tendency toward anti-intellectualism, particularly among the younger generation, that had displaced the earlier optimism of autonomous theoretical thinking. Thus, the illusion of a non-conceptual "history from below and within," a "neo-historicism with a leftist touch," had emerged, which in his view was not more convincing than "traditional historicism"; (3) the critical function of history in our times was being pushed back in favor of a quest for "collective identity of which we allegedly do not have enough."

Here, too narrow a notion of historicism was being used. The roots of historicism reached back not only to the irrationalism of romanticism, but also to the rationalism of the Enlightenment. We encounter a much broader concept of historicism among other participants in the Stuttgart discussions. Georg Iggers (U.S.) observed: "We must define historicism more broadly than Meinecke did, not as a concern with individuality and development, but as Troeltsch and Mannheim suggested, as an outlook on reality which sees all human affairs in historical perspective. Most nineteenth-century historians in this sense were historicists, not only Ranke, Droysen, and Dilthey, but also Guizot, Michelet, Fustel de Coulanges, Burckhardt, Tocqueville, Macaulay, and, I would stress, Karl Marx and Max Weber. And all historical thought, including that of Ranke, was guided by at least implicit theoretical assumptions."[59] In the context of this comprehensive notion of historicism, he understood "neohistoricism" as a "resuscitation of the narrative."

Jörn Rüsen proceeded from a similarly comprehensive understanding,[60] linking the historicist notion of development with the Enlightenment notion of progress. Referring to Ranke, he showed "that historicism did not simply reject the Enlightenment notion of progress, but rather preserved it within an extended notion of progress enclosing the intrinsic value of past cultural creations." His main concern was to identify the historical determinedness of the conception of history that was essential for historicism. He historicized historicism, so to speak, by pointing out that its guiding idea of liberty was based on a "middle-class view of life" that was shaped after the French Revolution and before the development of the modern industrial society. To the extent that industrialization and modern capitalism became the dominant experience of historians, "the attempt by historicism to conceive of history as a development of human liberty according to the norm system of middle-class emancipation has increasingly declined in plausibility." Historicism had not been able to "explicate the respective referential framework chosen for the interpretation of historical developments"; hence "the resistance of historicist historiography to the influence of social scientific theories and methods, which has lastingly informed the development of historical studies, particularly in Germany." This had led to neglect "of the non-intentional factors conditioning human action." Current historical thought and writing were located "beyond historicism," but at the same time they "were beholden to the legacy of historicism as a renewable tradition."[61] Historicism, which had attempted to develop categories essential for the study of history, had thus also "shown a path to a theory of history that wants to go beyond [historicism]." The most appropriate term for this transformation process appears to be "neohistoricism." This term means neither a new version of the old historicism nor the disruption of all links with it. Instead, it denotes a method receptive toward the social sciences and aware of the necessity of theoretical analysis, and combines it with the traditions of narrative art and individualizing approaches.

In Stuttgart, Ragner Björk reported on ways and means of combining structuralist research and historical narrative as exemplified by some Swedish studies.[62] In contrast to Kocka's verdict on the history of everyday life as neohistoricism, F. M. L. Thompson (London) did not see a rejection of structural history by this type of studies, at least not in England. In his view, structural history and the narrative approach were by no means mutually exclusive.[63] All in all, there was broad consensus regarding the possibility—if not the necessity—of a convergence of methods. One might argue that this insight resulting from the Stuttgart session of the historiographical commission was neither new nor spectacular. And yet, in regard to the theoretical and methodological discussion at the end of the Second World War, this outcome was indeed remarkable. It manifested a new awareness of a long tradition that lived in polarities and in continuous development, and comprised a positive perception of methodological pluralism and tolerance.

Propitiously, in Stuttgart the topic of "Max Weber and the Methodology of History" was discussed prominently over the course of several days. It had been selected because the person and work of Max Weber uniquely linked far-reaching historical research on world history with a challenging theoretical claim, and it corresponded to a broad "Weber Renaissance" in historiography.[64] At the same time, the choice of this subject matter made up for the previous omission of Weber's work at the International Congresses, aside from occasional references in individual contributions. This was certainly due above all to the inaccessibility of his language, and to the fact that even his writings on empirical research are densely permeated with epistemological and methodological reflections formulated in a degree of abstraction that lies beyond the empirical modes of thinking of the professional historian.

The reasons for the awakening interest in his work were revealed by the papers presented in Stuttgart. "He contributed more to the methodology and theory of modern historical studies than most historians of his own time and afterward," stated Jürgen Kocka, who had prepared this well attended section and himself chaired it.[65] Kocka located a historiography oriented on Weber somewhere "between historicism and nomothetic science." For Weber, the aim of the cultural sciences did not lie in "formulating general statements in the form of laws." Their "historicity" distinguished them from the nomothetic sciences. Like most historians, Weber regarded "the acting human being" as the true object of cognition. Thus, for him the method of "understanding" was crucial. On the other hand, Weber pleaded "for a conceptualized, to some extent theoretical historiography," i.e., "for the use of precisely defined concepts, models of probabilities, ideal types of various kinds, and for the use of nomological knowledge (knowledge of lawful processes, including those arising from political economy) as tools of historiography." Compared with preceding historians, Weber's nomological conceptual apparatus was a novelty in sofaras it was derived from the problems of modern economy and society and designed for comparative research. Furthermore, Weber never narrated history. He approached it analytically. In its essence, however, his analysis was concerned with historical, individual phenomena. While in regard to causal explanations, his studies were "nomologically striped," as Hans Freyer once put it, they were of a "narrative" nature in regard to the temporal sequence and the respective complexity of historical occurrences. I think Hans-Ulrich Wehler's formulation characterizing the advantages of Weber's "pragmatic-historical" approach is correct: Weber was leading "toward the combination of hermeneutic-understanding and analytically explanatory methods." Weber had recognized "that there was no path leading back to the time before historicism, but at the same time he wanted to overcome historical one-sidedness through methodical constructs and the supply of theory."[66]

Among the abundance of aspects discussed in the section on Max Weber, a recurring issue was Weber's place in the history of historiography—an issue that included the question of how to define the current position of the thought and writing on history. Pietro Rossi attempted to identify Weber's relationship to earlier theoreticians of historicism. Weber, he said, referred back to Dilthey, and in doing so he liberated the concept of "understanding" from "intuitionist interpretations ... in order to reconcile it with a causal explanation oriented toward individualization." In contrast to the neo-Kantians, for whom "the social sciences, as generalizing disciplines, [fell] into the category of the natural sciences," Weber considered nomological elements to be indispensable for historical knowing. He perceived them at first as auxiliary tools, but later on he arrived at a growing recognition of the "relative autonomy" of sociology with regard to history—with the result, however, that Weber's epistemological and methodological achievements should be assessed as more valuable for historical studies than for the social sciences.[67]

The Stuttgart commentaries on some of Weber's concrete research areas show that, guided by a disciplined formulation of questions, he succeeded like no one else in combining comparative, if heterogeneous, phenomena from the most diverse cultures into a conceptual nexus. In some areas he made statements that still remain valid today (as shown by Klaus Schreiner's comments on Weber's historical classification of the medieval city); in other areas he has become outdated by later research (as shown by Sir Moses Finley in regard to Weber's interpretation of the *polis*), or he arrived at his limits of understanding (as stated by Surendra Munshi in regard to Indian culture). However, in no way does this derogate the general methodological potency of his research approach. His analytical comparative approach represents a convincing method for the comprehension of world historical data and references.

Did Weber also see universal patterns of historical development? This question was discussed by Wolfgang J. Mommsen. He explained that Weber's interest in world historical comparison arose from his intention "to define the uniqueness and specific characteristics of occidental civilization by comparing it with the other world religions and civilizations." In his analysis of the Western rationalization process, the "model of a universal historical process" emerged, which Mommsen outlined as follows:

> At the beginning of the known history of mankind, magical worldviews and charismatic or patriarchal forms of political, religious, or ideological rule [arise], which in the course of their development are exposed to increasing routinization and, later on, advancing disenchantment, in order to yield finally to modern, rational, and bureaucratic types of rule, which make use of rational science and base themselves on purely legalistic systems of law. Within this context we find frequent allusions that at the end of this development, under the overwhelming pressure of increasing bureaucratization, the modern rationalistic civilization will freeze to death, like a second Late Antiquity.

Later on, Weber made a distinction between "formal" and "material rationality." In the disenchanted world, he envisaged the revival of the irrational struggle of the old gods, who would rise from their graves in the form of impersonal powers. Weber's view of the world was free of illusions, but at the same time, it was committed to "the great traditions of occidental individualism worthy of being defended at all costs," from which he derived the obligation to "contribute to the preservation of an optimum of freedom and dignity in today's world."[68]

Notes

1. *Première Conférence Internationale d'Histoire Économique. Août 1960, Stockholm*, vol. 1: *Contributions*, vol. 2: *Communications* (Paris, The Hague, 1960).
2. F. Braudel, "Stockholm 1960," *Annales: Économies—Sociétés-Civilisations* 16, no. 3 (1961): 497–500, quotation p. 498.
3. G. Manacorda, "L'XI Congresso internazionale di scienze storiche," *Studi Storici* 1, no. 4 (Rome, 1959/1960): 877.
4. J. Vicens Vives, "Estructure administrativa estatal en los siglos XVI y XVII," Congress Stockholm 1960: *Rapports*, vol. 4, pp. 1ff.
5. See p. 132 above. A special session had been devoted to this issue in Warsaw (contributions in Congress Warsaw 1933: *Rapports*, pp. 701–804).
6. Congress Rome 1955: *Relazioni*, vol. 4.
7. L. Febvre, "En lisant les revues allemandes: Deux articles de l'*Historische Zeitschrift*," *Annales: Économies—Sociétés—Civilisations* 5 (1950): 277f.
8. See J. Glénisson, "L'historiographie française contemporaine: Tendances et réalisations," in *La recherche historique en France de 1940 à 1965*, published by Comité français des sciences historiques (Paris, 1965), p. XXXVIIf.
9. Congress Rome 1955: *Atti*, p. 431.

10. A. Dufour, "XIe Congrès des Sciences Historiques," *Bibliothèque d'Humanisme et Renaissance* 23 (Geneva, 1961): 157–169.
11. Earl J. Hamilton, "The History of Prices Before 1750"; L. Henry, "Développements récents de l'étude de la démographie du passé," both in Congress Stockholm 1960: *Rapports*, vol. 1.
12. F. Rothacker, "Die Wirkung der Geschichtsphilosophie auf die neueren Geschichtswissenschaften"; F. Gilbert, "Cultural History and its Problems," both in Congress Stockholm 1960: *Rapports*, vol. 1.
13. Report on the meeting of the Commission Internationale d'Histoire Ecclésiastique Comparée in Congress Stockholm 1960: *Actes*, pp. 297ff., especially report by Hermann Heimpel on "Germania Sacra"; appreciation of Heimpel's report by Michele Maccarrone, "I lavori del XI Congresso Internazionale di Scienze Storiche," in *Rivista di Storia della Chiesa in Italia* 14 (Rome, 1960).
14. Glénisson, "L'historiographie française."
15. Ibid., p. XI, note 1; on the term "positivism" in its philosophical-systematic and empirical-historical meaning, see pp. 15–17 above.
16. Glénisson, "L'historiographie française," p. XXV.
17. Th. S. Kuhn, *The Structure of Scientific Revolutions* (Chicago, 1962).
18. Glénisson, "L'historiographie française," p. XVIII.
19. Ibid., p. LIII.
20. Congress Vienna 1965: *Actes*, p. 520f.
21. Ibid., p. 518.
22. For example, "Les classes dirigeantes de l'Antiquité aux temps modernes," Congress Vienna 1965: *Rapports*, vol. 1; "Structures sociales et littéraires aux XIXe et XXe siècles" and "La estructura politico-administrativa hispánica como base de las nacionalidades americanas," Congress Vienna 1965: *Rapports*, vol. 2; "Les bases économiques et sociales de l'absolutisme," "Mouvements paysans du centre et du sud-est de l'Europe du XVe au XXe siècle", and "Problèmes économiques et sociaux de la Ière guerre mondiale", Congress Vienna 1965: *Rapports*, vol 4.
23. ICHS, *Bulletin d'information* (1962–1964).
24. Congress Vienna 1965: *Actes*, pp. 231 and 264f.; Shafer (U.S.) to François, 13 Dec. 1965, Archives CISH, together with copies of letters from other American historians who sharply criticized the "Gaullism" of the Labrousse group. Graham wrote to G. Ritter, 19 Sep. 1965: "I was particularly piqued to learn, after writing Labrousse for the proofs of my contribution, that the Section of Theme One, Bilan 1815, had been abandoned; and only in Vienna did I learn that our places had been peremptorily taken by five Frenchmen under Labrousse's direction. I remonstrated with Engel Janosi to little effect, and I regret that you were not present to support me in condemning the worst case of bad manners, I have ever encountered.... In the opinion of the majority of the Committee I talked with during the Conference, we should have resigned as a body." Ritter papers, 354.
25. Congress Vienna 1965: *Rapports*, vol. 1, pp. 451–573.
26. Congress Vienna 1965: *Actes*, p. 261f.
27. *XIIe Congrès International des Sciences Historiques, Vienne 29 août 1965. Bilan du monde en 1815: Rapports Conjoints* (Paris, 1966).
28. D. Kosáry, "1815: Remarques sur son historiographie," in *Nouvelles Études Historiques, publiées à l'occasion du XIIe Congrès International des Sciences Historiques par la Commission Nationale des Historiens Hongrois*, 2 vols. (Budapest, 1965), vol. 1.
29. "Connaissances historiques—conscience sociale," in Congress Moscow 1970: *Doklady*, vol. 1.
30. Congress Moscow 1970: *Doklady*, vol. 1.
31. Ibid., p. 134. See also Hexter's brilliant essay on "The rhetoric of history," in *History and Theory* 6 (1967): 3–13.
32. "La méthode des sciences sociales dans la recherche historique," in Congress Moscow 1970: *Doklady*, vol. 1.

33. K. R. Popper, *The Poverty of Historicism* (London, 1957).
34. "L'histoire au carrefour des sciences humaines," Congress Moscow 1970: *Doklady*, vol. 1. Quotations pp. 148f. and 154.
35. Ibid., pp. 51ff. Schieder himself did not attend the Congress.
36. Congress Moscow 1970: *Doklady*, vol. 1; Congress San Francisco 1975: *Reports*, vol. 3.
37. Congress San Francisco 1975: *Reports*, vol. 3, p. 2023.
38. Ibid., p. 2018f.
39. Ibid., p. 2037.
40. Ibid., p. 2036f.
41. Ibid., pp. 1975ff.
42. Ibid., p. 1998, 2000 and 2005.
43. Th. Nipperdey, "Historismus und Historismuskritik heute," in E. Jäckel and E. Weymar, eds., *Die Funktion der Geschichte in unserer Zeit* [Festschrift for K. D. Erdmann] (Stuttgart, 1975), pp. 82–95, here p. 95.
44. H. Lübbe, *Geschichtsbegriff und Geschichtsinteresse* (Basel, 1977).
45. Congress Bucharest 1980: *Rapports*, vol. 1, pp. 421 and 422.
46. Congress Bucharest 1980: *Rapports*, vol. 1, p. 403f. In Bucharest there were a number of recommendations for how "to norm the language of the historian" through the creation of a uniform historical terminology, for instance, by Jean Bearten (Belgium), Congress Bucharest 1980: *Actes*, vol. 1, p. 380; Robert Fossier (France), ibid., p. 435; Eugen Stanescu and Aron Petric (Romania), Congress Bucharest 1980: *Rapports*, vol. 1, p. 435. The counterposition was taken inter alia by Wolfgang J. Mommsen and Gerhard Beier (Germany), Congress Bucharest 1980: *Actes*, vol. 1, pp. 386 and 389.
47. Congress Bucharest 1980: *Actes*, vol. 1.
48. Ibid., pp. 457ff.
49. "Oral History in Britain," Congress Bucharest 1980: *Rapports*, vol. 1.
50. *Storia della Storiografia* (Milan, 1982ff.).
51. One of the papers presented here: G. G. Iggers, "The 'Methodenstreit' in International Perspective: The Reorientation of Historical Studies at the Turn from the Nineteenth to the Twentieth Century," *Storia della Storiografia*, no. 6 (1984): 21–32.
52. See Vigezzi, *Chabod*.
53. W. J. Mommsen provided an introduction in Congress Stuttgart 1985: *Rapports*, vol. 2, pp. 839ff. The minutes of the sessions, which were to be published in Congress Stuttgart 1985: *Actes*, were not available during the writing of this study. Most of the papers were published in revised versions in W. J. Mommsen, ed., "Narrative History and Structural History: Past, Present, Perspectives," in *Storia della Storiografia*, no. 10 (1986): 1–194. Papers by the GDR historians H. Schleier, G. Lozek, W. Küttler, W. Schmidt, and R. Müller in *Zeitschrift für Geschichtswissenschaft* 34, no. 2 (1986): 99–132. Report on the discussion by A. Blänsdorf, "Methodologie und Geschichte der Geschichtswissenschaft," in "Bericht über den 16. Internationalen Kongreß für Geschichtswissenschaften in Stuttgart (25. 8.–1. 9. 1980)," *Geschichte in Wissenschaft und Unterricht* 37, no. 2 (1986): 81–87. The literary background of this issue includes the much-discussed essay by L. Stone, "The revival of narrative: reflections on a new old history," *Past and Present* 85 (1979): 3–24. For a critical view, see E. J. Hobsbawm, "The revival of narrative: some comments," *Past and Present* 86 (1980): 3–8, and the Stuttgart paper by F. M. L. Thompson, "The British Approach to Social History," in Mommsen, "Narrative History," pp. 162–169.
54. Quoted in Alfred Heuss, "Vom historischen Wissen," in *Erste Verleihung des Preises des Historischen Kollegs*, published by Stiftung des Historischen Kollegs (Munich, 1984), p. 35.
55. See Coutau-Bégarie, *"Nouvelle Histoire."*
56. Blänsdorf, "Methodologie," p. 85.
57. J. Kocka, "Theory Orientation and the New Quest for Narrative: Some Trends and Debates in West Germany," in Mommsen, "Narrative History," pp. 170–181.

58. G. A. Craig, *Der Historiker und sein Publikum* (Münster, 1982), address delivered at the bestowal of the Award for Historical Studies by the city of Münster/Westf., July 1982, for his work *Deutsche Geschichte 1866–1945* (Oxford, 1978).
59. G. G. Iggers, "Comment on Hans Schleier's paper," mimeographed MS; revised version under the title "Historicism (A Comment)" in Mommsen, "Narrative History," pp. 131–144; Schleier's paper "Narrative Geschichte und Strukturgeschichte im Historismus" ibid., pp. 112–130; under the title "Narrative Geschichte und strukturgeschichtliche Analyse im traditionellen Historismus," also in *Zeitschrift für Geschichtswissenschaft* 34, no. 2 (1986): 99–112.
60. J. Rüsen, "Narrative und Strukturgeschichte im Historismus," in Mommsen, "Narrative History," pp. 145–152.
61. He refers to W. J. Mommsen, *Geschichtswissenschaft jenseits des Historismus* (Düsseldorf, 1971) and to Nipperdey, "Historismus." See also Lübbe, *Geschichtsbegriff*, and the criticism of Lübbe's concept of an "analytical historicism" by J. Rüsen, "Zur Kritik des Neohistorismus," *Zeitschrift für philosophische Forschung* 33 (1979): 243–263.
62. R. Björk, "How to narrate a Structure or how to structure a Narrative," in Mommsen, "Narrative History," pp. 182–194.
63. Thompson, "The British Approach."
64. See the report on a conference held by the German Historical Institute in London in Sep. 1984 on "Max Weber and his Contemporaries," *Bulletin of the German Historical Institute London* (1985), p. 11; a critical complete edition of Weber's works under the direction of W. J. Mommsen et al., including previously unknown lecture manuscripts, is in progress.
65. The following contributions are available in abridged version in Congress Stuttgart 1985: *Rapports*, vol. 1, pp. 240–281: J. Kocka (Federal Republic of Germany), "Einleitung"; Pietro Rossi (Italy), "Max Weber und die Methodologie der Geschichts- und Sozialwissenschaften"; Wolfgang J. Mommsen (Federal Republic of Germany), "Max Webers Begriff der Universalgeschichte"; Sir Moses Finley (U.K.), "Max Weber and the Greek City-State"; Klaus Schreiner (GDR), "Die mittelalterliche Stadt in Webers Analyse und Deutung des okzidentalen Rationalismus"; Yoshinubu Shiba (Japan), "Max Weber's Contribution to the History of Non-European Societies: China"; Surendra Munshi (India), "Max Weber on India"; Wolfgang Küttler/Gerhard Lozek (GDR), "Der Klassenbegriff in der idealtypischen Methode Max Webers und im Marxismus"; Hans-Ulrich Wehler (Federal Republic of Germany), "Max Weber's Klassentheorie und die neuere Sozialgeschichte." The unabridged texts were published by J. Kocka, ed., *Max Weber, der Historiker* (Kritische Studien zur Geschichtswissenschaft, vol. 73). Göttingen, 1986.
66. Congress Stuttgart 1985: *Rapports*, vol. 1, p. 280f.
67. Congress Stuttgart 1985: *Rapports*, vol. 1, p. 253.
68. Ibid., pp. 255–257.

Chapter 18

Debates between East and West from the 1960s to the 1980s

Since the Second World War, Western historical scholarship has been under constant challenge from Marxist historicism. The latter made its first appearance as early as 1903 at the Rome Congress through scholars from the Naples School of Law and Economics. In Oslo in 1928 and in Warsaw in 1933, it laid claim, through Soviet Marxist historiography, to universal validity against what was believed to be a doomed "bourgeois" historicism. The metamorphosis of the latter into New Historicism occurred in an intellectual climate stimulated—along with social and economic-historical research, historical geography, and anthropology—by the new ideas and questions arising from Marxism. The challenge was mutual: the innovation of Western historical studies also had an impact on the Marxist historicism in Eastern Europe. The methodological yield of the New History, and particularly many of the stimuli associated with the *Annales* and the Historical Social Science in West Germany, were adopted, though often with critical demarcation. There appears to have been a certain readiness on both sides—clearly perceptible, albeit not universal—to deal frankly with each other and register positively that both sides could learn from each other. The ideological opposition, however, remained unchanged.

Western scholars, even those who are receptive to methodological stimuli from Soviet Marxist historicism, reject the latter's assertion that, as a historical "science," it can provide an objectively valid picture of the universal course of history, including the future. Conversely, Soviet historical scholarship is faced with the request from the West to account for the epistemological criteria of its interpretation of history, which is presented with a claim to objective validity. The International Historical Congresses are an arena for the debate over whether there exists a theoretically unambiguous distinction between historical scholarship and historical ideology, and whether it is possible—despite the contradictory answers to that question—to define clearly the limit up to

---

Notes for this chapter begin on page 310.

which there exists a pragmatic consensus concerning the principles of historical scholarship and beyond which the other's otherness has to be respected.

After Eastern and Western historians had promised in Rome to cooperate and learn from one another, Stockholm provided the test five years later. Here the warm sun of Rome no longer shone. But even if the meeting of the adversaries produced considerable disturbances, it is still worth trying to penetrate the ideological fog in order to make out the constellation of specifically academic arguments. Appropriate to this attempt are four closely related issues that gave rise to some particularly lively discussion in Stockholm: the periodization of history, the slaveholder society of Antiquity, the transition from Antiquity to the Middle Ages, and the concept of revolution.

Our starting point is a report presented in Stockholm by Evgenii M. Zhukov later to become president of the ICHS, on "The Periodization of World History."[1] Zhukov's position within the historical profession of the Soviet Union—as director of the Institute for World History, a member of the Academy of Sciences, and editor of a ten-volume world history[2]—gave an almost official stamp to his statements. In substance he simply presented the Marxist-Leninist schema, familiar to all historians, of sequential societal formations. But one thing was striking: Zhukov said nothing at all about the dilemma (otherwise vigorously discussed in Marxist research) of how to find a place in the Leninist-Stalinist periodization schema for "Asian" society, as addressed by Marx in the foreword to his *Political Economy*. Marx had defined "Asian" society as a most peculiar development characterized by the dual quality of an "oriental despotism" resting on the basis of a property-less, primitive cooperative economy, as it had existed everywhere at the beginning of social development. He had believed that the elements of this initial stage might be rediscovered in the historically fossilized form of Asian society, whereas he had explained the true course of history with the classical sequence of progressive stages of social development according to the specific model of Greco-Western evolution.[3]

Since Zhukov avoided the obvious historical and political questions posed by this issue and drew an overly harmonious picture of Marxist concepts of historical periodization, one may assume that Zhukov, who was well-versed in Asian history, was trying to get the Leninist-Stalinist conception of history away from the Europe-centered view of history cultivated by Marx and Engels,[4] even though in his Stockholm lecture he attempted to reconcile the assumption of a universally operative system of sequential stages of social development with the traditional periodization of European history into Antiquity, the Middle Ages, and the Modern Age. The problems inherent in this approach were brought up in the debates following Zhukov's lecture.[5] The sharpest reaction came from the British historian Peter Laslett, who said that Zhukov's whole report was "regrettable": "It seems to me that the Marxian sociology is now exhausted as a source of suggestion. It is out of date. We have got to find newer and subtler hypotheses."[6] This matched the tone of many commentaries in the Western press. Such judgements overlooked, however, that the proclamation of reduced and tersely presented theses and antitheses is capable of setting markers indicating what different general interpretations are still up for discussion.

First to take the floor was the indefatigable Polish émigré historian Halecki (New York), who had been actively involved in founding the ICHS. Halecki had his roots in Catholicism and contrasted his own Christian view of history as a clear alternative to the Marxist view. His yardstick was not economics but spiritual values; in place of quotations from Marx and Engels, he wanted scientific criteria for periodization. He called for belief not in historical but in moral laws, and questioned the idea of progress. He held up Christ's incarnation as the central event of history and advocated a periodization of the Christian era according to the stages of the spread of Christianity.[7] It was a notable indication of insouciance, even perhaps of civil courage, to come out with so full and unqualified a profession of faith in front of this gathering of skeptical historians—men who made doubt into a professional virtue.

Unlike Halecki, other Western historians were quite prepared to take economic production as the criterion of periodization. They saw the Industrial Revolution in particular as providing a turning point. According to Theodor Schieder (Cologne), for example, it constituted so profound a caesura in modern history that the importance of such forms of socioeconomic organization as capitalism and communism paled in comparison. Imanuel Geiss (Hamburg) supplemented this observation by pointing out that "the significance of this radical historical change in terms of world history ... [is] comparable only with the emergence of agrarian society and the advanced civilizations some 6,000 years ago." From this standpoint, he saw three great stages in the development of world history: the pre-agrarian, the agrarian, and the industrial.[8]

The problem of periodization presented itself from yet another perspective when one enquired into the significance of the "superstructure" in its effect on the course of world history. If, as was rightly stressed again and again, history was not to be explained mono-causally, why not ask with Erich Hassinger (Freiburg) how Soviet historians defined the interrelation between superstructure (e.g., the development of the fine arts) and base from the point of view of periodization? Also tending in an "idealistic" direction was a question raised by Robert R. Palmer (Princeton), namely, whether it might not be better to seek the basic factor of human development—the one shared by all human beings—not, as Zhukov did, in the "necessity" of producing food, clothing, and shelter, but in the "capacity" for doing so.[9]

What was the outcome of the Stockholm debate? How did Zhukov deal with the many questions put to him? He simply swept them aside with a grand gesture. His opponents, he said, were incapable of arguing scientifically; they were caught up in subjectivism, and their denial of a law-governed course of history meant the elimination of historical scholarship. Many a historian wondered how to get further under these circumstances. Had the idea of an academic dialogue between East and West turned out to be an illusion? The voices of resignation that expressed themselves in such terms were countered by a more optimistic and, it seems to me, more realistic assessment on the part of the Italian Marxist, Gastone Manacorda. Manacorda thought that the historians' search for a scientific basis for the explanation of world history corresponded to a genuine need. In Stockholm, the right conclusion had been reached, albeit with difficulty: that it was necessary to open up the large field of world historical developments to methodical investigation. "The territory best suited for further studies in this direction is the history of historiography, and not the confrontation of theoretical constructs: this is the essence that can be drawn from the debate."[10]

Indeed, it was already apparent at Stockholm that, to eyes focused on the history of historical research, real progress could be discerned behind contrasting ideologies. This applied particularly to a matter that was of central importance in the problem of periodization, namely, the transition from a "slaveholder society" to "feudalism." In the rigidly dogmatic Marxist-Leninist view of history, of course, the concept of the "slaveholder society," alongside the concept of "revolution" as a label to describe the transition from the slaveholder society of the Roman Empire to the feudal society of the Middle Ages, has its firm place. But the ideas associated with those concepts are in flux and have changed with the progress of research in West and East. Despite the vehemence of the controversies, this emerged clearly in the contributions by Siegfried Lauffer (Munich) and Friedrich Vittinghoff (Cologne) at the Stockholm Congress, and Ernst Engelberg (East Berlin) at the Vienna Congress five years later.[11] To Vittinghoff, the term "slaveholder society" was inaccurate as a general description of the socioeconomic circumstances in Greco-Roman Antiquity, let alone the whole of ancient history in the broader sense, both temporal and geographical; he restricted it to classical Athens and the late-Republican Rome of the second and first centuries BC. So far as research was concerned, he saw the nub of the problem as lying indisputably (and to my knowledge no one disputed him here) in the question: "Who in the various arenas and eras of history were the main producers in the key branch of production, namely, agriculture?"[12] However, despite differences of opinion concerning the accuracy and scope of the concept of the "slaveholder society," he stated with regard to Soviet research, to which history owed "some fertile new questions and answers," that agreement had been reached "that slavery was moribund in late Antiquity with new forms of ownership emerging, and that slaves did not constitute a unified, genuinely revolutionary class and were not the vehicle of a progressive mode of production, but also that the legal situation of slaves and above all their actual position in the socioeconomic process (e.g., as a result of the slave *peculium*) was substantially improved and the manner of exploitation had become less severe."[13]

The method used here, namely, to argue from the point of view of Marxist concepts, and to take the results of Marxist research seriously, evoked a certain amount of surprise. Thus, a Polish Congress report noted in regard to Vittinghoff's contribution:

> In many areas of our discipline, the representatives of Marxist scholarship have got used to fighting against familiar arguments by the enemies of Marxism.... In reality, the tactics of the conscious opponents of Marxism have changed. To see this change, it is sufficient to read the special issue of *Saeculum* (IX, nos. 1–2, 1961) edited by the West German historians for the purpose of the Congress, which is dedicated entirely to Soviet historical study. Our adversaries present themselves as the alleged proponents of "true" Marxism, and armed with single sentences from the works of Marx and Engels quoted out of context, they endeavor to prove that the works of the contemporary Marxist historians are not Marxist. The debate with such an attitude is unavoidable. However, it requires a deepened study of the genuine truth of a live Marxism.... At the Congress, not all participants in the discussion were up to this task.[14]

Along with the applicability of the concept of the "slaveholder society" to late Antiquity, various Western historians also questioned the applicability of the concept of revolution to the process of social and political transformation that had led from late Roman times to the founding of the early Germanic states. Others, however, pointed out that it was ultimately a merely terminological question whether this process, which resulted from diverse causal factors—the decline of the slave economy, the advent of the colonate, and above all the barbarian raids—was described as evolution or revolution. Of course, the expression of doubts concerning the validity of central notions of the Marxist historical nomenclature had its function within the ideological dispute. But did this mean that it was not legitimate to raise such objections on the forum of the International Congresses, provided that the controversy was conducted according to the rules of a fair intellectual discourse?[15] Even if the main stimuli of these controversies over central issues of historical knowledge stemmed from the ideological conflict, the decisive point ought to be whether or not they were conducive to the empirical investigation of fact.

It did indeed prove possible to make substantial progress and hence achieve a certain degree of convergence with regard to objective facts, despite the fiercely disputed terminology and diverging ideological interpretation. This is evident from the report that Ernst Engelberg presented to the Vienna Congress five years later.[16] Engelberg dealt with the questions of evolution and revolution from the standpoint of world history up to and including contemporary revolutions. In this context, he also examined the transition from late Antiquity to the society of the Middle Ages. He described it as a "revolution," although this transition was a process extending over several centuries. His report was characterized by the tension between the conceptual framework and the historical statements of the facts. Like Marx, Engelberg saw revolution as the "engine of history." He defined his conceptual starting point accordingly: "In the law-governed sequence of social formations, revolutions constitute the nodal points. They are culminations of the class struggle. Social revolution is connected with (often violent) political revolution."[17]

Obviously, these terms derive from the drama of the classic revolutions of the Modern Age. But since it was not possible to interpret the transition from the slaveholder society of Antiquity to feudal society as an abrupt social and political change arising out of a class struggle from the bottom up, Engelberg tried to extricate himself by saying that "the building of feudal states [constituted] what for those centuries was the specific form of political revolution." At the same time, he correctly stated that there had not "in the whole of the slaveholder society [been] a single class that pursued a consciously revolutionary goal." There had been no revolution in the sense of the French or Russian upheavals, although in those centuries "people had repeatedly banded together" who "with a truly dim desire attempted to free themselves from the chains of a miserable existence." Consequently, he continued, "the so-called barbarians, mainly Germans and Slavs, whose tribal order was breaking down, were assigned the task [by whom, one wonders?] of administering the death blow to the Western Roman Empire." But why, in so doing, did the barbarians finish off the slaveholder society, and why did they develop the feudal order in their states, rather than move from their tribal order to the next stage of social development allegedly demanded by the logic of history? Marxist historical theory was not short of an answer. It was sufficiently flexible to foresee the possibility that stages of development might be jumped here and there (Zhukov had suggested as much in his Stockholm lecture on the periodization of world history) or that outside military intervention might be the actual vehicle of a revolutionary change in social conditions. That flexibility accommodated certain contemporary legitimation requirements with respect to particular political-military interventions and invasions within the Soviet sphere of influence. Engelberg, however, was not content with an ad hoc legitimation of the barbarian invasion-revolution on the dividing line between Antiquity and the Middle Ages. He held that this too had happened according to rules and was thus logical and inevitable, turning it into a "law of history," which he defined as follows: "In the course of its historical development, a nation or people may jump a formation of society only if, from the standpoint of world history, that formation is already in decline or in a general state of crisis, and the new stage of development has begun to make head way or has already taken shape. Thus does the particular move in the wake of the universal and world-historical."[18]

Such conceptualizations and hypothetical constructions met with a number of objections in the Vienna discussions, partly in terms of critical comparison between Marx's concept of revolution and the Russian October Revolution or current events within the Soviet sphere of influence. Of particular relevance were the contributions of John L. Snell (New Orleans),[19] Jacob L. Talmon (Jerusalem),[20] and Adam Wandruszka (Cologne).[21] Engelberg believed that "the conflicts and differences of opinion in relation to the problem of revolutions" were partly explicable by the fact that "dialectical thought has suffered a decline since the last third of the nineteenth century, particularly in the countries of Western Europe." This was a very accurate observation. Used as an argument against his critics, however, it was unconvincing, because a dialectics of revolution and evolution obviously presupposes that the two concepts can be clearly distinguished, which was not the case in the description of the transition from the slaveholder society to feudal society given by the well-versed historian Engelberg. Translated into facts, this development appeared as an evolution that covered a long period and was punctuated by military incidents. Thus, it was not surprising that Engelberg was clearly criticized by the Soviet side, albeit in cautious terms. They agreed to his assertion of a dialectical relationship between revolution and evolution. Yet it should not be forgotten that revolution was "the driving force, the leading factor." When Mints pointed to the examples of the American and French revolutions in this context,[22] however, the problem was that no comparable events, in terms of their revolutionary character, were to be found in the transition period between Antiquity and the Middle Ages. It seems to me that Engelberg was right when he ended his closing statement with the comment that there was every reason for a "productive dissatisfaction."[23]

The theoretical and the empirical constitute complementary avenues of the study of history, in the field of Marxist-Leninist historicism as well as in New Historicism. This was evidenced particularly by a further report delivered by Ernst Engelberg in San Francisco on "Event, Structure, and Development in History."[24] He prefaced his paper with a remark that confirms my own observations, namely, that in non-Marxist history there was "an unmistakable tendency to bring together historicism and positivism, and particularly hermeneutics and neopositivism—despite all remaining differences and controversies."[25] For Marxists, however, both historicism and positivism are under suspicion of subjectivism. The same is true of a New Historicism that is open to theoretical thinking. In Engelberg's view, objectivity, i.e., the scientific nature of historical knowledge, was bound up with the dialectical principle of historical materialism. He thus referred the question about the relationship of structure and event, of theory and empirical experience, to the implicit epistemological problem of the interrelation between thought and existence. Using a methodologically convincing analysis of the strike as an example, Engelberg demonstrated how observations regarding event, structure, and development interpenetrate in the study of a concrete object. As a single event, circumscribed in space and time, he argued, a particular strike can be understood only in connection with the economic, social, and political conditions and effects of the general phenomenon of the strike in a particular historical situation, and that type of strike in turn can only be explained in connection with the temporal development of the strike movement.

But such an approach to a sociohistorical object of knowledge and its methodology is in essence, with regard to its techniques, by no means dependent on this or that ontological premise. The insight into the linkage of event and structure is not bound up with any particular philosophy of history. It is part of the common methodological inventory of modern historical research. Noteworthy in this context were Engelberg's remarks about the Marxist understanding of the relationship of thought to existence as a "mirroring," which basically represents an epistemological realism that as such is by no means confined to Marxism-Leninism. Engelberg described the relationship between the object of knowledge and the knowing subject as "dialectical," but at the same time emphasized the importance of the subjective side. He defined the acquisition of knowledge as a process beginning with the "selective" intellectual appropriation of particular parts of the object, and leading to results that did not "coincide with reality itself" and did not represent a "photocopy of the past." The concept of "mirroring" that Engelberg maintained is anchored in a materialist ontology, but it is not a necessary element of the definition of the historical method as a process, as Engelberg accurately elucidated in his San Francisco paper. A passage describing the path from historical "object" to historical "fact" seems to point to the notion that knowledge is produced through communicative processes: "All objective manifestations of material and intellectual life become facts for us only when there are statements about them that are true and certain, that is to say, that they have been verified, checked, and thus proven, according to a process of collecting evidence, which is subject to constant improvement."[26]

He portrayed this path of cognition in various stages. "Historical method stage one" was for him "source criticism in all its complexity."[27] What he set out in detail here was in the best tradition of historicism. In his critical appraisal of the quantitative method, he concurred with what had been said by others at earlier International Congresses.[28] The terminology of his methodological apparatus firmly included such classic concepts of early historicism as "understanding" (*Verstehen*) and "empathy" (*Einfühlen*). The same was true of his assessment of the "unique" as "event" and "individuality."[29]

According to Engelberg, discerning the dual aspect of the unique and of structures in event and individuality, i.e., recognizing historical connections, represents the second stage of the historical method. This is plausible, as is his reference to the function of theory for the elucidation of general contexts. It also certainly promoted the ecumenical climate of the historians' dialogue that he saw the "attempt to reduce the 'theory deficit'" in non-Marxist history as "an opportunity for further development of methodology," and emphasized that "materialist dialectics" were open to the integration of all "rational elements of newly developed methods." He registered with approval that Western scholars were taking into account various structures from the fields of politics, constitutional history, economics, and society, even including "concepts borrowed from Marxism, such as productive forces and conditions of production."[30] But that was not sufficient. What was needed, he said, was to "arrive at the nexus between and above the structures," to find a way out of the "structural chaos" that was no better than the "factual chaos of the individuality principle."[31] He considered this to be the third and highest stage of the historical method, and he stated: "It is only here that the academic dispute begins."[32]

Indeed, this is the point where minds part company. But over what? Engelberg asserted that "for the understanding of the basic social structure ... paths discovered long ago" must simply be "rediscovered." Having reached the heights of the third stage of historical initiation, the disciple under his guidance meets with a cross-section from the familiar conceptual world of dialectical and historical materialism. For the historian subscribing to New Historicism, this is where the problems begin. It is not that those concepts seem useless to him; concepts such as productive forces, conditions, and modes of production, as well as Engelberg's central concept of social formations, are certainly usable as part of the technical apparatus of New Historicism. But it is a different matter if we enquire about the validity of such concepts in terms of epistemology, about their scientific reliability. For the empirical historian and the skeptical philosopher of history, they are surely worth discussing as heuristic principles, hypotheses that can either be verified or proven wrong. But they are so no longer when, for the sake of Marxist-Leninist orthodoxy, they are defended against all the historical evidence, as, for example, in the attempt to impose the term "revolution" on the transition from the slaveholder society to feudalism,[33] or when it was said in San Francisco that the "dynamically moved structural nexus of society in its entirety" ruled out "monocausality," which is worth upholding as a generally valid methodological principle, while at the same time it was stated that only the economic base, not any "superstructural phenomenon, however important," was able to characterize "the essence of a society in its spatial and temporal structure."[34]

In regard to the question of how, in the cluster of plural causalities, the primacy of the mode of production is epistemologically justified, Engelberg's San Francisco contribution offers no answer. Nevertheless, it seems, if I understand him correctly, that for him the validity of the Marxist-Leninist view of history does not mean that assertions derived from it are equivalent to empirically proven statements. Perhaps we should speak of a theoretical postulate. This term is suggested by Engelberg's own choice of words. A characteristic feature of this theoretical postulate is that in Marxist-Leninist eyes it is rooted in the practical postulate of the class struggle as the driving force that steers world history in the direction of progress and bestows meaning upon it. In these ideological questions, basic anthropological convictions confront each other. It is inevitable that they are articulated, and where they are presented in a thoughtful way without reciprocal political accusations, this elucidates the simultaneously competitive and ecumenical character of the historians' community. However, the genuinely scholarly discourse, which is the lifeblood of the International Historical Congresses, presupposes as a common basis the mutual agreement about specific methodological standards that correspond to the first and second stages of the process of historical cognition, to borrow Engelberg's terms.

Continuing the efforts that had been so clearly evinced in San Francisco to sound out the extent of a possible methodological consensus over and above ideological cleavages, and influenced by a general reduction of tensions in the international political arena, the president of the ICHS set out in Bucharest in 1980 to remind the gathering of historians from all over the world of the fundamental rules of their ecumenical community.[35] What he said then comprises an account of the Congresses that has been confirmed by the subsequent study of their history. Therefore, in conclusion, parts from his address shall be presented here, with a few additions:

> In the light of the present international situation, it is undoubtedly important that historians from all over the world, who represent the broadest possible range of beliefs, should meet at our forum with the declared intention of discussing matters in such a way that they are not talking at cross-purposes but (to use a quaint old-fashioned notion) "understand" one another. But how is it to be done? This raises the question of the internal conditions under which the exchange of ideas between the adherents of New Historicism and historians of a historical-materialist persuasion takes place in the arena of the historians' ecumenical community. My concern here is with empirical observations that serve a pragmatic purpose.
>
> The experience of the Congresses has shown that there are some areas in this dialectical relationship where favorable conditions exist on both sides for a fruitful exchange of ideas, and others where any discussion almost inevitably reaches an impasse, with no epistemological benefit to either side. The latter include arguments of a teleological nature concerning the meaning and destination of the future course of history. Because such statements can neither be verified nor proved wrong, one side regards them as lying outside the sphere of empirical knowledge, and hence outside the study of history, while the other side maintains, based on an alleged regularity in the historical sequence of social formations, that such teleological statements can in fact constitute scientific statements. In this area, as the Congresses held up to now have shown, there is no getting beyond the declamation of controversial positions. So it would seem to be sensible to exclude that area as far as possible.
>
> That leaves the broad field of past history for a collaboration that has proved its worth repeatedly and is now more necessary than ever. It includes certain theoretical premises that can be deduced from the experience of the scholarly dialogue. These concern facts, causes, and values:
>
> 1. Discussion among historians is governed by the regulative idea of historical objectivity. This is the belief that it is possible to make intersubjectively valid statements about historical facts critically elaborated from the sources. They are valid irrespective of what particular national, political or social self-interests provided the motives for the scholarly consideration of those facts, and of what self-interest found them welcome or unwelcome. Objectivity and partisanship need not be in conflict with one another, whether such partisanship is based decisionally on personal values, or in an objectivistic approach on the assumption of historical laws. There is a temptation, of course, that partisanship will induce those concerned to avoid, conceal or even suppress embarrassing facts. A gauge of the scientific character of the historical exchange of ideas is the participants' readiness to mention precisely what is uncomfortable with regard to their own cause, in order to expose their own statements to the test of being proved false. Respect for the historical facts is and always has been a positivistic element in all historical research. That is why the demand made by Henri Houssaye at the first International Congress of Historical Sciences in Paris in 1900 is still valid today: "Facts, facts, facts, which contain within themselves their lesson

and their philosophy. The truth, the whole truth, nothing but the truth."[36] Thus, Mrs. Pankratowa, speaking about her experiences in Rome in 1955, saw "common ground for scholarly co-operation in the establishment of precise, verifiable historical facts."[37] Or in the words of a paper presented by Soviet historians in Vienna in 1965: "Facts are the bread of science ... experience shows that the difference in scientific and political views is no obstacle to a joint research of scientific truth."[38] The Hungarian historian Lajos Elekes, speaking in Moscow in quest of "elements of concordance," even felt able to say that "the facts as such surely speak for themselves."[39]

2. After the facts, causes. Inseparable though the two may be epistemologically, for practical historical research and for the methods of academic discourse, such a distinction is rather useful as a regulatory principle. The experience of our Congresses shows that the variety of views represented in discussions at the Congresses depends upon there being general recognition of the principle of multicausality in the explanation of historical facts. Marxist historians have repeatedly protested at our Congresses against the misunderstanding that ascribed monocausality to them. In Marxist terminology, they referred to the dialectics of base and superstructure, pointing out that the latter sphere of human activity, alongside social and economic factors, is indispensable to any explanation of history.[40] This idea was given its most crucial expression by Ernst Engelberg in San Francisco: "The mode of production as basis in the dynamically moved structural nexus of the social totality rules out the monocausality that is sometimes attributed to Marxism."[41] At whatever point the emphasis is laid in the system of determinants, on economic, social, political or cultural factors, and whatever differences of historical perspective may result from this, there is in any case a consensus in principle regarding a research into causes that is open in every direction.

3. Lastly, the question of values.[42] Is there agreement here, too? It goes without saying that opinions continue to differ concerning the problem of whether historical knowledge as such, through the discovery of lawful processes, can lead to logically compelling political and social values, or whether this is precisely what cannot be achieved through academic research. However, consensus can be reached in acknowledging that, like science as a whole, history too, and within it the International Historical Congresses, is based on a pre-scientific value decision. The maxim of the Congresses is that historical study should exist and that (in the words of our statutes) it should be promoted by "international co-operation." This is founded on the convening historians' willingness—which is essentially taken for granted—to submit the premises and results of their research and opinions to scrutiny through a discussion governed by the rules of critical scholarship. That is to say, the common study of history pursued in this organization rests on the mutual concession of freedom of scholarly convictions and expression. Without practicing this maxim, the International Historical Congresses would be futile. It goes without saying, yet it is of fundamental importance. The ICHS and the Congresses have been and remain, through the determination of historians coming together from all corners of the globe, a forum of intellectual freedom. In respecting the other's otherness, they serve the cause of peace.

Notes

1. Congress Stockholm 1960: *Rapports*, vol. 1.
2. *Vsemirnaja istorija* [World History] (Moscow, 1955–1965).
3. On the problems of interpretation touched on here, see K. D. Erdmann, "Die asiatische Welt im Denken von Karl Marx und Friedrich Engels" (first published 1961), in Erdmann, *Geschichte, Politik und Pädagogik: Aufsätze und Reden*, (Stuttgart, 1970), pp. 149–182, including a discussion of the ideas of K. A. Wittfogel, "The Ruling Bureaucracy of Oriental Despotism: A Phenomenon that paralysed Marx," *The Review of Politics* 15 (1953) and Wittfogel, *Oriental Despotism: A Comparative Study of Total Power* (Yale University Press, 1957).
4. See Erdmann, "Asiatische Welt," pp. 151ff.
5. W. Conze, Congress Stockholm 1960: *Actes*, p. 57; T. Yamamoto, ibid., p. 64; E. Hassinger, ibid., p. 65, among others, and the "Communication" of B. Djurdjev (Sarajevo), in Congress Stockholm 1960: *Communications*, p. 40; for a full treatment of the problem, see F. Vittinghoff, "Die Theorie des historischen Materialismus über den antiken 'Sklavenhalterstaat,'" in a special issue published for the Stockholm Congress of *Saeculum* 11 (1960): 89–131, esp. pp. 115ff.
6. Congress Stockholm 1960: *Actes*, p. 59.
7. Ibid., p. 56f.
8. Ibid., p. 65.
9. Ibid., p. 62.
10. Manacorda, "L'XI Congresso," p. 879.
11. S. Lauffer, "Die Sklaverei in der griechisch-römischen Welt," in Congress Stockholm 1960: *Rapports*, vol. 2; F. Vittinghoff, "Die Bedeutung der Sklaverei für den Übergang von der Antike in das abendländische Mittelalter," in Congress Stockholm 1960: *Communications*; see also Vittinghoff, "Sklavenhalterstaat"; E. Engelberg, "Fragen der Evolution und Revolution in der Weltgeschichte," in Congress Vienna 1965: *Rapports*, vol. 4.
12. Congress Stockholm 1960: *Actes*, p. 91.
13. Congress Stockholm 1960: *Communications*, p. 72.
14. Iza Bieżuńska-Małowistowa, "Historia starożytna na Kongresie sztokholmskim" [Ancient History at the Stockholm Congress], *Kwartalnik historyczny* 68 (1961): 562f.
15. In his survey on the slavery debate at the Stockholm Congress, *Ancient Slavery and Modern Ideology* (Cambridge, 1980), M. J. Finley criticizes the West German historians because they had conducted their side of the debate with "consciously polemical intent" (p. 73). There can be no denying that political motives were involved on their side, too, but the only thing that counts, as regards whether and to what extent discussions motivated by political ideology are legitimate or not, is whether, at a congress claiming to be scientific, political interests that influence the way questions are asked convert into verifiable scientific arguments or not. Finley's critique of Vittinghoff was criticized by E. Badian, "The bitter history of slave history," *New York Review of Books* 22 (1981), and H. W. Pleket, "Slavernij in de Oudheid: 'Voer' voor oudhistorici en comparatisten," *Tidschrift voor Geschiedenis* 95 (1982): 1–30. Fifteen years after Stockholm, the British Marxist E. J. Hobsbawm presented a report on "Revolution" to the San Francisco Congress. He restricted analysis and comparison essentially to the modern period and issued a warning, with reference to recent developments in Soviet research, against applying the concept to periods of history lying in the distant past. "Certainly the attempt to extend the 'system-changing' revolutions too far into the past breaks down, as witness the abandonment of the view that the transition from classical antiquity to feudalism was due to a 'slave revolution,' unsupported, incidentally, by Marx or Lenin" (Congress San Francisco 1975: *Rapports*, vol. 1, p. 268).

16. "Fragen der Evolution und Revolution in der Weltgeschichte," Congress Vienna 1965: *Rapports*, vol. 4.
17. Ibid., p. 22.
18. Ibid., p. 25 and 26.
19. Congress Vienna 1965: *Actes*, pp. 543–545.
20. Congress Vienna 1965: *Actes*, pp. 546–548.
21. Congress Vienna 1965: *Actes*, p. 548f.
22. Congress Vienna 1965: *Actes*, p. 542f.
23. Congress Vienna 1965: *Actes*, p. 553. Later, in the foreword to his essay collection *Theorie, Empirie und Methode in der Geschichtswissenschaft: Gesammelte Aufsätze*, ed. W. Küttler and G. Seeber (East Berlin, 1980), Engelberg fell back upon the conventional world-historical class struggle scheme. However, this did not prevent him from including his more problem-oriented Vienna contribution in this volume (pp. 101–115) and expanding it with his thoughtful and interesting essay "Zu methodologischen Problemen der Periodisierung" (1972, pp. 117–162). Here he called the new mode of production resulting from the "feudalization process" a "revolutionary process" or, using Engels's term, a "complete revolution," though it is not at all understandable how this "feudalization process," and the transformation of the mode of production caused by it, can be related to the dialectics of revolutionary class struggle. See also Peter Hassel, "Marxistische Formationstheorie und der Untergang Westroms," *Geschichte in Wissenschaft und Unterricht* 32 (1981): 713–725.
24. E. Engelberg, "Ereignis, Struktur und Entwicklung in der Geschichte," in Congress San Francisco 1975: *Reports*, vol. 3; reprinted in Engelberg, *Theorie*, pp. 59–93, with a supplement ("Nachtrag") reproducing his introductory remarks in the methodology section of the Congress (pp. 94–100).
25. Engelberg, *Theorie*, "Nachtrag," p. 94.
26. Engelberg, "Ereignis," in id., *Theorie*, p. 65.
27. Recent problems of sources and source criticism were comprehensively discussed in San Francisco by J. Topolski, "The historian in his quest for documentation," in Congress San Francisco: *Reports*, vol. 3. On Topolski, the Poznan School, and the moves being made there toward an open, undogmatic Marxist methodology of history including ideas from Western analytical epistemology (Popper et al.), see K. von Ascheraden, "Probleme der Theorie und Methodologie der Geschichtswissenschaft in der Volksrepublik Polen" (Ph.D. diss., Kiel, 1978), part 2.
28. See above the contributions on this subject at the Paris and Moscow Congresses, p. 211f. and pp. 285–288.
29. Engelberg, "Ereignis," in id., *Theorie*, p. 99.
30. Ibid., p. 80. At this point he cited a lengthy quotation from R. Koselleck, "Darstellung, Ereignis und Struktur," in G. Schulz, ed., *Geschichte heute: Positionen, Tendenzen, Probleme* (Göttingen, 1973), pp. 307–317.
31. Engelberg borrowed these terms from V. Rittner, "Zur Krise der westdeutschen Historiographie," in I. Geiss and R. Tamchina, eds., *Ansichten einer künftigen Geschichtswissenschaft*, vol. 1 (Munich, 1974), pp. 43–74.
32. Engelberg, "Ereignis," in id., *Theorie*, p. 80.
33. See above, pp. 303–305.
34. Engelberg, "Ereignis," in id., *Theorie*, pp. 86ff.
35. Erdmann, "Die Ökumene."
36. Cf. above, p. 15.
37. Pankratova, "K itogam."
38. Nechkina, Pashuto, and Chernyak, "Evolution of historical thought in the middle of the XXth century," in Congress Vienna 1965: *Rapports*, vol. 4, p. 65. In this connection, see also the comments in discussion by G. Lozek, Congress Vienna 1965: *Actes*, p. 516.

39. L. Elekes, "Connaissances historiques—conscience sociale," in Congress Moscow 1970: *Doklady*, vol. 1, p. 181.
40. J. Kladiva (Prague) and Ž. Kormanowa (Warsaw), Congress Stockholm 1960: *Actes*, p. 47.
41. "Ereignis, Struktur und Entwicklung in der Geschichte," in Congress San Francisco 1975: *Reports*, vol. 3, p. 1961. A similar statement was made by W. Küttler, "Wissenschaftssprache, Begriffs- und Theoriebildung in der historischen Forschung und Darstellung," in Congress Bucharest 1980: *Rapports*, vol. 1, p. 411.
42. See also above, p. 288.

Epilogue
After the End of the Great Schism—the International Historical Congresses from 1985 to 2000

Wolfgang J. Mommsen

Karl Dietrich Erdmann's plea for cooperation and understanding among historians from all over the world is governed by the maxim that historians form a sort of community that in principle transcends both national allegiances and ideological orientations. The search for the truth and the acceptance of the fundamental principles of historical research are common to all of them. This obligation establishes intellectual and often also personal links between the historians of various countries in a world full of strife and conflict. Two themes reverberate in Erdmann's history of the Congresses and the ICHS: the debate about alternative theoretical approaches to historical research, and the encounter between Western and Marxist-Leninist conceptions of history. These issues also overshadow the continuous efforts to engage historians from all countries in the activities of the ICHS.

At first, marked national differences stood in the way of establishing a genuine international organization of historical scholarship. In the last decades before 1914 it was the increasing rivalries between the European powers that hindered the international cooperation of the historians. After 1918 the bitter memories of the First World War and continuing nationalist conflicts initially prevented the participation of historians from the former Central Powers; later it was the mounting ideological conflicts between the democratic countries of the West, the fascist powers, and eventually the challenge to Western capitalism by the USSR that turned out to be serious hindrances to scholarly cooperation. Erdmann describes these obstacles in detail. Only with great difficulty could they be overcome to some extent and the idea of international historians' conferences revitalized. The historians who were involved in this

---

Notes for this section begin on page 358.

venture were motivated by the conviction that by promoting understanding and scholarly cooperation among different political respectively ideological camps, they might help to bring about a more peaceful world.

Erdmann argues time and again that scholarly activities can be pursued fruitfully across national or ideological boundaries, however strong the personal convictions of historians from different countries or, more importantly, their different ideological allegiances, might be. This is the central theme of his presentation. His favored term for describing this process, the ecumenical community of historians, is taken from the model of cooperation between the various Christian denominations; in his view the international community of historians is a spiritual community in much the same way as the ecumene of the Christian churches, which disagree on many things but not on the essential issue, belief in Christ. Erdmann considered it essential that Soviet historians should by all means be invited to participate in the International Congresses; otherwise their primary function, namely, to work for peace and understanding in a world full of strife and conflict, would be jeopardized. Hence, the later sections of his presentation are primarily concerned with this issue, even though he did his best to report in considerable detail on all the major international debates among historians, notably those on methodological issues.

His account covers events up to the International Historical Congress in Stuttgart in 1985. However, the collapse of the Soviet empire, associated with the disintegration of the Soviet satellite regimes in East-Central Europe, including the German Democratic Republic, brought a dramatic change of agenda. The deep cleavage among the international historical community, namely, the conflict between Marxist-Leninist and Western notions of history, suddenly lost the key importance that rightfully had been assigned to it by Erdmann.

It is significant that at the very end of his book Erdmann refers to the winding-up speech that he had presented as president of the ICHS to the Congress in Bucharest in 1980. In this message he emphasized the necessity of scholarly cooperation between Western and Soviet historians, but also listed essential preconditions for fruitful cooperation by the international community of historians. For one, he argued, all teleological arguments about the course and the eventual goal of history must be avoided, because on these issues no agreement could ever be reached. The mere declaration of controversial views on the sequence of social formations and the laws that govern the historical process was, in his view, pointless. Instead he demanded from the historians that they accept the essential multicausality that governs all historical processes. He sought support for this view in the writings of various historians, notably those from the Marxist-Leninist camp. Besides, he continued, historical discourse must adhere throughout to the regulative idea of objectivity. This postulate was valid even though no agreement could be expected about the fundamental values that guide the judgement of historians. Invoking the methodological principles of Max Weber, Erdmann emphasized that rational discussion of empirical facts and of different historical interpretations is possible in spite of the often sharp differences in the worldviews held by the historians engaged in such discourse. However, this is possible only if all partners are prepared to respect the freedom of scientific conviction for all. This was his final message to the international community of historians.

Karl Dietrich Erdmann presents a lucid description of the rifts and conflicts within the Western historical camp since the 1960s. He reports in considerable detail on the debate between the *Annales* school and conventional historiography, and also on the ongoing controversy between political history and New, Social History (which came to be known in the Federal Republic of Germany as "Historische Sozialwissenschaft"). For himself he claims a position in the middle ground that he calls "New Historicism," in part based upon Max Weber's methodological theory. Likewise he devotes attention to various new departures in the field, for instance, quantitative history or gender history. However, it is the ups and downs of the ongoing debate between Marxist-Leninist and Western historians that form the axis of his account of the Congresses from 1960 to 1985. For this reason this epilogue cannot merely continue the story at the point where Erdmann ends it. The secular conflict between Soviet Marxist-Leninism and Western pluralist historiography has faded away, and this withering coincided with substantial changes in the historical profession itself, regarding both subject matter and methods of historical research.

East-West Realignment: Madrid 1990

The seventeenth International Historical Congress in Madrid in 1990, at least in its initial stages, was prepared under the lingering impact of the international constellation prevailing before 1989. Soviet historians as well as historians from various East-Central European countries played a substantial role in the preparation of the Congress, in particular the selection of the themes to be presented. In a meeting of the Bureau of the ICHS at Athens on 25 September 1987, the scientific program of the forthcoming Congress in Madrid was debated at length. It was agreed, not least under the influence of Karl Dietrich Erdmann and Carl N. Degler (United States), that one of the "major themes" of the Congress ought to be a comparative analysis of "revolution and reform in modern and contemporary history." This was in line with Erdmann's desire to build bridges between scholars from East and West. The suggestion met with approval from the two representatives of Marxist-Leninist historiography in the Bureau of the ICHS, Sergei L. Tikhvinsky from the USSR, and Joachim Herrmann from the GDR. They suggested topics relevant to the Marxist-Leninist view of history, and they were seconded in these proposals by Karl Dietrich Erdmann, who as we have seen was interested in maintaining, if not intensifying, the dialogue between Marxist-Leninist and Western historians. This corresponded to the general political climate, insofar as the cleavage between the Soviet Bloc and the West was about to lose its stringency.

At any rate, the historians of Marxist-Leninist orientation were given considerable scope to pursue the themes favorable to them. The East-West dialogue was to be continued in three major sessions. The most important one, on "Revolution and/or Reform: Their Influence on the History of Society," was to be chaired jointly by Joachim Herrmann and Carl Degler; it was hoped that the session might lead to a genuine dialogue between East and West. Besides, the Eastern European historians could also make themselves heard in the session on "The Organization of Labor," likewise chaired by Joachim Herrmann jointly with Pere Molas Ribalta (Spain), and, somewhat surprisingly, also at a round table on "Historical Biography" that was apparently agreed upon in honor of the East German Ernst Engelberg, who recently had published a magisterial biography of Bismarck. This biography had been hailed by GDR historians as a major breakthrough; in fact it constituted a partial deviation from the course of a rigid Marxist interpretation of Bismarck and his times, and it was fairly well received also in the West German press. Besides, a round table on "Results of the New Research on Treaties on the Eve of and During the Second World War" provided the opportunity to defend the orthodox Soviet view of the famous "Non-Aggression Pact" of 23 August 1939 between Hitler's Germany and the Soviet Union. This considerable number of themes would allow the Soviet historians and their allies to voice their views on many controversial historical issues before an international audience.

The Eastern European group had enough clout in the ICHS to demand that the General Assembly of the ICHS should issue a public declaration in favor of coexistence and détente between the world powers, in the same vein as a resolution that had been adopted five years earlier at the Congress in Stuttgart. But the ICHS was reluctant to enter the public arena with a declaration that appeared to be in line with official Soviet propaganda. After long negotiations it agreed to issue instead a somewhat softened declaration, to be published in the next *Bulletin d'information*, a rather remote location not likely to find much resonance in the media. This resolution was directed against the "endless arms race" and asked all historians to work for the maintenance of peace. As "the study and use of history" offered historians a "deeper understanding" of the threats to world peace, they were entitled to urge "all people with responsibility for the preservation of human value" to speak up in this sense.[1]

However, the ICHS apparently was not prepared to go all the way in this direction. Prominent members wished to come clear of these versions of historiography loaded with ideological prejudices. At the meeting in Athens, they pleaded for a far more wide-ranging approach to the past that transcended the comparatively narrow issue of Marxism-Leninism versus liberal democracy. Theo C. Barker suggested pursuing an altogether new, global project, namely, the political, social, and cultural significance of the Megapolis; that is to say, of the big urban conglomerations throughout history. This was "thematic history" not limited to particular ages or regions. It could be considered a theme that would bring into play not only different times and ages, but more so the different continents and cultures throughout human history. The "giant cities" that represent a "large sample of the last three thousand years of human history" as centers of political and economic power, hubs of cultural and religious activity, and capitals of great kingdoms and large territories, represent world history perhaps better than any other subject.[2] Rightfully, this topic was chosen as one of the "major themes" to be discussed in Madrid, and it certainly proved a major success.

Madame Hélène Ahrweiler, the secretary-general, was even more determined that the Congress should be opened to themes of global history. Supported by Natalie Zemon Davis, she suggested that the discovery of America by the Europeans be made a "major theme" at the Madrid Congress, for one because of the upcoming fourth centenary of Christopher Columbus's famous voyage, but above all because such a theme would provide a first-class opportunity to widen the scope of the proceedings beyond Europe. This would provide impetus for a new, worldwide orientation in the proceedings, notably the integration of Latin America and the non-European countries, instead of the Europe-centered orientation predominant in earlier Congresses. This was in line with the longstanding demand that the ICHS should overcome its traditional European-American orientation once and for all. These arguments met with general approval, and hence "The Discovery of America by the Europeans and Its Consequences" was selected as the first major theme. The president of the ICHS, Ernesto de la Torre Villar, was chosen as its chairman, thereby giving it particular weight.

It is worth mentioning that a substantial group of members of the General Assembly in Athens, among them György Ránki (Hungary) and Natalie Zemon Davis (United States), wished to see the classical range of methodological themes, which traditionally formed an essential part of the Congress programs, further expanded. Historical anthropology and social history should be given adequate space in the proceedings. To this end a plenary session was scheduled to discuss "Anthropology and Social and Cultural History" under the chairmanship of György Ránki and Valerii A. Tishkov, one of the important figures of Soviet historiography. As vice-president of the ICHS Ránki had played an important role in preparing the Madrid Congress. He died in 1988. Ivan T. Berend was invited by the Bureau to take his place.[3]

Even the sections on methodology, which always had been given particular weight at the International Congresses, were now at least in part geared to concern themselves with issues and problems transcending the confines of traditional Europe-centered historiography. Masaki Miyake's suggestion was welcomed that a "major theme" should be devoted to the notions of "time" in different cultures throughout history. There was also agreement that more should be done in the chronological sections to address the history of the non-European world. Among other themes, a session on "The Decline of the Ottoman Empire" was suggested because it touched upon the histories of three continents. M. S. Chandra went even further; he proposed a session on "National Consciousness, Unity and People's Movements in Asia and in Africa." A less prominent session was devoted to Immanuel Wallerstein's theory of "Centre and Periphery," as explanatory model of colonial expansion and imperialist exploitation in the nineteenth and twentieth centuries. Likewise, a considerable number of themes referring to the non-European world were given an important place in the chronological sections. It can be said that this general line was maintained in Athens and at the following meetings of the Bureau on 27–28 May 1988 in Madrid and on 21–24 September 1989 in Vienna, although there were numerous requests to also consider other themes, among them gender history and the origins and diffusion of science.

However, the effort to widen the scope of the agenda of the forthcoming Congress in Madrid and open it to both universal historical themes and extra-European topics was in part hindered by structural and financial difficulties. There existed one fundamental problem: representation in the ICHS of scholars from non-Western countries was comparatively weak; such scholars were a small minority even in those sessions that directly concerned their problems. It goes without saying that the Bureau had made considerable efforts to alter this situation; the issue had been raised again and again in Bureau meetings before Madrid. But many "Third World" countries lacked sufficiently institutionalized national committees, which according to the statutes are alone entitled to nominate scholars for participation in the Congresses. Lack of funds prevented many non-Western historians from participating, even though the ICHS managed to get some financial support from UNESCO and other foundations for this purpose.

The task of the Bureau, and in particular of the secretary-general, was a huge one indeed. By September 1989 it had received no fewer than 700 propositions for papers from the various national committees, respectively affiliated organizations; these had to be processed carefully.[4] At a meeting in Vienna on 24 September 1989, the secretary-general Hélène Ahrweiler pointed out with considerable satisfaction that this strong interest in participation signified the vitality of the International Committee of Historical Sciences. On this occasion Madame Ahrweiler also notified the Bureau that she would not be able to serve as secretary-general in the forthcoming five-year period; her proposal to nominate as her successor Prof. François Bédarida was unanimously accepted. The choice of Bédarida was a most fortunate one. He had formerly been a researcher at the Institut français of Great Britain at London, and later he had been director of the Maison française at Oxford. Accordingly he was well familiar with the Anglo-Saxon academic milieu. His research on contemporary history during his years at the CNRS in Paris had established him as an eminent scholar, all the more since he also had published treatises on various aspects of methodology of history. His fluency in several languages, his pleasing manners, and his forthright personality were undoubtedly assets to his new job. A competent administrator, and a skillful negotiator, and last but not least a hard worker, he established himself quickly as the key figure in running the affairs of the ICHS.

As for the organizational procedures of future Congresses, the ICHS explicitly empowered the *rapporteurs* of the various sessions to organize matters according to their discretion, the intention being that instead of numerous papers being read in full length only summaries should be presented, in order to save time for a lively discussion. Thereby the Bureau sought to remedy the old complaint that at the International Congresses there never had been sufficient time for interventions from the floor. Besides, the more loosely organized round tables were intended to enliven discussion. Theo C. Barker suggested that in addition, special sessions on issues of general interest should provide outstanding scholars with the opportunity to invite about six to seven younger scholars of their own choice, in order to enliven the proceedings and to rejuvenate the participants. However, this proposal did not generate any following. Such a procedure would have impaired the dominant influence of the various national committees on the program and the selection of speakers at the Congresses. Perhaps it ought to be reported also that Barker exhorted the Bureau to open the Congress's doors as much as possible to the outside world. In particular the Bureau should invite representatives of the media, especially television, to take part in the Congresses and to get interested in the activities of the ICHS, thereby strengthening the interest of the public in history. Accordingly considerable efforts were undertaken by the organization committees to ensure adequate press coverage of the inaugural sessions of the Congress for these purposes.

Under the honorary presidency of the King of Spain, the seventeenth International Congress of Historical Sciences was opened on 26 August 1990 in a solemn procedure in the "Ramón y Cajal" Amphitheater of the Medical Faculty of the University of Madrid. Miguel-Angel Ladero Quesada presented an inaugural paper on "The Hispanic Environment of Christopher Columbus," thus reminding the 3,000 historians present that some 400 years ago Columbus had discovered America, and hence had taken the first step toward opening up, to Europe, an altogether new world.

The general political climate affected the proceedings at the Congress in Madrid a great deal. By then the international situation had changed dramatically. The Soviet hegemony over East-Central Europe had vanished; communist regimes had given way to new ones that were on their way to establishing democratic systems of rule. So far the institutional arrangements of the ICHS had not been affected by these momentous events; at the organizational level business went on as usual. In the years to come the ICHS had to adjust its membership regulations in order to account for the new territorial divisions in Eastern Europe, but for the moment this was not thought to have any urgency. As yet there was no change of personnel; the representatives in the Bureau and the ICHS, and the speakers in the individual sections selected by the old regimes respectively by their national committees, were still for the most part around, as if nothing had happened. In actual fact, historians from the former Marxist-Leninist countries were more strongly represented in Madrid than ever before.

As was reported before, at the General Assembly in 1987 at Athens some prominent members of the ICHS had already wished to come clear of themes loaded with ideological prejudices; they had pleaded for a global approach to the problems of the past that transcended the comparatively narrow issue of Marxism-Leninism versus Democracy. Hence, the session of "Revolution and/or Reform" now was relegated to third place in the program. The first plenary session, chaired by the ICHS president Ernesto de la Torre Villar, was devoted to the topic "The Discovery of America by the Europeans and Its Consequences." It was a suitable starting point for the Congress proceedings: the immediate, but more so the long-term, impact of these discoveries in the years from 1492 to 1498 and beyond obviously has been far-reaching up to our own day. During the proceedings Brian Tierney (United States) explicitly referred to John Locke, who had located the origins of the idea of "human rights" in colonial America, with reference to the indigenous Indian population on this new continent: "In the beginning of all the world was America."[5] The interchange between Europe and its colonial dependencies in Africa on the one hand, the new territories in the Americas on the other, proved to be of utmost importance for the development of their colonial institutions.

In the second plenary session Theo C. Barker launched a project of truly universal scope, namely, the political, social, and cultural significance of the Megapolis in universal history. This topic brought into play not only many historical periods from Antiquity to the present, but also different continents and cultures throughout human history. This session certainly proved a major success. Barker had succeeded in recruiting a sizeable group of eminent scholars from various countries; the panorama presented here extended from studies on Ancient Rome and Constantinople to St. Petersburg and New York, and last not least to cities like Shanghai and Sao Paolo. It was absolutely fascinating. The papers have since been published in a separate monograph.[6]

The plenary session on "Revolution and/or Reform" provided many historians of the former Marxist-Leninist camp with the opportunity to defend their views, but to some degree the heat was off; many historians from Western countries no longer felt obliged to speak up on this issue. Historians from the Marxist-Leninist camp were in the majority in the session, and almost exclusively they talked about the role of revolution, or, as it were, revolutions in modern and contemporary history. It was a strange apotheosis of "revolution," notably of those varieties that Ernst Engelberg called "social or total revolutions." Joachim Herrmann reiterated once again the theories of Marx and Engels on revolution, but he conceded that revolutions might be caused not only by objective economic conditions, as orthodox Marxists would have it, but also by subjective factors. From this follows that it is necessary to take into account the time and circumstances under which revolutions come about: "Historical Materialism holds that causes, content, course of events and results of a revolution can only be evaluated by a comprehensive historical scientific analysis. The tension between objective factors of social existence—first of all

[the] conditions of production—and subjective factors embodied in associated man with his views etc. play the paramount role."⁷ Pavel V. Volobuev and N. A. Simona (USSR) argued in a more flexible way; they were ready to acknowledge that there exists a plurality of types of revolution throughout contemporary history. However, the Russian Revolution of October 1917 was a different matter; it was a unique event in world history: "The Great October Socialist Revolution in Russia is undoubtedly the main revolutionary event of the twentieth century. It was this revolution that brought about a drastic change of the direction and the course of world history by marking the beginning of the [!] new socioeconomic formation. The October revolution together with the following ones denoted the main tendencies of the world's social evolution, putting on the agenda the task of elimination of the exploiter society."⁸ On the other hand, Volobuev and Simonya conceded that revolutionary reforms were necessary even in socialist countries. The only sober and differentiated interpretation of revolution was presented by Manfred Kossock (GDR), who presented an interesting comparative analysis of revolutions in Europe and Latin America since the French Revolution of 1789. Jerzy Topolski (Poland) struck a new, interesting note by pointing to the "myth of revolution," that is to say a mystified interpretation of actual events by historians who tend to inflate the significance of particular forms of social or political change in the course of time, thereby creating myths that then may have a substantial impact upon the political process.

In his introduction, the co-chairman of the plenary session Carl Degler expressed his dissatisfaction with the reports, inasmuch as the original intention, namely, to compare revolutions with reform processes, had largely been missed: "None of the papers ... compared reforms, either across nations or time. Nor were revolutions compared with reforms though this had been implicit in the goal of comparison." Furthermore, the American Revolution had been given almost no attention at all.⁹ The session had been dominated by contributions from historians from communist countries. In a way, the debates had turned out to be the swan song of orthodox Marxist-Leninist historiography, at any rate of its Soviet variety. Jin Chongji from China, the last speaker, struck a somewhat more balanced note. He argued that in the Chinese case revolution and reform were intertwined, and more recently revolutionary change had given way to "radical transformations."

The session on "Results of the New Research on Treaties on the Eve of and During the Second World War" led to a heated debate about the historical background of the German-Soviet Non-Aggression Pact of 23 August 1939. A masterly survey by Donald C. Watt (United Kingdom) of the diplomatic negotiations on the eve of and during the first stages of the war triggered passionate controversy. Alexander O. Chubaryan and Mikhail M. Narinsky argued that because Poland had refused to enter into an alliance with the USSR, the Soviets had no real alternative but to conclude the ominous Non-Aggression Pact with National Socialist Germany. Besides, Moscow was acting on the assumption that the Allied Powers were actively organizing an anti-Soviet intervention; they, not

Germany, were considered the main counterrevolutionary force. Chubaryan and Narinsky maintained that according to the view of most Soviet historians, the Soviet-German Non-Aggression Pact could not be considered "a decisive step toward the unleashing of the Second World War." On the other hand, they were unsparing in their sharp criticism of Stalin, insofar as he had perceived Hitler "as a more reliable partner than France and Great Britain." During the debate Klaus Hildebrand (West Germany) and others set the record straight on these issues. It may be said that these debates eliminated many prejudices on all sides. However, following the collapse of the Soviet Empire in 1989 it was less urgent to take issue in this matter then had been assumed by the organizers. This outcome presumably would have pleased Karl Dietrich Erdmann, who unfortunately did not live to be present at this session.

The session on "Forward in Peace and Backward in War," chaired by L. N. Niejinski, pursued essentially the same route. It had been planned to provide historical proof that now war had been supplanted by the peaceful competition of various countries. Of course, there was by now wide approval of the observation "that the deliberate launching of a war could now no longer be justified."[10] This thesis had been argued already after the end of the First World War, and now it seemed to be beyond doubt. Few participants, if any, disagreed with the finding by Niejinski: "War is declining as an institution not because it has ceased to be possible or fascinating, but because peoples and leaders in the developed world—where war was once endemic—have increasingly found war to be disgusting, ridiculous, and unwise." However, the Swiss scholar Georg Kreis cautiously warned that the forecast that war would gradually disappear altogether actually was a residual notion stemming from the nineteenth-century idea of progress. It could not be considered a valid prognosis for the future.

The first Methodology session was devoted to "Concepts of Time in Historical Writings in Europe and Asia." It was an interesting idea to discuss the widely diverging notions of historical time held in different ages and different cultural traditions: in Antiquity, in ancient Chinese philosophy, in early Indian cosmography, in the European Middle Ages, in European thought from Friedrich Nietzsche and Oswald Spengler to Arnold Toynbee. The point of departure was the observation that whereas in Antiquity historical thought preferably was oriented by cyclical notions of historical time, with the emergence of historicism the unilinearity of historical time came to be the generally accepted view. But the session did not get much farther than a mere enumeration of various notions of historical time, except for the contributions by Jerzy Topolski, who differentiated between three different concepts of time with respect to "durations," in the work of the historian, and by Ernst Schulin (West Germany), who pointed out that the historic notion of historical time in fact goes back to the Enlightenment concept of "structured linear time."

More rewarding was the session on anthropology and ethnology. One might have expected that anthropological and ethnological approaches to past history are especially fruitful in dealing with issues of non-Western history. The *rapporteurs* presented a somewhat inconclusive report on the development of anthropological research. Very interesting were the papers by Hans Medick (Göttingen) and Natalie Zemon Davis, who elaborated the historiographical potential of analyzing small groups with respect to social environments via the methods of close inspection and "thick description." The "return of narrative" was accepted by the participants as a matter of fact; it was considered a vital component in the writing of social history. Ton Nijhuis (Netherlands) made an elaborate theoretical attempt to build a bridge between anthropological research and the tradition of historicist thought. He emphasized that meaning cannot be extracted only from the self-knowledge of the human beings involved in a historical process, as the historicists assumed. Historical narratives are meaningful only if they are written from the viewpoint of an observer who envisages the eventual outcome of a particular sequence of events.

These sections were supplemented by a series of other gatherings whose agendas cannot be reported here in full. There were altogether twenty-six different sections, often overlapping in time and sometimes in substance also. All in all they represented a very impressive panorama of international research in history. In addition, the Congress provided ample chances for intensive communication between scholars from different countries and different fields of research. The sessions prepared by the ICHS itself were supplemented by the programs of fifteen affiliated and six "internal" commissions, all operating in areas of specialized research. It was helpful that in Madrid the traditional arrangement, which had reserved two specific days of the proceedings for the meetings of the affiliated and internal commissions, had been discontinued; at previous Congresses this arrangement had resulted in substantial overlapping of many meetings. Hence, the program was indeed a very rich, exceedingly diversified one. Some of the commissions did their best to adapt their programs to the overall program of the Congress. The Commission on the History of Historiography arranged a major conference on "The Encounter between Western and Non-Western Historiography," which explored the emergence and development of historical studies in the "Third World" during the nineteenth and early twentieth centuries. This program was in line with the ICHS Bureau's declared intention to transcend its traditional Eurocentric orientation and to enlist the participation of historians throughout the whole world. However, again it proved very difficult to invite scholars from non-European countries, and not only because of pressing financial difficulties. Among others, Zhang Zhi-Llan reported on "Chinese Historiography and the West," Sumit Sarkar on Indian historiography, and Sartono Kartodirdjo on contemporary Indonesian history. A. A. Duri and Tarif Khalidi spoke about Arab historiography; Ebiegberi J. Alagoa, Mumbanza mwa Bawele, and A. J. Temu about recent African historiography.[11]

The Congress in Madrid was undoubtedly a great success. The proceedings were attended by 2,500 historians from fifty-six countries. The sessions had covered a wide range of topics. The Congress had demonstrated that international scholarship in historiography was alive and well, and that in recent decades it had broadened its approaches to the past in a spectacular way. Regrettably, the goal to turn the Congress into a genuine worldwide gathering had not been achieved in full, largely because of difficulties beyond the control of the Bureau of the ICHS. Even so, the historical profession had presented itself as an international community of note. The old rift between Marxist-Leninist and Western historians had lost its significance, and other issues, notably the conflict between North and South, and between the industrialized countries and the relatively underdeveloped regions of the world, had moved to the forefront. But it may well be said that the historians had moved much closer to the aim that had been the governing idea of Karl Dietrich Erdmann's work as president of the ICHS, namely, the emergence of an "ecumene" of the historical profession.

The meeting of the General Assembly of the ICHS on 30 August 1990 had to settle various organizational issues. The first business at hand was the choice of the location of the next Congress, for which several national committees were competing. After a lengthy, highly emotional debate, Montreal, Tokyo, Glasgow, and Jerusalem won in the first round of the ballot, and eventually Montreal succeeded with 38 against 15 votes for Tokyo. The next meeting of the Bureau was to take place in 1991 in Berlin, the next General Assembly in 1992 in Prague. The elections for the members of the new Bureau brought no great surprises. The Bureau had suggested an improvement in international representation; however, it did nothing about the consequences of the political changes that had taken place in Germany and the former Soviet Union. Theo C. Barker was elected as president, Ivan T. Berend and Eloy Benito Ruano as vice-presidents, and Alain Dubois as treasurer, whereas François Bédarida was chosen as the new secretary-general. Natalie Zemon Davis, J. Karayannopoulos, M. Miyake, and S. Nurul Hasan were elected or reelected as Bureau members. Alexander O. Chubaryan was chosen to replace Sergei L. Tikhvinsky; Joachim Herrmann, the chairman of the national committee of historians of the GDR, also was reelected to the Bureau, though the German delegation had expected his resignation because by that time the GDR had ceased to exist. The Bureau intended, on the occasion of its forthcoming meeting in Berlin, to inquire into the situation of historical scholarship in the Eastern part of Germany.

In a second meeting on 2 September 1990 in Madrid, at the very end of the Madrid Congress, the Bureau resolved that potential reform measures concerning such procedures of future Congresses as had been tabled by Theo C. Barker and Ivan T. Berend would be discussed at a future date. Perhaps there had been a few too many round tables, which were not always well prepared. Likewise it was suggested that the nomenclature of the "*Grand Thèmes*" (major themes) be abandoned and replaced by "Plenary Sessions." More important was that it was agreed to alter the future composition of the Nomination Committee. So far, new members of the Bureau often had been selected through cooptations rather than open elections. Therefore, it was suggested that perhaps the number of outside members ought to be increased.

On the afternoon of 2 September 1990, Theo C. Barker closed the Congress in Madrid in a festive final session. He expressed his deep gratitude to all those who had assisted in making the Congress a great success, especially the Spanish national committee and the Bureau of the ICHS. He also thanked Hélène Ahrweiler for her work as secretary-general in the last decade, and he invoked the memory of Karl Dietrich Erdmann, who had died on 23 June 1990 shortly after his eightieth birthday. His warm words reminded the audience of Erdmann's great achievements, for the ICHS and for historical scholarship in general.

New Methodological Departures: Montreal 1995

The Bureau repeatedly had voiced concern about the ICHS's uneven representation of historians around the globe. Indeed, during the preparations for Madrid this had been a major issue. Undoubtedly the program of the Congress in Madrid had been more universal than all previous ones; however, the European-American predominance among ICHS members and Congress participants could not be altered overnight. The Bureau decided to intensify its efforts to motivate historians in countries outside Europe and North America to take an active interest in the activities of the ICHS. One instrument of pursuing this goal was the arrangement of smaller conferences between Congresses, usually in conjunction with the regular meetings of the Bureau and the General Assembly. The Bureau hoped thereby to broaden its own horizons regarding the state of affairs in the historical profession in those regions of the world which so far had been little or not at all represented.

It was chiefly Theo C. Barker who advocated for extending the activities of the ICHS beyond the organization of the Congresses every fifth year. However, François Bédarida was not so enthusiastic about these plans. For one, preparing them would lay further heavy burdens on the secretary-general and his small office, with Marianne Ranson as his only permanent assistant. Given the scarce financial resources at the disposal of the ICHS, there were limits to these endeavors. It was not easy to find outside funding for such ventures. Bédarida was strongly supported by the treasurer Alain Dubois in his reluctance to follow Barker's propositions. As a rule, the ICHS could operate only in conjunction with a national committee willing to act as a host organization. But in some countries such committees did not exist at all or were financially too weak to support such gatherings. For this reason the plan to extend the operations of the ICHS to African, Asian, and Latin American countries ran into considerable difficulties from the start.

In a Bureau meeting in Stockholm on 30 and 31 August 1996, the issue was once again discussed at length. While there was general agreement that smaller conferences in between the Congresses were in principle an advantage, the question was raised of whether the ICHS should interfere in the affairs of historical scholarship in individual countries. Perhaps the ICHS ought to restrict its activities to stimulating discussion about important new issues, meanwhile relegating the organization to the respective national committees. Bédarida argued that the individual members in any case "must feel free" to take their own initiatives.[12] More important was the financial aspect. To be sure, the finances of ICHS were in any case rather precarious. It relied primarily on the annual fees of the national committees and the affiliated international commissions. But as the treasurer, Pierre Ducrey, pointed out, the contributions could not easily be raised much further, given the fact that many national committees were short of funds. The dues of a considerable number of national committees were in arrears, and from some the annual fees could not be obtained at all. Besides, the subsidies that the ICHS received from UNESCO via its subsidiary, the International Council for Philosophy and Human Sciences (ICPHS), were tenuous and could not be relied upon with certainty.[13]

At the moment, however, the problems in East-Central Europe appeared to be more pressing than extending the activities of the ICHS to overseas regions. As has already been mentioned, the Bureau of the ICHS accepted the invitation of the West German national committee, the Verband der Historiker Deutschlands, to hold the next meeting of the Bureau on 12 to 15 September 1991 in Berlin, on the comfortable premises of the Wissenschaftskolleg (Institute of Advanced Study) at Berlin-Grunewald. Thus, the members of the Bureau were given the opportunity to inform themselves first-hand about developments in the former German Democratic Republic. It goes without saying that many of them shared the widespread concern about the alleged "colonization" of East Germany by the West, not least in the field of historical studies. On this occasion a small conference was arranged in order to discuss the present situation of historiography in the Eastern part of Germany with historians from the former GDR, including Fritz Klein and Bernd Florath from the Verband der unabhängigen Historiker (Association of Independent Historians), which had been founded in 1988 by a group of young historians from East Germany as a counterpart to the official Historikergesellschaft der DDR (Historical Society of the GDR). For the West, Winfried Schulze read a paper on the current state of historiography in the former GDR. A reception held for the Bureau members by the Regierende Bürgermeister of Berlin was a suitable way of wrapping up the proceedings.[14] The conference had been informative, and apparently it had been most welcome.[15] It helped to eliminate misunderstandings about the situation of historical studies in East Germany after unification.

This example encouraged the Bureau to organize, on the occasion of the next meeting of the Bureau in Prague, a similar though more extensive conference on "Historiography in the Countries of Eastern Europe: A Critical Summary, Prospects for the Future, International Comparisons." It should provide the opportunity "to reflect upon the conditions of historical research, the liberty of the historian, and the achievements of the various sections of historiography."[16]

In Berlin the Bureau undertook a critical assessment of the activities of the ICHS and in particular the organization of the International Congresses. The president Theo C. Barker presented a memorandum on the organization and structure of the International Congresses, authored by him jointly with Ivan T. Berend with the heading "The State and Future of the ICHS."[17] It amounted to a fairly radical self-critique of the ICHS, which allegedly had become "very a sleepy" and cumbersome institution in need of "awakening."[18] No longer was there sufficient outreach to the younger generation of historians. The sessions at the Madrid Congress had not been lively enough: many of them had been given over to an endless sequence of not always well-orchestrated papers, leaving little if any time for discussion. In particular the plenary sessions came under attack for their frequent failure to reflect the most important current research trends in history. "Choice of speakers is often haphazard and the presentation at the Congress itself can be boring in the extreme, papers sometimes being read out in full in a dull monotone."[19] Neither did the plenary sessions provide younger historians, who were often the most productive researchers, with the opportunity to appear on the platform. The current rules did not allow younger scholars to participate easily in the proceedings. "Rejuvenation" was the battle cry voiced by Barker, and he suggested a number of measures in order to remedy these shortcomings.

It was decided to forward the memorandum by Barker and Berend to all the members of the General Assembly, which was about to be convened on 3 September 1992 in Prague. Any major changes would have to be worked out in any case by the General Assembly and not by the Bureau. This postponement also allowed careful preparation of any resolutions to be taken.

There was a genuine willingness to modernize the procedures of the ICHS, which admittedly so far had the features of a honorific organization whose structure allows only slow movement and modest change. The main problem was (and still is) that the Bureau depended to an exceedingly high degree upon the initiative and the suggestions of the national committees, and there was little the secretary-general could do about it if individual committees failed in their functions. Moreover, in a way the national committees operated as a filter that did not easily allow young scholars working in not yet fully established research fields to be nominated to contribute to an International Congress. In fact, for the secretariat it usually was (and is) a heavy burden anyway to permanently maintain communication lines with the national committees (in 1995 there were fifty-three in all). It cannot be said that Bédarida had not maintained close links with the various national committees: on the contrary, he had adhered to the principle of *"fertilisation réciproque,"* which required "a straightforward and frequent co-operation between the center and the periphery."[20] But all the same Bédarida adhered to a healthy skepticism as to the efficiency of the national committees. "Whereas many of them (let us say, between a quarter and a third) are active and cooperate well, a good number of them are passive, falling prey to apathy and silence, not to mention those which exist only on the paper."[21] Whereas the efficiency of the national committees varied, the Bureau was not all that powerful either. It could encourage certain themes for proposals by the committees, but apart from exceptional cases, it could not propose its own. Its main way of influencing the proceedings was the selection of themes from the wide range of topics suggested by the national committees and the affiliated commissions.

The program for Montreal signified a radical shift of emphasis away from political history to new research fields. The first "major theme" drew attention to the political conditions of the host country Canada as a multinational state: "Nations, Peoples, and State Forms." It provided the opportunity to discuss the problems of multinational states and of nation-building on a global scale, an issue that up to a degree reflected current Canadian problems. The second theme was to be "Gender History." This session grew to enormous proportions; eventually it had to be divided into four subsections. The third "major theme" was loosely linked to the first: a historical account of the destinies of the manifold peoples that were living in a situation of "diaspora." The other "major themes" were later scaled down to "specialized themes," among them "Power and Liberty: The Freedom of Publication for Historical Research," and an entirely new topic: "Old Age and Aging." In the specialized themes suggested in Berlin the old quarrels between West and East that had dominated at former Congresses still continued, though in diluted form. It is significant that the proposal to hold a session on "The Historical Reassessment of the Russian Revolution: 1917" had disappeared from the agenda altogether. Instead, themes of a worldwide dimension, with a strong emphasis on social-historical rather than political approaches, won the day. The decisions regarding the program signified a shift away from "history of events" (*Ereignisgeschichte, histoire événementielle*) toward a focus on processes of long-term change in social structures or mental dispositions, with a comparative intent.

Two days before the opening of the General Assembly in Prague, on 31 August and 1 September 1992, the ICHS organized a conference in Prague on "Historiography in the East and Historiography in the West since 1945: Comparisons, Results, Perspectives." It was intended to help Czech historians to reestablish contacts with Western historiography, but also to inform the members of the Bureau about the state of historical studies in East-Central Europe after the fall of the Soviet regime. A remarkably high number of scholars of the Bureau contributed papers. Aleksander Gieysztor spoke about medieval historiography in the East and West since the 1950s, Natalie Zemon Davis about women's history, François Bédarida about "History, Memory, and Identity," Alexander O. Chubaryan on the past and future of Europe. Wolfgang J. Mommsen reported on theories and realities of imperialism, and Marie-Elisabeth Ducreux from Prague presented a paper on cultural history. The conference ended with a magisterial paper by Dusan Kovác, the director of the Institute of History at the Academy of Sciences in Bratislava, on the Czech and Slovak nations and the reasons why the Slovaks had decided after all to secede from Czechoslovakia and establish their own nation-state. In this context the classic principle of cultural ethnicity was articulated in a surprisingly straightforward manner. The members of the Bureau could not but accept this somewhat unexpected turn of events. All the same, a lively and fruitful round table was held on "Central Europe" (or rather, East-Central Europe).

The General Assembly was opened on 3 September 1992 with addresses by Viktor Knapp, the vice-president of the Czechoslovak Academy of Sciences, and Vilém Prečan, the director of the Institute of Contemporary History at the Czech Academy of Sciences. Prečan recalled the difficult years of conducting historical research under communist dictatorship, and once again expressed his thanks to the international community of historians for the aid granted to the dissident historians of Czechoslovakia in 1975 in San Francisco. In addition, a round table was arranged on "The Reconstruction of Historical Studies in Czechoslovakia: Problems and Perspectives," with presentations by Prečan and Kovác. There was a general feeling of relief that a long period of suffering and suppression of free historical scholarship in the Czech Republic and Slovakia had come to an end for good. On the other hand, with the separation of the two nations a new divide had opened between the Czech and the Slovak peoples, resulting in a redefinition of both Czech and Slovak national histories, that was manifested in the presentation made by Kovác at the final session of the conference preceding the General Assembly.

The proposals adopted by the Bureau in Berlin were presented to the General Assembly by François Bédarida. The secretary-general's report was geared to an optimistic note. Bédarida emphasized that the activities of the ICHS secretariat had followed the directives that had been agreed upon by the Bureau in 1990 and 1991, pursuing a path that "combined tradition and innovation." Three objectives had been paramount: the need to keep up with a changing world, the drive for rejuvenation in order to bring in new blood and stronger intergenerational continuity, and lastly, improvement of the circulation and exchange of information, both between and during the Congresses. He referred explicitly to the memorandum by Barker and Berend and expressed his satisfaction with the positive changes in the ICHS's organizational structure, which had given the organization fresh opportunities to become a genuine international community: "Not only has the East-West dialogue become active and productive again, but historians of the whole world are being united by the fact that they share the same scientific requirements and standards."[22]

Indeed, the secretary-general had undertaken considerable efforts to intensify contacts with historians on a worldwide scale at the institutional, but also at the personal, level. He pointed out that the *Bulletin d'information*, which regularly reported on the activities of the ICHS, had been made more attractive to the public; the latest issue was to include informative essays on the history of the ICHS since the 1920s.[23] All the same, Bédarida also referred to the enormous obstacles that stood in the way of the ICHS developing into a genuinely international institution. The new developments in Eastern Europe necessitated establishing connections with newly founded national committees, among others those of Slovenia and the Baltic states, while Croatia and

Ukraine waited in the wings. Even more difficult was the situation in Africa and the Arab countries, and also in Latin America, whose countries were underrepresented largely because as yet no national committees had been established on a permanent basis.

Besides, the General Assembly generally approved the amended Constitution of the ICHS, which had been worked out by the treasurer Alain Dubois to facilitate an orderly handling of its business in the future. The mission of the ICHS, namely, "to promote the historical sciences through international cooperation," was defined more clearly than before: it should do so by defending the principle of freedom of speech and uninhibited exchange of views between scholars. "It shall defend freedom of thought and expression in the field of historical research and ensure the respect of professional ethical standards among its members."[24] Otherwise it regulated the voting procedures of the affiliated and internal commissions, as well as the nomination procedure for new members of the Bureau. A modest increase in the number of outside members of the nomination committee should ensure a greater degree of transparency without restraining the initiative by the acting members of the Bureau.[25] The number of outside members was increased to five, and they now outnumbered the representatives of the Bureau by one.

The Bureau meeting of 16 to 19 May 1993 in Montreal was largely concerned with technical problems in the preparations for the forthcoming eighteenth International Congress. The secretary-general reported that the Bureau had to choose from about 550 proposals for particular sessions and 60 for round tables, far more than could possibly be accommodated in the program. Furthermore, the necessity and also difficulties of widening the scope of participating nations were pointed out once again. Considerable efforts had been undertaken by individual members of the Bureau to rally South Africa, China, and South Korea to the ICHS, and also to secure the cooperation of a number of Latin American countries, in particular Brazil. As to the ex–member states of the USSR, the situation was not clear; the Polish representative Aleksander Gieysztor promised to take care of this issue and collect the necessary information. The meeting of the Bureau was combined with a special conference on "Actual Tendencies in Canadian Historiography," which was held at the University of Quebec on 19 May 1993.[26]

At the next meeting of the Bureau, which took place from 8 to 11 September 1994 in Lausanne, the president Theo C. Barker presented a rather optimistic perspective regarding the forthcoming Congress in Montreal; it had been possible to recruit a most promising group of scholars for the sessions, and also for a substantial number of round tables. However, he again expressed his concern that so far the ICHS had not quite found the response to its activities in the international arena that he deemed necessary. Somewhat surprisingly, he suggested discontinuing the longstanding tradition that the secretariat always be located in France; perhaps the duties of the secretary-general ought to be divided instead between an administrative secretary and a general secretary whose task would be to focus on coordinating communication between the ICHS and leading historians in other countries, thereby establishing a worldwide network. However, these proposals were found to be impractical.

In the previous months tensions had arisen between Theo C. Barker and François Bédarida concerning the opening session of the Congress in Montreal. Barker suggested that in order to reach a wider audience for the activities of the ICHS, a film should be shown about the history of the twentieth century and its significance for the present. Bédarida was lukewarm to this suggestion. He doubted whether historians would be at all interested in such a "synthetic panorama of the twentieth century." It might be better to approach this theme from a particular viewpoint, for instance, the ways in which history had been instrumentalized by statesmen.[27] Eventually the Bureau agreed to prepare a video presentation of prominent public figures with interviews about their views on history and the historical profession. Interviews were planned with the French president François Mitterand, the economist and longstanding adviser to the British government Sir Alec Cairncross, the Polish historian and politician Bronisław Geremek, and the president of the South African Republic Nelson Mandela.[28] Bédarida managed to arrange the interview with Mitterand, and Barker did the same with Cairncross. Bédarida wrote a passionate letter to Geremek seeking his approval: "You who have the twofold experience of writing history and of making history are better qualified than anybody else to give first-rate testimony to the about 2,000 historians from all over the world who will assemble in Montreal.... [Y]ou will be the only voice combining scholarship and action and coming from the ex-communist world."[29] With the help of Aleksander Gieysztor Geremek was recruited, although in the form of a statement by Geremek, not as an interview as planned. The negotiations with Mandela eventually failed, and Bédarida decided (apparently on his own) to ask the Director General of UNESCO, Federico Mayor, instead. Initially these video interviews were to be supplemented by a panel discussion.[30] Later, the panel discussion was dissociated from the interviews; instead, it would discuss the significance of the twentieth century from a historian's viewpoint.

Theo C. Barker had placed the greatest hopes on this opening performance, and he wished to edit the videotapes himself. However, Bédarida did not agree to this, and neither was he prepared to accept that Barker should have the exclusive responsibility for arranging the inaugural session. Barker, on the other hand, suspected that the secretary-general had not done his utmost to realize the ambitious video project, which was in line with his far-reaching visions of the impact the Congress should have upon the public. There emerged a serious rift between both personalities that eventually was bridged again, in part thanks to an intervention by Ivan T. Berend. Barker retreated from his position and apologized to the secretary-general,[31] whereas Bédarida, having Ivan T. Berend and Alain Dubois on his side, eventually allowed the conflict to be dropped.[32] In substance, the clash between Barker and Bédarida reflected of two conflicting visions of the role of the ICHS vis-à-vis the public: Bédarida sought to organize this Congress as efficiently as possible while abstaining from pursuing any ulterior objectives; Barker intended to use it as an instrument in order to open up new public territories for historical thought.

On 27 August 1995 the eighteenth International Congress of Historical Sciences was opened at the Palais de Congrès in Montreal. The secretary-general François Béderida proposed that the Congress proceedings ought to be guided by three fundamental principles: universality, responsibility, and truth. He warned against a merely moralizing historiography, but likewise against a Machiavellian historiography reduced to *Realpolitik*. "History is a humanistic discipline and must remain so."[33] Contrary to some current tendencies to turn historiography into a "fiction-making operation," the principle of searching for the truth must be maintained throughout, because only in this way could its fundamental function as a scientific discipline be maintained.

In honor of the opening of the Congress, the video interviews that had been the cause of so much dispute were shown on screen, François Mitterand in an interview with François Bédarida, Sir Alec Cairncross with Theo C. Barker, the interview with Federico Mayor, and a video-recorded statement by Bronisław Geremek.[34]

President Mitterand found rather friendly, if noncommittal, words for the historians. He described in some detail the role that history had played in his own upbringing and in his early career as a politician. He agreed with Bédarida on the responsibility of historians in the present world. "The historians' theories carry a lot of weight for men like myself." In society the historian has "une sorte de magistère" (a position of high authority).[35]

Sir Alec Cairncross emphasized that the knowledge of history provides, above all, a sense of perspective, although it contains no recipes for future action: "as a discipline history is invaluable to somebody who is a political adviser.... [I]f you are advising on policy, it's no use doing it in a vacuum not knowing what has been going on. You really have to look back and have a sense of how things are shaping when you are putting forward your advice."[36] Cairncross then debated with Theo C. Barker on why historians are rarely asked to advise governments even though historical orientation is badly needed in the decision-making processes. Cairncross argued somewhat defensively that historians often are not sufficiently up-to-date with current developments.

Federico Mayor was somewhat more forthcoming in his statements: "History is of great importance for the formulation of our plan for the future." Historians "are the guardians of the past, and their help is needed for creating a more peaceful future world."[37] These statements did not necessarily live up to the expectations that had been harbored by Barker and Bédarida. Most impressive, however, was the message by Bronisław Geremek. The search for the truth as a fundamental directive had not only affected his own earlier work in history, but also his life as a political figure. In the course of his involvement in the struggle of Solidarnosc with the authorities, particularly during the famous Gdansk strike, he became acutely aware of the power of history, of "true history." The truth about the past could, and did, possess a subversive potential in confrontation with ideologies and totalitarian rule. Besides, for the active politician the experience of the historian can evoke a more humble mentality vis-à-vis politics, notably regarding the present-day actions of the politicians. "The historian may not be the bringer of hope—often he is subjected to grand deceptions himself, but the lessons of history are all the same lessons of hope."[38]

These presentations were followed by a panel discussion on the functions and future of the ICHS. Under the chairmanship of Theo C. Barker, the panel members were Ivan T. Berend, Ida Blom (Norway), Jürgen Kocka, and Eugène Weber. This was undoubtedly an impressive opening ceremony.[39]

Perhaps it was a symptom of the changed intellectual climate in the historical profession that at the Congress in Montreal "decline" and "decadence," not "modernization" and "progress," served as predominant paradigms of analysis. A new pensive mood prevailed that was prepared to inspect the past with a dispassionate approach rather than with political zeal. Certainly political issues were not left aside, but they were mostly discussed in a rather detached manner, something that had not been the case at previous Congresses. The comparative perspective was paramount.

The first session was devoted to a wide-ranging analysis of "Nationalism and the Nation-State," accompanied by presentations on "Minorities in the Diaspora" and reflections on the "Fall of Empires." A "major theme" was devoted to the problems of gender history and masculine versus feminine relations, both from the viewpoint of methodology and as a substantive object of historical inquiry. Likewise, the state of "Oral History" was given considerable attention. In the methodological sessions the dichotomy of political versus social historiography no longer maintained the prime importance it had once enjoyed at former International Congresses. Instead the problems of "fictionality" and "myth" in historical writing had moved to the top of the agenda, and in connection with them the issue of "objectivity" of historical writing. Only the session on "Power, Liberty, and the Work of the Historian" continued, however indirectly, the earlier discussions between Marxist-Leninist and Western historians, but it now took on the form of a sort of retrospective analysis. Many historians who had lived under totalitarian regimes in the past now exercised a sort of self-criticism, though perhaps in a rather mild fashion. It was acknowledged without any ado that under totalitarian rule, as Alexander O. Chubaryan put it in his report, "a significant number of researchers" had "willingly agreed to serve the regime and to prepare works to please the authorities."[40] But he also spoke about the prevailing "soft conformism," that is to say, the preparedness of historians "to adapt to an official line." "Although unwilling to serve power openly, they were keen on catching the upper strata's moods and attitudes carefully." However, Western historiography was not spared from criticism of this kind either, inter alia with regard to the policies of political orthodoxy or strategies of "political correctness" practiced by American university administrations. Besides these, a variety of themes on social history were offered, for instance, a "major session" on "Old Age and Aging" and a session on "Childhood in History," topics with a broad appeal to a variety of audiences. Finally, the still nascent field of "Environmental History" was given attention, not least because it paved the way for a return to macrohistory.

The first major theme, "Nations, Peoples, and State Form," was introduced by François Bédarida and Nicolas Roussellier (France). They presented a wide-ranging treatise on the meanings and emotions associated with the notions of "nation," "ethnicity," "nation-state," and "national identity" throughout history and in different regions of the globe. The *rapporteurs* argued that since the end of the Cold War and the dismemberment of the Soviet system, as well as the dissolution of the colonial empires and their frontiers, the nation-states had been stabilized again, if only up to a point. Among historians and politicians alike the opinion prevailed that the time of the nation-state was over and new federalist structures were on the ascendancy. However, they asked, why, contrary to the widespread talk about the alleged agony of the nation-state, was the nation still the most stable support of political power?

The question was raised when the nation-state actually came about. Was it, as Eric Hobsbawm and Ernest Gellner had argued, a phenomenon of the nineteenth and twentieth centuries, or did its origins reach back much farther in time, at least to the High Middle Ages? The contributions to the session from which Bédarida and Roussellier could draw their arguments indeed had made clear that during the medieval and early modern periods, nations and nationalism did not yet exist in the contemporary understanding. National identities, though, informed and influenced by specific cultural traditions and, still more often, by language and religion, have been around throughout history in a great many variants, not only in the Occident, but also in other regions of the globe. On the basis of these papers Bédarida and Roussellier presented a masterful analysis of the great variety of concepts of "nation" in different political and cultural settings. They singled out as particularly important the Central European notion of a "nation" defined by ethnic and cultural criteria, and the Western European state-oriented notion of "nation," which found its classic expression in Ernest Renan's writings. Bédarida and Roussellier went on to argue that whereas the great multiethnic empires of the past apparently were bound to collapse, this had not necessarily resulted in the strengthening of the nation-state. On the contrary, the nation-state had not been stabilized at all by the breakdown of the multinational empires. Bédarida and Roussellier referred to recent cases of the deconstruction of well established nation-states like Belgium and, as it were, of Canada, in favor of federalist structures that give leeway for a plurality of national entities within one and the same state; that is to say, classical nation-states may disintegrate into diverse nations or even nation-states just as well as the multinational empires. From this observation they concluded that national identities are very much alive under different social and political conditions, and also on different societal levels, and that they are constituted by a multitude of factors, among which ethnicity may not necessarily be the dominant one.

The second major theme, that on "Gender History," or rather the history of male and female relations throughout history, was divided up into four subsections. In the methodological section Yolande Cohen (Canada) argued with passion that in the wake of the collapse of the great ideological empires, gender studies came at the right moment as an alternative to traditional, ideology-oriented political history in that gender historians walked new methodological paths that have little in common with conventional national histories. Gender history stands for a historiography less distanced from its objects, closer to the lives, work, and everyday concerns of people. Through empathy gender historians are capable of apprehending the particular truth of their objects far better than conventional historiography. Cohen went so far as to claim that the papers presented in her section must be understood as contributions to a renovation of historiography through gender studies.

In its claim that there cannot be such a thing as objective truth, but only a plurality of historical insights, gender historiography comes close to the theories of poststructuralism. Deborah Gray White and Eileen Boris (United States) and Mary O'Dowd (Northern Ireland), to mention just a few contributors, demonstrated that gender history had moved far beyond being merely a "women's history." This point was argued even more stringently in the third subsection, introduced by Francisca de Haan (Netherlands). She took as starting point the assertion that by now "gender" had been acknowledged "as a fundamental category of history." She pinpointed one aspect, namely, the importance of overcoming the traditional viewpoint that concentrates on the question of how the lives and mentalities of women were shaped by historical events. The case studies of this subsection pursued an alternative path, namely, to ask in which respects general historical developments had been substantially influenced by women. They dealt inter alia with the impact of family farming on industrialization, the role of women in the welfare-state systems, and female-dominated family life in the context of the formation process of national identities. The positions of these historians varied considerably, not only in the details, but also as to the degree to which they required a radical "re-writing" of "traditional history" from a feminist point of view. On the other hand, there was general agreement that "the full potential of gender as an analytic category will not be realized until the masculinity of male historical subjects is also problematised and investigated."[41] For a segment of the history of Prussia, namely, the Prussian uprising against Napoleon Bonaparte from 1806 to 1815, Karen Hagemann did just that: she showed that the cult of masculinity during the Franco-Prussian war was an important ingredient of the nascent German national consciousness.

Far less controversial was the report on new developments in "Oral History" by Philippe Joutard (France). He provided a most informative survey on the contribution of oral history to the study of contemporary history. However, the debate between those oral historians who believe in the immediacy of their documents, and those who want to have them subjected to rigorous scientific scrutiny, seems to go on unabated. Indeed, it is an open question whether, in the public mind, powerful documents of oral history like those giving testimony of the Holocaust are about to take over altogether from traditional historiography in ascertaining the historical remembrance of such momentous events in contemporary history—to the detriment of regular historical research.

The session on "Fictionality, Narrativity, Objectivity (History and Literature, Historical Objectivity)" addressed the theoretical status of historiography in response to the challenge from Hayden White and the so-called linguistic turn in the literary disciplines. Historiography as a narrative is subject to the principles valid in the literary arts. This is to say that the specificity of a historical account is determined in each individual case by a particular mode of linguistic presentation. Given the plurality of possible linguistic modes that are in principle equally applicable, how is scientific objectivity still possible? The speakers' answers varied, but they all agreed that the acceptance of fictionality as an essential element of all narrative presentations does not necessarily imply that the link between historical observation and the objects is severed altogether. The narrative structure of historical reasoning, though involving fictionality as an essential component, does not necessarily mean that empirical reality is lost from sight. As Roger Chartier (Paris) put it, narrative constructions aim at reconstructing a past that really was. Thus, reference to a reality "pre-existing the historical text and situated outside it, of which the text has the function of producing an intelligible account, cannot be abandoned by any of the various forms of historical knowledge."[42] Accordingly historians are adamant about maintaining the principle of objective research based upon analysis of their sources. However, as Jörn Rüsen argued persuasively, they have to realize that "history as a cultural entity, as a specific representation of the past is constituted by mental operations" belonging to our own day, and not something outside of ourselves objectively given. "It has to be created, guided by the cultural value-system of the historians."[43] Hence, this session ended on a hopeful note, confident that history would not be thrown off its tracks by postmodern deconstructionist theory.

The debates that we have reported on so far dealt with key issues of international historiography after the end of the world's great divide between two ideological camps, the Soviet system and Western democracy. But the Congress proceedings also covered a great many other themes that can be mentioned here only in passing. The section on "Old Age and Aging" under the chairmanship of Paul Johnson (United Kingdom) tackled a theme of universal significance, relevant for many different cultures and times; from this point of view it was an ideal topic for an international congress of the historical sciences. Whereas "old age" had very different meanings in different historical time-frames, more recently the threshold of age seems to have come down slowly from the mid seventies to the sixties. Retirement as a retreat from active work was common in all ages, but in premodern societies everybody was expected to work until physical incapacity. Likewise, the social welfare systems expected workers to carry on working, regardless of age, until incapacity or sickness prevented them from doing so. The process of "aging"—rooted in demographic pressures in play in most societies—was associated with a growing awareness of the "aged" as a particular social group. Historians are divided as to whether there was a decline in the readiness of acceptance of the aged in society. Up to now the view has been widely held that in ancient times the social prestige of the aged was very high; however, as Pat Thane (United Kingdom) argued, it is rather the contrary that is true. With "age" about to become a major problem in all Western welfare systems, this theme deserves further investigation.

Another theme that has more recently attracted a considerable degree of attention was the relationship of "War and Culture" in Western history. Since Modris Eckstein's *Rites of Spring* and Paul Fussel's *The Great War and Modern Memory* the cultural dimensions of war and warfare have been made the subject of new departures in historiography. Under the chairmanship of Wolfgang J. Mommsen this issue was discussed in considerable detail by a multinational group of historians of different time spans. Two lines of approach were singled out as being of particular significance: first, war as a means of imposing a particular culture, as a rule closely associated with a religious faith, upon peoples to be subjected by force; second, war as an instrument for revitalizing high culture in situations of stagnation and petrification of cultural life.

Intellectuals and artists have been known to act as inventors and propagators of the national idea, and, still more often as proponents of war as an instrument for attaining national unity or, increasingly so, for extending the power position of one's own nation on the globe. After the so-called *fin de siècle*, another motive gained momentum as well, namely, that war, in embodying masculine values, imposing an ascetic, heroic life-style upon human beings, and demanding from them all their potential, would bring about a new, revitalized European culture that would replace the existing sterile, self-satisfied, materialistic bourgeois culture that allegedly had become devoid of all ideal content. The various avant-garde movements throughout Europe began to embrace war as a way to overcome the cultural stagnation they purported to suffer from. The Italian Futurists were the first to hail war as a force through which the solidified cultural life of their own day might be revitalized. Filippo Tommaso Marinetti revealed the "heroic apocalypse" of war as a way to provide innovative artistic and literary impulses as well as inject new vitality into the body politic of Italy. In other European countries these new ideas were taken up, though not with the same radicalism. Vitalism and symbolism began to praise the idea of war—initially merely in idealistic terms, but this soon spilled over into the political arena. In 1914 in most belligerent countries, a self-mobilization came about among the intellectuals and artists in favor of the war efforts of their own nation.

The conflict between those who opt, in the name of their own national culture, for war, or at any rate for violence, and those who tend to oppose the mighty can be observed even in our own day. Yves Brossart (Canada) demonstrated this in Montreal by describing the public career of Dimitrii Schostakovich and his dealings with the Soviet authorities during the Cold War. Jay Winter (United Kingdom), in his turn, pointed out that during and after war, cultural elites play an important role in providing language for the emotions of grief and mourning. In this respect culture relates to war in another, fundamentally humane way, deeply affecting the lives and memories of the men and women who live through war and communicate the experience of war to future generations.

The closing speech of the Congress in Montreal was presented by the Polish scholar and UNESCO representative Jerzy Kloczowski on "Historians and Culture."[44] He encouraged the ICHS to proceed with the work it had engaged in since its very beginnings after the First World War, namely, to promote understanding between the various nations of the world. Aware that modern war would be capable of destroying the world, historians associated with the ICHS Congresses in Oslo 1928 and in Warsaw 1933 had been determined to represent the conscience of humanity and belief in international law in the face of rising nationalistic tendencies. Their heritage deserved to be honored and continued by the work of today's historians. It would appear necessary to "disarm" the traditional historiography of war, violence, and nationalism and instead to create a new history of humanity, a genuine global history comprising men and women of all races and religions alike, born on all continents.[45]

Theo C. Barker, the outgoing president, had every reason to call the Congress in Montreal a great success and to praise the liveliness of the proceedings. Important business was handled at the second meeting of the General Assembly of the ICHS in Montreal on 31 August 1995 and the Bureau meeting immediately following the Congress on 3 September 1995, including a comprehensive account of the current state of ICHS affairs by the outgoing president. In his farewell message Barker strongly praised the achievements of the secretary-general, but at the same time he regretted that the ICHS had not, as had been suggested before, launched "some highly publicized panel debates on historical topics" in the years between the Congresses, with the purpose of promoting public interest in the study of history. He also suggested that English should be used alongside the French language throughout the activities of the ICHS, intimating that the predominant role of French was perhaps a cause of the still far too Eurocentric orientation of the ICHS.

The secretary-general François Bédarida struck a different note in his report. He pointed out that the activities of the ICHS had been intensified considerably, and that there had been continuous enlargement, although the membership from non-Western regions of the world still left much to be desired. The treasurer Alain Dubois supported this view. In his financial report he showed that the finances of the ICHS had improved a good deal. Although a substantial number of national committees were still in arrears with their payments, the ICHS now was—as he put it with his usual modesty—"in a slightly more comfortable financial position." Dubois received high praise for the responsible work he had done for the ICHS for so many years.

In the end, the controversy about the use of English rather than French was left undecided, whereas the thorny issue of whether the secretary-general should always be a French scholar was not even raised publicly. Most important was the election of the new Bureau in accordance with the proposals of the Nomination Committee. Ivan T. Berend (Hungary/United States) was elected president and Natalie Zemon Davis and Alexander Chubaryan (Russia) vice-presidents, whereas François Bédarida (France) was retained in his office as secretary-general. The job of treasurer was assigned to Pierre Ducrey (Switzerland). The new assessor members were Girolamo Arnaldi (Italy), Jürgen Kocka (Germany), Ravinder Kumar (India), Hiroyuki Ninomiya (Japan), Eva Österberg (Sweden), and Jean-Claude Robert (Canada). According to a well-established custom, Ernesto de La Torre Villar (Mexico) and the outgoing president Theo C. Barker (Great Britain) were retained as counsellors-members and Aleksander Gieysztor (Poland) as honorary counsellor.

The composition of the new Bureau was certainly as international as could be hoped for, although non-Western countries still were underrepresented. During his turn as first vice-president, Ivan T. Berend had already familiarized himself with the activities of the ICHS, so continuity was assured from the start. A Hungarian scholar who now held a position at UCLA, Berend was himself a model international scholar. He had started his career at the Eötvös Lóránd University in Budapest and earned there a high reputation as an economic historian specializing in East-Central Europe. More importantly, long before the fall of the Soviet system he jointly with György Ránki had established close links with Western scholarship, thereby earning a high reputation for Hungarian academia in the West. For his work he had been honored with Fellowships at St. Antony's and All Souls College in Oxford, as well as membership in a remarkable number of international academies, last but not least the Academia Europea. In sum, he was renowned as one of the leading experts on the economic and social history of Central and Eastern Europe.

After a heated debate, Oslo was chosen over Beijing and Jerusalem as the venue for the next Congress in 2000. Neither Beijing nor Jerusalem could qualify in the end; a majority still considered the hurdles in arranging an international gathering in one of these locations to be too high. The ICHS was ready for a new period of work, and the auspices for further augmentation of its international activities were, as François Bédarida pointed out in his closing message, good. He had every reason to be satisfied; the press coverage of the Montreal Congress had been very positive, not least regarding the role of French scholars.[46]

Oslo 2000

The Bureau of the ICHS met again in Stockholm on 30 and 31 August 1996. In the meantime the Bureau had received a detailed report about the Montreal Congress from the Canadian organizing committee; it was praised by the secretary-general François Bédarida "as a priceless reference and work tool for the history of the ICHS and for future organizers." On this basis an evaluation of the Congress in Montreal was undertaken. The objective of "rejuvenation" had been achieved in part. However, the attempts to involve scholars from Asia, the Middle East, and Africa had not been very successful. More important was the reassessment of the proceedings undertaken by the Bureau. The statement by the secretary-general was comparatively harsh; he argued that the program with its 274 papers, "despite its substantial content lacked theoretical thought." In the future an effort should be made to include more epistemology and theory. Other members of the Bureau thought that the round tables had not always lived up to ICHS standards; some round tables had been rather like specialized themes. Accordingly there should be fewer of them.

A controversial debate developed over the question of whether the ICHS should continue to run smaller conferences between the Congresses in order to mobilize interest and support in various regions of the globe, notably non-Western countries. There was general agreement that smaller conferences in between the Congresses were in principle desirable. However, it was doubted whether the ICHS should interfere with the affairs of historical scholarship in individual countries. Perhaps the ICHS ought to restrict its activities to stimulating discussion about important new issues in individual countries or regions, while leaving the responsibility of organizing conferences on these issues to the respective national committees. Bédarida objected to the proposal to arrange such conferences, notably in the overseas world; he, the secretary-general, had only "a limited capacity and could not, in any way, run all these projects."[47] Besides, he pointed out, the rights of the members must be respected. In any case they "must feel free" to take their own initiatives.[48] Catherine Coquery-Vidrovitch was skeptical as to whether the "occidental centralism" of the ICHS could be overcome by such pre-conferences.

Furthermore, Ducrey objected to these projects on financial grounds. In fact, the finances of the ICSH were rather precarious. It relied largely on the membership dues of the national committees and affiliated international commissions. The subsidies that the ICHS received from UNESCO via the "International Council for Philosophy and Human Sciences" (ICPHS) were tenuous and could not be relied upon with certainty. Theo C. Barker, however, was unrepentant. "He recommended leaving no stone unturned in the search for the outside funding needed to organize pre-conferences."[49]

More important was the issue of whether the ICHS should suggest themes and nominate speakers on its own, rather than working through the slow and cumbersome machinery of the national committees. After some discussion agreement was reached that the traditional procedures should not be changed fundamentally. However, following a proposal by the president, Ivan T. Berend, a Selection Committee consisting of François Bédarida, Jürgen Kocka, and Eva Österberg was asked to screen all incoming proposals. This committee took on the heavy burden of designing a scientific program for the next Congress on the basis of various proposals that had reached the ICHS secretariat. At its first meeting in Paris in March 1997, it drew up a provisional list of all the sessions and speakers to be presented to the next General Assembly, which was due to be held at Spoleto, Italy, on 1 and 2 September 1997.

The General Assembly at Spoleto discussed the proposals of the Selection Committee in considerable detail. In this context objections were raised from the floor against the procedure of selecting themes and/or speakers, which some members of the Assembly considered to be handled largely "from above." The national committees and affiliated commissions were all-important, whereas proposals from the rank and file had but a small chance of being accepted. Besides, the number of female scholars in the ruling bodies of the ICHS ought to be augmented. After a controversial debate it was agreed that the established ICHS rules were to be upheld; however, the Bureau declared that in the future the proposals ought to be published early on, via the Internet, so as to make it possible to take into account proposals by the membership at large. With this proviso the proposals by the Selection Committee were approved with only minor alterations. The Selection Committee was asked to carry on with its work and to present in due course a list of themes and speakers, balanced in its themes and geographical regions, in collaboration with the Norwegian organization committee.

Even Lange, the chairman of the Oslo organization committee, presented a detailed report on the planning for Oslo and the envisaged structure of the proceedings of the Congress. It should comprise no more than three sessions on "major themes" and twenty sessions on specialized ones, whereas the round tables should be limited to twenty. The proceedings should be organized in a more flexible way and the number of speakers be reduced to three or four, not, as had been the case so far, seven or eight. It was agreed that the Selection Committee should be entitled to ask individual scholars for contributions to particular sessions rather than always to have to operate in conjunction with the respective national committees. Above all it was held to be of utmost importance to find first-rate chairmen for the sessions, and to grant them authority to communicate directly with the respective speakers.

The first problem was that the national committees rarely replied to the secretary-general's requests in time; the final time limit for delivery of thematic proposals had been overstepped or neglected by many of them. Bédérida remarked sarcastically: "Unfortunately discipline is not among the principle qualities of our members."[50] The Selection Committee or, as Bédarida called it occasionally, the "Troika," worked hard to come up with a coherent list of proposals for the forthcoming Congress. On 23 November 1997 Bédarida, Österberg, and Kocka met for an intensive working meeting in Paris. The task was to find a "balance between [the] nations and regions of the world" and to try to increase the number of younger scholars, and that of women.[51] Even more difficult was culling a plausible list of themes from no fewer than 465 propositions. The Selection Committee was intent on integrating as many topics suggested by national committees as possible. In some cases this was done by amalgamating similar themes into a single one, although at times this strategy led to a diffuse handling of the topic in question, as was the case in the section on historiography chaired by Georg Iggers, who had been asked to tackle also the issue of the "responsibility of the historian," a theme close to Bédarida's heart. These decisions likewise included the—still preliminary—choice of chairmen, co-coordinators, conveners, and discussants. The Selection Committee felt free to deviate from the existing proposals, notably with regard to possible chairmen for the "major sessions," and in doing so in some cases its members relied on their own judgement and their knowledge of the field. The result was most satisfactory; after the meeting Bédarida drew up a final list of themes on which the Selection Committee had agreed.[52] A few days later Bédarida wrote to Berend: "We have worked hard, Eva, Jürgen, and I, the whole of last Sunday, for the choice of organizers and discussants. There were more than 480 proposals."[53] In another meeting in March 1998, the Selection Committee finalized the roster of organizers and discussants.

It might be argued that the creation of the Selection Committee could eventually mitigate the influence of the national committees and affiliated commissions, whose representatives have the exclusive right to suggest themes and to select organizers and speakers. However, proposals by the Selection Committee always require the approval of the General Assembly, which in this case was given with but a few minor amendments. It was a remarkable achievement to assemble a scheme of possible themes as a basis for an orderly process of decision from a huge quantity of often uneven and inhomogeneous proposals, and it could never have been brought about by one person alone.[54] Besides, Bédarida always relied on the advice of a small group of trusted personal friends and colleagues (who sometimes were members of the Bureau) to help him prepare the meetings of the Bureau or the General Assembly. As a rule he asked Natalie Zemon Davis to supply him with correct English titles for the themes in question, and he often accepted her advice in other matters. In Eastern-European matters Gieysztor was always at hand, and in later years "Sascha" Chubaryan. Catherine Coquery-Vidrovitch supplied information and assistance concerning African affairs. Undoubtedly Bédarida was delighted with the smooth and efficient cooperation with Jürgen Kocka and Eva Österberg; accordingly the "ad hoc Committee" (as it had been called in the files initially) became a permanent institution bound to assist an overburdened secretary-general in preparing the basis for the selection of themes and speakers. It helped that the issues at stake were less controversial than in the preparation of previous Congresses; politics were not as prominent on the agenda as in the 1980s.

Thanks to the efficient work of the Selection Committee and the Norwegian organizing committee, the program for Oslo was ready for presentation at the next Bureau meeting in Oslo from 20 to 22 June 1998, in a more or less definite form. The Oslo Congress was scheduled for 6 to 13 August 2000. The Norwegian organizing committee was planning to make all papers available to the participants before the Congress, on CD ROM and in printed form, including abbreviated versions of the contributions by the orators. It had entered upon intensive correspondence with all historians in question, making use of the Internet as a convenient and speedy means of communication. However, the communication process did not want for frictions, including those with North American historians who wanted to forward their proposals en bloc, and with some members who doubted whether forwarding abstracts of papers more than two years ahead of actual delivery would work in the end. But everything was arranged successfully, although ultimately, in spite of the endeavors of the organizers, many papers did not arrive in time to be published beforehand.

These activities had resulted in a substantial increase of the business of the general secretary, as François Bédarida pointed out: "The world is changing, so are the mechanisms and techniques of scientific life. We have advanced far from the 'artisanal' era of Michel François."[55] Since 1997 the correspondence of the Secretariat had quadrupled. Indeed, the ICHS had outgrown the stage of being an honorific institution run by a small group of scholars largely relying upon their personal connections within *academia*. Now Bédarida also warmed to the idea that the secretary-general possibly ought to be assisted by a second scholar who would take care of communications with historians overseas on a regular basis. The ICHS had become a scholarly enterprise that required a permanent institutional basis. However, it lacked sufficient financial resources, apart from the contributions by the national committees, the affiliated commissions, and some small subsidies from UNESCO supplied via the International Council for the Philosophy and Human Sciences.

Thanks to his excellent personal contacts Bédarida succeeded in establishing a Joint Committee of the ICHS and UNESCO under the chairmanship of Jerzy Kloczowski with Bédarida, Kocka, and Catherine Coquery-Vidrovitch as ICHS representatives. This turned out to be a decisive step. The committee was to arrange regional meetings on the history of areas blighted by ancient or recent conflict: Black Africa, Central/Eastern Europe, Latin America. First it arranged two conferences of ten to twelve specialists each. The first, which took place in Lublin, Poland, from 23 to 25 October 1998, dealt with "Borders, States, and National Land Areas" in Eastern Europe; the second, in Bamako, Mali, from 14 to 21 March 1999, was on "Reality and Perception of Borders in Africa." Other conferences were to follow, particularly in Latin America. These initiatives indirectly fulfilled an old demand of the Bureau, namely, to awaken interest in the work of the ICHS in less developed countries through regionally oriented conferences held between the Congresses.[56]

Before the Congress in Oslo, the Bureau of the ICHS had two more meetings, a one-day meeting in Paris on 9 January 1999 and a two-day meeting in Moscow from 27 to 28 August 1999. On these occasions the preparations for Oslo were finalized and in some cases modified. It was agreed that the official ceremonies of the opening session in Oslo should be followed by a panel discussion of three high-ranking international historians, Romila Thapar (New Delhi), Hans-Ulrich Wehler (Bielefeld), and Roger Chartier (Paris), under the chairmanship of the president Ivan T. Berend. The closing session was to include a panel discussion on "Historical Perspectives for the Next Century" that would be broadcasted by Norwegian television. The definitive program of the forthcoming Congress was approved by the Bureau and sent out to the national committees and affiliated commissions immediately afterward.

On 6 August 2000 the nineteenth International Congress of Historical Sciences was inaugurated with an impressive ceremony in the Oslo Concert Hall. After the opening address by Kirsti Kolle Grondahl, the president of the Norwegian Parliament, and the welcoming addresses, François Bédarida took the floor to greet all participants. More than 2,000 historians of 67 countries had come to Oslo. The proceedings comprised three "major" plenary sessions, twenty sessions on specialized themes, and more than twenty-five roundtable discussions. Besides, many historians cooperating in the affiliated international commissions had come to Oslo to meet and to hold conferences in their respective fields of research. All in all the Congress provided a most impressive survey of international historical scholarship.

The panel discussion on "The 20th Century as Seen by History and Historians" was devoted to an assessment of the century that had just passed by, viewed from different angles. Ivan T. Berend referred to Eric Hobsbawm, who had called the twentieth century "the age of extremes." He pointed out that it had been perhaps the cruelest century in the known history of mankind, with two bitterly fought world wars and a string of so-called local wars and civil wars, and above all systematic mass murder of a scale and a brutality that did not have a parallel in modern history. Yet at the same time the twentieth century was a period of unprecedented economic growth and wide-ranging improvements in living conditions. The average life expectancy more than doubled, and the education of the young made dramatic headway. Production rose thirty-fold on average, and the expansion of trade took on unprecedented proportions, eventually culminating in the emergence of an international economic system that provided a basis for further economic growth and social improvement, although global distribution of the benefits was exceedingly uneven. The European Union, which was created by formerly bitterly opposed nation-states, had to be seen as a hope for a better future. Berend wound up his ambivalent assessment by quoting Charles Dickens: we are living "in the best of times [and] the worst of times, in the season of Light and the season of Darkness."[57]

Chartier addressed a different aspect, namely, the radical changes and even ruptures that had occurred within the historical craft itself, inasmuch as the societies in which historians worked and wrote had been subjected to far-reaching alterations. For one the high self-confidence that had motivated historians during the nineteenth century was largely gone, and likewise their assuredness that by close reliance upon the sources they would deal with reality itself. Many factors came together: the permanent expansion of the field considered worthy of historical inquiry, the discovery that historical narratives are structured by linguistic modes implying that every historical account contains fictional components, the aesthetic revolution that changed the expectations of the public regarding the styles of presentation of the past, the rise of microhistory, and last not least the challenge to the conventional view that history is above all about state affairs and grand politics. Historians could no longer be sure that their narratives were "objective," even if the traditional standards of historical research were obeyed meticulously. No longer did they speak with one voice; whereas a few well-established schools of thought had heretofore dominated the field of historical research, by now the field was split up into numerous special approaches that likewise claimed to tell the historical truth.

Seen from this point of view, the twentieth century represents the end—or at any rate a deep-rooted crisis—of traditional historiography with its self-confidence and its predominant position in the public arena and in the educational system. Furthermore, it has brought home to historians that their work and their message can be abused for political or other purposes. The only consolation is that historical arguments do not necessarily favor only those who are in power; they may also be used to help the suppressed, the underdogs, the humiliated groups in society. Chartier's presentation ended with a cautious word of optimism: "the society of historians can be fraternal." Although the community of historians is deeply divided among itself due to the cleavages between the various states and cultures with which historians are aligned, it feels obliged to work jointly for a universal society of all human beings in the tradition of the Enlightenment.

In his talk under the heading "Consigning the 20th Century to History," Hans-Ulrich Wehler took as his point of departure Hobsbawm's concept of the "short" twentieth century, that is to say, the period that began with the First World War and ended with the breakdown of the Soviet empire. Wehler considered communism and fascism (including National Socialism) to be the two great counterrevolutionary forces against modernization and constitutional democratic government in the twentieth century, although both movements, in spite of being directed against it, themselves originated from the process of "modernization." Wehler named two major achievements of the twentieth century: the "*Rechtsstaat*," or the principle of the "rule of law," and the "welfare state." The steady growth of market economies had resulted in the disappearance of the traditional working classes and the language of class. Instead, "market-oriented classes" had emerged (referring to an ideal type posited by Max Weber), and class conflicts were moderated by welfare policies. Yet historians must not overlook the problematic consequences of the triumph of the "market economy," for instance, the worrisome ecological effects of progressive industrialization. As to the "worldviews dominant during the twenty-first century," Wehler forecasted the decline of nationalist ideologies and with it the gradual oblivion of the nation-state.

This was an opening worthy of a Congress devoted to a thorough review of worldwide developments in the historical sciences.

In the afternoon of 6 August 2000 the General Assembly of the ICHS sat for its statutory first meeting during the Congress. There was not much business outstanding besides the presentation of the list of nominations for the new Bureau. This had been a little more controversial than usual, in particular since a new secretary-general had to be found, and the question had arisen of whether a French scholar should be elected again, or whether candidatures from other countries might be considered as well. Furthermore, some new member states were admitted, in particular representatives from Chile and Peru. The key issue was the impending retirement of François Bédarida, who had reached the age of seventy-four and would no longer bear the heavy workload of the secretary-general.[58] He had run the ICHS for ten years. He now presented his last report as secretary-general. It was actually a "farewell address," even though it dealt with a variety of important business issues. With his usual modesty Bédarida had mailed the full text of his farewell address beforehand to all members of the Assembly; on this occasion he merely summarized it. It was, however, a major document, a kind of "*Staatsschrift*" (as one might put it in German) concerning the past and the future of the ICHS.[59]

Bédarida looked back to the origins and early stages of the ICHS. He referred to the principles that its "founding fathers" had put forward in the 1920s and concluded that by and large the ICHS had lived up to their expectations quite well. Bédarida invoked Henri Pirenne, who at the Congress in Brussels in 1923 had argued that only the comparative method could guarantee the spirit of objectivity and lift historiography beyond the level of prejudice. Likewise he quoted Marc Bloch's famous formula that the ICHS must work for "a comparative history of the European nations." This philosophy had always had a prominent place in the Bureau's directives for the organization of the Congresses. Meanwhile, the ICHS had always stayed in line with the different developments in international historical research.

> In a way, the ICHS is a perfect mirror that faithfully reflects the fully effervescent flows of historiography. Knowledge accumulation is on an accelerating track. Alongside it, three powerful movements are changing the work of practicing historians. These three movements are: changes in the historian's craft, expansion of the field of study, and globalization of research. As concerns the profession, the historian is, and should continue to be a "master of truth." This is both his vocation and his main *raison d'être*. According to Herodotus, the pioneer *histor*, his role is to present the results of his findings so that time does not abandon the works of man and great feats are not forgotten. But alongside these ageless dicta, immense mutations occur. A few years ago, Braudel pointed out that "the historian's profession has changed so dramatically during the last half century that images and problems of the past have turned themselves inside out. They, of course, are still being called into question, but now the terms are different."

The progressive professionalization of historians that stemmed from the emergence of a network binding the historians together, had resulted in a harmonization of scholarly standards and universal application of the critical method. At the same time the social responsibilities of the historian were considerably enhanced. Historians were expected to establish a "social memory" of mankind (with all the related dangers of instrumentalization). This involved the risk that "the historian may have to 'serve' memory although it may seriously cloud the relation between past and present." Bédarida welcomed the return of the "narrative" and the new importance given to the event and to contingency rather than to statistical curves. He expressed some satisfaction that historiography had been "de-fatalized" and that interpretation had regained primacy in historical writing.

The second major development in Bédarida's view was the enormous expansion of the field of historiography, at both ends of the time scale. Our knowledge of prehistoric times had been augmented dramatically, and this process was still going on with accelerating speed. Objects that seemed to be timeless now had come into the orbit of historical inquiry; even the biological evolution of man might now lie within the range of historical analysis. Besides, present-day historiography had grown rapidly in the last twenty years. The traditional saying that historians should not deal with open-ended subjects because this might cloud their vision would not do any longer. On the contrary, the presence of eyewitnesses and the interconnectedness of the historian's findings with contemporary debates and milieus enlivened historical interpretation a great deal.

The third major development in historiography was globalization. As such, this was not a new phenomenon; indeed, the very reason for establishing the ICHS was to advance globalization by institutionalizing it. "But in the world of today, it has become a major trend, traversing civilizations and continents. It tends to unify the historian's methods, approaches and practices, lines of questioning and scholarly discourse. He, whose function puts him at the epicenter of the institution, at the heart of its operations and mechanisms, is struck by the changes that have been occurring during the last decade. We clearly feel that we are on the road to the global village, which Marshall McLuhan already announced twenty-five years ago."

Bédarida pointed out that "the unity of the history of the world," which Lord Bryce invoked in 1913 as an ideal, was fast becoming a reality: "The march toward unity of the world of historians, despite the strength of national peculiarities and cultural specificities," was striking. A common code of ethics for historians, for which the ICHS stood since its early beginnings, was "clearly breaking ground." Henri Pirenne's plea expressed in 1921, "that there [be] no German, English, American, bourgeois or socialist science [of history], but only one science," had come to pass. Bédarida also voiced considerable satisfaction that during his ten years in office as secretary-general the policies of "innovation" and "rejuvenation" had been by and large successful. However, the third objective, namely, to overcome the respective Euro- and U.S.-centric orientations of the ICHS, had been achieved only in part despite considerable efforts by the secretary-general and the other members of the Bureau, primarily because the institutionalization of historical scholarship in large parts of the non-Western world still left much to be desired. Membership in the ICHS had grown considerably, but still in an uneven manner. It remained to be seen whether the current conjoint activities in conjunction with UNESCO to stimulate historical research in Asia, Africa, and Latin America would help to alter the present unsatisfactory state of affairs.

Finally, Bédarida formulated what amounted to an assignment for the new members of the Bureau, who would take over after the Congress. He suggested that the ICHS undertake a thorough survey of the state of the historical sciences in the various regions of the globe, and to analyze their specific achievements and trends as well as their deficiencies and mistakes. Secondly,

> an assessment of the way in which history, through its teachings, propagation, and representation of the—real or imagined—past, has been used, if not instrumentalised for good or for bad by the states and societies everywhere on the globe. On the eve of the new millennium might not an in-depth analysis of historical output during the last half century show … that the twentieth century transformed our planet by making it change from a finite world of certainties into an indefinite work of query and doubt. Whatever be the case, history will always be a major tool for better understanding our future within a plurality of cultures and a myriad of spiritual values from different civilizations.

Bédarida's satisfaction with the organization of the Congress in Oslo and the high quality of the program was well founded. Indeed, the Congress offered a comprehensive survey on the various trends of historical research worldwide and did its best to live up to the main theme, namely, global history. The organizers did so on the technical level, by providing adequate techniques of communication, including abstracts of the majority of papers, but more importantly by judicious composition of the sessions and round tables, which sought to bring together experts from various countries on a particular topic. The work of the Selection Committee in conjunction with the Norwegian organization committee and the various national committees had certainly been successful.

One of the highlights of the Congress in Oslo was undoubtedly the session on "Perspectives on Global History." Instead agglomerating papers from different regions and on different aspects, it attempted to present the issues in an integrated form that could genuinely be called global.[60] Patrick O'Brien (United Kingdom) tackled the difficult subject of whether "Universal History" is possible at all. He offered a comprehensive survey of different approaches to universal history, based in part upon the detailed reports of the other members on the panel. Starting out with Herodotus, he first gave a *"tableau"* of the classic examples of global and universal history by thinkers of the Enlightenment. He pointed out that since the beginning of the nineteenth century, universal history had come to be a sidetrack; most historians wrote within their national frameworks. Besides, they harbored the assumption that Europe had always been, or at any rate since the late eighteenth century had become, the core of the dynamic historical processes that terminated in the modern industrial system.

Accordingly, they tended to underrate, if not altogether failing to appreciate, the cultural achievements of non-European cultures, notably China (as was demonstrated in the exceedingly informative contribution by Gregory Blue, Canada). Only in the wake of the cultural shock of two World Wars did the "cultural arrogance" of Western universal historians give way to a sober or even deeply pessimistic account of the place of Europe and of Western civilization in a comprehensive account of universal history, as attested by the writings of Oswald Spengler, Arnold Toynbee, Dimitrii Sorokin, and H. G. Wells. However, in empirical respects these interpretations did not turn out to be a compelling framework for professional historians writing global history. The same is true for the attempt by UNESCO in the 1960s to put together a multivolume collaborative history of the world explicitly designed to promote universal history. Neither were the courses on Western Civilization at the great American universities satisfactory on this count. It was historians like Marshall Hodgson and William McNeill whose academic work made a difference, for here, notably in McNeill's *The Shape of European History*,[61] a far more balanced account of the place of Europe in the various world civilizations can be found.

The spectacular rise of the modern industrial system and the apparently unstoppable expansion of a worldwide market economy strengthened the conventional view that the world's history is in fact a history of Europe written large. The initial gap between the West and the non-Western regions of the world grew ever wider, even though many peoples at the periphery accepted Western technology and business methods. This gave rise to a new wave of self-assertion in the West. The invincibility of the Western path to modernity was more than ever before taken for granted, and other world cultures were considered old-fashioned, if not subjected to a slow death. O'Brien held against this the observation that today the younger generation is genuinely interested to learn about other cultures. The renaissance of global history is, O'Brien contended, "a rediscovery of the Enlightenment project and not a return to the arrogance of Rome or to Victorian triumphalism."[62]

O'Brien was not blind to the methodological weaknesses of universal historiography. But he maintained that "thick description" of narrowly defined fields of inquiry should not be the only path of contemporary historiography, however welcome microhistorical studies may be. He shared the view that teleological reconstructions of global history are unsatisfactory. Repeated attempts to elicit from the process of universal history the gradual unfolding of a single inherent principle like "rationality" or "competitiveness" would appear to be unconvincing. O'Brien also took issue with the still prevalent tendency to write global history in terms of a single pervasive process of technological and economic growth that allegedly originated in eighteenth- and nineteenth-century Europe exclusively. Instead, he proposed a cautious, descriptive approach that draws attention to the diversity of cultures and the multiplicity of causal factors.

Not all the discussants agreed with this plea for pragmatism. Graeme Donald Snooks (Australia) invoked the classic model of Auguste Comte; he presented an elaborate treatise that aimed at disclosing general laws underneath the ordinary regularities of historical events or, as it would appear in other words, revealing patterns of social behavior that are the determinant of the historical process, among which the "acquisitive nature" of human beings is named especially. But his arguments cut little ice with O'Brien. More plausible was the neo-Darwinian model, introduced into the debate by Christopher Lloyd (Australia) to help interpret the "Holocene," i.e., the long period in the history of mankind extending from its very beginnings at about 12,000 BC to the present, and integrate it into the study of history. This should be done, he argued, not in the conventional but instead in neo-Darwinian terms. During the debate it became clear that the early stages in the development of mankind must be seriously taken into account by the historians, instead of being discounted as phases of alleged stagnation. Likewise, biological factors play a decisive role in the prehistory of mankind. Given the fact that they have initiated historical change of substantive dimensions, they can no longer be left aside by universal historians as a marginal theme, or as one that concerns only the natural sciences.

The traditional eurocentricity of universal history was attacked from yet another angle, this time by emphasizing the cultural and technological transfer processes between Europe and the other continents since the fifteenth century. Jerry H. Bentley (United States) pointed out the substantial limitations of the traditional concepts of world history, referring in particular to Leopold von Ranke and Georg Friedrich Wilhelm Hegel, who both had considered the Asian cultures to be stationary and therefore merely marginal, from the point of view of a world history that primarily gives attention to intellectual and technological advancements.[63] In a special subsection on "Cultural Encounters between the Continents Over the Centuries," it was shown that these traditional views had been brought about by the historians' habit of thinking in individual units, notably the nation-state. For this reason these important transcontinental cultural and economic transfer processes had not been given sufficient attention. The exchange between Europe and the Ottoman Empire, which was often erroneously considered to have been a blatant form of tyrannical rule, was rather important, as were the relations between the various nations at the shores of the Pacific ocean. Yet another issue was the biological harmonization among the continents, a process that extended over a much longer time span. Given this state of affairs, it is apparently rather difficult, even impossible, to find a common denominator among these important transnational, if not global, processes. Catherine Coquery-Vidrovitch therefore suggested that for this sort of global history the traditional model of "master-narrative" would not do. What was required was a plurality of stories written from different viewpoints, which together would both account for alternative trajectories and developmental paths that transcend the notion of "exceptionalism," and place their findings into a global historical framework.

The second major theme was devoted to "Millennium, Time and History." This session dealt with a topic that had also been discussed at the Congress in Madrid, namely, the wide range of radically different time conceptions in various cultures over time and space.[64] An assessment of different notions of historical time can be used as a yardstick to measure the deep cultural differences between different regions of the globe. As a rule, conceptions of historical time were determined by religious tradition; God was considered the master of history, and theological assumptions therefore have been of the greatest importance in Buddhism, in Hinduism, and of course in Christianity as well. It was also customary to define different time segments according to particular dynasties or rulers, as, for instance, in China and Japan. Surprisingly, there was no mention of the practice in the French Revolution and later under the fascist dictatorships of introducing newly worded time schedules, mainly for propaganda reasons. The session demonstrated the breadth of the cultural divisions in world history. Only after the Second World War did the People's Republic of China eventually accept the Christian-era system of time, exclusively for pragmatic reasons.

On a more sophisticated level it is possible to ascertain a plurality of notions of time among philosophers and historians. These are determined by the different worldviews governing conceptions of historical change. This was shown by François Dosse (France) in an elaborate presentation that transcended the status of "commentary." Covering a wide range of different approaches,[65] he argued that every historian of note tends to have his own notion of time. To give but one example, Fernand Braudel distinguished between a plurality of sequences of time, inter alia the (relatively) "*longue durée*" and the fast-running but superficial "*histoire événementielle*." This aspect of the theme might have deserved somewhat greater attention from the *rapporteurs*. It was only Giuseppe Ricuperati (Italy) who took up this line of reasoning, by looking into the interrelationship of notions of time and periodization in early modern European philosophical and historical thought. This is, of course, not entirely new. Following in the footsteps of Reinhart Koselleck, historians nowadays are well aware of the "Gleichzeitigkeit des Ungleichzeitigen" (simultaneity of the non-simultaneous) as a widespread phenomenon in historical reality.

The third major theme concerned "The Uses and Misuses of History and the Responsibility of the Historian." In different ways this theme had been approached in most International Congresses, though at times it could not be discussed with the same frankness because the community of historians was divided among different ideological camps in the past. The demand that historians should respect the principles of objectivity and faithfulness vis-à-vis their sources had been raised time and again; Georg G. Iggers rehashed the story of how nineteenth-century historical writing had been subjected to nationalistic distortions of various sorts, in Germany and elsewhere.[66] However, there was no simple solution to the problem of objectivity. Iggers did not deny, indeed he emphasized, that the historian is always influenced by the dominant fashions and value attitudes of his own sociopolitical milieu, and that his intellectual energies are derived from them. Yet, he should maintain his independence and not act as a servant of the mighty or of the state. Iggers concluded that while historians cannot live up to Ranke's dictum to write history "wie es eigentlich gewesen" (how it actually was), at least they should show "wie es eigentlich nicht gewesen sei" (how it actually was not). From a theoretical point of view, this negative definition of objectivity is not very satisfactory; it does not solve the quandary of whether the relativity of the historian's standpoint makes it impossible to decide definitely once and for all about the right or wrong in a controversial historical issue. However, the principle may serve as a useful guideline for historical studies directed at disenchanting current ideological notions about recent history.

François Bédarida's comment was more pragmatic. Although history could be and indeed always had been instrumentalized for political purposes, this does not diminish the responsibility of the historian. His responsibility is of a threefold nature: it is the responsibility of the scholar, it is the responsibility of the citizen, and it is a moral responsibility. It has as one prerequisite a status of independence—conformist historiography is *quand même* suspect. Second, it requires freedom of thought. Third, the historian must not lose sight of the reality of the past. He must remain faithful to the facts. In a way, as Paul Ricoeur put it, he is "indebted to his sources." Furthermore, the historian must not succumb to a hopeless relativism or an unrestrained (*débridé*) subjectivism. This does not mean at all, however, that the postulate of objectivity is tantamount to neutrality.

In this context a series of notable examples of the instrumentalization of the past for political or ideological purposes was presented. Hans-Werner Goetz (Germany) demonstrated that the medieval historiography of the eleventh and twelfth centuries was largely determined by political considerations; historiography provided legitimacy for rulers, cities, and religious institutions.[67] Sergei Zhuravlev (Russia) reported about the endeavors by Maxim Gorky and his collaborators, with the active involvement of Stalin, to create a new multivolume history of Soviet Russia designed to legitimize the Stalinist dictatorship while eliminating as far as possible the remembrance of the Russian society's bourgeois past.[68] Objectivity would appear to be indeed "a noble dream" (Peter Novick), but undoubtedly there are to be found different degrees of falsification of the past in the service of present-day interests.

Apparently, the opposite approach, namely, a critical assessment of past events in order to emancipate the body politic from the burden of the past and to create a new identity, national or cultural, can be found as well, with far-reaching resonance on the body politic. A panel on "Memory and Identity" debated this issue at length on the basis of a series of remarkable cases. The most striking one comprised the activities of South Africa's Truth and Reconciliation Commission, about which the South African historian Brent Harris presented a detailed report. Through a thorough analysis of the atrocities of the Apartheid period, the Truth and Reconciliation Commission, under the chairmanship of Bishop Desmond Tutu, sought to lay the foundations for a new South African national understanding between all sections of South African society, from the ANC to the white nationalists.

Another fascinating case was presented in the contribution by François Hartog (France), "The Witness and the Historian."[69] He began with the contemporary situation in which the historian and his objective sources are progressively replaced by the witness who has observed the events in question personally or lived through them. The media, in particular film and television, rely increasingly upon such witnesses, often taking their reports or messages as indisputable truth, whereas the critical commentaries of historians who know better about the nature and the reliability of witnesses often are omitted, or listened to with dismay and irritation. Often the witness is himself a victim and his report therefore is held to be per se authentic and trustworthy. The emotional quality of testimony by witnesses is regarded by the audiovisual media as an advantage, rather than—as historians would argue—a factor that is likely to lead to distortion of the facts. This is particularly true with regard to controversial topics with a strong emotional dimension, for instance, the Holocaust or the bombing campaigns of the Allied Powers during the Second World War.

Hartog showed that the conflict between the witness and the historian, or initially, between the witness who purports to have seen things with his own eyes, the *martus* who has only heard things, and the *histor* who reports about the events in question on the basis of knowledge taken from written texts or from oral communication, is as old as history. We find it in Antiquity and in the Christian tradition, especially in ecclesiastical history, and likewise in medieval texts. The historian tends not to be the *auctor*, the compiler; his position is inferior to those of the witness and the *histor*. Only during the nineteenth century was this relationship reversed. Hartog wound up his observations by raising an open question, namely, whether we might experience a revival of the time-honored model of a history of witnessing and of witnesses.

In view of the findings of these papers it is doubtful whether the process of professionalization of historical studies, which presently is making headway on a worldwide scale—the topic of the first specialized theme discussed under the chairmanship of Rolf Torstendahl (Sweden)—will bring history nearer to the cherished ideal of objectivity. On the other hand, the emergence of a "worldwide profession of historians" that is increasingly subjecting historical analysis to universally established principles of historical research will eventually help to bring about the "ecumene of historians" that Karl Dietrich Erdmann considered to be the ultimate purpose of the ICHS.[70]

As this survey of the "major themes" has shown, the Congress in Oslo was primarily concerned with the theoretical status of the historical sciences at the turn of the twenty-first century. The ongoing debate on methodological issues and in particular on the intellectual orientation of historiography is a symptom of the latent crisis of the historical sciences at the present juncture. The traditional battles over political issues and their ideological ramifications have subsided since the end of the rivalry between the Soviet empire and the democratic West. Evidently the nation-state has reached the climax in its long history and can no longer serve as a signpost for the work of historians; however, the alternative, namely, a global reference point that would permit the writing of a genuine world history, has not yet been found.

The Congress in Oslo also sought to inform participants about the development of new subdisciplines such as environmental history, demography and migration studies, the history of tourism, and "gender" history. One aspect that received particular attention in Oslo was the expansion of the history of "gender" into "men's" (rather than "male") history, which so far had been rather neglected, by tackling a most sensitive topic, namely, "masculinity." Major wars have traditionally been breeding grounds for "masculinity," but it seems that the cultural milieu within the German Social Democracy was conducive to promoting masculinity as well. Still, the history of remembrance after the First World War, which of late has been the subject of innovative historical studies, should not be seen exclusively in terms of sustaining the ideology of male dominance. It was primarily a painful process of coping with the vivid memory of mass death and immense suffering in trench warfare.

War and mass killing in history was the theme of another section, which pursued the issue from the fourteenth to the twentieth century under the heading "Power, Violence and Mass Death in Pre-modern and Modern Times." It focused not only on death in war, but also on mass death caused by epidemics and famine. The long-term perspective applied to this theme was rewarding indeed. It is plausible to deal with these events in catastrophic terms, inasmuch as they involved suffering and death on a grand scale, transcending national boundaries. The "plague," or more precisely the "Black Death" that hit Europe in the mid fourteenth century, was not, as historical analysis proves in hindsight, a cosmic catastrophe beyond the control of the people; countermeasures were, at least in the longer run, quite effective. Ordinary people experienced war much as they did the plague or other epidemics: they were helplessly exposed to its devastating consequences. In war, for soldiers and the civil population alike, violence was always omnipresent, and hunger and suffering, if not death, were the logical consequences. During the Thirty Years' War looting and violence were always around, and given the widespread destruction of property, and more importantly of the crops, war was nearly always associated with hunger and extreme deprivation. It remains controversial whether there were, in the later Middle Ages, tendencies among the elites to domesticate war, at any rate up to some degree, by embracing an aristocratic way of life, as Johan Huizinga maintained half a century ago. The eighteenth and nineteenth centuries developed an idealized image of war, which later was cultivated by the nation-state; to die for one's own country was praised in glorious rhetoric.

Even so, the First World War must be considered a pivotal event. As Jay Winter put it: "War was now inseparable from mass death, from the conscription of unimaginable armies of the dead." Likewise Antoine Prost wrote: "After 1918, death is at the core of representations [of combat]. To make war is not to capture prisoners, take cities, conquer territory; it is to kill and be killed."[71] This assumption was corroborated by the experience of the Second World War. In the initial stages of the war the loss of soldierly lives was not as great as it had been in the First World War, but during the campaign against the USSR, its devastating nature became obvious in almost biblical proportions, including the murder of six million European Jews. It remains to be seen whether current attempts to propagate a new image of a "clean war" with just some "collateral damage" will be accepted by future historians.

It is impossible here to cover all the subjects that were discussed in Oslo. It proved not always possible to implement the general objective of the Congress, namely, to choose issues that carry significance in terms of global history. As a rule the organizers had given preference to themes with a global dimension. The section on "Changing Boundaries and Definitions of Work over Time and Space" chaired by Jürgen Kocka is a case in question. It did its best to cover a wide range of types of "work" throughout history in different regions of the world, but perhaps the topic was too general to get far beyond a delineation of the wide range of different definitions of work within a global context. One favored possibility was work as defined by the "market economy": (regular) employment for wage earnings. Karen Hagemann (Germany), however, would like to apply the notion of "work" to a much wider field of actions. In her view it is all-important to include the role of women within the household, and likewise in society at large. Eric Vanhaute (Belgium), in turn, holds the view that "labor" tends to radically change its significance in different economic contexts; under the conditions of urban industrial capitalism it shrinks to being almost an equivalent to employment, whereas all other forms of activities are excluded. Furthermore, work means rather different things in the core and in the periphery of a given social system. In Vanhaute's view a narrow definition of "labor" is a weapon in the struggle of different groups in society and therefore it should be avoided in a scholarly discourse.

In drawing up the program for Oslo the Selection Committee of the ICHS had gone beyond previous practice by organizing on its own initiative special sessions for new fields of historical research not suggested by any of the national committees. Franz-Josef Brüggemeier (Germany) had been asked to arrange a session on "New Developments in Environmental History," which provided information about a subject matter largely neglected in the agendas of the previous International Congresses. Brüggemeier presented an overview of recent developments in this discipline, which, as he pointed out, by now had become a mature discipline and was no longer a peripheral one. Even so, the subject matter of nature and the human being is vast and cannot be mastered easily in a single report. The papers presented by the discussants covered a wide range of cases, from the Eastern marches of eighteenth-century Prussia to the mountain ranges and lowlands of Switzerland, the great diversity of human interference with nature in China, and the environmental impact of colonization in Africa. From these observations it follows that environmental history is able to disprove many popular assumptions about environmental issues, for example, the "deforestation paradigm," whereas it allows a proper assessment of the impact of man upon nature, if seen in a long-term historical perspective. This session, like many others (for instance, those on "The Social Practices of Writing and Reading from Antiquity to the Present" or "The Transmission of Scientific Discoveries"), provided a valuable orientation for a new subject of historical research that can no longer be considered marginal.

Given the premise that the Congress in Oslo should primarily concern itself with global history, the number of sections dealing with non-Western issues was comparatively limited, and the representatives of these countries were regrettably few. An exception was the section on "Missions, Modernization, Colonization, and De-colonization," chaired by Jarle Simenson (Norway). It is well known that the Christian missions played an important role in early colonial expansion. The papers of this section are very valuable case studies that throw new light on the history of the encounter between the Western Christian culture and that of indigenous people in the early stages of penetration by the West. The section on "Muslim Societies," which represented only an early stage of a larger research project, was interesting and certainly most welcome. But it delivered only fragmentary pieces of information about a subject of great significance. It is to be hoped that the topic will be dealt with more prominently in future Congresses.

The General Assembly, which met after the end of the proceedings on 10 August 2000 in Oslo, turned its attention to the business of the next quinquennium of ICHS activities. A proposal to hold the next Congress in Sydney met with universal approval, as it corresponded with a longstanding wish to extend the activities of the ICHS beyond Europe and North America.

More important was the election of the new Bureau. The groundwork had been laid on 30 August 1999 in a somewhat stormy meeting of the Nomination Committee in which the votes of the three members of the Bureau were no longer automatically decisive. Initially it could not reach unanimity, not least because the old tradition that outgoing members of the Bureau were entitled to suggest their potential successors had not yet died out fully. Besides, the nominees were scrutinized in view of the likely future development of the ICHS. The key issue was its international standing. It was pointed out that now, since the East-West divide had come to an end, the North-South issue had become much more important for the ICHS; therefore this aspect should be given some weight in the selection of new members of the Bureau also.[72] Soon afterward, however, unanimous agreement as to the candidates to be presented to the General Assembly was reached, though only after a further exchange of views by mail among the members of the Bureau and the Nomination Committee.

When the General Assembly came to vote on this issue, everything had been sorted out. Jürgen Kocka (Germany) was elected president; Eva Österberg (Sweden) and Romila Thapar (India) were elected vice-presidents. Jean-Claude Robert (Canada), who had proven his excellent organizational skills as chairman of the Canadian organization committee in Montreal, was chosen for the position of secretary-general, to succeed François Bédarida. Quite a few members of the General Assembly voiced their concern that the secretariat of the ICHS, which for so many years, since its very inception, had had its domicile in Paris, would no longer be run by a French scholar. From this point of view also, the French-speaking Canadian Jean-Claude Robert was a good choice. The new assessor members were Gregorii Bongard-Levin (Russia), Catherine Coquery-Vidrovitch (France), Michael Heyd (Israel), William Chester Jordan (United States), Koichi Kabayama (Japan), and José Luis Peset (Spain). The office of treasurer was again entrusted to Pierre Ducrey (Switzerland). Ivan T. Berend (Hungary/United States) and Aleksander Gieysztor (Poland) stayed on as counsellors-members of the Bureau. This was not an altogether new, but a substantially rejuvenated team representing a new generation of scholars.

Jürgen Kocka (born in 1941) had studied in Marburg, Vienna, at the University of North Carolina (United States), and at the Freie Universität of Berlin. After his *Habilitation* in Münster in 1972 he had a meteoric career. In 1973 he was appointed Professor of General and Social History at the University of Bielefeld. Here he soon became one of the core members of the Editorial Committee of *Geschichte und Gesellschaft*, a journal that initiated a new form of social-scientific history ("Historische Sozialwissenschaft") in the Federal Republic of Germany. He became known as the author of various pioneering studies on the history of white-collar workers and on the German and European bourgeoisie in the nineteenth and twentieth centuries. His studies in the United States, along with numerous Visiting Professorships at overseas universities and Fellowships at renowned international research institutes qualified him exceedingly well for the presidency of the ICHS. As president of the Wissenschaftszentrum (Social Science Research Center) Berlin, he holds a key position in the academic system of the Federal Republic of Germany.

Jean-Claude Robert, the new secretary-general, was born in 1943. He studied at the University of Montreal and the École des Hautes Études en Sciences Sociales (Université de Paris I—Panthéon-Sorbonne). Here he finished his doctorate in 1977. From 1975 onward he taught as Professor at the Université du Québec à Montréal. In 1992 he was also *Directeur d'études associé* at the École des Hautes Études in Paris. He had published various studies on Canadian social history as well as on the culture of Quebec, and had held a responsible position in a large number of Canadian scientific research institutions.

On 13 August 2000, just after the Congress had ended, the new Bureau held its customary first meeting. Jürgen Kocka outlined the activities of the ICHS in the forthcoming years.[73] The primary tasks of the ICHS, as an organization of organizations, were to maintain close communication between its institutional members and to defend the principle of historians' freedom of thought and expression against any encroachments. Secondly, it was to prepare the next Congress in Sydney, in close cooperation with the Australian organization committee. Thirdly, it would try to help expand and deepen the international network of historians, notably in regions where so far the institutionalization of historical studies was weak. Within the limits of its financial and institutional resources, it would also organize regional conferences and workshops to promote historical research and build a basis for the ICHS in regions where it was not yet strongly represented. The joint ventures with UNESCO, in which François Bédarida, Catherine Coquery-Vidrovitch, and Jürgen Kocka had been particularly involved, should be continued as far as possible. This is to say that the activities of the ICHS were to undergo no radical change in their general direction under the new Bureau; but they were to be pursued with renewed vigor.

On the occasion of the next meeting of the Bureau in Princeton on 25 August 2001, Jürgen Kocka further elaborated this program in his message to the members.[74] Whereas the objectives of the ICHS would fundamentally remain the same ones they had been since its foundation in 1926, the altered conditions in the present world would necessitate "a change in our mode of action." The ICHS "should become more ecumenical." This would refer not just to expansion, but also to the need to take up new viewpoints, topics, and approaches. To become more ecumenical, the study of history would have to open up to a wider horizon. Special conferences between the Congresses should be held. "Broad questions, comprehensive approaches, and theoretical self-reflection are needed, developed and refined, at many places, but also at the ICHS." Achieving this required the active participation of historians from all parts of the world.

The future prospects of the International Committee of Historical Sciences and its Congresses appear to be promising. Karl Dietrich Erdmann's expectations that the "ecumene" of historians would acquire the status of an international scholarly community with moral clout, commanding high respect despite the ongoing ideological differences among nations, appear to have come much closer to their fulfillment, even as new fields and potentials broaden the approaching horizon.

Notes

1. ICHS, *Bulletin d'information*, no. 14 (1987), General Assembly, p. 115. However, in the end the *Bulletin d'information* did not publish the resolution. For 1985, see note 69 on p. 266 above.
2. See A. Sutcliffe, "Introduction: The Giant City as Historical Phenomenon," in Th. C. Barker and A. Sutcliffe, eds., *Megapolis: The Giant City in History* (Basingbroke, 1993), pp. 4f. The book is based upon a selection of the papers presented at the Madrid Congress.
3. Ránki's role in the session was taken over by Y. V. Bromley. See *XVIIe Congrès International des Sciences Historiques, Madrid 1990*. 2 vols. (Madrid, 1990), vol. 1: *Grands thèmes. Méthodologie. Sections chronologiques 1: Rapports et abrégés*, p. 175 [hereafter Congress Madrid 1990: *Rapports*].

4. Report of the secretary-general at Vienna, minutes in ICHS, *Bulletin d'information*, no. 16 (1989): 163f.
5. Congress Madrid 1990: *Rapports*, p. 24.
6. Barker and Sutcliffe, *Giant City*.
7. Congress Madrid 1990: *Rapports*, p. 60.
8. Ibid., p. 102.
9. Ibid., pp. 61f.
10. Congress Madrid 1990: *Rapports*, Section chronologique, p. 449.
11. The proceedings of the conference, containing most of the papers, were published in a special issue of *Storia della Storiografia* 19 (1991): 11–156.
12. ICHS, *Bulletin d'information*, no. 23 (1997): 51.
13. Ibid., p. 50.
14. Joachim Herrmann, who in the meantime had lost his position as chairman of the national committee of the historians of the GDR, initially had planned to organize a reception arranged by the Akademieverlag, the official publisher of the publications of the Akademie der Wissenschaften der DDR, on the premises of the former Prussian Academy. But this plan was forestalled by Bédarida, who realized that West German historians would see it as a provocative step. See letter to Barker, 10 July 1991, Archives Nationales, Fonds du CISH, cote 105, AS 272, correspondence Bédarida: "En ce qui concerne Herrmann … la situation est suffisamment délicate pour que Herrmann ne nous complique pas la tâche en se mêlant de l'organisation de la rencontre de Berlin (de mon côté j'ai reçu des échos très défavorables de plusieurs historiens allemands sur son compte). De toute façon il me paraîtrait particulièrement malvenu et inopportun qu'une réception soit organisée à l'initiative de Herrmann, et cela par une maison d'édition qui a été pendant des années l'éditeur de l'Academie des Sciences de Berlin et par conséquent la courroie de transmission du pouvoir et du régime…. Le Cish n'a guère intérêt à être entraîné dans les embrouilles germano-allemandes."
15. See letter of 26 Sep. 1991 by Barker to W. J. Mommsen (at the time chairman of the Verband der Historiker Deutschlands): "[W]e appreciated in particular the discussion … about the position of German historians. I hope that there are more than a few Dr. Floraths in the former eastern zone. He was most impressive and sincere." Bédarida wrote on 19 Sep. 1991: "La séance sur l'historiographie allemande d'aujourd'hui m'est apparue tout à fait passionnante. Tout en prenant mieux conscience de l'ampleur des problèmes intellectuels et scientifiques soulevés par la réunification, nous avons le sentiment que sont présents, en dépit des difficultés, des signes multiples de renouveau et nous vous souhaitons bonne chance dans votre effort pour rebâtir une science historique dans l'ex-Allemagne de l'Est." Both letters in the possession of the author.
16. Bédarida to Jaroslav Panek, secretary-general of the Czechoslovak national committee, 22 Nov. 1991, Archives Nationales, Fonds du CISH, cote 105, AS 272, correspondence Bédarida.
17. "A note from the President and Senior Vice President on the State and Future of CISH," in ICHS, *Bulletin d'information*, no. 19 (1993): 19–21.
18. Ibid., p. 21.
19. Ibid., p. 19.
20. Note of 10 Jan. 1990, Archives Nationales, Fonds du CISH, cote 105, AS 272, correspondence Bédarida.
21. Letter to Even Lange, 7 Apr. 1997, Archives Nationales, Fonds du CISH, cote 105, AS 275.
22. ICHS, *Bulletin d'information*, no. 19 (1993).
23. ICHS, *Bulletin d'information*, no. 23 (1997): 57–80; no. 24 (1998).
24. ICHS, *Bulletin d'information*, no. 19 (1993): 9, Art. 1. See appendix IVc below.
25. Ibid., Art. 5, second paragraph.
26. See ICHS, *Bulletin d'information*, no. 19 (1999): 115–157.
27. Letter to Berend, 30. Sep 1994, Archives Nationales, Fonds du CISH, cote 105, AS 277, correspondence Bédarida.

28. Mandela had been suggested by Natalie Zemon Davis.
29. Letter of 2 Aug. 1995, Archives Nationales, Fonds du CISH, cote 105, AS 276, correspondence Bédarida.
30. Barker to Bédarida, 9 May 1995, Archives Nationales, Fonds du CISH, cote 105, AS 461.
31. Agreement was also reached on a new compromise version of Barker's farewell message to the General Assembly.
32. A detailed account of the conflict drawn up by Bédarida, written on 27 June 1995, in Archives Nationales, Fonds du CISH, cote 105, AS 461, and in expurgated version in AS 180.
33. ICHS, *Bulletin d'information*, no. 22 (1996): 129.
34. Ibid., pp. 131–150.
35. Ibid., p. 137.
36. Ibid., p. 141.
37. Ibid., p. 143.
38. Ibid., pp. 147, 150.
39. The introductory papers were published in ibid., pp. 127–150.
40. Alexander O. Chubaryan, "Le pouvoir et la liberté de la recherche historique et ses moyens de diffusion / Power, Liberty, and the Work of the Historian: The Implications of Political, Economic, and Cultural Controls on the Organization of Historical Research and Publication," in *XVIIIe Congrès International des Sciences Historiques, du 27 août au 3 septembre 1995. Actes: rapports, résumés et présentations des tables rondes. 18th International Congress of Historical Sciences, from 27 August to 3 September 1995. Proceedings: reports, abstracts and introductions to round tables*. Claude Morin ed. (Montreal, 1995), p. 139.
41. Marilyn Lake, "Family, Sex, and Power," in ibid., pp. 91, 100.
42. Roger Chartier, "L'histoire, ou le passé composé: History between Narrative and Knowledge," in ibid., p. 174.
43. Jörn Rüsen, "Fictionality, Narrativity, Objectivity," in ibid., p. 181.
44. ICHS, *Bulletin d'information*, no. 22 (1996): 151–155.
45. Ibid., p. 154.
46. See, for instance, the report in *Le Monde*, 8 Sep. 1995.
47. ICHS, *Bulletin d'information*, no. 27 (2001): 51.
48. Ibid.
49. Ibid.
50. Letter to Natalie Zemon Davis, 8 Jan. 1997, Archives Nationales, Fonds du CISH, cote 105, AS 278.
51. See the handwritten record by Bédarida, Archives Nationales, Fonds du CISH, cote 105, AS 467.
52. Replies by Bédarida to letters from Österberg and Kocka, 9 Dec. 1997, Archives Nationales, Fonds du CISH, cote 105, AS 278.
53. 25 Dec. 1997, ibid.
54. A vivid example of Bédarida's meticulous attempts to develop sensible proposals may be found in the numerous handwritten drafts of a possible list of themes drawn up by him in Archives Nationales, Fonds du CISH, cote 105, AS 462 (1991) and AS 468 (1997).
55. ICHS, *Bulletin d'information*, no. 24 (1998): 100.
56. See Bédarida's report in the Bureau meeting in Moscow, 27–28 Aug. 1999, in ICHS, *Bulletin d'information*, no. 25 (1999/2000): 51–62.
57. This and all the subsequent quotations from the proceedings of the Oslo Congress are taken from *Papers for the 19th International Congress of Historical Sciences in Oslo 2000*, ed. Even Lange et al. (CD-ROM). Commemorative volume (Oslo, 2000).
58. François Bédarida died only one year later, on 16 Sep. 2001. Necrology by Jean-Claude Robert in ICHS, *Bulletin d'information*, no. 27 (2001): 213f.

59. Published in ICHS, *Bulletin d'information*, no. 27 (2001): 27–37, along with an English version which I quote here; some passages that seemed to have a somewhat obscure meaning were translated by me from the French original.
60. Revised version "The Status and Future of Universal History," in *Making Sense of Global History: The 19th International Congress of the Historical Sciences, Oslo 2000*. Commemorative volume. Ed. for the Organizing Committee by S. Sogner (Oslo, 2001), pp. 15–70 (hereafter Congress Oslo 2000: *Global History*).
61. W. H. McNeill, *The Shape of European History* (Oxford, 1974).
62. P. O'Brien, "Perspectives on Global History: Concepts and Methodology / Mondialisation de l'histoire: concepts et méthodologie," in *XIXe Congrès International des Sciences Historiques, Université d'Oslo, 6–13 août 2000. Actes: rapports, résumés et présentations des tables rondes. 19th International Congress of Historical Sciences, University of Oslo, 6–13 August 2000. Proceedings: reports, abstracts and round table introductions*, ed. A. Jølstad and M. Lunde (Oslo, 2000), p. 11 (hereafter Congress Oslo 2000: *Proceedings*).
63. Revised version: J. H., "Cultural Encounters between the Continents Over the Centuries," in Congress Oslo 2000: *Global History*, pp. 89–105.
64. See above, p. 322.
65. F. Dosse, "The Modes of Historicity as Experiential Traces," abstract in Congress Oslo 2000: *Proceedings*, p. 64. Extended version in Congress Oslo 2000: *Global History*, pp. 219–246.
66. Revised version: G. G. Iggers, "The Uses and Misuses of History: The Responsibility of the Historian. Past and Present," in Congress Oslo 2000: *Global History*, pp. 311–319.
67. H.-W. Goetz, "Historical Consciousness and Institutional Concern in European Medieval Historiography: Eleventh and Twelfth Centuries," in Congress Oslo 2000: *Global History*, pp. 350–365.
68. S. Zhuravlev, "Creating a Stalinist Model of Russian History in the 1930s. Maxim Gorky's Historical Initiatives," in Congress Oslo 2000: *Global History*, pp. 366–372.
69. F. Hartog, "The Witness and the Historian," in Congress Oslo 2000: *Global History*, pp. 320–337.
70. The papers of the section have been published in an enlarged version by R. Torstendahl, ed., *An Assessment of Twentieth-Century Historiography: Professionalism, Methodology, Writings* (Stockholm, 2000).
71. A. Prost, "*Representations of War and the Cultural History of France*," p. 11, quoted by J. Winter in Congress Oslo 2000: *Proceedings*, p. 415.
72. Somewhat acrimonious notes about the meeting by Bédarida are to be found in Archives Nationales, Fonds du CISH, cote 105, AS 177.
73. ICHS, *Bulletin d'information*, no. 27 (2001): 87–94.
74. Ibid., p. 104–120.

Appendices

I. Members of the Bureau of the International Committee of Historical Sciences, 1926–2000

1926	President:	Halvdan Koht	(Oslo)
	Vice-Presidents:	Alfons Dopsch	(Vienna)
		Henri Pirenne	(Ghent)
	Secretary-General:	Michel Lhéritier	(Paris)
	Treasurer:	Waldo G. Leland	(Washington, D.C.)
	Assessor Members:	Karl Brandi	(Göttingen)
		Bronisław Dembiński	(Poznan)
		Gaetano De Sanctis	(Turin)
		Harold W. V. Temperley	(Cambridge)
1928	President:	Halvdan Koht	(Oslo)
	Vice-Presidents:	Bronisław Dembiński	(Poznan)
		Alfons Dopsch	(Vienna)
	Secretary-General:	Michel Lhéritier	(Paris)
	Treasurer:	Waldo G. Leland	(Washington, D.C.)
	Assessor Members:	Karl Brandi	(Göttingen)
		Gaetano De Sanctis, until 1931	(Turin)
		Josef Šusta	(Prague)
		Harold W. V. Temperley	(Cambridge)
1933	President:	Harold W. V. Temperley	(Cambridge)
	Vice-Presidents:	Bronisław Dembiński	(Poznan)
		Karl Brandi	(Göttingen)
	Secretary-General:	Michel Lhéritier	(Paris)
	Treasurer:	Hans Nabholz	(Zurich)
	Assessor Members:	P. Hippolyte Delehaye	(Brussels)
		Sándor Domanovszky	(Budapest)

		Don Luis Nicolau d'Olwer	(Barcelona)
		Vincenzo Ussani, until 1936	(Rome)
	Counsellors-Members:	Halvdan Koht	(Oslo)
		Waldo G. Leland	(Washington, D.C.)
1938	President:	Waldo G. Leland	(Washington, D.C.)
	Vice-Presidents:	Nicolae Iorga	(Bucharest)
		Hans Nabholz	(Zurich)
	Secretary-General:	Michel Lhéritier	(Paris)
	Treasurer:	Ernest L. Woodward	(Oxford)
	Assessor Members:	François L. Ganshof	(Ghent)
		Marceli Handelsman	(Warsaw)
		Robert Holtzmann	(Berlin)
		Gioacchino Volpe	(Rome)
	Counsellors- Members:	Halvdan Koht	(Oslo)
		Harold W. V. Temperley	(Cambridge)
1948	President:	Hans Nabholz	(Zurich)
	Vice Presidents:	Sir Charles Webster	(London)
		Robert Fawtier	(Paris)
	Secretary-General:	Charles Morazé	(Paris)
	Treasurer:	Anton Largiadér	(Zurich)
	Assessor Members:	Axel Lindvald	(Copenhagen)
		Donald Mac Kay	(Cambridge, Mass.)
		Karel Stloukal	(Prague)
	Counsellors-Members:	Halvdan Koht	(Oslo)
		Waldo G. Leland	(Washington, D.C.)
1950	President:	Robert Fawtier	(Paris)
	Vice-Presidents:	Sir Charles Webster	(London)
		Nils Ahnlund	(Stockholm)
	Secretary-General:	Michel François	(Paris)
	Treasurer:	Anton Largiadér	(Zurich)
	Assessor Members:	Donald Mac Kay	(Cambridge, Mass.)
		Frans Van Kalken	(Brussels)
		Heinrich F. Schmid	(Vienna)
		Silvio Zavala	(Mexico)
		Luigi Salvatorelli, until 1952	(Rome)
		Federico Chabod (1952–55)	(Rome)
	Counsellors-Members:	Halvdan Koht	(Oslo)
		Waldo G. Leland	(Washington, D.C.)
		Hans Nabholz	(Zurich)

I. Members of the Bureau of the International Committee of Historical Sciences, 1926–2000 (cont.)

1955	President:	Federico Chabod	(Rome)
	Vice-Presidents:	Sir Charles Webster	(London)
		Nils Ahnlund, until 1957	(Stockholm)
		Torvald Höjer (1957–60)	(Stockholm)
	Secretary-General:	Michel François	(Paris)
	Treasurer:	Louis Junod	(Lausanne)
	Assessor Members:	Donald Mac Kay	(Amherst, Mass.)
		Izaak J. Brugmans	(Amsterdam)
		Gerhard Ritter	(Freiburg)
		Heinrich F. Schmid	(Vienna)
		Anna M. Pankratova, until 1957	(Moscow)
		Aleksandr A. Guber (1957–60)	(Moscow)
	Counsellors-Members:	Halvdan Koht	(Oslo)
		Waldo G. Leland	(Washington, D.C.)
		Hans Nabholz	(Zurich)
		Robert Fawtier	(Paris)
1960	President:	Heinrich F. Schmid (d. 1963)	(Vienna)
	Vice-Presidents:	Torvald Höjer, until 1962	(Stockholm)
		Gerhard Ritter (1962–65)	(Freiburg)
		Aleksandr A. Guber	(Moscow)
	Secretary-General:	Michel François	(Paris)
	Treasurer:	Louis Junod	(Lausanne)
	Assessor Members:	Ramon Carande	(Seville)
		Paul Harsin	(Liège)
		Ernest F. Jacob	(Oxford)
		Gerhard Ritter, until 1962	(Freiburg)
		Raffaello Morghen (1962–65)	(Rome)
		Boyd C. Shafer	(Saint Paul, Minn.)
		Kohachiro Takahashi	(Tokyo)
	Counsellor-Member:	Robert Fawtier	(Paris)
1965	President:	Paul Harsin	(Liège)
	Vice-Presidents:	Aleksandr A. Guber	(Moscow)
		Boyd C. Shafer	(Saint Paul, Minn.)
	Secretary-General:	Michel François	(Paris)
	Treasurer:	Louis Junod, until 1967	(Lausanne)
		Jean-Charles Biaudet (1967–70)	(Lausanne)
	Assessor Members:	Friedrich Engel-Janosi	(Vienna)
		Aleksander Gieysztor	(Warsaw)
		Ernest F. Jacob	(Oxford)
		Raffaello Morghen	(Rome)

		Jiorjio Tadić	(Belgrade)
		Kohachiro Takahashi	(Tokyo)
	Counsellor-Member:	Robert Fawtier (d. 1966)	(Paris)

1970	President:	Aleksandr A. Guber (d. 1971)	(Moscow)
		Evgenii M. Zhukov (1972–75)	(Moscow)
	Vice-Presidents:	Boyd C. Shafer	(Tucson, Ariz.)
		Karl D. Erdmann	(Kiel)
	Secretary-General:	Michel François	(Paris)
	Treasurer:	Jean-Charles Biaudet	(Lausanne)
	Assessor Members:	Kohachiro Takahashi	(Tokyo)
		Aleksander Gieysztor	(Warsaw)
		P. Miguel Batllori	(Vatican)
		Mihai Berza	(Bucharest)
		Lewis Hertzman	(Toronto)
		Folke Lindberg	(Stockholm)
	Counsellor-Member:	Paul Harsin	(Liège)

1975	President:	Karl D. Erdmann	(Kiel)
	Vice-Presidents:	Aleksander Gieysztor	(Warsaw)
		Gordon A. Craig	(Stanford)
	Secretary-General:	Michel François	(Paris)
	Treasurer:	Jean-Charles Biaudet	(Lausanne)
	Assessor Members:	P. Miguel Batllori	(Vatican)
		Mihai Berza (d. 1978)	(Bucharest)
		Lewis Hertzman	(Toronto)
		Satish Chandra	(New Delhi)
		Kåre D. Tønneson	(Oslo)
		Domenico Demarco	(Naples)
	Counsellors-Members:	Paul Harsin	(Liège)
		Evgenii M. Zhukov (d. 1980)	(Moscow)

1980	President:	Aleksander Gieysztor	(Warsaw)
	Vice-Presidents:	Gordon A. Craig	(Stanford)
		Domenico Demarco	(Naples)
	Secretary-General:	Hélène Ahrweiler	(Paris)
	Treasurer:	Alain Dubois	(Lausanne)
	Assessor Members:	Satish Chandra	(New Dehli)
		Kåre D. Tønneson	(Oslo)
		Theodore C. Barker	(London)
		Ernesto de la Torre Villar	(Mexico)
		György Ránki	(Budapest)
		Sergei L. Tikhvinsky	(Moscow)

I. Members of the Bureau of the International Committee of Historical Sciences, 1926–2000 *(cont.)*

	Counsellors-Members:	Karl D. Erdmann	(Kiel)
		Michel François (d. 1981)	(Paris)
1985	President:	Ernesto de la Torre Villar	(Mexico)
	Vice-Presidents:	György Ránki (d. 1988)	(Budapest)
		Theodore C. Barker	(London)
	Secretary-General:	Hélène Ahrweiler	(Paris)
	Treasurer:	Alain Dubois	(Lausanne)
	Assessor Members:	Eloy Benito Ruano	(Madrid)
		Carl N. Degler	(Washington, D.C.)
		Saiyid Nurul Hasan	(Calcutta)
		Joachim Herrmann	(East Berlin)
		Masaki Miyake	(Chigasaki City, Japan)
		Sergei L. Tikhvinsky	(Moscow)
	Counsellors-Members:	Karl D. Erdmann (d. 1990)	(Kiel)
		Aleksander Gieysztor	(Warsaw)
1990	President:	Theodore C. Barker	(London)
	Vice-Presidents:	Ivan T. Berend	(Budapest/Los
		Eloy Benito Ruano	(Madrid)
	Secretary-General:	François Bédarida	(Paris)
	Treasurer:	Alain Dubois	(Lausanne)
	Assessor Members:	Natalie Zemon Davis	(Princeton)
		Joachim Herrmann	(Berlin)
		Joannis Karayannopoulos	(Athens)
		Masaki Miyake	(Chigasaki City, Japan)
		Saiyid Nurul Hasan (d. 1993)	(Calcutta)
		Satish Chandra (1993–95)	(New Delhi)
		Alexander O. Chubaryan	(Moscow)
	Counsellors-Members:	Aleksander Gieysztor	(Warsaw)
		Ernesto de la Torre Villar	(Mexico)
1995	President:	Ivan T. Berend	(Los Angeles)
	Vice-Presidents:	Natalie Zemon Davis	(Princeton)
		Alexander O. Chubaryan	(Moscow)
	Secretary-General:	François Bédarida	(Paris)
	Treasurer:	Pierre Ducrey	(Lausanne)
	Assessor Members:	Girolamo Arnaldi, until 1998	(Rome)
		Rosario Villari (1998–2000)	(Rome)
		Jürgen Kocka	(Berlin)
		Ravinder Kumar	(New Delhi)

		after 1998 Romila Thapar	(New Delhi)
		Hiroyuki Ninomiya	(Tokyo)
		Eva Österberg	(Lund, Sweden)
		Jean-Claude Robert	(Montreal)
	Counsellors-Members:	Theodore C. Barker	(London)
		Ernesto de la Torre Villar	(Mexico)
	Honorary Counsellor:	Aleksander Gieysztor (d. 1999)	(Warsaw)
2000	President:	Jürgen Kocka	(Berlin)
	Vice-Presidents:	Eva Österberg	(Lund, Sweden)
		Romila Thapar	(New Delhi)
	Secretary-General:	Jean-Claude Robert	(Montreal)
	Treasurer:	Pierre Ducrey	(Lausanne)
	Assessor Members:	Gregorii Bongard-Levin	(Moscow)
		Catherine Coquery-Vidrovitch	(Paris)
		Michael Heyd	(Jerusalem)
		William Chester Jordan	(Princeton)
		Koichi Kabayama	(Tokyo)
		José Luis Peset	(Madrid)
	Counsellors-Members:	Ivan T. Berend	(Los Angeles)
		Theodore C. Barker (d. 2001)	(Faversham, U.K.)

II. Members of the International Committee of Historical Sciences, 1926–2003

1. National Committees

Listed according to information contained in the *Bulletin of the International Committee of Historical Sciences*, 1926–1939, *Bulletin d'information*, 1953–2003, and annual membership lists 1985–2003 arranged by secretary-general Jean-Claude Robert for this book. Up to 1939, this table shows the status at the time of the respective General Assembly; from 1953 to 1986, it shows the status in the year of appearance of the individual issues of the *Bulletin d'information;* from 1987 to 2002, when annual lists (with the exception of 1990) are available in the *Bulletin d'information* and the compilation by J.-C. Robert, the development is shown in one column (in parentheses: year of first appearance in the membership list). A complete list is presented for the years 1926, 1948, and 2003. For the intermediary years, only new members are shown.

a) 1926–1939

1926	1927	1928	1929	1930	1931	1932	1933	1938	1939
Argentina									
Austria[1]	Algeria/Tunisia								
Belgium									
Brazil									
Bulgaria									
Czechoslovakia		Chile						China	
Denmark	Danzig		Canada						
	Estonia					Egypt	Ecuador		
France	Finland								
Germany									
Great Britain	Greece								
	Hungary								
Italy				India					
Japan				Latvia	Lithuania			Indochina	Luxembourg
					Malta			Ireland	
					Mexico				
Netherlands									
Norway									
Poland									
Portugal									
Romania									
Sweden									
Switzerland									
Spain	Turkey								
United States		Uruguay	Ukraine					Vatican	
USSR[2]	Yugoslavia								

1. Included in the national committee of the German Reich in 1938.
2. Was invited to Geneva and recognized as a member in 1926, but only began active participation in the ICHS in 1928.

b) 1948–1954

For 1948–1950, the listed members were present at the meetings of the General Assembly of 1948 and 1950 (Paris, 5–6 April 1948, minutes in the Nabholz papers, 28,3; Paris, 28 August and 3 September 1950, minutes in Archives CISH, box 26). The actual membership of some national committees remained uncertain until 1952/53. In principle, the membership status of 1939 was to remain in effect. However, national committees that did not reassume their regular cooperation with the ICHS by 1952 were not included in the first published membership list in the *Bulletin d'information*, no. 1 (1953). They were later "reintegrated" by a readmission procedure. On Germany, Austria, Italy, and Japan, see pp. 191 and 202–204 above; on the Eastern Bloc nations, see note 2 below and under the years 1954–1955. The committees that were not named in the membership list of 1953 are shown in italics.

1948	1950	1953	1954
	Algeria/Tunisia[3]		
Austria	Argentina[4]		
Belgium			
Canada			
Czechoslovakia[2]			*Czechoslovakia*[2]
Denmark			
	Egypt[5]		
France	Finland		
Greece[1]		Germany[13]	
Great Britain			
Hungary[2]			
Italy	India[6]		
	Ireland[7]		
	Israel[8]		
Luxembourg			
	Mexico[9]		
Netherlands			
Norway			
Poland[2]	Portugal		*Poland*[2]
Sweden	Spain[10]		
Switzerland			
	Turkey[11]		
United States			
	Vatican[12]	Yugoslavia[14]	*Vatican*[12]

1. Reintegrated in 1956.
2. Participation in the ICHS until 1949/50. Then, like the USSR and the other Eastern Bloc nations, it no longer exercised its membership. Poland and Czechoslovakia were again named as members in the ICHS *Bulletin d'information* in 1954; Hungary, the USSR, and Romania followed in 1955; Bulgaria in 1956. After the dissolution of the Czechoslovakian state, the Czech Republic and Slovakia became members of the ICHS (see below 1993).
3. No longer listed as a member after 1956/57. Tunisia was readmitted in 1990.
4. Exercised its membership irregularly until 1974. Not included in the membership list from 1954 to 1964.

b) 1948–1954 *(cont.)*

5. Represented by the Ministry of Education in Cairo. In 1959 transformed into the "United Arab Republic" with the same contact office. See 1959 and 1985.
6. Not listed as a member after 1957; readmitted in 1960.
7. As before 1945, the Irish national committee represents both parts of Ireland.
8. Admitted as a new member at the General Assembly on 3 Sep. 1950.
9. Reintegrated in 1968.
10. Reintegrated in 1950.
11. Reintegrated in 1957.
12. Reintegrated in 1954. According to ICHS, *Bulletin d'information*, no. 2 (1954), the Vatican, which had been admitted as a member in 1950 (and in 1938) and was represented at the General Assembly of 1950, definitely joined the ICHS in March 1954.
13. The Verband der Historiker Deutschlands, which was readmitted to the ICHS in 1951, represented both parts of Germany until 1970.
14. Listed as a member until 1993; successor members after the dissolution of the Yugoslavian state listed in column 1986–2002.

c) 1955–2002

1955	1957	1959	1961	1964	1968	1973	1976	1985	1986–2002
				Australia	Albania[1]			Andorra[2]	Bielorus (1989)
Brazil[3]	Bulgaria[4]								Brazil (1989)[5]
				Cyprus	Columbia[6]			China PR[7]	Chile (2001)
					Cuba[8]				Croatia (1996)
						Ethiopia[9]		Egypt[10]	Czechia (1993)
		Greece				Germany FRG [11]			Georgia (2002)
Hungary[12]						Germany GDR [11]			Guinea (1990)[13]
Japan			India[14]				Iraq[15]		Iceland (1989)
						Korea North[16]		Kenya[17]	Latvia (1996)[18]
Malta[19]			Mongolia PR[20]		Mexico	Korea South[16]			Lithuania (1996)[18]
								Nigeria[17]	Morocco (1998)
					Paraguay[6]				Peru (2001)
Romania[12]									Russia (1992)[21]
									Slovakia (1993)
									Slovenia (1996)
									South Africa (1996)[22]
	Turkey								Tunisia (1989)[23]
USSR[12]	Uruguay[24]	United Arab. Republic[25]							Ukraine (1997)[26]
									Uruguay (1990)[27]
					Venezuela[28]				Vietnam (1990)
							Zaire		

c) 1955–2002 *(cont.)*

1. However, it did not exercise its ICHS membership until 1980.
2. No longer listed as a member after 2001.
3. No longer listed as a member after 1969 since the link to ICHS was not maintained. Readmitted in 1989.
4. See under 1955, note 12.
5. See under 1955, note 3.
6. Maintained no link to the ICHS, therefore no longer listed as a member after 1985.
7. Admitted already in 1938, but did not maintain the link to the ICHS from 1945 to 1980. Until 1999, the contacts with the ICHS remained unsatisfactory, but the ICHS continued to list China as a member.
8. Did not exercise its membership until 1982. Did not maintain its link to the ICHS after 1986, therefore no longer listed as a member after 1992.
9. No link to the ICHS after 1974, therefore no longer listed as a member in 1985.
10. Readmitted in 1980 following the expiration of the membership of the United Arab Republic in 1973. Did not maintain the link to the ICHS and therefore was no longer listed as a member after 1992.
11. The joint delegation of the two German states ended with the admission of the GDR in 1970; reunification in 1990.
12. See under 1948, note 2. The USSR and the other Eastern Bloc nations (with the exception of Bulgaria, see under 1957) reassumed their participation in the ICHS, which they had neither formally left nor been excluded from, on the occasion of the International Congress in Rome in 1955. In 1992, the place of the USSR was taken by the national committee of Russia.
13. Retained in the membership list, though it did not develop any activities. See ICHS, *Bulletin d'information*, no. 27 (2002): 32, report by the secretary-general.
14. See under 1950, note 6.
15. Did not exercise its ICHS membership, thus was not listed as a member after 1985.
16. The ICHS first insisted on allowing only one delegation for divided nations, and thus rejected North Korea's membership application since 1957. In 1970 it agreed to the admission of both Korean states. North Korea did not exercise its link to the ICHS from 1974 to 1980 and from 1989 to 2002; therefore it was no longer listed as a member after 2001.
17. Did not maintain the link to the ICHS, therefore no longer listed as members after 1992.
18. Already admitted in 1930 resp. 1931, no longer listed as a member after 1945 (see above, p. 196).
19. Represented by the Ministry of Education; no longer listed as a member after 1969.
20. Did not maintain its link to the ICHS after 1991, therefore no longer listed as a member in 2002.
21. Took the place of the USSR.
22. Retained in the membership list, though it withdrew in 1998 without explaining this decision. In 2001, it renewed its interest in the ICHS.
23. See under 1950, note 3. Until 2001, its membership "existed only on the paper" (report by the secretary-general, ICHS, *Bulletin d'information*, no. 27 [2001]: 32), but the ICHS continued to list it as a member.
24. Remained without regular links with the ICHS, no longer listed as a member after 1965. Readmitted in 1990.
25. Took Egypt's place, represented by the Ministry of Education in Cairo (see under 1950); no longer listed as a member after 1973.
26. Already admitted in 1929, but remained without any activity of its own; no longer listed as a separate member after 1945. After 1997, the contacts with the ICHS remained unsatisfactory.
27. See under 1957. Did not maintain the link to the ICHS after 1990, therefore no longer listed as a member after 2001.
28. Did not exercise its link to the ICHS until 1975; withdrew in 2002.

d) 2003

Albania	Croatia	Hungary	Mexico	South African
Argentina	Cyprus	Iceland	Morocco	Spain
Australia	Czechia	India	Netherlands	Sweden
Austria	Denmark	Ireland	Norway	Switzerland
Belgium	Finland	Israel	Peru	Tunisia
Brazil	France	Italy	Poland	Turkey
Bulgaria	Georgian Republic	Japan	Portugal	Ukraine
Bielorus	Germany	Korea South	Romania	United States
Canada	Great Britain	Latvia	Russia	Vatican
Chile	Greece	Lithuania	Slovakia	Vietnam
China PR	Guinea	Luxembourg	Slovenia	

2. International Commissions

Listed according to information contained in *Bulletin of the International Committee of Historical Sciences*, 1926–1939, and *Bulletin d'information*, 1953–2003. Up to 1939, this table shows the status at the time of the respective General Assembly; beginning in 1953, it shows the status in the year of appearance of the individual issues of the *Bulletin d'information*. Complete lists are shown for the years 1927, 1928, 1948, and 1953. For the intermediary years, only new members are shown. The names printed in italics denote the international commissions that are still in existence today. According to Art. 2 of the statutes adopted in 1992, new internal commissions were to be transformed into international affiliated organizations within ten years. The ICHS General Assembly at the Montreal Congress 1995 decided to convince the internal commissions constituted before 1992 to make this change. Most of these commissions implemented the resolution until 2002.

a) 1926–1939

Year	Internal Commissions	External Commissions
1926	Comm. de bibliographie pour la préparation de l'Annuaire int. de bibliographie historique	
1927	Comm. pour le projet d'une Revue internationale d'histoire (until 1928) Comm. spéciale pour l'enseignement de l'histoire	
1928	Comm. pour l'Annuaire int. de bibliographie historique	Comm. d'histoire des sciences
	Comm. de publication	Comm. d'histoire littéraire moderne
	Comm. pour l'enseignement de l'histoire	Comm. de géographie historique (1931 internal commission)
	Comm. pour la liste des diplomates (Comm. d'histoire diplomatique)	*Comm. de démographie historique (comparée)*
	Comm. pour le recueil des constitutions (Comm. d'histoire constitutionnelle)	Comm. pour l'histoire de la banque
	Comm. pour la bibliographie rétrospective de la presse (Comm. d'histoire de la presse)	Comm. du despotisme éclairé
	Comm. de chronologie	Comm. des grands voyages et des grandes découvertes
	Comm. d'iconographie	
	Comm. pour la coordination des recherches aux Archives Vaticanes (1932 external commission)	
1930	Comm. des Archives	
1931	Comm. de géographie historique	
	Comm. pour les abréviations	
1932		Comm. pour la bibliographie du pacifisme dans l'histoire

a) 1926–1939 (cont.)

1932	Comm. pour l'histoire des mouvements sociaux
	Comm. d'histoire coloniale
	Comm. internat. des Archives Vaticanes
1934	Comm. de numismatique
1936	Comm. pour l'histoire des assemblées d'états
1938	Comm. du Proche-Orient
	Comm. pour l'histoire de l'Extrême-Orient
	Comm. d'histoire militaire
	Comm. pour l'histoire de la Baltique
	Comm. d'histoire ecclésiastique

b) 1948–2003

	INTERNAL COMMISSIONS	INTERNATIONAL AFFILIATED ORGANIZATIONS
1948[1]	Comm. de Bibliographie (1953 internal commission) Comm. pour les listes diplomatiques (until 1951)	
1953	Comm. de Bibliographie internationale (until 1996)	Association int. des Etudes Byzantines
	Comm. d'Histoire diplomatique (until 1965)	Comm. Int. des Etudes Historiques Slaves
	Comm. Int. de Numismatique (1958 int. aff. organization)	Comm. int. des sciences onomastiques (until 1985)
	Comm. Int. pour l'Histoire des Assemblées d'Etats (1973 int. aff. organization.)	Instituto Panamericano de Geografia y Historia
	Comm. Int. d'Histoire Militaire Comparée (1972 int. aff. organization)	
	Comm. Int. d'Histoire Ecclésiastique (comparée) (1982 int. aff. organization)	
	Comm. Int. d'Histoire des Mouvements sociaux (after 1957: *et des Structures sociales;* 1965 int. aff. organization)	
	Comm. Int. de Démographie Historique (2000 int. aff. organization)	
	Comm. d'Iconographie (until 1955; renewed 1960–69)	
	Comm. d'Histoire de la Banque et des Changes (until 1955)	
	Comm. des Archives du Vatican (until 1955)	
	Comm. des sources de l'histoire des villes (until 1955; see 1968 below)	
	Comm. d'histoire des découvertes et de la colonisation (until 1954)	
	Comm. de chronologie (until 1954)	
1955		Unione Int. degli Istituti di Archeologia e Storia dell'Arte in Roma (later: … *Storia e Storia dell'Arte in Roma*)
		Association »Humanisme et Renaissance« (until 1957; then continued in the *Fédération int. des Instituts d'Histoire de la Renaissance*)

	INTERNAL COMMISSIONS	INTERNATIONAL AFFILIATED ORGANIZATIONS
1957		Fédération int. des Instituts d'Histoire de la Renaissance (after 1959: ... des Sociétés et Instituts pour l'étude de la Renaissance)
1959		Comm. Int. de Numismatique (previously internal Commission)
1961	Comm. int. d'histoire de la presse (until 1969)	Comm. int. d'Histoire Economique (after 1964: Association int. ...)
	Comm. Int. d'Histoire Maritime (1965 int. aff. organization)	
1964	Comm. Int. pour l'Histoire des Universités (1977 int. aff. organization)	Association Int. d'Histoire du Droit et des Institutions
1968	Comm. Int. pour l'Histoire des Villes (1977 int. aff. org.)	Association Int. d'Etudes du Sud-Est Européen
		Comm. Int. d'Histoire des Mouvements Sociaux et des Structures Sociales (previously internal commission; after 2002: Int. Social History Comm.)
		Comm. Int. d'Histoire Maritime (previously internal commission)
		Comm. Int. d'Histoire de la Deuxième Guerre Mondiale
1973	Comm. Int. de Diplomatique	Comm. Int. pour l'Histoire des Assemblées d'États/Int. Comm. for the History of Representative and Parliamentary Institutions (previously internal commission)
		Comm. Int. d'Histoire Militaire Comparée (previously internal commission)
1976	Comité Int. pour la Métrologie Historique	Association des Historiens Africains (1989 internal commission)
	Comm. Int. d'Histoire de la Révolution Française (2001 int. aff. organization)	
1977	Int. Association for Audiovisual Media in Historical Research and Education (after 1995: ... for Media and History)	Comm. Int. pour l'Histoire des Universités (previously internal commission)
		Comm. Int. pour l'Histoire des Villes (previously internal commission)
		Union des Historiens Arabes[2]
1986	Comm. Int. d'Histoire de l'Historiographie (admitted in 1980; 1985 int. aff. organization)	Int. Association of Historical Societies for the Study of Jewish History (admitted in 1980)
	Int. Comm. for the Application of Quantitative Methods in History (admitted in 1980; until 1999)	Comm. int. d'Histoire Ecclésiastique Comparée (internal commission until 1982)
	Comm. Int. d'Histoire des Relations Internationales (admitted in 1982; 1997 int. aff. organization)	Association Int. d'Histoire Contemporaine de l'Europe (admitted in 1980)
	Comm. Int. pour l'Histoire de la Révolution d'Octobre (1997: ... de la Révolution Russe; admitted in 1983)	Int. Gesellschaft für Geschichtsdidaktik / Int. Society for the History of Didactics (admitted in 1982)

b) 1948–2003 (cont.)

Year	INTERNAL COMMISSIONS	INTERNATIONAL AFFILIATED ORGANIZATIONS
1986	Société pour l'Histoire des Croisades et de l'Orient latin /Society for the Study of the Crusades and the Latin East (admitted in 1980; 2001 int. aff. organization)	Comm. Int. d'Histoire de l'Historiographie (internal commission until 1985; after 1996: Comm. Int. pour l'Histoire et la Théorie de l'Historiographie)
		Comm. Int. des Historiens Latino-Américanistes (admitted in 1985; until 1993)
1988	Comm. pour la Conservation et la Publication des Sources Contemporaines (until 1999)	
	Fédération Int. pour la Recherche en Histoire des Femmes	
1989	Association des Historiens Africains[3] (previously int. aff. org.)	
1991	Int. Standing Conference for the History of Education (2001 int. aff. organization)	
	Comité Int. de Paléographie latine	
	Majestas (Etudes de la Souveraineté)	
	Council on Peace Research in History (after 1994: Peace History Society)	
	Association contre la Manipulation de l'Histoire	
1998	Int. Comm. for Historical Journals	Comm. Int. d'Histoire des Relations Internationales (previously internal commission)
		Fédération Int. pour la Recherche en Histoire des Femmes (previously internal commission)
2001	Commission Int. pour l'étude de la Guerre froide	Comm. Int. de Démographie Historique (previously internal commission)
		Int. Society for the History of Physical Education and Sport
		Comm. Int. d'Histoire de la Révolution Française (previously internal commission)
		Int. Standing Conference for the History of Education (previously internal commission)
		Society for the Study of the Crusades and the Latin East (previously internal commission)
2002	Comm. Int. pour l'Histoire du Voyage et du Tourisme	

1. Status according to the first complete General Assembly of the ICHS after the war, Paris, 5–6 April 1948; minutes in Nabholz papers, 28/3.
2. Headquarters in Iraq; since 1999, no contacts with the ICHS, yet maintained in the membership list.
3. Maintained as a member, though it did not achieve significant activity. In 1999, the ICHS secretary-general Bédarida tried to stimulate its renaissance. ICHS, *Bulletin d'information*, no. 25 (1999): 43ff., "Report by the Secretary-General."

III. Participation of Individual Countries in the International Congresses, 1898–2000

1. Lectures, Reports, Communications

Statistics* drawn from the respectively most reliable information on papers actually presented at the Congresses: official reports in the proceedings of the Congresses, as far as they exist (1898–1903; 1923–65); for 1908, the published Congress program; for 1913, printed program in the Koht papers, Ms. Fol. 3668: 3; for 1970, contributions published in the Congress proceedings; for 1975, the program published under the title *Proceedings*; for 1980 and 1985, papers published in the Congress proceedings (*Rapports* and *Actes*); for 1990, 1995, and 2000, Congress programs (figures collected for this publication by the ICHS secretary-general J.-C. Robert). Titles: see bibliography, 3.

a) 1898–1938

Countries[1]	The Hague	Paris	Rome	Berlin	London	Brussels	Oslo	Warsaw	Zurich
	1898[2]	1900	1903	1908	1913	1923	1928[3]	1933[3]	1938[3]
Albania									1
Algeria							(1)	1	1
Austria[4]			5	15	7		8	4 (5)	7
Belgium	1	4	1	5	5	86	10	8 (9)	8
Brazil					1				
Bulgaria							1		1
Canada					1			1	
China									1
Columbia							1		
Czechoslovakia						3	8	10	13
Danzig							2	1	1
Denmark				3		3	3	1	1
Ecuador			1						
Egypt				2	4		2	1	1	2
Estonia								1	1
Finland					2		1	3	2	3 (2)
France	18	44	28	15[13]	15	121	77	51	53 (50)
Germany	8	6	18	69	28		42 (43)	23	13[9]
Great Britain	1	1	5	12	91	40	13 (14)	10 (9)	14

*Not included are discussion contributions, comments of "experts," and contributions to the meetings of international commissions within the framework of the International Congresses. For reports on which historians from various nations collaborated, the number of authors has been taken into consideration.

a) 1898–1938 (cont.)

Countries[1]	The Hague	Paris	Rome	Berlin	London	Brussels	Oslo	Warsaw	Zurich
	1898[2]	1900	1903	1908	1913	1923	1928[3]	1933[3]	1938[3]
Greece		2	2	4		4	1	1	
Iceland							1		
India					4	1		2	5
Ireland			1		2				
Italy	3	8	188	20	3	10	15	39	26 (27)
Japan	2								
Hungary[5]	2	5	1	1	1	3	3 (2)	13 (11)	13 (14)
Latvia								1	
Lithuania									3
Luxembourg		1							1
Malta								1	1
Monaco						2			
Netherlands	3	1		5	3	10	8 (5)	2	2
North Korea							2		
Norway				2	2	2	24	3 (4)	
Poland						18	33 (34)	73	28
Portugal		1					2		2 (1)
Romania			2			3	12 (11)	11 (13)	9 (8)
Russia/ USSR	4	6	5[6]	4	16[7]	9[8]	10	6 (10)	
Serbia	1		2						
South Africa			1				1		
Spain		3	2	2	1	7	1	3	1
Sweden	1	5	1	3	1	3	7		3
Switzerland	1	3	1	6	2	5	3	3 (4)	19 (18)
Syria									1
Turkey				1					2
United States	1	1	2	7	8	15	14 (16)	12 (10)	11
Vatican		2							1
Yugoslavia						4	3	2	1
Total	46	95	266	180	191	353	307 (308)	286 (285)	248 (243)

b) 1950–2000

Countries[1]	Paris	Rome	Stock-holm	Vienna	Moscow	San Francisco	Bucharest	Stuttgart	Madrid	Montreal	Oslo
	1950	1955	1960	1965	1970	1975	1980	1985	1990	1995	2000
Algeria	1										
Argentina									1	5	7
Australia	1						1		3	16	17
Austria	2	7	3	7	1		2	2	8	7	6
Bahrein									1		
Belgium	22	5	4	3	2		3	3	5	13	11
Benin								1			
Bolivia										1	
Brazil									1	4	7
Brunei										1	
Bulgaria					2	1	1	2	11	1	1
Burkina Faso								2			
Burundi											1
Cameroon										1	1
Canada		1			3	1	6	9	16	62	14
Chile									1		3
China (PR)							1	9	5	7	
Columbia								1			
Côte d'Ivoire										1	
Cyprus				1	1	1	3	1	2		
Czechoslovakia/Czechia			4	2	2	3	4	3	11	6	4
Denmark	4	3	2		1	1	5	5	6	4	9
Egypt	4								3		1
Ethiopia										1	
Finland		1	2	1	2		4	4	7	7	5
France	72	49	17	13	15	4	9	10	19	51	40
Germany/FRG[11]	[1][12]	22	14	7	7	9	12	14	25	49	37
Germany/GDR		1	1	4	4	3	8	8	33		
Great Britain	43	25	18	10	2	2	5	16	34	61	42
Greece							3	4	2	1	
Hong Kong									1		1
Hungary		1	3	1	3	5	7	3	17	7	10

b) 1950–2000 (cont.)

Countries[1]	Paris	Rome	Stockholm	Vienna	Moscow	San Francisco	Bucharest	Stuttgart	Madrid	Montreal	Oslo
	1950	1955	1960	1965	1970	1975	1980	1985	1990	1995	2000
Iceland									2	3	5
India							1	4	6	5	13
Ireland						1	2	1	3	4	6
Israel	2		2			1	1	3	19	22	8
Italy	48	33	12	6	7	5	10	6	9	36	22
Jamaica											1
Japan			4	3	4	2	7	6	19	30	21
Korea North								2	7		
Korea South						1	1	2	1	1	3
Latvia										2	1
Lebanon									1		
Malawi										3	
Malaysia										1	
Mali											1
Mexico		1		4					11	2	2
Mongolia				1		1	1	2			
Morocco										1	
Mozambique									1		
Netherlands	7	4	4		1	1	2	1	4	14	15
New Zealand										2	2
Nigeria							1		1	2	4
Northern Ireland										1	1
Norway	2	1	3			1	3	2	14	3	33
Pakistan										1	
Peru										3	1
Philippines											1
Poland	[2][10]	48	5		4	5	8	6	22	19	8
Portugal								1		2	
Romania			4	3	3	3	10	5	16	7	2
Russian Federation										36	19
Saudi Arabia									2		
Senegal							2			1	1

Countries[1]	Paris 1950	Rome 1955	Stock-holm 1960	Vienna 1965	Moscow 1970	San Francisco 1975	Bucharest 1980	Stuttgart 1985	Madrid 1990	Montreal 1995	Oslo 2000
Slovakia											2
Slovenia											1
South Africa										2	9
Spain	8	8	7	2	2	2	6	6	39	20	9
Sweden	8	5	8		2	2	2	2	1	13	14
Switzerland	8	7	3		1	1	4	4	10	9	10
Syria										1	1
Taiwan											1
Tanzania									1	1	
Tunisia									1		
Turkey	1		2	1		1	3			1	
U. A. E.									1		
Ukraine										1	
Uruguay		1								1	
United States	17	24	16	7	11	8	10	16	74	101	81
USSR		11	13	6	12	7	9	17	29		
Vatican		2	1			1	6	1	2	3	
Venezuela							2		3	1	
Vietnam										1	
Yugoslavia			4	7	2	1	2	4	4	6	
Zaire								3		1	
Zambia										1	
Zimbabwe										3	
N/A										13	1
Total	255	220	159	84	93	75	158	182	535	666	522

1. Understood as existing within their political boundaries at the time of the respective Congress.
2. Aside from the countries listed here, there was also one paper from Costa Rica (by the ambassador in Paris), which was not represented at the other International Congresses.
3. For 1928, 1933, and 1938, the respective organizing committees published statistics on participants and lectures, see ICHS, *Bulletin* 2 (1929/30): 21; 7 (1935): 139;11 (1939): 469f. Figures diverging from these statistics on the basis of the Congress proceedings are enclosed in parentheses.
4. Understood as Cisleithania until 1918, i.e., including the universities of Prague, Cracow, and Lemberg (Lvov). In 1908, one speaker from Lemberg was scheduled, in 1913 two speakers from Cracow.
5. Understood as Transleithania, i.e., including Agram, whose university was represented by one speaker in 1913.
6. Including four speakers from Russian Poland.
7. Including three speakers from Russian Poland.
8. Excluding emigrated historians, who are included with the countries at whose universities they taught.
9. Excluding Austrian historians, although they were included in the German national committee after the *Anschluß*.
10. Papers sent before the opening of the Congress, published in the Congress proceedings and considered at the Congress, whose authors—such as the other Poles who had registered for the Congress—were ultimately unable to attend.
11. Until 1990, the old FRG, including West-Berlin; after 1990, including the former GDR.
12. Communication of a historian from the Saarland.
13. See p. 45f. above.

2. Congress Participants

Figures derived from the sources listed below for the individual Congresses. The printed lists of participants refer to persons who registered. The actual number of participants cannot be determined exactly for the individual countries.

Sources:

1898:   Congress The Hague 1898: *Annales*, no. 1, pp. XI–XX (list of participants). In parentheses: information on actual participation from *Historisk Tidskrift* (Stockholm, 1898), 270.

1900:   Congress Paris 1900: *Annales*, vol. 1, pp. IX–XLIV (list of participants).

1903:   Congress Rome 1903: *Atti*, vol. 1, pp. 33–63 (list of participants).

1908:   "Mitglieder-Liste. Internationaler Kongreß für Historische Wissenschaften Berlin. 6.–12. August 1908." Supplement to *Kongreß-Tageblatt*, Nr. 6, 11 August 1908.

1923:   Congress Brussels 1923: *Compte rendu*, pp. 495–522 (list of participants).

1928:   ICHS, *Bulletin* 2: 20 (figures from organizing committee).

1933:   ICHS, *Bulletin* 7: 139 (figures from organizing committee).

1938:   ICHS, *Bulletin* 11: 467f. (figures from organizing committee, separated according to registered and, in parentheses, actually attending persons).

1950:   Congress Paris 1950: *Rapports*, pp. 305–324 (list of participants).

1955:   According to the files of the Giunta Centrale per gli Studi Storici, Rome, figures collected for this publication by its secretary-general, Prof. G. Vitucci. Considerably conflicting figures, based on a printed list of participants, in Mac Kay, "Tenth International Congress," p. 504; see pp. 221 and 240, note 3, above.

1960:   "XIe Congrès International des Sciences Historiques Stockholm, 21–28 Août 1960. Supplément: Listes des Membres. Circulaire Générale No. 4" (Rijksarkiv, Stockholm, files on the Stockholm Congress).

1965:   "Douzième Congrès International des Sciences Historiques Vienne, 29 Août–5 Septembre 1965: Liste des participants" and "Liste des participants (Annexe)" (Vienna, 1965); both made available from the files of the Austrian national committee by Dr. L. Mikoletzky.

1970:   Information based on files of the national committee of the USSR, made available by Prof. S. L. Tikhvinsky.

1975:   Congress San Francisco 1975: *Proceedings*, pp. 153–231 (list of participants).

1980:   "Quinzième Congrès international des Sciences historiques: Liste des participants" [Bucharest, 1980] and "Liste des Participants, Supplément nos. 1–2" (Bucharest, 1980), made available from the files of the Romanian national committee by Prof. D. Berindei.

1985:   "16. Internationaler Kongreß der Geschichtswissenschaften, Stuttgart 25. August–1. September 1985: Teilnehmerliste" and "1. Nachtragsliste" (Stuttgart, 1985). In parentheses: figures from a list of participants made during the Congress according to nations, status of 27 Aug. 1985.

1990:   Published list of participants. In parentheses, figures reported by the organizing committee.

1995:   Partial list of registered participants, in "Report of the Organising Committee," pp. 38–39. In parentheses, final figures from "Report of the Organising Committee," p. 24.

2000:   Computerized address list of participants. In parentheses, final figures from the "Report of the Organising Committee," p. 10 (figures for 1990–2000 made available by secretary-general Jean-Claude Robert).

a) 1898–1938

Countries[1]	The Hague	Paris	Rome	Berlin	London	Brussels	Oslo	Warsaw	Zurich
	1898	1900	1903	1908	1913[8]	1923	1928	1933	1938
Afghanistan									1
Albania									1
Algeria		1	1				3	2	4 (2)
Argentina		1	1				1	1	1 (1)
Australia		1	1						2 (2)
Austria[3]	3 (1)	10[15]	85[16]	30[17]	[25][10]		23	7	
Belgium	34 (10)	31	27	16		422	15	33	56 (31)
Brazil		10		1			3	2	1 (1)
Bulgaria							1		
Canada		1	1	1		3	2	2	1 (1)
Chile		1					2		2 (2)
China									1 (1)
Cuba		2							
Czechoslovakia						9	12	35	46 (31)
Danzig							5	6	6 (5)
Denmark		1	4	12		1	34	12	22 (17)
Dominican Rep.		2							
Egypt	1		8	7		3	1	3	5 (4)
Estonia						1	5	3	7 (6)
Finland[2]							10	8	7 (4)
France	118 (31)	540	194	22[24]	22	222	132	108	109 (67)
Germany	46 (22)	21	358	710	65		121	59	188 (104)[25]
Great Britain	7 (3)	17	74	33	450	137	56	51	83 (44)
Greece	1 (1)	3	8	4		4	3	3	7 (1)
Guatemala									1 (1)
Hungary[6]	6 (2)	11[21]	12[22]	13[23]	[25][10]	3	9	26	37 (25)
India			3			2		3	10 (7)
Iran	1	1							1 (-)
Ireland		1	4	3		5	2	1	10 (8)
Iceland							1		
Israel/Palestine									1 (1)
Italy		9 (2)	42	1144	57		34	28	86	89 (44)

a) 1898–1938 (cont.)

Countries[1]	The Hague	Paris	Rome	Berlin	London	Brussels	Oslo	Warsaw	Zurich
	1898	1900	1903	1908	1913[8]	1923	1928	1933	1938
Japan	2 (5)	1		4		6	2		1 (1)
Latvia							1	10	5 (2)
Lebanon				1		1			
Libya		1							
Liechtenstein									1 (1)
Lithuania						2			5 (3)
Luxembourg	2 (1)	3							3 (3)
Malta								2	3 (2)
Mexico		2						1	
Monaco		1				1		1	1 (1)
Netherlands	75 (15)	42	4	10		33	21	9	29 (21)
Norway			6	7		2	273	14	9 (4)
Peru			2						
Poland[4]						20	40	600	99 (87)
Portugal	4	5	9	2			2	1	2 (2)
Rhodesia						1			
Romania	8 (1)	12	12			4	18	25	46 (21)
Russia[5]/ USSR	6 (2)	26[18]	47[19]	43[20]	30	2	15	8	
San Marino			2						
Serbia	1 (1)	2	1						
South Africa		1		1		1	2		2 (1)
Spain	3	8	8	2		18	12	14	17 (9)
Sweden	3 (2)	14	13	30		5	30	7	9 (8)
Switzerland	8 (3)	12	16	14		18	8	10	204 (147)
Syria									1 (1)
Tunisia				1					
Turkey		2					1	3	5 (5)
Uruguay	1						1		2 (-)
United States	23 (12)	34	14	19	20	35	51	47	49 (30)
Vatican[27]								2	
Venezuela		1							
Yugoslavia						4	4	5	9 (5)
Total[7]	360 (115) (c.150)[11]	864 (100–200)	2060 (1500–1800)	1042 (c. 1000)	[680] (1000–1100)	999 (500)	950 (950)	1210 (1031)	1206 (770)

b) 1950–2000

Countries[1]	Paris	Rome	Stock-holm	Vienna	Moscow[9]	San Francisco	Bucharest	Stuttgart	Madrid	Montreal	Oslo
	1950	1955	1960	1965	1970	1975	1980	1985	1990	1995	2000
Albania				3			4	4 (4)	4	2	
Algeria	4								1	1	1
Andorra									2		
Argentina	2	1	3	3		6	16	7 (8)	5	18	17
Australia			5	3		6	6	13 (13)	12	22	27
Austria	15	49	26	168		16	26	33 (35)	17	15	20
Bangladesh								1 (1)		1	1
Barbados						1					
Belgium	96	53	32	43		18	37	30 (31)	24	26	29
Benin								2 (2)			
Bolivia						1				1	1
Brazil	4			7		6	7	4 (5)	5	15	15
Brunei										1	
Bulgaria		1	3	22	160	19	109	5 (41)	2	9	5
Burkina Faso							1				
Burundi						1	3				
Byelorussia										1	1
Cameroon							3	2 (2)			4
Canada	10		8	18	35	55	36	34 (37)	24	445	50
Central African Rep.										1	
Chile			3	5		1		2 (2)		2	3
China PR							14	25 (22)	2	24	23
Columbia			1			1				1	
Congo				1				2 (2)			
Costa Rica										1	1
Côte d'Ivoire									1	1	
Croatia										4	
Cuba		1	1	1	2		7	(3)		1	
Cyprus					1	2	14	3 (3)	2		
Czechia										10	9
Czechoslo-vakia	2[14]	7	34	74	91	11	57	53 (51)	17		
Denmark	34	54	45	38	43	13	25	19 (18)	19	10	74
Dominican Rep.						1		1 (1)			
Ecuador		1	1				1	1 (1)			
Egypt	34		1				1	6 (6)	1	1	1
Estonia										1	1

b) 1950–2000 (cont.)

Countries[1]	Paris	Rome	Stock-holm	Vienna	Moscow[9]	San Francisco	Bucharest	Stuttgart	Madrid	Montreal	Oslo
	1950	1955	1960	1965	1970	1975	1980	1985	1990	1995	2000
Ethiopia											2
Finland[2]	6	8	21	8	16	3	23	37 (38)	21	17	23
France	327	320	159	282	173	83	132	83 (92)	73	81	64
Gambia											1
Georgia											5
Germany/FRG	14[12]	150[13]	132	301	117	77	65	473 (534)	117	75	97
Germany/GDR		14[13]	61	56	130	22	86	61 (61)			
Ghana						1	1				
Great Britain	115	212	142	202	19	31	57	80 (84)	49	95	126
Greece		4	4	10		3	18	28 (30)	4	2	5
Greenland										1	
Guatemala			1								1
Hong Kong						3		1 (1)			1
Hungary[6]		5	15	46	110	20	86	80	41	34	19
India	6	2	2	4		4	7	8 (10)	4	6	14
Indonesia						1			1		
Iran						2	2				
Iraq						1	4	2 (2)	1	1	
Ireland	5	15	6	13		9	8	6 (6)	7	12	11
Iceland			1				1	5 (5)	6	6	11
Israel	13	3	7	10		6	8	17 (16)	16	24	25
Italy	138	318	130	187	97	72	73	100 (111)	103	123	120
Jamaica											1
Japan	1	4	16	26	84	78	101	104 (111)	113	108	100
Jordan							1				
Kenya						1	1				1
Korea North						1	6				
Korea South			3	1		27	26	28 (28)	2	2	12
Koweit									1		
Latvia										1	3
Lebanon	4	1				3	7				2
Libya											
Liechtenstein											
Lithuania											2
Luxembourg	1	3	2	4			1	2 (2)	1	4	2
Malawi										1	
Malaysia						2					
Mali											2

Countries[1]	Paris	Rome	Stock-holm	Vienna	Moscow[9]	San Francisco	Bucharest	Stuttgart	Madrid	Montreal	Oslo
	1950	1955	1960	1965	1970	1975	1980	1985	1990	1995	2000
Malta											2
Mauritius										1	
Mexico	3	1	5	1	11	20	8	2 (2)	7	9	15
Monaco								(1)			
Mongolia			2	1		3	6	1 (1)			
Morocco	5		1	2			3	2 (2)		3	2
Netherlands	52	42	38	65	63	39	29	41 (40)	36	35	41
New Zealand		1				1			1	5	2
Nicaragua						2					2
Nigeria				1		2	5			1	3
Norway	12	24	39	28		16	25	32 (32)	33	30	318
Pakistan			1								
Paraguay						1					
Peru	1					1	1			1	
Philippines						1					2
Poland	4	12	14	35	162	22	77	65 (74)	13	22	19
Portugal	10	5	8	8		2	4	6 (6)	16	11	6
Puerto Rico						2			3		
Rhodesia											
Romania		27	18	51	79	14	794	45 (57)	20	27	21
Russia										39	37
Saudi Arabia							1				
Senegal					1	2				2	1
Slovakia										5	3
Slovenia										2	3
South Africa				3		3		(1)		5	14
Spain	21	33	34	50	82	54	95	53 (60)	568	48	30
Sri Lanka						1					
Sudan											1
Sweden	40	40	192	49	68	43	83	51 (53)	45	53	144
Switzerland	64	48	26	52	13	20	27	39 (42)	30	21	25
Syria				1				1 (1)		1	
Taiwan						5		3 (5)		1	2
Tanzania								1 (4)	1	1	
Trinidad & Tobago											1

b) 1950–2000 (cont.)

Countries[1]	Paris	Rome	Stock-holm	Vienna	Moscow[9]	San Francisco	Bucharest	Stuttgart	Madrid	Montreal	Oslo
	1950	1955	1960	1965	1970	1975	1980	1985	1990	1995	2000
Tunisia	2			3		2	3	3 (31)	1	2	
Turkey	7	10	12	21	15	5	16	22 (25)	1	1	1
U. A. E									3		
Ukraine										2	1
Uruguay		1	1	1		1			1	2	
United States	74	80	167	153		488	126	104 (117)	91	202	208
USSR		13	48	58	1283	82	125	5 (68)	6		
Vatican[27]											
Venezuela		3	2	1		3	4	5 (5)	11	5	
Vietnam						2	4			6	2
Yugoslavia		68	31	67	119	23	68	27 (35)	3	1	
Zaire						1	2	8 (6)	2	1	
Zimbabwe										2	
Total[7]	1126 (c.1400)	1633 (c.1500)	1509 (1523)	2189 (c.2250)	3305	1465 (1473)	2713[26] (2713)	1878 (2150)	1590 (2380)	1754 (2109)	1838 (2109)

1. Understood within their political boundaries on the respective date.
2. Part of the Russian delegation until 1918, see there.
3. Understood as Cisleithania until 1918.
4. Listed as part of the Russian and Austrian delegations until 1918, see there.
5. Including Russian Poland and Finland until 1918.
6. Understood as Transleithania until 1918.
7. Sum of the individual numbers, with the exception of 1913 and 1970; in parentheses information from the literature on the number of participants (not including accompanying persons).
8. According to Jameson, "International Congress," p. 682. He derived his figures from an early, provisional list of participants with a total of 680 names distributed during the Congress (actual number of participants: 1,000–1,100).
9. According to information from the national committee of the USSR, fifty countries took part in the Congress. However, the documents of the national committee upon which our figures are based contain only statistics for 25 states. In particular, the countries of the Third World (apparently with the exception of socialist states), which were represented by only a few participants, are lacking.
10. Austria-Hungary is not listed separately in the source (see note 8).
11. Aside from the countries listed here there was also one paper from Costa Rica (by the ambassador in Paris), which was not represented at the other International Congresses.
12. Including 2 non-Germans residing in the Federal Republic and 2 participants from the Saarland. No participants from the German Democratic Republic.
13. The source used here (see above, 1955), in which the participants from the two German states are numbered together, is specified by information from Haun, "Der X. Internationale Historikerkongreß," pp. 303 and 306f.
14. No participants according to the literature.
15. 7 Austrians, 2 Bohemians, 1 Pole.
16. 61 Austrians, 11 Bohemians/Moravians, 12 Poles, 1 Dalmatian.
17. 19 Austrians, 8 Bohemians/Moravians, 2 Poles, 1 Dalmatian.
18. 22 Russians, 1 Pole, 2 Finns.
19. 24 Russians, 16 Poles, 7 Finns.
20. 35 Russians, 8 Finns.
21. 9 Hungarians, 2 Croatians.
22. Only Hungarians.
23. 11 Hungarians, 2 Slovaks.
24. See above, p. 56, note 18.
25. Including Austria.
26. Including 1 participant each from Gabon, Kuwait, Panama, and Sudan, along with 3 from Andorra.
27. Members of the Vatican delegation were included in the delegations of the individual countries.

IV. Development of the Constitution of the International Committee of Historical Sciences, 1926–2000

From 1926 up to the present, the statutes of the ICHS are laid down in French. Since 1987, however, an English translation is added to the French text in the ICHS *Bulletin d'information*, with a note: "The text in French is the only official one." In the following, this translation is used to present the development of the constitution since 1977, the amended constitution adopted then still being valid in 1987. For the period from 1926 to 1975, the constitution is presented in the official French version. Passages printed in italics denote modifications. For the years 1926, 1960, and 1977, the whole text is presented; for the intermediary years, only the modified passages are shown. The amended version of 1977, modified in 1992, is still valid today and printed in each issue of the *Bulletin d'information*.

a) 1926–1957

Constitution of 14 May 1926[1]	Modification of 1933[2]	Modification of 1950[3]	Modification of 1957[4]
Préambule.—Les soussignés délégués des corps savants et des institutions qui se consacrent aux sciences historiques dans les pays suivants: réunis par le Bureau du Ve Congrès international des sciences historiques, conformément à la résolution adoptée par le Congrès du 15 avril 1923, décident de constituer un Comité international des sciences historiques avec les statuts ci-après.		Préambule: Les *délégués des corps savants et des institutions qui se consacrent aux sciences historiques réunis par le Bureau du Ve Congrès International des Sciences Historiques à Genève, conformément à la résolution adoptée par le Congrès du 15 avril 1923 à Bruxelles, ont décidé* de constituer un Comité International des Sciences Historiques avec les statuts ci-après.	
Article Premier. But du Comité.—Le Comité international des sciences historiques est créé pour travailler au développement des sciences historiques, en procédant par voie de coopération internationale. Il organisera les Congrès internationaux des sciences historiques. Il établira le règlement des Congrès et en publiera le compte rendu; il fixera le lieu et l'époque de chaque Congrès, encouragera pour chaque Congrès la formation d'un Comité national d'organisation et préparera le programme du Congrès d'accord avec ce Comité.			
Art. 2. Composition du Comité.—Le Comité est composé de délégués de tous les pays qui sont admis à s'y faire représenter. Chaque pays ne peut avoir plus de deux délégués titulaires pourvus du droit de vote auxquels peuvent être associés toutefois des délégués adjoints. Le mot pays s'applique à la fois aux pays souverains et aux pays non souverains, tels que dominions, protectorats, colonies et territoires sous mandat; les pays non souverains n'ont droit chacun qu'à un seul délégué ayant droit de vote.	Deletion of Art. 2, par. 2	Art. 2.—Le Comité est composé de délégués de tous les pays qui sont admis à s'y faire représenter. Chaque pays ne peut avoir plus de deux délégués titulaires pourvus du droit de vote auxquels peuvent être associés toutefois des délégués adjoints.	Art. 2.—Le Comité est composé de délégués de tous les pays qui sont admis à s'y faire représenter, ainsi que des *délégués d'organismes internationaux se consacrant à des recherches et à des publications relevant des sciences historiques, et dont l'affiliation au Comité International des Sciences Historiques a été décidée par l'Assemblée Générale*, sur la proposition du Bureau. Chaque pays et chaque organisme affilié ne peuvent avoir plus de deux délégués titulaires pourvus du droit de vote auxquels peuvent être associés toutefois des délégués adjoints.

Constitution of 14 May 1926[1]	Modification of 1933[2]	Modification of 1950[3]	Modification of 1957[4]
Art. 3. Election des délégués.—Les délégués des pays qui désirent se faire représenter dans le Comité sont élus dans chacun de ces pays par les corps savants et les institutions qui se consacrent aux sciences historiques. Les dispositions prises pour le choix des délégués seront portées à la connaissance du Comité qui se réserve le droit d'apprécier les questions douteuses sans autre préoccupation que celle de son rôle purement scientifique.		Art. 3.—Les délégués des pays qui désirent se faire représenter dans le Comité sont élus dans chacun de ces pays par les corps savants et les institutions qui se consacrent aux sciences historiques. *Les délégués des organismes affiliés au Comité International des Sciences Historiques sont élus par ces organismes.* Les dispositions prises …	
Art. 4. Séances du Comité.—Le Comité tiendra une séance plénière au moins une fois par an dans la ville qui aura été choisie par le Comité dans sa réunion précédente. Une séance plénière devra être tenue à l'occasion du Congrès international, au même moment et dans la même ville.	Art. 4: Le Comité tiendra une séance plénière au moins *tous les trois ans* dans …		
Art. 5. Votes du Comité.— Le Comité ne peut délibérer valablement en séance plénière qu'en présence des délégués de plus de la moitié des pays représentés au Comité.		Art. 5.—Le Comité ne peut délibérer valablement en séance plénière qu'en présence des délégués de plus de la moitié des pays *ou organismes* représentés au Comité.	
En séance plénière, le premier vote a lieu par tête. Si la majorité des trois quarts ne peut être obtenue, un deuxième vote aura lieu par pays, chaque pays disposant d'autant de voix qu'il peut avoir de délégués ayant le droit de vote. Le vote par pays est à la majorité des deux tiers des voix.		En séance plénière, le premier vote a lieu par tête. Si la majorité des trois quarts ne peut être obtenue, un deuxième vote aura lieu par pays *ou organisme*, chaque pays *ou organisme* disposant d'autant de voix qu'il peut avoir de délégués ayant le droit de vote. Le vote par pays *ou organisme* est à la majorité des deux tiers des voix.	

a) 1926–1957 (cont.)

En cas d'urgence, à la demande du Bureau, le vote peut avoir lieu en dehors des séances et par correspondance. Le vote est alors par tête et à la majorité des deux tiers du nombre total des délégués. Si cette majorité n'est pas atteinte, le second vote aura lieu à la simple majorité des votants, à condition qu'elle représente plus de la moitié des pays.	En cas d'urgence, à la demande du Bureau, le vote peut avoir lieu en dehors des séances et par correspondance. Le vote est alors par tête et à la majorité des deux tiers du nombre total des délégués. Si cette majorité n'est pas atteinte, le second vote aura lieu à la simple majorité des votants, à condition qu'elle représente plus de la moitié des pays *ou organismes*.	
Art. 6. Le Bureau du Comité.—Le Bureau du Comité comprend un président, deux vice-présidents, quatre membres assesseurs, un secrétaire général et un trésorier. Le Bureau est élu dans la séance plénière du Comité qui a lieu à l'occasion du Congrès international. Il reste en fonctions jusqu'au Congrès suivant. Il doit comprendre des représentants de cinq pays au moins. Le président et trois autres membres du Bureau doivent être remplacés à chaque élection générale. Il sera pourvu aux vacances à l'intérieur du Bureau par des élections partielles ordonnées par le Bureau. Le Bureau prépare l'ordre du jour des séances et les communique aux délégués deux mois à l'avance. Il a qualité pour prendre dans l'intervalle des séances les mesures les plus urgentes, pour convoquer en cas de nécessité les délégués en séances extraordinaires, et pour requérir au besoin leur vote par correspondance. Le Bureau contrôle la gestion des fonds du Comité, lui soumet d'autre part les comptes de l'exercice de chaque année, et lui présente annuellement un projet de budget. Le Bureau est chargé de préparer un rapport annuel des travaux du Comité. Le Bureau, représenté par son délégué ou fondé de pouvoirs, aura le droit d'ester en justice pour le Comité. Il acceptera les legs ou les donations, et il assumera, conformément aux statuts, tous actes juridiques quelconques.	Art. 6, par. 1: Le Bureau du Comité comprend un président, deux vice-présidents, *cinq* membres assesseurs, un secrétaire général, et un trésorier.	Art. 6: ... deux vice-présidents, six membres assesseurs, ...

Constitution of 14 May 1926[1]	Modification of 1933[2]	Modification of 1950[3]	Modification of 1957[4]
Art. 7. Cotisations et contributions.—Le Comité a deux budgets, l'un administratif et l'autre scientifique. Pour le budget administratif, chaque pays verse une cotisation annuelle qui sera la même pour tous les pays. Le budget scientifique sera alimenté par les disponibilités éventuelles du budget administratif, par des contributions extraordinaires, par des dons, des subventions et des legs.		Art. 7, par. 2: Pour le budget administratif, chaque pays *ou organisme* verse une cotisation annuelle qui sera la même pour tous les pays *ou organismes*. Le budget scientifique …	
Art. 8. Siège du Comité.—Le siège du Comité est fixé provisoirement à Washington pour les actes juridiques, la gestion des fonds et le dépôt des archives.	Art. 8: Le Siège du Comité se trouve dans la ville où sont déposés les fonds du Comité International des Sciences Historiques.		
Art. 9. Modification des statuts.—Des modifications aux statuts peuvent être proposées par le Bureau ou par les délégués de trois pays différents; les modifications proposées doivent être notifiées aux membres du Comité deux mois avant la séance où elles figureront à l'ordre du jour.		Art. 9. … à l'ordre du jour. *Seuls les pays ont droit de vote lorsque l'Assemblée Générale délibère d'une réforme de statuts.*	
Art. 10. Dissolution du Comité.—Le Comité devra se déclarer dissous si le nombre des pays qui y participent descend au-dessous de cinq.			

1. ICHS, *Bulletin* 1 (1929): 24–26.
2. Adopted on 20 Aug. 1933. ICHS, *Bulletin* 7 (1935): 68f.
3. Adopted on 3 Sept. 1950. ICHS, *Bulletin d'information*, no. 1 (1953): 5–7.
4. Adopted on 19 June 1957. ICHS, *Bulletin d'information*, no. 4 (1957): 7–9.

b) 1960–1975

New version of 1960 *(changes in content printed in italics)*[1]	Modification of 1975[6]
Art. 1. But du Comité.—Le Comité International des Sciences Historiques (C.I.S.H.) constitué à Genève le 14 mai 1926, conformément à une résolution adoptée par le Congrès des Sciences historiques tenu à Bruxelles le 15 avril 1923, *est une organisation non gouvernementale en forme d'association au sens des articles 60 et suivants du Code Civil suisse,* créée pour travailler au développement des sciences historiques en procédant par voie de coopération internationale. Il organise *notamment tous les cinq ans et en liaison avec le Comité national d'historiens du pays intéressé,* un Congrès International des Sciences historiques dont il fixe le lieu et la date *et dont il détermine le programme. Il assure, d'autre part, la publication d'instruments de travail de portée générale dont il confie le soin de la préparation à des Commissions internes constituées à cet effet dans son sein.*	
Art. 2. Composition du Comité.—Le Comité est composé: a) de Comités nationaux qui représentent les institutions de recherche historique de leur pays respectif; b) d'organismes internationaux affiliés qui se consacrent *exclusivement* à des recherches et à des publications de caractère *strictement scientifique* relevant des sciences historiques. L'affiliation au Comité International des Sciences historiques des uns et des autres est décidée par l'Assemblée générale, sur la proposition du Bureau, conformément aux modalités précisées à l'article 4 ci-dessous. *Toute demande d'affiliation devra parvenir au Bureau six mois avant la date de sa réunion annuelle.*[2]	
Art. 3. Séances du Comité.—Le Comité tiendra une Assemblée générale au moins tous les trois ans. *Chaque Congrès sera immédiatement précédé et suivi d'une Assemblée générale, le Bureau ayant toute latitude de convoquer, le cas échéant, une Assemblée générale extraordinaire.*	
Art. 4. Votes du Comité.—Chaque Comité national comme chaque organisme international affilié est représenté aux Assemblées générales du C.I.S.H. par *un délégué titulaire* ayant droit de vote auquel peut être associé toutefois *un délégué adjoint* qui ne dispose pas du droit de vote; *en cas d'absence du délégué titulaire, le délégué adjoint se substitue à lui et dispose alors du droit de vote.* L'Assemblée ne peut délibérer valablement qu'en présence des délégués ayant droit de vote de plus de la moitié des pays ou organismes internationaux affiliés représentés au C.I.S.H. Les votes ont lieu par Comité national et par organisme international affilié.[3] *Les votes portant sur l'admission de nouveaux membres, sur l'exclusion de membres du C.I.S.H. et sur les modifications éventuelles des statuts doivent rassembler une majorité égale aux deux tiers des votants; toutefois, comme il est dit à l'article 9, alinéa 2 ci-dessous, seuls les Comités nationaux ont droit de vote lorsque l'Assemblée générale délibère d'une réforme des statuts. Toute autre question soumise au vote de l'Assemblée générale ne requerra que la majorité absolue des votants.*	

New version of 1960 *(changes in content printed in italics)*[1]	Modification of 1975[6]
En cas d'urgence *et à l'exclusion des trois cas prévus au paragraphe précédent*, un vote peut avoir lieu, à la demande du Bureau, en dehors de la réunion d'une Assemblée générale; le vote a lieu alors par correspondance. *Dans ce cas, le Président de chaque Comité national et de chaque Organisme international affilié ou, en cas d'empêchement, tout autre répondant habilité par ces organisations est invité à se prononcer, au nom de son organisation. Le vote est acquis à la majorité absolue des votants.*	
Art 5. Le Bureau du Comité.—Le Bureau du Comité comprend un président, deux vice-présidents, six membres assesseurs, un secrétaire général et un trésorier. Le Bureau est élu *dans la première des deux Assemblées générales* qui ont lieu à l'occasion du Congrès international quinquennal; *il entre en fonction à la fin de ce même Congrès* et le demeure jusqu'à la fin du Congrès suivant.[4] Les membres du Bureau sont rééligibles; toutefois le président et trois autres membres du Bureau doivent être obligatoirement remplacés à chaque élection générale. Il pourra être pourvu aux vacances survenues à l'intérieur du Bureau par des élections partielles ordonnées par le Bureau. *Du Bureau font également partie, à titre de membres conseillers et seulement avec voix consultative, les anciens présidents du C.I.S.H. pour une durée de dix ans, à compter du jour de l'expiration de leur mandat présidentiel. A l'issue de cette période de dix années, les anciens présidents prennent le titre de conseillers honoraires sans faire partie du Bureau.* Le Bureau assure le fonctionnement et la coordination des activités du C.I.S.H. Il prépare l'ordre du jour des Assemblées générales et le communique aux participants deux mois à l'avance. Il a qualité pour prendre, dans l'intervalle, les mesures les plus urgentes, pour convoquer, en cas de nécessité, des Assemblées extraordinaires et pour requérir, au besoin, le vote par correspondance des Comités nationaux et organismes internationaux affiliés. Le Bureau contrôle la gestion des fonds du Comité; il soumet à l'Assemblée générale le compte des exercices annuels et lui présente les projets de budget. Le Bureau, représenté *par le Président ou* par un fondé de pouvoirs, aura le droit d'ester en justice pour le Comité. Il acceptera les legs ou les donations et il assumera, conformément aux statuts, tous actes juridiques quelconques.	Art. 5. Le Bureau du Comité.—Le Bureau du Comité comprend un président, *un premier vice-président, un deuxième vice-président,* six membres assesseurs, un secrétaire général et un trésorier. Le Bureau est élu dans la première des deux Assemblées générales qui ont lieu à l'occasion du Congrès international quinquennal; il entre en fonction à la fin de ce même Congrès et le demeure jusqu'à la fin du Congrès suivant. Les membres du Bureau sont rééligibles; toutefois le président et trois autres membres du Bureau doivent être obligatoirement remplacés à chaque élection générale. *Nul ne peut être éligible ou rééligible s'il a soixante-dix ans révolus.* Il pourra être pourvu aux vacances survenues à l'intérieur du Bureau par des élections partielles ordonnées par le Bureau. *Toutefois, en cas d'empêchement pour le président d'exercer son mandat jusqu'à son terme, le premier vice-président deviendra président et exercera son mandat jusqu'à ce terme; au cas où celui-ci serait à son tour empêché, il serait remplacé dans les mêmes conditions par le second vice-président.* Du Bureau font également partie, à titre de membres conseillers, mais seulement avec voix consultative *et en dehors de toute considération d'âge,* les anciens présidents du C.I.S.H. pour une durée de dix ans, à compter du jour de l'expiration de leur mandat présidentiel. A l'issue de cette période de dix années, les anciens présidents prennent le titre de conseillers honoraires sans faire partie du Bureau. Le Bureau assure …

b) 1960–1975 (cont.)

New version of 1960 (changes in content printed in italics)[1]	Modification of 1975[6]
Art. 6. Cotisations et contributions.—Chaque Comité national ou Organisme international verse une cotisation annuelle dont le taux, fixé par l'Assemblée générale, sera le même pour tous les pays ou organismes internationaux affiliés. Les activités scientifiques du Comité seront alimentées par les disponibilités éventuelles du budget, par des contributions extraordinaires, par des subventions, des donations et des legs.	
Art. 7. Démissions et exclusions.[5]—*Tout Comité national ou Organisme international affilié qui n'aura pas payé sa cotisation durant trois années consécutives ne disposera plus du droit de vote. Après cinq années consécutives ce Comité national ou Organisme international affilié sera considéré comme démissionnaire de fait.* *D'autre part tout Comité national ou Organisme international affilié qui aurait gravement manqué aux principes de la coopération internationale en violation ouverte des articles 1 et 2 des statuts pourra être exclu du C.I.S.H. dans les conditions définies ci-dessus à l'article 4, alinéa 2.*	
Art. 8. Siège du Comité.—Le Siège du Comité se trouve dans la ville où sont déposés les fonds du Comité International des Sciences Historiques.	
Art. 9. Modification des statuts.—Des modifications aux statuts peuvent être proposées par le Bureau ou par les délégués de trois Comités nationaux différents. Les modifications proposées doivent être notifiées aux Comités deux mois avant l'Assemblée générale à l'ordre du jour de laquelle elles figureront: *la majorité des deux tiers des votants est requise pour leur adoption.* Seuls les Comités nationaux ont droit de vote lorsque l'Assemblée générale délibère d'une réforme des statuts. Tout conflit relatif aux statuts devra être porté devant le juge compétent au siège du Comité.	
Art. 10. Règlements intérieurs.[5]—*Toutes les questions relatives au fonctionnement du C.I.S.H. qui ne figurent pas dans les présents statuts pourront être définies par des Règlements intérieurs qui seront proposés par le Bureau à l'Assemblée générale et adoptés par elle à la majorité absolue.*	
Art. 11. Dissolution du Comité.—Le Comité devra se déclarer dissous si le nombre des pays qui en font partie est devenu inférieur à cinq. *Dans ce cas, le Comité nommera trois liquidateurs de nationalité différente et l'actif disponible sera remis à des institutions scientifiques désignées par lui.*	

1. Adopted on 16 Aug. 1960. ICHS, *Bulletin d'information*, no. 7 (1962–1964): 7–9.
2. Art. 3 of the old version (Élection des délégués) is void.
3. The other election modalities of Art. 5/par. 2 of the old text are voided. Art. 4/par. 2 has been inserted, except for the regulation contained in Art. 9/par. 2 (old and new version)
4. Void: (Le Bureau) doit comprendre des représentants de cinq pays au moins.
5. Art. 7 and Art. 10 are without equivalent in the old version.
6. Adopted on 21 Aug. 1975. ICHS, *Bulletin d'information*, no. 10 (1974–1976): 17–19.

c) 1977–2000

New version of 1977[1]	Modification of 1992[5]
ART. 1. Purpose of the Committee.—The International Committee of Historical Sciences (ICHS), organized in Geneva on May 14, 1926 in accordance with a resolution of the Congress of Historical Sciences meeting in Brussels on April 15, 1923, is a non-governmental organization established as an association within the meaning of articles 60 and following of the Civil Code of Switzerland, created to strive for development of the historical sciences through international cooperation. In particular it organizes every five years, in collaboration with the national Committee of historians of the host country, an International Congress of Historical Sciences. It sets the date of the congress and determines its programme. In addition, it undertakes to publish reference works of broad interest prepared by internal committees created for the purpose.	ART. 1, sentence 1: … created *in order to promote* the historical sciences. Sentence 3: *It may handle, patronize or support financially* the publication of reference works *of general interest and the organization of scientific symposia or of other events encouraging the spread of historical thought and knowledge. It may entrust such tasks to its members or* to Internal Commissions created for the purpose. *It shall defend freedom of thought and expression in the field of historical research and ensure the respect of professional ethical standards among its members.*[6]
ART. 2. Composition of the Committee.—The Committee shall be composed of: a) national Committees that represent the institutions of historical research in their respective countries; b) international affiliated Organizations which are oriented exclusively to research and to rigorously scholarly publication in the historical sciences. *The Committee is also authorized to set up internal Commissions to function in areas of special interest.* Admission to the International Committee of Historical Sciences within either category shall be decided by the General Assembly, upon proposal of the Board, in accordance with the procedures indicated in article 4 below. Requests for membership must be received by the Board six months before the date of its annual meeting.	ART. 2/par. 1: … b) International Affiliated Organizations which *are devoted* to research and *scholarly* publication in particular areas of historical study. *The Committee may set up Internal Commissions and assign to them the execution of scholarly projects or the organization of specific scholarly gatherings. It may also admit in quality of Internal Commissions, for a period not exceeding ten years and in view of a future admission as an Affiliated International Organization, new international associations which pursue, in their field, the same objectives as an Affiliated International Organization.* Admission to …
ART. 3. Meetings of the Committee.—The Committee shall hold a General Assembly at least every three years. Each Congress shall be immediately preceded and followed by a General Assembly. The Board at its discretion may in given circumstances summon an extraordinary General Assembly.	

c) **1977–2000** *(cont.)*

New version of 1977[1]	Modification of 1992[5]
ART. 4. Voting in the Committee.—Each national Committee and each international affiliated Organization shall be represented at General Assemblies of the ICHS by a principal delegate entitled to vote who may be accompanied by a non-voting alternate delegate. In the absence of the principal delegate, the alternate delegate may serve in his place and be then entitled to vote. A quorum of the Assembly shall consist of principal delegates from more than half of the countries and international affiliated Organizations represented in the ICHS. Voting shall be by national Committee and international affiliated Organization. *National Committees and international affiliated Organizations have equal standing in all votes.* Votes on the admission of new members, on the exclusion of members of the ICHS, and on constitutional amendments shall require a two-thirds majority. Any other matter before the General Assembly shall require only a simple majority vote.[2] Except in the three cases specified in the preceding paragraph, at the request of the Board a vote may, in urgent matters, take place outside of the meeting of a General Assembly, that is, by correspondence. In this case the president of each national Committee and of each international affiliated Organization shall vote in the name of his body. In case of disability, any other duly authorized officer may act in his place. Only a simple majority of the voting shall be required to pass a measure.	ART. 4/par. 1:… shall be represented at General Assemblies of the ICHS by *a delegate—who may be accompanied by a substitute—and is allowed one vote.* National Committees and International Affiliated Organizations have equal standings in all votes. A quorum of the Assembly shall consist of *the delegates—or their substitutes—from at least one-third* of the members of the ICHS. Votes on …

New version of 1977[1]	Modification of 1992[5]
ART. 5. The Board of the Committee.—The Board of the Committee shall consist of a president, a first vice-president, a second vice-president, six assessor members, a secretary-general, and a treasurer. The Board shall be elected at the first of the two General Assemblies which take place at each quinquennial international Congress. It shall assume office at the end of that same congress and serve until the end of the following congress. Members of the Board may be re-elected, but the president and three other members of the Board must be replaced at each general election. Persons who have reached the age of seventy may not be elected or re-elected. Vacancies within the Board may be filled by by-elections ordered by the Board. However, in case the president should be unable to serve his term to the end, the first vice-president shall become president and shall complete the term. In case the latter in turn should be disabled, he shall be replaced in the same way by the second vice-president. Past presidents of the ICHS shall also be members of the Board, as counsellor members without vote, for a period of ten years after their presidential office without consideration of age. Following the end of the ten-year period past presidents shall be deemed honorary counsellors.[3] The Board shall be responsible for the functioning and coordination of ICHS activities. It shall prepare the agenda of General Assemblies and distribute it to participants two months in advance. It shall be empowered between meetings to take necessary steps to summon, in case of urgency, extraordinary Assemblies and, if needed, to solicit votes by correspondence from national Committees and international affiliated Organizations. The Board shall supervise management of the Committee's finances. It shall submit accounts and budget proposals to the General Assembly. The Board, represented by the president or his proxy, shall have the right to go law on behalf of the Committee. It may accept legacies and gifts and may, in conformity with the constitution, fulfill all necessary legal formalities.	ART. 5/par. 1, after sentence 1:… and a treasurer. *The election of the Board shall be prepared by a Nominating Committee of seven members, three of them belonging to the Board. Membership of the Committee is proposed by the Board at the first meeting of the General Assembly convened between Congresses. Other candidates may be presented at the second meeting by the delegates of the National Committees or of the International Affiliated Organizations. The General Assembly will then proceed with the election of the Nominating Committee. If this procedure cannot be followed, the election will take place by correspondence as established in paragraph 3 of article 4 of the present constitution. Candidates for election to the Board may be proposed by National Committees, International Affiliated Organizations and the Board during the twelve months following the constitution of the Nominating Committee which shall present its proposals at the first of the two General Assemblies which take place at each quinquennial Congress. Counterproposals may be submitted to the Board between the first and the second Assembly. To be admissible, a counter-proposal has to be signed by the representatives of five National Committees or International Affiliated Organizations. The Board shall be elected at the second of the two* General Assemblies held at the quinquennial Congress. Members of the Board may be re-elected but the President and three other members of the Board must be replaced at each general election. Persons who have reached the age of seventy, are not eligible or re-eligible. *Should a vacancy occur within the Board during its term of office, the Board shall propose a substitute and organize a by-election at the next General Assembly or by way of correspondence. In the latter case, the procedure provided in par. 3 of art. 4 shall be applied.* However, in case the President … ART. 5/par. 5: The Board … shall submit to the General Assembly *the Treasurer's report, the accounts for the term since the previous General Assembly and the budget proposals for the coming year. The Board itself is responsible for budgets in other years.* The Board, represented by the President …

c) 1977–2000 (cont.)

ART. 6. Dues and contributions.—Every national Committee or international Organization shall pay annual dues in the amount determined by the General Assembly, which shall be the same for all countries and international affiliated Organizations. Scholarly activities of the Committee shall be funded by budgetary allocations, special contributions, subsidies, donations, and legacies.	ART. 6: Every National Committee or International *Affiliated* Organization shall pay annual dues determined by the General Assembly. *The amount shall be the same for all National Committees. It shall also be the same for all International Affiliated Organizations but lower than that paid by the National Committees. By way of exception the Board may concede duly motivated derogations to these rules. Proceeds of the dues shall be assigned in the first place to the international administration of the ICHS, and subsequently to its scholarly activities. These, however, shall be the first to benefit from extraordinary* contributions, subventions, gifts and legacies.
ART. 7. Withdrawals and exclusions.—Every national Committee or international affiliated Organization that has not paid its dues for three consecutive years shall lose its right to vote. After five consecutive years, that national Committee or international affiliated Organization shall be deemed to have withdrawn de facto. In addition, any national Committee or international affiliated Organization which shall have seriously violated the principles of international cooperation contrary to articles l and 2 of the constitution shall be liable to exclusion by the ICHS following the procedure provided in article 4, paragraph 2 above.	ART. 7/par. 1: … that has not paid its dues *for three years*, shall lose its right to vote. *After five years*, that National Committee …
ART. 8. Domicile of the Committee.—The domicile of the Committee shall be the city where the funds of the ICHS are deposited.	ART. 8: … shall be the *Swiss* city where the funds of the ICHS are deposited.
ART. 9. Amendment of the constitution.—Amendments to the constitution may be proposed by the Board or by the delegates of three different national Committees. Notice of proposed amendments must be made to national Committees two months before a General Assembly [for] inclusion [on] the agenda. A two-thirds majority of those voting shall be required for their adoption.[4] Any disagreement concerning the constitution shall be resolved by a competent judge of jurisdiction in the Committee's domicile.	ART. 9/par. 1: Amendments to the constitution may be proposed by the Board or by the delegates of three different National Committees *or International Affiliated Organizations*. Notice of proposed amendments must be made to National Committees *or International Affiliated Organizations* two months before a General Assembly …
ART. 10. By-laws.—All questions concerning the functioning of the ICHS, not dealt with by the present constitution may be regulated by by-laws which shall be proposed to the General Assembly by the Board and adopted in the Assembly by simple majority.	
ART. 11. Dissolution of the Committee.—The Committee shall be dissolved if the number of member countries falls below five. In such a case the Committee shall name three liquidators of different nationalities, and its assets shall be distributed to scholarly institutions that it shall have designated.	

1. Adopted on 28 July 1977. ICHS, *Bulletin d'information*, no. 11 (1977–1980): 7–9, official French version. In ICHS, *Bulletin d'information*, no. 14 (1987): 9–13, English version with the remark: "Unofficial English translation," alongside the French text. In the same manner, in all issues of the *Bulletin d'information* after 1987.
2. The restriction contained in the last part of Art. 4, par. 2 (modification of the constitution and reference to Art. 9, par. 2) is voided.
3. Art. 5, par. 2, sentence 2: the restriction "without being members of the Board" is voided.
4. Art. 9, par. 2 (restriction concerning modifications of the constitution) is voided. See note 2 above.
5. Adopted on 4 Sept. 1992. ICHS, *Bulletin d'information*, no. 19 (1993): 9–13. French text and English translation, with a note: "The French version is the only official one."
6. A modification of this sentence will be proposed by the Bureau to the ICHS General Assembly at Madrid in July 2005 as follows: "It shall defend freedom of thought and expression in the field of historical research *and teaching*, oppose the abuse *of history, and in all appropriate ways* ensure the respect of professional ethical standards among its members."

BIBLIOGRAPHY

1. Archival Sources

The documents used by Karl D. Erdmann are cited in this book according to the German edition of 1987. Some of them have been relocated or recategorized in the meantime. This applies particularly to the following archives (marked by *): (1) The ICHS archives from 1926 to 1945 are now deposited at the Bibliothèque cantonale et universitaire de Lausanne, under the title IS 4728; (2) the archives of the ICHS from 1950 to 1980, which had been deposited at the Archives Nationales in Paris in different places without being officially registered, are now categorized under the title 105 AS, Fonds du Comité International des Sciences Historiques; (3) The state archives of the GDR, located at Merseburg and Potsdam, were transferred to the Bundesarchiv in Berlin after the reunification of Germany. The documents cited by Erdmann as being in his own possession are included in the collection of his papers deposited after his death at the Bundesarchiv in Koblenz; the papers also contain his voluminous correspondence concerning the ICHS and a broad collection of sources on the history of the International Congresses.

(a) State Archives

Bundesarchiv Koblenz
    R 153/162   Publikationsstelle des Preußischen Geheimen Staatsarchivs, Berlin-Dahlem
    R 153/723
    R 153/755
    R 1131

    R 43/1, 559   Reichskanzlei, Akten betreffend Internationale Kongresse bzw. Interna-
    R 43/1, 817, vol. 1   tionale Wissenschaft

    R 73/19   Notgemeinschaft der Deutschen Wissenschaft, Internationale Kongresse
    R 73/52
    R 73/47–48

Politisches Archiv des Auswärtigen Amtes, Bonn
    Kulturabteilung, VI B: Kunst und Wissenschaft
    – Nr. 583 adh. I   Boykottierung der deutschen Wissenschaft, vols. 1–4
    – Nr. 607   Wiederaufnahme der Zusammenarbeit der internationalen Wissenschaft, vols. 1–2

- Nr. 607, VI w Wissenschaft. Institute und Vereinigungen. Die Internationale Historische Kommission (1923–1931), vol. 1.
Akten der ehemaligen Deutschen Botschaft in Paris, 1940–1943

Zentrales Staatsarchiv, Dienststelle Merseburg*
(Preußisches) Ministerium der geistlichen, Unterrichts- und Medizinalangelegenheiten, Unterrichts-Abteilung
- Rep. 76 V c, Sect. 1, Tit. 11, Teil VI: Acta betr. die intern. Ausstellungen und Congresse des In- und Auslands, vol. 7: oct. 1897 until dec. 1899
- Rep. 76 V c, Sect. 1, Tit. 11, Teil VI, no. 13: Die Historiker-Kongresse, 1900–1934

Zentrales Staatsarchiv, Potsdam*
49.01   Reichsministerium für Wissenschaft, Erziehung und Volksbildung
2842   Intern. Kongreß Zürich 1938
3089   Intern. Historische Vereinigung, 1930–1939
3190 and 3191 Intern. wissenschaftliche Verbände, Institute, Vereinigungen usw., 1939–1943

Algemeen Rijksarchief, Den Haag
Family archive Asser, nos. 148 and 149

Archive of the Ministerie van Buitenlandse Zaken, Den Haag
A¹   Congres van diplomatieke geschiedenis te s'Gravenhage in 1898

Archives Nationales, Paris
F^{17} 3092^{11} Congrès des historiens français
70 AJ 159 and 160 Comité français des Sciences historiques
105 AS   Fonds du Comité International des Sciences Historiques (CISH)

Archivio Centrale dello Stato, Rome
Presidenza del Consiglio dei Ministri, 1929, fasc. 14/3, no. 3432

Bibliothèque de l'Unesco, Division des archives et des Services de documentation, Paris
Holdings of the Institut international de Coopération Intellectuelle, DD XI, 3

Library of Congress, Washington, D.C.
Archives of the American Council of Learned Societies
- A 6 Union Académique Internationale, 1919–1927
- A 9 Admission of German Academies
- A 61 Intern. Commission of Historical Sciences

(b) Other Institutions

Institute of Historical Research, University of London
Papers of the British national committee

Deutsches Historisches Institut, Rome
Registratur No. 1, 1–217
No. 68

Giunta Centrale per gli Studi Storici, Rome
Comitato Internazionale di Scienze Storiche
Comitato Nazionale di Scienze Storiche, 1926–1945
Zurich (1938)
Paris (1950)
Rome (1955)

Historisches Archiv der Stadt Köln, Cologne
  Akten des Verbandes deutscher Historiker

Rockefeller Archive Center, Hillcrest, Pocantico Hills, North Tarrytown, N.Y.
  The Rockefeller Foundation Archives (cited as RFA)
  – Boxes 88 und 89, Series 100 R: Intern. Committee of Historical Sciences
  Laura Spelman Rockefeller Memorial (cited as LSRM)
  – Series III, Sub. 6: American Historical Association, Intern. Committee
  – RF, RG 2—1950/100: Intern. Congress, Paris 1950

(c) ICHS Archives (Cited as Archives CISH)

1. 1926–1945, files of secretary-general Michel Lhéritier, deposited in the Archives cantonales vaudoises, Lausanne*
2. Files from the years 1945–1950 in Archives Nationales, Paris, 70 AJ 159 and 160, under the title: Comité français des Sciences historiques (tenure of Robert Fawtier, Albert Depréaux, Charles Morazé)
3. 1950–1980, files of secretary-general Michel François, deposited in the Archives Nationales, Paris*
4. 1980–2000: see above, Archives Nationales (files of secretary-general François Bédarida)

(d) Private Papers

AUBIN, HERMANN (Bundesarchiv, Koblenz)
BRACKMANN, ALBERT (Geheimes Staatsarchiv Preußischer Kulturbesitz, Berlin)
BRANDI, KARL (Niedersächsische Staats- und Universitätsbibliothek, Göttingen)
BRANDI, KARL: "Aus 77 Jahren. Lebensgeschichte und wissenschaftliche Entwicklung." Typescript of memoirs, made available for the purposes of this study with the approval of Diez Brandi by Dr. Sabine Krüger, Max-Planck-Institut, Göttingen. Chapters 6–10, including the comments on the International Historical Congresses, collected after Brandi's death from his burned diaries and from the material in his private papers by Sabine Krüger.
DELBRÜCK, HANS (Bundesarchiv, Koblenz)
DE SANCTIS, GAETANO (Material on the subject of this study made available by Prof. Silvio Accame, Istituto Italiano per la Storia Antica, Rome)
DOMANOVSZKY, SÁNDOR (Manuscript department of the library of the Hungarian Academy of Sciences, Budapest. Material on the subject of this study made available by Prof. Ferenc Glatz)
DOPSCH, ALFONS (Material on the subject of this study made available by Prof. Erna Patzelt, Vienna)
ERDMANNSDÖRFFER, BERNHARD (Zentrales Staatsarchiv, Potsdam*)
FRIIS, AAGE (Rigsarkivet, Copenhagen)
HANDELSMAN, MARCELI (Archivum PAN, Warsaw [Polish Academy of Sciencess], III-10; Material on the subject of this study made available by Prof. A. Gieysztor)
JAMESON, JOHN FRANKLIN (Library of Congress, Washington, D.C.)
IORGA, NICOLAE (Library of the Academy of the Socialist Republic of Romania, Bucharest)
KOHT, HALVDAN (Universitetsbiblioteket, Oslo)
LAMPRECHT, KARL (Universitätsbibliothek, Bonn)
LELAND, WALDO G. (Library of Congress, Washington, D.C.)
MEINECKE, FRIEDRICH (Geheimes Staatsarchiv Preußischer Kulturbesitz, Berlin)
NABHOLZ, HANS (Zentralbibliothek, Zurich)
ONCKEN, HERMANN (Niedersächsisches Staatsarchiv, Oldenburg)

PIRENNE, HENRI (made available by Comte J.-H. Pirenne, Brussels, in the family archive in Hierges)
POLLARD, A. F. (University Library, London)
RITTER, GERHARD (Bundesarchiv, Koblenz)
ROTHFELS, HANS (Bundesarchiv, Koblenz)
SHOTWELL, JAMES T. (Columbia University Libraries, New York)
VILLARI, PASQUALE (Biblioteca Vaticana)
WEBSTER, SIR CHARLES (British Library of Political and Economic Sciences [London School of Economics and Political Science], London)

2. ICHS Publications

These do not include the publications of the international commissions affiliated with the ICHS, which have partially appeared under the auspices of the ICHS.

1. *Bulletin of the International Committee of Historical Sciences*. Edited by Michel Lhéritier, secretary-general of the ICHS. 47 issues in 12 volumes. Paris, 1926–1943 (vols. 1–5, nos. 1–21, 1926–1933, with Washington, D.C., as an additional place of publication).
   Bulletin d'information. Edited by Michel François, secretary-general of the ICHS. Nos. 1–11. Paris, 1953–1980.
   Lettre d'information. Edited by Hélène Ahrweiler, secretary-general of the ICHS. Nos. 1–2. Paris, 1982–1983.
   Bulletin d'information, nos. 12–16 (Série "Lettre d'information," nos. 3–7). Edited by Hélène Ahrweiler, secretary-general of the ICHS. Paris, 1985–1989.
   Bulletin d'information, nos. 17–26. Edited by François Bédarida, secretary-general of the ICHS. Paris, 1991–2000.
   Bulletin d'information, nos. 27–29. Edited by Jean-Claude Robert, secretary-general of the ICHS. Montreal, 2001–2003.

2. *International Bibliography of Historical Sciences*. Published by the ICHS, compiled by a bibliographical commission in collaboration with the national committees.
   Vols. 1–14, for the years 1926–1939. Paris, 1930–1941.
   Vol. 15, for 1940–1946, did not appear.
   Vols. 16–44, for 1947–1975. Paris, 1949–1979.
   Vols. 45–61, for 1976–1992. Munich/New York/London/Paris, 1980–1996. Continued with vols. 62–69 (for 1993–2000) by the same publishing company (K. G. Saur, München, 1999–2004) under the direction of Massimo Mastrogregori without involvement of the ICHS (despite the formulation "published under the auspices of the ICHS" on the title page).

3. *Catalogus mapparum geographicarum ad historiam pertinentium Varsoviae 1933 expositarum*. The Hague, 1934.

4. *Bibliographie internationale des travaux historiques publiés dans les volumes de "Mélanges."*
   Vol. 1: 1880–1939. Edited under the direction of Hans Nabholz by Margarethe Rothbarth and Ulrich Helfenstein. Paris, 1955.
   Vol. 2: 1940–1950. Edited under the direction of Gerhard Ritter by Th. Baumstark. Paris, 1955.

5. *Excerpta Historica Nordica*. Edited by Povl Bagge et al. 2 vols. Copenhagen, 1955–1959.

6. *Repertorium der diplomatischen Vertreter aller Länder seit dem Westfälischen Frieden (1648)*.
   Vol. 1: 1648–1715. Edited by Ludwig Bittner and Lothar Groß. Oldenburg, 1936.

Vol. 2: 1716–1763. Edited under the direction of Leo Santifaller by Frederic Haussmann. Zurich, 1950.

Vol. 3: 1764–1815. Edited under the direction of Leo Santifaller by Otto-Friedrich Winter. Vienna, 1965.

3. Proceedings of the International Historical Congresses (Lectures and Discussions)

1898: *Annales internationales d'histoire, Congrès de La Haye, les Ier, 2, 3 septembre 1898.* [Edited by René de Maulde-La Clavière, M. Boutry, and Comte de Tarade], 6 issues. Paris, 1899.

1900: *Annales internationales d'histoire, Congrès de Paris 1900*, 7 vols. Paris, 1900. Reprint in 2 vols. by Kraus Reprint (Nendeln/Liechtenstein, 1972). In this book, cited according to the reprint.

Congrès International d'Histoire comparée, tenu à Paris du 23 au 28 juillet 1900, Procès-verbaux sommaires. Published by Ministère du Commerce, de l'Industrie, des Postes et des Télégraphes. Paris, 1901.

1903: *Atti del Congresso Internazionale di Scienze Storiche, Roma 1–9 aprile 1903*, 12 vols. Rome, 1907. Reprint in 6 vols. by Kraus Reprint (Nendeln/Liechtenstein, 1972). In this book, cited according to the original edition.

1908: *Programm des Internationalen Kongresses für historische Wissenschaften, Berlin 6. bis 12. August 1908.* Berlin, 1908.

Kongreß-Tageblatt: Internationaler Kongreß für Historische Wissenschaften, Berlin 6.–12. August 1908, nos. 1–6. Published by the organization committee of the Congress. Berlin, 5–12 Aug. 1908. Contains lectures and speeches from the opening meeting and a brief report on the proceedings.

1913: *International Congress of Historical Studies, London 1913: Presidential Address by the Right Hon. James Bryce with suppl. remarks by A. W. Ward.* Oxford, 1913.

Naval and Military Essays, being papers read in the Naval and Military Section of the International Congress of Historical Studies, 1913. Edited by J. S. Cobett and H. J. Edwards. London, 1913.

Essays in Legal History read before the International Congress of Historical Studies. Edited by Paul Vinogradoff. London, 1913. Reprint of both volumes in one by Kraus Reprint (Nendeln/Liechtenstein, 1972).

1923: *Compte rendu du Ve Congrès International des Sciences Historiques, Bruxelles 1923.* Edited by Guillaume Des Marez and François-Louis Ganshof. Brussels, 1923.

La Pologne au Ve Congrès International des Sciences historiques, Bruxelles 1923. Published by Comité National Polonais du Ve Congrès d'Histoire, with assistance by the Ministry of Public Education of Poland. Warsaw, 1924.

1928: "VIe Congrès International des Sciences Historiques, Oslo 1928: Rapports présentés au Congrès." ICHS, *Bulletin* 1 (1929): 559–753.

———. *Résumés des Communications présentées au Congrès.* Oslo, 1928. Reprint by Kraus Reprint (Nendeln/Liechtenstein, 1972).

"Compte rendu du VIe Congrès International des Sciences Historiques." *Bulletin* 2 (1931): 25–211.

Rapports présentés au Congrès International des Sciences Historiques, publiés par Historisk Tidsskrift. Oslo, 1928.

La Pologne au VIe Congrès International des Sciences Historiques, Oslo 1928. Publisehd by the Société polonaise d'Histoire. Warsaw/Lemberg (Lvov), 1930.

La nationalité et l'histoire: Ensemble d'etudes par Halvdan Koht, Louis Eisenmann, Marcel Handelsman, Hermann Oncken, Harold Steinacker et T. Walek-Czernecki. Paris, 1929. Also in ICHS, Bulletin 2 (1931): 217–320.

1933: "VIIe Congrès International des Sciences Historiques: Rapports présentés au Congrès de Varsovie." ICHS, Bulletin 5 (1933).

———. Résumés des Communications présentées au Congrès, Varsovie 1933, 2 vols. Edited by Tadeusz Manteuffel. Warsaw, 1933. Reprint in 1 vol. by Kraus Reprint (Nendeln/Liechtenstein, 1972).

"Procès-Verbal du Septième Congrès International des Sciences Historiques, Varsovie 1933." ICHS, Bulletin 8 (1936): 361ff.

La Pologne au VIIe Congrès International des Sciences Historiques, Varsovie 1933, 3 vols. Edited for the Société polonaise d'Histoire by Oscar Halecki. Warsaw, 1933.

1938: "Eighth International Congress of Historical Sciences, Zürich 1938, Scientific Reports, I–II: Communications presentées au Congrès de Zürich, 1938." ICHS, Bulletin 10 (1938): 145ff. (Apparently identical with the 2 vols. of "Résumés" referred to in the proceedings cited below, which are not available.)

"VIII. Internationaler Kongreß für Geschichtswissenschaften, 28. August–4. September 1938 in Zürich: Protokoll." ICHS, Bulletin 11 (1939): 275ff.

1950: Comité International des Sciences Politiques [sic]—International Committee of Historical Sciences. IXe Congrès International des Sciences Historiques, Paris, 28 août–3 septembre 1950. I. Rapports. Paris, 1950. II. Actes. Paris, 1951. Reprint of both parts in one vol. by Kraus Reprint (Nendeln/ Liechtenstein, 1972)

1955: Comitato Internazionale di Scienze Storiche. X Congresso Internazionale di Scienze Storiche, Roma 4–11 settembre 1955. Vols. 1–6: Relazioni, Vol. 7: Riassunti delle Communicazioni. Florence, [1955].

———. Atti del X Congresso Internazionale, Roma 4–11 settembre 1955. Rome, [1957].

1960: Comité International des Sciences Historiques. XIe Congrès International des Sciences Historiques, Stockholm 21–28 août 1960.

———. Rapports, vols. 1–5. Uppsala, 1960.

———. Résumés des Communications Uppsala, 1960.

———. Actes du Congrès. Uppsala, 1962.

1965: Comité International des Sciences Historiques. XIIe Congrès International des Sciences Historiques, Vienne 29 août–5 septembre 1965.

———. Rapports, vols. 1–4. Vienna, [1965].

———. Bilan du monde en 1815. Rapports conjoints. Paris, 1966.

———. Actes. Vienna, [1968]

1970: XIII Meždunarodnyj kongress istoričeskich nauk. Moskva, 16–23 avgusta 1970 goda. Doklady Kongressa I, vols. 1–7. Moscow, 1973. Contains the presentations for the Congress as well as speeches and lectures at the opening and closing sessions. An intended second part with the discussion contributions did not appear.

1975: Proceedings: XIV International Congress Of The Historical Sciences. New York, 1976. Contains speeches and lectures of the opening and closing sessions, alongside the program and a list of participants.

Reports: XIV International Congress Of The Historical Sciences. Vols. 1–3. New York, 1977.

1980: Comité International des Sciences Historiques. XVe Congrès International des Sciences Historiques, Bucarest, 10–17 août 1980.

———. Rapports, vols. 1–3. Bucharest, 1980.

———. Actes, vols. l–2. Bucharest, 1982.

1985: Comité International des Sciences Historiques. XVIe Congrès International des Sciences Historiques, Stuttgart, du 25 août au 1er septembre 1985.

———. Rapports, vols. 1–2. Stuttgart, 1985.

———. Actes. Stuttgart, 1987.

1990:   Comité International des Sciences Historiques. XVII*e* Congrès International des Sciences Historiques, Madrid 1990: Rapports et abrégés, vols. 1–2. Madrid, 1990.
1995:   XVIII*e* Congrès International des Sciences Historiques, du 27 août au 3 septembre 1995. Actes: rapports, résumés et présentations des tables rondes. 18th International Congress of Historical Sciences, from 27 August to 3 September 1995. Proceedings: reports, abstracts and introductions to round tables. Edited by Claude Morin. Montreal, 1995.
2000:   XIX*e* Congrès International des Sciences Historiques, Université d'Oslo, 6–13 août 2000. Actes: rapports, résumés et présentations des tables rondes. 19th International Congress of Historical Sciences, University of Oslo, 6–13 August 2000. Proceedings: reports, abstracts and round table introductions. Edited by Anders Jølstad and Marianne Lunde. Oslo, 2000.
Papers for the 19th International Congress of Historical Sciences in Oslo 2000. Edited by Even Lange et al. (CD–ROM). Commemorative Volume. Oslo, 2000.
Making Sense of Global History: The 19th International Congress of the Historical Sciences Oslo 2000. Commemorative Volume. Ed. for the Organizing Committee by Sølvi Sogner. Oslo, 2001.
XIX*e* Congrès International des Sciences Historiques, mercredi 9 août. Table ronde: armée et pouvoir dans l'Antiquité. 19th International Congress of Historical Studies Oslo, Wednesday August 9. Round-table discussion: army and power in the ancient world. Oslo, 2000.

4. Other Publications

These do not include articles in newspapers, brief reports in professional journals or periodicals (if not cited more than once), and writings mentioned only in passing. A small selection of recent works dealing with the major topics discussed in this book has been added by the editors.

Académie Royale de Belgique: Bulletin de la Classe des Lettres et des Sciences Morales et Politiques 1919. Brussels, 1919.
Amouroux, Henri. La grande histoire des Français sous l'occupation, vol. 3: Les beaux jours des collabos juin 1940–juin 1942. Paris, 1979.
Ascheraden, Konstanze von. "Probleme der Theorie und Methodologie der Geschichtswissenschaft in der Volksrepublik Polen." Ph.D. diss., University of Kiel, 1978.
Bacha, Eugène. La Loi des Créations. Brussels/Paris, 1921.
Bariéty, Jacques. Les relations franco-allemandes après la première guerre mondiale. Paris, 1977.
Barker, Theo C., and Anthony Sutcliffe. Megapolis: The Giant City in History. Basingbroke, 1993.
Bauer, Stefan. "Ludo Moritz Hartmann." Neue Österreichische Biographie 1815–1918, Abt. 1, vol. 3. Vienna, 1926, pp. 197–209.
Bauerfeind, Alfred, et al. "Der XIV. Internationale Historikerkongreß in San Francisco." Zeitschrift für Geschichtswissenschaft 24 (1976): 442–467.
Becker, Gerhard. "Der XV. Internationale Historikerkongreß in Bukarest 1980." Zeitschrift für Geschichtswissenschaft 29 (1981): 507–537.
Becker, Gerhard, and Ernst Engelberg. "Der XII. Internationale Historikerkongress in Wien." Zeitschrift für Geschichtswissenschaft 13 (1965): 1309–1322.
Becker, Gerhard, Manfred Krause, and Dieter Lange. "Der XIII. Internationale Historikerkongress in Moskau." Zeitschrift für Geschichtswissenschaft 19 (1971): 165–179.
Bednarski, Ks. St. "VII Miedzynarodowy Kongres Nauk Historycznych" [VIIth International Congress of Historical Sciences]. Przegląd Powszechny 190 (1933).
Behrendt, Lutz-Dieter: "Die internationalen Beziehungen der sowjetischen Historiker (1917 bis Mitte der dreißiger Jahre): Zur internationalen Wirksamkeit der sowjetischen Geschichtswissenschaft in ihrer ersten Entwicklungsphase." Ph.D. diss., Univ. of Leipzig, 1977.

———. "Zu den internationalen Beziehungen der sowjetischen Historiker in den zwanziger und dreißiger Jahren." In Erich Donnert, Hans-Thomas Krause, and Hans-Werner Schaaf, eds., *Die sowjetische Geschichtswissenschaft: Leistungen und internationale Wirksamkeit*, part 4. Halle, 1979, pp. 29–37.
Below, Georg von. *Probleme der Wirtschaftsgeschichte: Eine Einführung in das Studium der Wirtschaftsgeschichte*. Tübingen, 1920.
Bémont, Charles. "Chronique: Le troisième congrès international d'histoire." *Revue historique* 113 (1913): 216–218.
Berger, Stefan, Heiko Feldner, and Kevin Passmore, eds. *Writing History: Theory and Practice*. London. 2003.
Bernheim, Ernst. *Lehrbuch der historischen Methode und der Geschichtsphilosophie*. Munich/Leipzig 1889, 6th ed. 1908.
Berr, Henri. "Sur notre programme." *Revue de synthèse historique* 1 (1900): 1–8.
———. "Le Ve Congrès international des sciences historiques (Bruxelles, 8–15 avril) et la synthèse en histoire." *Revue de synthèse historique* 35 (1923): 5–14.
———. "Les réfexions sur l'histoire d'un historien combattant." *Revue de synthèse historique* 36 (1923): 1–11.
———. "Quelques réflexions sur le VIe Congrès international des sciences historiques Oslo, 14–18 août 1928." *Revue de synthèse historique* 46 (1928): 5–14.
———. *La Synthèse en histoire*. New ed. Paris, 1953.
Berza, Mihai. "Nicolas Iorga, Historien du Moyen Âge." In *Nicolas Iorga, l'homme et l'œuvre*. Bucharest, 1972.
Bieżuńska-Małowistowa, Iza. "Historia starożytna na Kongresie sztokholmskim" [Ancient History at the Stockholm Congress]. *Kwartalnik historyczny* 68 (1961): 561–563.
Blänsdorf, Agnes. "Methodologie und Geschichte der Geschichtswissenschaft." In "Bericht über den 16. Internationalen Kongreß für Geschichtswissenschaften in Stuttgart (25. 8.–1. 9. 1980)." *Geschichte in Wissenschaft und Unterricht* 37, no. 2 (1986): 81–87.
Bloch, Marc. "Pour une histoire comparée des sociétés européennes." *Revue de synthèse historique* 56 (1928): 15–50. Reprint in Bloch, *Mélanges historiques*. Paris, 1963, pp. 16–42.
———. *Les Rois Thaumaturges*. Paris, 1924.
———. *La Société féodale*, 2 vols. Paris, 1939/40.
———. *L'Étrange Défaite. Témoignage écrit en 1940. Avant-propos de G. Altman*. Paris, 1946.
———. *Apologie pour l'histoire ou métier d'historien*. Edited by Lucien Febvre. Paris, 1949.
Boia, Lucian. "Nicolae Iorga si congressele internationale de istorie," *Revista de istorie* 31 (Bucharest, 1978): 1825ff.
Brackmann, Albert, ed. *Deutschland und Polen: Beiträge zu ihren geschichtlichen Beziehungen*. Munich, 1933.
———. "Über den Plan einer Germania sacra: Bericht über zwei Vorträge von P. Kehr und A. Brackmann gehalten auf dem Internationalen Kongreß für historische Wissenschaften in Berlin." *Historische Zeitschrift* 102 (1909): 325–334.
Brandi, Karl. "Karl V: Die Regierung eines Weltreiches." *Preußische Jahrbücher* 214 (1928): 23–31.
———. *Kaiser Karl V.* 2 vols. Munich, 1937, 1941.
Braudel, Fernand. *La Méditerrannée et le monde méditerranéen à l'époque de Philippe II*. Paris, 1949.
———. "Stockholm 1960." *Annales: Économies—Sociétés—Civilisations* 16 (1961): 497ff.
[Bryce, James]. *International Congress of Historical Studies, London 1913: Presidential Address by the Right Hon. James Bryce with suppl. remarks by A. W. Ward*. Oxford, 1913; also in *Proceedings of the British Academy* 6, 1913/14 (Oxford, 1920): 121–128.
Cantimori, Delio. "Epiloghi congressuali." In Cantimori, *Studi di Storia*. Torino, 1959.
Carbonell, Charles-Olivier. *Histoire et historiens: Une mutation idéologique des historiens français 1865–1885*. Toulouse, 1976.
Carbonell, Charles-Olivier, and Georges Livet, eds. *Au Berceau des Annales: Le milieu strasbourgeois. L'histoire en France au début du XXe siècle*. Toulouse, 1983.

Castelli, Clara. "Internazionalismo e Storia: Gli Storici Sovietici ai Congressi Internazionali di Scienze Storiche 1928–36." *Storia Contemporanea* 12 (1981).
Chakrabarty, Dipesh. *Provincializing Europe: Postcolonial Thought and Historical Difference.* Princeton, 2000.
The Congress of Vienna 1814–15 and the Conference of Paris 1919. 1. A comparison of their organization and results ... By Professor C. K. Webster. 2. Attempts at international Government in Europe; the period of the Congress of Vienna, 1814–15, and the period since the Treaty of Versailles, 1919–1922. By H. W. V. Temperley, Historical Association, Leaflet no. 56. London, 1923.
Coutau-Bégarie, Hervé: *Le phénomène "Nouvelle Histoire": Stratégie et idéologie des nouveaux historiens.* Paris, 1983.
Craig, Gordon A. *Der Historiker und sein Publikum.* Münster, 1982.
Croce, Benedetto. "L'histoire ramenée au concept général de l'Art." *Academia Pontaniana*, vol. 23 (1893).
———. *Materialismo storico ed economia marxista.* Bari, 1901; French edition *Matérialisme historique et économie marxiste: Essais critiques.* Paris, 1901.
———. "Les Études relatives à la théorie de l'histoire en Italie durant les quinze dernières années." *Revue de synthèse historique* 5 (1902).
———. *Lineamenti di una logica come scienza del concetto puro.* Naples, 1905.
———. *Ciò che è vivo e ciò che è morto della filosofia di Hegel.* Bari, 1907. German edition: *Lebendiges und Totes in Hegels Philosophie.* Heidelberg, 1909.
———. *Randbemerkungen eines Philosophen zum Weltkriege.* Zurich/Leipzig/Vienna, 1922.
———. "Entstehung und Erkenntnisse meiner Philosophie." *Universitas* 7 (Stuttgart, 1952): 1009–1020.
Dehio, Ludwig. "Der internationale Historikerkongreß in Paris (IX. congrès international des sciences historiques)." *Historische Zeitschrift* 170 (1950): 671–673.
"Den tredje internationella kongressen för historiska studier i London 1913," signed L. S. *Historisk tidskrift* (Stockholm, 1913): 97–104.
De Sanctis, Gaetano. *Ricordi della mia vita.* Edited by Silvio Accame. Florence, 1970.
Diels, Hermann. "Die Einheitsbestrebungen der Wissenschaft." *Internationale Wochenschrift für Wissenschaft, Kunst und Technik* 1 (1907): 3–10.
Dilthey, Wilhelm. *Texte zur Kritik der historischen Vernunft.* Edited by Hans-Ulrich Lessing. Göttingen, 1983.
Donnan, Elisabeth, and Leo F. Stock, eds. *An Historian's World: Selections from the Correspondence of John Franklin Jameson.* Philadelphia, 1956.
Dopsch, Alfons. *Die Wirtschaftsentwicklung der Karolingerzeit vornehmlich in Deutschland.* 2 vols. Weimar, 1912, 1913.
———. *Wirtschaftliche und soziale Grundlagen der europäischen Kulturentwicklung aus der Zeit von Cäsar bis auf Karl den Großen.* 2 vols. Vienna, 1918, 1920.
———. "Alfons Dopsch." In Sigfried Steinberg, ed., *Geschichtswissenschaft der Gegenwart in Selbstdarstellungen.* Leipzig, 1925, pp. 51–90.
———. "Naturalwirtschaft und Geldwirtschaft in der Weltgeschichte." *Archiv für Rechts- und Wirtschaftsphilosophie* 22/23 (1929), reprinted in Dopsch. *Beiträge zur Sozialgeschichte: Gesammelte Aufsätze, zweite Reihe.* Vienna, 1938, pp. 85–94.
———. *Naturalwirtschaft und Geldwirtschaft.* Vienna, 1930.
Dudzinskaia, E. A., *Meždunarodnye naučnye svjazi sovjetskich istorikov* [International scientific relations of Soviet historians]. Moscow, 1978.
Dufour, Alain. "XIe Congrès des Sciences Historiques." *Bibliothèque d'Humanisme et Renaissance* 23 (Geneva, 1961): 157–169.
Dupront, Alphonse. "Federico Chabod." *Revue historique* 85, no. 225 (1961): 261–294.
Düwell, Kurt. *Deutschlands auswärtige Kulturpolitik 1918–1932: Grundlinien und Dokumente.* Cologne, 1976.

Engelberg, Ernst. "Fragen der Evolution und Revolution in der Weltgeschichte" (1965), in Engelberg, *Theorie*, pp. 101–116.

———. "Ereignis, Struktur und Entwicklung in der Geschichte" (1975), in Engelberg, *Theorie*, pp. 59–93.

———. *Theorie, Empirie und Methode in der Geschichtswissenschaft: Gesammelte Aufsätze*. Edited by Wolfgang Küttler and Gutav Seeber. East Berlin, 1980.

Engel-Janosi, Friedrich. *... aber ein stolzer Bettler: Erinnerungen aus einer verlorenen Generation*. Graz, 1974.

Enteen, George M. "Marxists versus Non-Marxists: Soviet Historiography in the 1920s." *Slavic Review* 35 (1976): 91–110.

Erdmann, Karl Dietrich. "Geschichte, Politik und Pädagogik: Aus den Akten des Deutschen Historikerverbandes." *Geschichte in Wissenschaft und Unterricht* 19 (1968): 2–21.

———. "Die asiatische Welt im Denken von Karl Marx und Friedrich Engels" (1961), in Erdmann, *Geschichte, Politik und Pädagogik: Aufsätze und Reden*. Stuttgart, 1970, pp. 149–182.

———. "Fünfzig Jahre 'Comité International des Sciences Historiques': Erfahrungen und Perspektiven." *Geschichte in Wissenschaft und Unterricht* 27 (1976): 524–537.

———. "Die Ökumene der Historiker: Rede des Präsidenten des Comité International des Sciences Historiques zur Eröffnung des 15. Internationalen Historikerkongresses in Bukarest." *Geschichte in Wissenschaft und Unterricht* 31 (1980): 657–666. French text in Congress Bucharest 1980: *Actes*, vol. 1.

———. "Internationale Schulbuchrevision zwischen Politik und Wissenschaft." *Internationale Schulbuchforschung* 4 (Braunschweig, 1882): 249–260.

———. "Il contributo della storiografia italiana ai Congressi Internationali di Scienze Storiche nella prima metà del XX secolo." In Vigezzi, *Federico Chabod*.

———. "A History of the International Historical Congresses: Work in Progress." *Storia della Storiografia* 8 (1985): 3–23, German translation: "Zur Geschichte der Internationalen Historikerkongresse: Ein Werkstattbericht." *Geschichte in Wissenschaft und Unterricht* 36 (1985): 535–553.

———. "Genèse et débuts du Comité International des Sciences Historiques, fondé le 15 mai 1926." In ICHS, *Bulletin d'information* 13 (1986).

Febvre, Lucien. *La terre et l'évolution humaine: introduction géographique à l'histoire*. Paris, 1922.

———. *Combats pour l'histoire*. Paris, 1953.

Fellner, Günter. *Ludo Moritz Hartmann und die österreichische Geschichtswissenschaft*. Vienna/Salzburg, 1985.

Fester, Richard. *Die Säkularisation der Historie*. Leipzig, 1909.

Finley, Moses J. *Ancient Slavery and Modern Ideology*. Cambridge, 1980.

Firth, Charles H. *A Plea for the Historical Teaching of History: Inaugural Address*. Oxford, 1905.

———. "The study of modern history in Great Britain." *Proceedings of the British Academy* 6, 1913/14 (Oxford, 1920): 139–151.

Fischer, Fritz. *Deutschlands Griff nach der Weltmacht: Die Kriegszielpolitik des kaiserlichen Deutschland 1914–18*. Düsseldorf, 1961

Fling, Fred Morrow. "Historical Synthesis." *American Historical Review* 9 (1903): 1–22.

François, Michel. "Cinquante ans d'Histoire du Comité International des Sciences Historiques." In ICHS, *Bulletin d'information*, no. 10 (1976): 1ff.

Ganshof, François Louis. "Le Congrès historique international d'Oslo." *Revue belge de philologie et d'histoire* 4 (Brussels, 1928): 1685–1692.

Gay, Harry Nelson. "The International Congress of Historical Sciences," *American Historical Review* 8 (1902/03): 809–812.

Geiss, Imanuel. "Außereuropäische Geschichte." In "Bericht über den 16. Internationalen Kongreß der Geschichtswissenschaften in Stuttgart (25. 8.–1. 9. 1980)." *Geschichte in Wissenschaft und Unterricht* 37, no. 2 (1986): 105–115.

Gierke, Otto von. *Das deutsche Genossenschaftsrecht*. 4 vols. Berlin, 1868–1913.

Gieysztor, Aleksander. "Zagadniena archeologiczne na rzymskim kongresie historików" [Archaeological questions at the Historical Congress in Rome]. *Kwartalnik historyczny* 63, no. 3 (1956): 221–227.

———. "O kongressach historycznych nauk" [On the Historical Congresses]. *Kwartalnik historyczny* 73, no. 2 (1966): 481–495.

Glénisson, Jean. "L'historiographie française contemporaine: Tendances et réalisations." In *La recherche historique en France de 1940 à 1965*. Published by Comité français des sciences historiques. Paris, 1965.

Goldstein, Doris S. "The Professionalization of History in Britain in the Late Nineteenth and Early Twentieth Centuries." *Storia della Storiografia* 3 (1983): 3–27.

Gooch, George P. *History and Historians in the Nineteenth Century*. London 1913, 3rd ed. 1961.

Gothein, Eberhard. *Die Aufgaben der Kulturgeschichte*. Leipzig, 1889.

Grigulevich, Iosif R., Zinaida V. Udalcova, and Alexander O. Chubaryan, "Problemy novoj i novejšej istorii na XV Meždunarodnom kongresse istoričeskich nauk" [Problems of modern and recent history at the 15th International Historical Congress]. *Novaja i Novejšaja Istorija* 25, no. 4 (1981).

Grille, Dietrich. "Der XIII. Internationale Historikerkongreß in Moskau. Bericht und Kommentar eines Teilnehmers." *Deutsche Studien* 32 (Lüneburg, 1970): 406–416.

Guber, Aleksandr A. "Nekotorye problemy novoj i novejšej istorii na XI meždunarodnom Kongresse istorikov v Stokgol'me" [Problems of modern and recent history at the XIth International Historical Congress in Stockholm]. *Novaja i Novejšaja Istorija*, no. 1 (1961).

———. XIII *Meždunarodnyj kongress istoričeskich nauk v Moskve* [XIIIth International Historical Congress in Moscow]. *Voprosy istorii* 46, no. 6 (1971): 3–16.

Hajnal, St. "Über die Arbeitsgemeinschaft der Geschichtsschreibung kleiner Nationen." In Imre Lukinich, ed. *Archivum Europae Centro-Orientalis*, vol. 9/10. Budapest, 1943/1944, pp. 1–82.

Halecki, Oskar. *La Pologne de 963 à 1914: Essai de synthèse historique*. Paris, 1932.

———. "V Międzynarodowy kongres historyczny" [5th International Historical Congress]. *Kwartalnik historyczny* 37 (Lvov, 1923).

———. "VI Międzynarodowy kongres nauk istoryczny" [6th International Congress of Historical Sciences]. *Przegląd Powszechny* 180 (1928).

Hallgarten, George W. F. *Imperialismus vor 1914: Theoretisches, soziologische Skizzen der außenpolitischen Entwicklung in England und Frankreich, soziologische Darstellung der deutschen Außenpolitik bis zum ersten Weltkrieg*. Munich, 1951. 2nd rev. ed. under the title *Imperialismus vor 1914: Die soziologischen Grundlagen der Außenpolitik europäischer Großmächte vor dem ersten Weltkrieg*. 2 vols. Munich, 1963.

———. *Als die Schatten fielen: Erinnerungen vom Jahrhundertbeginn zur Jahrtausendwende*. Frankfurt a. M./ Berlin, 1969.

Harnack, Adolf von. "Vom Großbetrieb der Wissenschaft." *Preußische Jahrbücher* 119 (1905): 193–201.

———. "Der vierte Internationale Kongreß für historische Wissenschaften zu Berlin." *Internationale Wochenschrift für Wissenschaft, Kunst und Technik* 2 (1908): 512–519.

Harper, Samuel N. "A communist view of historical studies." *Journal of Modern History* 1 (Chicago, 1929): 77–84.

Hartmann, Ludo Moritz: *Über historische Entwickelung: Sechs Vorträge zur Einleitung in eine historische Soziologie*. Gotha, 1905.

Haskins, Charles H. "The International Historical Congress at Berlin." *American Historical Review* 14 (1908): 1–8.

Hassel, Peter. "Marxistische Formationstheorie und der Untergang Westroms." *Geschichte in Wissenschaft und Unterricht* 32 (1981): 713–725.

Hattenauer, Hans. *Die geistesgeschichtlichen Grundlagen des Rechts*. 2nd ed. Heidelberg, 1980.

Haun, Horst. "Der X. Internationale Historikerkongreß 1955 in Rom und die Geschichtswissenschaft der DDR." *Zeitschrift für Geschichtswissenschaft* 34 (1986): 303–314.

Hauser, Henri. "A propos d'un congrès." *Revue internationale de l'enseignement* 33, no. 2 (Paris, 1913): 2ff.
Heiber, Helmut. *Walter Frank und sein Reichsinstitut für Geschichte des neuen Deutschlands.* Stuttgart, 1966.
Heimpel, Hermann. "Internationaler Historikertag in Paris." *Geschichte in Wissenschaft und Unterricht* 1 (1950): 556–559.
Helmolt, Hans. "Nachrichten: Der IV. Internationale Kongreß für Historische Wissenschaften: Berlin, 6.–12. August 1908." *Historisches Jahrbuch der Görresgesellschaft* 30 (1909): 218–222.
Herre, Paul. "Bericht über den Internationalen Kongreß für historische Wissenschaften in Berlin, 6.–12. August 1908." *Historische Vierteljahrschrift* 11 (1908): 417–426.
Hexter, Jack H. "The rhetoric of history." *History and Theory* 6 (1967): 3–13.
Hill, David Jayne. "The Ethical Function of the Historian." *American Historical Review* 14 (1908): 9–20.
Hobsbawm, Eric J. "The revival of narrative: some comments." *Past and Present*, no. 86 (1980): 3–8.
Hofer, Walther. "IXe Congrès International des Sciences Historiques." *Schweizer Monatshefte* 30 (1950/51): 457–461.
Höjer, Torvald. "Den internationelle Kongressen för historiska vetenskaper i Berlin 1908." *Historisk tidskrift* (Stockholm, 1908): 145–169.
Hübinger, Paul Egon, ed. *Bedeutung und Rolle des Islam beim Übergang vom Altertum zum Mittelalter.* Darmstadt, 1968.
———, ed. *Kulturbruch oder Kulturkontinuität im Übergang von der Antike zum Mittelalter.* Darmstadt, 1968.
———, ed. *Zur Frage der Periodengrenze zwischen Altertum und Mittelalter.* Darmstadt, 1969.
———, ed. *Spätantike und frühes Mittelalter: Ein Problem historischer Periodenbildung.* Darmsatdt, 1972.
Hüffer, Hermann Joseph. *Lebenserinnerungen.* 2nd ed. Berlin, 1914.
Iggers, Georg G. "The 'Methodenstreit' in International Perspective: The Reorientation of Historical Studies at the Turn from the Nineteenth to the Twentieth Century." *Storia della Storiografia*, no. 6 (1984): 21–32.
———. "Historicism (A Comment)." In Mommsen, "Narrative History," pp. 131–144.
———. *Historiography in the Twentieth Century: From Scientific Objectivity to the Postmodern Challenge.* Hanover, N.H., 1997; 2nd rev. ed. 2004.
Ihering, Rudolf von. *Der Kampf ums Recht.* Vienna, [1872].
———. *Der Geist des römischen Rechts.* 4 vols. 1852–1865.
Iorga, Nicolae. *Essai de synthèse de l'histoire de l'humanité.* 4 vols. Paris, 1926–1929.
———. *1. Les bases nécessaires d'une nouvelle histoire du moyen-âge. 2. La survivance byzantine dans les pays roumains.* Bucharest/Paris, 1913.
———. "Les permanences de l'histoire." *Revue historique du Sud-Est européen* (Bucharest, 1938): 205–222.
Jäckel, Eberhard. "Der XI. Internationale Historikerkongreß in Stockholm." *Geschichte in Wissenschaft und Unterricht* 11 (1960): 700–705.
Jameson, John Franklin. "The International Congress of Historical Studies, held at London." *American Historical Review* 18 (1913): 679–691.
Jedruszczak, Tadeusz. "Sprawy niemieckie na XII Kongresie Nauk Historycznych" [German affairs at the XIIth Historical Congress]. *Kwartalnik historyczny* 73 (1966): 496–501.
———. "Z prac Komitetu Nauk Historycznych" [From the work of the Committee of Historical Sciences]. *Kwartalnik historyczny* 83 (1976): 476–480.
Kellermann, Hermann, ed. *Der Krieg der Geister: Eine Auslese deutscher und ausländischer Stimmen zum Weltkriege 1914.* Dresden, 1915.
Keylor, William R. *Academy and Community: The Foundation of the French Historical Profession.* Cambridge, Mass., 1975.

Kocka, Jürgen, ed. *Max Weber, der Historiker* (*Kritische Studien zur Geschichtswissenschaft*, vol. 73). Göttingen, 1986.
———. "Theory Orientation and the New Quest for Narrative: Some Trends and Debates in West Germany." In Mommsen, "Narrative History," pp. 170–181.
———. "Comparison and Beyond." *History and Theory* 42 (2003): 39–44
———. "Losses, Gains and Opportunities: Social History Today." *Journal of Social History* 37 (Fall 2003): 21–28.
Koht, Halvdan. "Le problème des origines de la Renaissance." *Revue de synthèse historique* 37 (1924): 107–116.
———. "The Importance of the Class Struggle." *Journal of Modern History* 1(Chicago, 1929): 353–360.
———. "Aus den Lehrjahren eines Historikers." *Die Welt als Geschichte* 13 (1953): 149–163. German-language exerpts from Koht. *Historikars laere*. Published by the Norwegian Historical Association. Oslo, 1951.
———. *The Origin and Beginnings of the International Committee of Historical Sciences: Personal Remembrances*. Published by the ICHS. Lausanne, 1962.
Kormanowa, Żanna. "Na marginesie obrad XI Międzynarodowego Kongresu Nauk Historycznych" [On the margins of the discussions of the XIth International Historical Congress], *Kwartalnik historyczny* 68, no. 1 (1961): 268–271.
Kosáry, Domokos. Introduction to *Études historiques hongroises publiées à l'occasion du XVIe Congrès International des Sciences Historiques*. Budapest, 1985.
———. "1815: Remarques sur son historiographie." In *Nouvelles Etudes Historiques, publiées à l'occasion du XIIe Congrès International des Sciences Historiques par la Commission Nationale des Historiens Hongrois*. 2 vols. Budapest, 1965, vol. 1.
Koselleck, Reinhart. Introduction to *Geschichtliche Grundbegriffe: Historisches Lexikon zur politischen Sprache in Deutschland*. Edited by Otto Brunner, Werner Conze, and Reinhart Koselleck. Vol. 1. Stuttgart, 1973.
———. "Darstellung, Ereignis und Struktur." In Gerhard Schulz, ed., *Geschichte heute: Positionen, Tendenzen, Probleme*. Göttingen, 1973, pp. 307–317.
Kramer, Lloyd, and Sarah Maza, eds. *A Companion to Western Historical Thought*. London, 2002.
Kuhn, Thomas S. *The Structure of Scientific Revolutions*. Chicago, 1962.
Lamprecht, Karl. *Deutsche Geschichte*. 2nd ed. Berlin, 1895.
———. "Die kultur- und universalgeschichtlichen Bestrebungen an der Universität Leipzig: Vortrag gehalten auf dem Internationalen Historikerkongreß zu Berlin am 11. August 1908." *Internationale Wochenschrift für Wissenschaft, Kunst und Technik* 2 (1908): 1142–1150.
Lavollée, René. "Les unions internationales." *Revue d'histoire diplomatique* 1 (1887): 333–362.
Le Goff, Jacques. "L'histoire nouvelle." In Le Goff, ed., *La Nouvelle Histoire*. Paris, 1978, pp. 210–241.
Leland, Waldo G. "The International Congress of Historical Sciences, held at Brussels." *American Historical Review* 28 (1922/23): 639–655.
Leuilliot, Paul. "Aux Origines des 'Annales d'histoire économique et sociale,' (1928): Contribution à l'historiographie française." In *Méthodologie de l'Histoire et des sciences humaines: Mélanges en l'honneur de Fernand Braudel*. Toulouse, 1973, pp. 317–324.
Lhéritier, Michel. "Henri Pirenne et le Comité International des Sciences Historiques." In *Henri Pirenne, Hommages et Souvenirs*, vol. 1. Brussels, 1938, pp. 88–89.
Lorenz, Chris. "Comparative Historiography: Problems and Perspectives." *History and Theory* 38 (1999): 25–39
Lübbe, Hermann. *Geschichtsbegriff und Geschichtsinteresse*. Basel, 1977.
Lukinich, Imre. *Les éditions des sources de l'histoire hongroise, 1854–1930*. Budapest, 1931.
Lyon, Bryce. *Henri Pirenne: A biographical and intellectual study*. Ghent, 1974.
———. "The letters of Henri Pirenne to Karl Lamprecht (1894–1915)." *Académie Royale de Belgique, Bulletin de la Commission Royale d'Histoire* 132 (1966): 161–231.

Lyon, Bryce and Mary, "Maurice Prou, ami de Henri Pirenne." *Le Moyen Age* 71 (1965): 71–107.
Maccarrone, Michele. "L'apertura degli archivi della Santa Sede per i pontificati di Pio X e di Benedetto XV (1903–1922)." *Rivista di Storia della Chiesa in Italia* 39 (Rome, 1985): 341–348.
Manacorda, Giuliano. "Le Correnti della storiografia contemporanea al decimo Congresso di scienze storiche." *Rinascita* 13, no. 9 (Rome, 1955); Russian translation in *Voprosy Istorii* 31, no. 2 (1956): 214–219.
———. "L'XI Congresso internazionale di scienze storiche." *Studi Storici* 1, no. 4 (Rome, 1959/1960).
Mac Kay, Donald C. "Tenth International Congress of Historical Sciences." *American Historical Review* 61 (1955/56): 504–511.
McNeill, William H. *The Shape of European History.* Oxford, 1974.
"XI Meždunarodnyj kongress istoričeskich nauk v Stokgol'me" [The XIth International Historical Congress in Stockholm, no author]. *Voprosy istorii* 35, no. 12 (1960): 3–29.
Marcks, Erich. *Bismarck: Eine Biographie.* Vol. 1: *Jugend.* Stuttgart, 1909.
Marrou, Henri-Irénéé. *De la connaissance historique.* Paris, 1954.
Meinecke, Friedrich. *Vom Weltbürgertum zum Nationalstaat* (vol. 5 of Meinecke. *Werke.* Edited by Hans Herzfeld et al. 8 vols. Stuttgart, 1957–1969).
———. *Zur Theorie und Philosophie der Geschichte.* Stuttgart, 1959 (vol. 4 of Meinecke. *Werke.* Edited by Hans Herzfeld et al.)
———. *Ausgewählter Briefwechsel.* Edited by Ludwig Dehio and Peter Classen. Stuttgart, 1962.
Merkle, Sebastian. *Die katholische Beurteilung des Aufklärungszeitalters* (*Kultur und Leben*, vol. 16). Berlin, 1909.
———. *Die kirchliche Aufklärung im katholischen Deutschland: Eine Abwehr und zugleich ein Beitrag zur Charakteristik "kirchlicher" und "nichtkirchlicher" Geschichtsschreibung.* Berlin, 1910.
Meyer, Arnold Oskar. "Charles I and Rome." *American Historical Review* 19 (1913/14): 13–26.
Michael, W. "Kongreß 1913," *Historische Zeitschrift* 111 (1913): 464–469.
Mints, Isaac I. "Marksisty na istoričeskoj nedele v Berline i VI Meždunarodnom kongresse istorikov b Norvegii" [Marxists at the historical week in Berlin and at the VIth International Historical Congress in Norway]. *Istorik Marksist* 9 (Moscow, 1928): 84–85.
Mommsen, Hans. "Der Internationale Historikertag in Moskau im Rückblick." *Geschichte in Wissenschaft und Unterricht* 22 (1971): 161–173.
Mommsen, Wolfgang J. *Geschichtswissenschaft jenseits des Historismus.* Düsseldorf, 1971.
———, ed. "Narrative History and Structural History: Past, Present, Perspectives." *Storia della Storiografia*, no. 10 (1986): 1–194.
Monod, Gabriel. "Avant-propos." *Revue historique* 1 (1876): 1f.
———. "Bulletin historique: Italie." *Revue historique* 82 (1903): 357–362.
———. "Bulletin historique: Le congrès historique de Berlin." *Revue historique* 99 (1908): 298–307.
Morazé, Charles. *Les méthodes en histoire moderne (Congrès historique du Centenaire de la Révolution 1848).* Paris, 1948.
Neck, Rudolf. "Alfons Dopsch und seine Schule." In Wolfgang Frühauf, ed. *Wissenschaft und Weltbild. Festschrift für Hertha Firnberg.* Vienna, 1975.
Neufeld, Karl Heinrich. "Adolf von Harnack." In Hans-Ulrich Wehler, ed., *Deutsche Historiker*, vol. 7. Göttingen, 1980, pp. 24–38.
"Niektore spostrzeżenia i wniowski z X Kongresu Nauk Historycznych w Rzymie" [Some comments and conclusions concerning the Xth Congress of the Historical Sciences in Rome], no author, *Kwartalnik historyczny* 63 no. 1 (1956): 3–11.
Nipperdey, Thomas. "Historismus und Historismuskritik heute." In Eberhard Jaeckel and Ernst Weymar, eds. *Die Funktion der Geschichte in unserer Zeit.* Festschrift für K. D. Erdmann. Stuttgart, 1975, pp. 82–95.
Oestreich, Gerhard. "Die Fachhistorie und die Anfänge der sozialgeschichtlichen Forschung in Deutschland." *Historische Zeitschrift* 208 (1969): 320–363.

Pais, Ettore. *Storia di Roma*. Vol. 1: *Critica della tradizione fino alla caduta del Decemvirato*. Vol. 2: *Critica della tradizione dalla caduta del Decemvirato all'intervento di Pirro*. Turin, 1898, 1899.
Pankratova, Anna M. "K itogam Meždunarodnova kongressa istorikov" [On the results of the International Historical Congress]. *Voprosy Istorii* 31, no. 5 (1956): 3–16.
———. "Unsere ruhmvolle Geschichte—wichtige Quelle des Studiums." In *Diskussionsreden auf dem XX. Parteitag der KPdSU 14.–25. Februar 1956*. East Berlin, 1956, pp. 364–375.
Pastor, Ludwig Freiherr von. *1854–1928: Tagebücher, Briefe, Erinnerungen*. Edited by Wilhelm Wühr. Heidelberg, 1950.
Petke, Wolfgang. "Karl Brandi und die Geschichtswissenschaft." In Hartmut Boockmann and Hermann Wellenreuther, eds. *Geschichtswissenschaft in Göttingen*. Göttingen, 1987, pp. 287–320.
Pirenne, Henri. "Die Entstehung und Verfassung des Burgundischen Reichs im XV. und XVI. Jahrhundert." *Jahrbuch für Gesetzgebung, Verwaltung und Volkswirtschaft* 33 (1909): 33–63. English translation: "The Formation and Constitution of the Burgundian State (Fifteenth and Sixteenth Centuries)." *American Historical Review* 14 (1909): 477–502.
———. "Stages in the Social History of Capitalism."*American Historical Review* 19 (1914): 494–515; completed French version in Pirenne, *Histoire économique*, pp. 15–50.
———. *Souvenirs de captivité en Allemagne: Mars 1916–Novembre 1918*. Brussels, 1920.
———. "De l'influence allemande sur le mouvement historique contemporain." *Scientia: Rivista Internazionale di Sintesi Scientifica* (Bologna, 1923): 173–183.
———. "Un contraste économique: Mérovingiens et Carolingiens." *Revue belge de Philologie et d'histoire* 2 (1923): 223–235. Completed version in Pirenne, *Histoire économique*.
———. "L'expansion de l'Islam et le commencement du Moyen-Age" (1928), in Pirenne, *Histoire économique*.
———. *Histoire économique de l'occident médiéval*. Edited by Emile Coornaert. Bruges, 1951.
Pleket, H. W. "Slavernij in de Oudheid: 'Voer' voor oudhistorici en comparatisten." *Tidschrift voor Geschiedenis* 95 (1982): 1–30.
Pokrovsky, Mikhail N. "Doklad o poezdke v Oslo" [Report on the trip to Oslo]. *Vestnik Kommunisticeskoj Akademii* [Bulletin of the Communist Academy] 30, no. 6 (Moscow, 1928): 231–237.
Pollock, Frederick. "Die Kommissionsverwaltung in England." *Jahrbuch für Gesetzgebung, Verwaltung und Volkswirtschaft im Deutschen Reich* 33 (Leipzig, 1909): 65–87.
Première Conférence Internationale d'Histoire Économique. Août 1960, Stockholm, vol. 1: *Contributions*, vol. 2: *Communications*. Paris/La Haye, 1960.
Rachfahl, Felix. "Alte und neue Landesvertretung in Deutschland." *Jahrbuch für Gesetzgebung, Verwaltung und Volkswirtschaft im Deutschen Reich* 33 (Leipzig, 1909): 89–130.
Raphael, Lutz. *Geschichtswissenschaft im Zeitalter der Extreme: Theorien, Methoden, Tendenzen von 1900 bis zur Gegenwart*. Munich, 2003.
Rauch, Georg von. "Der deutsch-sowjetische Nichtangriffspakt vom August 1939 und die sowjetische Geschichtsschreibung." *Geschichte in Wissenschaft und Unterricht* 17 (1966): 472–482.
Renouvin, Pierre. "L'histoire contemporaine des relations internationales: Orientation de recherches." *Revue historique* 211 (1954): 233–255.
Rhode, Gotthold. "Historiker am Pazifik—ganz unter sich." *Geschichte in Wissenschaft und Unterricht* 27 (1976): 420–435.
Rickert, Heinrich. *Die Grenzen der naturwissenschaftlichen Begriffsbildung*. 2 vols. Tübingen, 1896, 1902.
———. *Kulturwissenschaft und Naturwissenschaft*. 5th ed. Tübingen, 1921.
Riezler, Kurt [under the pseudonym of J. J. Ruedorffer]. *Grundzüge der Weltpolitik in der Gegenwart* (Berlin, 1914).
Ritter, Gerhard. *Der Oberrhein in der deutschen Geschichte* (Freiburger Universitätsreden 25). Freiburg i. Br., 1937.

———. *Zur politischen Psychologie des modernen Frankreich (Lehrbriefe der Philosophischen Fakultät der Universität Freiburg 2).* Freiburg i. Br., 1943.
———. "Zum Begiff der Kulturgeschichte: Ein Diskusionsbeitrag." *Historische Zeitschrift* 171 (1951): 293–302
———. "Der X. Internationale Historikerkongreß in Rom, 4.–11. September." *Historische Zeitschrift* 180 (1955): 657–663.
———. *Ein politischer Historiker in seinen Briefen.* Edited by Klaus Schwabe and Rolf Reichardt. Boppard, 1984.
Ritter, Gerhard A., "Internationale Wissenschaftsbeziehungen und auswärtige Kulturpolitik im deutschen Kaiserreich," *Zeitschrift für Kulturaustausch* 31 (1981): 5–16.
Rothbarth, Margarethe. "Die deutschen Gelehrten und die internationalen Wissenschaftsorganisationen." In Heinrich Konen and Johann Peter Steffes, eds. *Volkstum und Kulturpolitik* (Festschrift for Georg Schreiber). Cologne, 1932, pp. 143–157.
Rothberg, Michael D. "'To set a standard of workmanship and compel men to conform to it': John Franklin Jameson as editor of the American Historical Review." *American Historical Review* 89 (1984): 957–975.
Rüsen, Jörn. "Zur Kritik des Neohistorismus." *Zeitschrift für philosophische Forschung* 33 (1979): 243–263.
———. "Narrative und Strukturgeschichte im Historismus." In Mommsen, "Narrative History," pp. 145–152.
———, ed. *Western Historical Thinking: An Intercultural Debate.* New York, 2002.
Sakharov, Anatolii M., "O nekotorych metodologičeskich voprosach na XIV Mež." Indnom kongresse istorikov: zametke delegata" [On some methodological problems at the XIVth International Historical Congress: notes of a delegate]. *Vestnik Universiteta Moskovskovo*, no. 3 (1976): 3–22.
Sakharov, Anatolii M., and Semen S. Khromov, "XIV Meždunarodnyi kongress istoričeskich nauk" [XIVth International Historical Congress]. *Voprosy istorii* 51, no. 3 (1976): 14–32.
Schäfer, Dietrich. "Das eigentliche Arbeitsgebiet der Geschichte" [1888], in Schäfer, *Aufsätze, Vorträge und Reden,* vol. 1. Jena, 1913, pp. 264–290.
———. "Geschichte und Kulturgeschichte: Eine Erwiderung" [1891], ibid., pp. 291–351.
———. *Mein Leben.* Berlin, 1926.
Scheel, Otto. "Der Volksgedanke bei Luther." *Historische Zeitschrift* 161 (1940): 477–497.
Schieder, Theodor. "Der XI. Internationale Historikerkongreß in Stockholm: Ein Nachbericht." *Historische Zeitschrift* 193 (1961): 515–521.
Schleier, Hans. "Narrative Geschichte und strukturgeschichtliche Analyse im traditionellen Historismus." *Zeitschrift für Geschichtswissenschaft* 34, no. 2 (1986): 99–112.
Schmid, Heinrich Felix. "Zum Thema: 'Möglichkeiten und Grenzen west-östlicher Historikerbegegnung.'" *Geschichte in Wissenschaft und Unterricht* 10 (1959): 114–119.
Schröder-Gudehus, Brigitte. "Deutsche Wissenschaft und internationale Zusammenarbeit 1914–1928: Ein Beitrag zum Studium kultureller Beziehungen in politischen Krisenzeiten." Ph.D. diss., University of Geneva, 1966.
Schumann, Peter. "Die deutschen Historikertage von 1893–1937: Die Geschichte einer fachhistorischen Institution im Spiegel der Presse." Ph.D. diss., University of Marburg, 1974.
Schwabe, Klaus. *Wissenschaft und Kriegsmoral: Die deutschen Hochschullehrer und die politischen Grundfragen des Ersten Weltkriegs.* Göttingen, 1969.
Sée, Henri. "Remarks sur l'application de la méthode comparative à l'histoire économique et sociale." *Revue de synthèse historique* 36 (1923): 37–46.
Shteppa, Konstantin F.: *Russian Historians and the Soviet State.* New Brunswick N. J., 1962.
Siegel, Martin. "Henri Berr's 'Revue de synthèse historique.'" *History and Theory* 9 (1970): 322–334.
Silberschmidt, Max. "Wirtschaftshistorische Aspekte der neueren Geschichte: die atlantische Gemeinschaft." *Historische Zeitschrift* 171 (1951): 245–261.

Simiand, François. "Récents congrès internationaux: le Congrès historique de Berlin," *Revue de synthèse historique* 17 (1908): 222–223.
Slonimsky, A. G. "Učastie russijskich učënych v Meždunarodnych kongressach istorikov" [The participation of Russian historians at the International Historical Congresses]. *Voprosy istorii* 45, no. 7 (1970): 95–108.
Spahn, Martin. "Die Presse als Quelle der neueren Geschichte und ihre gegenwärtigen Benutzungsmöglichkeiten." *Internationale Wochenschrift für Wissenschaft, Kunst und Technik* 2 (1908): 1163–1170, 1202–1211.
Steinberg, Hans-Joseph. "Karl Lamprecht." In Hans-Ulrich Wehler, ed. *Deutsche Historiker*, vol. 1. Göttingen, 1971, pp. 58–68.
Stock, Leo F. "Some Bryce-Jameson Correspondence." *American Historical Review* 50 (1944/45): 261–298.
Stone, Lawrence. "The revival of narrative: reflexions on a new old history." *Past and Present*, no. 85 (1979): 3–24.
Stuchtey, Benedikt, and Eckhardt Fuchs. *Writing World History 1800–2000*. Oxford, 2003.
Stupperich, Robert. "Die Teilnahme deutscher Gelehrter am 200jährigen Jubiläum der Russischen Akademie der Wissenschaften, 1925." *Jahrbücher für Geschichte Osteuropas* 24 (Wiesbaden, 1976): 218–229.
Thieme, Karl. "Möglichkeiten und Grenzen west-östlicher Historikerbegegnung: Zu den 'Akten' des internationalen Historikerkongresses (Rom 1955)." *Geschichte in Wissenschaft und Unterricht* 8 (1957): 593–598.
Tikhvinsky, Sergei L., and Valerii A. Tishkov. "Problemy novoj i novejšej istorii na XIV Meždunarodnom kongresse istoričeskich nauk" [Problems of modern and recent history at the XIVth International Historical Congress]. *Novaja i Novejšaja Istoria* 20, no. 1 (1976).
———. "XV Meždunarodnyi kongress istoričeskich nauk" [XVth International Historical Congress]. *Voprosy istorii* 55, no. 12 (1980): 3–23.
Thompson, F. M. L. "The British Approach to Social History." In Mommsen, "Narrative History," 162–169.
Torstendahl, Rolf, ed. *An Assessment of Twentieth-Century Historiography: Professionalism, Methodology, Writings*. Stockholm, 2000.
Troeltsch, Ernst. "Der Krieg und die Internationalität der geistigen Kultur." *Internationale Monatsschrift für Wissenschaft, Kunst und Technik* 9 (1 Oct. 1915): 51–58.
Tout, Thomas F. "The present state of medieval studies in Great Britain." *Proceedings of the British Academy* 6, 1913/14 (Oxford, 1920): 139–151.
Tymieniecki, Kazimierz. "VII Miedzynarodowy kongres historyczny" [VIIth International historical congress]. *Roczniki Historyczne* 9 (1933).
Union Académique Internationale. Compte rendu de la Conférence préliminaire de Paris. Statuts proposés par le Comité des Délégués, 15 et 17 mai 1919. Paris, 1919.
———. *Compte rendu de la seconde Conférence académique, tenue à Paris les 15–18 octobre 1919*. Paris, 1919.
———. *Comptes rendus des sessions annuelles du Comité*, nos. 1–15. Brussels, 1920–1934.
Valota Cavalotti, Bianca. *Nicola Iorga*. Naples, 1977.
Vigezzi, Brunello, ed. *Federico Chabod e la "Nuova Storiografia" italiana*. Milan, 1984.
Vittinghof, Friedrich. "Die Theorie des historischen Materialismus über den antiken 'Sklavenhalterstaat.'" *Saeculum* 11 (1960): 89–131.
Volpe, Gioacchino. *Storici e Maestri*. 2nd ed. Rome, 1966.
Vom Brocke, Bernhard. "Hochschul- und Wissenschaftspolitik in Preußen und im Deutschen Kaiserreich 1882–1907: Das 'System Althoff.'" In Peter Baumgart, ed. *Bildungspolitik in Preußen zur Zeit des Kaiserreichs*. Stuttgart, 1980, pp. 9–118.
———. "Der deutsch-amerikanische Professorenaustausch: Preußische Wissenschaftspolitk, internationale Wissenschaftsbeziehungen und die Anfänge einer deutschen Kulturpolitik vor dem Ersten Weltkrieg." *Zeitschrift für Kulturaustausch* 31 (1981): 128–182.

———. "Wissenschaft und Militarismus. Der Aufruf der 93 'An die Kulturwelt!' und der Zusammenbruch der internationalen Gelehrtenrepublik im Ersten Weltkrieg." In William M. Calder III., Hellmuth Flashar, and Theo Lindken, eds. *Wilamowitz nach 50 Jahren.* Darmstadt, 1985.
Von Salis, Jean Rudolf. *Grenzüberschreitungen. Ein Lebensbericht. Erster Teil: 1901–1939.* Frankfurt, 1975.
Wang, Q. Edward, and Georg G. Iggers, eds. *Turning Points in Historiography: A Cross Cultural Perspective.* Rochester, 2002.
Ward, Adolphus W. "International Congress of Historical Studies, London 1913: Introductory words" and "Closing remarks on the speech by J. Bryce." *Proceedings of the British Academy* 6, 1913/14 (Oxford, 1920): 113–121; 129–132.
———. "The Study of History at Cambridge." In Ward, *Collected Papers*, vol. 5. Cambridge, 1921.
Wegeler, Cornelia. "… Wir sagen ab der internationalen Gelehrtenrepublik." *Altertumswissenschaft und Nationalsozialismus: Das Göttinger Institut für Altertumskunde 1861–1962.* Vienna/Cologne/Weimar, 1996.
Wehler, Hans-Ulrich. *Historisches Denken am Ende des 20. Jahrhunderts.* München, 2001.
Westrin, Th., "Den första diplomatisk-historiske kongressen i Haag den 1–4 September 1898," *Historisk tidskrift* (Stockholm, 1898): 267–275.
Westrin, Th., W. Sjögren, and E. Wrangel. "Den internationella Kongressen för jämförande historia: I Paris den 23–28 juli 1900." *Historisk tidskrift* (Stockholm 1900): 309–328.
Why We Are at War: Great Britain's Case. By Members of the Oxford Faculty of Modern History. Oxford, 1914.
Wiese-Schorn, Luise. "Karl Lamprechts Pläne zur Reform der auswärtigen Kulturpolitik." *Zeitschrift für Kulturaustausch* 31 (1981): 27–42.
Wilamowitz-Moellendorff, Ulrich von: *Erinnerungen 1848–1914.* Leipzig, 1928.
———. "Der Krieg und die Wissenschaft." *Internationale Monatsschrift für Wissenschaft, Kunst und Technik* 9 (15 Oct. 1914): 101–106.
Windelband, Wilhelm. "Geschichte und Naturwissenschaft." In Windelband, *Präludien: Aufsätze und Reden zur Philosophie und ihrer Geschichte.* 2 vols. Tübingen, 1919.
Xenopol, Alexandru. *Les principes fondamentaux de l'histoire.* Paris, 1899; 2nd ed.: *La Théorie de l'histoire.* Paris, 1908.
Zöllner, Erich. "Bericht über den 12. Internationalen Historikertag." *Mitteilungen des Instituts für Österreichische Geschichtsforschung* 73 (1965): 437–445.

Index

Acton, Lord, 64–65
Adler, Viktor, 34
Adoratsky, Vladimir V., 132
Ahnlund, Nils, 234, 242n50, 363–64
Ahrweiler, Hélène, 219n80, 271–72, 317–18, 325, 365–66
Alagoa, Ebiegberi J., 271, 277n29, 323
Alatri, Paolo, 235, 243n67
Alföldi, Andreas, 178n33
Almquist, Johan A., 103
Althoff, Friedrich, 43–44, 55n10
Amino, Yoshihiko, 271, 277n28
Anrich, Ernst, 171
Ansprenger, Franz, 269, 276n16
Archimedes, 54
Arnaldi, Girolamo, 339, 366
Aron, Raymond, 282
Asoka, Emperor (Japan), 94
Asser, Tobias Michael Carel, 7
Atatürk, Kemal, 271
Aubin, Hermann, 145, 153
Aulard, Alphonse, 95
Aymard, André, 207, 212

Bacha, Eugène, 89, 99nn89–90
Badian, Ernest, 310n15
Bakunin, Mikhail A., 161n54
Baráth, Tibor, 158
Barbagallo, Corrado, 77
Barkai, Ron, 272
Barker, Ernest, 77
Barker, Theo (Theodore) C., 266n69, 272, 290, 316, 319–20, 324–25, 327, 329–33, 338–40, 357–60, 365–67

Barral, Pierre, 270
Barrère, Camille, 39n34
Barry, Boubacar, 271, 277n29
Bárta, Drahomir, 269
Barthold, Vasilii Vladimirovich, 81
Batllori, Père Miguel, 365
Battenberg, Prince Ludwig von (Mountbattan), 61
Bautier, Robert-Henri, 281
Baxter, John Houston, 120n59
Bearten, Jean, 297n46
Beazley, Sir Charles R., 90, 94
Beck, Ludwig, 162
Becker, Gerhard, 248–49, 261, 263nn14–15, 266n63
Bédarida, François, 262, 318, 324–32, 334, 338–44, 346–48, 352, 357–58, 359nn14–15, 360n54, 360n58, 366
Beethoven, Ludwig van, 30
Beier, Gerhard, 297n46
Below, Georg von, 8–10, 13, 33, 89, 92, 95, 98n53
Bémont, Charles, 66n4, 66n6
Benedict XV (pope), 242n59
Benito-Ruano, Eloy, 324, 366
Bentley, Jerry H., 350
Berend, Ivan T., 317, 324, 327, 329, 331, 333, 339–40, 342–44, 357, 359, 366–67
Bergson, Henri, 88
Berindei, Dan, 260
Berlin, Heinrich, 268, 276n9
Bernal, Ignazio, 268, 276n9
Bernheim, Ernst, 64, 86

– 419 –

Berr, Henri, 18–19, 45, 50, 66n5, 85, 88–89, 91–92, 95, 130–31, 141, 150, 153, 155–56, 172–73, 209, 227, 281
Berthelot, Daniel, 16
Berthier, Louis-Alexandre, 113
Bertolini, Ottorino, 178n33
Berza, Mihai, 365
Bethmann Hollweg, Theobald von, 1, 46, 251
Bhalla, Gurdarshan S., 272
Bhattacharya, Sachchidananda, 272
Bianco, Lucien, 270–71
Biaudet, Jean–Charles, 364–65
Bickermann, Elias, 222
Bidlo, Jaresław, 151
Bieżuńska-Małowistowa, Iza, 302–3
Bira, Šagdaryn, 268
Bismarck, Otto von, 30, 37, 53–54, 77, 171, 214, 316
Bittner, Ludwig, 160n36
Björk, Ragnar, 293
Björnson, Bjornstjerne, 78
Blänsdorf, Agnes, 291, 297n56
Bloch, Marc, 91–93, 95, 109–10, 126–31, 150, 172, 196–98, 204, 207, 211, 217n2, 346
Blom, Ida, 333
Blondel, Georges, 90
Blue, Gregory, 349
Bogaevsky, Boris L., 132
Boissier, Gaston, 14–15
Bongard-Levin, Gregorii, 357, 367
Boniface VIII (pope), 233
Bonjour, Edgar, 174–75, 179n56
Bonnard, Abel, 195n48
Bonnet, Henri, 186–87
Boulanger, Georges, 2
Bourgin, Georges, 228
Boutroux, Émile, 88
Boutruche, Robert, 207
Brackmann, Albert, 54, 145–46, 159n3, 160n29
Brandenburg, Erich, 146, 152
Brandi, Karl, 109, 111–15, 129–31, 139, 144–47, 150, 159n 3, 163, 170–71, 175, 177n21, 178n41, 186–88, 362
Brandt, Willy, 255
Braudel, Fernand, 204, 209, 223, 229, 279, 282, 287, 346, 351
Breßlau, Harry, 24, 54
Breysig, Kurt, 49–50

Brezzi, Paolo, 288
Briand, Aristide, 112, 122, 139, 143
Broglie, Albert Duc de, 6–7
Bromley, Yulian Vladimirovich, 358n3
Brossart, Yves, 337
Brown, William Norman, 263n11, 268, 276n6
Brüggemeier, Franz-Josef, 355
Brugmans, Izaak J., 234, 264n29, 364
Brunetière, Ferdinand, 18
Bryce, Viscount James, 25, 58–59, 65, 75, 347
Bubnov, A. S., 61
Bukharin, Nikolai Ivanovich, 156
Buck, Solon J., 193n15
Bücheler, Karl, 24
Bücher, Karl, 130
Buckle, Henry Thomas, 16
Bujak, Fransciszek, 87–9, 99n83
Burckhardt, Jacob, 47–48, 168, 208, 292
Burg, Maclyn P., 290
Burke, Edmund, 151
Byrnes, James F., 191

Cagatay, Nechet, 271
Cairncross, Sir Alec, 331–32
Calvin, Jean, 51
Cam, Helen M., 241n28
Cantimori, Delio, 242n54
Carande, Ramon, 364
Carbonell, Charles-Olivier, 291
Cardenas, Edoardo, 272
Carducci, Giosuè, 27
Caron, Pierre, 110, 165, 177n8, 177n14, 198
Catullus, Gaius Valerius, 35
Ceaușescu, Nicolae, 260
Ceci, Luigi, 23
Chabod, Federico, 110, 151, 220, 234, 237–40, 241n43, 242n61, 246, 252, 256, 278, 287, 290, 363–64
Chamberlain, Houston Steward, 50, 53, 90
Chamberlain, Sir J. Austin, 122
Chandra, Satish, 267, 271–72, 317, 365–66
Charles I (Great Britain), 63
Charles V (Holy Roman emperor), 129
Charles VIII (France), 29
Chartier, Roger, 336, 343–45
Chernyak, Efim Borisovich, 249, 263n16, 309, 311n38
Chevalier, Louis, 207, 218nn40–41

Index | 421

Chubaryan, Alexander O., 255, 261, 266n64, 321–22, 324, 328, 333, 339, 342, 366
Churchill, Sir Winston Spencer, 191
Cipolla, Carlo, 207
Clark, George N., 77
Clemenceau, Georges, 96n7
Cochran, Thomas C., 227
Cohen, Yolande, 335
Colenbrander, Herman Theodor, 114
Coligny, Gaspard de, 53–54, 56n18
Collingwood, Robin G., 227, 281–82, 286
Columbus, Christopher, 317, 319
Comte, Auguste, 16, 349
Condorcet, Antoine Marquis de, 16
Constantine (Roman emperor), 54
Conze, Werner, 310n5
Coornaert, Émile, 211
Coquery-Vidrovitch, Catherine, 340, 342–43, 350, 357–58, 367
Coutau-Bégarie, Hervé, 291
Coville, Alfred, 164, 177n9
Craig, Gordon A., 266n69, 291, 298n58, 365
Crawley, Charles W., 284
Croce, Benedetto, 3, 22, 25, 33, 35–38, 40n49, 40n57, 69, 86, 89, 131, 140, 153, 169, 224, 232–34, 239, 282, 286, 288–89
Curschmann, Fritz, 151, 170
Czartoryski, Prince Adam, 151, 161n50

Dabrowski, Jan, 202
Danielsson, Olof A., 54
D'Arms, Edward, 217n1, 217n6
Darvaï, Maurice (Móricz), 17
Darwin, Charles, 32, 34
Dawes, Charles G., 104, 122
Day, Edmund E., 119n27
de Beaufort, Willem, 7–8, 12
de Boer, Michael G., 84, 98n70, 93, 100n107, 100n116
Deborin, Abram Moisevich, 165
de Crue, Francis, 82, 118n11
Degler, Carl Neumann, 315–16, 321, 366
de Haan, Francisca, 335
Dehio, Georg, 17–18
Dehio, Ludwig, 218n29, 224
Deißmann, Adolf, 53
de Lagarde, Georges, 210, 219n51
de la Torre Villar, Ernesto, 267, 317, 320, 339, 365–67

Delbrück, Hans, 8, 48, 55n7
Delcassé, Théophile, 23
Delehaye, Père Hippolyte, SJ, 118n11, 362
Delitzsch, Friedrich, 31
Demarco, Domenico, 228, 365
de Maulde-La Clavière, René, 6–9, 11n1, 12–14, 24, 26, 65
Dembiński, Bronisław, 82–83, 103, 109, 115, 124, 135, 139, 149, 151, 153, 163, 362
de Montemayor, Giulio, 33
Denifle, Friedrich Heinrich Suso, 52
Depréaux, Albert, 189, 194n44
de Roover, Raymond, 207
Dery, Tibór, 240
De Sanctis, Gaetano, 82–83, 103, 109, 114, 140, 165–66, 190–191, 239, 362
Des Marez, Guillaume, 76
Dhont, Jean (Jan), 207
Dickens, Al., 264n26
Dickens, Charles, 344
Diehl, Ernst, 254
Diels, Hermann, 44
Diez del Coral, Luis, 266n62
Dilthey, Wilhelm, 47, 51, 282, 286, 288, 292, 294
Djurdjev, Branislav, 310n5
Dollfuss, Engelbert, 148
d'Olwer, Don Luis Nicolau, 363
Domanovszky, Alexander (Sándor), 158, 164, 168, 177n9, 177n20, 185, 190, 195n55, 362
d'Ormesson, Jean, 253–54
Dopsch, Alfons, 63, 67n23, 80, 87, 102, 105, 109, 111–12, 114, 126–27, 129–31, 135, 136n19, 136n30, 147, 166, 177n20, 191, 217n19, 362
Dosse, François, 351
Droysen, Johann Gustav, 292
Droz, Jacques, 251, 270
Dubois, Alain, 324–25, 330–31, 338, 365–66
Dubrovsky, Sergei M., 115, 132, 152, 161n54
Dubuc, Alfred, 286
Duchesne, Abbé Jean Baptiste, 25–26
Ducreux, Marie-Elisabeth, 328
Ducrey, Pierre, 326, 339–40, 357, 366–67
Dürer, Albrecht, 136n29
Dufour, Alain, 280
Dupré (Italy, National Committee), 185, 193
Duri, Abdal Aziz ad, 323

Durkheim, Émile, 18, 87
Duroselle, Jean-Baptiste, 251

Eckhart, Ferenc, 202
Eckstein, Modris, 337
Edward VII (Great Britain), 58
Egorov, Dimitrii N., 115
Eguchi, Bokuro, 271, 277n28
Einstein, Albert, 80
Eisenmann, Louis, 123, 125, 135n6, 152
Elekes, Lajos, 285, 309
Elizabeth I (England), 53
El-Shakandiri, Mohamed, 271, 277n31
Engelberg, Ernst, 246, 248–49, 263nn14–15, 302–7, 309–11, 316, 320
Engel-Janosi, Friedrich, 250–52, 264n31, 296n24, 364
Engels, Friedrich, 35, 247, 300–301, 303, 310n3, 311n23, 320
Epting, Karl, 187–88
Erdmann, Karl Dietrich, x, xiin1, xix, xvin3, 251, 254, 256, 258–61, 266n67, 289, 307–8, 310–11, 313–15, 322, 324–25, 353, 358, 365–66
Erdmannsdörffer, Bernhard, 8, 13, 20n8
Esmein, Adhémar, 14–15, 17, 62
Espinas, Georges, 93
Eucken, Rudolf, 154

Faber, Karl-Georg, 289
Fagniez, Gustave, 89
Fairbank, John King, 268, 276n5
Fawtier, Robert, 189, 191–92, 198–205, 215–16, 230, 235, 238–40, 241n43, 281, 363–65
Febvre, Lucien, 91–93, 95, 109–10, 126, 128, 189, 204, 209, 211, 213–14, 223, 279–80, 282
Fedele, Pietro, 140, 152, 164
Fellner, Fritz, 260
Ferrabino, Aldo, 230
Ferrero, Guglielmo, 184, 193n18
Ferro, Marc, 291
Fester, Richard, 49, 51–52
Finke, Heinrich, 52–53, 57n40
Finley, Sir Moses I., 294, 298n65, 310n15
Fiorini, Vittorio, 27
Firth, Charles H., 64, 67n26, 74, 77, 97n29
Fischer, Fritz, 251
Fish, Carl R., 95

Fling, Fred Morrow, 153–55
Florath, Bernd, 326, 359n15
Ford, Guy Stanton, 107, 119n26
Fossier, Robert, 297n46
Fourastié, Jean, 207, 211
Francastel, Pierre, 207–9
François, Michel, xiv, 216, 217n16, 219n80, 234, 237–40, 241n43, 246–47, 252–53, 256, 281, 343, 363–366
François-Poncet, André, 204
Frank, Walter, 170–71, 178n41
Frederic II (Holy German emperor), 136n29
Frederick William IV (Prussia), 52
Fredericq, Paul, 73
Freeman, E. K., 226
Freyer, Hans, 294
Frick, Wilhelm, 147
Friedmann, Franz, 152
Friedmann, Georges, 207, 209
Friis, Aage, 77–79, 103, 109–10, 117–18, 121n76, 135, 138n53, 139–40, 143, 145, 146–47, 164, 166, 168, 175–77, 183–84, 202
Fussel, Paul, 337
Fustel de Coulanges, Numa Denis, 153, 215, 292

Gabrieli, Francesco, 268, 276n5
Gaeta, Franco, 232
Gans, Eduard, 30
Ganshof, Francois-Louis, 76, 118n11, 131, 150–51, 167, 169, 177n21, 189, 194n48, 200, 363
Gay, Jules, 95
Geiss, Imanuel, 269, 276n16, 301
Gellner, Ernest, 334
Gentile, Giovanni, 35, 37–38, 140, 169, 174
George I (Greece), 58
Geremek, Bronisław, 331–32
Gerhard, Dietrich, 227
Gibbon, Edward, 3, 227
Gierke, Otto von, 24–25, 41, 45, 62
Gieysztor, Aleksander, 206, 231, 260, 328, 330–31, 339, 342, 357, 364–67
Gilbert, Felix, 296n12
Giurescu, Constantin C., 271
Gladstone, William Ewert, 214
Glénisson, Jean, 281–83, 291
Glinkin, Anatolii Nikolaevich, 276n19

Glotz, Gustave, 111–13, 119n36
Gobineau, Joseph-Arthur Comte de, 90
Godart, Justin, 19
Godechot, Jacques, 228–29, 282–83
Goderic, Saint, 63
Godlewski, archbishop (Warsaw), 150
Goerdeler, Carl Friedrich, 203, 225
Goethe, Johann Wolfgang von, 17
Goetz, Hans-Werner, 352
Gökbilgin, Tayyib, 271
Gollancz, Israel, 60
Gooch, George Peabody, 64, 77, 223
Goonawardhane, L., 383
Gorky, Maxim, 352, 361n68
Gorrini, Giacomo, 24
Gothein, Eberhard, 8–9, 47, 51, 56n22
Gottschalk, Louis, 269, 283
Graham, Gerald S., 283–84, 296n24
Gray White, Deborah, 335
Gregory I (pope), 33
Grey, Sir Edward, 58
Grigulevich, Iosif R., 261, 266n64
Grimm, Jacob, 30
Grisar, Hartmann, SJ, 52
Grondahl, Kristi Kolle, 344
Grotius, Hugo, 10, 209
Grousset, René, 188
Guber, Aleksandr A., 253, 256, 262n5, 264n46, 269, 276n13, 364–65
Guerlac, Henry, 211
Guizot, François, 292
Gunkel, Hermann, 53
Gustav Adolf (King of Sweden), 54

Haber, Fritz, 105–6
Haag, Henri, 263n10
Haebler, Konrad, 54
Hagemann, Karen, 335, 355
Hajnal, István, 161n69
Halecki, Oscar, 80, 82, 91, 98n65, 99, 126, 145, 151, 160n29, 160n40, 210, 212, 231, 248, 301
Hallgarten, George W. F., 169, 171–72, 174, 178n35, 179nn46–47
Halpérin, Jean, 211
Halphen, Louis, 95, 168
Hamilton, Earl J., 263n10, 296n11
Handelsman, Marceli, 95, 124, 126, 135n6, 149, 151, 161n72, 163, 168, 177n21, 196, 363

Handfest, Carl (Karl), 218n28
Handlin, Oscar, 226–27
Haneda, Akira, 271
Hansy, Alfred, 90
Harnack, Adolf von, 24–25, 30–31, 41–42, 44–45, 55n14, 68
Harris, Brent, 352
Harrison, Frederic, 9
Harsin, Paul, 247, 252–54, 364–65
Hartmann, Ludo Moritz, 25, 33–34, 92, 131
Hartog, François, 353, 361
Hartung, Fritz, 145, 279–80
Hasan, Saiyid Nurul, 267, 272, 324, 366
Haskins, Charles H., 49, 54, 57n52
Hassinger, Erich, 301, 310n5
Haupt, Paul, 53
Hauser, Henri, 66n5, 171
Haushofer, Karl, 173
Hegel, Georg Wilhelm Friedrich, 35–36, 350
Heigel, Karl Theodor Ritter von, 44
Heimpel, Hermann, 204, 218n25, 296n13
Helbig, Wolfgang, 23
Heller, Gerhard, 194n41
Helmolt, Hans, 49, 52, 57n40
Henry, Louis, 296n11
Herder, Johann Gottfried, 30, 36, 124, 169, 211
Herodotus, 346, 348
Herre, Paul, 49, 54, 57n51
Herrmann, Joachim, 315–16, 320, 324, 359n14, 366
Hertzman, Lewis, 283–84, 365
Herzen, Aleksandr I., 30
Hexter, Jack H., 285, 296n31
Heyd, Michael, 357, 367
Hildebrand, Klaus, 322
Hill, David Jayne, 24, 51
Hintze, Otto, 43
Hirschfeld, Otto, 55n7
Hitler, Adolf, 145–46, 148, 162, 174, 186–87, 194n48, 202–3, 225, 231, 262, 316, 322
Hobbes, Thomas, 209
Hobsbawm, Eric J. E., 206, 212, 229, 249, 297n53, 310n15, 334, 344–45
Hodgson, Marshall, 349
Hoetzsch, Otto, 115, 145
Hofer, Walther, 207, 218n39, 231–32, 242n49

Hoffmann, Georg, 178n26
Höjer, Torvald, 49, 57n54, 246, 364
Holtzmann, Robert, 143, 145–46, 159n17, 160n29, 168, 185–89, 193n30, 363
Homer, 38
Homolle, Théophil, 69, 82–83, 103
Hopkins, John, 223
Horvath, Eugen, 95
Houssaye, Henri, 15, 59, 308
Hrushevsky, Mikhailo S., 166, 188
Hua, Q., 272
Huizinga, Johan, 208, 354
Hülsen, Christian, 23, 25
Humboldt, Wilhelm von, 153
Husowa, Marie, 202

Ibsen, Henrik, 78
Iggers, Georg G., 292, 297n51, 298n59, 342, 351–52
Ignatius of Loyola, Saint, 47, 51
Ihering, Rudolf von, 32
Imahori, Seiji, 269–270, 276n18
Imanaga, Seiji, 271
Iorga, Nicolae, 16, 50, 62, 99n78, 126–27, 152, 163–64, 172–74, 177n9, 179n50, 179n54, 180, 186, 188–89, 196, 224, 363

Jäckel, Eberhard, 247, 254, 263n8
Jacob, Ernest, 364
James I (Grat Britain), 136n29
Jameson, John Franklin, 60, 65, 72–79, 81–82, 84, 95, 97n29, 101, 104, 109
Jaryc, Marc, 177n8, 187
Jedruszczak, Tadeusz, 251, 258, 264n24, 265n55
Ji Xian-Lin, 272
Jiménez Moreno, Wigberto, 268, 276n9
Jin Chongji, 321
Jobbé-Duval, Émile Louis Marie, 19
Johannesson, Gösta, 263n10
Johnson, Paul, 336
Jonas, Franz, 249
Jordan, Karl, 256
Jordan, William Chester, 357, 367
Joutard, Philippe, 335
Juan Carlos (King of Spain), 319
Junod, Louis, 364

Kabayama, Koichi, 357, 367
Kádár, János, 240

Kaehler, Siegfried A., 175
Kahle, Günther, 270, 276n19
Kahrstedt, Ulrich, 147
Kampschulte, Friedrich Wilhelm, 51
Kanda, Fumihito, 272
Kann, Robert A., 284
Kant, Immanuel, 30, 129
Karayannopoulos, Joannis, 324, 366
Kartodirdjo, Sartono, 323
Kaser, Kurt, 54
Katz, Henryk, 263n17
Kautsky, Karl, 1
Kehr, Paul F., 24–25, 54, 73, 97n22
Keilhau, Wilhelm, 154–55
Kellogg, Frank B., 122
Khalidi, Tarif, 323
Khrushchev, Nikita Sergeevich, 230, 234, 245, 248
Khvostov, Vladimir Mikhailovich, 229, 241n37, 263n11
Kimbara, Samon, 270, 277n24.
Kinal, Füruzan, 271
Kirchhoff, Paul, 268, 276n9
Ki-Zerbo, Joseph, 272
Kjellén, Rudolf, 173
Kladiva, J., 312n40
Klein, Fritz, 260, 326
Kloczowski, Jerzy, 338, 343
Knapp, Viktor, 329
Kobata, Atsushi, 270, 277n21
Koch, Franz, 169, 171, 174
Kocka, Jürgen, 291–93, 298n65, 333, 339–43, 355–58, 360, 366–67
Koebner, Richard, 147, 176n3
Kohn, Hans, 246, 250
Koht, Halvdan, xivn50, 57n36, 57nn78–79, 81, 83–84, 91, 103–4, 109, 112, 114–17, 122–25, 132–33, 135n5, 137n35, 140, 142–43, 147, 149, 153, 157, 162, 164, 166, 177n21, 184, 188–89, 194n48, 198, 200–201, 205, 219n78, 238, 248, 362–64
Kolbenheyer, Erwin Guido, 169
Kondo, O., 272
Kormanowa, Żanna, 245, 312n40
Kosáry, Domokos, 161n71, 176n2, 202, 239–40, 243n83, 284
Koselleck, Reinhart, 99n84, 311n30, 351
Koser, Reinhold, 11, 44–45, 55n7
Kossuth, Lajos von, 151
Kot, Stanisław, 166

Kotani, Hiroyuki, 272
Kovác, Dušan, 328–29
Kowalski, Józef, 263n17
Kozłowski, Władysław M., 89–90
Kozminsky, Evgenii A., 132
Kreis, Georg, 322
Kropilák, Miroslav, 262
Kuhn, Thomas S., 281
Kula, Witold, 206, 218n37
Kumar, Ravinder, 339, 366
Küntzel, Georg, 105
Kuroda, Toshio, 272
Küttler, Wolfgang, 297n53, 298n65, 312n41

Labriola, Antonio, 35, 131
Labrousse, Ernest, 204, 211, 214, 224, 228, 232, 241n31, 249, 278, 283, 296n24
Lackó, Miclos, 255
Lacombe, Paul, 90
Ladero Quesada, Miguel-Angel, 319
Lake, Marilyn, 335, 360n41
Lalande, André, 16
Lamarck, Jean Baptiste de, 88
Lamprecht, Karl, 9–10, 28, 46–50, 56nn23–24, 57n36, 59, 63–64, 90, 99n78, 164
Lancini, Rodolfo, 29
Landes, David S., 229
Lange, Even, 341
Langlois, Charles-Victor, 153, 282
Lapi, Scipione, 27
Lappo-Danilevsky, Aleksandr Sergeevich, 62, 72–73
Largiadér, Anton, 215, 363
Laslett, Peter, 300
Lattimore, Owen, 226
Lauffer, Siegfried, 302
Lavollée, René, 1–2, 6
Le Bras, Gabriel, 263n10
Lecca, Baron Octav-George, 90, 99n92
Lee, Ki-Baik, 272
Lefebvre, Georges, 207
Leland, Waldo, 75–77, 79–84, 93–94, 97n33, 100n110, 100n116, 101–14, 117, 118n12, 119n17, 140, 142–44, 147–48, 150, 163, 166, 176, 176n6, 180–81, 183–91, 193n14, 194n48, 198, 200–201, 215, 362–64
Lenin, Vladimir Ilich, 1, 247, 254–56, 310n15
Lenz, Max, 48, 55n7, 68

Leo XIII (pope), 26, 52, 150
Leśnodorski, Bogusław, 229–31, 241n40
Lew, Young Ick, 272
Lewinski, Jan Stanisław, 88–89
Lhéritier, Michel, 98n72, 103, 105, 107–9, 111–13, 116–17, 118n9, 121n76, 122, 132, 134–35, 137n39, 140, 142–44, 148–50, 164–65, 167, 177n21, 180–83, 185–89, 193n34, 194n44, 194n48, 198, 201, 205, 279, 362–63
Lindberg, Folke, 365
Lindvald, Axel, 363
Linné, Carl von, 88
Lloyd, Christopher, 350
Locke, John, 209, 320
Loehr, August von, 178n41, 191, 203
Louis XIV (France), 136n29
Lousse, Émile, 152, 161n56
Lozek, Gerhard, 297n53, 298n65
Lübbe, Hermann, 297n44, 298n61
Lüders, Heinrich, 120n59
Lukin, Nikolai M., 137n46, 152, 155, 160n37, 161n54, 165
Lukinich, Imre, 158, 161n71
Lunacharsky, Anatolii Vasilevich, 156, 161n65
Luther, Ernst, 105
Luther, Martin, 30, 52, 152, 170, 223
Lüthy, Herbert, 269
Luxemburg, Rosa, 254
Lyell, Charles, 88

Macaulay, Lord Thomas, 292
Maccarrone, Michele, 242n59, 296n13
Macek, Josef, 246, 262n3
Machiavelli, Niccolò, 24
Mac Kay, Donald, 229, 240n3, 241n17, 363–64
Mackinnon, James, 94, 100n114
Mafulu, Uyind-a-Kanga, 272
Mahler, Rafael, 152
Maîtron, Jean, 228
Malowist, Marian, 206, 212, 218n37
Maltzan, Ago von, 105
Manacorda, Gastone, 243n67, 249, 279, 302
Mandela, Nelson, 331, 360n28
Manfred, Albert Zakharovich, 284
Mann, Thomas, 169
Mannheim, Karl, 292
Manselli, Raoul, 266n62

Manteuffel, Tadeusz, 149, 202
Marcks, Erich, 53, 120n63
Marinetti, Filipo Tommaso, 337
Markov, Walter, 269–70, 276n18
Marolles, Vicomte de, 19
Marongiu, Antonio, 241n28
Marrou, Henri-Irénée, 212, 214, 215, 219n73, 222, 282
Marshall, Georges, 191
Marshall, John, 194n37, 194n48, 199–200, 217n4, 217n6, 217n8
Martier, French general, 113
Marx, Karl, 33–36, 154–55, 157, 161n54, 197–98, 210, 246–47, 292, 300–301, 303–4, 310n3, 310n15, 320
Masabuchi, Tatsuo, 268, 276n8
Mashaury, Kule Tambite, 272
Maspéro, Gaston, 54, 56n18
Masson-Oursel, Paul, 212
Matl, Josef, 264n22
Matsuoka, Hisato, 270, 277n20
Mayer, Hans, 171
Mayor, Federico, 331–32
Mazzini, Giuseppe, 178n37
McLuhan, Marshall, 347
McNeill, William H., 349, 361
Medick, Hans, 323
Mehring, Franz, 47–48
Meier, Christian, 261
Meinecke, Friedrich, 36, 40n55, 77, 109, 124, 170, 175, 224, 233–34, 288, 292
Melik-Taikazov, N. N., 235
Menelsohn, E., 272
Merkle, Sebastian, 53, 57n41
Metternich, Klemens Lothar Wenzel, Fürst von, 175, 284
Meyer, Arnold Oskar, 63
Meyer, Eduard, 23, 43–45, 64, 68
Meyer Paul, 25
Michelet, Jules, 16, 29–30, 45, 136n29, 292
Mickiewicz, Adam, 30
Mikoletzky, Hanns Leo, 195n60
Milhaud, Gaston, 16
Miller, A. F., 269, 276n13
Mints, Isaac I. 115, 133–34, 305
Minocchi, Salvatore, 31
Mirot, Léon, 118n11
Mitterand, François, 331–32
Miyake, Masaki, 317, 324, 366
Modestov, Vasilii Ivanovich, 25

Molas Ribalta, Pere, 316
Momigliano, Arnaldo, 221–22, 278
Mommsen, Hans, 263n19, 264n46
Mommsen, Theodor, iii, 3, 22–23, 25, 22–23, 25, 33, 44, 55n7
Mommsen, Wilhelm, 146, 170
Mommsen, Wolfgang J., xii, 295, 297n46, 297n53, 298n61, 298nn64–65, 328, 337, 359n15
Moniot, Henri, 268, 276n10
Monod, Gabriel, 6, 8–10, 13, 18, 25, 27, 29–30, 41, 45, 48, 50, 56n18, 65, 86
Montesquieu, Charles de, 32, 173
Morazé, Charles, 189–90, 192, 198–201, 204–5, 209, 213–16, 217n17, 218n36, 219n69, 219n76, 363
Morén, Guillermo, 271, 277n30
Morghen, Raffaelo, 168, 364
Morley of Blackburn, John Lord (Viscount), 64
Mörner, Magnus, 270, 276n19
Möser, Justus, 48, 291
Mostovac, Milivoj, 250
Mousnier, Roland, 272, 279, 280
Munshi, Surendra, 272, 294, 298n65
Muratori, Ludovico Antonio, 26–27
Mussolini, Benito, 175
mwa Bawele, Mumbanza, 323

Nabholz, Hans, 156–58, 163, 165–68, 171, 175, 176n6, 177n8, 178n34, 180, 186–87, 189–191, 194n48, 198, 200, 203–4, 218n31, 362–64
Nadler, Josef, 145
Näf, Werner, 175
Nagahra, K., 272
Napoleon Bonaparte, 136n29, 335
Narinsky, Mikhail M., 321, 322
Narochnitsky, Aleksei L., 264n46, 283–84
Narul, D. D., 272
Natsagdorj, Sh., 271
Nechkina, Milica Vasil, 249, 263n16, 309, 311n38
Niebuhr, Barthold Georg, 36, 48, 291
Niejinski, L. N., 322
Nietzsche, Friedrich, 322
Niida, Noboru, 268, 276n8
Nijhuis, Ton, 323
Ninomiya, Hiroyuki, 339, 367
Nishijima, Sadao, 268, 276n8

Nishikawa, Yoichi, 271, 277n28
Nitobe, Inazo, 112
Nixon, Richard, 259
Norden, Eduard, 120n59
Novick, Peter, 352

O'Brien, Patrick, 348–50, 361
O'Dowd, Mary, 335
Oldenburg, Sergei F., 105, 114–15, 141
Oncken, Hermann, 105–6, 123–24, 135, 145, 170
Orano, Paolo, 31
Österberg, Eva, 339–42, 356, 367
Ots Capdequi, José María, 268, 276n11
Ottokar, Nicola, 81

Pagès, Georges, 103, 152
Painlevé, Paul, 69
Pais, Ettore, 22–23, 25–26
Palanque, Jean-Rémy, 212
Palat, A., 269–270, 276n18
Palmer, Robert R., 228–29, 301
Panek, Jaroslav, 359n16
Pankratova, Anna Mikhailovna, 152, 232, 234, 236–38, 242n54, 309, 364
Papadopoulos, Theodore, 271, 285
Pashuto, Vladimir T., 249, 263n16, 309, 311n38
Pastor, Ludwig von, 25–26
Patzelt, Erna, 177n20, 178n41
Pélinier, L., 56n18
Perényi, József, 271
Pergameni, Charles, 91
Peset, José Luis, 357, 367
Pétain, Henri Philippe, 187
Petit-Dutaillis, Charles, 194n48, 195n57
Petric, Aron, 297n46
Philip of Macedonia, 136n29
Philip II (Spain), 136n29, 224
Piganiol, André, 282
Pilsudski, Józef Klemens, 109
Pirenne, Henri, 46, 50, 54, 57nn36–37, 59, 63, 71, 73, 75–78, 80, 83–90, 92–96, 101–5, 107, 109–10, 114, 117, 119n36, 121n76, 125–31, 135, 136n14, 143, 150, 153–54, 346–47, 362
Pius IX (pope), 52
Pius X (pope), 52
Pius XI (pope), 150
Pius XII (pope), 26, 233, 242n59

Planck, Max, 68
Platonov, Sergei F., 115, 141
Platzhoff, Walter, 178n41, 188
Pleket, Henri Willy, 310n15
Pohlenz, Max, 120n59
Pokrovsky, Mikhail N., 115, 132–34, 137n43, 141, 159nn12–13, 236–37
Pollard, Albert F., 77, 97n41, 119n17
Pollock, Sir Frederick, 25, 31–32, 54, 62, 66n17
Poniatowski, Stanisław II. Augustus (Poland), 151, 161n50
Popper, Karl R., 285, 311n27
Postan, Michael, 207, 211, 279
Powicke, Frederick Maurice, 103
Prečan, Vilém, 265n56, 329
Preobrazhensky, Evgenii A., 154–55
Pribram, Franz, 26
Prinetti, Giulio, 29, 39n34
Prost, Antoine, 354
Prothero, George W., 60, 67n36, 74–75, 97n29
Prou, Maurice, 46, 99n81

Rabelais, François, 223
Rachfahl, Felix, 54
Racine, Jean Baptiste, 37
Rafto, Torolf, 255
Ranke, Leopold von, 3, 25, 28, 36, 47–48, 60, 147, 156, 174, 208, 211, 233, 250, 282, 292, 350, 352
Ránki, György, 317, 339, 358, 365–66
Ranson, Marianne, 325
Ratzel, Friedrich, 91
Rein, Adolf, 171, 175
Reincke-Bloch, Hermann, 111–13, 119n19, 119n41, 120n74
Reinhard, Marcel, 264n30, 283
Reisch, Emil, 120n59
Reitzenstein, Richard, 120n59
Renan, Ernest, 334
Renouard, Yves, 207, 212–13, 223
Renouvin, Pierre, 82, 94, 142, 148, 168, 171, 175, 204, 213–14, 216, 217n22, 221, 225–28, 240, 241n15, 251, 278, 283
Richelieu, Cardinal, 179n48
Rickert, Heinrich, 37, 51, 87–88, 153, 155, 282
Ricoeur, Paul, 352
Ricuperati, Giuseppe, 351

Riezler, Kurt, 1
Ritter, Gerhard, 145, 152–53, 170–71, 174–75, 203–4, 208–9, 217n22, 218n26, 218n44, 221, 223–25, 227, 233–35, 242n59, 246, 251, 278, 296n24, 364
Robert, Jean-Claude, 339, 356–57, 360n58, 367, 376
Rörig, Fritz, 168
Rosenberg, Alfred, 170
Rossi, Pietro, 289, 294, 298n65
Rostovtsev, Mikhail, 54, 81, 105, 133, 222
Rothacker, Erich, 296n12
Rothfels, Hans, 145–47, 166, 175, 177n16, 263n12, 286
Roussellier, Nicolas, 334
Ruisbroeck, Johannes van, 136n29
Rüsen, Jörn, 292, 298nn60–61, 336
Rüter, Adolf J. C., 212

Sagnac, Philippe, 95
Saint-Saëns, Camille, 136n29
Sakharov, Anatolii M., 258, 265n52, 265n54
Saleilles, Raymond, 32–33
Salvatorelli, Luigi, 220, 363
Salvioli, Giuseppe, 93
Sapori, Armando, 168, 207
Sasaki, Jumosuke, 272
Savigny, Friedrich Karl von, 32, 36
Savonarola, Girolamo, 24
Schäfer, Dietrich, 43, 45, 47, 55n7
Scheel, Otto, 170–71, 174,
Scheel, Walter, 255
Scheffer-Boichorst, Paul, 33
Schieder, Theodor, 247, 269, 286–88, 297n35, 301
Schiller, Friedrich, 124
Schlatter, Richard, 257
Schleier, Hans, 297n53, 298n59
Schmid, Heinrich Felix, 232, 235, 242nn50–51, 256, 273, 363–64
Schmitt, Bernadotte E., 241n27, 242n47
Schmitt, Carl, 195n48
Schmittlein, Raymond, 203–4
Schostakovich, Dimitrii, 337
Schramm, Percy Ernst, 175
Schreiner, Klaus, 294, 298n65
Schröder, Gerhard, 178n41
Schulte, Aloys, 25
Schulze, Winfried, 326

Schuschnigg, Kurt Edler von, 166
Seeley, John Robert, 60
Seignobos, Charles, 213–14, 282
Sellin, Ernst, 53
Semkovicz, Władysław, 151
Servet (Serveto), Miguel, 54
Sestan, Ernesto, 263n10, 287–88
Seton-Watson, Robert William, 77
Seton-Watson, G. Hugh N., 242n47
Shafer, Boyd Carlisle, 252, 256–57, 296n24, 364–65
Shakespeare, William, 30
Shiba, Yoshinubu, 272, 298n65
Shimokawa, K., 272
Shotwell, James T., 75–76, 79, 82–84, 94, 101, 104–5, 107, 118n11, 183, 186
Sidorov, Arkadii Lavr., 230, 232, 237, 241n40, 263n11
Silberschmidt, Max, 229
Simenson, Jarle, 356
Simiand, François, 45, 49–50, 56n18, 222
Simonya, N. A., 321
Simonsohn, Shlomo, 272
Sismondi, J. C. Léonard Simonde de, 136n29
Snooks, Graeme Donald, 349
Soboul, Albert, 249, 270, 283
Solmssen, Georg, 172
Sombart, Werner, 63, 130, 168, 226
Sorokin, Dimitrii, 349
Spahn, Martin, 54
Spengler, Oswald, 232, 322, 349
Spuler, Bertold, 271
Srbik, Heinrich Ritter von, 40n55, 175, 284
Stalin, Iosif V., 156, 230–31, 234, 236, 262, 322, 352
Stanescu, Eugen, 297n46
Steensgard, Niels, 272, 277n33
Stein, Arthur, 178n33
Steinacker, Harold, 124–25, 160n35, 175
Stelling-Michaud, Sven, 263n10
Stevens, David Harrison, 195n63, 200
Stille, Hans, 120n59
Stloukal, Karel, 177n9, 363
Stökl, Günther, 241n28
Stolz, Otto, 159n17
Stone, Lawrence, 297n53
Stresemann, Gustav, 112, 122, 143
Struve, Peter, 81
Stubbs, Charles Williams, 60
Šusta, Josef, 362

Sverdrup, Johan, 78
Syme, Ronald, 222

Tadić, Jiorjio, 365
Takahashi, Kohachiro, 267, 364–65
Talleyrand, Charles Maurice de, 188
Talmon, Jacob L., 210, 304
Tangl, Michael, 43
Tarle, Evgenii Viktor, 81, 114, 141
Tavernier, Yves, 270
Tawney, Richard H., 223
Teano, Caetani Principe di, 54
Temperley, Harold W. V., 62, 77, 95, 105, 109, 162–64, 166–68, 177n9, 180, 184–85, 191, 200, 362–63
Temu, A. J., 323
Thane, Pat, 337
Thapar, Romila, 343, 356, 367
Thayer, William R., 38
Thieme, Karl, 242n49, 242n51
Thiersch, Hermann, 113, 120n59
Thistlethwaite, Frank, 263n10
Thomas of Bradwardine, 136n29
Thompson, Francis Michael Longstreth, 293, 297n53, 298
Tierney, Brian, 320
Tikhvinsky, Sergei Leonidovich, 265n52, 266n64, 266n69, 315, 324, 365–66
Tishkov, Valerii A., 265n52, 266n64, 317
Tisserand, Cardinal Eugène, 163
Tocqueville, Alexis Comte de, 28, 292
Tokody, Gyula, 249
Tønneson, Kåre D., 365
Topolski, Jerzy, 311n27, 321–22
Torstendahl, Rolf, 353, 361
Toscano, Mario, 241n27, 242n47
Tosti, Amadeo, 134, 137n48
Tout, Thomas F., 64, 82– 83, 103, 105, 118n11, 119n17, 121n74
Toynbee, Arnold J., 77, 209–10, 214, 322, 349
Trénard, Louis, 283
Trevelyan, George M., 77, 212
Troeltsch, Ernst, 15, 69, 157, 288, 292
Trotsky, Lev Davidovich, 165
Truyol Serra, Antonio, 266n62
Tshund'olela, Epanya Sh., 272
Tsuda, Hideo, 272
Turner, Frederick Jackson, 226–27
Tutu, Bishop Desmond, 352

Udalcova, Zinaida V., 261, 266n64
Ussani, Vincenzo, 120n59, 165, 177n21, 363

Valentin, Veit, 171
Valiani, Leo, 249
Vanhaute, Eric, 355
Van Kalken, Frans, 193n22, 363
Van Raalte, Ernst, 90
van Thieghem, Paul, 177n8
Varagnac, André, 207, 209–10
Vercauteren, Fernand, 221–23, 225
Vergil, 29
Verlinden, Charles, 272, 277n33
Vesnitsch, Milenko R., 9
Vicens Vives, Jaime, 279–80
Vico, Giambattista, 29, 32–33, 37
Vidal de la Blache, Paul, 25, 91
Viénot, John Emanuel, 56n18
Vigander, Haakon, 149
Vigier, Philippe, 270
Vilar, Pierre, 206, 211–12, 249, 270, 276n19, 279
Villari, Pasquale, 24–25, 27–28, 31, 85
Villari, Rosario, 366
Vinogradoff, Sir Paul (Pavel G.), 61–62, 81–83, 93, 103, 105, 119n17
Vittinghoff, Friedrich, 302, 310n15
Vitucci, Giovanni, 252–253, 264n31, 264n40
Volgin, Vyacheslav P., 132, 155
Volobuev, Pavel V., 321
Volpe, Gioacchino, 61, 66n9, 134–35, 151, 165, 177n8, 182, 184, 189, 191, 234, 363

Waitz, Georg, 17
Walek-Czernecki, Tadeusz, 124–25, 178n33
Wallerstein, Immanuel, 318
Wandruszka, Adam, 304
Wangzhi, G., 272
Ward, Adolphus W., 60, 64, 66n1, 77
Watt, Donald C., 321
Weber, Max, 51, 63, 156, 210, 214, 272, 282, 285–86, 288, 292–95, 298nn64–65, 314–15, 345
Weber, Eugène, 333
Webster, Sir Charles, 62, 95, 168, 184–85, 187, 192, 194n48, 205–6, 214, 216, 232, 235, 237–38, 246, 256, 363–64
Weech, Friedrich von, 13

Wehler, Hans-Ulrich, 294, 298n65, 343, 345
Weiler, Anton G., 288
Weizsäcker, Richard von, 261
Wells, Herbert George, 349
Westergaard, Waldemar, 98n44, 98n51
White, Hayden, 336
Whitwell, R. J., 64
Wilamowitz-Moellendorff, Ulrich von, 24–25, 41, 44–45, 61, 65, 68–69, 114, 120n59
Wilhelmina, Queen (Netherlands), 7
William I (Germany), 53
William II (Germany), 31, 46
William the Conqueror, 54
Windelband, Wilhelm, 51, 155, 188
Winter, Jay, 337, 354
Withney, James P., 60
Wittfogel, Karl August, 310n3
Wolff, Philippe, 207
Woods, Frederick A., 64
Woodward, Ernest Llewellyn, 73, 97n27, 176n6, 180, 185–87, 189, 192, 193n34, 194n48, 198, 200, 201, 215, 363

Wormald, Francis, 264n26
Wrede, Ferdinand, 54

Xenopol, Alexandru D., 16–17, 37, 173

Yamamoto, Tatsuro, 268, 276n7, 310n5
Yangasa, Eyi Engusa, 271

Zaidel, Grigorii S., 152, 161n54
Zakrzewski, Kasimierz, 178n33
Zavala, Silvio, 267, 363
Zechlin, Egmont, 251
Zeiss, Hans, 178n33
Zemon Davis, Natalie 317, 323–24, 328, 339, 342, 360n28, 366
Zhang Zhilian, 323
Zhukov, Evgenii M., 255–56, 258, 300–301, 304, 365
Zhuravlev, Sergei, 352